Fundamentals of
Media Effects

Second Edition

Jennings Bryant
University of Alabama

Susan Thompson
University of Montevallo

Bruce W. Finklea
University of Montevallo

WAVELAND

PRESS, INC.

Long Grove, Illinois

For information about this book, contact:
Waveland Press, Inc.
4180 IL Route 83, Suite 101
Long Grove, IL 60047-9580
(847) 634-0081
info@waveland.com
www.waveland.com

10-digit ISBN 1-57766-785-9
13-digit ISBN 978-1-57766-785-8

Printed in the United States of America

7 6 5 4 3

About the Authors

Jennings Bryant (PhD, Indiana University, 1974) is Distinguished Professor Emeritus at The University of Alabama (UA). Prior to his retirement in 2010, he was CIS Distinguished Research Professor, holder of the Reagan Endowed Chair of Broadcasting, and Associate Dean for Graduate Studies and Research in the College of Communication and Information Sciences at UA. He received the university's Burnum Distinguished Faculty Award in 2008, the Blackmon-Moody Outstanding Professor Award for 2000, and was President of the International Communication Association (ICA) in 2002–2003. In 2006 he received a Distinguished Scholar Award from the Broadcast Education Association, was elected a Fellow of the International Communication Association, and a Research Pioneer Tribute Essay was published in his honor in the *Journal of Broadcasting & Electronic Media* ("Jennings Bryant—The 'Compleat' Scholar"). In 2011 he received the Steven Chaffee Career Productivity Award from ICA. He was Advisory Editor of the 12-volume *International Encyclopedia of Communication*, which was published by Wiley-Blackwell in 2008 and is updated quarterly. Bryant is author or editor of 26 scholarly books or textbooks in communication.

Susan Thompson (PhD, University of Alabama, 2002) is an Associate Professor of Communication at the University of Montevallo. She received several awards while completing her doctoral studies, including the college's Outstanding Graduate PhD Research Assistant Award in 1997, the Knox Hagood Award as outstanding graduate student in 1999, and the University of Alabama's Outstanding Dissertation Award in 2002. At the University of Montevallo, Thompson often mentors McNair scholars. Thompson has authored or coauthored several books, including *The Penny Press* (2004), *Reinventing Media* (1996), and *Introduction to Media Communication* 5th edition (1998), and has written several book chapters related to media history. She has also presented papers at national and international conferences.

Bruce W. Finklea (BS, University of Montevallo, 2007) is a doctoral candidate at the University of Alabama and is a Mass Communication instructor at the University of Montevallo. Finklea teaches a variety of courses related to broadcast news production. He worked for several years as a news producer at the Birmingham, Alabama, NBC affiliate before returning to the classroom. His research focuses on gender portrayals in children's media, particularly masculinity in Pixar films. Finklea has presented several research papers and posters at national conferences.

Contents

SECTION TWO
Theory and Concepts 55

SECTION THREE
Key Areas of Research   153

Preface

In the third edition of *Cognitive Psychology of Mass Communication*, Richard J. Harris noted, "The most common general perspective in studying the media is a search for the *effects* of exposure to mass communication. In the general public, the major concerns about the media probably center on their effects" (p. 17). Given such interest in media effects by scholars and the public, one might expect that basic textbooks on the topic would abound. But that is not the case. Although scholarly volumes analyzing media effects, including many focusing on specialized effects topics, have traditionally assumed an important place in the literature of mass communication, basic textbooks about media effects are quite scarce.

A Vital Issue for Those Coming of Age in an Information Society

This paucity of textbooks in media effects is particularly problematic in our modern information age. College students are socialized into an environment in which media permeate their lives and are so omnipresent as to be essentially invisible—like water to those proverbially oblivious fish. Moreover, today's typical undergraduate students are so routinely exposed to inaccurate hype about media effects in popular culture fare, that setting the record straight about media effects has become an increasingly important part of a liberal arts education—a phenomenon often called *media literacy* or *media education*.

Our Goal and Challenge

Our primary goal in this volume is to represent the massive body of literature about media effects in such a way that undergraduate students can comprehend, manage, and appreciate this vitally important topic. To that end we have been ably assisted by literally thousands of our students who have eagerly raised their hands (or, less to our liking, put their heads on their desks) whenever we dared to trot out overly technical terms or ambiguous concepts. To them, and to our exceedingly fine reviewers, who willingly served as student surrogates as well as peer consultants, we are extremely grateful.

Special Features

In order to assist instructors who teach courses in media effects, we are pleased to offer several supplemental features to this textbook in an accompanying *Instructor's Manual* on CD-ROM.

Key Terms

In each chapter, key terms that need to be understood in order for students to fully comprehend the material are identified by bold typeface and are defined in the accompanying discussion. A glossary of these terms is provided on the CD.

Test Bank

Instructors are provided with numerous multiple choice and true/false questions. We have provided these in both Word and PDF formats.

PowerPoint Slides

PowerPoint slides are available for those who find them useful for class. Organized on a chapter-by-chapter basis, they include summaries of chapter concepts and key figures.

Discussion Questions

To spark lively class discussions, you'll find chapter questions that encourage students to think about the roles and effects of mediated communication in their lives.

Acknowledgments

Over the years, numerous instructors and students who have used various editions of a volume one of us (JB) co-edited entitled *Media Effects: Advances in Theory and Research* have encouraged us to write this textbook (sometimes sounding downright urgent in their pleas), and they have offered very specific suggestions for how the book should be structured and what should be included and excluded. To them we are extremely grateful.

We had a team of exceptionally fine reviewers for the First Edition of this text. They made the book better than it would have been without them. Sincere thanks to:

Oscar Patterson III, *University of North Florida*
George Comstock, *Syracuse University*
Daniel Riffe, *Ohio University*
Elizabeth Perse, *University of Delaware*
James Weaver, *Emory University*
Mary Cassata, *SUNY—Buffalo*
David J. Atkin, *Cleveland State University*
Michael Meffert, *University of Maryland*
Mike Basil, *University of Lethbridge*
John Chapin, *Pennsylvania State University*
Randyll Yoder, *Ohio University*
Donald Singleton, *Salisbury State University*
Diane Furno Lumade, *University of New Mexico*
Susanna Priest, *University of Nevada, Las Vegas*

As we were working on revisions for the Second Edition, we also received valuable feedback from the following First Edition adopters. Our sincere appreciation to:

William Christ, *Trinity University*
Aysel Morin, *East Carolina University*
Sriram Kalyanaraman, *University of North Carolina*

And our publisher and editor at Waveland Press have been superlative. Thank you, Neil Rowe and Laurie Prossnitz.

In closing, we would like to encourage readers of this book to become a part of our editorial team also. Let us know your specific suggestions and how we may serve you better in understanding the roles and effects of media in our society.

Jennings Bryant
Susan Thompson
Bruce W. Finklea

Overview and History

one

Understanding Media Effects

Whoever controls the media, controls the mind.
—Jim Morrison, American musician, 1943–1971

In 1995 a Louisiana couple, 18-year-old Benjamin Darras and 19-year-old Sarah Edmonson, became obsessed with *Natural Born Killers,* a violent movie about a young duo who engage in a random killing spree after taking hallucinogenic drugs. Darras and Edmonson watched the video up to six times a day. They wanted to become the main characters, Mickey and Mallory, who murder innocent people for the sheer thrill of it, apparently feel no remorse, and ultimately escape punishment for their evil deeds.

One day in early March, Darras and Edmonson smoked some grass, dropped some acid, loaded some guns, and went out joy riding in search of a Grateful Dead concert. Like their heroes in the film, they also went looking for victims. They never found the concert, but they did find victims, the first of them in rural Mississippi. There, Darras gunned down a cotton gin manager named Bill Savage. The next day, after traveling to Louisiana, Edmonson put a bullet in the throat of Patsy Byers, a Louisiana grocery store clerk and mother of three, and left her for dead. Life imitated "art."

Instances of imitation of mass media fare are rare, but they usually receive tremendous attention in the press because of their sensational nature. As you will learn in the chapters throughout this book, a great deal of research has revealed that people learn from mediated communication (Bandura, 1977, 1986, 1994, 2009), and numerous studies have found a causal link between the viewing of media violence and an increase in aggressive behavior (Bandura, 1978, 1979, 1982, 1986; Centerwall, 1989; Liebert & Schwartzberg, 1977; Williams, 1986). Interestingly, no research findings or theoretical formulations have adequately explained why the great majority of people who watch violent movies seemingly exhibit no ill effects, whereas a few go out and imitate the actions they see on the screen, no matter how gruesome those actions. Our knowledge of the link between media violence and aggression is growing, however, and several different theories explaining why media violence may result in real-world violence have been proposed and tested.

Measuring the effects of viewing screen violence represents one important facet of media effects research, but the study of media effects encompasses many other types of research as well. Social scientists are also interested in the persuasive powers of mass mediated messages (advertisements, propaganda, communication campaigns, etc.), the impact of new communication technologies, the effects of viewing sexually explicit media fare, reactions to frightening or disturbing media content, effects from political communication, and much more, as you will learn.

This chapter provides a foundation for the concepts, theories, and research studies covered throughout the remainder of the text. This book is divided into three sections. In the first—in addition to this introductory chapter—we explore the importance of media effects in historical perspective. We provide historical evidence for media effects (and for societal concern about them) since the dawn of mass communication, and we offer our version of the history of media effects research. The next section includes several of the concepts and theories that serve as the basis for different types of media effects research. Social cognitive theory, priming, agenda setting, framing, cultivation, uses and gratifications, and various persuasion theories are covered, along with some of the relevant research in each of the areas. The final section covers key areas of media effects research, including media violence, effects of sexual content, reactions to disturbing or frightening media content, political communication effects, effects on health, effects of stereotyping, educational effects, video game effects, Internet effects (i.e., impact of social networking sites), and the effects of mobile communications.

Following a review of communication processes, we turn in this chapter to a discussion of different types of communication models. We then explore the means social scientists use to measure media effects—both quantitative and qualitative research methodologies. We close with a word about the importance of studying media effects in today's information society.

Processes of Communication

> Communication can be any or all of the following: an *action on* others, an *interaction with* others, and a *reaction to* others. (McQuail & Windahl, 1993, p. 5)

Communication may take several different forms. It may be interpersonal in nature, it may involve the use of a personal communication medium, or it may be described as mass communication. When two people have a conversation, they are engaging in *interpersonal communication*. When two people talk to each other on the telephone or by means of electronic mail, *media (or mediated) communication* occurs. When a news anchor talks to a camera and his or her image and voice are transmitted to a large number of viewers watching in homes scattered throughout the land, *mass communication* takes place.

The act of communicating by way of interpersonal face-to-face interactions or mass media channels involves a *process*. In its simplest form, communication historically has been perceived as a sender delivering a message via a channel to a receiver, *usually* producing some kind of effect. We hear a joke and we laugh. We see a sad movie and we cry. We listen to a lecture and we learn—or we become confused. These examples illustrate that communication may be thought of as a *cause* that produces some kind of *effect*. Another view of communication is that of symbolic interaction, whereby meaning is shared through the use of symbols, which can be either words or images.

We emphasize the word *usually* in the previous paragraph because not all communication produces effects. The effects of any communication are subject to the conditions under which the communication occurs: the receptivity of listeners, readers, or viewers as well as numerous other factors. Certain factors may keep us from attending to the messages as we should, thereby mitigating effects or preventing them entirely. Someone may whisper something to us and cause us to miss the punch line of a joke. We may be more interested in our date than in the movie and not pay any attention whatsoever to the actions on the screen. We may sit through a lecture with our mind on an upcoming exam and walk out of the classroom without a clue as to what we just heard.

Even in its simplest form, communication between even two people is rarely simple and typically takes on an *interactional* or *transactional* dimension. In an interpersonal conversation, the listener may offer immediate feedback to the initial talker. In the course of a conversation or discussion, direct or electronically mediated senders and receivers may alternate repeatedly in their respective roles, and all of them as communicators.

In contrast, the process of mass communication involves a single source (usually a complex entity such as a television network) reaching thousands or millions of people with the same institutionalized message. The audience members are often heterogeneous, or demographically diverse, and typically are unknown to the message source. An interpersonal relationship between a network or station and any one audience member usually does not occur, although it should be noted that program websites and, especially, interactive television and other new media technologies are beginning to offer a new, interpersonal dimension to mass communication. Mass communication also has been revolutionized during the past 20 years with the widespread adoption of the Internet, cell phones, and smart phones. These media have shattered some of the previous ideas held about mass communication. Rather than consuming media produced by television and film studios, today's consumer is also a mass media producer. For example, the infamous "Charlie Bit Me" YouTube video went viral after the children's mother posted it online. Blogs allow anyone to write posts about any topic of their choosing, from documenting the daily happenings of a stay-at-home mom to writing reviews of popular films and television shows to discussing ways to care for your pet parakeet. Moreover, smart phones allow us to be media producers/consumers on the move, always in touch with the world around us. With your phone, you can text your mom while you walk on the treadmill, shoot a video as you walk down the Vegas strip and post it on your Facebook page, and watch the latest episode of *30 Rock* while riding the bus.

Communication Models

To understand processes of communication and effects from communication, some scholars have developed pictorial models to explain their theories and illustrate abstract notions regarding communication behavior. These models make it easier for us to identify the similarities and differences among the various types of communication. Models also help demonstrate the different processes of communication, whether linear, interactional, or transactional in nature.

A simple search for the phrase "communication model" in an academic database such as ERIC results in hundreds of hits. The ubiquity of the phrase has made it something of a cliché in academia. Models of communication have been employed in disciplines from psychiatry to parapsychology and just about everything in between.

Even in the field of communication, the phrase "communication model" may be used in several different ways. In this chapter, we define the term **model** as a pictorial means of explicating, or facilitating the understanding of, an abstract process such as communication. (In Chapter 3 "model" is used in another sense, to describe a prevailing paradigm or overall trend in scholarly thought, such as the powerful effects model, the limited effects model, and so forth.)

The successful pictorial models identified in this chapter offer three major advantages: They *organize* concepts, they *explain* processes, and they *predict* outcomes (Deutsch, 1966). These models range from the very simple to the very complex, but all attempt to make abstruse concepts readily understandable. A familiarity with these models may prove beneficial when the various instances of media effects are described throughout this book.

In this section we will examine two broad categories of pictorial models: those that describe various communication processes and those that explicate some kinds of media effects. The examples we offer represent only a few of the many different kinds of communication models that scholars have developed. For a more comprehensive catalog of communication models, you are encouraged to consult McQuail and Windahl's *Communication Models for the Study of Mass Communication* (1993).

Models to Depict Communication Processes

A number of pictorial models illustrate the various processes of communication. In this section, we discuss and reproduce graphic models that depict three different ways of viewing communication processes: linear, interactive, and transactional representations.

Linear Models

Linear models are based on the principles of stimulus-response psychology, in which a receiver is affected (response) by a message (stimulus) that emanates from a communication source. These models depict the communication process as a series of progressive, linear steps in the transmission of ideas from one person to another.

One of the first linear models of communication, known as the **Shannon-Weaver model**, described the process of telecommunication. Claude Shannon and Warren Weaver, researchers in the Bell Telephone laboratory in the 1940s, developed a model (see Figure 1.1) that depicts a message emanating from an information source, which becomes a signal after passing through a transmitter. Depending upon the amount of noise or interference present, the signal passes through to a receiver, where it is decoded as a message.

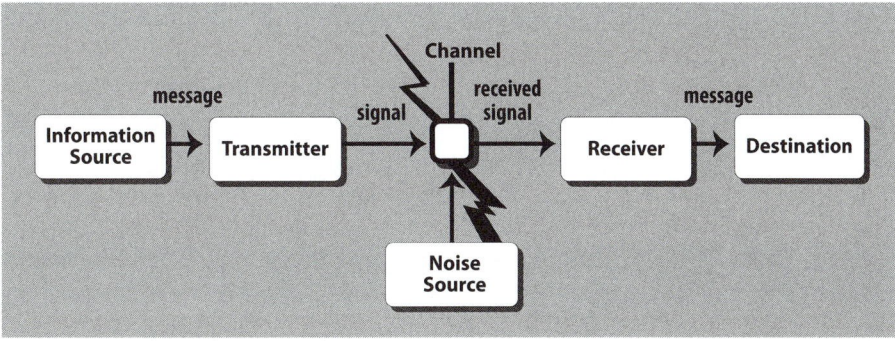

Figure 1.1   Shannon and Weaver's model describes communication as a linear, one-way process.

Source: From *The Mathematical Theory of Communication.* Copyright 1949, 1998 by the Board of Trustees of the University of Illinois. Used with permission of the author and the University of Illinois Press.

In the 1950s, Bruce Westley and Malcolm S. MacLean, Jr., sought to expand upon the Shannon-Weaver model. They developed a sender-receiver model to explain types of communication other than telecommunication, such as interpersonal and mass mediated. The various versions of the **Westley-MacLean model** (see Figures 1.2a and 1.2b) differ from the Shannon-Weaver model in that they include mechanisms for *feedback,* or return flow of information from a receiver to the original source, and *gatekeeping*, a mechanism (usually a person) that has the power to control information and even prevent it from reaching a destination. The gatekeeper was thought to be an important new dimension of communication models to many in mass communication because it addresses the role of editors, for example, who control and select the messages that ultimately get read in newspapers or watched on the news.

Interactive Models

One of the best definitions of communication as an *interactive* process comes from the United States Office of Technology Assessment (OTA). A 1990 report from the now-defunct OTA defined communication as "the process by which messages are formulated, exchanged, and interpreted" (U.S. Congress, 1990).

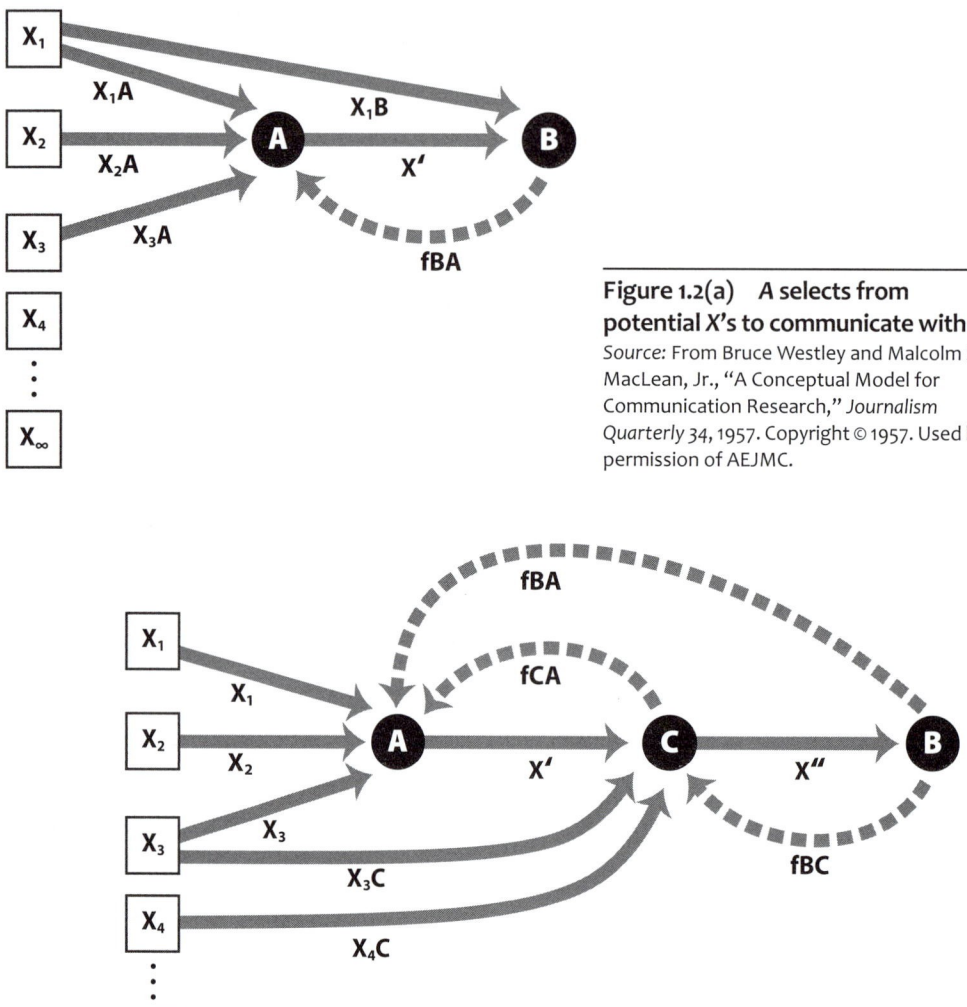

**Figure 1.2(b)   Westley and MacLean's conceptual model of mass communication,
in which a second type of communicator, C (channel role), is introduced.**

As with the Westley-MacLean linear model, our example of a model that
depicts communication as an interactive process also originated in the 1950s.
The **Schramm interactive model** emphasizes the sharing of information
between communicators, who give and receive information interactively. Developed by communication theorist Wilbur Schramm (1954), the circular model
describes communication as interactive and interpretive, with communicators

almost simultaneously sending and receiving messages. Each person alternates in his or her role as encoder, interpreter, and decoder of shared messages (see Figure 1.3).

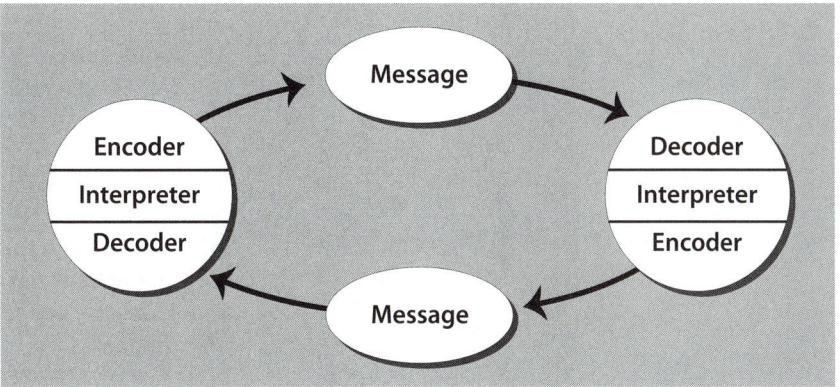

Figure 1.3   In Schramm's model both parties in, for example, a conversation fulfill the same functions.

Source: From Wilbur Schramm, "How Communication Works," in *The Processes and Effects of Mass Communication,* p. 8, ed. Wilbur Schramm. Copyright © 1954. Reprinted by permission of the Estate of Wilbur Schramm.

Transactional Models

The same OTA report that offered the interactive definition of communication also offered one of the few models ever advanced that reveal the *transactional* nature of communication. As with a business transaction that involves exchange, the word "transactional" in describing communication implies the giving and receiving of something—in this case, information—in order to create meaning. This model takes into consideration both the character of the message and the psychological orientation of the audience member as factors influencing the power of media effects. According to Bell, Ford, and Ozley (2010), transactional communication focuses on both the verbal and nonverbal choices we make. Essentially, we have the ability to choose what we say and how we say it, as well as having the ability to choose how to create meaning from the messages we receive.

The model reproduced here offers different views of communication as a transactional process, from microanalytical and macroanalytical levels. The **OTA transactional model** (see Figure 1.4) separates communication into three distinct processes—message formulation, message interpretation, and message exchange—and emphasizes the interdependencies of the processes. This model offers a microanalytical view of the transactional and multidimensional nature of communication.

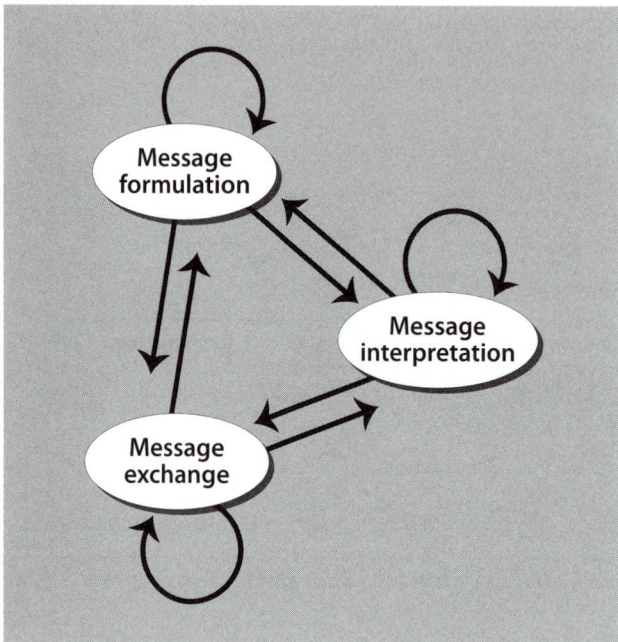

Figure 1.4   The Office of Technology Assessment model reveals the transactional nature of communication theories. The formation, exchange, and interpretation of messages and the interdependencies of these processes are key features of this model.

Source: Office of Technology Assessment, *Critical Connections: Communication for the Future*, OTA-CIT-407 (Washington, DC: U.S. Government Printing Office, January 1990).

Models to Explain Media Effects

In addition to models that describe the overall processes of communication, scholars have advanced other models to depict the effects that may result whenever media communication occurs. Both micro- and macroanalytical models have been used to describe the different types and levels of media effects, from purely individual effects to influences on groups of people or even society at large.

Individual Effects

One of the most useful models to illustrate direct effects on individuals from mass mediated communication is the **Comstock psychological model** (see Figure 1.5). Comstock and his associates (1978) developed this model to describe certain mental processes that occur while watching television. The model shows that the behavior of an individual viewer may be influenced by televised actions. A person learns some behavior by watching it presented on television, and the person may adopt the learned behavior, depending upon the salience (or psychological importance) and the personal excitement or motivation (called *arousal* in this model) gained by engaging in such behavior. The perceived reality of the mediated action is an important mitigating variable (i.e., the more realistic the media portrayal, the greater the psychological effect on the viewer and the greater the potential influence on the viewer's behavior).

Another good example of a model that shows individual psychological effects from media communication is the **Thorson cognitive processing model**

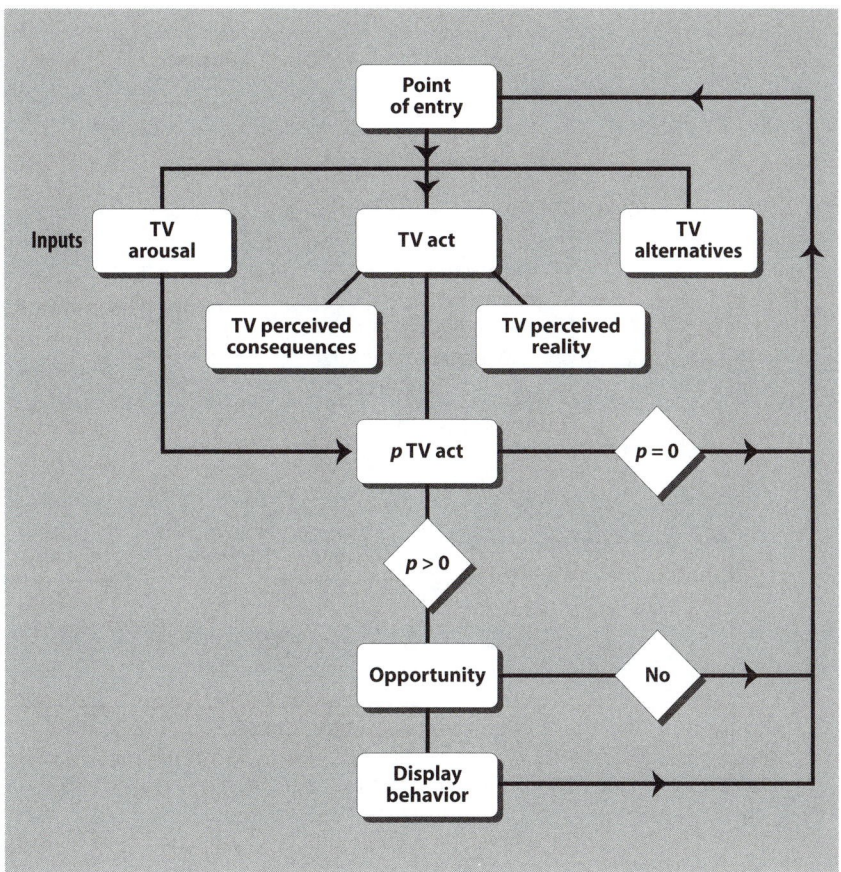

Figure 1.5   A simplified version of Comstock's psychological model of television's effects on individual behavior. The model is given in the form of an "itinerary" of an individual in time, starting with exposure to a given television portrayal.
Source: From G. Comstock, S. Chaffee, N. Katzman, M. McCombs, & D. Roberts, *Television and Human Behavior.* Copyright © 1978. Reprinted by permission of Rand Corporation.

(see Figure 1.6). Whenever cognitive (or mental) dimensions are under consideration, models are sometimes rather complex; however, such complexities are necessary to accurately depict the many factors and steps involved in the processing of mediated information. The Thorson model concentrates on the steps taken in the processing of television commercials. It takes into consideration the individual viewer's personal interest in and attention to the commercial message, the person's memory, and even language capacity, in determining the potential effects of the messages. For example, a foreign student who does not yet have a thorough command of English would have more trouble processing commercials than a native speaker, and would not remember the commercial message as well.

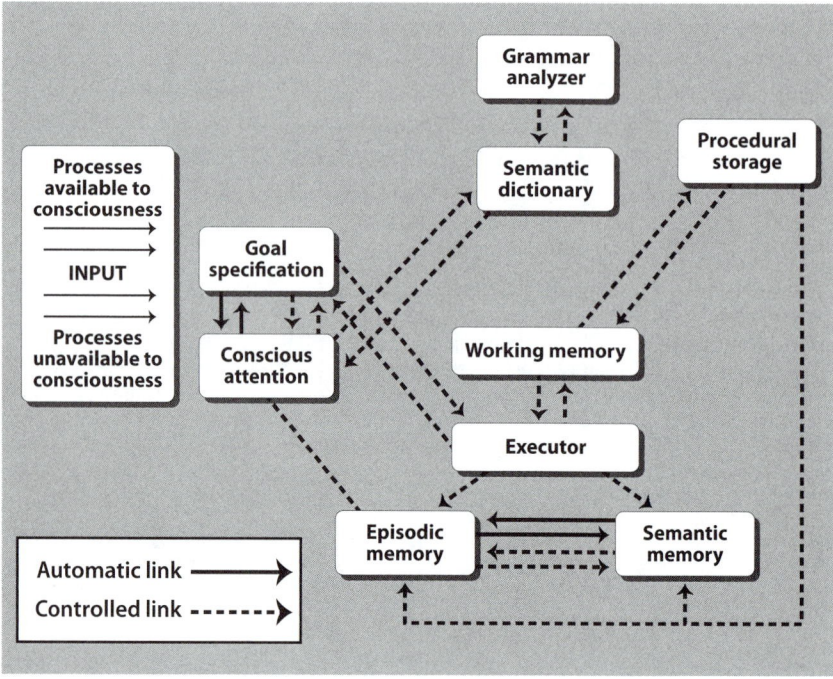

Figure 1.6   Thorson's cognitive processing model.

Source: B. Derwin, L. Grossberg, B. J. O'Keefe, and E. Wartella, eds., *Rethinking Communication: Paradigm Exemplars*, vol. 2, pp. 397–410, copyright © 1989 by Sage Publications, Inc. Reprinted by permission.

Social Effects

As an example of a model of media effects at the societal level, we have selected the **media system dependency model** advanced by Ball-Rokeach and DeFleur (1976). This model (see Figure 1.7) focuses on the relationships between the mass media entity (information system) and society itself (social system). It assumes that individuals in modern society become increasingly dependent upon mass media as a source of news and information. The level of the dependency relationship and the strength of the media effects hinge on the stability or instability of the society and the degree of societal importance placed upon mass media as an information source. Relationships and interactions among media, society, and audience are demonstrated, along with media effects. News in times of crisis serves as a good example of dependency theory in action. Whenever a crisis occurs (e.g., the terrorist attacks of September 11, 2001, or the tornadoes that ravaged Tuscaloosa, Alabama, and Joplin, Missouri, in early 2011) people turn to the news media as a source of information and even comfort. Their dependency on the media increases during times of crisis.

These examples represent only a few of the large and growing number of pictorial models used to illustrate communication processes and effects from

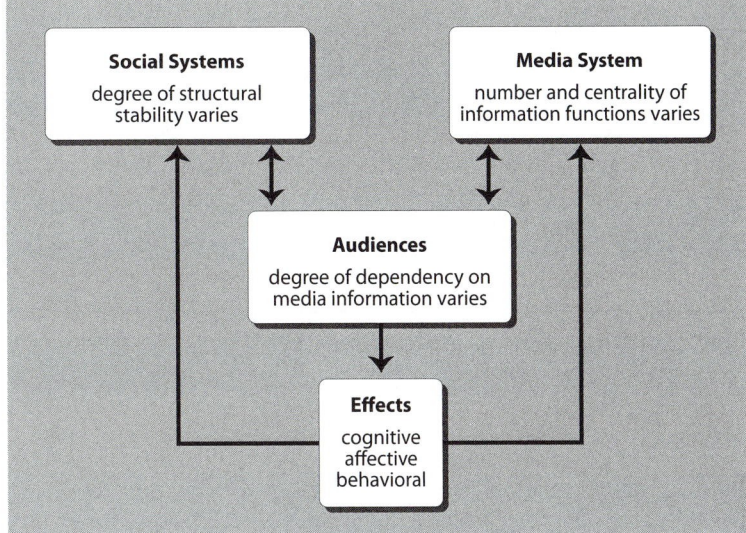

Figure 1.7 The dependency state.

Source: From M. L. DeFleur and S. J. Ball-Rokeach, eds., *Theories of Mass Communication.* Copyright © 1982. Used by permission of Pearson Publishing.

media communication. With this basic foundation, we now turn specifically to the topic of media effects. In these final sections, we discuss the various means of measuring or assessing media effects and consider the social relevance of media effects research.

Measuring Media Effects

The study of media effects typically assumes a basic cause-and-effect relationship. It does not, however, completely disregard the role of chance in the unfolding of events. Social scientists employ statistical tools to account for chance while accepting the notion of causality. In fact, most contemporary communication scholars accept a view of causation that indicates that cause and effect cannot be determined exactly, only probabilistically (e.g., Born, 1949). According to Perry:

> Any discussion of media effects requires a concern with causation. Before a researcher can conclude that one concept is a cause of another, the researcher must establish three things. First, the presumed cause and the presumed effect must covary, or go together. For example, people who are heavily exposed to mediated violence should tend, on the average, to be either more or less aggressive than those who are less exposed. . . . Second, the presumed cause must precede the presumed effect. Finally, a researcher must eliminate plausible rival (i.e., third variable) explanations for the observed covariation of the presumed cause and effect. (1996, pp. 25–26)

Throughout this text, you will read about the results of many studies that have been conducted to test for evidence of media effects. Most effects research involves the use of quantitative research methods, but studies employing more qualitative measures, or some combination of the two, have also been used. In this section we examine four research methodologies that have been used to study media effects: the laboratory experiment, survey research (often called cross-sectional research), field experiments, and a form of longitudinal research known as the panel study. We also mention the importance of statistical methods in assessing the presence of media effects. Table 1.1 provides a list of terms used in the discussion of media effects.

Table 1.1   Terms Used by Social Scientists

Throughout the text, we will use various terms in our discussions of concepts and theories related to media effects. The following list should provide a useful review.

Theory	Systematic explanations and predictions of phenomena. More formally, a theory is a systematic and plausible set of generalizations that explain some observable phenomena by linking constructs and variables in terms of organizing principles that are internally consistent.
Concept	A general idea derived from many specific particulars; for example, *social class* is a concept generalized from particulars like income, education, status, occupation, and esteem.
Hypothesis	A specific statement or proposal that can be tested by means of gathering empirical evidence.
Qualitative	Research methods that allow the investigator to describe a phenomenon without relying heavily on numbers. Qualitative methods allow the researcher to interpret a phenomenon more holistically using words rather than numbers.
Quantitative	Research methods that use numbers to describe the relative amount of something.
Triangulation	Use of multiple types of research methods to address questions of media effects.
Deductive reasoning	From the general to the particular; the process by which theory is tested. The researcher begins with a general idea or theory and asks a specific statement or hypothesis, then tests the hypothesis with the collection of data.
Inductive reasoning	From the particular to the general; the process by which theory is generated. The researcher begins with a simple research question and collects data that describe a particular case, and then develops a theory based upon findings.
Variable	Anything to which more than one value can be assigned; for example, hair color is a variable that can have values of black, brown, blond, red, and so forth.

Laboratory Experiments

By far the most popular method for measuring media effects in its most simple form, the experimental method involves having people watch or listen to or read a certain type of media fare (violent, sexually explicit, frightening, or something else) while other people watch, read, or listen to innocuous content, then comparing any measurable changes exhibited by individuals from the two groups. The measurement tool may be either the self-reports of participants on questionnaires or automated instruments (e.g., preference analyzers), observation of participants' actions, assessments of various activities performed by the individual, or some sort of physiological measure (e.g., blood pressure, heart rate, skin conductance) or cognitive assessment (e.g., brain waves) as the participant is viewing the content.

In more complex formulations, experiments often include control groups (e.g., people who did not read, hear, or see a media message). Complex research designs also are employed so that researchers can examine the effects of several variables simultaneously—for example, the impact of (a) frightening versus nonfrightening media content on (b) boys versus girls (c) at different ages (e.g., 3, 6, 9).

Wimmer and Dominick (1994) listed four major advantages and two disadvantages of laboratory experiments in media research. On the positive side, the experiment represents "the best social science research method for establishing causality" (p. 85). The experiment also affords the researcher much control, especially in the presentation of the variables in proper time order so that the cause is shown to precede the effect, and in the manipulation of variables. In terms of cost, experiments also involve less expense than most other research methods. Finally, the step-by-step techniques make laboratory experiments easier for others to replicate than other types of research methods. As for disadvantages, the artificial surroundings of lab experiments may affect a research participant's behavior, including the very variable that researchers are attempting to observe and measure. Another problem, experimental bias, occurs when the researcher influences the results either intentionally or unintentionally. Many researchers avoid the problem by conducting double-blind experiments, in which neither the research participants nor the researchers know which participants are part of the control group and which belong to the experimental group.

Survey Research

Another common means of measuring effects from media fare uses written questionnaires, telephone interviews, face-to-face interviews, or Web surveys to gauge (1) the type and extent of media exposure of an individual (e.g., number of hours the person watches violent television programs per week, or the number of pornographic websites the person visits each week), and (2) the respondent's self-reported attitudes and tendencies toward antisocial or prosocial behaviors. For the latter measure, researchers may employ any of several scales or inventories that have been refined over time. These studies often search for specific demographic or sociographic factors that might affect the relationship between variables because surveys are commonly conducted with representative samples of the population of interest.

One caveat about using survey research to determine media effects should be noted. If you recall Perry's (1996) three criteria for causation, you can see that the first criterion—that the presumed cause and the presumed effect must covary—can be readily accommodated through survey research. The third criterion—the elimination of rival causes—can also be addressed somewhat by survey research. Indeed, using a well-designed survey, a number of different potential contributors to a particular media effect can be evaluated in the same survey. For this reason, researchers conducting an experiment also frequently administer a survey to their research participants. In this way, they can use various statistical controls and partially account for rival causes at the same time as they determine cause-and-effect relationships by way of the tight research designs that experiments typically permit. However, Perry's second criterion for causation—that the presumed cause must precede the presumed effect—is the potential trouble spot in using survey research to determine media effects. This issue of time sequence or time order cannot be determined if the questionnaire or interview assesses the presumed cause (e.g., the number of hours of violent television watched) and the presumed effect (e.g., the level of fear for personal safety) at the same time. To attempt to get around the time-sequence issue, researchers often administer the same survey (or similar surveys) on multiple occasions, or they administer different portions of the instrument at different times. However, because such control typically is not considered to be as certain or as effective as that exerted by tight research designs and a properly conducted experiment, the determination of causation from such procedures is frequently called into question if surveys are the only means to assess media effects. In other words, surveys are very good for determining associations or relationships between and among variables, but they are less compelling for determining cause and effect.

Field Experiments

Experiments conducted "in the field," or in real-world settings, have not been used to study media effects to the extent that laboratory and survey research methods have been employed, but a handful of important studies have been conducted in this manner (e.g., Williams, 1986; Parke, Berkowitz, & Leyens, 1977). Field experiments do not allow as much physical control as experiments conducted in the laboratory; however, the use of statistical controls in the field has allowed researchers to gain more control over extraneous or intervening variables. Field experiments rate high in *external validity,* or the measure of a particular study's generalizability. The attitudes or behaviors of research participants are measured in real-life settings rather than in the often sterile environment of a laboratory; therefore, the behaviors of participants are thought to be more natural. In some cases, people being studied in the field may not be aware that they are being measured and therefore may behave more naturally, although such approaches raise ethical issues. An additional advantage of the field study may be found in its expediency for studying rather complex social situations, such as the impact of television on a community receiving it for the first time.

Panel Studies

Panel studies require the researcher to either interview or send questionnaires to the same respondents at different times. This method is not employed as often in the study of media effects as other methods; however, one of the major studies in the history of media effects (Lazarsfeld, Berelson, & Gaudet, 1944) made use of a panel. Panel studies are inherently longitudinal in nature, meaning that the same respondents provide information at more than one point in time. This means that respondents must be recruited and retained over time, a situation that makes demands on the researcher's time and may involve considerable expense. However, the benefits of panel studies often outweigh these human and fiscal costs.

Triangulation

Because each of these primary research methodologies for establishing media effects has limitations, researchers often try to utilize several different methodologies to address a question or issue. For example, to determine whether watching a great deal of television drama in which the lead characters are generous and altruistic causes viewers to increase their charitable giving, it is possible to use a laboratory experiment, a field experiment, or a survey. However, it would be even better to utilize all three methodologies; that is, a so-called triangulation of methodologies. If the results of the three separate studies are similar, the cumulative findings are much more compelling than the findings from any of the independent investigations. Scholars who approach media effects questions utilizing complementary methodologies (or who use several different experiments or surveys to answer similar research questions) are often said to conduct *programmatic* research in media effects. This greatly increases the credibility of their findings not only among their peers, but also for news reporters and policy makers.

Other Research Methodologies of Media Effects

A number of other research methodologies are also useful in understanding and predicting media effects. Two of them, content analysis and meta-analysis, are briefly profiled because of their prevalence in media effects research.

Content Analysis

Content analysis has often been used to examine the presence, absence, or quantity of certain attributes of media messages that allegedly contribute to certain types of media impact. For example, as a part of its program designed to highlight "the importance of entertainment media in shaping people's awareness of health issues" (Kaiser Family Foundation, 1999, p. 2), the Kaiser Family Foundation commissioned several content analyses of sex on television, including assessments of the prevalence of sexual messages, the types of talk about sex, the types of sexual behaviors presented or discussed, and the prevalence of messages about sexual risks or responsibilities (Kunkel et al., 1999). It should be noted that the presence or absence of such message features does not provide any direct evidence of media effects on sexual behavior; instead, such content analyses can provide a valuable profile of the type of content that might be expected to lead to prosocial or antisocial media effects. Other research methodologies must be used in conjunction with content analyses to provide evidence of effects per se.

Meta-Analysis

Throughout this textbook you will find the results from various meta-analyses of media effects. Meta-analysis is a relatively new methodology in media effects research, and it is unusual in that it does not contribute any new "primary" evidence regarding media effects. Instead, **meta-analysis** is a means of systematically integrating the extant findings from a large number of empirical studies on any given topic. Statistical methods are used to provide a "big picture" in terms of the magnitude as well as the direction of the effects attributable to the media in a particular area of inquiry (e.g., stereotyping, pornography, video games). Because the procedures employed in meta-analysis are relatively objective and are designed to be quite comprehensive, a well-conducted meta-analysis can give an analytical interpretation of a body of media effects literature. This information can then be combined with traditional narrative literature reviews to provide further insight into the effects of media in society.

Statistical Methods

Most media effects studies make use of *statistics,* "the science that uses mathematical models to collect, organize, summarize, and analyze data" (Wimmer & Dominick, 1994, p. 205). Statistical methods may be *descriptive,* such as this sample result: "Readers of *six* or more mystery novels per month performed *three* times as well on problem-solving tasks as their peers who did not read mystery novels." However, probably the most common use of statistical tools in communication research involves the use of *inferential* statistics. The science of statistics assumes that random samples from populations take on the same distribution properties of the larger population; thus tests conducted upon a random sample may be generalizable to the overall population within certain well-defined limits. Statistical methods are based upon laws of probability. The methods make allowances for errors in sampling, as well as provisions for chance. Errors due to chance, whether sampling errors (e.g., the chance selection or assignment of a sample that is not representative of a population) or something else, become part of the overall equation. Research designs allow investigators to isolate particular causes for media effects; statistical methods permit us to assign values to the strength of those causes.

Importance of Studying Media Effects

We live in a world in which we receive a multitude of mediated messages daily. As you will learn in the next chapter, the concern about effects from media communication, as well as evidence for effects, are as old as mass communication itself. People have always wondered how media messages are affecting them and, especially, their children. They have always been concerned for the negative effects of a particular message, or message systems, and they have been curious about the potential prosocial effects of others.

As we move further into a new millennium, the knowledge of effects from mediated communications assumes increasing importance. We have become so information oriented and information dependent that some have dubbed ours an "information society." Computers, mobile technology, and mass media are vital cogs in our societal infrastructure. With so much of what is perceived to be wrong in today's world blamed on media communications of some sort or another, the issue of mass media effects has become one of paramount social relevance. But effects from mediated violence, pornography, advertising, video games, or news are but the most visible surface of this fascinating and important research domain. As we hope you will discover as you read the chapters of this text, knowledge of the power of mediated communications is important for us all. It is often said that we are the "sovereign consumers" of the information age. But if our consumption is to be fruitful, we must be extremely knowledgeable about the effects of media in our lives.

Summary

Measuring the effects of viewing on-screen violence represents one important facet of media effects research, but the study of media effects encompasses many other types of research as well. Social scientists are also interested in the persuasive powers of mass mediated messages (e.g., advertisements, propaganda, communication campaigns), the impact of new communication technologies, the effects of viewing sexually explicit media fare, reactions to frightful or disturbing media content, effects from political communication, and much more.

Communication may take several different forms. It may be interpersonal in nature, it may involve the use of a personal communication medium, or it may be described as mass communication. The act of communicating via interpersonal, media, or mass media channels involves a process or series of stages. Even in its simplest form, communication between a source and a receiver may take on an interactional or transactional dimension. In the case of an interpersonal conversation, the receiver may offer immediate feedback to the source. In the course of a conversation or discussion, senders and receivers may alternate repeatedly in their respective roles. Mass communication involves one or more institutional sources (usually complex entities such as production houses in conjunction with a television network) reaching thousands or millions of people with the same transient message. The audience members are heterogeneous, or demographically diverse, and unknown to the message source.

Scholars have developed models to explain their theories and illustrate abstract ideas regarding communication processes and behavior. Models may also be used to explain media effects. Models help demonstrate the different processes of communication, whether linear, interactional, or transactional in nature. Successful pictorial models offer three major advantages: They organize concepts, they explain processes, and they predict outcomes.

The study of media effects assumes a basic cause-and-effect scenario. Social scientists employ statistical methods to account for chance as an important component of the notion of causality.

Researchers often measure media effects in laboratory settings using experimental methods. Other research methods include surveys, field experiments, and panel studies. Triangulation is the use of several research methods to address questions of media effects. Content analysis is used to examine the presence, absence, or quantity of certain attributes of media messages that allegedly contribute to certain media effects. Meta-analyses are useful for systematically integrating extant findings from a large number of empirical studies on any given topic. Most media effects studies employ statistical methods.

With so many of the problems in today's world being blamed on media communications, the issue of mass media effects has become one of paramount social relevance. Media effects is an important and fascinating research domain. A fundamental knowledge of media effects is a necessary criterion for excelling in the information age.

chapter two

Media Effects
Historical Overview

> *Among the most alarming evils of our age and country is the injurious tendency of the publications that are daily flowing from the press.*
> —*U.S. Catholic Magazine,* 1847

Since the invention of the printing press in 1450, people have suggested that mass media have important effects on their audiences. Sometimes historical evidence has been utilized to chronicle pronounced changes in public opinions or behavior after widespread exposure to certain media content. At other times, media effects have been less obvious, but *concern* of the critics for media effects on others has prompted various actions against mass media. Such concerns for generalized "others" rather than self have been systematically explained as *third-person effects,* which are said to occur whenever individuals believe other audience members are more susceptible than they are to persuasive, violent, or objectionable media content (Davison, 1983).

This chapter examines the concern for media effects in historical perspective and the historical evidence for actual media effects on opinions and behaviors since the invention of the printing press. The chapter also documents selected popular concern about media effects prior to and after social scientific measurement of such effects became an area of scholarly enquiry.

The existence of media effects ultimately requires a cause-and-effect perspective, with the most common "cause" being some kind of message conveyed by way of a communication medium (i.e., message effects). When social and behavioral scientists enter their media effects laboratories, they typically exercise tight control to ensure that extraneous influences are minimized and that precise measurement of influences on individuals can be accomplished. They are thereby equipped to assess actual media effects on individuals in a variety of ways. In contrast, historians are usually limited to assessing cause-and-effect relationships involving media only when the effects, as indicated in recorded opinions and actions, seem obvious and powerful in retrospect.

Moreover, whereas social and behavioral scientists typically amass evidence for or against media effects by treating or examining individuals, often one at a time, historians sometimes examine aggregate data from public records and the like, thereby focusing on societal-level effects. It should be noted that the various historical examples we cite provide evidence for media effects among great numbers of people rather than individual and isolated cases of the "man bites dog" variety. We will emphasize major trends rather than idiosyncratic events of media impact that may be newsworthy because of their human interest value.

Many scholars might argue that historical examples do not provide adequate, scientific evidence of a cause-and-effect relationship. As a University of Chicago social scientist once stated:

> [T]he case method and the collection of anecdotes do not supply proof of a generalization; rather they provide illustrations, and such illustrations can be deceptive if they lead the author or others to accept them as proof. (Stouffer, 1942, p. 144)

In answer to this argument, we emphasize that historical methods are different from other research methods. The historian looks for a preponderance of evidence, usually various concurring indications of influence, that suggest cause-and-effect relationships. A book such as Harriet Beecher Stowe's *Uncle Tom's Cabin* (1852), for example, is known to have been influential because of its high sales figures and from discussions about its influence among writers and orators of the period. It should be remembered that scores of examples of null or minimal media effects may never show up on a historian's radar screen.

As will be shown, obtrusive examples of what certainly appear to be media effects on opinions and behavior are rather plentiful throughout modern history, especially when people reacted to frightful or disturbing media content and persuasive messages. Historical evidence for popular public concern about media effects also abounds and has manifested

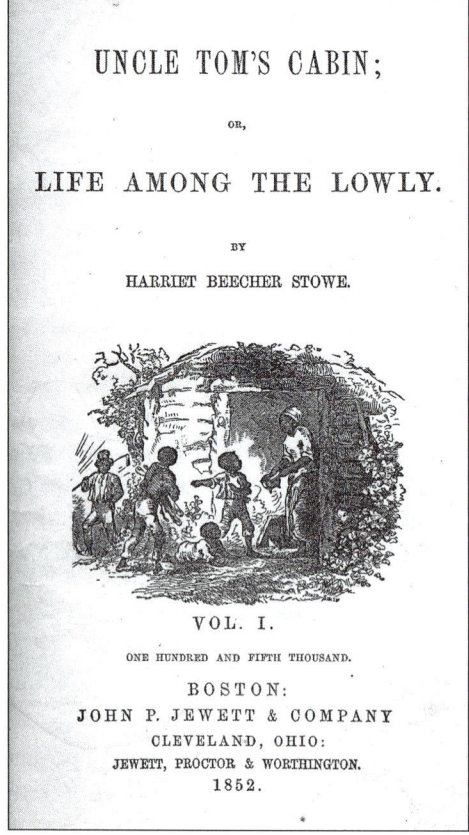

Uncle Tom's Cabin was recognized as influential in swaying public opinion toward the abolitionist cause.

itself in different ways. The many instances of suppression of the press by authorities can be viewed as evidence of their concern for powerful media effects on the masses, as can instances of individual efforts against violent or sexually explicit material due to their suspected harmful effects on the masses, especially children.

Historical Concern for Media Effects

The modern-day emphasis on quantitative, experimental measures in media effects research has obscured the obvious bond that exists between the study of media history and that of media effects. Like scientific effects researchers, many media historians also search for evidence of media effects. However, the historian's "laboratory" is the past—the centuries since humans first used mass media to communicate with each other. Therefore, the historian's subjects can speak only through records that have survived.

Historical evidence reveals that, at first, only society's elite recognized potential societal influences from exposure to the printed word. Many leaders, due to their fear of effects from literacy and reading on the masses, sought to control publications and thereby silence opposition voices. Such fear of media influences lingers today in many totalitarian societies, in which leaders suppress or control media to maintain their power.

In the 19th century, new technologies and the spread of literacy made possible the development of remarkable new forms of communication: mass communication. Since that period, concern for powerful media effects has been expressed not only by society's educated elite, but also has been shared by individuals and groups from all strata of the population, from presidents to parents, from the intelligentsia to beginning students. These historical instances of the concern about detrimental societal impacts of media messages have been strong enough and loud enough to influence lawmakers, shape public policy, and attract the interest of numerous scholars.

Western history provides many examples of attempts to control the press due to the supposed power of its messages over its audience. The control has taken various forms, such as suppression or censorship of information, use of propaganda, or physical violence against editors or reporters. The agents of control have included government officials, the clergy, and others. This section offers a brief survey of some of the more memorable instances in history when concern for media effects caused actions against the press or other media.

Suppression Due to Concern for Media Effects

The most compelling examples of the concern for powerful media effects on the masses might be found in the many instances in which authorities have taken preemptive measures to suppress mass media messages. Soon after the appearance of the printing press, the ecclesiastical and governmental elite showed concern for the power of the printed word. They used the press for their own ends and attempted measures of censorship to prevent the publishing of opposition views. For example, in the mid-16th century, Catholics wanted Protestant material banned. In 1559, Pope Paul IV began issuing an *Index of Prohibited Books,* a listing of forbidden works. In addition to Protestant books, the list included pornography, occult books, and opposition political works. Protestant leaders such as Martin Luther defied the pope and used the printing press to spread Reformation literature to the masses. As this reform literature was disseminated to print shops throughout Europe, the repercussions against the rebels who used media without authority were extremely severe: Printers caught spreading propaganda often were imprisoned or burned at the stake.

In early 16th-century England, King Henry VIII was so concerned about the printed word that he created the Court of the Star Chamber, which prosecuted those who published material offensive to the Crown. Henry also insisted upon a system of licensing that held the English press under strict control.

In the late 1700s in the United States, Benjamin Franklin Bache's *Philadelphia Aurora* provided a leading voice for the cause of Republicanism in the United States. His inflammatory writings galvanized public opinion and produced a number of different, notable reactions:

> On one occasion or another, Treasury Secretary Oliver Wolcott threatened to investigate the *Aurora* for treason, Federalist Speaker of the House Jonathan Dayton barred Bache from the House floor, Federalist editors and politicians subjected him to written and verbal attacks, Federalist merchants imposed an advertising boycott on the *Aurora* and barred the paper from their establishments, the government tried Bache for sedition, and individuals and mobs physically attacked him. (Sloan, 1998, pp. 130–131)

In an effort to control opposition voices such as Bache's, the Federalists passed one of the most oppressive government measures in U.S. history, the Sedition Act of 1798. The act was passed at the time of the French Revolution in an effort to keep pro-French voices from being heard in American newspapers. "Give to any set of men the command of the press and you give them the command of the country, for you give them the command of public opinion, which commands everything," wrote Judge Alexander Addison in the *Columbian Centinel* on January 1, 1799 (Sloan, 1998, p. 119).

> Federalists by 1799 had come to realize a fact that had been at the essence of American public life almost since the first colonists had stepped ashore in the early 1600s. Public opinion was the basis for public policy, and the printing press was the means that provided a forum for it. (p. 119)

From the 1830s until the Civil War, many feared the powerful effects of abolitionist messages. Southerners objected vehemently to publication and circulation of such material because they believed it would encourage slave revolts. President Andrew Jackson urged Congress to pass a law to prevent incendiary material regarding the slavery debate from being circulated in the mails.

During World War I, Congress passed both the Espionage Act of 1917 and the Sedition Act of 1918. These acts made it illegal to publish information critical of the U.S. government or in support of any of the enemy powers. The government feared the effects of voices that opposed the war effort.

Mob Violence as Media Effect

Another historical indicator of suppression due to concern for media effects might be instances of mob violence directed against mass media offices or editors in response to the publishing or showing of incendiary material. History is filled with such outbreaks of violence directed against the press (Nerone, 1994). One of the nastiest antipress mobs in history attacked producers of the Baltimore *Federal Republican,* a radical Federalist paper that opposed American participation in the War of 1812. Several people died and at least one editor was maimed for life.

Many examples of mob actions against the expression of race-related messages abound (Grimsted, 1998). During the abolitionist movement, a mob attacked and killed Elijah Lovejoy in Illinois. Frederick Douglass, the African American editor of *The North Star,* was continually harassed and even had his house burned by those who opposed his views. During the civil rights movement of the 1950s and 1960s, Mississippi editor Hazel Brannon Smith spoke out against racial injustices against African Americans and, as a result, faced considerable opposition from local residents and local government officials alike. A white citizens' council urged local businesses to stop advertising in her paper, subscribers canceled their subscriptions, and one white official brought a libel suit against her—all in reaction to her stand against the unfair treatment of Blacks (Davies, 1998).

Not all of the mob incidents related to racial issues involved the press. At least one instance of mob action came in response to a major motion picture. In the early 20th century, release of the film *The Birth of a Nation* caused race riots and mob actions against Blacks by arousing emotion and controversy. Produced by D. W. Griffith, the father of American film, *The Birth of a Nation* told the story of the Civil War, Reconstruction, and the rise of the Ku Klux Klan from a white supremacist perspective.

Public Concern for "Indecent" Material

The public concern for the ill effects of media violence and sexually explicit material is not exclusive to the 20th century. In the early 19th century, a new type of journalism emerged in England, one that would soon be copied successfully by penny dailies in the United States. In the English press, humorous reports on the activities of arrested thieves, drunks, prostitutes, and other miscreants and lowlifes of society became immensely popular among many readers, but elicited severe criticisms from social critics. In the United States, the appearance of New York's *The Sun* in 1833 and its similar reports of police and courtroom activities in New York City resulted in the same mixed response: The articles made the penny sheets very popular among their devoted readers, but the emphasis on violence, sexuality, and unseemly conduct also caused many to criticize the sheets and express concern for the effects of such material on an innocent and expanding reading public.

The second successful penny paper, James Gordon Bennett's *The New York Herald,* though immensely popular, attracted controversy almost from the start due to Bennett's habit of ridiculing his competitors in print, his language (which was not always respectable by 19th-century standards), and his extensive coverage of sensational trials that involved scandal, illicit sex, and murder. Competitors and opponents thrashed him in print and in person. On several occasions angry readers physically attacked Bennett on the streets of New York. The "moral war" on Bennett is a good 19th-century example of society's concern for printed material it considered indecent. Prominent citizens called for a boycott against the *Herald* and businesses that advertised in it. As a result, the *Herald* lost some of its mammoth circulation and Bennett soon modified the tone of his paper.

The readable style of *The Sun*, the *Herald*, and the other penny dailies, as well as their sensational and sometimes titillating news stories, made them popular and profitable. Critics continued to complain about the suspected negative effects on society, especially as other newspapers began to copy the *Herald's* techniques and a new style of journalism emerged. A commentator in 1847 complained about the sorry state of the periodical press as a purveyor of immorality. The article "Pernicious Literature" called for press reforms to avoid rather serious effects from such "contamination."

> Among the most alarming evils of our age and country is the injurious tendency of the publications that are daily flowing from the press. The licentious and anti-social works which are so profusely scattered throughout the length and breadth of the land, in the shape of annuals, brochures, and family newspapers, are sowing a seed of corruption which will bring disgrace and wretchedness upon thousands, if not lay the foundation of that sensual and selfish spirit which will contaminate the nation at large, and threaten the downfall of its free institutions. . . . In this state of things the secular press must be reformed itself. . . . Until this be done, the spirit of our newspapers and the depravity of the popular appetite will exert a reciprocal influence;—one will encourage the other, and both will combine to swell and precipitate that torrent of licentiousness which is beginning to excite the profound and just apprehensions of all good men. (*U.S. Catholic Magazine*, 1847, pp. 46, 48)

After film became popular in the early 20th century, public concern for negative effects of violent and sexually explicit film presentations on youngsters prompted the Payne Fund studies. These studies examined the influence of motion pictures on juvenile delinquency, attitudes, and other factors.

In the 1950s, Fredric Wertham's *Seduction of the Innocent* (1954) expressed an anti-comic-book sentiment that resulted in the inclusion of comic book content in the meetings of the Senate Subcommittee to Investigate Juvenile Delinquency. The comic book industry began measures of self-regulation to ward off government intervention. The Comics Magazine Association of America was formed and issued the Comics Code Authority, which prohibited graphic violence and erotic depictions, among other things.

In recent years, novels such as *The Catcher in the Rye*, movies like *Natural Born Killers*, musical recordings, and video games have been blamed for influencing audience members to commit horrible acts of violence or for causing "copycat crimes." The concern for the ill effects of viewing violence and sexual content on television and in motion pictures has led to countless studies and government-sponsored inquiries. The debate over the strength of these effects rages to this day.

Historical Evidence for Changes in Behavior and Opinion Due to Mass Media

Although actual media effects are impossible to demonstrate empirically in a historical context—owing to the difficulty of controlling for or eliminating rival causes, among other limitations—Western history is rich with more general, anecdotal examinations of media effects. Such effects include the social changes that occurred after the introduction of new communication technologies, the many instances when individuals and groups used mediated messages to achieve certain goals, and instances in which citizens took actions due to their fear of the power of media messages to sway audiences in some undesirable manner. Long before media effects were studied scientifically and measured analytically, they were assumed, felt, witnessed, and recorded.

Effects from the Printing Press

Through the years, historians have examined new media technologies as they developed and have uncovered what they considered to be evidence for rather powerful effects at societal and cultural levels. Many studies have explored the advent of the printing press and the many societal changes it brought about (Eisenstein, 1979, 1983; Febvre & Martin, 1984). With the introduction of the printing press, paper, and movable type, more books appeared, prices fell, and literacy spread. The societal impact was considerable. Within approximately one hundred years, the audience for books exploded from a select, elite few to masses of people. By 1500 printers throughout western Europe had established more than 250 presses that produced some 35,000 editions and from 15 to 20 million copies (Febvre & Martin, 1984). Specific historical studies on the diffusion of innovations have looked at the spread of other new media technologies, such as the telegraph and the phonograph, and have also included research examining social effects from the use of the new technology (Hyde, 1994). Other historical studies have explored dynamics and changes in social processes brought about by new media technologies (Pool, 1977; Marvin, 1988).

Media Effects on Public Opinion

The influence of the abolitionist press in the years prior to the Civil War illustrates the power of the press (in this case, an alternative press) to sway public opinion. African American newspapers such as *Freedom's Journal, The Colored American,* and *The North Star* advanced the cause of Blacks, attacked slavery, and contributed to the growing abolitionist sentiment in the North. In the long run, the effects of such printed material served to educate, mobilize, and motivate Blacks and to cultivate attitudes that were much less tolerant of human slavery and more sympathetic to the rights of African Americans among Whites in the northern United States.

> Gunnar Myrdal, in *An American Dilemma,* called the black press the most important educational agency for blacks. One of the most powerful arenas in which political, economic, and cultural battles could be fought, it provided a way to tell the black experience: African-American life, concerns, achievements. It was a forum to air blacks' views and discuss issues concerning blacks. Further, coverage of blacks' achievements instilled pride and a sense of progress, identity and hope for the future. The black press also was an educator and aid to readers' intellectual development at a time when blacks were barred from formal education, and it served a vital political function. That is, it helped blacks first understand and then find their political potential. Black editors informed, inspired, unified, and mobilized readers, directing them to act on information and how. (Dicken-Garcia, 1998, p. 154)

History provides a number of other examples of media messages that seemingly proved powerful enough to influence public opinion. In the newly formed United States, a series of articles called "The Federalist Papers" appeared in the *New York Independent Journal* and were widely reprinted. This series, written by Alexander Hamilton, James Madison, and John Jay, has been credited with garnering support for adoption of the new constitutional form of government (Bent, 1969).

Another example from the antebellum period is *Uncle Tom's Cabin,* which we mentioned previously in this chapter. Historians have generally agreed that Harriet Beecher Stowe's classic novel was instrumental in fueling the fires of the abolitionist movement in the antebellum United States and helped turn public opinion against the continuance of slavery in the South.

> Stowe's novel *Uncle Tom's Cabin* originally appeared in serialized form in 1852–1853 in the *National Era,* an abolitionist newspaper. It was the most widely read literature of the time. Within months of publication in book form, sales reached 300,000. The book was the single most important writing in increasing the demand that slavery be abolished. (Dicken-Garcia, 1998, p. 155)

Several other works published about this same time eventually had significant effects on thoughts and actions in the 19th and 20th centuries. These included Karl Marx and Friedrich Engels's *Communist Manifesto,* published in 1848, Charles Darwin's *Origin of Species,* and John Stuart Mill's essay "On Liberty," both published in 1859 (Cowley & Smith, 1939).

After the Civil War, William Tweed and his political machine, the Tammany Ring, took control of municipal government in New York City and eventually stole hundreds of millions of dollars from the city coffers. The stinging caricatures of Thomas Nast, an illustrator for the *New York Times,* were especially powerful in gaining public support that eventually brought down the party boss. The *New York Times's* successful crusade against the Tweed Ring and municipal corruption set the stage for the muckraking era in American journalism that soon followed (Bent, 1969).

The sensational yellow journalism of the newspapers owned by Joseph Pulitzer and William Randolph Hearst in the late 1800s resulted in great increases in circulation (over 1 million) for both newspapers—evidence of powerful media effectiveness if not effects per se. Some historians have claimed that Hearst's cries of Spanish atrocities in Cuba were responsible for turning public opinion and causing the Spanish-American War, especially after a mysterious explosion sank the U.S. battleship *Maine* near Havana.

> Hearst has been credited with inflaming public opinion and ultimately starting the war with jingoistic headlines such as "THE WHOLE COUNTRY THRILLS WITH THE WAR FEVER!" Whether or not he deserved such dubious credit, he certainly believed his newspaper was instrumental in the U.S. intervention and actually published the query "HOW DO YOU LIKE THE JOURNAL'S WAR?" in a box next to the masthead for two days. (Hoff, 1998, p. 247)

Two interesting instances of powerful media effects on public opinion in the 20th century involved a significant shift in the public perception of Standard Oil Company magnate John D. Rockefeller. One of these shifts was the result of work during the "muckraking"[1] years at the turn of the century—the Progressive Era—when a group of magazine journalists wrote series after series of scathing articles to expose a number of social ills. The muckraking journalist Ida Tarbell painted Rockefeller as a ruthless capitalist who used shady methods to gain advantages over his competitors. Tarbell's articles in *McClure's Magazine* soon made the ultrarich Rockefeller one of the most hated figures in America, as evidenced in disparaging news cartoons and articles from the period. Ironically, a few years later, Rockefeller hired public relations expert Ivy Lee to improve his public image. Lee made Rockefeller's philanthropic activities more visible to the press and public and presented him as a kindly old man—grandfatherly and fun loving—and helped change public opinion favorably toward the former robber baron. The media giveth and the media taketh away!

The works of other muckraking journalists during the Progressive era have been credited with arousing public opinion and forcing social changes. The articles of Lincoln Steffens led to a focus on local corruption and a demand for better city government. Leaders in the campaign against patent medicine advertisers were the *Ladies' Home Journal,* which ran strident editorials, and *Collier's Weekly,* which published in 1905 a series of exposés under the title "The Great American Fraud." These articles contributed to a "truth in advertising" campaign that resulted in the establishment of the Federal Trade Commission and better business bureaus. Upton Sinclair's exposure of the horrible conditions of the meatpacking industry in Chicago spawned a government inquiry that led to passage of the Pure Food and Drug Act of 1907, which formed the Food and Drug Administration. The orchestrated media efforts of others precipitated improved industrial relations, child labor laws, workmen's compensation laws, and general social reform measures.

Powerful Effects: Widespread Fright Reactions to Media Content

Fright reactions in the modern sense usually involve the media presentation of monsters or supernatural beings or real-world occurrences that cause fear, especially in children. As will be shown in Chapter 13 on the effects of frightful or disturbing media content, the work of Joanne Cantor is typical of modern-day studies. Her work and that of several of her prominent students have focused on measuring the fright reactions of individual children to scary movies or television programs or to disturbing news reports. These experiments have contributed much to our knowledge about the kind of program content that frightens children at different ages, and about ways for parents to reduce the effects of frightening program content on their children.

The Great Moon Hoax of 1835

The first penny newspaper, New York's *The Sun*, concocted a hoax in 1835 that proved so disturbing and entertaining to its audience that circulation for the paper increased to more than 19,000, the largest of any newspaper in the world at that time. Reporter Richard Adams Locke wrote that a British astronomer had discovered life on the moon while peering through his giant telescope. Readers requested reprints of the articles and other newspapers throughout the world republished the stories. Women in Bible societies talked about traveling to the moon to convert the lunar beings to Christianity. Edgar Allan Poe said the hoax "was, upon the whole, the greatest hit in the way of sensation—of merely popular sensation—ever made by any similar fiction either in America or Europe" (Poe, 1902, p. 134).

Media history provides numerous earlier instances of powerful effects from frightful or disturbing media content at a more societal level. *The New York Herald* on November 9, 1874, included a frightening hoax that caused audiences to react in hysteria. Reporter T. B. Connery felt that animals at the Central Park Zoo were not as secure as they should be, so he concocted a story about their escape. "The list of mutilated, trampled and injured in various ways must reach nearly two hundred persons of all ages, of which, so far as known, about sixty are very serious, and of these latter, three can hardly outlast the night," he wrote. "Twelve of the wild carnivorous beasts are still at large, their lurking places not being known for a certainty . . ." (Hoff, 1998, p. 239). The final paragraph explained that the story was "pure fabrication" and "a huge hoax," but not everyone read the entire article. A number of people took to the streets with their guns to hunt down the killer animals.

The best known historical example of fright reaction from media content is that of the *War of the Worlds* broadcast. On Halloween in 1938, Orson Welles and the Mercury Theatre on the CBS radio network presented an original adaptation of H. G. Wells's science-fiction thriller *The War of the Worlds,* in which beings from Mars invade the world and kill millions with poison gas. Many listeners were enjoying another program when the theatre presentation began, then switched their radio dials to the Mercury Theatre broadcast after the original announcement had been made that the presentation was fantasy. CBS made the announcement four times during the program, but these occurred

> (1) at the beginning of the broadcast (when most people were not listening), (2) before the station break, about 8:35 (by this time, most of those who panicked were no longer listening, but fleeing), (3) right after the station break, and (4) at the end of the broadcast. Moreover, the most terrifying part of the broadcast, it should be remembered, came *before* the station break. Those listeners who failed to hear the original announcement therefore had ample opportunity to become frightened. (Lowery & DeFleur, 1995, p. 51)

Of the several million people who listened to the broadcast, about 1 million were estimated to have been frightened, and some of them actually panicked and left their homes in an effort to escape the sinister invaders (Cantril, Gaudet, & Herzog, 1940).

Widespread panic from the radio broadcast of *War of the Worlds* contributed to early models of powerful media effects.
© *Bettmann/CORBIS*

Evidence for Effects from Persuasive Messages

Throughout history people have been convinced of the power of particular media messages to persuade others. This singular recognition has served to shape the evolution of American media systems because advertising is predicated on the assumption of media effects. Long before the first mass-circulation newspapers appeared, advertising had gained a foothold as a major revenue producer. As the years advanced, advertising profits became the lifeblood of newspapers, magazines, and, later, of commercial radio and television.

Other types of persuasive messages have proven important and effective throughout history. In Europe during the 17th century, despite tight restrictions on printing by the authorities, new ideas and renegade views found their way into print. An intellectual movement known as the Enlightenment created a revolution in thought in 18th-century Europe. Restrictions on the printed word loosened somewhat. A literate middle class emerged, and the works of Voltaire, Jean-Jacques Rousseau, and others had the persuasive power to move people to seek more individual freedoms and rebel against tyranny.

In the 16th and early 17th centuries, noblemen and investors began to recognize the influential power of the printed word. Many books, pamphlets, and tracts promoting colonization in America circulated at this time and throughout the colonial years. Earlier printed works such as *Divers Voyages* (Hakluyt, 1582, 1850), *A Briefe and True Report of the Newfound Land of Virginia* (Hariot, 1590, 1972), *Nova Britannia* (Johnson, 1609), *The Description of New England* (Smith, 1616), *A Relation of Maryland* (1635, Hall & Jameson, 1910), and *Some Account of the Province of Pennsylvania* (Penn, 1681) outlined the advantages of colonization and presented favorable accounts of life in America. If population growth in the New World is any indication, these promotional materials and advertisements produced powerful media effects (Thompson, 1998).

On the American frontier, editors used newspapers to promote their towns and to attract potential settlers. Throughout the 19th century, as pioneers moved west, newspapers appeared in the burgeoning towns and cities. Frontier editors became known as "town boosters" due to the promotional services they performed in an effort to increase population and economic prosperity. Their efforts proved effective. One historian called the California gold rush "one of the most effective promotional campaigns in history" (quoted in Huntzicker, 1998, p. 198). During the second half of the 19th century, the number of newspapers west of the Mississippi River increased from less than 50 to more than 650.

P. T. Barnum and promotion were synonymous in mid-19th-century America. Long before the days of the public relations "fathers," Ivy Lee and Edward Bernays, Barnum mastered the art of successful publicity campaigns. Swedish singer Jenny Lind was unknown in the United States throughout most of the antebellum period, although she was famous in Europe. Barnum issued press releases, wrote letters to the editors, printed pamphlets, and even sponsored a songwriting contest, so that by the time Lind arrived in New York in 1850, more than 40,000 excited fans greeted her at the docks (Hume, 1977; Applegate, 1998). In another example, Barnum was so successful in publicizing his acquisition of Jumbo the Elephant that in the first week of Jumbo's display he earned back the $30,000 it cost him to buy and transport the animal from London to the United States (James, 1982; Applegate, 1998).

During the two world wars of the 20th century, the U.S. government took measures to spread propaganda in support of the war effort. In World War I, President Woodrow Wilson set up the Committee on Public Information (CPI), which engaged in propaganda and censorship activities. The CPI, under the direction of the muckraker George Creel, produced articles, advertisements, press releases, films, and hired speakers to promote the war effort throughout the country. Many of the scholars who served in a similar "public information" effort during World War II later became the founders of modern media effects research.

In the late 1930s, a number of newspapers began vigorous campaigns to encourage traffic safety; as a result, fatalities decreased substantially. An earlier newspaper campaign had successfully promoted a "safe-and-sane" Fourth of July. Newspaper editor James Keeley has been credited with initiating the crusade (Bent, 1969).

> On the evening of July 4, 1899, when he was beside a child gravely ill, the thunder of giant firecrackers outside disturbed her, and he telephoned his office to collect figures from thirty cities on fatalities and accidents that day. The figures showed that the celebration of a national holiday had cost more in suffering and life than the Spanish-American War. The next year the *Tribune,* demanding a "sane Fourth," presented a similar table of statistics, and thereafter other newspapers followed suit, until mortality and casualties were reduced by more than nine-tenths. (p. 220)

Summary

Since the invention of the printing press in 1450, people have acknowledged the potential influence of mass media communication on audiences. The concern for powerful media effects has not been exclusive to society's elite, but has been felt by all strata of society. This concern has influenced lawmakers, shaped public policy, and attracted the interest of scholars.

History is replete with examples of media effects. These include changes that occurred due to the spread of new media technologies, instances of suppression of the press by authorities, instances of public reaction against violent or sexually explicit material, reactions against producers of inflammatory material, and reactions from frightful media content. The many successful publicity and advertising campaigns throughout history attest to the power of media communications to persuade audiences.

▣ NOTE

[1] The journalists were labeled "muckrakers" by President Theodore Roosevelt, who compared them to a character in John Bunyan's book *Pilgrim's Progress*—a man who raked muck or filth and refused to look up from his task.

three

History of the Scientific Study of Media Effects

Tantalized fascination surrounds all efforts to study the effects of mass media.
—Paul F. Lazarsfeld, 1949

If one were to judge from the preceding chapter, effects from media communications would appear to be rather powerful. The reason for this is obvious: History is biased toward recording instances when mediated communications seem to provoke action. Major reactions that can be traced to mediated communication are much easier to locate. Except for the existence of a very detailed personal diary or some other trustworthy personal account, instances of limited media effects are difficult for the historian to identify.[1]

Several late 19th-century studies in psychology and sociology involved research on mass media and presaged the theoretical bases for more sophisticated and numerous studies in the decades to follow, but media effects research emerged categorically in the 20th century. Since 1960, graduate programs in mass communication have sprung to life at major research universities throughout the country, and the study of media effects has quickly matured and diversified. Researchers now search for evidence of media effects in a number of distinct research branches such as persuasion, media violence, sexually explicit material, fright reactions, agenda setting, new media technologies, uses and gratifications, cultivation research, and other areas.

Several communication scholars have offered excellent historical studies of communication (Dennis & Wartella, 1996; Rogers, 1994; Heath & Bryant, 2000). Katz (1980, 1983) examined the media effects research tradition from a conceptual standpoint, offered an interesting analysis of media effects research issues, and suggested significant points of connection among the various theories of media effects.

This chapter relates the history of media effects research. We identify some pioneers and more recent scholars of media effects who contributed significantly to our knowledge of media effects. We discuss the notions of powerful, limited, and varying effects levels. Finally, we offer some suggestions for advancing the knowledge of media effects in the future.

Nineteenth-Century Beginnings

Several 19th- and early 20th-century studies in psychology, sociology, and social psychology involved the examination of particular mass media effects. Some studies were philosophical in nature and offered comments on the suspected influence of mediated communications on audiences and public opinion, rather than isolating particular social effects on mass media audiences in a controlled design or a laboratory setting. The handful of experimental studies conducted usually focused on the measure of very specific physical or psychological effects from media exposure.

We cite these studies for two reasons. Because of their emphasis on mass media and their introduction of ideas that would later become the theoretical bases of particular media effects studies, they should be considered precursors to the mass media effects studies that would arise in the 20th century. Additionally, two of these precursory studies reveal that the models for suspected powerful and limited effects from mass media communications developed almost simultaneously.

Two articles in the *American Journal of Sociology* in the late 19th century illustrate early differing views on the power mediated communications exerted on audiences. They introduced ideas that other social scientists would explore more fully in theoretical formations and controlled experiments during the next century. It is interesting that of these two articles, the "limited effects" view preceded the "powerful effects" view. Jenks (1895) doubted the influence of newspapers of the period on the formation of public opinion, and he proposed that the individual differences of audience members modified the influential power of communications:

> One chief reason, perhaps, of the comparatively small influence of our press is that the people know the fact that the papers are run from motives of personal profits, and that the policy of the paper is largely determined by the amount to which its opinions will affect its sales and advertising. . . . [A]ll of us doubtless have our opinions formed from former prejudices, we ourselves unconsciously selecting the facts and statements that fit into these former prejudices, and thus tend to conform to our own beliefs. . . . It is probably not too much to say that not 25 percent of our adult voting population have deliberately made up an opinion on a public question after anything like a reasonably full and fair study of the facts in the case. Public opinion, then, seems to be a mixture of sense and nonsense, of sentiment, of prejudice, of more or less clearly defined feelings coming from influences of various kinds that have been brought to bear upon the citizens, these influences perhaps being mostly those of sentiment rather than those acting upon the judgment. (p. 160)

Yarros took the opposite view by emphasizing the power of the newspaper as an organ of public opinion; however, he bemoaned the "mendacity, sensationalism, and recklessness" (1899, p. 374) that characterized most of the newspapers of his day. He also regretted that so many editors of the day were so incompetent yet wielded so much power over an unsuspecting public:

> The editor is glad to have the support of authority, but he is not daunted or disturbed at finding recognized authority against his position. The mature opinions of scholars and experts he treats with a flippancy and contempt which the slightest degree of responsibility would render impossible. But the editor is irresponsible. The judicious and competent few may laugh at his ignorance and presumption, but the cheap applause of the many who mistake smartness for wit and loud assertion for knowledge affords abundant compensation. Controversy with an editor is a blunder. He always has the last word, and his space is unlimited. He is adept at dust-throwing, question-begging, and confusing the issue. In private life he may be intellectually and morally insignificant, but his readers are imposed upon by the air of infallibility with which he treats all things, and the assurance with which he assails those who have the audacity to disagree with him. The average newspaper reader easily yields to iteration and bombast. He believes that which is said daily in print by the august and mysterious power behind the editorial "we." His sentiments and notions are formed for him by that power, and he is not even conscious of the fact. (p. 375)

The debate about the power of newspapers to either direct or reflect public opinion, which is the forerunner of the mirror/lamp metaphor of the popular culture debate of the 1950s, as well as an antecedent of the modern-day argument for and against the agenda-setting hypothesis, continues to this day. In the 20th century, articles in the *American Journal of Sociology* and elsewhere kept the debate alive (Angell, 1941; Orton, 1927; Park, 1941; Shepard, 1909).

Several early experimental studies deserve mention as precursors to modern-day media effects investigations, especially in the area of entertainment. These include a study of the effects of music on attention (Titchener, 1898), the effects of music on thoracic breathing (Foster & Gamble, 1906), and a study of musical enjoyment as measured by plethysmographic and pneumographic records of changes in circulation and respiration (Weld, 1912). Another early study, more theoretical than experimental, examined the nature and origin of humor as a mental process and the functions of humor (Kline, 1907).

One of the earliest (perhaps the first) studies of the effects of consumption of media violence on behavior was a doctoral dissertation by Frances Fenton. The partial and summary findings of her study appeared in two issues of the *American Journal of Sociology* in November 1910 and January 1911. Fenton pointed out that the popular notion that newspaper accounts of antisocial activities had suggestive powers on readers was well established prior to her thesis (see Fenton, 1910, pp. 345 and 350 for lists of articles). She defined *suggestion* as

> the process by which ideas, images, impulsive tendencies, or any sort of stimulus, enter from without into the composition of the neural make-up or disposition and, at times more or less in the focus of consciousness, at other

times not in the focus at all, are transformed into activity by the agency of a stimulus which bears an effective though unrecognized relation or similarity to the image or neural set, and in which there is in large part, or wholly, failure to anticipate the results of the suggested act. (pp. 364–365)

Fenton argued "on the basis of the psychology of suggestion" that a direct causal relationship could be assumed between reading newspaper articles on crime and on antisocial activities and subsequent criminal or antisocial acts. In her dissertation, she identified numerous cases in which individuals were known to have committed copycat-type crimes or other antisocial acts after getting ideas from a newspaper article. Due to lack of available space, the journal articles included only summary headings to describe the nature of the cases, but these headings were said to represent

a mass of both direct and indirect evidence of the suggestive influence of the newspaper on antisocial activity gathered from a wide range of territory and from many different sources. (1911, pp. 557–558)

Fenton also measured the amount of such material appearing in several large-circulation newspapers of the "yellow" variety, although she emphasized that

this was undertaken not because the actual amount of antisocial matter in a newspaper is known to bear a direct relation to the growth of crime, or because we have any evidence to show that changes in the two bear a constant relation to one another. (1911, p. 539)

The Notion of Powerful Effects

Because of the historical bias toward chronicling powerful media effects and the concern about media's impact, it should not be surprising that in the early days of scientific effects studies in the 20th century, powerful effects were assumed by many. During World War I, social scientists were concerned about propaganda spread by the military and, after the war, by corporations (in the form of advertising and public relations efforts).

People in the United States (including most social scientists) believed that mass media, especially electronic media such as film and radio, had incredible powers to influence their audiences. The immense power of media messages on unsuspecting audiences was described in colorful ways: Mass media supposedly fired messages like dangerous bullets, or shot messages like strong drugs pushed through hypodermic needles. These descriptions gave rise to the "bullet" or "hypodermic-needle" theory of powerful media effects.

Carey (1996) provided an eloquent summary of the bullet theory:

As the "jazz age" turned into the Great Depression, the fears of propaganda and the media were confirmed by the mass movements in politics and culture typical of that period and by a series of specific and startling events of which Orson Welles' radio broadcast "The War of the Worlds" stood as an archetype. In the standard history, this random assortment of fears, alarms, jeremiads, political pronouncements, and a few pieces of empirical research were collapsed into the "hypodermic-needle model" or "bullet theory" or "model of unlimited effects" of the mass media, for they converged on a common conclusion: The media collectively, but in particularly the newer, illiterate media of radio and film, possessed extraordinary power to shape the beliefs and conduct of ordinary men and women. (p. 22)

Early theorists focused on the phenomenal changes in society from the late 19th to early 20th century and the resulting influences on the masses. Blumer (1951), noting the importance of mass behavior, wrote that due to urbanization and industrialization of the early 20th century,

mass behaviour has emerged in increasing magnitude and importance. This is due primarily to the operation of factors which have detached people from their local cultures and local group settings. Migrations, changes of residence, newspapers, motion pictures, the radio, education—all have operated to detach individuals from customary moorings and thrust them into a wider world. In the face of this world, individuals have had to make adjustments on the basis of largely unaided selections. The convergence of their selection has made the mass a potent influence. At times its behaviour comes to approximate that of a crowd, especially under conditions of excitement. At such times it is likely to be influenced by excited appeals as these appear in the press or over the radio—appeals that play upon primitive impulses, antipathies and traditional hatreds.[2] (pp. 187–188)

Early books were written with an underlying acceptance of the bullet or hypodermic-needle theories;[3] that is, the immense power of mass communication messages on their audiences. These included Walter Lippmann's *Public Opinion* (1922), Harold Lasswell's *Propaganda Technique in the World War* (1927), and G. G. Bruntz's *Allied Propaganda and the Collapse of the German Empire in 1918* (1938). The bullet theory served as the basis for a series of studies sponsored by the Payne Fund from 1929–1932. These studies sought to determine the influence of the motion picture on children and found that

as an instrument of education it has unusual power to impart information, to influence specific attitudes toward objects of social value, to affect emotions either in gross or in microscopic proportions, to affect health in a minor degree through sleep disturbance, and to affect profoundly the patterns of conduct of children. (Charters, 1950, p. 406)

One media historian called journalist Walter Lippmann's *Public Opinion* "the originating book in the modern history of communication research"[4] (Carey, 1996, p. 28). Another prominent media scholar viewed it as a founding work for agenda-setting research (Rogers, 1994). In this classic work, Lippmann called upon his experiences with propaganda during World War I. The book became "a key intellectual influence in creating public apprehension about the role of propaganda in a democratic society" (Rogers, 1994, p. 236). Lippmann emphasized the role of the news media in influencing the perceptions of audiences about issues of importance.

The reaction of children to movies was the focus of the Payne Fund studies of the late 1920s and early 1930s. © *Bettmann/CORBIS*

The Notion of Limited Media Effects

The hypodermic-needle theory remained dominant until after the Depression, when empirical studies began to indicate that effects from mass media were not as powerful as originally thought. Rather than a society of fragmented individuals receiving all-powerful messages from mass media, the view shifted to one of a society of individuals who interacted within groups and thus limited the effects of media messages. Studies by Paul Lazarsfeld at Columbia University's Bureau of Applied Social Research and by other social scientists such as Carl Hovland working for the U.S. War Department, indicated that mass media had only limited effects on individuals in their audiences (Carey, 1996).

> What was also discovered, in the standard rendition, was that individuals, the members of the audience, were protected from the deleterious possibilities inherent in the mass media by a group of predispositional or mediating factors. . . . Some individuals (a few) under some circumstances (rare) were directly affected by the mass media. Otherwise, media propaganda and mass culture were held at bay by an invisible shield erected by a universally resistant psyche and a universally present network of social groups. (Carey, 1996, p. 23)

The limited effects model became thoroughly established in 1960 with the publication of Joseph Klapper's *The Effects of Mass Communication*. This classic work, based on his doctoral dissertation at Columbia University, reviewed hundreds of media effects studies from the 1920s through the 1950s and attempted to make blanket generalizations on the subject of mass media effects. Klapper called for a new approach to research in the field, a "phenomenistic approach," which emphasized particular factors that limited the effects of mass media messages on individuals.

> In a well-known line, interest shifted from what it was that the media did to people toward what it was people did with the media. This was then a shift in interest and attention from the source to the receiver and a relocation of the point of power in the process: The audience controlled the producers. Except for some special problems (violence and pornography are the best-known examples) and some special groups (principally children), interest in direct effects and propaganda withered away. (Carey, 1996, pp. 23–24)

Effects of Varying Levels

Researchers began to focus experiments on the different reactions of individuals to the same media presentations. Rather than viewing audiences as passive victims who could be manipulated by mass media messages, scholars soon realized that individual differences and environmental factors were important moderators in the process of mass media effects.

> Experiments in behaviorism, motivation, persuasion, and conditioning led researchers to examine the processes of habit formation and learning. Differences among individual personality traits and psychological organization were found to be affected by the social environment in which people were raised. Moreover, studies in human perception showed that an individual's values, needs, beliefs, and attitudes were instrumental in determining how stimuli are selected from the environment and the way meaning is attributed to those stimuli within an individual's frame of reference. (Heath & Bryant, 2000, p. 347)

Studies with theoretical bases in psychology and sociology found that audience members selectively attended to media messages, depending upon their predispositions, interests, attitudes, social category, and a number of other factors. Similar variables were found to influence an individual's perception of a media message and what the person remembered about the message. These concepts were later defined as selective exposure, selective perception, selective retention, and the social categories perspective, which posits that people with similar demographic characteristics react similarly to media messages.

In the decades following the 1960s, mass media research thrived as the field of mass communication became firmly established at research universities throughout the nation. Certain new theories and research findings did not fit neatly into the limited effects paradigm; therefore, the history was amended to include new studies that indicated moderate to powerful media effects were indeed possible (Ball-Rokeach, Rokeach, & Grube, 1984a, 1984b; Blumler & McLeod, 1974; Maccoby & Farquhar, 1975; Mendelsohn, 1973; Noelle-Neumann, 1973).

Many research studies through the years have indicated different levels of media effects. From the beginning, overwhelming evidence accumulated for *significant* effects from media communications on audiences, based for the most part upon scientific methods and traditional statistical models. The recounting of the history makes apparent an immediate need for clarifications, standardizations, and additional research in the field of mass media effects (Thompson & Bryant, 2000).

Without standard lines of demarcation, media effects researchers have often made qualitative judgment calls about the power of effects. Based upon these qualitative verdicts, what emerges is a history of research that states conclusively that, yes, various kinds of mass media effects do occur, but the levels of influence have been assumed to vary from limited to rather powerful; furthermore, researchers have recognized this—mostly they have argued this—from the beginning.

The intense debate about the power or limits of media effects still rages to this day, but knowledge in the field continues to advance. For example, as is delineated in subsequent chapters, we have discovered that media effects may be cognitive (affecting thoughts or learning), behavioral (affecting behavior), or affective (affecting attitudes and emotions). Effects may be either direct or indirect, and they may be short term, long term, or delayed. They may be self-contained or cumulative. We have learned much about individual differences, psychological factors, environmental factors, and social group characteristics that cause audience members to perceive and react to media messages in specific ways. Still, much remains to be discovered.

Some Pioneers in Media Effects Research

In the years following World War I, innovative scholars from various disciplines at several particular institutions of learning conducted pioneering studies to examine the fledgling domain of scientific research on the effects of mass communication. These scholars, who came from disciplines outside journalism or mass communication, hailed principally from the University of Chicago, Columbia University, and Yale University. They included (among a number of others) the following: Carl Hovland, an experimental psychologist from Yale University; Paul F. Lazarsfeld, a sociologist at Columbia University; Harold Lasswell, a political scientist at the University of Chicago and, later, Yale University; Kurt Lewin, a social psychologist at the University of Iowa and, later, MIT; Samuel A. Stouffer, a sociologist from the University of Chicago; and Douglas Waples, a "professor of researches in reading" (Waples, 1942, p. xi) at the University of Chicago.[5] The importance of the first four of these scholars to the history of mass communication research has been firmly established by Wilbur

Schramm prior to his death in 1987 (Rogers & Chaffee, 1997) and reiterated by Rogers (1994), and for this reason alone we greatly condense our discussion of them. We concentrate more on the final two scholars who have not received much recognition in either the standard or other revised versions of communications history, even though they made significant contributions to the media effects tradition.

Carl Hovland

Carl Hovland studied the effects of training films on the attitudes of American soldiers during World War II (Hovland, Lumsdaine, & Sheffield, 1949), and later directed experimental research that explored media effects on attitude change.[6] The tight design of the experiments conducted by Hovland became the model for much future research in media effects. Wilbur Schramm, a principle "mover and shaker" of mass communication research in the United States, said that Hovland's body of research from 1945 to 1961 constituted "the largest single contribution . . . to this field any man has made" (Schramm, 1997, p. 104).

Carl Hovland. *Courtesy of Katharine Walvick*

Paul Lazarsfeld

Paul F. Lazarsfeld earned a PhD in mathematics, but his diverse research interests included social psychology, sociology, and mass communication. Lazarsfeld and his research institute at Columbia University pioneered research in the effects of radio and introduced the notion that interpersonal communication was an important moderating factor in certain mass media effects. In the 1940s Lazarsfeld and his colleagues examined the influences of mass media on public opinion during a presidential campaign. They found that most people were influenced primarily through interpersonal contacts rather than by what they read in newspapers and magazines or heard on the radio, although those media were found to have some influence in and of themselves.[7] Particular individuals whom the researchers called "opinion leaders," who were often heavy users of mass media, were found to pass along information to others in the community who looked to them for guidance. This finding led to establishment of a two-step flow model of mass communication, in which media effects were perceived as being modified by interpersonal communication about those media messages. Subsequent research expanded the two-step flow model into one of multistep flow:

> Later studies concluded that the influence of opinion leaders was not always "downward," as in the interpretation of news events for a less informed audience. Opinion leaders were found to communicate "upward" to the media gatekeepers (i.e., newspaper editors and radio programmers) as well as share information "sideways" with other opinion leaders. Further studies of

interpersonal communication showed that an individual's personal identification with an organization, religion, or other social group has a strong influence on the type of media content selected. . . . Group norms apparently provide a type of "social reality" check built on similar and shared beliefs, attitudes, opinions, and concerns that tend to form barriers against mediated messages contrary to the group's point of view. Likewise, mediated messages in agreement with the group or provided by the group are usually attended to and utilized to reinforce the status quo. (Heath & Bryant, 2000, pp. 349–350)

Harold Lasswell

Harold D. Lasswell made many contributions to the study of media effects, the most notable being his five-question model—"Who says what in which channel to whom with what effects?" (Lasswell, 1948)—his studies of propaganda, and his identification of three important functions that mass communications serve in society: surveillance of the environment, correlation of society's response to events in the environment, and transmission of the cultural heritage.[8] Rogers (1994) listed five major contributions that he believed Lasswell made to communication study:

1. His five-question model of communication led to the emphasis in communication study on determining effects. Lasswell's contemporary, Paul F. Lazarsfeld, did even more to crystallize this focus on communication effects.

2. He pioneered in content analysis methods, virtually inventing the methodology of qualitative and quantitative measurement of communication messages (propaganda messages and newspaper editorials, for example).

3. His study of political and wartime propaganda represented an important early type of communication study. The word *propaganda* later gained a negative connotation and is not used much today, although there is even more political propaganda. Propaganda analysis has been absorbed into the general body of communication research.

4. He introduced Freudian psychoanalytic theory to the social sciences in America. Lasswell integrated Freudian theory with political analysis, as in his psychoanalytic study of political leaders. He applied Freud's id-ego-superego via content analysis to political science problems. In essence, he utilized intra-individual Freudian theory at the societal level.

5. He helped create the policy sciences, an interdisciplinary movement to integrate social science knowledge with public action. The social sciences, however, generally resisted this attempt at integration and application to public policy problems (pp. 232–233).

Kurt Lewin

Social psychologist Kurt Lewin instituted pioneering studies in the dynamics of group communication. While at the University of Iowa, he conducted a famous group of communication experiments to explore the differences in persuasive power on audiences in different group conditions. In the best known of these experiments, "the sweetbreads study," groups of housewives reluctant to serve glandular meats to their families learned about the benefits of beef hearts, thymus (sweetbreads), liver, and kidneys by either attending a lecture or a discussion group. The discussion group situation proved far more effective in changing the behavior of the housewives (making them more likely to serve glandular meats to their families).

According to Rogers, Lewin's "greatest academic influence was through the brilliant students whom he trained" (1994, p. 354). One of his students, Leon Festinger, directed a study to identify communication network links among married students living in a set of apartments (Festinger, Schachter, & Bach, 1950). Later, Festinger advanced his famous theory of cognitive dissonance, which proposes that whenever an individual's attitudes and actions are in conflict, the person will adjust cognitions in an attempt to resolve the conflict.[9]

Samuel Stouffer

Paul Lazarsfeld dedicated to Stouffer his report of the Columbia University voting studies, "which profited from his skillful procedures of survey analysis" (1962, p. xxxi). He also cited Stouffer's influence on Carl Hovland's studies on attitudes and communications conducted at Yale University after World War II. Stouffer pioneered the use of empirical research, especially survey research, for social enquiries, and the use of precise statistical methods. He directed research for the Division of Information and Education of the United States Army during World War II.

After the war, Stouffer conducted several studies of communications media, but these studies deal more with the effectiveness of media and often are not labeled as effects studies.[10] His importance to the history of media effects research lies in his empirical expertise, his influence on early communication researchers such as Hovland and Lazarsfeld, and his insistence that communication research adhere to strict empirical standards. In a 1942 chapter called "A Sociologist Takes a Look at Communications Research," Stouffer applauded the careful methods of the investigation by Peterson and Thurstone (1933), one of the famous Payne Fund studies that examined the effects of movies on children.

> A classic example of a complete experimental study in communications research was Thurstone and Peterson's study of the effects of specific motion pictures on social attitudes. . . . Subsequently there have been several other studies more or less similar to Thurstone's and Peterson's, but it is surprising that there have not been more. . . . This experiment demonstrated that a single movie has measurable and relatively lasting effects on children—but did anybody doubt that? Why spend a lot of money and time to demonstrate the obvious? There are two answers to this. In the first place, Thurstone showed that the direction of the effect (whether toward or against a given set of values) was not always predictable on a common-sense basis. A film glorifying a gambler had the unpredicted effect of making children feel more than ever that gambling was an evil. In the second place, Thurstone and Peterson were able to prove that effects of single films lasted over

a long period of time and also that certain combinations of films had mutually reinforcing effects. It is true that they left hundreds of interesting questions unanswered. What types of children were affected most? What types of scenes within a given picture had the most effect? Were there differences in the kind of effect which would require a multidimensional rather than unidimensional attitude continuum for description? Such questions call for further research, and the Thurstone-Peterson method shows a way of answering them. (pp. 138–141)

Stouffer emphasized the importance of controlling for variables such as educational status, age, or other differences among audiences that could account for differences between the groups tested—variables that might make a difference in media effects. When the researcher does not control for confounding variables, he warned, "we can only hope and pray that we are controlling all the factors which would tend to differentiate" (p. 139) the control and experimental groups.

Finally, Stouffer's empirical expertise and prescience allowed him to identify problems in 1942 that continue to plague communication researchers in the 21st century—namely, the accurate measure of cumulative effects of mass media communications:

> It is a difficult matter to design an experiment which will measure the cumulative effect of, say, a year's exposure to a given medium of communication. . . . The difficulty of evaluating cumulative effects of many small stimuli in the field of communications is all the more serious because there is good basis for the belief that it is in just this way that communications have their principal effect. One soft-drink ad may not invite the pause that refreshes, but hundreds, and even thousands of them, confronting the consumer in as many different social situations evidently help sell the product. (pp. 141–142)

Douglas Waples

Douglas Waples was a professor in the Graduate Library School at the University of Chicago. In 1940, at the same time that Lazarsfeld was conducting radio studies at Columbia University, Waples, Bernard Berelson, and Franklyn Bradshaw published their work on the effects of print media, *What Reading Does to People*. The work revealed much about print media effects on attitude change.

> The studies have repeatedly shown that reading can change attitudes. They have also shown that certain reader traits and certain content elements will modify the effect of the reading. For example, the effects are modified by differences in what the readers already know about the subject. The less the reader knows about the complexities of and objections to issues discussed in the text, the greater the change in attitude will be. (pp. 108–109)

More significantly, Waples offered the earliest published version of the most famous statement about the process of communication in the history of effects research, and he added an important phrase that the later versions neglected. "Who says what in which channel to whom with what effect?" (Lasswell, 1948,

p. 37) has always been credited to Lasswell. Joseph Klapper (1960) indicated the statement originated with Lasswell in 1946 (Smith, Lasswell, & Casey, 1946), but an article by Waples in the *American Journal of Sociology* in 1942 begins with the following quotation: *"Who* communicates *what* to *whom* by *what medium,* under *what conditions,* and with *what effects?"* (p. 907). Rogers (1994) credited the "who says what" statement to Lasswell, spoken during a Rockefeller Communication Seminar in 1940, a conference also attended by Waples, but the quote is not recorded in the rather detailed conference papers.[11] Lerner and Nelson (1977) said that Lasswell's *Propaganda Technique in the World War* "set forth the dominant paradigm" (p. 1) of the five-question line, but nothing resembling the "who says what" statement appears in that text. As for the Waples quote, whether he was quoting Lasswell, himself, or someone else is unclear; neither scholar provided a citation for the words, either in 1942 or 1948.

The identity of the speaker is less important than the substance of the Waples quote; namely, the inclusion of the "under what conditions" phrase. This phrase, absent from any of the published Lasswell versions, adds a sophistication to the process that is essential to the sorting out of media effects at their various levels. Waples wrote the following after the quote:

> Reliable answers to this complex question at regular time intervals would greatly clarify the process of social change via communications and would simplify predictions of impending changes. (1942, p. 907)

Wilbur Schramm

Though Schramm did not specialize exclusively in media effects (one of his principal areas of interest was in international communication and the role of mass communication in developing third-world nations), his importance must not be overlooked due to his role as consolidator and legitimizer of mass communication study—including media effects.

> Schramm was the first professor of communication so-designated; his was the first communication research institute and the first doctoral program awarding degrees in communication; and Schramm presided over the first academic unit (a "division") of communication in the world. (Rogers & Chaffee, 1997, p. 7)

Schramm initiated the first PhD program in mass communication in 1943, when he served as director of the journalism school at the University of Iowa. Three years later, he had founded the Bureau of Audience Research at Iowa, one of several communication research institutes that sprang to life during the 1940s and 1950s. These institutes were patterned somewhat after Lazarsfeld's Bureau of Applied Social Research at Columbia.

Bernard Berelson

Bernard Berelson, another pioneer in media effects research, was a colleague of Waples at the University of Chicago, where Berelson served as dean of the Library School, and later a colleague of Lazarsfeld's at Columbia University and the Bureau for Applied Social Research. He coauthored with Lazarsfeld the classic voting study, *The People's Choice.*

Berelson was perhaps the first researcher to attempt to make umbrella generalizations about mass communication effects when he suggested the following formulation for research. His concern was for the influence of communication effects on public opinion, rather than media effects overall, yet his formulation could be applied to other research in media effects:

> Some kinds of *communication* on some kinds of *issues,* brought to the attention of some kinds of *people* under some kinds of *conditions,* have some kinds of *effects.* This formulation identifies five central factors (or rather groups of factors) which are involved in the process, and it is the interrelationship of these variables which represents the subject matter of theory in this field. At present, students can fill out only part of the total picture—a small part—but the development of major variables and the formulation of hypotheses and generalizations concerning them are steps in the right direction. (1948, p. 172)

Several years later Berelson noted the many complex findings that had emerged from research studies that would have to be considered in the development of any overarching theory of mass communication effects:

> The effects of communication are many and diverse. They may be short-range or long-run. They may be manifest or latent. They may be strong or weak. They may derive from any number of aspects of the communication content. They may be considered as psychological or political or economic or sociological. They may operate upon opinions, values, information levels, skills, taste, behavior. . . . Because of the variety and the complexity of the effects of communications, this topic probably represents the most neglected area in communication research. (Berelson & Janowitz, 1950, p. 395)

Joseph Klapper

Ten years later, one of Lazarsfeld's students, Joseph Klapper, produced his still valuable and classic work, *The Effects of Mass Communication* (1960). In this book, Klapper offered several overarching generalizations "in their bare bones" (p. 7) about the effects of mass media messages. Unfortunately, through the course of history, the ideas in Klapper's book have been greatly reduced to a "limited effects" notion that encouraged a "phenomenistic approach" that would identify moderating factors involved in effects, even though Klapper warned repeatedly about the grave danger in "the tendency to go overboard in blindly minimizing the effects and potentialities of mass communications" (p. 252).

Klapper's generalizations have usually been overlooked or quoted only in partial form. In most cases, only the first two generalizations have been reproduced—the two that, not surprisingly, emphasize the many studies that show limited or indirect effects of media communications. Generalizations 3, 4, and 5—those that emphasize that direct effects from media communications are indeed possible—have been ignored by the standard history. For this reason, we include all five generalizations in our sidebar.

Klapper's Generalizations

1. Mass communication *ordinarily* does not serve as a necessary and sufficient cause of audience effects, but rather functions among and through a nexus of mediating factors and influences.

2. These mediating factors are such that they typically render mass communication a contributory agent, but not the sole cause, in a process of reinforcing the existing conditions. Regardless of the condition in question—be it the vote intentions of audience members, their tendency toward or away from delinquent behavior, or their general orientation toward life and its problems—and regardless of whether the effect in question be social or individual, the media are more likely to reinforce than to change.

3. On such occasions as mass communication does function in the service of change, one of two conditions is likely to exist. Either:

   a. The mediating factors will be found to be inoperative and the effect of the media will be found to be direct; or

   b. The mediating factors, which normally favor reinforcement, will be found to be impelling toward change.

4. There are certain residual situations in which mass communication seems to produce direct effects, or directly and of itself to serve certain psychophysical functions.

5. The efficacy of mass communication, either as a contributory agent or as an agent of direct effect, is affected by various aspects of the media and communications themselves or of the communication situation, including, for example, aspects of textual organization, the nature of the source and medium, the existing climate of public opinion, and the like.

Albert Bandura

In the 1970s, the decade following the appearance of Klapper's (1960) book, psychological theories arose that had strong implications for the understanding of mass media effects. The theories of Albert Bandura (1973, 1991)—social learning theory and, later, social cognitive theory—opened up alternative lines of inquiry for communication researchers.[12] Rather than focus primarily on mass communication's effects upon attitude change, scholars in the 1970s and beyond began for the most part to examine more complex behavioral responses, changes in cognitive patterns, and media effects on learning and knowledge (Becker, McCombs, & McLeod, 1975; Chaffee, 1977; Clarke & Kline, 1974). Many of the most important of these findings are discussed throughout the remainder of this text.

Albert Bandura. © *Albert Bandura*

Social learning theory explains how viewers learn and model behaviors they see in the mass media, based upon their environmental and cognitive predispositions. It began to serve as the basis for a bevy of research that examined the effects, especially among children, of viewing violence on film and television, the latter medium fast coming into dominance.

The Legacy of the Pioneers

In the years since the 1960s, as the field of mass communication research continued to blossom and attract more scholars interested specifically in media effects, other areas of media effects research were either born or developed into maturity. These included cultivation analysis and other sociological procedures that attempt to measure the cumulative effects of mass communication, research to examine the agenda-setting hypothesis that mass media are responsible for bringing public awareness to particular issues, research to explore the reasons why audience members used particular mass media, and the many other areas of media effects.

Future of Effects Research

The challenges for media effects researchers of the 21st century are great, but they will eventually be met if scholars continue to approach the problems with "tantalized fascination" (Lazarsfeld, 1949, p. 1). First and foremost, if we are to continue to describe media effects as either powerful, moderate, or limited, we must come up with standard, empirical lines of demarcation to separate the levels. In his influential article on "The Myth of Massive Media Impact," McGuire (1986) based his definition of small effects sizes on the percentage of variance accounted for by several dependent variables of effects; certainly statistical effect sizes would be one basis for delineating the standards. McGuire argued that powerful media effects were exaggerated, based on review of a handful of important studies in a variety of areas.

> A formidable proportion of the published studies (and presumably an even higher proportion of the unpublished studies) have failed to show overall effects sizable enough even to reach the conventionally accepted .05 level of statistical significance. Some respectable studies in several of the dozen impact areas reviewed . . . do have impacts significant at the .05 level, but even these tend to have very small effect sizes, accounting for no more than 2 or 3% of the variance in dependent variables. . . . (p. 177)

Although we respect the forcefulness of McGuire's argument, we must point out that a number of studies have shown media effects significant at not only the .05 level, but at the .01 and the .001 level and beyond, and with effects sizes that account for substantial amounts of the variance (Bryant & Zillmann, 1994). Moreover, meta-analyses (statistical studies that make generalizations about effects by examining and comparing findings from many different completed research studies) reveal relatively robust effects sizes within entire genres of media effects investigations and more modest effect sizes associated with other genres (Preiss et al., 2007). Other studies, although recording effects in the small-to-moderate range, gain significance when one considers the vast sizes of media audiences (Andison, 1977; Wood, Wong, & Chachere, 1991). Neither these studies nor their robust effects are "mythical," but in order to classify them as "powerful" effects, a precise classification schema must first be established.

In another example, Hovland (1959) described the divergence in results from correlational studies and experimental studies on attitude change from exposure to mass communication in simple terms of *percentages of people found to be affected.* This represents another method that could be used to classify the appropriate types of studies into the various levels.

> Lazarsfeld, Berelson, and Gaudet estimate that the political positions of only about 5 percent of their respondents were changed by the election campaign, and they are inclined to attribute even this small amount of change more to personal influence than to the mass media. . . . Research using experimental procedures, on the other hand, indicates the possibility of considerable modifiability of attitudes through exposure to communication. In both Klapper's survey (1949) and in my chapter in the *Handbook of Social Psychology* (Hovland, 1954) a number of experimental studies are discussed in which the opinions of a third to a half or more of the audience are changed. (p. 440)

Another challenge for media effects researchers will be to identify the circumstances, conditions, or variables that account for media effects at all their various levels and forms and offer generalizations—perhaps very complex ones, even typologies of effects—that will explain the complex phenomenon of mass media effects. These are the theoretical generalizations that will advance understanding in the field of media effects. To advance such theories, communication scholars will need to use either quantitative meta-analysis techniques (when feasible) or more qualitative, intensive examination of studies in the different areas of effects research (such as that employed by Klapper), grouping the studies on the basis of their effects levels (based upon the to-be-established schema or on other theoretical criteria).

In 1960 Klapper insisted that the time for media effects generalizations had arrived. Fifty-plus years after Klapper's insistence, we can say that we know much more about the effects of media communications, but precise, blanket generalizations remain elusive, owing to the complex nature of the subject. One obvious omission in the effects literature to date is the conspicuous absence of a "no-effects model." Academic journals are severely biased toward publishing studies that show the occurrence of statistically significant media effects. Studies that find no significant effects do not normally appear—a 1944 study by Mott was a notable exception. Most studies examine a number of factors or variables, and statistically significant relationships are usually found for some but not others. No scholar has yet sifted through the thousands of effects studies to identify those particular variables or instances—reported in many studies—when no noticeable effects occurred. The statistically significant results are the ones that attract the most attention, yet the instances when media effects do not occur should be of as much interest to communication scholars as the instances when effects do occur—the no-effects scenario is, thus far, a missing piece of the effects puzzle.[13]

In recent years, a research technique known as meta-analysis has been useful in making generalizations about the different genres of media effects. For example, Paik and Comstock (1994) conducted a major review of studies on the effects of television violence and produced a useful meta-analysis by partitioning variables (e.g., viewer attributes and types of antisocial behavior) in their research design. Meta-analysis involves finding common statistical ground among a large number of same-genre studies and then offering summary findings based on all the available evidence. Throughout this book, we include discoveries from recent meta-analyses in the various types of effects research.

Meta-analyses may be the best hope of producing blanket generalizations similar to those proposed by Klapper. If such generalizations are indeed possible, they would need to sufficiently explain the circumstances and conditions necessary for powerful or limited, direct or indirect, short-term or long-term, cumulative, cognitive, affective, or behavioral effects from mass media communications and, if possible, the factors present in a no-effects scenario. The enormity of the task stands apparent when one realizes that Klapper (1960) seems to be the only scholar in the history of media effects research who has even attempted to make such blanket generalizations on media effects across the board. Klapper offered a good starting point for those scholars of the 21st century brave enough to tackle the job of sorting through and studying the thousands of media effects studies that have been conducted through the years.

Klapper (1960) emphasized that he was "in no way committed to these particular generalizations, let alone to the exact form in which they here appear" (p. 9). He hoped that additional thought and research on the subject would "modify and perhaps annihilate the schema," and pointed out that he was "far less concerned with insuring the viability of these generalizations" than with "indicating that the time for generalization is at hand" (p. 9). "For certainly these particular generalizations do not usher in the millennium. They are imperfect and underdeveloped, they are inadequate in scope, and in some senses they are dangerous" (p. 251). It seems that, contrary to Klapper's view, his generalizations *do* usher us into the millennium. More than 50 years after Klapper insisted that generalizations needed to be made, the challenge remains unmet. It is our hope that this text will pique the interest of future media effects scholars who will meet the challenge of developing the long-awaited, overarching theory of media effects.

Summary

Several late 19th-century studies in psychology and sociology involved research on mass media and presaged the theoretical bases for more sophisticated and numerous studies in the decades to follow, but media effects research emerged categorically in the 20th century.

One of the earliest (perhaps the first) studies of the effects of consumption of media violence on behavior was a doctoral dissertation by Frances Fenton. The partial and summary findings of her study appeared in two issues of the *American Journal of Sociology* in November 1910 and January 1911. Fenton pointed out that the popular notion that newspaper accounts of antisocial activities had suggestive powers on readers was well established prior to her thesis.

During the early years of scientific effects studies in the 20th century, powerful effects were assumed by many. The powerful impact of media messages on audiences was likened to firing a bullet or injecting a drug, which gave rise to the bullet theory or hypodermic needle theory of mass communication.

The hypodermic-needle theory remained dominant until after the Depression, when empirical studies began to indicate that effects from mass media were not as powerful as originally thought. Rather than a society of fragmented individuals receiving all-powerful messages from mass media, the view shifted to one of a society of individuals who interacted within groups and thus limited the effects of media messages. Studies by Paul Lazarsfeld at Columbia University's Bureau of Applied Social Research and by other social scientists such as Carl Hovland working for the U.S. War Department, indicated that mass media had only limited effects on individuals in their audiences.

The limited effects model became thoroughly established in 1960 with the publication of Joseph Klapper's *The Effects of Mass Communication*. Klapper made blanket generalizations about media effects, but interestingly, only two mentioned indirect effects.

Researchers began to focus experiments on the different reactions of individuals to the same media presentations. Rather than viewing audiences as passive victims who could be manipulated by mass media messages, scholars soon realized that individual differences and environmental factors were important moderators in the process of mass media effects.

Certain new theories and research findings did not fit neatly into the limited effects paradigm; therefore, the history was amended to include new studies that indicated moderate to powerful media effects were indeed possible. From the beginning, overwhelming evidence accumulated for *significant* effects from media communications on audiences, based for the most part upon scientific methods and traditional statistical models.

Without standard lines of demarcation, media effects researchers have often made qualitative judgment calls about the power of effects. The intense debate about the power or limits of media effects still rages to this day, but knowledge in the field continues to advance.

Important scholars in the area of media effects include Carl Hovland, Paul F. Lazarsfeld, Harold Lasswell, Kurt Lewin, Samuel Stouffer, Douglas Waples, Wilbur Schramm, Bernard Berelson, Joseph Klapper, and Albert Bandura.

If we are to continue to describe media effects as either powerful, moderate, or limited, we must come up with standard, empirical lines of demarcation to separate the levels. This could be based upon the percentage of variance accounted for by several dependent variables, percentages of people affected, or some other measure.

▓ NOTES

[1] Difficult but not impossible: F. L. Mott (1944) conducted a historical study and found "no correlation, positive or negative, between the support of a majority of newspapers during a campaign and success at the polls" (p. 356). Another instance of limited effects that could be argued is indicated by Isaiah Thomas's *History of Printing*, which offered state-by-state counts on the number of newspapers for and against ratification of the Constitution. In some cases, newspapers seemed to have little or no effect upon the outcome of the vote. In Delaware, for example, no newspapers favored adoption and two opposed adoption, yet Delaware was the first state to adopt the Constitution—and by unanimous vote at its convention.

[2] Blumer's statement, originally written in 1939, was later called by Denis McQuail (1972/1969) "the most influential single statement of the concept of the mass, looked at from the perspective of the sociology of collective behaviour" (p. 100).

[3] None used these terms, however. Many have attributed the "hypodermic needle" phrase to Lasswell, but a re-reading of Lasswell's works revealed he used no such phrase (Chaffee & Hochheimer, 1985).

[4] Carey wrote: "Lippmann, in fact, redefined the problem of the media from one of morals, politics, and freedom to one of psychology and epistemology. He established the tradition of propaganda analysis and simultaneously, by framing the problem not as one of normative political theory but as one of human psychology, opened up the tradition of effects analysis that was to dominate the literature less than two decades after the publication of *Public Opinion*" (Carey, 1996, p. 30).

[5] Rogers (1994) offers information about many others who made important contributions to communication study, including mass media effects research. The student is encouraged to refer to this work.

[6] It should be recalled that Hovland's U.S. Army studies reportedly showed limited media effects; however, the limits of the effects extended only to attitude change—the films proved to have much stronger effects on learning; that is, the soldiers learned a great deal from the films.

[7] More recent findings (Blumler & McLeod, 1974; McLeod & McDonald, 1985; Ranney, 1983) suggest that the influence of mass media may be more powerful in the political communication process than the findings of *The People's Choice* indicated.

[8] Wright (1960) added "entertainment" as another important function of mass media.

[9] Rogers (1994, p. 352) offered this example of cognitive dissonance: "One effect of dissonance is for an individual to avoid exposure to conflicting messages. For example, once an individual purchases a new car, that individual tends to avoid advertisements for competing makes of cars."

[10] One explored the different advantages of radio and newspaper as news sources, and identified preferences for one or the other among various classes and groups of people. Another examined the effect that radio was having on newspaper circulation. Both were included in Lazarsfeld's *Radio and the Printed Page* (1940).

[11] The conference proceedings are included in the papers of Lyman Bryson at the Library of Congress (Rockefeller Foundation, "Needed Research in Communication," "Public Opinion and the Emergency," and "Memorandum on Communications Conference," U.S. Library of Congress: Papers of Lyman Bryson, Box 18, October 17, 1940, November 1, 1940, and January 18, 1941).

[12] Bandura began studying children and teens and the learning of antisocial behavior by viewing models' actions on films or on television during the 1960s (e.g., Bandura, 1965b; Bandura, Ross, & Ross, 1963a; Bandura & Walters, 1963).

[13] Some of the works of Cantor and her associates (Cantor, Sparks & Hoffner, 1988; Cantor & Wilson, 1984) have explored ways in which effects may be diminished, but a "no effects" model has never been advanced.

Theory and Concepts

chapter four

Social Cognitive Theory

*Social cognitive theory embraces an interactional model of causation
in which environmental events, personal factors, and behavior
all operate as interacting determinants of each other.*
—Albert Bandura, 1986

For many years, psychologists, especially social psychologists, have advanced various theories about why people behave the ways that they do. Some say behavior is based upon a person's motivations. Others propose that behavior is a response to external stimuli and subsequent reinforcements. Still others point out that people react differently in different situations, and these scholars think that the *interaction* between a person and a situation produces a particular behavior.

It may seem strange that such issues from social and behavioral psychology would appear in a media effects textbook. Yet, as subsequent chapters will reveal, the study of effects of mediated communication often is a specialization in the social science research domains of communication, psychology, anthropology, and sociology.

One theory undergirds a great deal of the media effects literature. It serves as at least a portion of the theoretical basis for several other media effects theories, including those in the critical and highly scrutinized area of media violence. For this reason, an acquaintance with this important theory, called *social cognitive theory,* is essential for a basic comprehension of media effects.

Social cognitive theory provides a framework that allows us to analyze the human cognitions (or mental functions) that produce certain behaviors. Social cognitive theory explains human thought and actions as a process of *triadic reciprocal causation* (Bandura, 1994). This means that thought and behavior are determined by three different factors that interact and influence each other with variable strength, at the same time or at different times: (1) behavior, (2) personal characteristics such as cognitive and biological qualities (e.g., IQ, gender, height, or race), and (3) environmental factors or events.

Albert Bandura's social cognitive theory of mass communication and his earlier social learning theory constitute a major portion of the foundations for volumes of research in several areas of media effects study—effects of media violence and sexually explicit material, prosocial or positive media effects, health communication effects, persuasion, and so forth. For the student of media effects, an understanding of Bandura's theory is therefore essential because the concepts serve as a common denominator among other media effects theories and hypotheses.

In this chapter we examine the various dimensions of social cognitive theory, including the cognitive characteristics distinct to humans, the dynamics of observational learning, the effects of modeling, and the ways we learn from media content. The theory provides a framework to explain prosocial effects from mass media, social prompting or persuasion, and diffusion of an idea, message, or belief by way of symbolic modeling. The overall objective of the chapter is to provide an explanation of social cognitive theory, and significant studies that have drawn heavily upon the theory are also discussed.

Distinctly Human Traits

Many animals have the ability to learn, but several distinct cognitive traits set human beings apart. Social cognitive theory emphasizes the importance of these uniquely human characteristics, known as the *symbolizing, self-regulatory, self-reflective,* and *vicarious* capacities (Bandura, 1994).

Symbolizing Capacity

Human communication is based upon a system of shared meanings of various symbols known as language. These symbols occur at more than one conceptual level—letters of the alphabet are symbols used to construct words, for example, and words serve as symbols to represent specific objects, thoughts, or ideas. The capacity to understand and use these symbols allows people to store, process, and transform observed experiences into cognitive models that guide them in future actions and decisions.

Self-Regulatory Capacity

The self-regulatory capacity includes the concepts of motivation and evaluation. People have the ability to motivate themselves to achieve certain goals. They tend to evaluate their own behavior and respond accordingly. In this way, behavior is *self-directed* and *self-regulated.*

For example, a young father and mother are motivated to achieve the goal of providing for the emotional and material needs of their toddler. If they find that they are not earning enough money to achieve their goal, they may evaluate the situation and decide to look for higher-paying jobs or supplemental second jobs. They may then realize that the child's emotional needs are not being fulfilled because of their absence. In this case, one of the two may decide to start a home-based business in order to spend more time with the child. In either case, the couple evaluated, regulated, and directed their behavior in response to a common motivation or goal.

Self-Reflective Capacity

This capacity involves the process of thought verification. It is the ability of a person to perform a self-check to make sure his or her thinking is correct. Bandura identified four different self-reflective "modes" used in thought verification: the enactive, vicarious, social, and logical modes (1986, 1994, 2009).

In the *enactive* mode, a person assesses the agreement between thoughts and the results of actions. For example, a young girl may think she has the potential to be an Olympic gymnast, but when she goes for her first gymnastics lesson she discovers that she is a hopeless klutz. The instructor encourages her to concentrate on her studies at school and forget about sports. In this case, her actions do not verify her thoughts and she must reassess her thinking. If, however, she shows incredible natural talent in the gym, the instructor might tell her that with hard work the Olympics might someday be possible. In this scenario, the girl's actions corroborate her thoughts and provide verification.

With the *vicarious* mode, observation of another's experiences and the outcomes of those experiences serve to confirm or refute the veracity of thoughts. Perhaps the same gymnast (the one who initially thought she had considerable talent) enters the gym and sees a world-class gymnast working on her routines in preparation for the Olympic Games. After joining the gym and seeing the Olympic-bound gymnast working day after day for months or years, the younger girl sees that with talent and hard work, the realization of her big dreams are possible.

With *social* verification, a person compares his or her beliefs with what others believe, and from that comparison, determines if his or her thinking is correct. For example, when a young person reaches college, exposure to new ways of thinking and mores may cause the person to do things previously unthinkable. Consider, for example, the young woman raised in a nondrinking Baptist family who has been home schooled until going away to college, where she is exposed to many other young people who encourage her to change her beliefs.

The last mode of thought verification within the self-reflective capability, the *logical* mode, involves verification by using previously acquired rules of inference. The young woman may decide that the rules that were set in her strict religious upbringing are more important to her than popularity at school. She remembers times when she strayed from those rules and regretted it later, so she chooses to avoid drinking and find a small set of friends with similar views to hers.

Vicarious Capacity

This human characteristic, vicarious capacity, which is the ability to learn without direct experience, emphasizes the potential contributions of mass media messages—for better or worse. As an example of positive social impact, the vicarious capacity allows a person to learn all sorts of beneficial things by simply reading or watching a television program presenting these prosocial behaviors. On the negative side, people may witness and learn certain *antisocial* behaviors to which they might not otherwise have been exposed.

> Much social learning occurs either designedly or unintentionally from models in one's immediate environment. However, a vast amount of information about human values, styles of thinking, and behavior patterns is gained from the extensive modeling in the symbolic environment of the mass media. (Bandura, 2009, p. 98)

Observational Learning and Modeling

Social learning and social cognitive theories place much emphasis on the concept of *observational learning.* A person observes other people's actions and the consequences of those actions, and learns from what has been observed. The learned behavior can then be reenacted by the observer.

Modeling

The phenomenon of behavior reenactment, called **modeling**, includes four component processes: *attention, retention, motor reproduction,* and *motivation* (Bandura, 1986, 1994). These can be explained by using a simple example of observational learning, such as learning how to swing a golf club.

Attention

A person must pay attention to any behavior and perceive it accurately in order to model it successfully. The beginning golfer must watch the actions of the teacher and listen carefully to instructions—in short, pay close attention to the actions to be modeled.

Retention

Modeled behavior must be remembered or retained in order to be used again. The permanent memory stores the information by means of symbolic representations that subsequently can be converted into actions. The beginning golfer must understand the instructor's comments and remember them, along with demonstrations and corrections, as well as what he sees other golfers do—either in person or on television.

Motor Reproduction

At first, motor reproduction may be difficult and even faulty, as the beginner has to "think through" all the various steps involved in making a successful swing. As the golfer practices the modeled swing, however, the cognitive process becomes less tedious. If the beginner possesses the necessary component skills, observational learning occurs at a much faster rate. In other words, the natural athletic ability or the superior motor memory of the beginner largely determines the length of time required for mastery of the modeled swing.

Motivation

For various reasons, people are not always motivated to model the behaviors they learn. Using the golfer again as an example, the beginning golfer might notice that his instructor cannot drive the ball nearly as far as Phil Mickelson can. The beginner may also notice that the two stand differently, hold the club differently, and move different parts of the body whenever they swing the club. In this case, the beginner may choose to model his behavior after the more successful Mickelson. Or the student golfer may realize that green fees and cart fees are too expensive, and that the years it will take to master a swing like Mickelson's will be hard and costly, and thus never utilize his or her newfound knowledge. Motivation becomes a major factor in the decision to use modeled behavior.

Some instances of modeling result in actions far more consequential than the innocuous golf swing. Different learning situations dictate the importance of the four component parts. Consider, for instance, the young intern learning to perform surgery, or the fearful child learning to swim. In each case, the actual *motor reproduction* of the modeled behavior assumes paramount importance. The significance of *motivation* in the learning process may be illustrated by two people learning to speak a foreign language: an American student learning Russian for a degree requirement would not have the same motivation as a Russian immigrant learning English to survive in the United States.

Three types of situations provide the incentives that motivate a person to model learned behavior: (1) positive outcomes through direct performance of the behavior, (2) observation of another's behavior and the subsequent outcomes, and (3) evaluation based upon personal values or standards of behavior (Bandura, 1989, 1994). For instance, a child who learns a song from *Blue's Clues,* then performs the song for her parents and receives much praise and encouragement, is motivated to model that learned behavior in the future. In this case, the child performed the behavior and experienced the outcome directly.

The successful Nickelodeon program *Blue's Clues* also serves as a good example of the more vicarious, second type of motivational situation. In every show, the human character solves a mystery message from his animated puppy Blue. As they sing and play games, three clues are discovered, then the young man sits in his chair to think through the problem and solve the mystery. The child sees that the technique is always successful, and therefore the child is likely to model such "thinking chair" behavior whenever faced with solving his own mysterious problem.

To illustrate the third motivational situation, consider a young boy who views and imitates the violence he sees on reruns of *Power Rangers.* Perhaps he is a sensitive child who does not wish to hurt anyone physically, and he has been told that violence is wrong, yet his ability to imitate the Red Ranger impresses the other children and makes him very popular at day care. One day he jumps, kicks his friend a little too hard, and knocks him onto the pavement, breaking the friend's arm badly. The scene is a frightful one—the bloody bone protrudes from the skin and the arm dangles. The child who kicked his friend is devastated. He cries intermittently for a week and never again imitates a Power Ranger. In this case, the child is motivated to avoid modeling the violent behavior because he has witnessed a horrible outcome. His internalized standard of conduct has become more strict.

Abstract Modeling

Rules of behavior learned in the past serve as a *guide* for new life situations (Bandura, 1994). These rules often provide an abstract framework for decision making in new situations. In other words, existing standards of behavior are not perfect or constant for each new situation. A person is merely guided by the outcomes of his or her own past experiences or the observed experiences of other people.

Abstract modeling takes learning to a higher level than mere mimicry of observed behavior. New situations generate new behaviors based upon the rules of behavior learned previously. These behaviors are themselves learned and stored in memory for future adaptation in other situations.

The use of abstract modeling offers many practical advantages (Bandura, 1986, 1994; Rosenthal & Zimmerman, 1978). One acquires personal standards for judging one's own motivations and behavior and those of others. Abstract modeling also boosts critical thinking, communication skills, and creativity.

Consider, for example, the creativity of the Beatles or other artists. Paul McCartney often said that he and John Lennon tried to imitate the work of other musical groups or soloists, but also drew from their personal knowledge, experience, and preferences, only to put their own personal stamp on their popular music. They were performing *abstract modeling*.

Effects of Modeling

Sometimes a person observes behavior or receives information that conflicts in some way with that person's established pattern of behavior. Two major effects are associated with such situations—**inhibitory** and **disinhibitory effects** (Anderson et al., 2003; Bandura, 1973, 2009; Berkowitz, 1984; Malamuth & Donnerstein, 1984; Zillmann & Bryant, 1984). The inner conflict causes a person to reexamine his or her motivations to perform the established behavior.

Inhibitory Effects

Most studies on inhibitory and disinhibitory effects have examined transgressive, aggressive, or sexual behavior (Berkowitz, 1984; Liebert, Sprafkin, & Davidson, 1982; Malamuth & Donnerstein, 1984; Zillmann & Bryant, 1984). In each case, inhibitory effects occurred whenever a person refrained from reprehensible conduct for fear of the consequences, such as formal punishment by society or censure from one's own conscience.

Inhibitory effects occur whenever new information or the observation of new behavior *inhibits* or *restrains* a person from acting in a previously learned way. Disinhibitory effects *disinhibit* or lift previously learned internal restraints on certain behaviors. A smoker might decide to change his behavior if he sees his favorite uncle (who smoked all his life) suffer miserably and die of emphysema. He has experienced inhibitory effects. On the other hand, consider a teenage girl from a strict family who counts the use of alcohol and tobacco among the ultimate of taboos. Then she goes away to college and makes friends with other students who drink and smoke. Her established mores become more relaxed. When she decides to try a beer for the first time, she has experienced disinhibitory effects.

For another example of inhibitory effects, imagine that two college students are taking an introductory communication course during their first semester. The two young women are friends. One watches television while studying, a habit of behavior she developed in high school. She reads during the commercials. The other student isolates herself in her room, and reads and studies without distraction. The student who works in quiet seclusion receives an "A" on the first exam, whereas the other student gets an "F." After recovering from the initial shock, the second student decides to *inhibit* her usual behavior and to model the behavior of her friend while reading and studying.

Disinhibitory Effects

A 1963 study by Bandura and his colleagues serves as an excellent example of disinhibitory effects. The researchers showed nursery school children a film in which an adult performed physically aggressive actions (such as pounding an air-filled, vinyl punching bag called a Bobo doll). The children who watched later imitated those aggressive acts. Moreover, the researchers found that the children who had watched the violent film were less inhibited about performing *other* violent acts they had learned in the past—acts that were not demonstrated on the film (Bandura, Ross, & Ross, 1963a). The film therefore had a *disinhibitory* effect upon the children who saw it. (See the Research Spotlight for a discussion of the Bobo Doll experiment.)

Disinhibitory Devices

Many types of behavior are not socially acceptable. Murder, rape, physical violence against others, and other criminal acts serve as extreme examples of impulses that must be restrained. Other less sensational behaviors also qualify.

Research has shown that people who engage in reprehensible behavior often use cognitive techniques to justify their actions to themselves. In other words, they lose their inhibitions (become disinhibited) about acting in a certain way even if those actions conflict with their internal moral standards. Researchers have identified eight such cognitive techniques or devices: moral justification, exonerative comparison, euphemistic labeling, displacement of responsibility, diffusion of responsibility, distortion of the consequences of action, dehumanization, and attribution of blame (Bandura, 2009).

The first three techniques—moral justification, exonerative comparison, and euphemistic labeling—are the most powerful of the eight in terms of cognitive and moral restructuring. This means that a person may actually change or restructure the way he or she views the undesirable behavior. Through use of disinhibitory devices, reprehensible conduct might be seen as not only *acceptable,*

Research Spotlight

Imitation of Film-Mediated Aggressive Models
Albert Bandura, Dorothea Ross, and Sheila A. Ross (1963)
Journal of Abnormal and Social Psychology, 66(1), 3–11

In this research classic, published in 1963, Bandura and his associates tested children to determine if watching aggressive actions on film caused the children to imitate the behavior displayed by the film characters in real-life situations.

Subjects

Children ranging in age from about 3 to 5 years old (mean age of 4 years 4 months) from the Stanford University Nursery School were tested. The subjects consisted of 48 boys and 48 girls.

Procedure

Three experimental groups and one control group consisted of 24 subjects each. One group saw real-life aggressive models. A second group saw the same models portraying aggression on film. The third group watched a film with an aggressive cartoon character. The control group subjects had no exposure to aggressive models.

Two adults served as models, a male and a female, in the real-life aggression and human film-aggression conditions. The children were subdivided by gender so that they would be exposed to either same-sex models or opposite-sex models.

The children were rated on their aggressive behavior by the experimenter and a nursery school teacher. They used scales that measured how much physical aggression, verbal aggression, aggression toward inanimate objects, and aggressive inhibition the children displayed prior to the experiment.

Subjects in the real-life aggression condition were brought individually into the room and taken to one corner and seated at a small table that contained potato prints, multicolor picture stickers, and colored paper. The experimenter demonstrated to the child how to make pictures with the materials provided. The model was brought into the room and taken to another table with a tinker toy set, a mallet, and the 5-foot inflated Bobo doll. The experimenter told the child that this was the model's play area. After the model was seated, the experimenter left the room.

The model began the session by assembling the tinker toys but soon turned attention to the Bobo doll and started punching it, sitting on it and punching it, pummeling it on the head with a mallet, tossing the doll up in the air and kicking it about the room. The sequence of aggressiveness was repeated about three times. As the model aggressed toward the doll, the model used verbally aggressive phrases such as "Sock him in the nose" or "Hit him down" or "Kick him" or "Pow."

Subjects in the human film-aggression condition were also taken individually into the experiment room, to the table with the materials for making pictures, and told that while they worked on their pictures a movie would be shown on a screen about 6 feet from the subject's table. The film was shown for a duration of 10 minutes while the child was alone in the room. The models used for the first condition were also used in the filmed condition. The aggressive behavior in the film was identical to the real-life aggressiveness they displayed toward the doll.

In the cartoon film-aggression condition, the subject was taken individually into the room and seated at the table with the picture construction material, then the experimenter walked over to a television console about 3 feet in front of the subject's table and said, "I guess I'll turn on the color TV," and turned on the cartoon program. The aggression toward the Bobo doll was performed by one of the female models in a black cat costume. The verbal aggression was repeated in a high-pitched, animated voice.

In both film conditions, the experimenter entered the room at the conclusion of the movie and escorted the subject to another room that contained toys outside the actual test room. The child was allowed to play with the toys for a while, and then was stopped by the experimenter, who explained to the child that these were the very best toys and should be reserved for other children. The child was told to enter the next room (the actual test room) and play with the toys there. The toys in the test room consisted of a 3-foot Bobo doll, a mallet and peg board, two dart guns, a tether ball with a face painted on it that hung from the ceiling, and nonaggressive toys including a tea set, crayons and coloring paper, a ball, two dolls, three bears, cars and trucks, and plastic farm animals.

Each subject spent 20 minutes in the experimental room while judges observed through a one-way mirror in an adjoining room. Acts of aggression were coded.

Results

The results showed no difference in total aggressiveness for the subjects who viewed the real-life models and the film-mediated models. All three groups were significantly more aggressive than the control subjects. The subjects in the first three groups performed considerably more imitative physical and verbal aggression than the control group. The data suggested that exposure to humans on film portraying aggression was the most influential in eliciting and shaping aggressive behavior, even more so than the real-life condition.

The researchers noted that boys exhibited significantly more total aggression, imitative aggression, more aggressive gun play, and more nonimitative aggressive behavior than girls. The sex of the model was shown to have some influence in promoting social learning, by the sex appropriateness of the model's behavior.

Subjects exposed to the human and cartoon models on film showed nearly twice as much aggression as subjects in the control group who were not exposed to the film content.

The famous Bobo doll study showed that children often imitate violence they see on the screen. © *Albert Bandura*

but actually *desirable*. As an example of such restructuring, consider the case described previously—the girl with the strict upbringing who decided to try a beer with her college friends. Certainly she may have experienced some degree of cognitive and moral restructuring that made beer drinking seem to be a desirable behavior.

Moral justification occurs whenever a person believes his or her otherwise culpable actions are serving some moral, noble, or higher purpose and are therefore justified. In such cases, inhibitive restraints on certain behaviors are released or relaxed. In the mind of the transgressor, a greater good is served. A good example of moral justification is soldiers during wartime who legitimize aggression based on the "greater good" of protecting freedoms. A more common example would be that of a mother who spanks a misbehaving child.

Exonerative comparison also involves seeing one's own bad actions serving the greater good of society. A modern-day Robin Hood-type thief would exonerate himself for stealing because he gives what he steals to the poor.

Euphemistic labeling offers not only a means of camouflaging reprehensible conduct, but may even make the conduct respectable or at least acceptable. For example, the girl who watches television while studying might euphemistically consider her viewing as an *educational* rather than a *recreational* (or mindless) experience. She convinces herself that watching television keeps her abreast of current events, and therefore it is just as important as her textbook reading assignment. The teenage girl who starts smoking cigarettes euphemistically labels the activity as "cool" or "sexy" in her mind, rather than viewing the activity as a health hazard and a nasty habit.

Two disinhibitory techniques or devices cause a transgressor to shift the responsibility for wrongdoing to another. **Displacement of responsibility** occurs when someone in authority directs a person to act in a certain reprehensible way, and the authority figure accepts responsibility for the actions. With **diffusion of responsibility**, a transgressor acts within a group and therefore does not feel personally responsible for the subsequent act. Again, soldiers at war serve as excellent examples of such devices in action.

Another device, **disregard or distortion of the consequences of action**, refers to situations in which a person performs an act without thinking about the harm that act may cause, or with the belief that the act will cause only minimal harm (Brock & Buss, 1962, 1964). The teenager who accepts the dare of his buddies and throws bricks through a store window is concerned only with the thrill of the moment—the idea of "getting away with" the wrongdoing and meeting the challenge of the dare. He gives no thought to the poor store owner who must have the window replaced, or the jail time he will serve if caught.

The final devices, **dehumanization** and **attribution of blame**, focus upon the attitudes of transgressors toward their victims. Dehumanization occurs whenever a person is divested of human qualities and considered no better than a beast. Nazi soldiers dehumanized Jewish people during World War II; therefore, they were able to commit unspeakable atrocities without feelings of remorse. In the United States prior to the civil rights movement, many Whites dehumanized Blacks and thus prevented them from voting and enjoying advantages known by White people. Belligerent Whites attacked peaceful civil rights demonstrators and justified their hostilities by attributing blame to the demonstrators or the situation rather than to themselves—they blamed the demonstrators for causing trouble and "provoking" them to hostile actions.

Learning from Media Content and Modeling

Remember the death scene in the film *E.T.: The Extra-Terrestrial* when the alien died and the boy delivered the sad soliloquy? It was one of those "lump in the throat" scenes for audience members. Then, when ET came back to life and the child experienced such marvelous joy, it became difficult for audience members to hold back the happy tears.

When the thriller *Jaws* played in theaters in the 1970s, audiences throughout the country actually applauded after the sheriff took aim, fired, and blasted the monster shark out of the water. In the summer months that followed, newscasters reported that many people at beach resorts were afraid to set foot in the ocean because they had seen the film and feared a shark attack.

As these examples show, whenever a person sees a character on the screen expressing some strong emotion or performing some powerful action, the viewer is affected or *aroused.* The viewer remembers similar experiences and emotions, and these thoughts and images serve as cues that trigger self-arousal (Bandura, 1992; Wilson & Cantor, 1985).

Such experiences of arousal are not always fleeting in nature. Several studies have shown that audience members sometimes develop lasting emotional reactions, attitudes, and behaviors after viewing emotional content that arouses them. Vivid memories of the killer Great White shark from *Jaws* kept many people out of the ocean for years, and many who did brave the waves were cautious and uneasy. A decade earlier, the shower scene in Alfred Hitchcock's *Psycho* made many people throw back their shower curtains and opt for a much safer bath!

Examples of such fear reactions abound, but research has shown that people also learn many other reactions from media content, some of them lasting. Coping skills portrayed on the screen help people deal with their fears and phobias by lessening them and making them more tolerable (Bandura, 1982). Audience members learn to dislike whatever screen characters dislike, and they like whatever pleases or gratifies those characters (Bandura, 1986; Duncker, 1938).

Viewing Disinhibitory Devices

Media effects scholars are also interested in what happens whenever viewers see television and film characters acting in violent ways and employing the disinhibitory devices described in the previous section. How do viewers respond? How are they affected?

Research has shown that whenever viewers see television or movie characters injuring their victims and engaging in one or more of the devices, those viewers are then more likely to inflict punishment or penalty on others. Injurious conduct on the part of the viewer is linked to the sanctioned social behavior depicted on the screen (Bandura, Underwood, & Fromson, 1975).

Social Construction of Reality and Cultivation

Studies show that the "realities" depicted on television programs do not always reflect the true state of affairs in the real world. Some scholars believe that heavy viewing of television tends to shape or cultivate viewers' perceptions and beliefs so that they are more in line with the world portrayed on television than with that of the real world. Media scholars call this media effects phenomenon the **social construction of reality**. As you will learn in Chapter 8, one research tradition associated with such effects is known as **cultivation**.

Some of the best examples of television's power to alter viewers' perceptions are revealed whenever regular television viewers are asked to estimate their chances of being aboard a plane that will crash, or their chances of being a victim of a violent crime. In the "real world" such events are extremely rare, whereas in the "world of television" they occur frequently. Most people, especially those who are heavy viewers of particular types of television programs, grossly *overestimate* their chances of being in a plane crash or becoming a victim of some criminal.

Some studies have shown that viewers tend to have misconceptions due to stereotypical portrayals on television (Buerkel-Rothfuss & Mayes, 1981; McGhee & Frueh, 1980; Tan, 1979). In 1981, Buerkel-Rothfuss and Mayes tested 290 college students who reportedly watched, on average, seven episodes of daytime serial dramas, or "soaps," each week. Students were asked to estimate the occurrence in society of certain occupations (e.g., doctor, lawyer, businessman, blue-collar worker, housewife), health concerns (e.g., nervous breakdown, major operation, abortion), and other life issues and crises (e.g., having an affair, being happily married, getting divorced). Students estimated how many women of every 10 and how many men of every 10 could be classified in the various categories. The researchers *controlled* for factors such as intelligence, sex, age, and self-concept; in other words, they designed their investigation in a way to make sure that any exaggerated estimates were not due to these factors rather than the viewing alone. As the researchers expected, the students who watched the most soap operas were more likely than light viewers or nonviewers to perceive the real world as similar to that of television. These students overestimated the number of doctors and lawyers, the number of extramarital affairs and divorces, the number of illegitimate births and abortions, and other events that occurred on soap operas far more frequently than in the real world.

Effects of Viewing Televised or Film Violence

Through the years, many media effects studies have examined the negative effects that result from the vicarious capacity, such as the learning of aggressive behavior by viewing televised or filmed violence. Critics point out that millions of viewers who watch violent programming are *not* inspired to imitate such violent behavior. This suggests that individual factors such as a person's disposition (or predisposition to violent behavior), state of mind, emotional stability, and personal circumstances play a major role in determining whether that person will resort to aggression after viewing violent fare.

Social scientists often are concerned with more subtle media effects—those that they can measure through strictly controlled experiments that do not involve harm or injury to anyone. Most studies have concentrated on identifying the effects of media violence as *cognitive, affective,* or *behavioral.* Each of these will be discussed in detail in Chapter 11 on media violence.

Learning Good Things from Mass Media

In recent years, a growing body of research that examines children's television programming has yielded promising findings (see Chapter 17 on educational effects). These studies have shown that many children's television shows have *prosocial* or positive learning effects. In general, research has shown that through watching educational and nonviolent programs such as *Sesame Street* (Fisch, 2002; Fisch & Truglio, 2001), children improve literacy, science, and mathematics skills, and learn positive social behaviors, enhance their imaginative powers, and develop problem-solving skills.

Studies of *Sesame Street* suggest positive gains in cognitive skills and other prosocial effects for viewers compared to nonviewers, both in the United States (Wright & Huston, 1995; Wright, Huston, Scantlin, & Kotler, 2001) and abroad (UNICEF, 1996; Brederode-Santos, 1993; Ulitsa Sezam Department of Research and Content, 1998). Longitudinal studies have revealed that positive effects, especially in terms of academic achievement and reading skills, from viewing *Sesame Street* as preschoolers continued as the children advanced to grade school (Zill, 2001; Zill, Davies, & Daly, 1994) and even high school (Anderson, Huston, Wright, & Collins, 1998).

Studies show that children learn a great deal from educational television. © *Heather Swolsky*

Studies have also found beneficial effects from programs such as *Barney & Friends* (Singer & Singer, 1994, 1995, 1998), *Gullah Gullah Island* and *Allegra's Window* (Bryant et al., 1997; Mulliken & J. A. Bryant, 1999), *Blue's Clues* (Anderson et al., 2000; Bryant et al., 1999), *Mister Rogers' Neighborhood* and *The Electric Company* (Rice, 1984; Rice & Haight, 1986; Ball & Bogatz, 1973; Ball, Bogatz, Karazow, & Rubin, 1974), *Between the Lions* (Linebarger, 2000), *Reading Rainbow* (Leitner, 1991), *Square One TV* (Hall, Esty, & Fisch, 1990; Hall & Fisch et al., 1990), and *3–2–1 Contact* (Cambre & Fernie, 1985; Johnston, 1980; Johnston & Luker, 1983; Wagner, 1985). Positive benefits of educational programming for children are enhanced whenever parents or caregivers view programs with the children and reinforce the messages (Singer & Singer, 1983).

In a two-year assessment of Nickelodeon programs *Gullah Gullah Island* and *Allegra's Window,* children who watched regularly were able to solve problems with greater ease and exhibit more flexible thinking skills than children who did not watch the program. In addition, regular viewers learned more about appropriate social behaviors than children of similar ages who did not watch the programs (Bryant et al., 1997) and performed better on three types of problem-solving tasks (Mulliken & J. A. Bryant, 1999).

Another two-year assessment targeted viewers of *Blue's Clues,* an educational program on Nick Jr. (Nickelodeon's network for preschoolers), and found effects for viewers were beneficial compared to effects for nonviewers (Anderson et al., 2000; Bryant et al., 1999). Nonverbal problem solving and non-humorous riddle solving on standardized Kaufman tests were two areas that showed statistically significant differences in favor of viewers of *Blue's Clues.*

Language development, literacy, mathematics and problem solving, science and technology, civics, and social studies are other areas that have shown positive effects for viewers of educational programming (Fisch, 2002).

Social Prompting or Persuasion

Advertising campaigns and other persuasive efforts serve as excellent examples of social prompting, another example of modeled behavior. Social prompting does not involve learning new behavior, and therefore it differs from observational learning and disinhibition. **Social prompting** implies that a person is offered an *inducement* (an incentive) to act in a particular way that has already been learned.

Most people are not inclined to try a new product unless, of course, the new product is shown to offer great benefits or inducements. Using toothpaste as an example, a viewer might be prompted to switch brands if a new, whitening toothpaste promises a beautiful smile, popularity, love, and happiness (as indicated by the actions of the attractive models in the commercial); a technique we see far too often in the advertising of categories of products that have few if any real advantages over others of the same class.

Many Influences Cause Persuasion

According to social cognitive theory, many different influences of varying strengths often determine human behavior. No single pattern of influence exists to explain every instance of persuasion or modeling or adoption of a new behavior. Sometimes people are influenced by what they see on television, sometimes they are persuaded by interpersonal communication, and sometimes by a little of both. In all cases in which behavior is influenced, a combination of outside factors and personal characteristics are at work. The dynamics of those combinations differ with each person.

You will recall from Chapter 3 that the indirect influence hypothesis characterized the tradition. The limited effects hypothesis held that influential people in the community, called opinion leaders, are influenced by mass media. These opinion leaders in turn influence the majority of others through interpersonal contact.

A substantial body of evidence debunks the idea that media can *only* reinforce changes in behavior rather than initiating them. Research has shown that in some cases media influences *do* initiate change (Bandura, 1986; Liebert et al., 1982) and have direct effects on viewers (Watt & van den Berg, 1978). Media influences vary in strength as do influences from other sources that ultimately determine a person's behavior (Bandura, 1994).

With the proliferation of new media technologies, the impact of communications media in influencing behaviors has become even more significant. Bandura (2009, p. 113) summarized the findings in this way:

> On the input side, communications can now be personally tailored to factors that are causally related to the behavior of interest. Tailored communications are viewed as more relevant and credible, are better remembered and are more effective in influencing behavior than general messages (Kreuter, Strecher, & Glassman, 1999). On the behavioral guidance side, interactive technologies provide a convenient means of individualizing the type and level of behavioral guidance needed to bring desired changes to fruition (Bandura, 2004). In the population-based approaches the communications are designed to inform, enable, motivate, and guide people to effect personal and social changes. In implementing the social linking function, communications media can connect people to interactive online self-management programs that provide intensive individualized guidance in their homes when they want it (Bandura, 2004, 2006; Taylor, Winzelberg, & Celio, 2001; Munoz et al., 2006).

Diffusion by Way of Symbolic Modeling

One important area of media effects research involves the study of diffusion or spread of an innovation—a new technology, tool, behavior, farming technique—throughout a society or a large group of people. Communication scholar Everett Rogers (1983) is well known for his scholarship in this area, which is called **diffusion of innovations**.

Research has shown that successful diffusion of an innovation follows a similar pattern each time, an S-shaped distribution. It is the normal bell curve plotted over a period of time.

Social cognitive theory views diffusion of innovations in terms of symbolic modeling, persuasion, social prompting, and motivation. Three major events define the diffusion process:

1. When the person learns about an innovation (a new behavior, tool, product, and so on).

2. When the person adopts the innovation or performs the new behavior.

3. When the person interacts with others in a social network, either encouraging them to adopt the new behavior or confirming their own decision to adopt the behavior.

Diffusion of innovations research examines the different strengths of media and interpersonal influences in adoption of new behavior. The symbolic world of television is broadcast to masses of viewers at the same time. Satellite telecommunications carry television programs to millions of viewers in different countries throughout the world. Social changes have occurred due to the influences of television on entire societies of viewers who model the various behaviors, styles, and ideas that they see and learn (Bandura, 1986; Singhal & Rogers, 1989; Winett et al., 1985).

Recent Research

Social cognitive theory, as mentioned earlier in this chapter, comprises the theoretical basis for many types of media effects research covered within this text—from media violence studies and fright reactions to media content to effects from sexually explicit content and effects from persuasive media messages.

In recent years, social cognitive theory of mass communication has proved especially useful as the theoretical underpinning for communication campaigns and their design (Lapinski & Witte, 1998). Mass media campaigns intended to change health behaviors (Marcus et al., 1998; Clark & Gong, 1997; Maibach et al., 1996) have drawn heavily from social cognitive theory.

The theory has also served as a key part of the foundation for the study of media effects in a variety of other areas. These include the study of effects from news frames during the coverage of election campaigns (Rhee, 1997), the study of priming effects of media violence on aggressive constructs in memory (Bushman, 1998), the study of children's acceptance of safety rules after exposure to accidents in television dramas (Cantor & Omdahl, 1999), and even a historical content-analysis study of infant feeding messages in magazines (Potter & Sheeshka, 2000).

Summary

Albert Bandura's social cognitive theory serves not only as a major, independent theory of media effects, but also as a component of many other theories of media effects. It provides a framework to analyze human cognitions that produce certain behaviors and describe mental processes at work whenever a person learns. Social cognitive theory explains behavior by examining the triadic reciprocal causation process, or the interaction among cognitive, behavioral, and environmental factors.

Social cognitive theory emphasizes the importance of several distinct cognitive traits that set human beings apart. These include the symbolizing, self-regulatory, self-reflective, and vicarious capacities. The self-reflective capacity includes four different modes used in thought verification: the enactive, vicarious, persuasory, and logical modes.

Observational learning and modeling are key elements in social cognitive theory. Whenever a person observes other people's actions and the consequences of those actions, the person may learn from what has been observed. Modeling is the reenactment of learned behavior and includes four component processes: attention, retention, motor reproduction, and motivation.

New life situations require people to apply the rules of behavior learned in the past to the new and different situations. Abstract modeling takes learning to a higher level than mere mimicry of observed behavior and therefore offers many practical advantages.

Whenever a person observes behavior or receives information that conflicts with established patterns of behavior or principles of conduct, the inner conflict causes a reexamination of motivations to perform the established behavior. Inhibitory effects occur whenever a person refrains from reprehensible conduct for fear of the consequences. Disinhibitory effects lift previously learned internal restraints on certain behaviors.

People who engage in reprehensible behaviors often use cognitive techniques or devices to justify their actions. Eight such disinhibitory devices have been identified: moral justification, exonerative comparison, euphemistic labeling, displacement of responsibility, diffusion of responsibility, distortion of the consequences of action, dehumanization, and attribution of blame.

Viewers are affected or aroused by much that they see on the screen. Some experiences of arousal are not fleeting in nature. Fear reactions, coping skills, and likes and dislikes may all be learned, with lasting results, from media characters.

Social cognitive theory helps explain cultivation effects, priming effects, and prosocial effects in terms of cognitions, observational learning, and modeling. The basis for many persuasion effects or social prompting from mass media can be found in social cognitive theory, which recognizes that motivations or influences to model new behavior or adopt new ideas are dynamic and usually a combination of outside factors and personal cognitions and characteristics.

Diffusion of innovations research also finds a conceptual basis in social cognitive theory. Diffusion of an innovation throughout a society or a large group of people is explained in terms of symbolic modeling, persuasion or social prompting, and motivation. Successful diffusion of an innovation requires three steps: learning about the innovation, adoption of the innovation, and the development of social networks after initial adoption.

five

Priming

It is assumed that concepts that have some relation to each other
are connected in some mental network, so that if one concept
is activated, then concepts related to it are also activated.
—Entry on "Priming,"
University of Alberta's *Cognitive Science Dictionary*, 1998

Suppose someone in your family once battled cancer and overcame it through conventional treatment. Years later, a Hollywood star appears on the television news and in the tabloids, suffering from the same cancer that your family member had. Chances are you would be more interested in reading about the star's plight with the disease, curious about treatment, and so forth. You would already have certain information stored in your memory about that particular kind of cancer due to personal experience with someone who battled the disease. Your memories would be activated by the new information.

Priming is the study of this activation of related concepts archived in the mind of a media consumer. Studies of priming usually test priming activation from the introduction of information from media messages.

Many priming studies, for example, have looked at media content related to political issues and tested how exposure to that content affects presidential performance ratings or other measures of public opinion. In the case of these studies, the media are said to "prime" certain information in the minds of audience members, which can cause them to give more importance to one issue (i.e., agenda setting, see Chapter 6), or even influence their judgments on important matters (i.e., persuasion, see Chapter 10).

Consider the example of viewing media content. What mental associations would you expect such content to prompt in viewers? Does media violence cause viewers to make associations with angry or critical thoughts stored in their own memories? More significantly, does the viewing of mediated violence and the mental associations it arouses make viewers more likely to commit acts of violence themselves?

These types of questions lie at the heart of many social scientific investigations of media effects, as well as questions related to the psychological processes present whenever media effects do indeed occur. Cognitive research typically explores *short-term* media effects that sometimes have long-term implications. Historically, such research has employed strong experimental designs and tight controls that lend rigor and specificity to the research, although at the expense of generalizability to "real-world" media-violence issues.

The cognitive theoretical emphasis involves application of theories from psychology, including social psychology, to explain media effects phenomena, including social cognitive theory and priming, the subject of this chapter. **Priming** is a popular area of media effects research based upon the psychological principles of information processing by means of cognitive components. Priming theory often serves as a theoretical basis for particular studies in other areas of media effects research, including agenda setting and other political communication issues. As with the other major theories in the body of media effects research, so many studies have focused on the priming mechanism itself that an entire body of media effects literature related to priming now exists.

This chapter examines the theoretical underpinnings of priming and reviews some of the important studies that have measured priming effects resulting from mediated communication. Following a description of the priming mechanism and factors that may determine its activation, the chapter provides a glimpse into the conceptual foundations for the theory, examines a research tradition rooted in principles of cognitive psychology, and explores variables that enhance priming effects. Finally, the most recent research studies involving priming mechanisms and future directions in priming research are considered.

Activation of Priming

Priming occurs when exposure to mediated communication activates related thoughts that have been stored or "archived" in the mind of an audience member. Media message content triggers concepts, thoughts, learning, or knowledge acquired in the past that are related to the message content. In this way, message content is connected, associated, or *reinforced* by related thoughts and concepts that it brings to mind. For a certain period of time after viewing such content, a person is more likely to have thoughts about the content, related thoughts, or memories. In some instances, the related thoughts or memories become permanently associated with the message content or *stimulus* (Fiske & Taylor, 1991).

For example, a network newscast that features a story on the U.S. recession may cause a viewer to remember her grandparents' horror stories of life during the Great Depression. Any knowledge already acquired regarding economic depressions would be associated with new information gathered from the newscast. The viewer's interest in the news story and reaction to it may well be affected by existing knowledge and previous experiences. If, for example, depression stories heard during childhood caused much anxiety, the story of current economic hardships might cause the recollection of such feelings. In other words, the news story *primed* a particular reaction.

> As applied to the media, priming refers to the effects of the content of the media on people's later behavior or judgments related to the content that was processed. . . . [I]t is important to understand that, with priming, the effect of the priming event is time bound. For example, in media priming focused on violence, studies often find that the priming effect fades quickly—oftentimes within the time course of the experimental setting (Farrar & Krcmar, 2006; Josephson, 1987; Roskos-Ewoldsen, Klinger, & Roskos-Ewoldsen, 2007). For political priming, the effects are often argued to last for perhaps two months. . . . (Roskos-Ewoldsen, Roskos-Ewoldsen, & Carpentier, 2009, pp. 74–75)

The priming activation may also influence a person's behavior, causing a particular reaction, sometimes with undesirable consequences. For most people, priming effects cause only mild reactions that usually diminish in time and may even pass unnoticed. Nevertheless, the overall evidence for priming has been substantial. The strength of the activation, the types of thoughts provoked, and the behavioral results of the activation depend upon a number of contingent factors.

Conceptual Roots

Media violence priming has been based upon two models, *cognitive neoassociation* (Berkowitz, 1984, 1990, 1994, 1997) and the *general affective aggression model* (Anderson, 1997). Political priming has also been explained by a network model that takes into account the accessibility or frequency of primed information from mass media, along with the applicability of such information in the mind of the viewer (Price & Tewksbury, 1997; Scheufele & Tewksbury, 2007).

Whereas Roskos-Ewoldsen and his associates (2009) point out that "priming, as conceptualized by network models of memory, clearly occurs with the media" (p. 84), they also note the shortcomings of the network models for explaining the different areas of priming and argue for the use of *mental models* as an alternative approach for understanding the mechanisms present in priming effects.

Cognitive Neoassociation

The concept of **cognitive neoassociation** is a social psychological perspective that attempts to explain a portion of the phenomenon of memory (Anderson & Bower, 1973; Landman & Manis, 1983). To understand cognitive neoassociation, one must picture the brain as a complex network of pathways that connect associative ideas, thoughts, feelings, and concepts. *Memory* can be described as the overall network. When a person watches a television program or reads a newspaper, the information being processed triggers or activates certain pathways throughout the network. Individual thoughts or feelings from past experiences are *remembered* and associated with the new information. These ideas and thoughts may stimulate other, related ideas and they may influence a person's actions.

When audiences are presented with a certain stimulus that has a specific meaning, they are "primed" to related concepts. Ideas connected to emotions trigger associated feelings and responses. For example, research has shown that *thinking* depressing thoughts can actually cause *feelings* of depression (Velten, 1968), and exposure to ideas of aggression can produce feelings of anger or even aggressive acts under some circumstances (Berkowitz & Heimer, 1989).

Audience members are likely to have thoughts with meanings similar to what they are viewing or *semantically* similar thoughts. In short, the primed ideas activate semantically related thoughts (Collins & Loftus, 1975). Watching a love scene in a movie, for instance, causes audiences to remember similar moments in their own lives and recall emotions associated with the events.

Research shows that thinking depressing thoughts can actually trigger feelings of depression.

Individual differences in perceptions, of course, cause priming activation strengths to vary considerably from person to person (Bargh & Chartrand, 2000). Priming effects appear to be mitigated by the recency of each individual's experiences that are called into recollection and thus their individual perceptions of the priming mechanism. More recent research has delved further into the effects of priming, showing that access to related memories provides only part of the picture—the application of related knowledge constructs also occurs (Althaus & Kim, 2006).

General Affective Aggression Model

Another network model, the **general affective aggression model**, explains priming as a three-step process. In the first step, arousal is increased when exposure to mediated violence primes hostile thoughts and anger. In step two, a primary or automatic appraisal is made in the mind of the viewer; and in the third step, a secondary appraisal is made in which the viewer thinks more carefully about reactions to the prime.

Mental Models

"A **mental model** is a dynamic mental representation of a situation, event, or object" (van Dijk & Kintsch, 1983). We may use these mental models as a way to (1) process, organize, and comprehend incoming information (Radvansky, Zwann, Federico, & Franklin, 1998; Zwann & Radvansky, 1998), (2) make social judgments (Wyer & Radvansky, 1999), (3) formulate predictions and inferences (Magliano, Dijkstra, & Swann, 1996), or (4) generate descriptions and explanations of how a system operates (Rickheit & Sichelschmidt, 1999). A key notion of the mental model approach is that there is some correspondence between an external entity and our constructed mental representations of that entity (Johnson-Laird, 1983, 1989; Norman, 1983). An important element of mental models is the sense that they are "runable" (Williams, Hollan, & Stevens, 1983) in that elements of the model can be changed to see how other elements of the mental model or relationships between elements of the model would change (Roskos-Ewoldsen et al., 2009, pp. 84–85).

Researchers have identified the differences between mental models, situation models, and schemas. A **situation model** is a type of mental model that is less abstract than mental models or schemas. A person creates a situation model in memory to represent a particular story or episode viewed via mass media, whereas a person would create a mental model based on a number of related stories or episodes. A **schema** is "a cognitive structure that represents knowledge about a concept or type of stimulus, including its attributes and the relations among those attributes" (Fiske & Taylor, 1991, p. 98). Schemas are similar to mental models, but are more abstract, less contextualized, and less mutable (Roskos-Ewoldsen et al., 2009).

Mental models are time-bound, like priming activations, but exist for longer periods of time than network models of priming. They are "mutable, dynamic, and contextualized" (Roskos-Ewoldsen et al., 2009, p. 87). Mental models therefore can explain priming effects of political communications that last weeks or even months. At some point, however, the repeated priming of concepts via mass media passes the threshold into cultivation effects rather than priming effects. Currently, precise time lines that would differentiate these models are in question.

Variables That Enhance Priming Effects

The connection between the *priming* of aggressive thoughts and the *actual display of aggression* is, generally speaking, a tenuous one, but it is substantially strengthened whenever certain variables are present. Research has shown that these **intervening variables**, or variables that strengthen and serve as catalysts for the cause-effect phenomenon when they are present, include the following:

1. The perceived meaning of the communication.
2. The perceived justifiability of the witnessed aggression.
3. The extent to which audiences identify with the characters.
4. The perceived reality of the mediated communication.
5. The stimulus of prior experiences.

Perceived Meaning

Berkowitz and Alioto (1973) angered male participants and then showed them either a professional prizefight or a professional football game. The participants were given information that would enable them to interpret the events in one of two ways: either the athletes were intent on hurting each other or the athletes were simply performing their professional jobs without emotion. After watching the event, the participants had the opportunity to shock the person who had provoked them earlier. The men who had been led to believe that the athletes were intent upon hurting each other showed evidence of being "primed" with more aggressive thoughts, because they administered more punishing electrical shocks.

Contact sports have the potential to prime thoughts about hostile and aggressive behaviors. *Daniel Padavona/shutterstock.com*

Perceived Justifiability

Research has shown that viewers of mediated violence are also influenced in their actions by the *outcomes* of the situations they see. Several studies have revealed that viewers believe what happens on television or in movies could also happen to them if they behave in ways similar to the characters depicted (Bandura, 1977; Comstock, 1980; Comstock et al., 1978; Huesmann, 1982). When viewers see aggressors suffering as a result of their behavior, they are less likely to imitate the aggressive behavior (Bandura, 1965b, 1977). Also, when viewers are reminded of the serious and unfortunate consequences of violence, aggression is usually restrained. Goranson (1969) gave angry participants a chance to punish their provocateur after viewing a film in which a man received a bad beating in a prizefight. One group of participants was told the beaten man subsequently died from his injuries; the other group did not receive this information. The participants who were led to believe that the fighter died showed more restraint in punishing the provocateur than did participants in the other experimental condition.

Character Identification

Research has also shown that identification with a media character enhances priming effects. In one study, three groups of male participants were angered, then asked to watch a prizefight (Turner & Berkowitz, 1972). The members of one group were told to think of themselves as the winner. The men in the second group were told to think of themselves as the referee. The third group did not receive any instructions. In each group, half the participants were directed to think of the word "hit" each time the winner punched his opponent. After the movie, each participant had the opportunity to shock the person who had angered him. The most severe punishment was administered by the group of men who had pictured themselves as the winner and had purportedly thought "hit" with each punch.

Researchers have advanced various hypotheses to explain the strength of identification in causing priming effects. The "hit" word may have served as a cue from memory to retrieve combative experiences from the past. The inducement of such memories, along with the thoughts and feelings associated with them, would only serve to intensify aggression. Jo and Berkowitz (1994) wrote:

> It could be that the viewers who identify with (or think of themselves as) the movie aggressor are especially apt to have aggression-related thoughts as they watch the violent events. In their minds they strike at the film victim along with the movie aggressor so that these aggression-related thoughts then prime their aggression-associated mental networks relatively strongly. (p. 54)

Perceived Reality

The perceived reality of media depictions can also intensify the strength of priming effects. Research has shown that priming effects are strongest when audiences believe they are witnessing *actual* rather than *fictional* events. In one study, angered participants saw the same war film, but only half were told it was a fictional movie (Berkowitz & Alioto, 1973). The other half was led to believe that the film depicted actual combat. When given the opportunity afterward to punish their provocateur with electrical shock, members of the latter group administered shocks that were longer in duration. Another study found similar results among three groups of fifth- and sixth-grade children (Atkin, 1983). The first group of children saw a fight being reported realistically on the news. The second group viewed the fight in the context of fantasy entertainment. The control group viewed an ordinary commercial. When tested, the first group scored significantly higher on an aggression index than did the other two groups.

Memories of Prior Experiences

Another factor identified with enhancing priming effects is that of *prior learning* or *remembered experiences.* As an audience member views a violent act, he or she remembers other occasions when semantically similar thoughts or feelings cropped up. The memory reactivates a neural network or a mental model and strengthens the effects of priming.

> ### Research Has Shown . . .
>
> Priming effects are most enhanced when audience members:
> - *Interpret* the *meaning* of a film or communication in a particular way.
> - *Believe* that the violent behavior they are seeing is *justified* for some reason.
> - *Identify* with the characters they see.
> - *Believe* they are seeing *actual* events rather than fiction.
> - See the portrayed violence and *remember* experiencing similar feelings and thoughts in the past.

Research Tradition

Psychologists began studying the effects of priming on social interactions several decades ago. Many of these studies have used similar procedures to examine various aspects of priming. Researchers have subtly introduced certain thoughts into the minds of the people being studied; then they have tested those people to determine the extent of the priming effect.

Many early priming studies focused upon the psychological phenomenon itself rather than the media effects dimension, but the findings of these studies have proven very useful for media effects scholars. Wyer and Srull (1981) gave study participants word sets from which they were instructed to make sentences. Some participants were given words with meanings semantically related to aggression, whereas others received only neutral words. When evaluating a targeted person, participants who had constructed aggression-related sentences were far more critical.

Some early studies showed that priming can even occur without a person's awareness. Bargh and Pietromonaco (1982) exposed their study participants to certain words, some of which were semantically related to the idea of hostility, and then asked them to evaluate a targeted person. Those who were primed with more hostility-related words were far more negative in their evaluations of a target person than were those who had not received the hostility priming.

Wilson and Capitman (1982) asked male participants to read one of two stories—a romantic "boy-meets-girl" story or a control story. Those who had read the romantic story were observed afterward to pay much closer attention to a female confederate than were those who had read the control story.

A number of media effects studies have shown strong evidence for priming, especially for the priming of ideas related to aggression. One study found that children who read comic books with violent contents were more likely to have aggressive thoughts than children who read comic books with more neutral contents (Berkowitz, 1973). Another study (Berkowitz, 1970) examined the effects of listening to aggression-related humor. Young women who heard either the hostile humor of Don Rickles or a nonaggressive comedy routine by George Carlin were then asked to rate a job applicant. The women who had listened to Rickles evaluated applicants more harshly than did the women who had heard Carlin.

Recent Research

Media effects scholars continue to study priming effects, especially those that result from exposure to media violence, but recently the focus has changed from television and movies to the impact of video games. Political priming has shifted to investigate how movies and television and websites prime political information. Also, many studies in recent years have examined the priming of racial stereotypes in media content (Roskos-Ewoldsen et al., 2009).

Studies have shown that playing violent video games primes aggression, but on a short-term basis only (Anderson, 2004; Anderson & Dill, 2000; Anderson & Murphy, 2003; Carnagey & Anderson, 2005; Uhlmann & Swanson, 2004). Other studies have not found such a link (Cooper & Mackie, 1986; Graybill, Kirsch, & Esselman, 1985; Scott, 1995). Three meta-analyses of such priming studies found that video game violence primes aggression and aggression-related concepts in memory (Anderson & Bushman, 2001; Roskos-Ewoldsen et al., 2007; Sherry, 2001). Other researchers noted that the earliest two meta-analyses did not include longitudinal studies (Dill & Dill, 1998). Another problem with the research that social scientists have identified is that there are so many different kinds of games available, and each one has potentially different effects.

Williams & Skoric (2005) selected the violent video game *Asheron's Call 2*, that involves repetitive killing of monsters to advance. They hypothesized that over time, players would come to approve of aggression as a response in a social situation. They found that the amount of game play over a month's time did not predict whether or not participants answered on a questionnaire that they had had an "argument with a friend" during that time, and as such found that "there were no strong effects associated with aggression caused by this violent video game" (p. 228).

A more recent study of the use of avatars in virtual settings found that avatars can prime negative attitudes and thoughts. Those using black-cloaked avatars showed more aggressive intentions and attitudes and less group cohesion than those using white-cloaked avatars (Pena, Hancock, & Merola, 2009).

In the area of political news coverage, studies have usually focused on media coverage of particular issues and subsequent presidential performance ratings among audiences, to see if the media primed the audiences to make certain judgments. In one famous study, researchers examined people's opinions of President Ronald Reagan before and after the Iran-Contra scandal of 1986. If you recall, the U.S. sold weapons to Iran and gave the profits to the Contras in Central America. Before the event, the overall evaluations of Reagan were predicted by domestic issues, but after the Iran-Contra affair, people based their evaluation of Reagan on foreign affairs issues, particularly those in Central America (Krosnick & Kinder, 1990). In a more recent study in South Korea, researchers also found that television news coverage affected evaluations of their president, but they pointed out that the priming was largely due to the recency rather than the frequency of the coverage (Kim, Han, & Scheufele, 2010).

In a 2005 study, Holbrook and Hill found that content in entertainment media as well as news media can serve as primes for political concerns. In particular, viewing of prime-time crime dramas (*Third Watch, NYPD Blue, Robbery Homicide Division,* and *Without a Trace)* is a significant indicator of people's concerns about crime in the real world, and these primes caused people to judge the president based on his performance in addressing crime.

A study of the documentary film *Fahrenheit 9-11* showed that viewing the movie had significant effects on people's evaluations of President George W. Bush (Holbert & Hansen, 2006). This study found support that ambivalence—the presence of both positive and negative evaluations—sometimes exists in the minds of the electorate, especially political Independents. When they were presented with the strong, anti-Bush message of the movie, those identifying themselves as Republicans, Democrats, and Independents reacted in different ways. The Democrats and Independents decreased in ambivalence and had more negative attitudes toward Bush than did the Republicans, who increased in ambivalence.

Another study involved a telephone survey prior to the 2008 presidential primary election. Respondents were primed to think about the war in Iraq and the president (Bush) before they were asked for their candidate choice. The priming more than doubled the support for Barack Obama and hurt support for the Republican front-runner (Cassino & Erisen, 2010).

In addition to movies and crime dramas, late-night talk shows have also been shown to be responsible for political priming (Moy, Xenos, & Hess, 2006; see the Research Spotlight box in Chapter 14). Viewers of *The Late Show with David Letterman* were more likely than nonviewers to evaluate George W. Bush's character traits based on his appearance on the show.

Political sophistication of voters affects media priming. One study found that those who are moderately sophisticated in their knowledge of political affairs were more likely to be primed by mass media than were those who were most or least sophisticated (Ha, 2011).

Stereotype priming is a growing area of priming research and includes the study of priming stereotypes related to gender and race. In one study, some participants viewed video segments of three different stereotypes of African American women: a mammy, a jezebel, or a welfare queen. Then they were asked to rate a well-groomed African American woman on a mock job interview. Those who saw the videos of specific stereotypes were more likely than those who did not see them to use stereotype-consistent adjectives to describe the interviewee (Monahan, Shtrulis, & Givens, 2005).

Research Spotlight

Priming Mammies, Jezebels, and Other Controlling Images: An Examination of the Influence of Mediated Stereotypes on Perceptions of an African American Woman
Sonja M. Brown Givens and Jennifer L. Monahan (2005)
Media Psychology, 7, 87–106

After showing participants images of a mammy, jezebel, or nonstereotypic image of African American females on video, participants observed mock interviews with African American and White women. The African American interviewee was associated more readily with negative terms (such as "aggressive") than with positive terms (such as "sincere"). Participants who saw the jezebel stereotype video were more likely to associate the African American interviewee with jezebel-related terms (such as "sexual") than with positive, negative, or mammy-related (such as "maternal") terms.

Hypotheses

H1a: Response times will be faster to negative words and slower to positive words when evaluating an African American woman.

H1b: Response times will be faster to positive words and slower to negative words when evaluating a White woman.

H2a: Exposure to stereotypic portrayals of an African American woman will result in stereotype-consistent judgments of another African American woman.

H2b: Response times will be faster to stereotype-consistent adjectives than to stereotype-inconsistent adjectives after viewing a stereotypic image of an African American woman.

Method

Undergraduate students from introductory speech communication courses participated in the study. Of the 182 students, 70% were between the ages of 18 and 21, with 158 who classified themselves as White, 13 as Black, 2 as Hispanic, 8 as Asian, and 1 as "other." About half (48.4%) were male.

Participants viewed a 3–minute videotaped segment of a movie clip that represented either a mammy (a nurturing Black woman), a jezebel (a sexually aggressive African American woman), or a nonstereotype control condition (no references to African American women or female sexuality). The "mammy" condition was taken from the 1959 film *Imitation of Life.* The "jezebel" condition was from the 1999 biographical film of Dorothy Dandridge's life, played by

Halle Berry. The control condition was a segment of the movie *Better off Dead,* and featured a middle-aged White man having difficulty retrieving the morning newspaper from his lawn.

After viewing one of the tapes, participants watched one of two 3–minute mock employment interviews. The interviewees were female, either White or African American. Great care was taken so that the interviewees responded to interviewer questions in very similar ways.

A list of adjectives was developed, 40 in all, with eight being stereotypically positive (such as sincere, friendly, intelligent), nine stereotypically negative (aggressive, hostile, lazy), eight related to the mammy stereotype (maternal, loyal, devoted), and nine related to the jezebel stereotype (sexual, alluring, erotic). The remaining terms were used as fillers (shy, fun, organized, etc.).

Participants were asked whether the character traits fit the person they observed on the interview tape, and the speed at which they responded with each adjective was timed and recorded in milliseconds. Participants also responded to 40 items that indicated the suitability of the African American or White woman for the position of sales representative.

Results

Participants who viewed the African American female interviewee responded significantly faster to negative adjectives than positive ones, and those who viewed the White female interviewee responded significantly faster to positive adjectives than negatives ones. Hypotheses 1a and 1b were supported.

Hypothesis 2a was not supported by the evidence, but Hypothesis 2b received partial support. Participants who saw the jezebel prime responded significantly faster to jezebel-related terms than to mammy terms when evaluating the African American interviewee. Those who viewed the mammy prime responded faster to mammy-related terms than to jezebel-related terms but the difference was not statistically significant.

One study examined television portrayals of Asian Americans to see if they would affect viewers' judgments of both Asian and African Americans and whether or not viewers were inclined to endorse affirmative action. Studies have shown that television portrayals usually stereotype Asian Americans as hardworking and skilled in business and technology. The study found that exposure to positive portrayals of Asian Americans led to more positive perceptions of them, and more negative stereotypical perceptions of African Americans. The positive portrayal of Asian Americans were associated with less endorsement of affirmative action (Dalisay & Tan, 2009).

Another study (Dixon, 2007) revealed that when the race of the officer and the criminal are not revealed in a crime news story, heavy viewers of news were more likely than light news viewers to think of the arresting officer as White and the criminal as Black.

As the examples have shown, priming theory has become a viable theoretical basis for the explanation of many different types of media effects. The theory has found successful application in a variety of domains of media effects research, and study after study records support for the principles of the theory. In addition to violent media content, researchers now often measure the extent to which other types of media content, such as political communications and minority stereotypes, also serve to prime media audiences. The number of media effects studies based upon priming theory continues to increase as more researchers seek to identify the links between media priming and the subsequent attitudes and behaviors of audience members.

Summary

Priming is a popular area of media effects research that explores the cognitive components of information processing. Priming occurs when exposure to mediated communication activates related thoughts in the mind of an audience member. In other words, media content triggers concepts, thoughts, learning, or knowledge acquired in the past and related to the message content. For a certain period of time after viewing, a person is more likely to have thoughts about the content, related thoughts, or memories than a person who does not view the content.

Priming may influence a person's thoughts or behavior, but only for a brief time. For most people, priming effects cause mild reactions that diminish in time or may pass unnoticed. The priming effects from media violence often pass very quickly, whereas political priming effects can last for weeks or months.

Most studies investigating the priming of media violence have been based upon one of two models, cognitive neoassociation or the general affective aggression model. Political priming has additionally been explained by a network model that takes into account the accessibility or frequency of primed information from mass media, along with the applicability of such information in the mind of the viewer.

The use of mental models to explain priming effects offers an alternative to network models of memory. Mental models differ from situation models or schemas. Mental models are time-bound, like priming activations, but exist for longer periods of time than do network models of priming. Mental models therefore can explain priming effects of political messages that last weeks or even months. At some yet undefined point, however, the repeated priming of concepts via mass media passes the threshold into cultivation effects rather than priming effects.

The connection between the priming of aggressive thoughts and the actual display of aggression is not particularly strong unless certain variables are present. These include (1) the perceived meaning of the communication, (2) the perceived justifiability of the witnessed aggression, (3) the extent to which audiences identify with the characters, (4) the perceived reality of the mediated communication, and (5) the stimulus of prior experiences.

Psychologists began studying the effects of priming on social interactions several decades ago. Many of these studies have used similar procedures to examine various aspects. Researchers subtly introduce certain thoughts into the minds of the people being studied; then they test those people to determine the extent of the priming effect.

Media effects studies have shown strong evidence for priming, especially for the priming of ideas related to aggression. In recent years, media effects scholars have continued to study priming effects, especially those that result from exposure to media violence, but the focus has changed from television and movies to the impact of video games. Political priming has shifted to investigate how movies and television and websites prime political information. Also, many studies in recent years have examined the priming of racial stereotypes in media content.

Agenda Setting

*I am one of those who believe that at least in America the press
rules the country; it rules its politics, its religion, its social practices.*
—Edward Willis Scripps, from *Damned Old Crank* (1951)

Does the news tell us what to think as a society? Or, in an oft-quoted remark by a communication scholar, is it "stunningly successful" in telling us "what to think about" (Cohen, 1963, p. 13)? The strong link between the importance that news media place on particular issues and the importance that the public places on those same issues demonstrates a type of communication effect called **agenda setting**.

Numerous studies have shown that news media do set the public agenda, but only in recent years have media effects researchers been able to solve empirical problems that had made it difficult for them to address agenda-setting issues in compelling ways. For years, critics of agenda setting pointed out that the methods employed in agenda-setting research only indicated that a relationship existed between the media agenda and the public agenda. The causal direction, they said, could not be established. Do the media always set the agenda for the public, they asked, or does the public sometimes set the media agenda? This led to ongoing research that asks the question: Who sets the agenda?

Using precise statistical methods, causal directions are now much clearer. Agenda-setting effects are clearly indicated only when researchers are able to measure public opinion before and after media coverage of specific issues and to control or account for additional factors. For this reason, election campaigns have been popular among researchers because of their periodicity and other characteristics that make them suitable for agenda-setting research designs.

Initially, agenda-setting research examined in fairly global terms the influence of news media in shaping people's perceptions of varied issues and events. Since the seminal study of public issues in the 1968 presidential campaign

(McCombs & Shaw, 1972), studies have confirmed the strong correspondence between news stories and the salience of issues covered to the public.

In recent years, agenda-setting research has expanded to ask the question: "Who sets the media agenda?" Each day, hundreds of news stories occur around the world, throughout the nation, in individual regions and states, and at local levels. News professionals cannot possibly examine, organize, and pass along to the public *all* the news of the day. Space and time limitations preclude doing that. Instead, journalists and news editors must decide which stories to cover, which to run, and which to ignore. In making such decisions, news professionals invariably *set the agenda* for news consumers. They gauge the value of news on the basis of their perceptions of its importance to their readers and viewers.

Control over the flow of news information by media professionals is an important function called **gatekeeping**. Simply put, journalists, editors, and broadcasters allow a certain amount of news to pass through to the public each day, but time and space constraints force them to shut the gates and stop the flow of most information to news consumers. Scholars have been aware of this powerful gatekeeping function for many years, but only recently have they begun to examine the many factors that influence the gatekeeping process.

More recent research has identified a **second level of agenda setting** called **attribute agenda setting** (McCombs & Reynolds, 2009). This research strongly resembles framing research in many ways (see Chapter 7). Researchers study the attributes of different elements related to media stories—such as the attributes of issue coverage, attributes of candidates, or of their images. Studies have shown that people tend to attribute to candidates that which the press tells them to attribute (Becker & McCombs, 1978; Kim & McCombs, 2007; King, 1997; McCombs, Lopez-Escobar, & Llamas, 2000). The way the press covers attributes of issues has also been found to influence voters. In one Japanese study, the media emphasized the importance of traditional government mechanisms in initiating political reforms, and the more people used the media, the more they cited this as an issue of importance (Takeshita & Mikami, 1995).

Attributes can be *cognitive* in nature, meaning that the media user thinks about the issues or candidates and their attributes, or attributes can be *affective* in nature, meaning that the media user notices the tone in which the attributes are portrayed. If the media portray candidates or issues in negative or positive tones, they can actually influence what voters think, rather than simply what they think about.

This makes **framing** of a news story very important. Journalists can use particular viewpoints from various sources or even particular word choices to "frame" a story in a particular light. Frames "invite people to think about an issue in a particular way" (Tewksbury & Scheufele, 2009, p. 19).

This chapter identifies the conceptual foundations of agenda setting and provides a brief history of the agenda-setting research tradition. It also takes a look at recent trends in agenda-setting research, such as attribute agenda setting, and studies that examine who sets the media agenda, including intermedia agenda setting. It examines the scholarly controversy over agenda setting, framing, and priming, noting similarities and differences in these three related areas of media effects research.

Conceptual Roots

Bernard Cohen (1963) was not the first to describe the notion of the press setting the public agenda. The concept can be traced to Walter Lippmann, a famous newspaper columnist and social commentator of the early 20th century. Lippmann's book, *Public Opinion* (1922), has been called the most influential, nonscholarly work in the history of the academic study of mass communication (Carey, 1996). Lippmann wrote about how the news media are responsible for shaping the public's perception of the world. He emphasized that the pictures of reality created by the news media were merely *reflections* of actual reality and therefore were sometimes distorted. Lippmann said that the news-media projections of the world create a **pseudo-environment** for each news consumer. The pseudo-environment exists in addition to the *actual* environment, and people react to this pseudo-environment that media create. "For the real environment is altogether too big, too complex, and too fleeting for a direct acquaintance" (p. 16).

Other scholars also described the concept of agenda setting in their writings prior to empirical assessment of the concept in the early 1970s. In 1958 Norton Long wrote:

> In a sense, the newspaper is the prime mover in setting the territorial agenda. It has a great part in determining what most people will be talking about, what most people will think the facts are, and what most people will regard as the way problems are to be dealt with. (p. 260)

The following year, Kurt and Gladys Lang wrote: "The mass media force attention to certain issues. They build up public images of political figures. They are constantly presenting objects suggesting what individuals in the mass should think about, know about, have feelings about" (1959, p. 232).

The Cognitive Paradigm

According to Kosicki (1993), agenda-setting research evolved into its present form for several reasons. During the 1960s and 1970s, researchers rejected using the persuasion paradigm to explain agenda-setting effects, and began taking notice of the emerging cognitive paradigm.

> Agenda setting, with its apparently simple, easy-to-explain, and intuitively appealing hypothesis, seemed right for the time. On its face it is a rejection of persuasion, a "reframing" of the basic research question from "telling people what to think" to "telling them what to think about" (Cohen, 1963). This seemingly small, but clever, twist of phrase focuses attention away from persuasion and onto something new. The freshness of the model has obvious appeal. It signals not only a move away from persuasion toward other cognitive factors (Becker & Kosicki, 1991), but a move toward a particular kind of cognitive factor: an agenda of issues. (Kosicki, 1993, p. 231)

In the cognitive paradigm, three primary factors influence each other bidirectionally: a person's behavior, a person's cognitive abilities, and environmental events to which a person is exposed. "Reciprocal causation provides people with opportunities to exercise some control over events in their lives, as well as set limits of self-direction. Because of the bidirectionality of influence, people are both products and producers of their environment" (Bandura, 1994, p. 61).

The need for orientation, for example, is based upon the idea of cognitive mapping, in which people strive to orient themselves whenever they find themselves in unfamiliar settings. Agenda-setting researchers have found that voters with high need for orientation (a high degree of interest in the election and a high degree of uncertainty about key issues) are more likely to be influenced by media messages. According to McCombs and Reynolds (2009), "The concept of need for orientation provides a richer psychological explanation for variability in agenda-setting effects than simply classifying issues along the obtrusive/unobtrusive continuum" (p. 8).

Priming

Priming is another strong conceptual basis for the agenda-setting phenomenon, as it is considered by researchers to be one of the outcomes of agenda setting (McCombs & Reynolds, 2009; see Chapter 5). When the news media report on particular attributes of certain issues or emphasize particular characteristics of political candidates, for example, news consumers are "primed" to associate those characteristics with those candidates or identify certain attributes to particular issues.

"By calling attention to some matters while ignoring others, television news [as well as other news media] influences the standards by which governments, presidents, policies, and candidates for public office are judged" (Iyengar & Kinder, 1987, p. 63).

Research Tradition

The first empirical test of Lippmann's ideas about agenda setting was published in 1972 by two University of North Carolina researchers, Maxwell McCombs and Donald Shaw, in what came to be known as the Chapel Hill study.

In 1968 the Vietnam conflict raged, African Americans struggled for civil rights, the country's youth rebelled against authority, and drug abuse became a serious problem. Robert F. Kennedy's bid for the presidency ended tragically when an assassin gunned him down in California. Hubert H. Humphrey emerged as the Democratic nominee instead, challenging Republican Richard M. Nixon and the independent candidate, George C. Wallace.

In this tempestuous social climate, as the nation prepared to select a new chief executive, McCombs and Shaw designed a study to test the influence of campaign coverage on public perceptions of the importance of several crucial social issues. Prior to the election, they asked Chapel Hill voters: "What are you most concerned about these days? That is, regardless of what politicians say, what are the two or three main things which you think the government should

The first agenda-setting study was conducted in the tempestuous social climate of 1968.

concentrate on doing something about?" (McCombs & Shaw, 1972, p. 178). The issues that respondents identified—foreign policy, law and order, fiscal policy, civil rights, and public welfare—were ranked according to the percentage of respondents identifying them.

The actual content of local news media served as a measured independent variable in the Chapel Hill study, and the dependent variable, issue salience, was compared to topic coverage. The researchers analyzed the contents of local newspapers, television, and radio stations for three weeks during the campaign to identify issues that were receiving the most media attention. When McCombs and Shaw compared these results to the public responses, they found almost identical "agendas" on the part of the public and the news media. They named this "transfer of salience" of issues from the media to the public "the agenda-setting influence of mass communication" (McCombs & Bell, 1996, p. 96).

After this groundbreaking study, it might be said that agenda-setting research caught fire among communication investigators, with hundreds of studies being conducted throughout the ensuing decades. McCombs and Shaw (1993) reviewed the abundant research findings and identified four phases of growth in agenda-setting research: (1) publication of their original study in 1972, (2) replication and examination of contingent conditions, (3) an expansion of the original idea of agenda setting into the areas of candidate characteristics and other political aspects, and (4) a focus upon the sources of the media agenda.

In 1973, G. Ray Funkhouser replicated the Chapel Hill study and identified a strong correspondence between public opinion trends in the 1960s and coverage of issues in the news media during that period. Funkhouser assessed public opinion using answers to a Gallup Poll question regarding the most significant problem in the nation. He analyzed the content of issues of *Time, Newsweek,* and *U.S. News and World Report* to determine the media agenda. He then compared these findings with official statistics (e.g., the actual number of U.S. soldiers in Vietnam, number of demonstrations on campus or on behalf of civil rights) to gauge congruence between *actual* reality and *perceptions* of reality on the part of the public and the media. He found a strong correlation between the amount of media coverage of an issue and the public's perceived importance of that issue; moreover, he also found that media coverage did not always represent the actual reality of issues and situations (Funkhouser, 1973).

McCombs and Shaw's second study (Shaw & McCombs, 1977) examined the causal directions for agenda-setting effects and contingent conditions for such effects during the 1972 presidential election campaign. Voters in Charlotte, North Carolina, were surveyed before and after the election to reveal short-term agenda-setting effects. The researchers found that voters with a greater need for orientation to their world and voters who used the mass media more frequently than others were more likely to have agendas that corresponded to the news media agenda. As for causation, the researchers claimed to find evidence to support the agenda-setting influence of the press, but the evidence was not overwhelming (1977; Westley, 1978).

In an attempt to provide stronger evidence for causal direction, the next major study of agenda setting was conducted in a laboratory setting where the researchers manipulated videotaped network television newscasts to vary the placement and emphasis given to the stories (Iyengar, Peters, & Kinder, 1982). Each day for a week, research participants viewed the altered newscasts, which were presented to them as actual and unaltered. Participants were divided into two groups. One group was shown newscasts that emphasized the weak nature of U.S. military defenses; the other group saw newscasts that did not contain these particular stories. The researchers surveyed participants before and after the weeklong experiment and found statistically significant agenda-setting effects. At the end of the week, the group that had seen the "weak defense" stories rated the issue of military defense significantly higher than the group that had not been shown the stories (Iyengar et al., 1982). Follow-up experiments provided additional empirical evidence for the agenda-setting effects of mass media (Iyengar & Kinder, 1987; Wanta, 1988).

Another phase of agenda-setting research began during the 1976 presidential campaign when the agenda of candidate characteristics and the alternative agenda of political interest were examined (Weaver, Graber, McCombs, & Eyal, 1981). The researchers analyzed the dynamics of how voters perceived candidate characteristics and the images of candidates portrayed in the media (McCombs, 1992). Voters in six locations—three sites in the Northeast and three in the Midwest—participated in the longitudinal study to assess contingent factors at work in the agenda-setting process. The voters' occupations, education levels, and geographic locations were found to affect the degree to which the media were responsible for setting their issue agendas at various times during the election campaign.

Agenda-Setting Research

Four Phases at a Glance

Phase 1: Initial Study

Chapel Hill Study (1972), McCombs & Shaw.

Findings: The issues considered important by the news media were also considered important by the general public.

Phase 2: Replication

Charlotte Voter Study (1977), Shaw & McCombs.

Findings: Voters with greater orientation needs and those who used mass media more often than others were more likely to have agendas (issue salience) that matched the media agenda.

Laboratory Study (1982), Iyengar, Peters, & Kinder.

Findings: Research participants who viewed stories about the weak nature of United States defense capabilities rated the issue significantly higher than those who did not see the stories.

Phase 3: Contingent Factors

1976 Candidate Study (1981), Weaver, Graber, McCombs, & Eyal.

Findings: Dynamics of voters' perceptions of candidates and their images as portrayed by news media were examined. Contingent factors were found to affect the agenda-setting process. Voters' occupations, education levels, and their geographic locations played a part in determining whether voters' issue agendas matched the media agenda.

Phase 4: Who Sets The Media Agenda?

Media Agenda Sources (1991), Shoemaker & Reese.

Findings: Many influences are at work creating the media agenda each day. These include, for example, sociological factors related to the news organization and external organizations, ideological factors, individual differences among reporters and editors, and the routine of media work.

A fourth phase began in the 1980s when researchers began investigating sources of the media agenda. A number of influences that create the media agenda each day were identified (Shoemaker & Reese, 1991). These included sociological factors related to the news organization and external organizations, the routine of media work, ideological concerns, and individual differences between reporters and editors.

Recent Research

The current state of agenda-setting research expands on all four phases, but many recent studies have focused on attribute agenda setting and who sets the media agenda. There has been an explosion of framing studies in recent years, along with the argument that framing should be considered a separate area of media effects research; consequently, we have provided a separate chapter on framing in this volume.

McCombs and Reynolds noted in 2009 that since the Chapel Hill study, "more than 425 empirical studies on the agenda-setting influence of the news media" have been conducted by researchers (p. 2). This section will examine several studies conducted since the turn of the century.

One avenue that agenda-setting researchers have begun exploring is the various effects of Internet news coverage. Wang (2000) conducted an experiment in which certain groups were shown an online newspaper containing articles on racism, and other groups were shown online newspapers not containing the racism articles. The groups who read the racism articles subsequently identified racism as an important public issue.

In 2003, Ku, Kaid, and Pfau published a study that looked at the importance of website campaigning on both public opinion and setting the traditional media agendas. They noted that "there is strong evidence of a convergence of the public's attention to the issues on the Web sites," and that the candidate websites had a "direct agenda-setting impact on the public" (p. 544).

Another study of agenda setting tested readers of the online version of *The New York Times* (Althaus & Tewksbury, 2002). For five days, some readers examined the print version of the newspaper whereas others examined the online version. Both experienced agenda-setting effects, and their perceptions of important issues were different, corresponding to the differing issues of importance in the print and online versions.

Attribute Agenda Setting and Framing

Hester and Gibson (2003) used a content analysis and a time-series analysis to study second-level agenda-setting effects of news about the economy and its influence on people's perceptions and actual economic conditions. They found that negative economic news was much more likely to occur than positive news, and that the negative news coverage had no effect on individuals' evaluations of *present* economic predictions. Instead, people seem to rely more on "day-to-day personal experiences with the economy and real-world economic indicators when making assessments of current economic conditions" (p. 85). The researchers did find that the negative news coverage was a strong factor in shaping opinions of the public regarding *future* economic conditions. In the words of the researchers, "Increased unfavorable news coverage of the economy was related to lowered evaluations of future economic performance" (p. 85). They noted that time-series analysis allowed them to confidently say that the media influenced people's evaluations and not the other way around.

An attribute agenda setting study conducted by Kim and McCombs (2007) found that media portrayal of candidates' attributes had a strong influence on voters in the 2002 elections for Texas governor and U.S. senator. These researchers content analyzed a daily newspaper in Austin, Texas, and identified attributes that were strongly covered in the press, including "general political descriptions, specific issue positions, personal qualifications and character, biographical information, campaign conduct, and support and endorsements" (p. 303). Then they

Research Spotlight

News Story Descriptions and the Public's Opinions of Political Candidates
Kihan Kim and Maxwell McCombs (2007)
Journalism & Mass Communication Quarterly, 84(2), 299–314

In this 2007 study, the researchers combined a content analysis of the local daily newspaper in Austin, Texas, with a telephone survey of Austin residents during the 2002 elections for Texas governor and U.S. senator to discover agenda-setting effects. "Correlation and regression analyses support the central proposition of attribute agenda setting and indicate that attributes positively or negatively covered in the news are related to opinions about each candidate. Attributes receiving extensive media attention were more likely to affect attitudinal judgments for heavy newspaper readers than for light newspaper readers" (p. 299).

The Hypotheses

H1: The public's attribute agenda for a political candidate reflects the media's attribute agenda. These attribute agendas are defined in terms of two dimensions, the substantive attributes on the agenda and the affective tone of each substantive attribute.

H2: The affective tone of the attributes in the public's mind for a candidate predicts opinions about the candidates.

H3: The substantive and affective aspects of attributes emphasized in the media are significant elements in the public's attitudinal judgments.

The Content Analysis

The content analysis focused on news stories, editorials, and opinion articles that asserted various attributes for four candidates (Rick Perry and Tony Sanchez for governor and John Cornyn and Ron Kirk for U.S. senator) during a four-week period in September 2002. They identified 298 assertions that included 83 specific or discrete attributes. The 83 attributes fell under six major attribute categories:

- General political descriptions
- Specific issue positions
- Personal qualifications and character
- Biographical information
- Campaign conduct
- Support and endorsements

Of the six, the personal qualifications and character category accounted for 42.1% of all the assertions. This category included 11 specific attributes:

- Leadership
- Experience
- Competence
- Credibility
- Morality
- Caring about people
- Communication skills
- Pride in family/background, roots, and race/ethnicity

(continued)

- Nonpolitician
- Style and personality
- Other comments about the candidate's personal qualifications and character

The researchers further coded the tone of the attributes, noting if they were positive, negative, or neutral.

The Survey

A telephone survey was conducted between September 26 and October 11, 2002, with 417 adults, randomly selected from the Austin metropolitan area. Students were trained to conduct the interviews via the telephone. Of the 417 randomly selected, 45% completed the survey.

Among those who completed the survey, 47% were male and 35% were between the ages of 18 and 34; 27% were between 35 and 44; 22% were between 44 and 54, and 16% were 55 or older. Whites accounted for 78% of respondents, African Americans, 7%, and Hispanics, 15%. Half of the sample reported annual incomes of $50,000 or higher and 60% of the sample had at least some college education or a college degree.

Variables of major interest included the public's attribute agenda for each of the four candidates and attitude toward each of the four candidates. Respondents were asked the following question to measure attribute agenda:

"Suppose that one of your friends has been away a long time and knows nothing about the candidates for governor of Texas and U.S. Senator from Texas. What would you tell your friend about (Cornyn, Kirk, Perry, and Sanchez)?"

Descriptions of the candidates were dominated by assertions about personal qualifications and character, ranging from 70% to 72% of the attributes.

To measure respondents' attitudes toward each of the candidates, they were asked:

"How do you feel about Rick Perry (Sanchez, Kirk, and Cornyn)?" They were offered a five-point scale ranging from "strongly favorable" to "strongly unfavorable."

The researchers measured three control variables: age, party identification (Republican, Democrat, and Independent) and ideological orientation (conservative, moderate, and liberal). They measured frequency of newspaper reading on a five-point scale from "never read the newspaper" to "read the newspaper every day." Respondents were asked which newspaper they read.

The Findings

The most visible candidates were described in most detail, and descriptions of all candidates focused on comments about their personal qualifications and character. The media's attribute agenda and the public's attribute agenda were found to correspond significantly, and thus hypothesis 1 was supported.

Regression analysis was used to test hypothesis 2. The positive attributes predicted attitude toward each candidate in positive directions, and negative attributes predicted attitude toward each candidate in negative directions, above and beyond the effects of political identity, ideology, age, and frequency of newspaper reading. The findings supported hypothesis 2.

To test hypothesis 3, regression analysis was used again, but this time respondents were divided into two groups of heavy and light newspaper readers. Party identification, ideological orientation, and age served as control variables. Results supported hypothesis 3, with heavy newspaper readers more likely to have attitudes toward candidates predicted by the tone emphasized in the media, whereas light newspaper readers were less likely.

conducted telephone interviews of a sample of residents in the area. Those people who read the newspaper were found to be more likely to have their judgments affected by what they read in the press regarding the attributes of the candidates.

Wu and Coleman's 2009 study of the two levels of agenda setting focused on the 2004 presidential election. The researchers found that the attributes describing the candidates had a strong influence on voter perceptions of the candidates and actually predicted their voting intentions. The study also confirmed that negative media coverage of a candidate's image influences the public more than does positive coverage.

Ha (2011), Rhee (1997), and Shen (2004) found that people's existing attitudes influence the impact of news framing. Ha found that a person's level of political sophistication was the key to understanding agenda-setting effects of campaign news coverage. The least politically sophisticated and most politically sophisticated audience members were less likely to accept the news agendas than were the moderately politically sophisticated. Shen (2004) tested research participants to see if they had preexisting beliefs and attitudes about the economic and environmental dimensions of two types of news stories, one on stem cell research and the other on oil drilling in Alaska. The participants who already had existing beliefs and attitudes on the topics were more likely than non-predisposed participants to accept new constructs that applied to the issues at hand.

The Media Agenda

Investigation of news sources that may set the media agenda has continued to interest scholars (Wanta, Stephenson, Turk, & McCombs, 1989). Several recent studies have focused on the influence of a particular U.S. president on the news media agenda. In particular, these studies have identified issues covered prominently in the news media a month before and after the President's State of the Union Address to determine any influence the speech may have had.

Wanta and Foote (1994) examined presidential documents related to various issues, then employed a time-series analysis to compare news coverage of those issues on the three national networks. The researchers identified 16 issues that they categorized into four groups: international problems, the economy, social problems, and social issues. They found significant correlations between media coverage and presidential emphasis on the issues in all categories except that of the economy.

Another important finding of the Wanta and Foote (1994) study was that media coverage was most often influenced by the president. In other words, the president's issue agenda strongly influenced the media agenda. The news media appeared to influence the president on only 3 of the 16 issues examined: East-West relations, crime and drugs, and environmental concerns.

Agenda-setting researchers have often used the metaphor of peeling an onion to describe the process of setting the media agenda, with the different layers representing different influences. These layers range from "prevailing social ideology to the beliefs and psychology of an individual journalist" (McCombs & Reynolds, 2009).

In addition to the president of the United States, other public officials and individuals have been found to influence the media agenda—even media outlets themselves, such as *The New York Times* (Mazur, 1987; Ploughman, 1984; Reese & Danielian, 1989). Public relations news releases, political advertisements, and websites have also been shown to set the agenda for other news outlets (Boyle, 2001).

Agenda Setting, Framing, and Priming

The most recent debate among mass communication scholars has to do with the similarities and differences of agenda setting, framing, and priming. Some say framing and priming should be included beneath the heading of agenda setting (Ghanem, 1997), whereas others argue that these three areas of research should be distinct from one another (Scheufele, 2000; Scheufele, 2004; Scheufele & Tewksbury, 2007).

Framing studies have escalated in recent years, but more research needs to be done to make the distinctions between framing and agenda setting clearer. Weaver (2007) wrote of agenda setting and framing: "Both are concerned with ways of thinking rather than objects of thinking. But framing does seem to include a broader range of cognitive processes—such as moral evaluations, causal reasoning, appeals to principles, and recommendations for treatment of problems—than does second-level agenda setting (the salience of attributes of an object)" (p. 146).

Framing studies are focused not only on media frames of particular issues or objects, but on the way that audience members receive and interpret those frames or develop a "schema" that can be stored in memory and activated for later judgment. Schemata are related to mental models in the way they are formed, activated, and stored (Scheufele, 2004).

Part of the problem that scholars have not addressed may have to do with semantics. Priming and agenda setting are phrases that denote active influence of one thing on another, or a media effect. The mere word *framing* suggests the activity of putting something in a particular light or saying it in a particular way, but "framing" in and of itself does not suggest an effect of any kind, even though most framing studies test for effects of the news frame. In other words, people can be "primed" and their agendas can be "set" by mass media, but a mass media consumer cannot be "framed" (except for a crime). The name does not suggest an effect, only a preliminary activity.

Summary

Agenda setting is often described in Cohen's quote that the press "may not be successful much of the time in telling people what to think, but it is stunningly successful in telling its readers what to think *about*." Recent research has identified "second-level agenda-setting effects" that reveal mass media are also successful in telling people what to think.

One serious problem that agenda-setting researchers have faced is the control of extraneous variables. Agenda-setting effects are clearly indicated only when researchers are able to measure public opinion before and after media coverage of specific issues. Strong and reliable statistical tools have helped media researchers identify the direction of the agenda-setting influence.

Initially, agenda-setting research examined the influence of news media in shaping people's perceptions of the world. In recent years, agenda-setting research has expanded to ask: Who sets the media agenda? Control over the flow of news information by media professionals is an important function called gatekeeping.

Walter Lippmann was the first to describe the agenda-setting process in *Public Opinion* (1922). He wrote about the news media's responsibility for shaping the public's perception of the world and creating a pseudo-environment for each news consumer.

The first empirical test of Lippmann's ideas about agenda-setting was Maxwell McCombs and Donald Shaw's Chapel Hill study (1972), which tested the influence of campaign coverage on public perceptions of issue importance.

Hundreds of agenda-setting studies were conducted in the years following the Chapel Hill study. The growth in the research tradition has been divided into four phases: (1) publication of the Chapel Hill study, (2) replication and examination of contingent conditions, (3) an expansion of the original idea of agenda setting into the areas of candidate characteristics and other political aspects, and (4) a focus on the sources of the media agenda.

Scholars are divided on whether agenda setting, priming, and framing should be considered different areas of media effects research.

Framing

> *Frames are seen as patterns of interpretation through which*
> *people classify information in order to handle it efficiently.*
> —Dietram Scheufele (2004), p. 402

Each day, we as news consumers are bombarded with stories from news media—television, newspapers, magazines, the Internet, mobile phones—and we form attitudes and opinions and make judgments based in part on the information we consume. In the agenda-setting chapter, we learned that mass media have the power to set our issue agendas, or tell us what to think about, and they also have the power, through the way they put together stories with words and images, to *frame* that information in such a way that can actually affect the way we think.

In recent years, media effects researchers have turned their attention to the power of the way information is put together or framed, and the effects that it has in the minds of media consumers. You will recall from the agenda-setting chapter that "attribute" agenda setting focuses on the media not only telling viewers what to think *about* but also telling them what to think. This type of research has developed into an entirely new area, called **framing**, that some media effects scholars believe should be distinguished from agenda-setting research and priming research both theoretically and experimentally.

This chapter examines the theory of framing, the effects of framing, frame-building and frame-setting approaches, and types of frames. Then we take a look at relevant recent research in framing.

Framing Theory

Framing theory finds its roots in the fields of psychology and sociology. Psychologically oriented research typically has featured micro-level studies of individuals, whereas sociologically oriented research has generated macro-level studies of society.

According to Tewksbury and Scheufele (2009), the psychological perspective of framing comes from Sherif's (1967) work on "frames of reference," and from prospect theory (Kahneman, 2003; Kahneman & Tversky, 1979, 1984). Individuals make judgments and perceive the world within certain frames of reference, and these frames of reference can be set up in such a way to impact individual judgments and perceptions. *Prospect theory* expands this idea by noting that perceptions are dependent upon the point of reference of the information that is being given. In other words, framing a message in different ways will result in different interpretations.

The sociological approaches to framing are drawn from attribution theory (Heider, 1959; Heider & Simmel, 1944) and frame analysis (Goffman, 1974). *Attribution theory* states that people simplify their perceptions of social reality by making judgments about what causes others to act in particular ways. They attribute the actions they observe to either personal, social, or environmental factors (Tewksbury & Scheufele, 2009). In *frame analysis theory*, people do not simply attribute the cause of actions, but they rely on socially shared meanings to categorize information into "schemas" (Tewksbury & Scheufele, 2009, p. 18) or "primary frameworks" (Goffman, 1974, p. 24) in their minds.

Effects of Framing

Framing can result in several types of effects, including having an impact on knowledge, persuasion, or agenda setting. "At their most powerful, frames invite people to think about an issue in particular ways" (Tewksbury & Scheufele, 2009, p. 19).

For example, if a news story contains information on an issue that has never been covered before, people will learn the facts about that issue from the presentation. If people already have set ideas about a particular issue that the news covers, the manner in which a story is framed may cause them to rethink that issue or react in some way to the information that is being presented. In some cases, the information is framed in such a way that the audience member is persuaded to a particular point of view. In the agenda-setting chapter, we learned that coverage of certain issues by news media set the agenda for the public, or made those issues salient in the minds of the audiences. Framing theorists distinguish framing effects from agenda-setting effects by pointing out that framing goes beyond the mere accessibility of particular issues in the news by inviting audience members to apply the information or ideas in particular ways.

> The basis of a psychological difference between agenda setting and framing, therefore, lies in this accessibility/applicability distinction. Ironically, perhaps the best way to conceive of the difference between the two is to recognize that accessibility and applicability go hand-in-hand in everyday information processing. (Tewksbury & Scheufele, 2009, p. 21)

Framing researchers have found evidence for both accessibility and applicability as important processes in framing effects.

Framing researchers also distinguish framing studies from persuasion studies because some framing studies focus on the origin or evolution of news frames. Persuasion studies involve the presentation of persuasive information that audiences usually recognize as having persuasive appeal. Framing studies usually deal with news presented by journalists who are supposed to be objective in their presentations, and audiences usually do not suspect that the information may be persuasive or at least influences the way they perceive certain issues.

Another important difference between persuasion research and framing research is the effects that are measured. Persuasion researchers try to measure changes in *attitudes* due to exposure to persuasive messages. Framing researchers seek to discover audience *interpretations* of news information (Tewksbury et al., 2000).

Using a study cited in the chapter on priming can serve to demonstrate framing effects at work. Simon and Jerit's 2007 study found that people exposed to a news story about a new abortion procedure were affected by the way the story was framed. When presented with a news story that referred to the fetus as a "baby," people were more likely to support regulation of the new abortion procedure. Those presented with a news story that used the terms "fetus" and "baby" equally in the story also experienced these framing effects. Audiences who read the "fetus"-only story were significantly more likely *not* to express support for regulation of the procedure.

Frame Building and Frame Setting

Framing studies come in two types. The first includes studies that examine the way frames are put together by news professionals. These studies are included under the heading of "frame building." The second type is comprised of studies that examine the effects on audiences from news frames. These are referred to as "frame-setting" studies.

Frame Building

Studies that examine frame building focus on the way frames are constructed—by journalists, by politicians, and by culture. Issues come to be framed in a particular manner because of the way elites present the information, or the way the media present the information in line with events and popular culture (Scheufele & Nisbet, 2007).

Research on framing by journalists has identified five factors that can influence how journalists frame the information they present (Tewksbury & Scheufele, 2009). Journalists may be influenced by

- societal norms and values
- the pressure and constraint of news organizations
- pressures from interest groups or policy makers
- their professional routines
- each journalist's own political orientation or ideology (Shoemaker & Reese, 1996; Tuchman, 1978)

The elite in society—interest groups, politicians, government agencies—routinely attempt to frame issues that the media cover (Scheufele, 1999; Gamson & Modigliani, 1987; Miller, Andsager, & Riechart, 1998; Nisbet, Brossard, & Kroepsch, 2003; Nisbet & Huge, 2006). Research has shown that the elite are sometimes successful (Andsager, 2000) but at other times are not (Miller et al., 1998) in influencing journalists on the way issues are framed.

The surrounding culture also plays a part in the way journalists frame issues. Journalists are a part of the culture in which they work, and their stories reflect that culture. Because of this, frames "often are unnoticed and implicit, their impact is by stealth" (Van Gorp, 2007, p. 63). For example, the cultural movement to separate church and state matters in this country has been taken seriously by journalists, who do not frame stories from a religious standpoint.

Frame Setting

Frames can influence individuals to make connections in their minds that can result in four outcomes—defining the issue, determining the causes for an issue, noting the implications for an issue, and the treatment of an issue (Entman, 1993; Tewksbury & Scheufele, 2009).

A frame can wield its influence cognitively—in the way the individual thinks about an issue, or affectively—the way the person feels about an issue. It all depends on the way a story is constructed, whether it focuses on conflicts among elite policy makers, the results of certain policy changes on individuals, or stirs the emotions of individuals by focusing on a human interest angle (Price, Tewksbury, & Powers, 1997).

In one study, researchers presented individuals with two identical stories, except the stories had different lead (or beginning) sentences and different headlines. One story's headline and lead paragraph favored the economic benefits of large farms that raised hogs, whereas the other story pointed out serious environmental concerns with such farms. The way the story was framed significantly affected individuals' opinions on large hog farms, and the effect remained weeks after the people read the stories. The ones who read about the economic benefits of the farms showed support for the farms, and those who read about the environmental problems associated with the farms were significantly less likely to support them (Tewksbury et al., 2000).

Such research makes it clear that journalists need to take seriously their duty to present all sides of an issue and not focus on only one aspect. It also demonstrates the power that reporters have to influence the public in the way they frame stories.

Another study tested tolerance for a Ku Klux Klan rally by presenting individuals with stories framed in different ways. The people who read articles that framed the rally in terms of free speech were significantly more tolerant when asked about Klan speeches and rallies (Nelson, Clawson, & Oxley, 1997) than were those who read articles that framed the rally in terms of racism.

Studies also have shown that individual differences among audience members affect the power of the framed information. People with particular beliefs and attitudes or "schema" on a particular topic tend to accept new information on the topic more than those without such existing schemas (Rhee, 1997; Shen, 2004). People react differently to news stories, depending upon their personal knowledge, experiences, and attitudes. For example, someone who has suffered with asthma for many years would accept information about new treatment options for the condition. They would attend to the information and possibly store the information based on their existing schema.

Research has shown that frames can have effects on attitudes—either formation of attitudes or change of attitudes (Nelson & Oxley, 1999; Brewer, 2002)—and sometimes on behaviors (Valentino, Beckmann, & Buhr, 2001; Boyle et al., 2006).

Most studies of framing effects have focused on short-term evaluations, and for that reason they resemble priming studies. Framing theorists point out that the best way to show that people apply the information they learn in frames is through longitudinal research (Price & Tewksbury, 1997; Tewksbury & Scheufele, 2009). These studies test for applicability of the frame weeks or months after exposure, and therefore differ from priming studies.

Types of Frames

Researchers have tended to test for specific types of frames in audience reactions. "This includes sets of frames, such as gains vs. loss frames [i.e., losses that hurt more than gains feel good] (Kahneman & Tversky, 1979), episodic vs. thematic frames [i.e., *episodic* in that news is reported in terms of a specific event or a typical case, versus *thematic*, in which news is reported within a more general context] (Iyengar, 1991), strategy vs. issue frames (Cappella & Jamieson, 1997), or human interest, conflict, and economic consequences frames (Price et al., 1997)" (Tewksbury & Scheufele, 2009, p. 28).

Tewksbury and Scheufele (2009) pointed out that this practice has a limiting effect on framing research, in that it ignores the possibility of "master frames" (Snow & Benford, 1992) or frames that might exist in the culture that could apply across issues.

Recent Research in Framing

As stated previously, some framing studies are concerned with the way messages are framed by news media (frame building) and others are more concerned with the effects those frames have on audiences (frame setting). In one frame-building study, researchers examined the *Washington Post*'s coverage of the Abu Ghraib prison incident that involved abuse of Iraqi prisoners by U.S.

Research Spotlight

Abuse, Torture, Frames, and the *Washington Post*
Douglas V. Porpora, Alexander Nikolaev, and Julia Hagemann (2010)
Journal of Communication, 60, 254–270

In this study, the researchers provided evidence that disputed findings that other researchers had published in a journal article and a book regarding news frames in the *Washington Post* that related to the Abu Ghraib incident. The earlier study had contended that the newspaper had framed the mistreatment of prisoners in the same manner as the Bush administration; that is, as "a few bad apples" and averted blame to higher authorities or administration policy.

Method

Straight news stories and opinion pieces regarding Abu Ghraib in the *Washington Post* were examined from April 1 through August 31, 2004. They coded the straight news stories for the presence of two types of slants: (1) the mistreatment was neither systematic nor widespread but the work of a few ("bad apples") and (2) higher level responsibility. The title and first three paragraphs of the news stories were examined.

With opinion pieces, the researchers coded for the placement of the words *abuse* and *torture*, or whether the words did not appear. Opinion pieces were also coded for whether the piece defended the mistreatment as the work of a few (supported the Bush administration's framing of the incident) or charged the administration with responsibility and accused the administration of lying.

Findings

The most frequent frame found in the headlines and first three paragraphs of the news stories was for higher-level responsibility for the incident. This was found in 44% of the straight news pieces. The "bad apples" frame was suggested in less than 12% of the pieces. In examining headlines alone, 63 of them (26%) suggested higher responsibility for the incident (counterframing of the administration view) as opposed to 12 (5%) that suggested the prisoner abuse was the result of a few bad apples.

As time passed, the counterframing in the *Post* grew stronger. Coverage of the incident fell off in July, but it resumed in mid-August, when half the headlines implicated higher responsibility in comparison with only one that suggested a few bad apples.

In opinion pieces, only three opinion pieces (out of 56) supported the bad apples defense, whereas 85% of the pieces implicated that high levels of command, including the administration, should be held accountable. The "bad apples" frame of the administration was explicitly rejected in 44% of the opinion pieces examined.

The researchers concluded that the earlier study, which had coded for instances of the words *abuse* and *torture*, had not delved deeply enough into the content of the *Washington Post* during the period of investigation. Counterframes to the administration's view were present and abundant.

military personnel. Previous studies (Bennett, Lawrence, & Livingston, 2006, 2007) had suggested that the newspaper accepted the Bush administration's framing of the incident as an isolated instance of wrongdoing perpetrated by a few bad individuals and did not suggest that administration policy had anything to do with the scandal. In a content analysis of the *Post*, Porpora, Nikolaev, and Hagemann (2010) found evidence to the contrary. They said that the newspaper did engage in counterframing measures.

Another frame-building study focused on the framing of two conflicts in the Middle East covered by *The New York Times*. The researchers found that the experience of the reporters involved affected the depth of the coverage and framing of the stories. A conflict in one location was covered by a veteran *Times* correspondent, whereas the other conflict was covered primarily by local journalists. "Thus, in both cases, *NY Times'* framing cast the armies' actions against the militants in unambiguous moral terms, as either pointless destruction or justified and decisive. Interestingly, in both cases, the assessments were soon proven incorrect" (Evans, 2010, p. 224).

Entman (2010) studied news frames of Sarah Palin during the 2008 presidential election campaign. He found evidence of slanted framing and expanded framing theory to include systematic studies of bias in news reporting. "Slanted framing results from the interaction of real world developments, cultural norms, and journalistic decision rules with the sometimes proficient and other times maladroit efforts of competing elites to manage the news" (p. 389).

Other frame-building studies have examined media framing of illegal immigration (Kim, Carvalho, Davis, & Mullins, 2011), of nonverbal actions in the 2008 Democratic primary (Manusov & Harvey, 2011), of news related to energy

Some candidates, such as 2008 vice-presidential candidate Sarah Palin, allegedly are framed negatively in the news media. *Steve Broer/shutterstock.com*

conservation in the United States (Bolsen, 2011), of the long conflict between BP and Greenpeace (Garcia, 2011), of U.S. media coverage of terrorism since 9/11 (Powell, 2011), and of how opinion page and editorial writers discussed the subprime mortgage crisis in terms of racial aspects (Squires, 2011).

A study that involved frame-building and frame-setting effects conducted by Slothuus (2010) involved a natural experiment using data from the 2005 Danish National Election Study. The study showed how people reacted toward the Social Democrats in Denmark when the group suddenly changed its stance on early retirement benefits. The way the Social Democrats framed the issue, at first, was in terms of assisting workers. When a new party leader took over, the issue was framed as an economic one—the growing number of retirees meant the benefit system needed reforms for economic reasons. The data from the survey revealed that the shift in framing of the issue increased public support overall for an abolishment of the early retirement benefits, but the policy support changed more for respondents who identified themselves as Social Democrats than as affiliates of other political parties (Slothuus, 2010).

Other frame-setting studies have been conducted on public support for Turkey joining the European Union (de Vreese, Boomgaarden, & Semetko, 2011), on viewer evaluations of Sarah Palin's vice presidential debate performance following negative framing of Palin by the media (McKinney, Rill, & Watson, 2011), and on the attribution of blame in the Hurricane Katrina aftermath in terms of news images and race (Ben-Porath & Shaker, 2010).

Summary

In recent years, media effects researchers have turned their attention to the power of the way information is put together or framed, and the effects that it has in the minds of media consumers. Framing research can be distinguished from agenda-setting research and priming research both theoretically and experimentally.

Framing theory finds its roots in the fields of psychology and sociology. Studies are distinguished between micro-level studies of individuals (psychology) and macro-level studies of society (sociology).

Framing can result in several types of effects, including knowledge, persuasion, or agenda setting. Framing studies usually deal with news created by journalists who are supposed to be objective in their presentations, and audiences usually do not suspect that the information may be persuading them or at least influencing the way they perceive certain issues.

Framing studies come in two types. The first type includes studies that examine the way frames are put together by news professionals. These studies are included beneath the heading of "frame building." The second consists of studies that examine the effects on audiences from news frames. These studies are referred to as "frame setting" studies.

eight

Cultivation

We have found that long-term exposure to television tends to cultivate the image of a relatively mean and dangerous world.
—Morgan, Shanahan, & Signorielli, 2009

Do you watch a lot of television? Cultivation research throughout the past few decades has shown that if you do, then chances are high that if someone asked you to estimate crime rates in the United States you would grossly overestimate the frequency of crime in the real world. You would probably be more fearful of falling victim to a crime than a person who does not watch much television.

Since the dawn of mass mediated entertainment, people have feared powerful and harmful media effects, especially on that segment of the population considered most vulnerable—the nation's children. As a result, the media effects tradition has been one of the most prolific, socially important, and highly scrutinized areas of mass communication research.

In the 1920s and 1930s, before television became a household fixture, feature films thrilled audiences by the millions in theaters across the country; however, those same films raised public concerns because of their violent and sometimes sexually explicit content. The Payne Fund studies brought together a group of social scientists who examined the effects of movies on the nation's youth. The results were alarming for Americans, in that children were experiencing negative effects from movies filled with violence and booze.

Once television became entrenched in the American way of life, apprehension about negative media effects assumed a dominating presence on the public and political agenda. In the 1960s and 1970s, U.S. presidents appointed commissions and charged them with studying television violence and assessing its effects on young people.

Through the years the research findings have varied, but many studies have shown that the connection between viewing television and developing a distorted image of reality (closer to what is depicted on television) often occurs.

The Cultural Indicators Project

Cultivation theory developed as one attempt to explain the influence of television on its viewers. The cultivation tradition grew out of a media violence research project called the Cultural Indicators Project, headed in the 1960s by George Gerbner (1919–2005), a University of Pennsylvania (and later Temple University) communication scholar. Cultivation analysis is one of three components in the Cultural Indicators Project. The other two research activities include institutional process analysis and message system analysis. **Institutional process analysis** examines the production, management, and distribution of media messages. **Message system analysis** involves the investigation of images in the media content, such as gender roles, portrayal of minorities, and the way certain occupations are depicted.

Since the early days of the project, cultivation research has expanded to encompass many topics in addition to media violence. Investigators now explore the relationship of long-term television viewing to the inculcation of various perceptions, values, and beliefs on the part of audiences.

Simply stated, *cultivation* proposes that over time, heavy viewers of television develop or cultivate views of the world similar to what they see on television, generally a "mean" world filled with violence and crime. Cultivation researchers call this the **mean world syndrome**.

People who watch a lot of television tend to overestimate the frequency of crime in the real world and tend to view the world as a more dangerous place than those who watch less television.

Cultivation research has typically involved two research methods: content analysis of television programs and survey methods to assess viewer perceptions of the world. In measuring cultivation effects related to violence, researchers developed the Mean World Index, a tool for measuring perceptions of the prevalence of violence and danger in the world (Signorielli, 1990). Among various demographic groups, heavy viewers of television score consistently higher on the Mean World Index than do light viewers.

The "symbolic world" of television is very different from objective reality, and this disparity has been a major point of interest for cultivation researchers. Examples of the distorted realities presented on television abound. Analyses of network television programs have revealed that most TV characters are young, energetic, and appealing. Few shows feature elderly people (age 65 or older) in starring or important roles, and when older people are used as characters they often portray sick or dying people. Needless to say, television does not accurately reflect the true proportions, conditions, or health status of the elderly population in American society today.

Violent crime serves as the most obvious example of television's distortion of reality. With all the gun battles, fist fights, karate chops, and high-speed chases that occur as standard fare on most programs, it should come as no surprise that in a given week, more than half of all the leading characters on television are involved in some kind of violent act. Actual crime statistics from the FBI tell a much different story. In a single year, less than 1 percent of the population in the United States actually fall victim to criminal acts.

Research has shown that among certain groups of people, heavy viewers of television tend to cultivate the same distorted pictures of reality that they see on television. Using the examples of the condition of the elderly and the frequency of criminal acts, heavy viewers tend to *underestimate* the number of elderly people in the U.S. population as well as their health status. In addition, heavy viewers consistently *overestimate* real-world crime statistics.

Since the Cultural Indicators Project began, most studies have revealed only low-level statistical evidence of a cultivation effect, but the consistency of such findings offered credence to the theory. Gerbner and his associates insisted that cultivation has considerable implications for society, despite low-level statistical correlations and effect sizes. They often made (and still make) the analogy between cultivation effects upon society and global temperature changes upon climate—a variance of only a few degrees in temperature would result in another ice age, they say (Morgan, Shanahan, & Signorielli, 2009).

Cultivation used to be described as a *hypothesis* rather than a formal media effects *theory* due to a lack of theoretical and supporting, empirical evidence to explain how the cultivation process occurs. In particular, early studies did not reveal the psychological dimensions of cultivation—how television viewers learn to construct their views of social reality.

Through the years, most explanations of media effects have been firmly grounded in theories of cognitive psychology. Media effects scholars trained in this tradition criticized the work of Gerbner and his associates for their lack of emphasis on cognitive processes (Hawkins & Pingree, 1990; Potter, 1994; Bry-

> **The Cultural Indicators Project**
>
> - Initiated in 1967 by George Gerbner.
> - First study conducted for President Johnson's National Commission on the Causes and Prevention of Violence.
> - Introduced the Mean World Index, an instrument used to measure people's perceptions about violence and aggression in the world.
> - Performs content analysis of televised violence each year.
> - Focuses on content of network television, both prime-time dramas during the week and daytime programming on weekends.
> - Investigates the "cultivation" effect on audiences due to television portrayals with regard to issues of gender, age-role stereotypes, the family, and so forth.

ant, 1986). Much of the criticism was constructive, leading Gerbner and other cultivation researchers to make revisions and improvements in their explanation of cultivation.

More recent studies have begun to fill this void and answer the critics. In recent years Shrum (1995, 1999, 2007) and others have done much to explore the psychological dimensions of cultivation and the mediating factors present. Research that explores the cognitive dimensions of cultivation continues.

Research has shown that certain characteristics among audiences tend to make cultivation effects more or less pronounced; for example, educational level has been shown to affect cultivation effects. Among heavy viewers of television, those with higher levels of educational attainment are less likely to have their views of the world influenced by television. Age has been shown to be another mediating factor, as has need for cognition.

In this chapter, we delve into the research domain of cultivation analysis. In addition to the concepts and criticisms associated with cultivation, we examine how recent research is attempting to answer the critics. We also look at the theoretical bases for cultivation, and we close with some of the most recent studies in cultivation research.

Concepts and Criticisms

Cultivation adherents argue that television, as a "wholesale distributor of images," is different from other mass media (Morgan & Signorielli, 1990, p. 13). It serves as the *great storyteller* of our age. Programs are produced to appeal to the entire population. Even very young viewers find it easy to become enthralled by an entertaining television show.

According to these researchers, the diverse publics that make up the United States—the poor children living in a housing project in Georgia, the wealthy families living in an exclusive neighborhood in New York, the farm families in middle America, and the sorority sisters on a West Coast campus—all tend to think more alike when watching television because they all receive similar messages. All television programs, from entertaining action programs to news programs, possess similar, repetitive patterns, sometimes called myths, "facts," or ideologies. These patterns are thought to influence viewers' perceptions of the world. Long-term exposure to these overall patterns of television programming is most likely to result in "the steady entrenchment of mainstream orientations for most viewers" (Gerbner et al., 1994, p. 25).

Mainstreaming is one of the principal concepts that underlie cultivation analysis; another is *resonance*. The concept of **mainstreaming** assumes that dominant sets of attitudes, beliefs, values, and practices exist within cultures. Patterns also emerge across the spectrum of television programming—patterns regarding outcomes to various situations, gender roles, minority representations, and so forth. These patterns result in a "mainstream" set of attitudes, beliefs, and values that are repetitively presented on television. Heavy television viewers tend to cultivate similar mainstream views. Cultivation researchers Nancy Signorielli and Michael Morgan (1996) defined the concept in this way:

> Mainstreaming means that heavy viewing may absorb or override differences in perspectives and behavior which ordinarily stem from other factors and influences. In other words, differences found in the responses of different groups of viewers, differences that usually are associated with the varied cultural, social, and political characteristics of these groups, are diminished or even absent from the responses of heavy viewers in these same groups. (p. 117)

Resonance occurs when real-world events support the distorted image of reality shown on television. Whenever direct experience is in agreement with the messages from television, the messages are reinforced—they *resonate*—and the cultivation effect is amplified. For example, research has shown that the heavy television viewers who are most likely to fear crime are those who live in inner-city areas where crime rates are high (Morgan, 1983).

Cultivation researchers stress that the concept of cultivation assumes that television and its publics *interact* in a dynamic process. The extent to which a person cultivates the messages seen on television depends upon a number of factors. Some people are more susceptible to cultivation influence due to per-

---

Key Concepts of Cultivation

- Television serves as the great storyteller—the wholesale distributor of images—with programs designed to appeal to the entire population
- Mainstreaming
- Resonance
- Interaction
- Complex psychological processes

sonality traits, social background, cultural mores, and even their past television viewing experiences. Gerbner and colleagues (1994) explained the interaction process in this way:

> Although a viewer's gender, or age, or class makes a difference in perspective, television viewing can make a similar and interacting difference. Viewing may help define what it means, for example, to be an adolescent female member of a given social class. The interaction is a continuous process (as is cultivation) beginning with infancy and going on from cradle to grave. (p. 23)

Cultivation scholars define television exposure in terms of time. They assume that television messages are relatively *uniform* in nature and that viewing of television is *nonselective*. In other words, the narrative structure of various types of programs—cartoons, dramatic movies, crime shows—often resemble each other in terms of casting, action, and other factors. In this sense, scholars say, the messages are uniform. The concept of nonselective viewing is based on the idea of *ritualized viewing* or habitual viewing—watching television at certain times and being confined to whatever programs are offered for viewing at those times. Some networks actively promote habitual viewing, like NBC's long-running shows that were dubbed "Must See TV." (Of course, DVRs and streaming websites like hulu.com are making the notion of ritualized viewing increasingly uncommon.)

As mentioned previously, many have argued that complex psychological processes form the basis for cultivation effects, but most early studies were criticized because they were not directed toward identifying the cognitive components that would *explain* cultivation effects rather than *merely showing* the connection between television viewing and beliefs about social reality (Hawkins & Pingree, 1990; Potter, 1993). The ways in which cognitive mechanisms involved in cultivation resemble those of social learning theory needed to be examined, critics said (Bryant, 1986). A number of scholars expressed concerns about statistical controls and interpretation of cultivation findings (Hirsch, 1980; Hughes, 1980; Wober, 1978). Still others questioned the causal order of effects in cultivation research and objected to certain theoretical formulations (Doob & MacDonald, 1979; Zillmann, 1980).

Theoretical Bases for Cultivation

Cultivation assumes that television has become a primary source of shared meanings and messages for people in the United States and throughout the world. It has evolved into a medium with many functions for people in modern society. According to Signorielli and Morgan:

> Television has thus become our nation's (and increasingly the world's) most common and constant learning environment. It both mirrors and leads society. It serves, however, first and foremost as our storyteller; it has become the wholesale distributor of images which form the mainstream of our popular culture. The world of television shows and tells us about life—people, places, striving, power, and fate. It presents the good and bad, the happy and

> sad, the powerful and the weak, and lets us know who or what is successful or a failure. (1996, p. 114)

In the words of Morgan and Signorielli (1990), cultivation analysis "is designed to understand gradual, long-term shifts and transformations in the way generations are socialized (not short-term, dramatic changes in individuals' beliefs or behaviors)" (p. 19).

Gerbner and colleagues (1994) elaborated on the differences in theoretical bases for cultivation and other types of media effects research:

> Traditional effects research is based on evaluating specific informational, educational, political, or marketing efforts in terms of selective exposure and measurable differences between those exposed and others. Scholars steeped in those traditions find it difficult to accept the emphasis of cultivation analysis on total immersion rather than selective viewing and on the spread of stable similarities of outlook rather than on the remaining sources of cultural differentiation and change. . . . Cultivation theory is based on the results of research finding a persistent and pervasive pull of the television mainstream on a great variety of conceptual currents and countercurrents. The focus on broad commonalities of perspective among heavy viewers of otherwise varied backgrounds requires a theoretical and methodological approach different from traditional media effects research and appropriate to the distinct dynamics of television. (pp. 20–21)

Other researchers insist that psychological processes underlie the cultivation process, and therefore the *cognitive paradigm* should serve as the theoretical base. Hawkins and Pingree (1982) have theorized that the cultivation process involves *learning* and *construction*. The viewer learns by watching television, perceiving and remembering the contents. The viewer constructs an outlook regarding the real world based upon what has been learned from television viewing.

The social cognitive theory, advanced by Bandura (1986), states that the actions and behavior of a person are determined by both internal factors (intelligence and biological factors) and external factors (such as environmental events). Three components—behavior, internal factors, and external factors—interact at varying degrees and varying levels. The effects of mass communication are also influenced by the presence and interaction of the three components (Bandura, 1994).

Recent research has attempted to understand the cognitive processes at work in cultivation and answer some of the criticism. Shrum (1995, 1999, 2007) determined that the images and messages on television that are remembered by audience members are readily available in their memory when they are asked a question off the cuff. These memories operate under an *availability heuristic*, as he put it, or provide a cognitive shortcut for audience members. In various studies, he found that heavy viewers of television tended to give quick responses to questions about social reality, and this indicated that an answer was more readily accessible to them.

Shrum (2004) said that television messages should be viewed as persuasive communications and, as such, cultivation effects on attitudes and beliefs can result from one of two routes to persuasion—the *central* and *peripheral* (or heuristic) routes. The central route involves much cognitive effort. The person listens carefully to arguments and thinks things through deliberately before arriving at a judgment. The peripheral route does not involve that much cognitive effort. People base their attitudes and beliefs on what is said by an attractive spokesperson or an expert, for example.

Additional research has revealed that people who view more crime dramas or other TV genres are more likely to store in their memories scenes and messages from those particular genres, and those memories are accessible to them when they make judgments about the social world around them. Such memories are called into play in the way they perceive the real world (Shrum, 2002).

Shrum's (2004) work identified first- and second-order measures in the cultivation effects—the first being demographic judgments (the percentage of people who will be victims of crimes) and the second being value judgments (focus on materialism, for example). Effects on first-order measures are explained by the availability of TV messages that are in the memories of viewers. Second-order measures operate within the bounds of persuasion theory. According to Shrum,

> When motivation or ability to process information *during viewing* is high, the cultivation effect is *increased*. Note that the very same variables (motivation and ability) are thus shown to moderate the cultivation effect for both first-

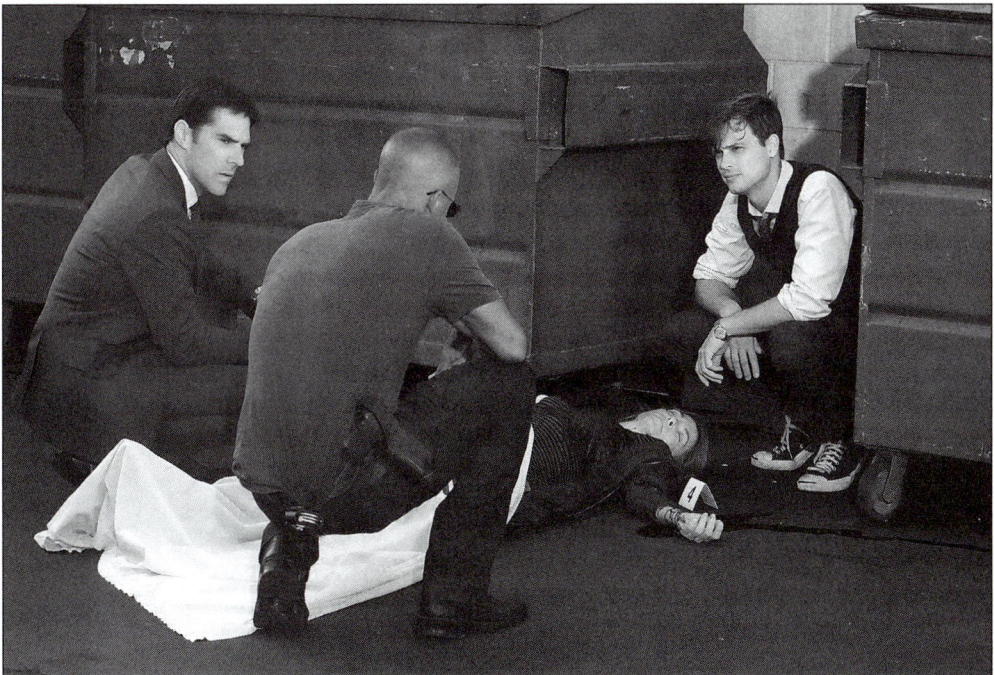

Many procedural dramas on television today are centered on violent crimes, such as murder and sexual assault. Each episode of *Criminal Minds* depicts grisly crime scenes, which could contribute to cultivating ideas about real-world violence. *CBS/Monty Brinton/Landov*

and second-order judgments. The key is that they exert their effects at different times (during viewing versus during recall) and in the opposite direction (decrease the effect for first-order, increase the effect for second-order). (2004, p. 337)

Other media effects researchers have argued for the "mental models" approach to understanding cultivation (Roskos-Ewoldsen, Davies, & Roskos-Ewoldsen, 2004). Mental models, put simply, focus on the dynamics of the way we construct thoughts about certain things—real or imagined situations, objects, events, familiar territory and unfamiliar territory, complex systems, and so forth. Mental models are not rigid and concrete; rather, they are malleable. As far as cultivation is concerned, the concept of mental models takes into consideration the interaction of our memories, our reasoning power, our real-life experiences, and our viewing experiences. The stories viewed on television may be thought of as *situation* models that involve a particular story or situation. "The basic idea is that people construct situation models of TV programs as they watch them. These situation models are stored in memory and, if activated, can be used to interpret new situations" (p. 351).

Recent Research

Cultivation researchers continue to answer their critics and to collect evidence for cultivation effects. In recent years, researchers have expanded their domain to include countries throughout the world. Some of these studies attempt to determine "global" perceptions of social reality attributed to television viewing (Morgan, 1990), but such attempts have not addressed particular empirical problems, such as the development of simple quantitative indicators of culture that would allow researchers to apply the indicators across cultures.

Still, cultivation researchers argue that, "In fact, such study is the best test of system-wide similarities and differences across national boundaries, and of the actual significance of national cultural policies" (Morgan et al., 2009).

Studies have examined cultivation effects in foreign countries that import considerable television programming from the United States. Findings have varied, but most indicate interactions between television viewing and cultural contexts. Most reveal a cultivation of attitudes toward violence, values, social stereotypes, and other areas of interest similar to the distorted pictures of reality shown on television. Sweden (Reimer & Rosengren, 1990), Argentina (Morgan & Shanahan, 1995), and Japan (Saito, 2007) are among the several countries that have been the focus of such cultivation analyses.

In Australia, Pingree and Hawkins (1981) found that students with high levels of exposure to television programming from the United States were more likely to rate Australia as a dangerous place to live.

A study in South Korea found that Korean women with high levels of exposure to U.S. television programs were more likely to have liberal views regarding marriage, clothing, and music, but Korean males who were heavy viewers of U.S. programming supported traditional Korean cultural values and expressed hostility toward the United States (Kang & Morgan, 1988). A more recent Korean study examined the cultivation effect of viewing particular television dramas and people's perceptions about the number of single adults and the number of children in married families. Jin and Jeong (2010) found that heavy viewers of dramas that positively depicted the life of singles and families with fewer children tended to cultivate overrated perceptions about the number of unmarried Koreans and the number of Korean married couples having no children.

In Japan, Saito (2007) found that heavy viewers of television demonstrated traditional views about gender in society, except among the most conservative viewers, whereas in Korea (Kang & Morgan, 1988), heavy viewers cultivated more liberal ideas about family values and women in society.

Researchers found that heavy viewing of exported U.S. television programs in the countries of South Korea and India resulted in feelings of deprivation among heavy viewers in those countries (Yang, Ramasubramanian, & Oliver, 2008). Heavy viewers among South Koreans reported more dissatisfaction with their own society, as did heavy viewers in India, who also reported dissatisfaction with their personal lives.

In Israel, heavy viewers of American programming tended to give estimations of certain occupations in the United States in accordance with what they viewed on television, whereas viewers of Israeli programs did not (Hestroni, 2008; Hestroni, Elphariach, Kapuza, & Tsfoni, 2007).

Other studies have updated findings from earlier investigations by collecting data from more recent television programming. For example, one study (Shanahan & Morgan, 1999) confirmed evidence from earlier studies that heavy viewing of television is associated with people overestimating the incidence of real-world violence and holding many other inaccurate beliefs related to criminal activity and crime statistics. Signorielli and Kahlenberg (2001) found that despite significant role changes for women in the real world, television continues to depict a world where males fill the majority (60–65 percent) of roles; this does represent an improvement from depictions in the 1970s and 1980s, when television programs contained three men to every one woman.

Research Spotlight

The Effects of Viewing *Grey's Anatomy* on Perceptions of Doctors and Patient Satisfaction
Brian L. Quick (2009)
Journal of Broadcasting & Electronic Media, 53, 38–55

This study examined the effect that watching *Grey's Anatomy* could have on viewers' attitudes and beliefs about their real-world doctors. Cultivation theory has been used primarily in a broad context (i.e., overall television consumption); however, Quick examined the cultivation effects of watching a single series. Because TV doctors are often seen performing risky operations and choosing unconventional treatments, Quick noted that television doctors are often

(continued)

seen as courageous. But do those feelings about TV doctors carry over to one's own real-life doctor? Citing research that found cultivation effects were greater after watching programs with which the audience had little personal experience (e.g., the daily activities of a hospital emergency room), Quick formulated the following hypotheses and research question.

Hypotheses and Research Question

H1: The viewing of Grey's Anatomy is positively associated with perceived credibility of this program.

H2: Perceived credibility of Grey's Anatomy is positively associated with perceived courageousness of real-world doctors.

H3: The viewing of Grey's Anatomy is positively associated with perceived courageousness of real-world doctors.

RQ1: Does perceived credibility of Grey's Anatomy mediate the relationship between Grey's Anatomy viewing and perceived courageousness of real-world doctors?

H4: Perceived courageousness of real-world doctors is positively associated with patient satisfaction with their real-world doctors.

Method

Two hundred sixty-nine participants took part in a paper-and-pencil survey regarding their television viewing habits—particularly of the second season and first five episodes from season three of Grey's Anatomy—and their beliefs about doctors.

Grey's Anatomy was selected to be the focus of this study due to its popularity. During the 2005–2006 season, the show averaged 19.9 million weekly viewers, making it the fifth most-watched series of the season.

To measure viewing habits, two questions specifically asked participants how many of the 32 episodes in the sample they watched. Credibility was asked by having participants rate answer choices to complete the following sentence: "In general, images and story lines communicated in medical dramas like Grey's Anatomy are _____." Participants then used a 5-point scale to rate realism, credibility, and believability. Courageousness was measured with questions asking participants to rate doctors on a scale of one to five for characteristics like heroism, bravery, courageousness, cleverness, and brilliance. Lastly, to measure patient satisfaction, participants responded to two questions: (a) "In general, I am satisfied with my physician," and (b) "On average, my physician meets my health needs." These questions were also answered using a 5-point scale.

Results

On average, participants reported watching almost 13 episodes of Grey's Anatomy during the second and third seasons. Seventy-eight participants reported watching all 32 episodes, although 95 never saw the show.

Analyses showed support for Hypothesis 1; viewing Grey's Anatomy was associated with stronger perceptions about the show's credibility. Secondly, Hypothesis 2 was also supported. The belief that the show was credible was positively related to the perception that real-world doctors are courageous. Hypothesis 3, however, was not supported; simply being a heavy viewer of Grey's Anatomy did not positively relate to perceptions of real-world courageousness. Thus, answering the research question with a "yes," perceived credibility appeared to be a key factor for cultivating ideas about real-world doctors' courageousness. Lastly, Hypothesis 4 was supported; the more courageous participants perceived their real-world doctors to be, the more satisfied they were with them.

Overall, the findings do support cultivation theory. This study contributes to the area of cultivation research by highlighting the importance of perceived credibility in promoting cultivation effects. It also showed that cultivation effects are created just by watching a single series.

Researchers have also tested the cultivation effects of heavy television viewing on attitudes toward family values, the environment, and health-related topics. As for family values, one interesting study found that television depictions of the American family in the 1990s did not reflect reality, but overrepresented single-parent households (Morgan, Leggett, & Shanahan, 1999). Moreover, single parents on television were usually males with live-in help, unlike real-world situations. The research found that heavy television viewers possibly romanticize single parenthood, as they tend to be more accepting of single-parent households and unwed mothers. Other research indicated that heavy viewing of television cultivated views related to material values—that luxury items and services were more available than they really are in society (Shrum, Burroughs, & Rindfleisch, 2005).

On the issue of the environment, heavy viewers tended to cultivate a fearful withdrawal from scientific issues in general (Shanahan, Morgan, & Stenbjerre, 1997). Heavy television viewers were less likely than others to have knowledge of environmental issues. More recent research has shown conflicting results as far as indicating that exposure to diverse content on television is associated with the cultivation of concern for environmental risks (Dahlstrom & Scheufele, 2010; Good, 2007, 2009). As for health-related topics, heavy television viewing was related to children's erroneous and unhealthy views about nutrition (Signorielli & Staples, 1997), earlier onset of smoking (Gutschoven & Van den Bulk, 2005), and greater acceptance of gender and sexual stereotypes (Ward & Friedman, 2006). Diefenbach and West (2007) found that people with mental disorders are portrayed on television as being violent and prone to criminal behavior. Heavy viewers of television had more negative perceptions of the mentally ill than light viewers.

Several recent studies have explored the cognitive processing involved in cultivation. Shapiro and Lang (1991) suggested that cultivation of beliefs that are incorrect or exaggerated stems from the tendency of heavy viewers to forget that television programming is not real. One study confirmed the hypothesis (Mares, 1996), but another interpreted the data differently (Shrum, 1999, 1997, 1995). Mares found that viewers who confused fictional programs with fact were more likely to cultivate a view of the world in line with the world shown on television. Shrum contended that viewers do not consider whether what they are watching is fact or fiction, but viewers use television images whenever making cognitive judgments about social issues. Heavy television viewers answer questions more readily than others, indicating that some sort of cognitive shortcut has been forged and that answers are more readily accessible. Shrum's explanation suggests that the cultivation process strengthens a viewer's beliefs rather than changing them.

Bradley (2007) found support for Shrum's heuristic model of cultivation effects, and found that the ability to systematically process information can make cultivation effects disappear. For example, priming people with non-TV examples and asking them to think carefully before answering the questions usually posed by cultivation researchers, and asking them to attempt to answer correctly, greatly diminishes any cultivation effects even among heavy viewers of television. Shrum (2007) found that people tend to think more carefully about questions cultivation researchers ask when responding to mail surveys rather than telephone inquiries. He found that cultivation effects were strongest among those who responded to telephone surveys.

More recent research has explored the heavy exposure to specific television genres. High exposure to television news, for example, cultivated perceptions among those viewers that juvenile crime was on the increase (Goidel, Freeman, & Procopio, 2006). Those who watch reality crime shows expressed perceptions that crime overall is on the increase, and they also perceive that more juveniles are imprisoned for violent crimes than is actually the case.

Other research on the heavy viewing of crime dramas indicates that it leads to concern about crime in society (Holbrook & Hill, 2005; Busselle, 2003). Another study found that heavy viewing of crime shows on television is associated with support for the death penalty (Holbert, Shah, & Kwak, 2004). Riddle (2010) found that vivid portrayals of crime on crime dramas were connected with viewers' tendency to give a higher estimate of crime's prevalence in the real world. Grabe and Drew (2007) explored differences in television genres and noticed that exposure to televised nonfiction (news and reality cop shows) provided more evidence of a cultivation effect of falling victim to an actual crime than did the viewing of crime dramas.

Appel (2008) found that German and Austrian viewers of televised fiction that portrays the world as a reasonable and fair place showed significant cultivation effects related to the belief in a just world. In the same study, the number of hours spent viewing television was found to be related to a belief in a mean or scary world.

Cultivation research in the 21st century will need to consider the growing popularity of cable and satellite networks, use of digital video recorders (DVRs) and the Internet, and the impact of these on the traditional network television audience. So far, no studies have determined great differences in viewing habits or content for heavy viewers despite the proliferation of viewer choices (Morgan, Shanahan, & Harris, 1990).

Williams (2006) conducted "the first longitudinal, controlled experiment of a video game" (p. 69) and found that players of *Asheron's Call 2* experienced significant cultivation effects. Those players in the treatment condition were more likely than those in a control group to overestimate real-world tendencies for armed robbery.

Cultivation researchers point out that, despite the diversity of choices in media entertainment, concentration of ownership will continue to produce similarities across media and channels. Nonetheless, cultivation research should expand its horizons to include investigations into the impact of messages from these new avenues and new media technologies (Morgan et al., 2009).

Summary

Simply stated, *cultivation* proposes that over time, heavy viewers of television develop or cultivate views of the world similar to what they see on television, generally a "mean" world filled with violence, crime, and other negatives. Cultivation analysis is one of three components in the Cultural Indicators Project. The other two research activities include institutional process analysis and message system analysis. Institutional process analysis examines the production, management, and distribution of media messages. Message system analysis involves the investigation of images in the media content, such as gender roles, portrayal of minorities, and the way certain occupations are depicted.

Cultivation research has typically involved two research methods: content analysis of television programs and survey methods to assess viewer perceptions of the world. The "symbolic world" of television is very different from objective reality, and this disparity has been a major point of interest for cultivation researchers. Violent crime serves as the most obvious example of television's distortion of reality. Research has shown that among certain groups of people, heavy viewers of television tend to cultivate the same distorted pictures of reality that they see on television.

Since the Cultural Indicators Project began, most studies have revealed only low-level statistical evidence of a cultivation effect, but the consistency of such findings offered credence to the theory. *Mainstreaming* is one of the principal concepts that underlie cultivation analysis; another is *resonance.*

Through the years, most explanations of media effects have been firmly grounded in theories of cognitive psychology. Media effects scholars trained in this tradition often criticized cultivation researchers for not explaining the underlying processes at work, but in recent years, scholars have begun to explore these processes in terms of cognitive psychology and persuasion. Other researchers have argued for a mental models approach to understanding cultivation.

Cultivation researchers continue to answer their critics and to collect evidence for cultivation effects. In recent years, researchers have expanded their domain to include countries throughout the world. Studies have examined cultivation effects in foreign countries that import considerable television programming from the United States. Findings have varied, but most indicate interactions between television viewing and cultural contexts.

Researchers have also tested the cultivation effects of heavy television viewing on attitudes toward family values, the environment, and health-related topics.

Recent studies have explored the cognitive processing involved in cultivation. Bradley found support for Shrum's heuristic model of cultivation effects, and that the ability to systematically process information can make cultivation effects disappear. More recent research has explored the heavy exposure to specific television genres.

Cultivation research in the 21st century will need to consider the growing popularity of cable and satellite networks, use of DVRs and the Internet, and the impact of these on the traditional network television audience.

Uses and Gratifications

Television is becoming a collage—there are so many channels that you move through them making a collage yourself. In that sense, everyone sees something a bit different.
—David Hockney, *Hockney on Photography*, 1988

In the checkout line at the grocery store, one young woman reaches for the latest copy of *Cosmo* because she is interested in the new styles of bikinis that are going to be popular that season. Another woman, much older and a gardening enthusiast, picks up the current issue of *Better Homes and Gardens* to get the latest tips on spring planting arrangements. The woman's 13-year-old granddaughter begs for the latest copy of her favorite teen magazine with Justin Bieber on the cover.

In front of the television one evening, a couple and their children are arguing over which program to watch. The father wants to see the popular *60 Minutes* because it is featuring a story about a scandal that affected someone in his profession. The mother wants to watch a Paula Deen cooking show to learn how to make a Southern apple pie. The young daughter is dying to see if *iCarly* is on Nickelodeon. The young son is anxious to pop the latest Harry Potter movie into the DVD player for an evening of magic and adventure.

These examples demonstrate how people seek out certain kinds of media content to satisfy a variety of very personal needs. Their behavior is often goal oriented when they select media fare. Their selections are based on the information or satisfactions they anticipate they will receive by viewing a certain program or selecting a certain magazine.

The **uses and gratifications** approach assumes that individual differences among audience members cause each person to seek out different messages, use those messages differently, and respond to them uniquely. Many social or psychological factors cause audience members to select different media fare as well as to experience divergent if not idiosyncratic media effects. The approach assumes that a person's social and psychological makeup is as responsible for media uses and effects as are the media messages themselves.

Rather than focus upon the direct effects from mass media on audience members, uses and gratifications research examines the *motivations and behavior of viewers,* or *how* and *why* they use the media. It always assumes that viewers actively choose programs or other media content to gratify their individual needs.

This chapter examines the uses and gratifications approach to media effects. After a brief look at the functions of mass media in society and the communication models used to explain uses and effects, we discuss several basic assumptions of the uses and gratifications perspective. We then trace uses and gratifications research historically, examine recent research, and note criticisms of the approach.

Societal-Level Functions of the Mass Media

To understand why individuals use the media, it may be helpful to examine the reasons why societies use the media. Lasswell (1948) identified three major functions that the media serve in society. First, the media keep viewers aware of what is going on in the world around them by *surveying the environment.* Second, by providing an explanation of how various components of the environment operate, the media help audience members make sense of it all, so to speak. This second function, *correlation of environmental parts,* allows audience members to form a more accurate and perhaps a more holistic view of the world around them. Finally, media messages serve to *transmit social norms and customs* to new generations of viewers. Transmission of the social heritage is a powerful and controversial function. For example, people in countries throughout the world who receive programs produced in the United States have complained of Western cultural imperialism, or the imposition of Western social norms and values on citizens with very different cultural norms.

Researchers have identified several other functions of mass media. Wright (1960) named another function that media serve in society, that of *entertainment.* This important function recognizes that many people use mass media for personal enjoyment. Another function, called *parasocial interaction* (Horton & Wohl, 1956), describes the phenomenon that occurs when viewers feel as though they personally know certain television personalities (e.g., talk show hosts Jay Leno and Ellen DeGeneres) and film characters and share their worlds simply because they see and hear them so often. *Escapism,* another function, assumes that television entertainment allows viewers to escape from real-life problems (Pearlin, 1959). Other related functions that have been identified include *anxiety reduction* (Mendelsohn, 1963) and *play* (Stephenson, 1967), two escapist functions that allow audience members to put aside the pressures and tensions of real life and experience enjoyment while being entertained with fantasy.

Models to Explain Uses and Effects

Communication scholars have developed several different models that attempt to explain individual-level media uses and effects, which is the principal focus of uses and gratifications research. These include the transactional model (McLeod & Becker, 1974), the gratification seeking and audience activity model (Rubin & Perse, 1987), the expectancy-value model (Palmgreen & Rayburn, 1982), and the uses and dependency model (Rubin & Windahl, 1986).

Transactional Model

In the transactional model, two factors in combination produce an effect: the characteristics of the message and the psychological orientation of the audience member. This model combines the direct effects model and an individual differences model. Exposure to a media message has powerful effects to the extent that an audience member's psychological orientation permits (McLeod & Becker, 1974). For example, a news report about severe budget cuts to a state's institutions of higher learning would be more likely to produce an effect on people involved in higher education than those with no involvement. Such a report would be very disturbing to administrators who would be forced to make reductions and to professors who might not receive pay raises or might even lose their jobs. Such news would also be disturbing to students and parents, who may face higher tuition bills.

Gratification-Seeking and Audience Activity Model

In the gratification-seeking and audience activity model, many different factors and elements come to bear on the uses and effects process. Particular kinds of gratifications sought by the viewer, as well as the viewer's attitude, determine the viewer's attention to the content of those messages. Effects on viewers' thoughts, emotions, or behavior depend on their degree of involvement with the message and behavioral intentions of the viewer (Rubin & Perse, 1987). For example, a person with asthma would pay more attention to a commercial for an asthma medication than a person who does not have asthma.

Expectancy-Value Model

The expectancy-value model examines the use of the media in terms of the gratifications sought and obtained in addition to the outcomes that are expected at the onset. Palmgreen and Rayburn (1982) proposed that the model explains a person's behavior, intentions, and attitudes as a function of two separate components: expectancy and evaluation. They defined *expectancy* as "the probability that an attitude possesses a particular attribute or that a behavior will have a particular consequence," and *evaluation* as "the degree of affect, positive or negative, toward an attitude or behavioral outcome" (pp. 562–563). For example, people might watch a presidential debate expecting their favorite candidate to win, only to witness the opposing candidate do a much better job. They may or may not

Viewers who tune in to a presidential primary debate have an opportunity to evaluate the performance of each candidate. These evaluations may or may not be in line with viewers' original expectations. *AP Photo/Paul Sancya*

change their attitude toward their favorite candidate, but their evaluation of the candidates' performances might well affect their subsequent political behaviors.

Uses and Dependency Model

Research has shown that dependency on a medium is the result of two major factors: viewer motives for obtaining gratifications and the availability of viewing alternatives. Each of these factors may be affected by any number of social or psychological characteristics. For example, a person with poor health and limited mobility would be more likely to be dependent upon a medium such as television for entertainment and diversion than would a healthy person who enjoys many different types of activities. Furthermore, the person with limited mobility would be more likely to become dependent upon a medium such as television if he or she did not have access to other media options—such as a personal computer, a DVD or Blu-ray player, computer games, and so forth—in the home.

The **uses and dependency model** (Rubin & Windahl, 1986) proposes that certain elements in a media system (e.g., the system itself, the structure of society, individual differences that result in highly personal motives) cause people to use and depend upon the media. Dependency upon the media may lead to effects in itself. For example, such dependence could produce an attitude change and thus affect the other elements in the model.

The greater the dependency upon a medium, the more likely that medium will have effects upon the viewer. Miller and Reese (1982) studied political effects and found that effects were more likely to occur among those who relied more upon the medium rather than those who did not rely upon the medium.

Assumptions of Uses and Gratifications

Several basic assumptions lie at the heart of the uses and gratifications perspective. Scholars identified most of these assumptions in 1974. Since then, others (e.g., Palmgreen, 1984; Palmgreen, Wenner, & Rosengren, 1985; Rubin, 1986; Rubin, 2002; Rubin & Windahl, 1986) have learned more about media audiences and have expanded the list of assumptions inherent in uses and gratifications. Alan Rubin (2009) provided a concise list of these assumptions.

The Active Audience

This uses and gratifications perspective assumes that viewers are active participants in the communication process, but they are not all equally active; in other words, audience activity varies. The communication behavior of audience members is goal directed, purposive, and motivated. They make viewing selections based on personal motivations, goals, and needs; these same factors influence what they actually see and hear.

Additional research has attempted to explore audience involvement with the media (Rubin & Perse, 1987). Studies have found that audience members differ in the level of activity (media use or involvement) and that individual members experience variability in their media activity levels and their reasons for viewing at various times. One study showed that viewers are not particularly active when they seek programs for the motive of diversion, but they do actively seek out information when they watch news programs (Levy & Windahl, 1984).

The uses and gratifications approach assumes an actively involved audience, as is often the case with those who play video games. © *Heather Swolsky*

Media Use for Gratifications

This perspective emphasizes that viewers use the media for a variety of reasons, sometimes to obtain information about something that interests or troubles them, or sometimes to simply entertain them. It is always used or selected to gratify the needs or wants of the audience member.

Finn (1992) described the motives for media use as falling under one of two headings: proactive or passive. Examples of proactive media use are watching a particular television program in order to learn more about a specific subject of interest, watching a certain movie for the express purpose of being entertained, or using the Internet to find information for a project at school or work. In other words, the media user actively seeks something from the media based upon his or her wants, needs, and motives. As the name suggests, passive motives describes the use of media in a lackadaisical (passive) sense, what we could consider "mindless consumption." For example, sometimes we turn on the television simply because it is there, just to "see what's on." We are not actively seeking information, entertainment, or anything in particular. This does not mean that we will not be entertained or learn something—we very well might. It only suggests that we did not begin the viewing experience with a particular, proactive motive in mind.

Media use orientations can be described as either ritualized or instrumental (Rubin, 1984). Ritualized use describes habitual use of the media to pass time or divert one's attention from real-life concerns. Instrumental use characterizes active and goal-oriented use of the media. Watching news programs or a particular documentary because of a desire for news and information is an example of instrumental media use; listening to favorite music to calm one's nerves before playing a big game is another.

Social and Psychological Factors

A host of social and psychological factors mediate people's communication behavior. When someone watches a newscast or dramatic program, his or her reaction to the information depends upon individual personality, social circumstances, psychological disposition, and so forth. For example, people who are not particularly mobile and those who are lonely have been found to rely heavily on media use (Perse & Rubin, 1990; Rubin & Rubin, 1982).

Competition and Mediation

Media compete with other forms of communication (i.e., functional alternatives) for selection, attention, and use to gratify our needs or wants. A viewer must pay attention to media messages in order to be influenced or affected by them. Personal choices and individual differences are strong influences that mitigate media effects. One's initiative mediates patterns and consequences of media use. For example, if you plan on auditioning for *American Idol* next year, it is likely that you will watch every episode of this and related television talent shows (e.g., *The Voice, America's Got Talent*) this season. Lack of sufficient individual initiative results in stronger influences from media messages.

Uses and Gratifications Research: A Brief History

Most research activity in the area of uses and gratifications has examined the motives behind media use. In other words, researchers have sought to find out why people watch the television programs they watch, or why they are influenced by some commercials but not by others. Instead of focusing on what the media do to people, these studies ask the question: What do people do with the media? (Klapper, 1963; Rubin, 2009).

A series of studies in the 1940s sought to identify people's motives for listening to certain radio programs and for reading the newspaper. Some scholars conducted their studies before the phrase "uses and gratifications" was utilized (Lazarsfeld, 1940; Herzog, 1940, 1944; Berelson, 1949), typically using the labels "functionalism" or "functional analysis" for this early empirical research. These researchers were more interested in the motives of audience members than the effects of the media content, and their findings were quite revealing. Their studies examined (1) radio quiz shows to determine their various appeals among audiences, (2) daytime serials to find out what gratifications women received from listening to them, and (3) newspaper readership to determine readers' motives for reading or subscribing. They found that listeners enjoyed the programs for various reasons, from the educational appeal of quiz shows to the opportunity for emotional release of daytime serial listeners.

By the 1970s researchers had begun to categorize the various motives for media use (Katz, Gurevitch, & Haas, 1973). Needs were found to be related to social and psychological factors. Katz and his colleagues found that viewers used the media to help them gain more understanding of themselves, the people close to them, or society at large. Also, the media were used to increase personal status and to strengthen relationships.

Other researchers developed their own typology for audience gratifications (McQuail, Blumler, & Brown, 1972). They found that people use television to be diverted, to fulfill the need for personal relationships, to reinforce personal identity, and to keep abreast of happenings in the world around them.

Rosengren and Windahl (1972) were among the first to suggest that media uses and effects should be linked. Research should ask what effects particular gratifications may result in, or what effects particular uses of the media may have. They found that people depend upon the media to fulfill certain needs, such as vicarious experience and escapism, or involvement or interaction, and they explored how these lead to particular effects.

Other researchers have also suggested that a synthesis of the two research realms would be logical and beneficial. These research domains have some obvious similarities in that each examines the consequences of mass communication from an individual or societal level—changes in attitudes, perceptions, or behavior.

Since the mid-1970s, research has provided a greater understanding of the uses and effects of mass media. In answer to criticisms regarding lack of uniformity, uses and effects researchers have adapted similar measures for viewer motives. Based upon work by Greenberg (1974) and Rubin (1979), most uses and gratifications scholars now recognize the following motives for media use among audience members: learning, habit, companionship, arousal, relaxation, escapism, or a way to pass time (Rubin, 1994). The studies by Greenberg and Rubin produced similar results. Both found, for example, that motives for viewing changed with a person's age. Most habitual viewers liked watching comedies rather than news. Most viewers seeking excitement tended to watch action/ adventure programs.

Criticisms of Uses and Gratifications

Rubin (1994) reviewed the literature on uses and gratifications and identified several major criticisms of the approach. Some of the criticisms were aimed at the results of early research. Additional research has served to answer the critics on several issues.

Too Individualistic

The focus upon individual differences makes the findings of uses and gratifications research difficult to extend to other people or to society as a whole (Carey & Kreiling, 1974; Elliott, 1974). In recent years, however, the consistency of findings in replicated studies (including standardization of measures in terms of viewer motives) has contributed to the generalization of results.

Lack of Synthesis of Research Findings

The various typologies that have been developed to describe audience uses and gratifications had initially been criticized as difficult to synthesize (Anderson & Meyer, 1975; Swanson, 1979). Since the 1970s, the efforts toward consistency in typologies have produced more systematic categorizations, but differences in typologies still exist. This criticism should guide future research toward a more synthesized level.

Lack of Clarity among Key Concepts

Some researchers have argued that key concepts such as needs, motives, behavior, and so forth have not been clearly explicated (Anderson & Meyer, 1975; Blumler, 1979; Elliott, 1974). Since the 1970s these concepts have been studied and described more explicitly, but the criticism still has some validity.

Differences in the Meaning of Key Concepts

Other critics have pointed out that researchers have offered different definitions for various concepts such as motives, uses, and gratifications (Elliott, 1974; Swanson, 1977, 1979). Comparisons between studies become difficult when one investigator defines a key concept in one way and another defines it in another way.

The Active Audience and Use of Self-Reporting

These two related notions have been criticized for a perceived lack of accuracy and consistency (Elliott, 1974; Swanson, 1977, 1979). For the most part, studies have answered the criticisms by using validating scales (Rubin, 1979, 1981), experimental methods (Bryant & Zillmann, 1984), and other means. Other critics have pointed out that self-reports might be affected by individual interpretations and perceptions (Babrow, 1988); therefore, some caution is warranted.

Recent Research

Many recent research studies have involved expansion of uses and gratifications into other domains, in combination with third-person effects, cultivation, and parasocial interaction. Uses and gratifications researchers have also expanded their inquiries into the uses and effects from social media, including the Internet and social network sites, reality television programming, and MP3 players.

One of the areas of expansion has to do with third-person effects from the uses and gratifications perspective. *Third-person effects* occur when media consumers perceive that media content affects others more so than it affects them personally. (For example, when asked if watching a violent movie might cause you to act aggressively, you would probably say "no," but when asked if the same movie might cause others to act aggressively, you are more likely to say "yes.") Banning (2007) found that continued exposure to a public service campaign resulted in a third-person effect, and that other studies might demonstrate such a link, with uses and gratifications causing third-person effects. Haridakis and Rubin (2005) also connected uses and gratifications with third-person effects.

Other researchers have linked uses and gratifications with cultivation (Bilandzic & Rossler, 2004), information processing (Eveland, 2004), and an integrated model of active audience exposure to television (Cooper & Tang, 2009).

Another area of expansion has been with parasocial interaction, the feeling of media consumers that media celebrities are more like friends than strangers. One study found that talk-radio listeners parasocially interacted with the host of the program, and this behavior predicted the frequency with which they listened to the show and whether or not they made plans to listen. Listeners were also found to view the host as an influential opinion leader (Rubin & Step, 2000).

In a study of Internet uses and gratifications, Ko, Cho, and Roberts (2005) discovered that people with strong motives to seek information are more likely to interact with others via a website than those who had strong motives for social interaction, who were more likely to prefer face-to-face contact. Another study found that people who were motivated to use the Internet experienced more dependency than others, and that motivation and Internet dependency was mediated by how cognitively and affectively they were involved (Sun, Rubin, & Haridakis, 2008).

Talk show hosts and other media celebrities interact with their audiences parasocially. *AP Photo/Photo courtesy of Rush Limbaugh*

One study compared the uses and gratifications of Facebook and instant messaging (Quan-Haase & Young, 2010). The researchers found that Facebook users enjoyed sharing with their friends in the network, while instant messaging was used to maintain and develop relationships. Another Facebook study examined students' motives for using the social network. Sheldon (2008) determined that the primary motive of women for using Facebook was to maintain relationships; for men it was to develop new relationships. A study of MySpace (Ancu & Cozma, 2009) found that people visited MySpace profiles of primary political candidates in 2008 so that they could interact with other supporters.

Focus groups were used to determine college students' uses and gratifications from watching reality television programs (Lundy, Ruth, & Park, 2008). The researchers found that students were, for the most part, embarrassed by the amount of time they spent watching reality programming. The students noted that viewing such programs provided an excellent means to escape from the pressures of life and live vicariously through the lives of people featured in the programs. They said that reality television did not require their full attention, and therefore the convenience of watching such programs while multitasking was determined to be a major gratification from viewing. Students reported enjoying watching such programs in the presence of other students, and talking about the programs afterward. Another focus-group study (Barton, 2009) examined competition reality programs and suggested that people watch the shows to be gratified on an individual rather than social level.

Another study examined the uses and gratifications of using MP3 players. Zeng (2011) found that people use MP3 players for various reasons, but usage was significantly predicted by use for entertainment and use for concentration.

Research Spotlight

The Uses and Gratifications of Online Care Pages: A Study of CaringBridge
Isolde K. Anderson (2011)
Health Communication, 26, 546–559

Since 1997, CaringBridge.org has provided free online web pages for patients and family members to communicate about various types of situations, such as serious illness, childbirth, adoption, hospitalization, and military deployment. These pages function similarly to many social network sites, allowing users to post photos and updates in addition to leaving comments on others' pages. In this study, Anderson examined the uses and gratifications that motivate people to use CaringBridge (CB), which differs from "traditional" social network sites in that CB pages are set up most often during times of a medical crisis. Additionally, unlike Facebook or Twitter, CB pages are often set up and managed by someone other than the patient (e.g., a mother may start a page dedicated to her small child, who is battling leukemia). Anderson referred to the creators and managers of these pages as *authors*.

Research Questions

To explore uses and gratifications related to CaringBridge, Anderson developed the following research questions:

RQ1: What gratifications do CaringBridge authors receive from their sites?

RQ2: How does the purpose for setting up the site affect the gratifications CB authors obtain from their sites?

RQ3: How does setting up a site for oneself or others affect the gratifications CB authors obtain from their sites?

RQ4: How does sufficiency of information from health care providers affect gratifications authors obtain from their CaringBridge sites?

RQ5: How does the outcome of the illness affect the gratifications authors obtain from their CaringBridge sites?

RQ6: How does an author's age affect the gratifications obtained from his or her CaringBridge site?

RQ7: How do gratifications obtained from CaringBridge sites differ for male and female authors?

RQ8: How do gratifications obtained from CaringBridge sites differ depending on the author's frequency of Internet usage?

RQ9: How do gratifications obtained from CB sites differ depending on the author's religiosity?

Method: Pilot Study

Because little research has been conducted about the use of CaringBridge, Anderson began by implementing a pilot study of CB authors. With the help of CB administrators, Anderson sent the pilot survey to 1,646 CB authors who started pages between January and March 2006. The survey included 14 general uses and gratifications categories, including entertainment, to pass time, information-gathering, social interaction, and surveillance. Anderson also developed a spirituality category based on previous CB research, and interviews with two CB administrators were used to develop additional uses and gratifications categories, such as helping others, convenience, and having a creative outlet. The survey also included an opened-ended question that allowed CB authors to write in additional answers.

The pilot survey was e-mailed to the 1,646 authors, of whom 378 completed the survey, resulting in a 22.4 percent response rate. Of those who responded, 80 percent were women, and the participants' average age was 39 years old.

After the survey responses were collected, Anderson analyzed them to find which categories were rated as most important. Items that participants rated with a 4 or 5 (on a 5-point scale) were included in the survey used during the main study, while items of low importance were discarded. Additionally, responses to the opened-ended question were coded, and if three or more people described a similar benefit (e.g., CB provides a record of my experience), it was included in the second survey.

Method: Main Study

Based on the responses to the pilot study, Anderson developed a second questionnaire, which consisted of 45 questions about perceived gratifications from using CB. (Anderson used the word *benefits* instead of *gratifications* in the survey.) The survey also included demographic and open-ended questions, for a total of 145 questions.

For this study, the survey invitation was e-mailed to new CB authors who started pages between April and November 2006 (n=4,681). Of those, 1,035 filled out the survey, resulting in a 22.1% response rate. Respondents were mostly female (85%), between 20 and 39 years old (51%), White (93%), and religious (90%).

Results

Analyses of the data revealed that a majority of CB pages were created in response to a serious illness (67.4%) or hospitalization (22.5%). Most sites were set up for a child (50%) or other relative (33%). A majority of authors (57%) read comments from others daily, while updating their page several times a week (32%).

CB was also reported as the preferred method of contact during the health crisis, followed closely by cards and e-mails. Anderson said this finding suggests CB is not a substitute for other types of communication (since cards and e-mail were also rated highly); it is simply the preferred method of contact, which may suggests that CB users derive different gratifications from the site.

To answer RQ1, Anderson found the top four gratifications from CB use to be providing others with information, receiving encouragement from reading the posts others made on their page, the convenience factor, and receiving psychological support (which is derived from the general awareness that others care about the situation). For RQ2, those who set up sites because of serious illness rated the ability to provide information to others higher than those who set up a CB site for other reasons (e.g., hospitalization, premature birth).

RQ3 found no significant relationship between gratifications and whom the CB site was created for, such as a child or other family member. Those who reported receiving more information from health care providers rated providing others with information, the convenience factor, and psychological support gratifications more highly than those who did not receive as much information from health care providers, thus answering RQ4.

RQ5 sought to find if there was a relationship between the outcome of the illness (i.e., recovery versus death) and gratifications from using CB; however, of the four main benefits, providing others with information was only found to be marginally significant, while there was no significance for the other benefits. For RQ6, older authors rated convenience more highly than did younger authors, but no other significant relationships were found for the age variable.

RQ7 focused on gender differences, and the only significant differences in perceived gratifications were that women rated encouragement from reading others' posts and psychological support more highly than men. RQ8 found no significance for the impact of authors' Internet usage; however, psychological support did approach significance. Lastly, RQ9 found that an author's religiosity was related to higher gratifications for sharing information, encouragement from reading posts, and psychological support.

Because the top four benefits remained the same for all groups in the sample, Anderson said this could reveal that most people in a health-related situation have the same fundamental needs.

Summary

The uses and gratifications approach assumes that individual differences among audience members cause each person to use media messages differently and react to them differently. It assumes that a person's social setting and psychological makeup are as responsible for producing certain effects as are the media messages themselves.

Uses and gratifications research examines the motivations and behaviors of viewers, or how and why they use the media. It always assumes that viewers actively choose which programs or other media content they will use to gratify their individual needs.

Several basic assumptions lie at the heart of the uses and gratifications perspective. Some of these include the assumption that the audience is an active one, that they seek out media use for specific gratifications, and that viewer reactions are dependent upon social and psychological factors.

A series of studies in the 1940s sought to identify people's motives for listening to certain radio programs and for reading the newspaper. By the 1970s, researchers had begun to classify the various motives for media use. Needs were found to be related to social and psychological factors.

Many researchers have believed that a synthesis of media effects research and uses research would be logical and beneficial. Such research would explore what effects particular gratifications might have, or what effects particular uses of the media might produce.

Since the mid-1970s research has provided a greater understanding of the use of mass media and the effects of that use. In answer to one of the criticisms of such research in previous years, uses and effects researchers have adapted similar measures for viewer motives. Most uses and gratifications research now recognizes the following motives for media use among audience members: learning, habit, companionship, arousal, relaxation, escapism, and a way to pass time.

Communication scholars have developed several different models that attempt to explain media uses and effects. These include the transactional model, the gratification-seeking and audience-activity model, the expectancy-value model, and the uses and dependency model.

Several components and characteristics of uses and gratifications research have been criticized through the years. The more substantial criticisms include the following: findings that are too individualistic and not easily generalized, lack of synthesis among research findings, lack of clarity among key concepts, differences in the meanings of key concepts, the notion of the active audience, and the perceived lack of accuracy of self-reporting measures.

A great deal of uses and gratifications research since the 1970s has served to answer the critics on several issues. In addition, uses and gratifications researchers have expanded their views to link the uses and effects approach with cultivation, parasocial interaction, and third-person effects. Studies involving new communication technologies and social media have been abundant in recent years.

Persuasion

> *The real persuaders are our appetites, our fears and above all our vanity.*
> *The skillful propagandist stirs and coaches these internal persuaders.*
> —Eric Hoffer, *The Passionate State of Mind*, 1955

Persuasion research in mass communication examines the process of attitude formation and change in audience members and the modification of behavior based upon attitude change. Its roots are in antiquity, and it remains one of the most prolific realms of modern communication scholarship.

Any individual or group that has some stake in influencing mass audiences stands to benefit from this particular arm of communication research. Advertising agents, consumer product manufacturers, politicians, and public service organizations are a few of the groups that use research findings to their practical advantage. Knowledge of persuasive influences is also important for consumers, voters, and other audience members who wish to protect themselves from being manipulated.

Persuasion research differs in an important way from most other areas of media effects research. Most persuasive messages are intentional; that is, they are designed to have an *intended effect*. Media effects in other realms of effects research (e.g., aggressive behavior after viewing violence) are usually *unintended*. The exceptions to this would be some instances of fright reactions in horror films and certain gratifications obtained from media use.

Persuasion involves certain processes of attitude change. Psychologists Petty and Cacioppo have created a popular model to explain the processes that audience members experience as they are persuaded. Their **Elaboration Likelihood Model (ELM)** of persuasion identifies two separate "routes to persuasion" or one of two bridges that must be crossed before persuasion can occur (Petty & Cacioppo, 1981, 1986b; Petty & Wegener, 1999; Petty, Briñol, & Priester, 2009). In addition to ELM, this chapter also discusses other theories of persuasion, such as the Theory of Planned Behavior and Theory of Reasoned Action.

Following a review of the research tradition associated with studies of persuasion, we discuss the importance of attitudes, emotions, and behavior in the persuasion process. We then take a look at various models of persuasion, including models that link attitudes and actions. Finally, we examine recent trends in persuasion research.

Research Tradition

When radio became popular in the early 20th century, psychologists and sociologists began investigating the persuasive power of mass media. In the 1920s and 1930s, a respected social scientist found that propaganda messages had had *powerful* effects upon audiences during World War I (Lasswell, 1927).

In the years between the world wars, several events provided additional evidence for the power of the media to influence the masses: In 1929, news of the crash on Wall Street brought nationwide panic; in 1938, Orson Welles's *War of the Worlds* broadcast resulted in cases of hysteria that received much publicity; finally—perhaps most significantly—Adolf Hitler's rise to power in Germany underscored the frightening potential for mass persuasion by means of media communication.

During World War II, researcher Carl Hovland continued to investigate the effects of persuasive messages on attitude change through his study of soldiers who viewed military training films. Hovland found that the soldiers learned new information from the films, but the persuasive power of the films in effecting changes in attitudes and behavior was rather limited. Persuasion, Hovland found, was contingent upon any number of variables that served to moderate the effects (Hovland, Lumsdaine, & Sheffield, 1949).

After the war, Hovland continued his research on persuasion at Yale University. His research priority became the identification of the moderating variables that acted upon the persuasive process. Hovland found that successful persuasion involved a process of three important steps: (1) listeners must pay attention to a message, (2) they must comprehend the message, and (3) they must accept the message. He identified a number of variables that affected the power of a persuasive message. These included the credibility of the message source, the type of message appeal (e.g., did it arouse fear or motivate the listener?), the order of the arguments presented (e.g., the different power of one-sided arguments compared with two-sided arguments), identification of the audience member with certain groups, and specific personality characteristics of audience members.

Much of the evidence for powerful and direct media effects during the early years was not based on the best research designs. For example, little effort was expended toward measuring people's attitudes *prior to* receiving the propaganda messages—a crucial factor in proving that attitude change had actually occurred due to the propaganda message.

Social scientists continued to study the effects of persuasive messages in the 1940s and 1950s, using more rigorous empirical methods. Hyman and Sheatsley (1947) found that to be successful in changing attitudes, persuasive messages had to overcome certain psychological barriers. Other social scientists reported that persuasive campaign messages from the media had little effect on changing people's preferences for candidates in the 1940 presidential election (Lazarsfeld, Berelson, & Gaudet, 1948).

Paul Lazarsfeld and his colleagues determined that media messages served primarily to reinforce existing attitudes rather than to change anyone's opinion. Media messages did seem to influence certain members of the community who were respected for their knowledge of current affairs. These *opinion leaders,* as the researchers called them, had the personal influence to change the attitudes of others in the community. Thus, media influence was described as a *two-step flow* or *indirect effects* situation in which media messages influenced opinion leaders who, in turn, influenced others in the community via interpersonal communication (Katz & Lazarsfeld, 1955).

Through the years, communication scholars have debated the extent to which mass mediated messages have the power to persuade audiences. Most recent research has shown that persuasion is not simply a stimulus-and-response-type situation, but a more complicated process that emphasizes the *receptivity* of the receiver, or his or her willingness to receive the message.

Attitude, Emotions, Behavior, and Persuasion

To understand the persuasion process, one must first understand the concept of *attitude.* A person's attitude can be defined as that person's "abstract evaluation of an object" (Chaiken, Wood, & Eagly, 1996, p. 702). Others have defined attitudes as "people's general predispositions to evaluate other people, objects, and issues favorably or unfavorably" (Petty, Briñol, & Priester, 2009, p. 127).

Whatever the definition, most contemporary research involving persuasive effects places much importance on the critical role of attitudes in the persuasion process. Attitude is viewed as the all-important mediator that stands between the acquisition of new persuasive information and subsequent behavioral change. If the new information changes a person's attitude, then behavioral change is more likely.

What actually causes a change in attitude? What internal processes come into play? Are people motivated to change their attitudes and behavior to gain rewards or avoid punishment, or do they make the change due to some other reason?

One explanation of this complex process is the **theory of cognitive dissonance** (Festinger, 1957). The best way to understand this theory is to define each of its components. We have already learned that the term "cognitive" is used to describe mental processes or thoughts. "Dissonance" in this case refers to something being *inconsistent.* Cognitive dissonance occurs when attitude and action become inconsistent with one another. For example, someone who is forced to make major dietary changes for health reasons would also have to make significant adjustments in his or her attitude, especially if the old way of eating was believed to be a "healthy" diet. According to Festinger's theory of cognitive dissonance, this inconsistency causes the person anxiety that must be resolved. The way it is resolved is to bring the attitude in line with the actions. The new diet is soon believed to be healthier than the old one.

For example, consider the person who has been brought up to believe that homosexuality is sinful. Perhaps the person has carried strong prejudices toward homosexuals, and has even cracked jokes about homosexuals, using derisive names. Suppose such behaviors would not be tolerated in the person's work-

---

Research Spotlight

Happiness versus Sadness as a Determinant of Thought Confidence in Persuasion: A Self-Validation Analysis
Pablo Briñol, Richard E. Petty, and Jamie Barden (2007)
Journal of Personality and Social Psychology, 93(5), 711–727

The researchers used the self-validation hypothesis to predict that emotion (happiness or sadness) plays a role in evaluative judgments by affecting the confidence people have in their thoughts about a persuasive message. The study, published in 2007, consisted of four experiments. We discuss the first of these experiments below.

The Self-Validation Hypothesis

This hypothesis (Petty et al., 2002) states that thought confidence is important in determining which thoughts predict attitudes, just as attitude confidence determines which attitudes predict behavior. It predicts that people in a happy state of mind should be more influenced by the quality of a persuasive argument than people who are in a sad state of mind.

Method

Ohio State University undergraduate psychology students, 92 of them, were randomly assigned to the argument quality conditions (strong or weak), emotional conditions (happy or sad), and the message focus conditions (argument focus or control). The students were told that they were to give reactions to a change in the university's academic policy, specifically the possibility of instituting senior comprehensive exams in the students' major. All received a message in favor of the comprehensive exams, but some messages contained strong arguments and some weak arguments.

The students were told that as a second part of the research project, they were to think and write about either happy or sad personal experiences. After this, the students were asked to think back to the original message and write down their thoughts about it. Some students were asked to rate the strength of the arguments; others were not.

Results

Using analysis of variance, the researchers found that they had successfully manipulated emotion. Students reported feeling significantly better after writing about happy rather than sad personal episodes. Their thoughts were more favorable toward the proposal after receiving the strong version of the message rather than the weak version. Their attitudes were also more favorable toward the proposal after receiving the strong argument. The two-way interaction between argument quality and emotion was significant. For happy participants, the strong message resulted in significantly more favorable attitudes toward the proposal than those who received the weak message. Attitudes of sad participants did not differ for the strong and weak messages. The three-way interaction between argument quality, emotion, and message focus was not significant.

place, where coworkers, clients, or subordinates might be gay or lesbian. The person may even come to like and respect some coworkers who have different sexual preferences, adding to the dissonance between attitude and behavior. Rather than continue with absolute intolerance, the person might ease cognitive dissonance by changing attitudes toward the gay community.

Many social scientists emphasize the connection between attitudes and *emotions* or affective components. Persuasive messages that contain emotional appeals can be powerful. Studies have found that emotions are very important in the formation and change of attitudes (Jorgensen, 1998). A happy or sad state of mind can determine how confident one is in one's attitudes, and therefore affect persuasive processes (Briñol, Petty, & Barden, 2007; DeSteno, Petty, Wegener, & Rucker, 2000; DeSteno et al., 2004).

Persuasion Models

Through the years, a number of researchers have developed various models to explain the persuasion process. Special emphasis is given to the Elaboration Likelihood Model (ELM), which provides one of the most comprehensive explanations for persuasive processes in terms of mediated communications. However, ELM is just one method of understanding persuasion; therefore we will also examine other theories that contribute to our understanding of how we are influenced by mediated messages.

McGuire's Communication/Persuasion Matrix Model

McGuire (1985, 1989) introduced a model to explain persuasion effects by identifying *inputs* and *outputs*. Inputs, or independent variables, include the source, the message, the recipient, the channel, and the context of the presentation of the message. Inputs are variables controlled by the person or group attempting to persuade or influence audience members. Outputs, or dependent variables, are variables that fall under the control of the individual audience members. These variables include exposure to the information; attention to the information; interest, comprehension, and acquisition of new knowledge; yielding to the weight of the message and changing the attitude; remembering of the information and new attitude; retrieval of the information; the conscious decision to act according to the new attitude; action based upon that decision; reinforcement of the new behavior; and consolidation of the new attitude.

McGuire's model has several shortcomings (Petty & Priester, 1994). The first is its lack of detail regarding the process of actual *yielding* to a new attitude. Second, the model assumes that the input and output variables are *sequential*; that is, they must occur in the order listed in order to have persuasive effects. Yet subsequent research has shown that the variables do not need to be sequential for persuasion to occur. The acquisition (or learning) and remembering of new information have been found to be independent of each other and even unnecessary steps in the persuasion process (Greenwald, 1968; McGuire, 1985;

> ## McGuire's Matrix Model
>
> **Variables that Affect the Persuasive Power of a Communication Message**
>
> **Input Variables (Controlled by Communicator)**
> Source   Message   Recipient   Channel   Context
>
> **Output Variables (Controlled by Receiver)**
> Exposure   Attention   Interest   Comprehension
> Acquisition   Yielding   Memory   Retrieval
> Decision   Action   Reinforcement   Consolidation

Petty & Cacioppo, 1981). For example, a person might acquire and learn new information but refuse to change his or her attitude, or a person might conceivably misunderstand the information, learn it wrong, but still change his or her attitude in the intended way.

Cognitive Response Theory

In an attempt to explain the shortcomings of the matrix model, several researchers developed the theory of cognitive response (Greenwald, 1968; Petty, Ostrom, & Brock, 1981). According to this theory, an audience member does not yield to a new attitude after simply learning a new message. Yielding depends upon cognitive responses to the message—or what he or she *thinks* about the message. The memory of what is thought about a message is much more important than a memory of the message itself.

Another theory, *self-validation theory* (Petty, Briñol, & Tormala, 2002), posits that persuasion is dependent upon the amount of confidence people have in their thoughts in response to a persuasive message. When people think favorably of a persuasive message, increasing the validity of the message causes persuasion to increase, while increasing doubt about the validity of the message causes persuasion to decrease. When people think unfavorable thoughts in response to a persuasive message, increasing the validity of the message causes persuasion to decrease, while increasing doubt about the validity of the message increases persuasion (Petty et al., 2002; Briñol & Petty, 2004).

In some cases, however, persuasion has been shown to occur even when an audience member does not think carefully about the content of a message. Cognitive response theory could not explain such instances (Petty, Cacioppo, & Goldman, 1981).

The Elaboration Likelihood Model

Petty and Cacioppo (1981, 1986a, 1986b) extended the theory of cognitive response and developed a theoretical model to explain the processes that occur when a person yields to a persuasive message. Their *Elaboration Likelihood Model* explains the process of persuasion by identifying the likelihood of a person to elaborate cognitively or think very carefully about a persuasive message.

The model proposes two distinct routes that may be taken in order for persuasion to result: central and peripheral. The *central route* to persuasion requires much cognitive effort on the part of the audience member in order to judge the merit of the advocated position or persuasive message. The message recipient listens closely to what is said and then evaluates the information in light of past experiences and previous knowledge. During this process, the person forms opinions about the message—either favorable or unfavorable—and these play a major part in determining the success of the persuasive message. For example, news reports that cover debates on important national and international issues usually require a great deal of cognitive processing on the part of the viewer or reader. Whether or not a spokesperson for a particular side in an issue persuades the reader or viewer to advocate a particular position depends upon central route processing of the information.

As mentioned, the central route necessitates considerable cognitive effort on the part of the audience member. As a result, attitude changes resulting from the central route have shown several common characteristics, including: (1) accessibility, (2) persistency, (3) predictability of behavior, and (4) resistance to change (Petty & Priester, 1994, pp. 100–101).

The *peripheral route* to persuasion may occur in any number of ways, none of which involves considerable cognitive effort. *Simple cues* in the context of the message are more responsible for the change in attitude than a purposeful effort to process and understand information. For example, a relaxing scene by a calm, crystal-blue mountain lake in a television commercial might cause the viewer to experience a nice, contented mood that becomes associated with the mountain-

Prescription drug advertisements have become commonplace on television today. Their persuasive appeal is apparent in the popularity of the advertised drugs. *LUNESTA and the LUNESTA moth are registered trademarks of Sunovion Pharmaceuticals Inc. © 2012 Sunovion Pharmaceuticals Inc. All rights reserved.*

fresh scented detergent that is being pitched. The viewer is persuaded to try the detergent because the commercial has conditioned a certain affective response—the nice, contented mood—that is associated with the product.

The *use of experts* to pitch particular products is another example of the peripheral route to persuasion. More doctors use this pain reliever . . . , more hospitals use this brand . . . , more dentists recommend this toothpaste—are all examples of cues used to effectively shortcut the route to persuasion. The viewer infers that experts are supposed to be correct; therefore, the message is judged as truthful and the viewer is persuaded to use the product (Chaiken, 1987).

Another example of the peripheral route, the *bandwagon effect,* was identified by researchers for the Institute for Propaganda Analysis in the 1930s (Lee & Lee, 1939). Audience members were made to believe that many other people already supported the position of a speaker. They inferred that with so many people in agreement, the speaker's message must be true. Such an inference served as a cue that the message of the speaker was valid, and the bandwagon effect occurred (Axsom, Yates, & Chaiken, 1987).

In contrast, persuasion by way of the central route has been shown to be more successful in long-term attitude change than persuasion through more peripheral routes. Peripheral route persuasion has been shown to be successful in the short run, but over a period of time the strength of the peripheral cues weakens. A person's mood and feelings may change, for example, or cues are no longer associated with certain messages. Petty and Cacioppo (1986a) found that in terms of resistance to attack and durability, attitude changes that occurred through the peripheral route were much weaker than those that occurred through the central route.

In summary, as the likelihood of mental elaboration (careful processing of a persuasive message) increases, the central route to persuasion is dominant. As the likelihood of mental elaboration decreases, the peripheral route to persuasion becomes more important in the persuasion process.

Predictions of the Elaboration Likelihood Model

When the likelihood for elaboration is high (e.g., when the message has personal relevance for the audience member, when there are few distractions), a person is motivated to listen to the message, mentally process, and evaluate the information. Peripheral cue variables are likely to have less impact in such a situation.

When the likelihood for elaboration is low (e.g., when the message has low personal relevance or there are many distractions), the importance of peripheral variables increases significantly. Under such circumstances, the audience member is not likely to be motivated or able to process the message with careful thought.

When the likelihood for elaboration is moderate (e.g., when the audience member has some knowledge of the issue but uncertainty about its personal relevance), the recipient may evaluate the context of the message to determine whether the message should be processed. A contextual component would be, for example, the credibility or the attractiveness of a source.

Variables that Motivate

The strength of the central route to persuasion has led researchers to examine the variables that motivate a person to think carefully about a message. One of the most important of these variables is that of *personal relevance* of the message (Brickner, Harkins, & Ostrom, 1986; Leippe & Elkin, 1987; Petty, Cacioppo, & Haugtvedt, 1992).

Whenever information is perceived as personally relevant to the listener, he or she will process the information more carefully. When this happens, strong arguments become more persuasive and weak arguments become less persuasive (Petty & Cacioppo, 1979).

One study found that personal relevance could be increased by simply using the second person pronoun "you" rather than the third person pronouns "he" or "she." Those who received messages containing "you" were shown to listen and process the information more carefully. Those who processed the information more carefully were more persuaded by strong arguments and less persuaded by weak arguments (Burnkrant & Unnava, 1989).

Researchers have identified other variables that provide the necessary motivation for a receiver to think carefully about a message. One of these involves formulating a question rather than making an assertion in a message to provoke more thought processing on the part of the receiver (Howard, 1990; Petty, Cacioppo, & Heesacker, 1981; Swasy & Munch, 1985). For example, rather than say "Vote for John Doe" at the end of a campaign commercial, it is more effective to present arguments and say "Shouldn't you vote for John Doe?" at the end.

Another way to increase the personal relevance of the message is to frame it in concert with a person's values or self-perceptions (Petty & Wegener, 1998; see Petty, Wheeler, & Bizer, 2000, for review). In one study, students were given a test to determine if they had outgoing or shy personalities. The introverts were shown ads for a VCR that promised "you can have all the luxuries of a movie theater without having to deal with the crowds" while the extroverts were shown ads that promised "you'll be the life of the party, whether the party's in your home or out of it" (Wheeler, Petty, & Bizer, 2005, p. 789). The researchers found that by matching the persuasive message content with the individual's self-perception, persuasion was enhanced or reduced, depending upon the quality of the argument.

"Peripheral Cue" Variables

A number of variables have been shown to affect the persuasion process by means of the peripheral route. According to researchers, a *peripheral cue* can be defined as "a feature of the persuasion context that allows favorable or unfavorable attitude formation even in the absence of an effortful consideration of the true merits of the object or issue" (Petty, Briñol, & Priester, 2009, p. 141). As the likelihood of mental elaboration (careful cognitive processing of a message) decreases, peripheral cues become more potent. Petty and Priester (1994) reviewed the research findings to identify several variables that serve as simple cues. These included:

1. The likability or attractiveness of the message source.
2. The credibility of the source.

Many advertisements make use of persuasive devices such as use of experts, testimonials, and attractive sources to sell products.

3. The number of arguments the message contained.

4. How long the arguments were.

5. How many other people were perceived by the viewer to agree with the position, also known as the bandwagon effect.

The Role of Variables

For persuasion to occur, three factors must be present. A *source* must deliver a persuasive *message* to a *recipient*. Variables that affect the persuasion process may take on different roles and impact any of the three factors.

Source factor variables would include characteristics such as the attractiveness or credibility of the source. Research has shown that such variables serve as peripheral cues when the likelihood of elaboration is low, but are not as important as the quality of the argument itself when the likelihood of elaboration is high (Petty, Cacioppo, & Goldman, 1981). Such variables either enhance or weaken the likelihood for persuasion, depending upon the strength of the argument (Moore, Hausknecht, & Thamodaran, 1986; Heesacker, Petty, & Cacioppo, 1983; Puckett, Petty, Cacioppo, & Fischer, 1983). An attractive or expert source made a strong argument stronger and more persuasive, but the same type of source made a weak argument weaker and even less persuasive.

In one study of source credibility, people were presented either strong or weak arguments for a new pain relief medicine. After the presentation of the persuasive messages, audience members were told that the source of the information was either (1) a federal agency that does research on such products or, (2) a 14-year-old student's class report. Those who believed the message came from the highly credible source showed more favorable attitudes and evidence of persuasion—when the arguments of the message were strong. Less favorable attitudes and less likelihood of persuasion occurred when they were presented with weak arguments from the credible source (Tormala, Briñol, & Petty, 2006).

Variables that could be considered message factors would include all the informational items included in a message. When the likelihood for elaboration is low, the informational items in the message serve as peripheral cues. When the likelihood for elaboration is high, the items are processed carefully and are not merely peripheral cues. Research has shown that the addition of weak arguments in support of a position for each of the low and high ELM conditions results in a different outcome. When informational items are peripheral cues, the addition of weak supporting arguments makes persuasion more likely, but when informational items are evaluated cogently as arguments themselves, weak additional arguments are less likely to affect persuasion (Alba & Marmorstein, 1987; Petty & Cacioppo, 1986a).

An example of a recipient factor would be a person's mood at the time the message is received. An experiment by Petty, Schumann, Richman, and Strathman (1993) revealed several ways in which the recipient's mood influenced the persuasion process. Participants saw a product advertisement while watching one of two television programs, either a pleasant situation comedy or a neutral documentary. In the high involvement or high elaboration likelihood condition, participants were told they could select a free gift afterward from several brands of the product in the commercial. In the low involvement or low elaboration likelihood condition, participants could select from several brands of another kind of product than that depicted in the commercial. The study revealed that viewing the pleasant program not only made people evaluate their own moods more positively, but it made them evaluate the commercial product more positively as well. This was true for both the high- and low-involvement conditions, though it must be pointed out that more positive thoughts about the product were generated when the elaboration likelihood was high rather than low. Generally speaking, mood tended to affect a person's attitude directly when involvement (elaboration likelihood) was low, but when involvement was high, the effect of mood upon attitude depended upon the number of positive thoughts generated.

Social Judgment Theory

Although **social judgment theory** is viewed as a "historical relic" (O'Keefe, 2009, p. 277), its contributions to our understanding of persuasion make it worthy of discussing here. One of the main factors in social judgment theory is the idea that people make various judgments about the differing views that could be held about a particular issue (Sherif, Sherif, & Nebergall, 1965). Take the issue of abortion, for example. Although a person most likely has a certain belief about abortion, he or she may view other positions as acceptable, others as unacceptable, and still some may be viewed neutrally. These various mind-sets "represent the person's latitudes of acceptance, rejection, and noncommitment" (O'Keefe, 2009, p. 276) about the issue. The latitude we give to various viewpoints is influenced by the degree to which a person's identity is tied to his or her viewpoint on a particular issue. The stronger the connection between one's belief about an issue and their concept of self-identity, the more likely they are to reject differing viewpoints.

Models That Link Attitudes and Actions

A large body of persuasion research has addressed the connection between a person's attitude and his or her actions or behavior. Whether or not a person changes his behavior to come into line with a change in attitude depends upon a number of factors. Most of these factors are related to particular situations or the person's disposition (Ajzen, 1988).

Scholars have developed two general purpose models that serve to explain the process that links a new or changed attitude with appropriate action or behavior. One model holds that behavior is a result of thoughtful reasoning; the other proposes that behavior is more spontaneous and is activated automatically. These two models are called, respectively, the *reasoned action and planned behavior model* and the *automatic activation model.*

Theories of Reasoned Action and Planned Behavior

Fishbein and Ajzen (1975) introduced the **theory of reasoned action (TRA)** with the assumption that "people consider the implications of their actions before they decide to engage or not engage in a given behavior" (p. 5). The model hypothesizes that people make the decision to behave or not to behave in a certain way based upon two criteria: (1) the person's attitude toward the behavior itself is one important criterion and (2) the person's perceptions about how others will view the behavior. Essentially, "the TRA depicts behavioral intentions as potentially shaped by both personal (attitudinal) and social (normative) influences" (O'Keefe, 2009, p. 273). These personal and social factors allow persuaders to better tailor their messages to audiences depending on which factors influence the audiences' intentions to do something (e.g., vote for a particular candidate, buy a certain brand of car) (O'Keefe, 2009). Before the person engages in a particular behavior, he or she carefully weighs the personal advantages or disadvantages of doing so. If engaging in the behavior comes at a cost, that cost is considered and carefully weighed against the perceived benefits of engaging in that behavior.

Ajzen (1991) revised the TRA to include the **theory of planned behavior (TPB)**. In addition to basing intentions for action upon attitudes and the behavioral norms of others, the expanded model reveals that intentions to act are also based upon the perceived *control* the person has over the behavior. This factor essentially examines whether a person thinks the action is easy or difficult to perform.

It is easy to see how the TRA and TPB work when we look at health-related behaviors, such as dieting or exercise. An overweight person would probably think that dieting is desirable (which is a positive attitude toward the behavior) and that person's friends and family would also think it is a good idea (which means there is a positive social norm); however, the overweight person may believe that he or she is not able to go on a diet—healthy food is often more expensive, healthy food takes too long to prepare, he or she does not like the taste of broccoli and squash, and so on (which shows that the overweight person believes the change is too difficult to perform).

In these types of situations, creators of persuasive messages need to work on finding ways to change a person's perceptions about their behavioral control, rather than focusing on the benefits of changing their behavior (because the people already have a positive attitude toward the behavior). Imagine that a mattress company was trying to persuade you to buy a new mattress. Research had shown that audiences and society at large had positive attitudes about getting a good night's sleep, but audience and society members also believed that it was impossible for them personally to achieve this because quality mattresses were too expensive. In this case, the mattress company should focus its persuasive message on the cost factor, showing audiences that they could, in fact, afford the mattress.

Thus, by using the three factors (personal attitude, societal norms, and perceived behavioral control) associated with the TRA and TPB, persuaders can tailor their messages to better influence their audience.

Protection Motivation Theory

Similar to TRA and TPB, **protection motivation theory (PMT)** was developed to better understand what influences people to engage in protective behaviors, such as practicing safe sex, taking measures to prevent skin cancer, and ceasing to smoke (Rogers, 1975; Rogers & Prentice-Dunn, 1997). Two main factors are examined when looking at PMT: (1) threat appraisal (what a person thinks about the threat) and (2) coping appraisal (what a person thinks about the protective behavior).

Two sub-factors of threat appraisal include perceptions about how serious the threat is (e.g., breast cancer, obesity-related illnesses) and how likely one is to suffer from the threat (e.g., family history of cancer or obesity). The coping appraisal is also made up of two sub-factors: perceptions of how effective the protective behavior is (e.g., chemotherapy and radiation, diet and exercise) and how capable one believes herself to be to perform the protective behavior (e.g., undergoing chemo treatments, the ability to lose weight).

Research has shown that when a threat is seen as more severe or when a protective behavior is seen as more effective, people are more likely to engage in the protective action (e.g., Floyd, Prentice-Dunn, & Rogers, 2000; Witte & Allen, 2000).

Stage Models

Persuading someone to change a behavior is not as simple as flipping a switch. In fact, behavior change is often thought of as a process in which a person passes through several distinct stages. The **transtheoretical model of health behavior change**, developed by Prochaska and colleagues (Prochaska, 1994;

Prochaska, Redding, & Evers, 2002) identifies these stages as precontemplation, contemplation, preparation, action, and maintenance.

Let us use the example of running for exercise to illustrate the progression through the stages in this model. Chuck wants to get in better shape, but in the precontemplation stage he is not even thinking about starting to run. When Chuck starts seriously thinking about running—researching the best brand of running shoes and thinking about where he could run—he is in the contemplation stage. Then Chuck actually buys the running shoes and maps out his route, entering the preparation stage. After lacing up his shoes and hitting the pavement, Chuck enters the action stage, where he is actually running. Lastly, as Chuck continues to go for daily runs for several months, he enters the maintenance stage.

With this model, every stage is influenced by different considerations. To persuade someone to move from the precontemplation stage to the contemplation stage, a persuader must be able to get his or her audience to at least *think* about making a behavioral change. Whereas moving from the preparation to action stage involves considerations about how to turn plans into reality. Slater (1999) found that matching considerations to a particular stage was more successful than when they were mismatched.

Automatic Activation

The **automatic activation model** proposes that behavior follows automatically whenever an attitude comes to mind. The process is spontaneous and does not involve any extended reflection or reasoning on the part of the individual. Fazio (1990), the originator of the model, offered two contingent circumstances that allow attitudes to guide behavior automatically: (1) if there is spontaneous access to the attitude whenever the object of the attitude is present, and (2) if the object is perceived according to the attitude (if the attitude is favorable, it is perceived favorably; if unfavorable, it is perceived unfavorably).

More recent research has shown that people sometimes need time to adjust to their new attitudes, to become more confident in them (Rucker & Petty, 2006), or rehearse the new attitude in new situations until it replaces the old attitude (Petty, Gleicher, & Jarvis, 1993; Wilson, Lindsey, & Schooler, 2000).

Recent Research

Wood (2000) reviewed recent research on message-based persuasion and identified different types of motives that produce attitude change or resistance. Research studies on these motives have examined the functions of attitude, sometimes using cognitive dissonance theory as a basis for investigation.

Gender differences and emotions and their influence in the persuasion process have also interested researchers. Burgoon and Klingle (1998) reviewed research on the importance of gender differences in persuasive communications. They argued that, generally, men are more persuasive and women are more persuadable, but the sex of the communicator and the strategies of the persuasive message are important determinants. As for the connection between emotion and persuasion, Jorgensen (1998) discussed the importance of emotions in the formation and change of attitudes in the persuasion process.

The link between attitudes and persuasion has received attention in recent years. Petty and Cacioppo (1996) surveyed the different theories related to persuasion and changes in attitudes and beliefs. Roskos-Ewoldsen (1997) reviewed research on attitude accessibility as a factor in persuasion and argued that some attitudes are remembered more than others. Those that are highly accessible from memory are more likely to influence a person's reception of various messages. He also proposed a model to demonstrate the transactive relationship between persuasion and attitude accessibility.

Researchers have developed new measures to study the availability of automatic attitudes (Fazio, Jackson, Dunton, & Williams, 1995; Greenwald et al., 1998; Petty, Fazio, & Briñol, 2008; and Wittenbrink & Schwarz, 2007). At first, researchers thought that automatic attitudes might show more resistance to change, but studies have shown that even long-held attitudes can be subject to change via classical conditioning and exposure to the new information and the processing of it (Briñol, Petty, & McCaslin, 2008; Fazio & Olson, 2003).

The new information can be presented in the form of advertisements, mass mediated campaigns, or other means of verbal communication (Briñol et al., 2008; Czyzewska & Ginsburg, 2007; Maio, Haddock, Watt, & Hewstone, 2008; Park, Felix, & Lee, 2007; Gawronski & Bodenhausen, 2006).

For example, Park and associates (2007) used implicit measures to determine that people held automatic attitudes toward Arab-Muslims, in that they associated them with terrorism. When presented with positive information about Arab-Muslims, the attitudes were moderated.

In the future, persuasion researchers will continue to identify and study the many variables at work whenever persuasive messages reach audience members. The important influences of individual attitudes and individual emotions on the power of persuasive messages appear to be especially illuminating in our ever-increasing understanding of the persuasion process.

Summary

Persuasion research in mass communication examines the process of attitude change in audience members and the modification of behavior based upon attitude change. Persuasion is an intentional process.

Research on the persuasive power of mass media began in the 1920s and 1930s when radio and films were popular. Lasswell found that propaganda messages had had powerful effects upon audiences during World War I. Several events provided evidence for the influential power of the media: news of the Wall Street crash in 1929, Orson Welles's *War of the Worlds* radio broadcast in 1938, and Adolf Hitler's rise to power in Germany. During World War II, Hovland found persuasion was contingent upon any number of moderating variables.

Hovland found that successful persuasion involved three steps: (1) listeners must pay attention to a message, (2) they must comprehend the message, and (3) they must accept the message. The credibility of the message source, the type of message appeal, the order of the arguments presented, identification of the audience member with certain groups, and specific personality characteristics of audience members all affected persuasive power of media messages.

In the 1940s and 1950s, persuasion was studied using more rigorous empirical methods. Hyman and Sheatsley found that attitude change required persuasive messages to pass over certain psychological barriers. Katz and Lazarsfeld described media influence as a two-step flow or indirect effects situation in which media messages influenced opinion leaders who in turn influenced others in the community through interpersonal communication. Recent research has shown that persuasion is not simply a stimulus-and-response-type situation, but a more complicated process that emphasizes the receptivity of the receiver. Most contemporary research places considerable importance on the critical role of attitudes in the persuasion process. Attitudes can be defined as "people's general predispositions to evaluate other people, objects, and issues favorably or unfavorably." Attitude is the mediator between the acquisition of persuasive information and behavioral change.

McGuire's model explained persuasion effects by identifying inputs (variables controlled by the persuasive source) and outputs (variables controlled by audience members). The model has been criticized for its lack of detail regarding the process of actual yielding to a new attitude and its assumption that the input and output variables are sequential.

The theory of cognitive response holds that yielding to persuasive messages depends upon audience members' cognitive responses to the messages. The memory of what is thought about a message is much more important than a memory of the message itself. Cognitive response theory does not explain instances when persuasion occurs even when an audience member does not think about the content of a message.

Petty and Cacioppo's Elaboration Likelihood Model extends the theory of cognitive response and explains the processes that occur whenever a person yields to a persuasive message. It identifies the likelihood of a person to elaborate cognitively or think very carefully about a persuasive message.

The ELM proposes two distinct routes—central and peripheral. The central route requires much cognitive effort. Attitude changes resulting from the central route have shown several common characteristics: (1) accessibility, (2) persistency, (3) predictability of behavior, and (4) resistance to change. When persuasion occurs by means of the peripheral route, simple cues in the context of the message, the use of experts to pitch products, and the bandwagon effect are more responsible for attitude change than any considerable cognitive effort. As the likelihood of mental elaboration (careful processing of a persuasive message) increases, the central route to persuasion is dominant. As the likelihood of mental elaboration decreases, the peripheral route to persuasion becomes more important in the persuasion process.

The theory of reasoned action (TRA) hypothesizes that people make the decision to behave or not to behave in a certain way based upon two criteria: (1) the person's attitude toward the behavior itself and (2) the person's perceptions about how others will view the behavior.

The theory of planned behavior (TPB) reveals that intentions to act are also based upon the perceived *control* the person has over the behavior. This factor essentially examines whether a person thinks the action is easy or difficult to perform.

It is easy to see how the TRA and TPB work when we look at health related behaviors, such as dieting or exercise. An overweight person would probably think that dieting is desirable (which is a positive attitude toward the behavior) and that person's friends and family would also think it is a good idea (which means there is a positive social norm); however, the overweight person may believe that he or she is not able to go on a diet due to concerns about cost, time, aversion to some healthy foods, and so on (which shows that the overweight person believes the change is too difficult to perform).

Similar to TRA and TPB, protection motivation theory (PMT) was developed to better understand what influences people to engage in protective behaviors like practicing safe sex, taking steps to prevent skin cancer, and quitting smoking.

THREE

Key Areas of Research

eleven

Effects of Media Violence

By the time the average child is eighteen years old,
he or she will have witnessed 16,000 murders.
—Facts and Figures About Our TV Habit, TV Turnoff Network
www.tuneintokids.org/docs2007/rm2.pdf

One of the most important social issues of our time has been the public concern for the negative effects of exposure to media violence, especially among children. Most studies on violent media fare have focused on movies, television dramas, cartoons, and other fantasy shows, as well as news reports, violent video games, and websites.

Through the years, many studies have revealed that viewing mediated violence leads to or causes aggressive behavior. Adults and children have been the research participants in these numerous experiments and studies. Despite the findings, critics of these studies and the research methods they employ abound. Due to the implications for society as a whole, the entire media violence issue has been one of major concern for public policy makers over the years. This chapter will review the important studies and the voice of the critics from a public policy standpoint. We will take a brief look at the research methods used to study the effects from mediated violence, including the ways media violence is measured. Then we turn to the various types of effects from violence, including behavioral, emotional, and cognitive effects. Finally, we note new directions that media violence researchers are taking.

Media Violence Research and Public Policy: History and Future

Through the years, numerous studies of media effects have examined the negative effects on behavior that result from consuming media violence, whether reading, viewing, or listening to it. Since the beginning of radio, movies, and television, concern about media violence has been a major force in public policy making. The struggle for lawmakers has always been maintaining balance between First Amendment rights in a free society and concern for the public welfare.

In her book *Violence on Television,* author Cynthia A. Cooper (1996) identified three phases in the public policy debate that emerged through the years. In the first phase, the debate focused upon the rising rate of juvenile delinquency. Next, the boundaries of the debate expanded to include concern about the effects of television violence on the social behavior and well-being of society in its entirety. In the third phase, the concern of policy makers shifted from identification of detrimental effects on viewers to a proactive attempt to reduce televised violence through legislative restrictions.

Social scientists coordinated their efforts in the 1920s and 1930s to investigate the behavioral and social influences of viewing motion pictures. The Payne Fund studies were a series of tests conducted on adults and children who went to movies. The studies found that the violent and sexual content of movies did not match conventional social mores, but the research evidence did not provide any wholesale support for popular public contentions of detrimental effects upon the social standards of adult movie audiences. The findings did suggest, however, that particularly "vulnerable" children who were prone to juvenile delinquency were influenced by violent and criminal behavior they watched on the screen (Blumer & Hauser, 1933; Dysinger & Ruckmick, 1933).

The next major study to gain public attention appeared in the mid-1950s. This time, the comic book industry came under intense scrutiny. A popular book, *The Seduction of the Innocent* (Wertham, 1954), contended that comic books offered children a distorted picture of reality and were responsible for problems with reading and even instances of juvenile delinquency. The author's methods and interpretations were questioned by the social scientific community, but the general public and the press challenged the findings far less rigorously.

In the 1950s and early 1960s, when television became a popular medium for entertainment, communication researchers in the United States and Great Britain became curious about the effects of exposure to the new medium, especially among young audiences. In their studies, researchers in the United States (Schramm, Lyle, & Parker, 1961) found a connection between viewing televised violence and aggressive behavior among youngsters, whereas a British group (Himmelweit, Oppenheim, & Vince, 1958) did not find evidence of such a causal relationship and contended that such a link would be difficult to prove.

Later, in the socially turbulent and violent 1960s, two more important reports again produced findings that conflicted with one another. First, President Lyndon Johnson's National Commission on the Causes and Prevention of Violence (1969) studied the issue and found that television could not be implicated as a primary cause for violence in society. Soon thereafter, the U.S. Surgeon General's Scientific Advisory Committee on Television and Social Behavior issued its five-volume report. According to the Surgeon General's committee, the evidence indicated that viewing violence on television *did* increase a viewer's tendencies to behave aggressively (1972).

Throughout the 1980s, the Federal Communications Commission loosened earlier restrictions that had been placed on broadcasters to operate "in the public interest." Although the relaxing of restrictions signified a victory for broadcaster's First Amendment rights, the resulting changes in programming caused considerable public concern. Many children's programs disappeared, for example, and those that remained were more violent or highly commercial. A 1982 report from the National Institute of Mental Health, called *Television and Behavior*, did little to settle the issue, but only fueled more public controversy.

Congress reacted to the lowering of program standards with the Children's Television Act of 1990, which required broadcasters to air a certain amount of educational programming suitable for young viewers. It also placed time limits on the amount of commercials shown on children's programs.

Three years later, Congress began hearings to explore the subject of media violence and its effects on children. Due to increased public awareness and concern over the issue, the television networks decided to begin labeling programs to warn parents about violent and unsuitable content. This led to the suggestion for some device that would permit parents to control which programs could be seen on their television sets.

The Telecommunications Act of 1996 made installation of the V-chip mandatory on new models of televisions. This device allows parents to block signals and prevent certain undesirable programs containing violence, sex, or strong language from being received in their homes. The act also required the television industry to rate programs based upon suitability for certain age levels (see Figure 11.1).

Whereas many saw these developments as positive steps, others pointed to problems inherent in such attempts to limit or prohibit children's exposure to undesirable programming (Potter & Warren, 1996). According to some, advisory warnings and blocking devices created a "forbidden fruit" effect, causing children to be extremely interested in seeing the very programs their parents were trying to block (Christenson, 1992).

At the end of the century, a three-year study on television violence conducted by researchers at several leading universities again confirmed the link between viewing violence and subsequent aggressive behavior. Released in 1998, the *National Television Violence Study* found that not only had the proportion of violent prime-time network and cable shows increased since 1994, but the *way the violence was portrayed* on these programs actually encouraged children to imitate the behavior they saw. The study also found that age-based ratings did not indicate the amount of violent content in a program (Federman, 1998).

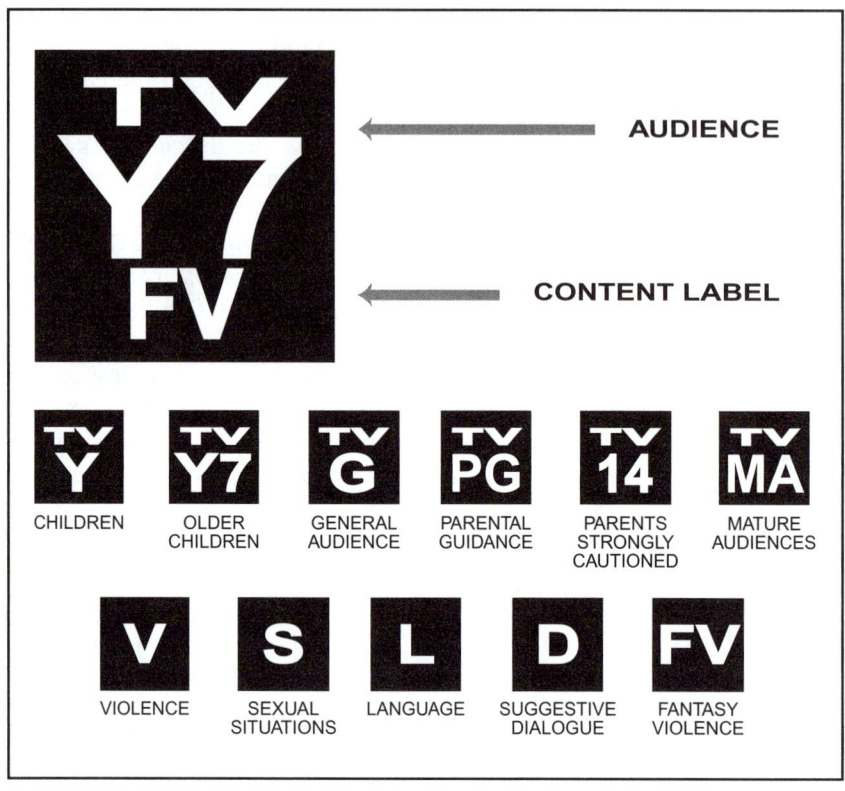

Figure 11.1   The Federal Communications Commission's *TV Parental Guidelines*.

After the Columbine High School shootings in Littleton, Colorado, in April 1999, the perceived link between media violence and murderous behavior thrust itself squarely into the public eye once again. The reactions of horror to the senseless slayings resulted in congressional actions and a subsequent report on violence from the U.S. Surgeon General ordered by President Clinton. *Youth Violence: A Report of the Surgeon General* found a strong relationship between consumption of media violence and short-term aggression, but the aggressive behavior that typically resulted stopped far short of breaking limbs or committing murder.

In 2000, the American Academy of Pediatrics, American Academy of Child and Adolescent Psychiatry, American Psychological Association, American Medical Association, American Academy of Family Physicians, and American Psychiatric Association issued a Joint Statement on the Impact of Entertainment Violence on Children. It pointed to 30 years of research that had suggested that viewing violent media content could lead to aggression, especially among children, but it qualified its stance on the issue by pointing out that other important factors contribute to youth aggression, such as the influence of peers, the situation at home, and the easy availability of weapons in this country (Joint Statement, 2000).

In the first issue of *Annual Review of Public Health* in 2006, Huesmann and Taylor wrote:

> Media violence poses a threat to public health inasmuch as it leads to an increase in real-world violence and aggression. Research shows that fictional television and film violence contribute to both a short-term and a long-term increase in aggression and violence in young viewers. Television news violence also contributes to increased violence, principally in the form of imitative suicides and acts of aggression. Video games are clearly capable of producing an increase in aggression and violence in the short term, although no long-term longitudinal studies capable of demonstrating long-term effects have been conducted. The relationship between media violence and real-world violence and aggression is moderated by the nature of the media content and characteristics of and social influences on the individual exposed to that content. Still, the average overall size of the effect is large enough to place it in the category of known threats to public health. (p. 393)

Other studies continued to confirm "real and strong" effects from media violence (Murray, 2008). Barrie Gunter, in a study that appeared in *American Behavioral Scientist,* concluded that studies on media violence should not be dismissed, but he advised caution in accepting "blanket conclusions about harmful effects of media violence" (Gunter, 2008, p. 1061). He also said that some people who watch violent media fare may be more susceptible to harmful effects than others, and that media depictions of violence also play a role in the mix.

Despite the enormous number of studies linking mediated violence to aggression, critics point to statistical problems within the studies that have to do with effects sizes, which tend to be small to moderate. Researchers usually respond by pointing out that even small effects sizes could be detrimental when considering that mass media audiences number in the millions.

Savage (2004) conducted a methodological review of the literature on media violence and concluded that a clear causal relationship between viewing violence and subsequent criminal behavior does not exist (see also Savage, 2008, and Grimes & Bergen, 2008). Reports such as these, however, make a giant leap when linking viewing violence to criminal behavior. The vast majority of studies on mediated violence do not make such a jump. They only point to aggressive predispositions and tendencies being measured after viewing mediated violence. Aggressive tendencies do not equal criminal behavior. Other critics point to the nature of the experiments in an artificial setting and the use of college students as subjects, as well as the short-term nature of the effects usually measured.

Zillmann and Weaver (1999) answered some of these criticisms:

> It seems that critics of media-violence research could only be satisfied with longitudinal experimental studies in which, within gender and a multitude of personality variables, random assignment is honored and exposure to violent fare is rigorously controlled—that is, with research that in a free society simply cannot be conducted. (p. 147)

Media Violence Research Methods

When carried to perhaps its worst extreme, the modeling or imitation of screen violence has been linked to violent and brutal "copycat" crimes—rapes and even murders. As we discussed in Chapter 5 on priming, violent copycat crimes are among the most disturbing examples of imitative behavior.

The sensational nature of copycat crimes attracts the notice of print and electronic news media, and therefore examples of such crimes abound in the public's memory; in reality however, copycat crimes are extremely rare. Millions of other viewers who watch the same film or program are *not* inspired to imitate such extreme violent behavior. This suggests that other individual factors, such as a person's disposition (or predisposition to violent behavior), state of mind, emotional stability, and personal circumstances play a major role in determining whether that person will resort to aggression after viewing violent fare.

Social scientists attempt to record more subtle media effects—those that they can measure through strictly controlled experiments and studies, which do not involve actual harm or injury to anyone. These researchers concentrate their efforts on several major issues related to media violence. Many studies are designed to measure the *amount* of violence that occurs on various media. Other studies explore the *contexts* in which the violence occurs, as research has shown that such contexts are very important in determining the extent of harmful effects. (Examples of such contexts would be whether or not the violence was accidental in nature or performed with malicious intent, whether or not the perpetrator was punished, or whether or not the consequences of the violence were shown.) Most importantly, these and other studies examine viewers' exposure to such violence and attempt to answer the difficult question: What effect does media violence have on those who consume it?

Research studies on the effects of viewing violent media fare have employed a number of different methodologies. Gunter (1994) reviewed the vast body of research and identified six major research methods that have been used to study the question. These include laboratory experiments, field experiments, correlational or cross-sectional surveys, longitudinal panel studies, natural experiments, and intervention studies. To that list we also add meta-analysis, a statistical technique that allows researchers to combine various studies to reveal significant results in the area of media violence research. We will discuss each in turn.

Laboratory Experiments

Strictly controlled experiments in a laboratory setting have provided compelling evidence that watching media violence may cause a viewer to behave more aggressively. Such experiments are constructed to show a *causal relationship* between viewing TV violence and behaving aggressively. Critics point to the unnatural circumstances surrounding the viewing in such experiments and question whether the results have any meaning in the real world.

One recent experiment tested the role of song lyrics, video clips, and musical tone on aggressive tendencies. The researchers found that the individuals exposed to violent lyrics, whether or not violent images were shown with the music, showed the highest level of aggression (Brummert Lennings & Warburton, 2011).

Field Experiments

Most of these studies have taken place among children in an institutional setting, such as a nursery school. Prior to viewing violence, the children are randomly assigned to groups (one group views violence and another sees nonviolent programming). Their levels of natural aggressiveness and attitudes are measured, then compared to measures taken *after* viewing violent fare. Field experiments avoid the problem of unnaturalness associated with laboratory experiments.

One field study worth noting (Williams, 1986) provided strong evidence for the connection between viewing violent content and behaving aggressively. Of the three communities in Canada selected for study, one did not have television (notel), the second received only one channel (unitel), and the third had access to several channels (multitel). The study showed that the children in the community without television at the outset showed significant increases in aggressive behavior over a two-year period after TV was introduced. The aggressiveness of children in the other two communities did not change over the same period.

Correlational Surveys

In these cross-sectional studies, typically viewers are asked to read a list of program titles and select those programs that they watch regularly. Researchers rely on content analyses of the amount of violence in potential programs to develop a measure of the amount of violent programming exposure per viewer. Viewers are also asked about their attitudes and behavior in order to gauge some measure of aggressiveness or hostility. The two measures are then correlated to ascertain any relationship between the viewing of violence and subsequent aggressive behavior or attitudes. The major problem with such studies is that they are ultimately unable to demonstrate a causal relationship with any degree of certainty. Statistically significant correlations have been found between consumption of violent media fare and aggressive or hostile behaviors and attitudes, but most of those associations have been relatively weak.

One recent study made use of survey research in a short-term longitudinal design. Third and fourth-graders, their peers, and teachers were surveyed twice in the school year to determine if various forms of aggression might be predicted by violent media exposure. "Children's consumption of media violence early in the school year predicted higher verbally aggressive behavior, higher relationally aggressive behavior, higher physically aggressive behavior, and less prosocial behavior later in the school year" (Gentile, Coyne, & Walsh, 2011, p. 193).

Longitudinal Studies

These studies attempt to identify relationships that may develop over a period of time between consumption of violent fare and antisocial attitudes and behaviors. According to Gunter (1994), such studies "represent perhaps the best kind of studies of TV effects. They can test causal hypotheses and they usually employ sound sampling methods" (p. 174). Researchers remain in contact with particular viewers and test them at various intervals over time to determine whether or not consumption of media violence is affecting them. Longitudinal studies take into account the assumption that exposure to media violence has a *cumulative* effect over time; in other words, repeated exposure to media violence has an increasing effect on aggressive behavior or attitudes as the years pass by.

In particular, children who have consumed a heavy diet of media violence in their most formative years are more likely than their peers to behave aggressively as adolescents and adults. In one longitudinal investigation, researchers found that children who watched a lot of violent media at ages 8 to 10 were significantly more aggressive 15 years later, when they were adults (Huesmann, Moise-Titus, Podolski, & Eron, 2003).

Natural Experiments

With these studies, researchers make use of a natural setting in which television is being introduced into the community for the first time. Through *longitudinal assessment* (similar evaluations made over a period of time), documented conduct such as criminal statistics are examined and compared before and after television becomes available in a country or community.

The results of natural experiments have varied. Through studying crime rates from 1949 to 1952, Hennigan and colleagues (1982) found that the introduction of television in certain American communities did not bring significant increases in homicides or other violent or serious crimes. Centerwall (1989) examined homicide rates from 1945 to 1975 among Whites in three countries: the United States, Canada, and South Africa. He found that in the United States and Canada the murder rate among Whites increased dramatically about 15 years after the rate of television set ownership in those countries increased, while homicide rates in South Africa (where TV ownership was very limited) were not so affected.

Intervention Studies

Just as vaccinations are used to inoculate people to protect them from dangerous or deadly diseases, intervention studies are designed to *intervene* and inoculate viewers against the harmful effects of viewing televised violence. With these studies, the harmful effects of viewing violence is assumed to be prevalent in the population; researchers then attempt to alleviate the negative effects in some way—that is, through some intervention strategy. Some intervention studies have indicated that increased television literacy (critical understanding of television content and production methods) may reduce the negative effects of TV violence (see, for example, Webb, Martin, Afifi, & Kraus, 2010).

Meta-Analyses

The technique of meta-analysis allows media effects researchers to combine the large number of studies that have been done on media violence and its effects in a statistical study that measures overall effects sizes (Sparks, Sparks, &

Sparks, 2009). A number of meta-analyses have confirmed that exposure to mediated violence and subsequent aggression are indeed related (Christensen & Wood, 2007; Hearold, 1986; Paik & Comstock, 1994; Sherry, 2001; Wood, Wong, & Chachere, 1991).

These studies have shown evidence for several major types of effects. The most prevalent effect is that of *imitative behavior* (Liebert & Schwartzberg, 1977). Children especially are likely to learn aggressive behaviors by watching them on television. After the behaviors are learned, they are subsequently imitated. Children are also vulnerable to another effect, *fear,* when viewing violent or disturbing subject matter (Cantor, 1994; Gunter & Furnham, 1984). *Desensitization,* a third prominent effect identified in the literature, may occur after repeated exposure to violence (Greenberg, 1975) or after only brief exposure (Drabman & Thomas, 1974; Linz, Donnerstein, & Penrod, 1988).

To better understand these categories of effects as well as others, we will examine them in greater depth in the next section. The various levels of psychological effects are explained, and the different types of effects common to each are discussed in detail.

Measuring Violent Content

How does one define media violence? Is it harmful physical contact? Can it be verbal in nature? What about a car crash or an accidental death? What about news footage of a suicide? What about a bomb threat? Should these be considered violent?

Social scientists must address these and other highly specific questions before they can even begin to measure the amount of violence present in mass media, much less assess the effects of this violence. The research method used to determine the amount of violent content is called **content analysis**. In using this methodology, researchers must first clearly define violent content, and then carefully watch various programs to code each instance of violence as it occurs. Sometimes content is classified according to program type, character type, weapon type, and the type of physical harm or damage that results.

The first content analyses of prime-time television programs were conducted in the 1950s and 1960s (Schramm et al., 1961; Smythe, 1956). These studies found that violence and criminal activities appeared frequently on the popular new medium; unfortunately, however, these early studies used different definitions and methods of measurement, making comparisons and trend studies impossible for the formative years of television.

Systematic analyses of television violence gained prowess and popularity in the 1960s programmatic study conducted by George Gerbner and his associates. Beginning in 1967 and for many years thereafter, these cultivation researchers have analyzed and coded samples of prime-time and daytime dramas from all the major networks in the United States. Their technique of measurement, called *message system analysis,* has become one of the most widely used measures of violence on network television.

Gerbner and his colleagues defined violence as "the overt expression of physical force against self or other compelling action against one's will on pain of being hurt or killed or actually hurting or killing" (Gerbner, 1972, p. 32). Coders use the definition to generate very specific coding categories, with which they assess the number of violent acts they witness on the programs, the type of violence, the victims, the perpetrators, and the settings. The information from the coders is then synthesized to provide a **violence profile** for each program. The profile provides an objective appraisal of the amount of violence contained in each televised drama.

During the first 10 years of message system analysis, Gerbner and his associates found that the vast majority of network television programs (8 of 10) contained violent content, and a majority of characters (6 of 10) were involved in the violent acts. Children's cartoons contained more violence than all other types of shows, including action-adventure programs for adults and crime-detective programs.

In the 1990s, two Finnish researchers developed a coding scheme to measure the obtrusiveness of TV violence and to classify the *context*—the circumstances surrounding the violence or the message the violence conveys. The study examined violence present in fictional and nonfictional programs (Mustonen & Pulkkinen, 1997).

Other research on "reality" programming, or nonfictional television, revealed that the content of such programs was more similar to television drama than to an accurate portrayal of violence in the real world. Reality programming includes national and local newscasts, police news programs, documentaries,

Violent content is present in nonfictional programming like newscasts, police news programs, documentaries, and the like.

public affairs shows, tabloid news programs, and the like. In terms of context, the violent acts shown on such programs were rarely punished and negative consequences of violence were rarely shown (Federman, 1998; Potter et al., 1997).

It should be remembered that content analysis is simply a system of coding and describing content. The perceptions of audience members and effects of the content are entirely different questions, and researchers must employ different research strategies to answer them (Gunter, 1988; Gunter & Wober, 1988).

Measuring Viewers' Perceptions

Another method of classifying televised violence is by measuring viewers' perceptions of it. Different people react differently to television programs because each person possesses a unique set of psychological traits. Their judgments about violence do not always match those of researchers (Gunter, 1985; Van der Voort, 1986). Most people—adults and children—perceive violence in the context of a program genre and personal preferences. For example, if a program is one that parents enjoy watching, they generally perceive it as being harmless to themselves and their children. This means that programs that have been labeled as highly violent by trained content analysts may be perceived as rather harmless by actual viewers.

Despite individual differences among viewers, research has shown that people often experience similar, harmful effects after viewing certain types of violence portrayed in certain contexts. Social scientists have identified five key elements of context that make people susceptible to negative effects. Children, especially, are at high risk for learning aggressive behaviors from portrayals that feature all five of the following elements:

1. A perpetrator who is an attractive role model.

2. Violence that seems justified.

3. Violence that goes unpunished (no remorse, criticism, or penalty).

4. Minimal consequences to the victims.

5. Violence that seems realistic to the viewer. (Federman 1998, p. 33)

"High Risk" Contexts
Depictions that Encourage Aggressive Attitudes and Behaviors

- Perpetrator is an attractive role model
- Violence seems justified
- Violence goes unpunished (no remorse, criticism, or penalty)
- Consequences to the victims are minimal
- Violence seems realistic to the viewer

Source: Joel Federman, Ed., (1998). *National television violence study, Vol. 3, Executive summary* (Santa Barbara: Regents of the University of California).

Research has shown that in recent years many television programs include these "high-risk" contexts. In a four-year study of television programming, researchers from the University of California at Santa Barbara found that most violence on the screen is initiated by the "good guys," the screen characters that are most likely to serve as role models. Moreover, only about 15 percent of the prime-time programs from 1995 to 1998 revealed the long-term, negative consequences of violent behavior. Approximately three out of four violent acts were performed without remorse or penalty, and the "bad guys" went unpunished in about 4 of 10 programs (Federman, 1998).

The Psychological Impact of Media Violence

In terms of effects research, communication scholars have identified three different levels of psychological impact that violent media fare may have upon viewers. These levels—behavioral, affective, and cognitive—simply refer to the different types of effects that violence may have upon viewers. In this section, studies from the various methodologies described earlier will be used to illustrate each of the levels.

Behavioral Effects

When a four-year-old boy watches an old episode of the *Power Rangers,* then pretends he is the Red Ranger while kicking and hitting "the villain" (his two-year-old brother), that child is exhibiting a *behavioral effect* from viewing televised violence. Specifically, the child is using the mechanism of *imitation,* one of five major mechanisms through which behavioral effects may occur that we will discuss in this section. The other important mechanisms include *catharsis, arousal, disinhibition,* and *desensitization.*

Catharsis

The catharsis mechanism purportedly allows viewers to vent their aggressive impulses harmlessly through viewing televised violence or by fantasizing about violent acts. In the 1950s and 1960s, Feshbach (1955, 1961) reported the existence of a cathartic effect when participants in his experiments were able to release aggressive urges nonviolently by viewing acts of televised violence or by fantasizing about violence. In 1971, Feshbach and Singer observed teenage boys in natural settings—residential schools and homes—for six weeks. During the experimental period, the researchers controlled the boys' exposure to televised violence. They found that the boys who had watched mostly nonviolent television behaved *more aggressively* toward their peers than the boys who had watched violent programming, thus presumably indicating some sort of catharsis effect.

It should be noted that very few of the hundreds of experimental studies have replicated Feshbach's findings or have supported the catharsis mechanism. Despite this weak body of scientific evidence, a substantial portion of the lay public believes that catharsis occurs through watching film, television, or video

> ## Psychological Effects from Exposure to TV Violence
>
> **Cognitive**
> Watching TV violence influences a viewer's beliefs about the real world.
>
> **Affective (Emotional)**
> Watching TV violence causes an immediate or long-term emotional reaction.
>
> **Behavioral**
> Watching TV violence influences a person's behavior. Five major categories of behavioral effects:
>
> - Arousal
> - Desensitization
> - Imitation
> - Catharsis
> - Disinhibition

game violence. Media industry spokespeople happily remind the public and its elected representatives of the alleged benefits of catharsis every time a public investigation of the effects of media violence is undertaken.

Because of the popularity of the notion of catharsis and the lack of empirical support for cathartic or pseudocathartic effects, investigators have often tried to find some perhaps very limited conditions under which catharsis can be demonstrated. For example, Gunter (1980) suggested that certain human cognitive skills are responsible for limited catharsis effects. One study revealed that people with strong imaginations or fantasy skills were able to relieve their anger by viewing a violent film, whereas those subjects who did not possess a vivid imagination were unable to experience such a cathartic effect (Biblow, 1973).

Arousal

The behavioral effect of this mechanism is that of excitement or, as the name says, arousal. Whenever a viewer watches a violent scene (or a particularly funny or sexually explicit scene), he or she becomes excited or emotionally aroused, and this arousal can be measured physiologically. Viewers usually do not attribute their elevated arousal to what they are viewing. For example, if a teenage boy who is already mad about something is watching a violent program, he interprets his heightened arousal, which is in part due to excitation from the television program, as intense anger. He may therefore respond more aggressively than he would if he had not watched the violent program, particularly if an opportunity to become aggressive occurs shortly after viewing (Tannenbaum & Zillmann, 1975; Zillmann, 1988, 2000).

Disinhibition

The disinhibition mechanism operates under the assumption that as viewers grow more accustomed to seeing violence on television, especially violence that is justified by the situation or is socially sanctioned, they become less inhibited by social sanctions against committing violent acts. Research has shown that viewers do behave more aggressively after watching a program presenting sanctioned violence, especially if they were angry when they began watching

(Berkowitz, 1962, 1965, 1974); however, more specialized investigations are required to indicate whether these results are due to disinhibition.

In one group of laboratory studies, a confederate angered research participants who then watched a clip from a violent film (usually a boxing match, which is a socially sanctioned form of violence). The same participants were then allowed to administer electric shocks to the person who had angered them. Other research participants were angered and shown a nonviolent film, and still other participants assigned to a control group were not angered. The researchers found that those who had seen the violent clip delivered harsher shocks than those who had not viewed violence, and that those who had been angered beforehand and viewed the sanctioned violence were the most aggressive of all. The investigators interpreted these results as providing evidence that watching sanctioned violence in the film clips served to remove some of the research participants' inhibitions, therefore permitting them to be more aggressive (Berkowitz & Alioto, 1973; Berkowitz, Corwin, & Heironimous, 1963; Berkowitz & Geen, 1966; Berkowitz & Rawlings, 1963).

Evidence for the disinhibition mechanism has also been found in longitudinal studies. In one such study, researchers collected data from about 800 eight-year-olds regarding their TV viewing habits and their levels of aggressiveness. Ten years later, when the children were 18, the researchers located about half of the original group and obtained additional information. They found a strong positive correlation between viewing televised violence when young and measures of aggression as adults (Eron, Huesmann, Lefkowitz, & Walder, 1972).

Imitation

This mechanism assumes that viewers learn from what they see on television and sometimes try to mimic the actions themselves. This is especially true for young children who identify with the characters they see on television and try to imitate them. (Chapter 4 discusses the concept of *observational learning,* the essence of the imitation mechanism.)

You will recall from Chapter 4 that the laboratory experiments of Albert Bandura (1965a, 1978, 1979, 1982, 1986) and Bandura, Ross, and Ross (1963a, 1963b) found that children imitate the aggressive behaviors they witness on the screen. One group of children watched a film of someone hitting and knocking about a plastic, air-filled Bobo doll. Another group watched a film that showed a person in a cat costume performing the same violent acts on the doll, and yet another group was not shown any film. The researchers then took the children to a playroom with a large number of toys—and one plastic Bobo doll. The children who had seen on film the Bobo doll being battered were not only more aggressive toward the Bobo doll than the other children, but they actually copied the violent behaviors they had witnessed in the film. Bandura attributed the copycat behavior in part to the disinhibition mechanism and in part to observational learning or the imitation mechanism.

Several intervention studies with children have attempted to mitigate the imitation effect. These studies have revealed that instructing children about television procedures, making them aware that viewing violence may have harmful effects on them, and teaching them critical viewing skills may reduce aggressive tendencies as they grow older (Singer & Singer, 1983; Huesmann & Eron, 1986). Some significant research in recent years has focused on reducing the negative consequences of consuming mediated violence. Nathanson (1999) found that parental involvement, whether limiting programming, talking to their children, or teaching them critical viewing skills, tends to reduce aggressive effects.

Desensitization

As viewers repeatedly witness violent acts on the screen, they become less and less sensitive through the years to seeing violence, less sympathetic to the victims of violence (Linz et al., 1988), and more likely to accept real-life violence. Laboratory studies, in particular, have provided enough evidence to give some credence to the hypothesis. In one study, children who viewed a violent program beforehand were less likely to go for adult help when they witnessed a playroom fight between two other children (Drabman & Thomas, 1974; Thomas, Horton, Lippincott, & Drabman, 1977). The other study found that children who watched 25 or more hours of television per week experienced less physiological arousal when viewing TV violence than children who watched less than four hours per week (Cline, Croft, & Courrier, 1973).

Similar desensitization effects have been observed among children who play a lot of violent video games. In particular, playing violent video games seems to have a pronounced effect on diminishing the empathy players feel for victims of violence (e.g., Bushman & Anderson, 2009; Funk, Baldacci, Pasold, & Baumgardner, 2004).

Affective, or Emotional, Effects

Research has shown that everyone, regardless of age, experiences an emotional reaction when viewing violent content on television and in films. Studies have examined reactions to programs that depict violence: either physical injury or threat of bodily harm. The emotional effects from watching such violence may be immediate (e.g., fright, anxiety) or long term (e.g., persistent fear of becoming a victim of crime).

Palazzolo and Roberto (2011) showed study participants media news messages about intimate partner violence "containing information designed to increase or decrease attributions of responsibility both toward the perpetrator and toward the victim" (p. 1). The viewers experienced many emotions, but only certain emotions were triggered related to whether or not the viewers saw the perpetrator or the victim as being responsible for the violence.

The reactions of children have been of particular interest to social scientists involved in this realm of media effects research. Studies have revealed that children become very frightened when viewing certain kinds of programs. These fright reactions, which are sometimes very intense, have been observed by a number of researchers (see Blumer & Hauser, 1933; Himmelweit et al., 1958; Preston, 1941; Schramm et al., 1961). The reactions range from loss of control over their feelings (Blumer & Hauser, 1933) to horrible nightmares (Singer, 1975).

The most extensive research on children and their fright reactions has been done by Cantor and her associates (1998). Their studies have examined the effects of viewing different types of program content on various fright responses among children (Cantor & Hoffner, 1987; Cantor & Reilly, 1982; Cantor & Sparks, 1984; Cantor, Wilson, & Hoffner, 1986; Sparks, 1986; Sparks & Cantor, 1986; Wilson & Cantor, 1985). The research also explored the differences in various fright reactions of children at different ages and developmental levels. At a very young age, for example, children are more likely to be frightened by *threatening characters* and *situations*. Older children are more frightened by *threats of either realistic or abstract stimuli* rather than scary images alone.

The experiments of Cantor and associates have usually involved 3- to 11-year-olds who are randomly assigned to various groups. The children in the control group are simply shown a violent or frightening scene. The other groups of children are given certain strategies beforehand that should help them cope with the content they are about to view.

In all the studies, fright reactions are measured using one or more of four different methods. Immediately afterward, the children are asked to assess the extent of their fright by choosing one of four responses, from "not at all scared" to "very, very scared." Additionally, the researchers record and code fright reactions by evaluating the child's facial expression from a videotape made while the child is watching the program. As another supplementary measure, small sen-

Moviemakers use frightful scenes to entertain audiences. Sometimes fright reactions to mediated content can last from childhood into adulthood. © *Sunset Boulevard/Corbis*

sors are attached to the child's fingers and physiological data are collected. Finally, some studies have shown behavioral measures of fear. Wilson and Cantor (1987), for example, measured fear by a child's willingness to see a live snake after watching the snake scene from *Raiders of the Lost Ark.*

Coping strategies may be cognitive or noncognitive in nature. Cognitive strategies involve changing the child's mental conceptions of the frightening content. A thorough explanation of the fantasy nature of a character or situation is one form of cognitive coping strategy. Cantor, Sparks, and Hoffner (1988) found that by showing children a behind-the-scenes video that explained and showed the makeup preparation for the actor in *The Incredible Hulk,* the children were far less fearful during the program than those children who had not seen the video. Cantor and Wilson (1984) examined the reactions of young and older children while watching the witch in the classic, *The Wizard of Oz.* Some of the children were told beforehand that the witch was "just a regular person dressed up in a costume," and were reminded that the story was "make believe." Other children were not given such coping strategies. Results were different among the children. Older children were able to use the coping strategy to reduce their fears. They were significantly less frightened by the witch than other older children who had not received the explanations. The coping strategy did not work so well with the younger children. The scary witch frightened those who had received the fear-reducing strategy (the explanation) as much as those who had not. The researchers attributed the results to developmental differences in children of different ages.

An example of a noncognitive strategy is **desensitization**, which involves repeated exposure to the frightening matter in a secure and nonthreatening atmosphere; in therapy, this is called a "flooding" method. Several studies have shown that such desensitization procedures work to reduce fright reactions in children (Wilson, 1987; Wilson & Cantor, 1987).

Research has also revealed that children experience fright reactions to television news as well as to fictional drama. In a survey, Cantor and Nathanson (1996) found that almost 40 percent of the children of those parents surveyed had been frightened or upset by something seen on newscasts. The most fear-producing stories were those that involved violence among strangers, wars and famines abroad, and natural disasters. Younger children tended to react emotionally to upsetting images such as weapons and people dying, whereas older children were more troubled by abstract issues—fears of nuclear wars, bombing, and the reality of death (Cantor & Nathanson, 1996).

Research has shown that fright reactions to scary movies that occur in childhood and adolescence often linger into adulthood (see Chapter 13). Using a methodology called "recollective or retrospective reports," or "autobiographical memory," two independent teams of investigators found evidence for lingering fright reactions (Harrison & Cantor, 1999; Hoekstra, Harris, & Helmick, 1999; Cantor, 1999). Both studies involved content analyses of college students' reports of something that had frightened them in the mass media during their childhood. Remarkably, between 90 and 100 percent of the college students recalled such experiences, many poignantly. In both studies, the younger the child had been when he or she was frightened by something watched on television or film, the more intense the fright reaction was reported to be. In one investigation, more than 25 percent of the college students reported still experiencing residual anxiety from their childhood exposure to frightening media portrayals (Harrison & Cantor, 1999).

Cognitive Effects

When viewing mediated violence influences a viewer's beliefs about the real world, that viewer has experienced a *cognitive* effect. Indeed, many of the affective fright reactions just discussed may have become cognitive effects over time. The most extensive research on such cognitive effects has been performed by George Gerbner and his associates.

In the 1970s, Gerbner and his colleagues analyzed data from national public opinion surveys to gauge some of the cognitive effects of television viewing. The surveys contained a large amount of useful information from each of the participants, such as how much time they spent watching television and their perceptions about the world in which they lived. The researchers found a positive correlation between the amount of time spent watching television and the prevalence of certain beliefs about the world; those who watched the most television perceived the world as a more dangerous place than light viewers (Gerb-

Mediated violence can cause viewers to think more aggressive thoughts. © *Etienne George/Sygma/ Corbis*

ner, 1972; Gerbner & Gross, 1976; Gerbner et al., 1977; Gerbner et al., 1978; Gerbner, Gross, Morgan, & Signorielli, 1980). This is called *cultivation analysis*.

Through analysis of the content of network television programs, Gerbner and his associates showed the prime-time dramatic world of television to be an exceedingly violent place. They hypothesized that regular exposure to mediated violence made viewers develop an exaggerated view of real-life dangers in society.

Although widely accepted, Gerbner's methods and results have been challenged by a number of researchers (Blank, 1977a, 1977b; Coffin & Tuchman, 1973; Hirsh, 1980; Hughes, 1980; Wober & Gunter, 1988). Several of the researchers used the same database but exercised statistical controls for extraneous demographic variables and found no significant evidence for cultivation. (An extraneous demographic variable might be, for instance, the type of neighborhood in which the person lived—was it a high-crime district such as an urban ghetto or a low-crime area of affluence?)

Wober and Gunter (1982) found that a person's perception of the real world was related more to viewing certain types of programs than to the total time spent viewing. These researchers' findings indicated that people select particular types of programs that agree with, or reinforce, their personal beliefs. Such a hypothesis stands in opposition to the cultivation hypothesis.

The strength of television's influence on viewers' perceptions of the world can be mitigated by many factors. Gunter (1987) identified four leading categories of these factors which he called **levels of judgment**: program specificity, viewer perceptions or interpretations, personal judgments about crime, and situation specificity.

Program specificity means simply that television's influence on perceptions about the real world may have more to do with the types of programs watched rather than the total time spent viewing. For example, two people might watch the same amount of television each week, but one may view only violent programs, while the other watches nonviolent educational shows. The perceptions of real-world crime on the part of the two viewers might be vastly different, even though both watch the same amount of TV (Weaver & Wakshlag, 1986).

The influence of television also may depend upon how viewers perceive what they are viewing, and how they interpret it (Collins, 1973; Pingree, 1983; Teevan & Hartnagel, 1976). *Viewer perceptions and interpretations* may conceivably render the most violent programs rather innocuous in their effects.

Personal judgments about crime may also modify television's influence on viewers of violent programming. Examples of such judgments would be beliefs about the prevalence of crime in society or beliefs about one's own chances of becoming a victim of crime. Tyler (1980, 1984; Tyler & Cook, 1984) found that such judgments often were not connected to viewing behavior at all, but to a person's particular, personal encounters with crime.

Situation specificity means that television's influence on personal perceptions about crime may also be moderated by the person's individual situation or setting. For example, those who live in urban areas tend to fear crime more than those who live in rural, low-crime areas (Tamborini, Zillmann, & Bryant, 1984).

In recent years, researchers have turned their attention to video games and the Internet as sources of mediated violence to investigate. The evidence suggests that those who play violent video games are more likely to have aggressive thoughts and behaviors afterward (Anderson, Gentile, & Buckley, 2007; Anderson, 2004; Anderson et al., 2004; Anderson & Dill, 2000; Bartholow & Anderson, 2002; Bushman & Anderson, 2009; Irwin & Gross, 1995). Repeated exposure can cause desensitization to violence (Bartholow, Bushman, & Sestir, 2006).

New Directions for Media Violence Researchers

Sparks, Sparks, and Sparks (2009) identified five areas of research that have emerged as promising for media effects scholars in recent years. These include: individual differences, enjoyment of media violence, violent video games, effects on variables other than aggressive behavior, and advances in brain research.

Individual Differences

Several studies have identified that individual differences among consumers of mediated violence have a great bearing on the effects of exposure. Children diagnosed with Disruptive Behavior Disorders reacted physiologically to viewing mediated violence more so than undiagnosed children (Grimes et al., 2004). People who exhibit low levels of empathy tend to consume more media violence (Sigurdsson et al., 2006).

Enjoyment of Media Violence

One meta-analysis on the enjoyment of media violence found that males tended to enjoy violence more than females, and viewers who measured high on sensation seeking and exhibited a low measure of empathy also enjoyed violence more (Hoffner & Levine, 2005). Sparks and Sparks (2002), however, found little data to support that media violence is enjoyed more than programs that do not contain violence. In one study, Sparks, Sherry, and Lubsen (2005) showed some participants the movie *The Fugitive* unedited, and showed other participants the movie with violence expurgated. They found that the inclusion of violence had no effect on the enjoyment of the movie—those who saw the edited version enjoyed the movie just as much as those who saw the violent version.

Weaver and his colleagues (2011) manipulated violence and action in slapstick cartoons using animation software. Elementary school children in various groups watched the programs, and it was found that violence did not have a direct effect on whether or not the children liked the cartoon.

Violent Video Games

Several studies on the effects of violent video games have already been mentioned. Most of the research in this area focuses on the connection between exposure to video game violence and subsequent aggressive behavior (Anderson & Dill, 2000; Anderson, Gentile, & Buckley, 2007; Bushman & Anderson, 2009; Dill

& Dill, 1998), but some studies have examined enjoyment of violence (Jansz, 2005) and the issue of desensitization (Bartholow, Bushman, & Sestir, 2006).

Möller and Krahé (2009) conducted a longitudinal study among German adolescents and found a link between playing violent video games and physical

---

Research Spotlight

The Appeal of Media Violence in a Full-Length Motion Picture: An Experimental Investigation

Glenn G. Sparks, John Sherry, and Graig Lubsen (2005)
Communication Reports, 18(1), 21-30

For this study, researchers edited out all the violence in a full-length motion picture to see if students would enjoy the film as much as students who saw the unedited version.

Participants

A total of 134 undergraduate students at a large midwestern university (41 males, 93 females) served as participants. Most of the participants were Caucasian and ranged in age from 18 to 22 years.

Method

Participants saw one of two versions of a full-length Hollywood film, *The Fugitive*. One version was edited to remove violence and the other version was in its original form. After watching the film, respondents rated the film on a variety of questions that were converted to scales, including overall enjoyment, desire to see the movie again, degree of entertainment, how much fun it was to watch, and other measures of the perceived quality of the movie and perceived violence.

The participants were randomly assigned to one of the two groups. Those who saw the original film version consisted of 15 males and 51 females. The edited version was shown to 26 males and 42 females.

The original film ran for 2 hours, 11 minutes, and 5 seconds and included 104 separate acts of physical violence. The edited version without the violent scenes lasted 2 hours, 0 minutes, and 49 seconds. Participants saw the films at the same time in different rooms and were asked to avoid talking during the film.

In order to disguise the purpose of the experiment, researchers asked the respondents to guess the hypothesis. Seven participants indicated that they thought the experiment involved some sort of editing of the film to test differences in perceptions of the movie. Those seven were eliminated from subsequent analysis. The final design of the study included 64 participants who watched the original movie (15 males and 49 females) and 63 participants who watched the edited version (24 males and 39 females).

Results

Using analysis of variance (ANOVA), no significant differences emerged on any of the enjoyment measures by version or by gender. Results were also analyzed for ratings of suspense. No significant differences were found by condition, but women found the film significantly more suspenseful than men did.

The results showed that the violent version of the movie was no more enjoyable than the nonviolent version. Although supporting the null hypothesis leaves open a wider range of interpretations than might be desirable, the results raise questions about the media industry's frequent claims that violence is a critical ingredient of audience enjoyment.

aggression. Anderson and his colleagues conducted a meta-analytic review of the effects of violent video games on aggression, empathy, and prosocial behavior. "The evidence strongly suggests that exposure to violent video games is a causal risk factor for increased aggressive behavior, aggressive cognition, and aggressive affect and for decreased empathy and prosocial behavior" (Anderson et al., 2010, p. 151).

Researchers have also studied the features that allow players of violent video games to design their own characters or avatars in the game. Fischer, Kastenmüller, and Greitemeyer (2010) suspected that this added feature would make the psychological effects of the video game more intense. Their study confirmed that the players with personalized characters showed higher levels of aggression.

Effects on Variables Other than Aggressive Behavior

The cultivation tradition asserts that consumption of news of violent crimes is related to fear of being an actual victim. Smolej and Kivivouri (2006) found this to be true in a study in Finland. In another study, children proved vulnerable to fear and anxiety related to coverage of terrorist attacks on the news (Fremont, Pataki, & Beresin, 2005). Anastasio (2005) exposed experimental participants to several minutes of justified violence and noticed an increased tendency to devalue others.

In addition to aggression, European researchers have measured the effects of habitual use of media violence on empathy. More than 1,200 seventh- and eighth-grade German students were measured for aggression, media use, and empathy. The researchers found that use of violent media led to higher levels of physical aggression and lower empathy (Krahé & Möller, 2010).

Advances in Brain Research

New research studies in media effects of viewing violence have used Magnetic Resonance Imaging (MRI) to examine the brain as it is exposed to violent programming. One study found differences in brain activity among children who viewed violence as opposed to children who did not view violence (Murray et al., 2006). In another study, 13 males were scanned with MRI while playing a violent video game. The images showed low activity in the areas of the brain related to affect or emotion (Weber, Ritterfield, & Mathiak, 2006).

Other researchers have taken notice of this new trend in media violence research and noted that the tools of neuroscience should prove helpful (Carnagey, Anderson, & Bartholow, 2007; see also Kalnin et al., 2011).

Summary

Public concern for the negative effects of exposure to media violence has been one of the most important, ongoing social issues of the 20th and 21st centuries. Through the years, many studies have established a causal link between viewing media violence and subsequent aggressive behavior or attitudes.

Concern about media violence has always been a major issue for public policy makers. Despite the great number of studies that have shown a link between viewing mediated violence and subsequent aggression, critics point to statistical problems within the studies.

Media effects researchers are interested in several issues related to media violence. They measure the amount of violence that occurs in various media, the context in which the violence occurs, and viewers' perceptions of the content.

Researchers have employed many different methods for studying the effects of exposure to media violence. Six of these are laboratory experiments, field experiments, correlational surveys, longitudinal panel studies, natural experiments, and intervention studies.

In measuring violent content, researchers must first define media violence. The method used to assess the amount of violence is called content analysis. Each instance of violence is coded using this technique.

Content analyses have shown that prime-time television programs contain a great deal of violent content, as do nonfictional programs. Content analyses provide a system for coding and describing content; they do not measure audience perceptions. Contextual content analyses examine the situations surrounding the portrayals of violence. Research has shown that contextual features are most important in determining what effects violence will have upon audience members.

Meta-analyses use statistical methods to combine a great number of different research studies to find overall indications of effects and general trends. Meta-analyses that examine media violence have consistently found a causal link between viewing violence and aggressive behavior. The major effects have been imitative behavior, fear, and desensitization.

Violent media fare may affect audiences at three different psychological levels: behavioral, affective (emotional), and cognitive. Behavioral effects may be exhibited through one of five different mechanisms: imitation, catharsis, arousal, disinhibition, and desensitization. Emotional effects may be immediate or extended, long-term reactions. Fright reactions of children are one example of emotional effects. Cognitive effects occur whenever viewing violent content influences a person's beliefs about the real world. The approach of cultivation analysis examines such cognitive effects.

Television's influence on viewers' perceptions can be mitigated. Four leading mitigating factors, called levels of judgment, include program specificity, viewer perceptions or interpretations, personal judgments about crime, and situation specificity.

The debate has advanced through several stages. Most recently, the Telecommunications Act of 1996 made installation of the V-chip blocking device mandatory on new models of television sets, and required broadcasters to rate their programs based upon suitability for certain age levels.

twelve

Media Effects from Sexual Content

*Listen, I'm no social scientist and I haven't done a survey. I don't pretend
to know what John Q. Citizen knows about this. But I've lived in prison for
a long time now and I've met a lot of men who were motivated to commit
violence just like me. And without exception, every one of them was deeply
involved in pornography; without question, without exception, deeply influenced
and consumed by an addiction to pornography. There's no question about it—
the FBI's own study on serial homicide shows that the most common
interest among serial killers is pornography.*
—Ted Bundy, serial killer, January 23, 1989, Interview

Whatever the medium—television, movies, magazines, music videos, the Internet—media users, including children, are inundated daily with sexually oriented messages and images. These messages range from the mildly suggestive to various levels of the **sexually explicit**, a term used to describe media depictions of individuals engaging in various kinds of sexual activities.

In Chapter 11, we explored the issue of media violence and discovered that significant links exist between the viewing of violence and subsequent acts of aggression. Sexual content in electronic and print media also has important implications because of its perceived connection with serious social concerns, such as teenage pregnancy and the numbers of people contracting sexually transmitted diseases such as AIDS.

In the early 1990s, researchers determined that 7 of 10 girls and 8 of 10 boys in the United States engaged in sexual intercourse by the time they had reached the age of 20, and one-fourth of all pregnant women were teenagers (Greenberg, Brown, & Buerkel-Rothfuss, 1993). Almost 20 years later, a government study indicated that the number of teens engaging in sexual intercourse was down slightly (from 78 percent in 2001 to 72 percent in 2011). The report also said that vaginal intercourse has been on the decline among teens and young adults since the late 1980s (Stobbe & Johnson, 2011). Interestingly enough, a recent longitudinal meta-analytic review revealed that sexual content on network television declined from 1975 to 2004 (Hestroni, 2007). The same meta-analysis showed that the exception to the sexual content decline was homosexuality, which "considerably" increased from the 1980s to the present. A 2010 study on homosexual activity among teens showed that 9.3 percent of teenagers—nearly one in 10—reported having sex with someone of the same gender, double the number reported in 2002 (Donaldson-Evans, 2010; see also Pathela & Schillinger, 2010).

Juxtaposing studies such as these amounts to "anecdotal" evidence in the eyes of scholars and other critics, simply because no causal relationship can be established. Yet plenty of studies on sexually explicit content have been documented that do show causal evidence for harmful effects.

This chapter examines the media effects from sexual content. It reveals the nature and extent of sexual content in mass media. We review results from studies that examine exposure to highly explicit sexual content, and we point out the importance of context. We also look at recent research that reveals the harmful effects of sexual content on the Internet. We then examine the evidence for effects from sexually violent media fare with respect to sex offenders.

The Nature of Sexual Content

Whenever you use the word "sexual" to describe media content, you must clearly define what it means, as it occurs at many levels of intensity. In its broadest sense, it includes *all* types of media products that either show or imply sexual acts or make sexual references or innuendoes, whether in humorous or dramatic context, from X-rated materials to general-audience sitcoms. Sexual content may range from rather mild sexual comments on network television to unabashedly blatant XXX videos with themes of sadomasochism, bondage, or bestiality.

The degree of sexual explicitness in media content usually depends upon how much is left to the imagination. Highly explicit materials such as X-rated[1] movies or XXX videos leave nothing to the viewer's imagination. R-rated movies contain nudity and a moderate degree of explicitness, but sexual activities are less explicit than those depicted in X-rated films. Frontal nudity does not appear on broadcast network television in the United States; therefore, the sexual explicitness of network programs is rather tame when compared to R- and X-rated movies; however, the sizzling sex scenes on daytime soap operas or prime-time serial programming or "reality fare" should leave no doubt in anyone's mind that television contains much sexual content. Moreover, premium cable series (e.g., Starz's *Spartacus*, HBO's *Game of Thrones* or *True Blood*) often contain graphic sex scenes, often with full frontal nudity of both male and female characters.

Surveys and studies reveal the pervasiveness of mass media as a source of sexual information, especially for adolescents and teenagers. A Time/CNN poll

(Stodghill, 1998) reported that almost 30 percent of teenagers in the United States said they get most of their information about sex from watching television. In contrast, 45 percent said "friends" served as their source for learning about sex, but only 7 percent identified "parents" and only 3 percent identified sex education as a source of information. A 1992 study in Toronto (Russell, 1998) revealed that 9 out of 10 adolescent boys and 6 out of 10 adolescent girls had viewed at least one pornographic movie in their lives. Another study showed that almost 30 percent of adolescent boys listed pornography as their most significant source of information on sex, and pornography rated higher than schools, parents, peers, books, and magazines (Check, 1995; Harris & Scott, 2002).

The pervasiveness of pornography is indisputable. According to an Internet Filter Software Review (Ropelato, 2011; see also DeAngelis, 2007), a pornographic video is created in the U.S. every 39 minutes. Pornographic websites account for about 12 percent of all websites. About 40 percent of teens or younger children view sexually explicit websites either on purpose or accidentally each year. In 2006, revenues from pornography worldwide hit $97 billion, nearly double the amount from 1999 (Morais, 1999).

Even though most programs on television leave much more to the imagination than do these more explicit materials, their potential for negative effects is not necessarily diminished. The availability of television to all ages makes that medium a particularly dangerous one when considering the damaging social effects that result from the consumption of sexual content.

In any discussion of sexual content in mass media, particular terms appear from time to time and therefore need explication. *Pornography* and *obscenity* are two such terms.

Pornography

The extreme class of sexually explicit materials is commonly referred to as erotica or **pornography**, which is defined as "the graphic and explicit depictions of sexual activity" (Cline, 1994). X-rated movies or videos, certain sex magazines, sexually explicit computer and video games, and so forth belong to this class. Such materials are supposedly restricted to adult audiences only and are produced for the express purpose of pandering sexual content. They are usually considered devoid of literary merit or artistic value. Exceptions often include the magazine *Playboy*, which is also known for respectable reading content and educational materials such as sex manuals.

Playboy brought pornography into mainstream America in the 1950s. *AP Photo/Damian Dovarganes, File*

In 1986, the Meese Commission classified five types of materials as pornography. These included (1) materials that depict sexual violence such as rape or other violent sex crimes, (2) nonviolent sexual materials that depict instances of degrading or humiliating activities, or scenes of domination and subordination, (3) nonviolent sexual materials without degrading activities (usually portraying a couple having consensual and nonviolent intercourse), (4) materials that depict nudity, and (5) child pornography (the sexual exploitation of children in media content) (*Final Report,* 1986).

The Meese classifications are not without controversy, because the term "pornography" is difficult to define in a standard way. Each person's definition may be different, depending upon his or her values. For example, some people do not consider nudity to be pornographic. Others may not consider consensual and nonviolent intercourse to be pornographic.

Obscenity

Pornographic material is not always considered to be obscene. The term **obscenity** is a legal one that has been defined by the United States Supreme Court. The *Miller v. California* case in 1973 set the criteria for proclaiming material legally "obscene." Three criteria, as judged by a jury representative of the community, must be present. These include (1) the material appeals to a prurient (shameful, sick, morbid, or lustful) interest in sex, (2) the material is patently offensive or beyond the contemporary community standards regarding depictions of sexual content or activity, and (3) the material as a whole lacks "serious literary, artistic, political, or scientific value" (Cline, 1994, p. 230).

The Extent of Sexual Content in the Media

In recent decades, researchers have studied the extent and the explicitness of sexual content in mass media. Many of these studies have been content analyses that focus on various types of sexual media fare that children and teens are likely to see, such as Internet sites, R-rated movies, sex magazines, and, especially, network television programming.

Harris and Bartlett (2009) observed that although sex magazines have been declining in circulation since the 1990s, other media have stepped up to make sexual content even more pervasive in our society. The sale and rental of videos, whether X-rated or R-rated or highly suggestive music videos, the proliferation of cable and pay-per-view TV, the explosion of Internet pornography, and "sexting" (texting or sending sexual messages and photos via cell phones and social media)—all have contributed to a sexually charged media environment.

> Sex in media is not limited to explicit portrayals of intercourse or nudity, however, but may include any representation that portrays or implies sexual behavior, interest, or motivation. Sex also occurs in many other places besides explicitly sexual materials. Many news stories, including reports of sex crimes, sex scandals, celebrity starlet social gossip, or tragic excesses like the

Abu Ghraib prison abuses, involve sexual content. Sex is rampant in advertising, particularly for products like perfume, cologne, and aftershave, but also for tires, automobiles, and kitchen sinks. (Harris & Bartlett, 2009, p. 305)

A number of content analyses have identified that, aside from explicit sexual portrayals, *talk about sex* has been on the increase, especially on network television, and the effects of this can be equally as harmful (Kunkel et al., 2003; Hestroni, 2007).

Greenberg (1994) examined the sexual content trends in several types of media, including music videos, X-rated videos, and television. He found that the amount of sexual content and the degree of explicitness varied considerably among the media.

Music Videos

Several content analyses have measured the amount of sexual content contained in music videos. Two major studies in the 1980s examined MTV and other televised music programs during 1984. The first study (Baxter et al., 1985) found that well over half of the 62 videos analyzed contained sexual content. Sexually suggestive actions such as embraces, provocative dancing, kisses, and the wearing of sexy clothing occurred frequently. The researchers concluded that "sexually oriented suggestive behavior is portrayed frequently in music videos" (p. 336).

In another study that involved content analysis, Sherman and Dominick (1986) examined the visual aspects of 166 videos that featured a "concept," such as a story line, drama, or narrative (for at least half the video), rather than a studio performance alone. The videos were taken from MTV and the programs *Night Tracks* and *Friday Night Videos.* The researchers found that three of every four videos contained sexual content, and that the average number of sexual acts in each video was almost five. In terms of sex and violence, the study revealed that 80 percent of the videos that contained violence also contained sexual content.

X-Rated Videos

In a content analysis of sexual activities in X-rated videos, researchers found that almost 450 sexually explicit scenes appeared in the 45 videos analyzed in the study (Cowan, Lee, Levy, & Snyder, 1988). Overall, the scenes depicted one of four major themes: domination, reciprocity, exploitation, or autoeroticism. Scenes featuring satisfying and consensual sex (*reciprocity*) were the most numerous of the four types, occurring in 37 percent of the 450 scenes; however, the themes of either domination or exploitation (mostly men over women) accounted for more than 50 percent of the scenes. *Domination,* or sexual control by one person over another, occurred in 28 percent of the scenes. *Exploitation,* where one coerced another or used status to get what was wanted, was present in 26 percent of the scenes. *Autoeroticism,* which means some form of self-stimulation such as masturbation, was the least frequent theme, occurring in 9 percent of the scenes studied.

Another study compared the differences in content of X-rated videos to triple-X titles. Palys (1986) found that the XXX videos contained a much larger

---

X-Rated Videos

The Four Major Themes

- Domination—sexual control of one person over another
- Reciprocity—consensual sex, satisfying to both individuals
- Exploitation—coercion of one over another, or use of status to make another perform as desired sexually
- Autoeroticism—self-stimulation such as masturbation

More than half of all scenes in X-rated films feature themes of domination or exploitation, usually men over women.

---

number of scenes depicting oral-genital sex, the touching and fondling of breasts or genitals, genital-genital sex, masturbation, and anal sex. Surprisingly, the XXX videos contained less violence and less sexual violence than the X titles.

More recent content analyses have confirmed the earlier findings. Bridges and her associates (2010) found high levels of aggression, both verbal and physical, in their study of popular pornographic videos. They analyzed 304 scenes and found that 88.2 percent featured spanking, gagging, slapping, and other acts of physical aggression, and 48.7 percent of scenes contained name-calling and other acts of verbal aggression. The perpetrators of aggressiveness were usually male and their targets were overwhelmingly female.

In another recent content analysis, Cowan and Campbell (1994) examined interracial X-rated pornography videocassettes and coded 476 characters in sexually explicit scenes in 54 videos. Black women were the targets of more acts of aggression than White women, and Black men showed fewer intimate behaviors than White men. Further, cross-race sexual interactions contained more aggression than same-race sexual interactions. "These findings suggest that pornography is racist as well as sexist," the authors wrote (p. 323).

The areas of gay porn (and child porn, for obvious ethical reasons) have been virtually ignored by researchers. An article in the *British Medical Journal* in 2009 did point out that condoms were not used in gay pornographic videos (Hurley, 2009).

Television

R-rated movies, sex magazines, and the Internet have been found to contain far more explicit sexual content than network television, but sexual comments and overtures are numerous and frequent on network programming (Greenberg et al., 1993a; Greenberg & Hofschire, 2000; Kunkel et al., 1999). Most of the sexual innuendoes on TV occur in humorous scenes. One content analysis of network and cable television programs during the 1997–1998 season revealed that 56 percent of the shows included sexual content, with 23 percent depicting sexual behaviors (Kunkel et al., 1999). Another content analysis showed that 68 percent of network and cable programs in 1999–2000 contained sexual content. Of that content, 65 percent included talk about sex and 27 percent of it showed actual sexual behaviors (Kunkel et al., 2003). References to sex between the unmarried outnumber references to sex between the married by a ratio of 6 to 1 on television programs (Greenberg & Hofschire, 2000), 24 to 1 on television soap operas (Lowry & Towles, 1989), and 32 to 1 in R-rated movies (Greenberg, Brown, & Buerkel-Rothfuss, 1993).

A more recent meta-analysis of sexual content on television showed that the amount of sex talk on prime-time network programming increased steadily from 1999 to 2004, and the amount of unmarried intercourse and prostitution portrayed increased from 2000 to 2004 (Hestroni, 2007).

Another study published in 2004 found that the amount of sexual content that children watch on television (whether viewing physically sexual scenes or hearing talk about sex) actually may cause adolescents to begin engaging in sex sooner. The study also found that the negative consequences could be mitigated by reducing the amount of sexual content in entertainment programs or by parents watching with their teenaged children and discussing their beliefs about sex and what is being portrayed (Collins et al., 2004; see also Kim et al., 2006).

Other studies have confirmed that the more sexual content exposure among adolescents, the more likely the adolescents are to experiment with sexual activity (Bleakley, Hennessy, Fishbein, & Jordan, 2008; Fisher et al., 2009; Collins et al., 2004; Bryant & Rockwell, 1994).

The Internet

Researchers are only beginning to explore the consequences of exposure to sexually explicit material on the Internet and forms of social media. The findings so far are alarming. The studies show that adolescent males are more likely to seek out sexually explicit Internet material, and their exposure to this material has a direct effect on males' tendency to view women as sex objects. Viewing highly realistic portrayals of online sexual material is also associated with more recreational attitudes toward sex (Peter & Valkenburg, 2006, 2009).

A study published in *Pediatrics* in 2007 found that in a nationally representative sample of young Internet users between the ages of 10 and 17, 42 percent had been exposed to Internet pornography in the past year, and of those, 66 percent said the exposure was unwanted or accidental. Moreover, those exposed were likely to be vulnerable individuals, either suffering from depression, sexual victimization, or having tendencies toward delinquency (Wolak, Mitchell, & Finkelhor, 2007). The authors concluded:

> More research concerning the potential impact of Internet pornography on youth is warranted, given the high rate of exposure, the fact that much exposure is unwanted, and the fact that youth with certain vulnerabilities, such as depression, interpersonal victimization, and delinquent tendencies, have more exposure. (p. 247)

Effects of Exposure to Highly Explicit Sexual Content

When a person thumbs through the pages of *Playboy*, calls up a website that features child pornography, or watches an X-rated video that depicts a sexually violent crime such as rape, how does it affect that person? How is the person changed by the exposure to highly explicit sexual content? More importantly, is it possible to mitigate or lessen any negative effects of viewing such material?

Researchers have found that highly explicit sexual content may affect media users in one or more of several ways. One type of effect, of course, is sexual arousal. Other effects include changes in attitudes, values, and behaviors. Each of these areas has been studied extensively, especially the behavioral changes that result from viewing pornography (Gunter, 2002; Huston, Wartella, & Donnerstein, 1998; Linz & Malamuth, 1993; Malamuth, 1993; Malamuth & Impett, 2001; Mundorf, D'Alessio, Allen, & Emmers-Sommer, 2007; Oddone-Paolucci, Genuis, & Violato, 2000; Pollard, 1995).

Sexual Arousal

A number of studies have demonstrated that sexually oriented media content does tend to sexually arouse the viewer or user (Abramson et al., 1981; Eccles, Marshall, & Barbaree, 1988; Malamuth & Check, 1980a; Schaefer & Colgan, 1977; Sintchak & Geer, 1975). These studies have used different types of measures. In some cases, viewers were asked to rate their level of sexual arousal after seeing sexually explicit material. In other instances, researchers used physiological measures to determine arousal, such as the measurement of penile tumescence or vaginal changes. Thermography has also been used.

Gender differences usually show up in terms of usage of sexually explicit materials and whenever arousal measures are recorded. Estimates reveal that more than 70 percent of sexually explicit videos are viewed by men rather than women (Gettleman, 1999). The industry caters to male consumers, but evidence shows that women react more positively to sexually explicit material written and directed by women, especially when themes are romantic (Mosher & Maclan, 1994; Quackenbush, Strassberg, & Turner, 1995). Regardless of content, however, evidence suggests that men are more purposive seekers of sexually explicit fare, and they tend to be more aroused by it (Malamuth, 1996), especially depictions of sexual violence or dehumanization (Murnen & Stockton, 1997).

Researchers have also studied the relationship between the explicitness of sexual content and the extent of sexual arousal. These studies have shown that less explicit materials are sometimes *more* arousing than the highly explicit ones (Bancroft & Mathews, 1971). Scenes that leave much to the viewer's imagination may arouse the viewer more than those that leave no questions unanswered.

Different individuals are "turned on" by different sexual stimuli. Classic conditioning studies have shown that sexual arousal can sometimes be *learned*. This may explain the many individual differences in sexual orientation and arousal. In the 1960s researchers showed heterosexual men photos of nude women

Some movie stars are glamorized for their sexual appeal, such as Marilyn Monroe and her iconic image from the film *The Seven Year Itch*. *AP Photo/ Matty Zimmerman*

paired with boots and actually taught the men to be aroused by only the sight of women's boots (Rachman, 1966; Rachman & Hodgson, 1968).

Studies have also revealed that over time, viewers of common pornography (nonviolent sex between a man and woman) become habituated and tend to seek more uncommon porn (e.g., bondage, sadomasochism, bestiality) in order to find stimulation (Zillmann & Bryant, 1986). Also over time, heavy consumption of pornography causes viewers to report less sexual satisfaction with their intimate partners and to assign increased importance to sex without emotional involvement (Zillmann & Bryant, 1988b).

Changes in Values and Attitudes

Repeated exposure to explicit sexual materials usually results in *desensitization* of a person's attitudes and values. Desensitization is a change in values or attitudes that occurs over time as a previously taboo behavior is gradually accepted because of repeated exposure to mass media. For example, if a man watches a number of X-rated movies that depict women enjoying being raped, he may soon change his perceptions about the frequency of the occurrence of that behavior in the real world as well as his attitude about the amount of social and psychological harm rape causes, and even his beliefs about the likelihood that he would commit such a crime.

Research has revealed that exposure to sexually explicit materials produces significant changes in attitudes. For six weeks, Zillmann and Bryant (1982, 1984) showed sexually explicit films to one group and nonexplicit films to a second group. When they tested the groups, they found that the first group overestimated the popularity of the sexual activities they had viewed in the movies (e.g., fellatio, cunnilingus, anal intercourse, sadomasochism, and bestiality). The estimates of the second group were much more conservative. Later, the same researchers (Zillmann & Bryant, 1988b) used similar methods to determine if the viewing of such films caused changes in attitudes toward their sexual partners, or changes in basic values such as a desire for marriage, monogamy, children, and so forth. They found that changes did occur. Those who saw the explicit films reported less satisfaction with their real-life partners than those in the control group. In addition to rating their partners lower in terms of physical appearance and sexual performance, the group shown explicit films was more accepting of premarital sex and extramarital sex. They reported less of a desire for marriage, monogamy, and children than the control group. The researchers explained these findings in this way:

> Only pornography shows men and women to experience the greatest sexual pleasures from coition with many partners, one after the other, or from sexual activities with several partners at the same time. . . . And only this genre provides specifics such as fellatio in which women make entire male organs vanish or coition in which penises of extreme proportion cause women to scream in apparent painful ecstasy. The sexual experience of normals must pale by comparison. Partners must seem prudish, insensitive, inhibited, frigid . . . and deficient in endowment and skill. And who, confronted with the bounty of readily attainable sexual joys that are continually presented in pornography and nowhere else, could consider his or her sexual life fulfilled? (p. 452)

Research has also provided evidence that sexual content need not be overtly explicit or pornographic to have detrimental psychological effects. For example, in three studies of 13- and 14-year-old boys and girls, Bryant and Rockwell (1994) found that under certain circumstances, massive exposure to sexual content on prime-time television (in particular, intimate sexual relations between unmarried couples) caused significant shifts in the teens' moral judgment. The studies also showed that three mitigating factors could serve to diminish or eliminate the harmful effects. In the words of the researchers:

> First, having a clear and well-defined family value system—a value system that teenagers can know and use—mediates potentially harmful media

---

Research Spotlight

It Works Both Ways: The Relationship between Exposure to Sexual Content in the Media and Adolescent Sexual Behavior
Amy Bleakley, Michael Hennessy, Martin Fishbein, and Amy Jordan (2008)
Media Psychology, 11, 443–461

This study, published in 2008, made use of a longitudinal Web-based survey of 14- to 16-year-olds and regression models to determine that sexually active adolescents are more likely to expose themselves to mediated sexual content, and those exposed to sexual content in media are more likely to progress in sexual activity.

Participants

The Web-based survey was conducted with a quota sample of adolescents from the greater Philadelphia area. Data collection for the first wave was in the spring and summer of 2005; wave two data were collected one year later in the spring and summer of 2006. The researchers recruited participants through print and radio ads, direct mail, and word of mouth. Written parental consent and teen assent were collected for all participants.

Design

The survey took about an hour to complete and participants were compensated with $25 each. For the first wave, 547 adolescents (40.4 percent male and 42.7 percent African American, 41.2 percent White, 13.4 percent Hispanic, and 2.8 percent other) completed the survey. Of the 547 participants in wave one, 501 were retained for wave two. These 501 consisted of 38.3 percent males, 33.1 percent age 15, 34.7 percent age 16, and 32.1 percent age 17.

Measures

Respondents were asked to indicate how often (during lifetime, more than a year ago, or within the past year) they engaged in the following sexual behaviors: deep kissing, touching breasts, breasts touched, genital touching, oral sex (receive), vaginal sex, oral sex (give), anal sex (receive), and anal sex (give).

Respondents were also asked about exposure to selected media titles in four media (television, music, magazines, and video games). Respondents also rated sexual content exposure to each of the media titles (never, rarely, sometimes, often) indicating how frequently within the last year they watched each show, listened to each artist, read each magazine, or played each video game.

Results

Sexual activity successfully predicted exposure to sexual content in the media and sexual content exposure predicted a progression of sexual activity. Increased sexual activity was also found to be related to a mature physical development, having ever had a boyfriend or girlfriend, and friends' approval of sex. Parental disapproval was associated with increased exposure to sexual content: the more the parent disapproves of sex, the higher adolescents' exposure to sexual content. Other variables associated with higher exposure to sexual content include having a television in the bedroom, and total time spent with television, music, video games, and magazines.

The results showed that adolescents who engage in sexual activity seek out media with sexual content and those who are exposed to more sexual content are more likely to engage in sexual behaviors.

effects; the second mitigating factor we found is coming from a family in which free and open discussion of issues is encouraged and practiced . . . third, active critical viewing, or the active viewing and analysis of program content, is a most desirable trait for teenagers to have and is to be encouraged. Again, it can make a big difference in mediating the cognitive effects of mass media consumption as far as moral judgment is concerned. (p. 194)

Other studies also support the evidence for attitudinal changes related to consumption of sexually explicit material. As some have pointed out, most pornography conveys an ideological message that degrades or dehumanizes women as victims or playthings (Buchwald, Fletcher, & Roth, 1993; Russell, 1998).

Changes in Behavior

Behavioral effects from the consumption of sexually explicit media content may occur at several levels. For better or worse, people often *learn* when they consume sexual content. The learning may be highly constructive, as in a couple undergoing sexual therapy, or it may be extremely destructive, as in copycat sexual offenses that involve violence.

Disinhibition causes changes in behavior in much the same way that desensitization causes changes in attitudes and values. After seeing an R-rated movie or an X-rated video, a person becomes less inhibited about performing the sexual behaviors witnessed—behaviors that were previously taboo. Again, when taken to an extreme, disinhibition may reduce moral judgment constraints that result in an individual committing some type of violent sex crime.

The relationship between the viewing of sexually explicit materials and the occurrence of sex crimes has received much attention through the years. Many studies have examined the numbers of rape and child molestation cases in a particular locale in relation to the amount of sexually explicit ma-

Sexual content is found in all types of media, including action films targeted at boys and teenagers. In *X-Men: First Class*, January Jones's character is often seen scantily dressed and using her sexuality to manipulate male characters. *Murray Close/Getty Images*

terials available there. After reviewing these studies, Court (1984) found a statistically significant correlation between the availability of explicit materials and the occurrence of violent sexual crimes.

The relationship between sexually explicit materials and the occurrence of rape in particular has been difficult to prove, however, because of several confounding variables: the variety of sexual materials, changing social norms, and the increasing number of such assaults actually being reported. Several studies have found a relationship between the crime of rape and the availability of one particular medium—sex magazines. In one study, researchers found a high correlation in all 50 states between the number of rapes and the circulation numbers for eight sex magazines (Baron & Straus, 1987). The correlations were particularly high for magazines that contained sexual violence.

Effects of Erotica on Aggression

A number of studies have shown that when individuals who had been provoked as part of the experimental protocol were exposed to sexually explicit materials, they were more likely to retaliate against or "get back at" the person who provoked them (Baron, 1979; Cantor, Zillmann, & Einsiedel, 1978; Donnerstein & Hallam, 1978; Meyer, 1972; Zillmann, 1971). In other words, viewing arousing erotic material tended to enhance aggressive tendencies in individuals. The process by which the effect occurs is known as *excitation transfer* (Zillmann, 1978, 1979, 1982b). Zillmann and Bryant (1984) explained the role of excitation transfer from erotica on aggression in this way:

> Exposure to erotica fosters increased sympathetic activity as an accompaniment to more specific genital responses . . . and that, after sexual stimulation, residues of the slowly dissipating nonspecific sympathetic activity enter into unrelated affective states and potentially intensify them. If the subsequent state is one of annoyance and anger, residual sympathetic excitation from sexual arousal thus is likely to intensify these experiences and to energize the hostile and aggressive actions incited by them. (p. 116)

When the erotic material was pleasing and nonarousing (e.g., photographs of nudes), the aggressive tendencies of provoked individuals were actually *calmed* (Baron, 1974a, 1974b; Baron & Bell, 1973; Donnerstein, Donnerstein, & Evans, 1975; White, 1979). Based on these findings and others, Zillmann and Bryant (1984) developed a model called the *excitation-and-valence model* of the effects of erotica on motivated aggression. The model makes the following four predictions: (1) pleasing and nonarousing erotica reduces aggressiveness because it counteracts the provoked person's feelings of anger; (2) displeasing and nonarousing erotica increases aggressiveness because it adds to the provoked person's feelings of annoyance; (3) displeasing and nonarousing erotica increases aggressiveness because the enhanced feelings of annoyance are retained by the person and transferred to situations afterward; and (4) pleasing and arousing erotica create a situation in which calmness rather than excitation is transferred, therefore canceling out negative effects such as aggressiveness.

Importance of the Prevailing Tone

The effects of viewing sexual content in the media are also determined by context—both the context of the material and the context in which the person is exposed to it. These contextual variables, when considered as a whole, constitute what is known as a **prevailing tone**. Harris (1994) listed the following contextual variables that contribute to the prevailing tone of sexual content.

The *seriousness or triviality of the treatment* is one major aspect of the prevailing tone. Controversial topics such as rape or incest are acceptable when given serious treatment (as in a documentary) but become offensive if treated flippantly (e.g., in a comedy).

Another aspect, *artistic value and intent,* also contributes to the prevailing tone. The Bible's Song of Solomon contains many references to sexual activities, but these are a vital part of a beautiful work that carries the theme of love as shared by a married couple. The same holds true for certain works by Chaucer and Shakespeare. At the other end of the spectrum are XXX videos or films such as *Debbie Does Dallas*, which are largely devoid of artistic merit.

The prevailing tone is also affected by whether or not a sex scene is *necessary to the plot,* and by the *degree of explicitness* of the sex. Scenes of explicit sex become more acceptable to a viewer if they are important in the development of the plot.

Another aspect of the prevailing tone lies within the *context of viewing.* A man's reactions when thumbing through the pages of *Hustler* are likely to be very different if (1) he is alone, or he is sitting beside (2) his wife, (3) a male friend, (4) his grandmother, or (5) his preacher. The man may view the material as highly offensive or highly exciting, depending upon his context of viewing.

Cultural context also affects the prevailing tone. What may be considered inappropriate in one culture may be commonplace in another. Many men and women in primitive tribes throughout the world walk about scantily dressed or completely naked, and the behavior is entirely appropriate for that culture. In marked contrast, in certain Islamic cultures women must cover themselves from head to toe before appearing in public.

Impact of Exposure to Sexually Violent Material

In recent years much more than in years past, the media have begun to portray sex in combination with violent acts. Magazines that portray sexual violence have appeared and joined old standards like *Penthouse* and *Playboy* in depicting more images of domination and bondage (Malamuth & Spinner, 1980). Also, the horror movies of old have evolved into a new genre called *slasher films* (very popular among teenagers despite their R ratings), which depict much brute violence against women in combination with sexual acts or in a sexual context (Yang & Linz, 1990).

Should we be concerned about this tendency to mix sex with violence? Judging from the research findings, the answer is indisputably yes.

Studies using both normal populations or convicted sex offenders have shown that the mixture of sex and violence has potentially harmful effects. In one of these studies, researchers found that convicted rapists were aroused by viewing both rape and consenting sex, whereas normal participants were aroused only by depictions of consenting sex (Abel, Barlow, Blanchard, & Guild, 1977; Barbaree, Marshall, & Lanthier, 1979). A later study revealed that normal males could be aroused by depictions of rape if the victim appeared to enjoy it and experienced an orgasm (Malamuth, Heim, & Feshbach, 1980). The arousal of the males was equal to or exceeded what they experienced while viewing a film of consensual sex; however, females in the study were not aroused by the rape film.

Importance of Individual Differences

Individual differences account for great variances in the effects of sexually explicit material. A person who is more likely to use force in situations of conflict is more likely to experience the harmful effects from viewing sexually explicit material. In a study of college males, Malamuth (1981) separated force-oriented men (those who reported they would be likely to use force in their lives) from nonforce-oriented men in order to determine if sexually violent media fare affected them similarly or differently. The force-oriented men were more aroused by a rape scene in which a woman was depicted as finally enjoying the assault, whereas a film of consensual sex proved to be more arousing for the nonforce-oriented men.

In another study of force-oriented and nonforce-oriented males by Malamuth and Check (1983), participants listened to tapes of either consenting sex, rape with the woman eventually becoming aroused (rape-arousal), or rape with the woman being disgusted during the assault rather than aroused (rape-disgust). Arousal for both groups of men, measured by self-reports and penile tumescence, was greater for the consenting sex version than for the rape-disgust version; however, the rape-arousal version proved to be a "turn on" for both groups. The nonforce-oriented group became as aroused with the rape-arousal tape as with the consensual sex tape, while the force-oriented group was even more aroused by the rape-arousal tape than by the consenting sex version.

Other studies (Donnerstein, 1980; Donnerstein & Berkowitz, 1981) have involved the viewing of sexual violence and the subsequent administration of electric shock by the viewer on a confederate. These studies have concluded that a link exists between the viewing of sexual violence (especially a rape in which the woman is depicted as becoming aroused) and a propensity to inflict pain upon females.

In summary, the research findings show that harmful effects occur whenever sexually violent materials depict a woman who becomes aroused by an assault. Also, individual differences in disposition (e.g., being force-oriented or nonforce-oriented) cause different people to react differently when viewing sexually violent media fare. As discussed earlier, the prevailing tone of the material is always an important consideration.

Sexual Violence in Slasher Films

The studies cited above made use of pornographic material; however, sexual violence is not limited to films exclusively for adult audiences. The highly popular, R-rated slasher movies contain a great deal of violence, usually in a sexual context (Weaver & Tamborini, 1996). According to Harris (1994):

> The main concern with such films is the juxtaposition of erotic sex and violence. For example, one scene from *Toolbox Murders* opens with a beautiful woman disrobing and getting into her bath, with the very romantic music "Pretty Baby" playing in the background. For several minutes she is shown fondling herself and masturbating in a very erotic manner. Suddenly the camera cuts to the scene of an intruder breaking into her apartment, with loud, fast-paced suspenseful music in the background. The camera and sound track cut back and forth several times between these two characters until he finally encounters the woman. He attacks her with electric tools, chasing her around the apartment, finally shooting her several times in the head with a nail gun. The scene closes after seeing her bleed profusely, finally lying on the bed to die with the sound track again playing the erotic "Pretty Baby." (pp. 261–262)

One of the main concerns regarding slasher films is their ready availability to teens. Many of these films are not rated and therefore not restricted to adult audiences; those that do receive the R rating are available to youngsters in video stores where restrictions often are not applied, as well as on cable and satellite television.

Teens take full advantage of the availability of slasher movies. A survey of 4,500 children in the United Kingdom in the 1980s found that about one in five young teenage boys (aged 13–14) had seen an illegal and sexually violent film called *I Spit on Your Grave* (Hill, Davis, Holman, & Nelson, 1984). In another study of American college students, Greenberg and associates found that two of three watched slasher movies on a regular basis (1993b).

Researchers have also studied slasher movies for the effects of the sexual violence on young audiences. Findings suggest that men become desensitized when they repeatedly watch slasher films (Linz, Donnerstein, & Penrod, 1984), but women do not (Krafka, 1985). Over time, the men found the slasher movies to be less degrading to women, more enjoyable, less offensive, and less violent.

Reducing the Negative Effects

The negative effects of viewing sexual violence can be mitigated or lessened. In several studies, participants were trained prior to viewing in an effort to reduce desensitization effects (Intons-Peterson & Roskos-Ewoldsen, 1989; Intons-Peterson et al., 1989; Linz, Donnerstein, Bross, & Chapin, 1986; Linz, Fuson, & Donnerstein, 1990). Some procedures have proven more successful than others; for example, men were found to be most affected by learning that women are not responsible for sexual assaults against them.

Other researchers have given extensive debriefings to participants to make them aware of the horrors of rape and the absolute inability of a woman to be able to enjoy it (Malamuth et al., 1980; Donnerstein & Berkowitz, 1981; Malamuth & Check, 1980b). Evaluations have revealed that these debriefings make participants less susceptible to rape myths (e.g., a woman's enjoyment of rape).

Allen and his associates (1999) conducted a meta-analysis of 10 studies that had used educational briefings to mitigate the harmful effects of sexually explicit material. Their analysis found overwhelming support for the effectiveness of debriefings in lessening harmful effects.

More on Behavioral Effects of Pornography: The Study of Sex Offenders

The link between exposure to pornography and the commission of sex crimes is a controversial one. In 1996 one researcher reviewed the many correlational studies that attempted to link sexual aggression with use of pornography and concluded that statistically significant correlations between the two do not exist, although particular subsets of sex offenders may use pornography in significant ways (Bauserman, 1996). Other scholars and clinicians have studied the issue and found positive correlational links between the consumption of pornography and criminal sexual aggression (Marshall, 1989; Malamuth & Donnerstein, 1984).

In 1994 Cline examined data from experimental laboratory studies, field studies, and clinical case histories and found four major behavioral effects that result from the consumption of pornography. As a clinical psychologist, Cline had treated hundreds of people (mostly men) who suffered from serious sexual disorders and many who had committed sex crimes such as child molestation, rape, exhibitionism, and so forth. "With only several exceptions," Cline wrote, "pornography has been a major or minor contributor or facilitator in the acquisition of their deviation or sexual addiction" (p. 233).

The Four-Factor Syndrome

The four major effects of consuming pornography are *addiction, escalation, desensitization,* and the *tendency to act out or copy* what had been viewed. Cline (1994) called these four effects the **four-factor syndrome**, because the effects occurred in the same sequence over time. Almost all his clients had experienced the four-factor syndrome.

Addiction to pornography was the first effect that Cline (1994) noticed. Once his clients began viewing pornography, they soon found themselves wanting more of it. Most of them experienced sexual stimulation followed by sexual release from masturbation.

Once addicted, an *escalation* effect occurred as time passed. As with a drug addict, the pornography addict began craving stronger (i.e., more explicit or more deviant) sexual materials to achieve the same stimulation as the initial experience. Cline (1994) found that over time, most of his clients preferred masturbating while viewing pornography to sexual intercourse and intimacy with a partner.

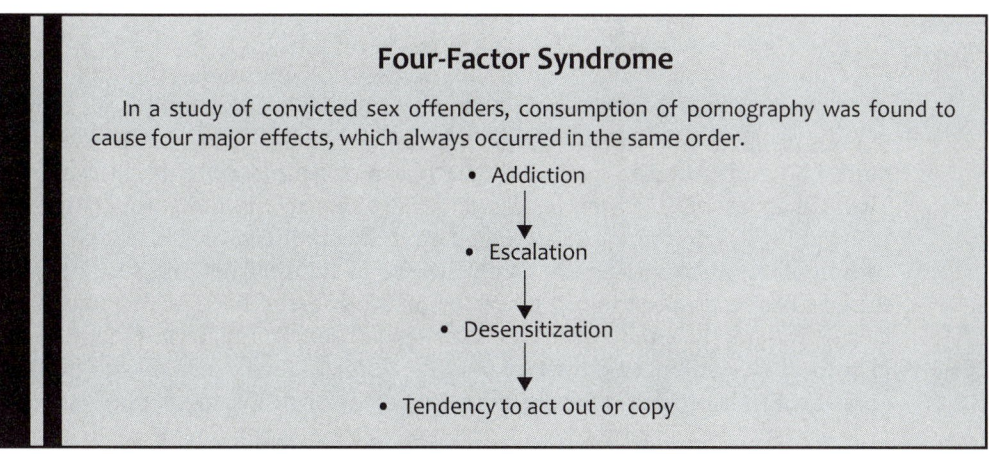

Desensitization was the third effect. Over time, shocking, antisocial, illegal, immoral, and deviant sexual behavior came to be viewed as acceptable and legitimate. The morals and standards of pornography addicts tended to sink lower and lower as more and more material was consumed. The addicts began to believe that deviant sexual behaviors were more commonplace than they had originally thought.

The final effect was the tendency to *act out sexually* or copy the sexual acts they had seen in pornographic materials. These activities included deviant and illegal behaviors such as sex with children, rape, sadomasochism, exhibitionism, and so forth. According to Cline (1994), these deviant behaviors "frequently grew into a sexual addiction that they found themselves locked into and unable to change or reverse—no matter what the negative consequences in their life" (p. 234).

Correlation between Sex Crimes and Sexually Explicit Materials

More recent research has also suggested a connection between sex crimes and the use of sexually explicit materials. Zgourides, Monto, and Harris (1997) conducted a study of 176 males from the ages of 13 to 19. Of the 176 males, 80 were convicted sex offenders and 96 were not. The study found a significant positive correlation between the use of sexually explicit materials and the commission of sex crimes. In other words, far more sex offenders than nonoffenders reported using sexually explicit materials. Another study (Allen, D'Alessio, & Emmers-Sommer, 1999) did not find significantly different results in a comparison of pornographic consumption among sex offenders and nonoffenders, but it did find significant differences in terms of arousal and behavioral consequences. Sex offenders were more likely to become aroused and more likely to perform some sort of sexual act (whether masturbation, consensual sex, or coercive sex) after consuming sexually explicit material.

Summary

Sexual content in media ranges from the mildly suggestive to various levels of the sexually explicit. Sexual content in electronic and print media has important implications due to its perceived connection with serious social concerns. The availability of television to all ages makes that medium a particularly dangerous one when considering the damaging social effects that result from the consumption of sexual content. With the rise of the Internet and social media, the effects of exposure to sexually explicit material are only beginning to be realized. Pornography is the extreme class of sexually explicit materials that is available to adult audiences only. Pornography, largely devoid of literary merit or artistic value, is produced for the express purpose of pandering sexual content.

Obscenity is a legal term that describes certain pornographic material that must meet three criteria as judged by a jury representative of the community: (1) the material appeals to a prurient (shameful, sick, morbid, or lustful) interest in sex; (2) the material is patently offensive or beyond the contemporary community standards regarding depictions of sexual content or activity; (3) the material as a whole must lack serious literary, artistic, political, or scientific value.

Many studies have examined the extent and explicitness of sexual content in mass media. These studies have found that music videos, X-rated videos, television, R-rated movies, and the Internet contain varying amounts and types of sexual content.

Exposure to highly explicit sexual content may affect media users in one or more of several ways. These include sexual arousal and changes in attitudes, values, and behaviors.

When provoked individuals are exposed to sexually explicit materials, they are more likely to engage in retaliatory behavior. In other words, viewing arousing erotic material tends to enhance aggressive tendencies in individuals. This effect is known as excitation transfer.

The effects of viewing sexual content in the media are altered by the context of the material and the context in which a person is exposed to it. The seriousness or triviality of the material, the artistic value and intent of the material, the degree of explicitness and the necessity of the sex scene to the development of the plot, the cultural context, and the context of viewing are contextual variables that constitute the prevailing tone.

Harmful effects occur whenever sexually violent materials depict a woman who becomes aroused by an assault. Individual differences in disposition (e.g., being force-oriented or nonforce-oriented) cause people to react differently when viewing sexually violent media fare.

R-rated slasher movies, highly popular among teenagers, contain much violence, usually in a sexual context. Men become desensitized when they watch slasher films repeatedly.

The negative effects of viewing sexual violence can be mitigated. Training sessions prior to viewing or extensive debriefing sessions proved successful in lessening negative effects.

In a study of convicted sex offenders, a clinical psychologist found that use of pornography produced four major behavioral effects that occurred in the same sequence over time. These effects, known as the four-factor syndrome, included addiction, escalation, desensitization, and the tendency to act out or copy what had been viewed.

▣ NOTE

[1] Technically, the X-rating has not been used since 1990, when the Motion Picture Association of America began exploring less sensational NC-17 and NC-18 ratings.

thirteen

Reactions to Disturbing or Frightening Media Content

Fear is a darkroom where negatives develop.
—Usman B. Asif, photo critic

In 1975, the hit movie *Jaws* appeared in theaters across the United States. That summer, the press reported that the movie had caused many people to suddenly be very afraid of swimming in the ocean or even in lakes. On beaches throughout the country, sunbathers avoided stepping too far into the water. They feared that ravenous Great Whites were lurking nearby, ready to clamp their razor-sharp teeth on the unsuspecting.

The emotional response that many moviegoers experienced after seeing *Jaws,* while anecdotal in nature, is a good example of a **reaction of fright or anxiety** to media content. Other anecdotal examples of fright reactions to feature films abound. In 1974, *The Exorcist,* with its disturbing scenes, brought intense responses among audiences of all ages. Other films, such as *Indiana Jones and the Temple of Doom, Invasion of the Body Snatchers,* and *Gremlins,* contained content that was especially disturbing to children, and actually caused the Motion Picture Association of America (MPAA) to come up with the PG-13 rating so parents would know that the contents of the film might be inappropriate for children under 13 (Zoglin, 1984).

Since the mid-1970s, Hollywood has continued to produce thrillers that contain graphic and intense content. The proliferation of cable and satellite television in millions of homes and the addition of new channels has brought many of these thrillers directly into the homes of American families. Research on exposure to disturbing content has practical benefits for society's children, especially if such research can show ways to predict when fears will be strongest or

The summer blockbuster film *Jaws* caused swimmers to clear the surf in 1975. *AP Photo*

effects will be most negative. Such knowledge might allow the prevention or the reduction of fears.

In recent years, media effects researchers have learned a great deal about fright reaction to media content, including the reasons for it and ways to control it. This chapter will identify some of the more important findings from fright-reaction studies that have been conducted through the years. Children especially have been the focus of much of this research, but adults have not been ignored. For both age groups, many studies have explored fright as an immediate response that is rather short lived, but studies exploring long-term emotional responses that continue for hours or days or longer have popped up in recent years.

Throughout this chapter, we will refer to the substantial work done by media effects researcher Joanne Cantor and her associates. For the past few decades, Cantor's studies have appeared in numerous journals and books, and most of what we know about fright reactions to media fare comes from her work. She is considered the leading expert on the subject of fright reactions to mass media. The definition she uses for "fear" comes from the writings of Izard (1977). *Fear is generally conceived of as an emotional response of negative hedonic tone related to avoidance or escape, due to the perception of real or imagined threat* (Cantor, 2009, p. 290). (Hedonics is the branch of psychology that deals with the pleasant or unpleasant states of consciousness.)

Following a brief historical look at the study of frightening media fare, we turn to the different ways in which fright is measured. Then we focus on the reasons for fright reactions to media content. We assess the importance of age and gender differences in gauging fear reactions, and we close with research-directed strategies for coping with fear.

The Study of Fright

Fright reactions have been measured for many years. In the 1930s and 1940s, several studies examined reactions of fear among mass media audiences, especially children (Dysinger & Ruckmick, 1933; Eisenberg, 1936; Preston, 1941). You will recall from a previous chapter that the Payne Fund studies of the late 1920s and early 1930s examined the effects of motion pictures on young people. One of the experimenters, Herbert Blumer (1933), discovered that 93 percent of the children in his study reported being frightened by a film.

The modern horror genre developed throughout the 20th century. Classic films such as *Dracula* and *Frankenstein* appeared in 1931. The most famous incident of media-induced fright, which we mentioned previously, occurred on October 30, 1938, when thousands of people panicked during the dramatic *War of the Worlds* radio broadcast. The radio drama, set up as a series of news announcements that interrupted "regular" programming, alarmed Depression-era listeners by reporting an invasion from the planet Mars. Cantril (1940) studied the reactions of people throughout the country and could not pinpoint a single variable that caused the fear reaction, but he found that a lack of critical ability on the part of listeners did seem to contribute. Cantril discovered that personality influences and other psychological differences tended to influence whether listeners believed what they were hearing was an actual broadcast of news.

Most studies in the 1950s and early 1960s followed the lead of earlier studies by focusing upon the content of motion pictures and television and their effects upon viewers (Wall & Simson, 1950; Himmelweit, Oppenheim, & Vince, 1958; Schramm, Lyle, & Parker, 1961). One famous study, however, broke with tradition and examined the harmful effects of comic books on American youth (Wertham, 1954). In the 1950s, comic books took on a more frightful aspect. Scary stories such as those from the *Tales from the Crypt* series entertained a generation of young boys in the 1950s. In the 1950s and 1960s, horror films such as Alfred Hitchcock's *Psycho* were immensely popular among audiences.

Throughout the remainder of the 1960s, 1970s, and 1980s, researchers often concentrated their efforts on the *long-term effects* of mass media rather than short-term emotional effects. Enduring fright reactions, the kind that cause nightmares or long-term effects, became the focus of surveys and experiments. Hess and Goldman (1962) found that three of four parents interviewed said their children sometimes react with nightmares after viewing disturbing programs on television. Singer (1975) showed that children are in danger of having terrifying nightmares after watching disturbing media content. Years after seeing a frightening movie, children may experience such night "terrors" or, at the least, have strange or weird fantasies. Sarafino (1986) argued that frightening media content not only caused fear reactions in children, but threatened to impair psychological development. Enduring reactions of fright were also measured by Cantor and Reilly (1982) and Palmer, Hockett, and Dean (1983).

Much research in the 1970s and 1980s underscored the prevalence of media fright reactions among children. In one study, almost 50 percent of the first graders in the study group reported having been sometimes frightened or often frightened by television programs (Lyle & Hoffman, 1972). In 1977, a national survey found that one in four of the children questioned responded that shooting and violent fighting on television had frightened them (Zill, 1977).

Hoffner and Cantor (1985) found even more startling results. Three of four elementary school children and preschoolers in their sample reported having been frightened by a program on television or action in a movie. In 1987, researchers found that about 75 percent of the preschool and elementary school children sampled in Wisconsin reported being frightened by something they witnessed on television or in a movie (Wilson, Hoffner, & Cantor, 1987).

Since the 1990s, a number of different types of studies have offered compelling evidence for problems associated with media-induced fright among children, including lasting, detrimental effects (Cantor, 1998; Harrison & Cantor, 1999; Hoekstra, Harris, & Helmick, 1999). Singer and colleagues (1998) conducted a survey of more than 2,000 Ohio children in the third through eighth grades and found that students who watched more hours of television each day reported more symptoms of anxiety, depression, and post-traumatic stress. Another survey of parents found that the more television a child watched, the more likely the child was to have a sleep disturbance. Children with television sets in their bedroom were significantly more likely to experience sleep disturbances and other problems than children without televisions in their bedrooms (Cantor et al., 2010; Owens et al., 1999).

Researchers in Europe have reported similar findings. About one-third of a sample of 13-year-olds in Belgium reported having nightmares at least once a week after watching frightening or disturbing media content (Van den Bulck, 2004). In Finland, passive TV exposure among 5- and 6-year-olds (the time they were awake while the television was on) was found to correlate with sleep problems, and the study controlled for things like psychiatric problems and family influences (Paavonen et al., 2006).

Back in the U.S., one survey conducted in 2004 found that children who watched more than three hours of television per day at the age of 14 were likely to have sleep problems at ages 16 and 22, suggesting that the effects of watching television and having sleep disturbances may be cumulative. Those who reduced the amount of television viewing from ages 14 to 16 were less likely to have sleep problems at ages 16 and 22. Light viewers of television were the ones who reported the least problems with sleep (Johnson et al., 2004).

Another study found that children exposed to a destructive and deadly house fire in an episode of *Little House on the Prairie* were less likely to want to learn about building a fire in a fireplace than children who had not watched the episode (Cantor & Omdahl, 1991). A similar study showed children a scene involving a drowning; those children showed more concern about water accidents and were less likely to want to learn about canoeing than children not exposed to the scene (Cantor & Omdahl, 1999). The researchers took care in the later study to debrief the children and teach them water safety guidelines so that effects would not be long lasting.

Recent years have brought more graphic depictions—more blood, gore, and realism—in books and on the screen, and audiences seem to love it. On the big screen, box office classics such as *Friday the 13th, Halloween, Nightmare on Elm Street,* and *Scream* continue to thrill audiences in sequels, remakes, and on DVD, along with more current hits such as the *Paranormal Activity* and *Saw* movie franchises. Advances in the art of special effects have enhanced the graphic and realistic nature of horrible scenes in these popular films. Even on television, special effects create frightening content (especially for young viewers) on hits such as *Fringe, Criminal Minds, The Walking Dead,* and the *CSI* dramas.

Many researchers have documented the effects of frightening films through the years. Buzzuto recorded incidents of neurosis following viewing of *The Exorcist* (1975). Mathai (1983) noted an acute state of anxiety in an adolescent who viewed *Invasion of the Body Snatchers.* Cantor, Wilson, and Hoffner (1986) found that after watching a television movie called *The Day After,* about the results of a nuclear holocaust, young children were least frightened while teenagers were more disturbed and their parents were the most frightened. (Developmental differences due to age will be discussed in another section.) In 1994, Simons and Silveira found evidence of post-traumatic stress disorder in viewers of a television program in Britain called *Ghostwatch*. For a review of such studies and others, see Cantor (2009).

In recent years, researchers have turned their attention to fright reactions, especially among children, to news broadcasts. News events such as 9/11, the Virginia Tech massacre, the kidnapping and rescue of Elizabeth Smart, and other events have provided researchers with rich opportunities to study this domain (Bond & Harrison, 2008; Cantor, Mares, & Oliver, 1993; Cantor & Nathanson, 1996; Wilson, Martins, & Marske, 2005).

In addition to studying effects of actual films or programs on television recently viewed, researchers have discovered that fright reactions often linger and can be recalled years later by older children and adults (Hoekstra et al., 1999; Cantor, 1998; Johnson, 1980). The researchers examine these self-reports by participants in studies to determine the severity and duration of fright reactions. Two studies in 1999 found that undergraduates reported having vivid memories of media-related fright reactions as children or adolescents or more recently (Harrison & Cantor, 1999; Hoekstra et al., 1999). One of the studies found that more than a quarter of the respondents still had emotional feelings about the episode even though it had occurred, on average, six years earlier. So fright reactions to media fare tend to linger.

Through the years, a body of research has examined immediate and short-lived reactions of fright or anxiety among children, as well as reactions of extended duration to media content, whether movies, radio, or television. After a thorough review of the literature, Cantor (2009) assessed the findings in this way:

> In summary, research shows that children often experience anxiety and distress while watching mass media presentations and that these feelings, in varying intensities, often linger on after exposure. Recent surveys demonstrate that media-induced fears often interfere with children's sleep, and retrospective reports suggest that the negative effects of scary media can endure for years, even into adulthood. (p. 300)

Explanations for the Appeal of Fright

Horror has been described as stories "characterized by fear of some uncertain threat to existential nature and by disgust over its potential aftermath . . . perhaps the source of threat is supernatural in its composition" (Tamborini & Weaver, 1996). In other words, horror stories cause extreme fear. A monster or some other terrible source threatens lives, and the manner of death or the aftermath of death causes disgust.

Despite the feelings of fear and disgust, audiences are entertained—they actually seek out such experiences. This fright-as-entertainment phenomenon has piqued the interest of several communication researchers. Attempts have been made to explain the complexities that make unpleasant and horrible stories enjoyable entertainment.

Scientists have advanced a number of other theories to explain the appeal of frightening stories among audiences. Zillmann and Gibson (1996) provided an excellent summary of these views.

The most popular view has been that of catharsis. This view holds that when audience members witness graphic violence on the screen or read about it in books, they purge or rid themselves of their own violent tendencies or inclinations. Some have argued that such purgation is enjoyable (Clarens, 1967). Some have extended the notion of catharsis to include purgation of personal fears and anxieties (Douglas, 1966; Tudor, 1989). Also, the transformations that monsters, such as humans changing into werewolves, undergo in many horror films supposedly provide cathartic relief for teens who are experiencing physical changes as they mature sexually (Evans, 1984).

Researchers sometimes use terms like "identification" or "vicarious experience" to explain cathartic effects from horror. Some say that viewers are able to gain sadistic pleasure by identifying with the monsters and killers (King, 1981). Viewers are able to enjoy certain taboo experiences in a vicarious manner (Wood, 1984). Deep anxieties about certain acts (especially sexual acts that frequently occur in horror films) find expression and even resolution through the entertaining horror book or movie (Derry, 1987).

Another suggestion about the appeal of horror comes from Berlyne (1967, 1971), who believed that horror serves as a necessary, noxious experience that provides the viewer with feelings of gratified relief once it is finished. Of this view, Zillmann and Gibson (1996) wrote:

> It is the *termination* of this aversive state that is expected to prompt pleasurable relief. In this view, the enjoyment of horror is akin to the pleasures of

the sudden end to a bad toothache—which should leave people in hopes for recurrences. (p. 26)

Rosenbaum (1979) provided an explanation of the appeal of frightening content with distinctly religious overtones: People enjoy horror because it encourages a belief in a superior spiritual being capable of destroying evil forces. Ultimately, they experience feelings of "spiritual safety" (Zillmann & Gibson, 1996, p. 27).

Zillmann (1991a, 1991b) described horror as frightening because it releases empathetic responses toward victims and makes viewers apprehensive about becoming victims themselves. In other words, viewers identify with the victims and experience their terror vicariously. Horror also frightens viewers because of their apprehensions; they fear being victims themselves. Finally, horror usually features a satisfying ending that viewers enjoy.

Research Spotlight

Enjoyment of Mediated Fright and Violence: A Meta-Analysis
Cynthia A. Hoffner and Kenneth J. Levine (2005)
Media Psychology, 7, 207–237

The researchers selected studies that examined frightening or violent media content, used self-report measures of enjoyment of the content, and included independent variables such as negative affect and arousal during viewing, empathy, sensation seeking, aggressiveness, gender, and age. Once the studies were selected, the researchers synthesized the data in a meta-analysis.

Method

The researchers searched computer databases to identify articles for the study. They used multiple search terms related to media type (film, mass media, motion picture, television, TV), frightening or violent content (fright, frightening, horror, scary, violence, violent), and enjoyment (affect, appeal, enjoy, enjoyment, entertainment, like, liking). To qualify for the study, the researchers selected studies that were classified as scary media, horror, or violent media, that also included a self-report measure of enjoyment or preference for fright or violence as the dependent variable. Also, each study in the meta-analysis had to include at least one of the following independent variables: negative affect and arousal during viewing, empathy, sensation seeking, aggressiveness, and gender and age of respondent. Finally, each study had to contain enough information so that an effect size could be computed. The meta-analysis was based on data from 35 journal articles.

Analysis

The results of the studies had to be converted into a common effect-size metric using statistical tools.

Results

Male viewers, individuals lower in empathy, and people higher in sensation seeking and aggressiveness reported more enjoyment of fright and violence. The researchers noted the need for additional research to examine how empathy influences viewers' responses to violence and victimization. They also suggested that further research should take a look at how gender difference in the enjoyment of fright and violence changes from childhood to adulthood.

Zillmann (1991a, 1991b) called his view for the enjoyment of horror a "gender-socialization approach." This explanation differed considerably from previous views. Zillmann noticed that males and females reacted very differently to horror films, and part of the enjoyment obtained from watching the film had to do with acting or reacting in those predictable ways. Zillmann and Gibson (1996) wrote:

> The precept for boys and men stipulates that exposure to horror be nondistressing. Their show of mastery of distress in the face of terror should please them and favorably impress others. Gratification is thus self-generated and of a social nature. The precept for girls and women, in contrast, stipulates that exposure to horror be distressing and duly expressed as such. Their show of appropriate sensitivity—dismay, disgust, and contempt—should give them pleasure and favorably impress others. Gratification is again self-generated and social in kind. (p. 28)

Hoffner and Levine (2005) conducted a meta-analysis of the literature on enjoyment of fright and found that male viewers enjoyed being frightened by media depictions more than did females, as did people who scored low on empathy and high on sensation seeking and aggressiveness. They stressed the need for additional research to sort out the reasons for enjoyment that have been theorized.

Measuring Fright

Social scientists use a variety of research methods to measure responses of fear or anxiety when a person is viewing media content. Whether studying adults or children, researchers have found that **self-reporting measures** and **measures of physiological responses** have been most useful.

With self-reporting measures, adult participants are shown frightening or disturbing content, then asked to select words or phrases that best describe their reactions to the content. Adults, for example, are asked to report levels of anxiety or states of anxiety they experienced (Lazarus, Speisman, Mordkoff, & Davidson, 1962). Other descriptors such as the amount of tension or emotional arousal provide additional information. Studies have also asked adults to recall media content that frightened them as children (Hoekstra et al., 1999; Harrison & Cantor, 1999) or report on fright reactions of their children to mediated content (Cantor & Sparks, 1984; Sparks, 1986). The self-reports for children must be more simply stated. Usually, researchers ask the children to express reactions in varying degrees—for instance, how scared or upset they felt after viewing the disturbing scene or content (Sparks & Cantor, 1986).

Several physiological responses have been used to measure fright reactions. Among adults, the most common have been the measures of heart rate and palmar skin conductance (Falkowski & Steptoe, 1983; Koriat, Melkman, Averill, & Lazarus, 1972). When the participants are children, experimenters have used heart rate, skin temperature (Wilson & Cantor, 1985; Zillmann, Hay, & Bryant, 1975), and facial expressions of fear (Wilson & Cantor, 1987).

Reasons for Fear Reactions to Media Content

Media effects researchers have debated the reasons for fear reactions among audiences, especially those that have the age and developmental capacity to understand that what they are witnessing never actually happened. Fright occurs despite the fact that the viewer is not in danger and understands that he or she is not in danger. Why is this? Most social scientists explain the reaction in terms of classical conditioning (Pavlov, 1960). According to classical conditioning, certain stimuli cause certain responses, and similar stimuli evoke similar, albeit less intense, responses.

Fear-Producing Stimuli

According to Cantor (2009), three categories of stimuli that recur in media content usually result in fear responses in real life. These include (1) dangers and injuries, (2) distortions of natural forms, and (3) the experience of endangerment and fear by others (p. 291–292).

Dangers and Injuries

Many different kinds of events that threaten harm pop up repeatedly in scary programs. These might include natural disasters (e.g., earthquakes and tornadoes), violent confrontations between people such as interpersonal conflicts or major wars throughout the globe or even the universe, animal attacks, or major accidents (Cantor, 2009). Depictions of dangerous stimuli in mass media have produced measurable fright reactions in a number of experimental and survey research studies (Cantor, 1998; Harrison & Cantor, 1999).

Distortions of Natural Forms

Another stimulus that tends to produce a fear response occurs when familiar sights or organisms are shown with a deformity, distortion, or mutilation. Movie monsters, for example, fall into this category.

Throughout the research literature, monstrous characters are frequently mentioned as causing fear in children. Surveys and reports have revealed such fears in children (Cantor, 1998; Cantor & Sparks, 1984).

Endangerment and Fear by Others

Dramatic movies and television programs are designed to involve the audience in the situation of characters who are sometimes responding to frightful situations. The audiences are thus drawn into the plot and establish *empathy* with the characters with whom they are able to identify. Empathy is one of two primary mechanisms of this third category of responses to frightful stimuli.

This final category is the only one which involves an *indirect* response to scary content being viewed. In other words, fear is produced when audience members see characters afraid while in fearful situations.

Laboratory research studies have revealed that empathy is something that must be developed with age and is associated with the acquisition of role-play skills (Feshbach, 1982; Selman & Byrne, 1978). Research has shown that pre-

Freddy Krueger is the vengeful spirit of *The Nightmare on Elm Street* films.
AP Photo

school children are not nearly as frightened by a character's fear than by the actual frightening stimulus, while older children (ages 9 to 11) are known to experience fear simply by seeing a character's fearful expression and without witnessing the frightening stimulus itself (Wilson & Cantor, 1985).

The other mechanism that produces an indirect response of fear is that of *vicarious involvement*. This mechanism explains the fear of audiences in situations in which characters are unafraid because they are unaware that any danger is impending. Suspenseful dramas rely upon audience tensions and worries that something terrible might happen to characters with whom the audience identifies or develops an affective attachment (Cantor, 1998; Cantor & Omdahl, 1991). Examples of this include when moviegoers talk to the characters on the screen, saying things like "Don't go upstairs!" or "Look behind the door!"

Emotional Response Factors

Cantor (2009) also identified three important factors that cause viewers to react emotionally whenever they see fearful situations on the screen: (1) realism of depiction, (2) motivations of the viewer, (3) and other factors that affect a viewer's emotionality (pp. 292–294).

Realism of Depiction

Whenever viewers witness highly realistic, scary action on the screen, their fright responses tend to be intensely emotional. This is known as **stimulus generalization**. This notion refers to the similarity between conditioned or unconditioned stimuli from real life and what is seen on the screen. The greater the similarity between real life and screen drama, the stronger the generalization stimulus will be, and thus the fearful or emotional response to that stimulus.

The stimulus generalization notion explains why people react more intensely to violent scenes that involve live action or real-life depictions, rather than, for example, violence in cartoons or between puppets (Gunter & Furnham, 1984; Osborn & Endsley, 1971; Surbeck, 1975).

Particular fears of individuals in the audience also affect the intensity of emotional responses that screen depictions evoke. Children, for instance, are more frightened by screen incidents that they can identify with—those that come within personal experiences. Experimental research has confirmed that individual fears and associated real-life experiences cause the affected individuals to react more intensely when related material is shown on the screen (Hare & Bevings, 1975; Sapolsky & Zillmann, 1978; Weiss, Katkin, & Rubin, 1968).

A process called *stimulus discrimination* has also been identified as affecting the emotional reactions of audience members. This refers to the ability of audience members at various ages to be able to (or not be able to) distinguish screen events from real-life occurrences. In young children who lack developmental maturity, for example, realizing that a TV or screen monster is not actually real or that a brutal shooting on a dramatic thriller is not indeed taking place can be very difficult and emotionally disturbing (Door, 1980). Young children lack the developmental capacity to understand that the world of motion pictures and television is a distinctly different place from the real world (Cantor & Hoffner, 1990; Cantor & Wilson, 1984). The notion of stimulus discrimination is not entirely supported by research evidence because many adults have been shown to exhibit fear to media portrayals despite their understanding that the material is fictional (Johnson, 1980). Additional research has shown that even habitual viewing of frightening material among adults does not necessarily lessen fright responses (von Feilitzen, 1975; Cantor & Reilly, 1982; Sapolsky & Zillmann, 1978).

Motivations of the Viewer

Researchers have argued that the mature adult viewer possesses a fair amount of control over responses to media content. Certain cognitive measures can be taken to enhance or to minimize fright responses (Zillmann, 1978, 1982a). For example, viewers who want to be entertained and aroused by a screen drama might purposely "forget" that the events are being staged in order to enhance enjoyment. On the other hand, viewers who want to keep fright reactions to a minimum might continue to remind themselves that the actions are only mediated. This ability is especially difficult for young children (Cantor & Wilson, 1984).

Another motivation for viewing is that of acquisition of information. Studies have shown that audience members who watch for this motivational reason tend to pay more attention to the program and thus may become more aroused by what they see. Considerable research has involved documentaries as stimulus films, as studies have shown that portrayals of violence that actually happened are significantly more arousing than programs that are known by the viewers to be purely fictional (Geen, 1975; Geen & Rakosky, 1973). Cantor and Hoffner (1990) found that children who see something frightening in a movie—something that they think could affect them in their own environment—were more frightened than children who did not think that it could happen in their lives.

Factors Affecting Viewers' Emotional Responses

Research has shown that audience members who are previously aroused before viewing an exciting or disturbing scene retain some "arousal residue," which combines with new responses to film scenes to produce more intense emotional reactions. The theory that explains this phenomenon is called *excitation transfer* (Zillmann, 1978; Cantor, Zillmann, & Bryant, 1975; Zillmann, Mody, & Cantor, 1974). The arousing incidents may or may not be related to one another, and may or may not occur simultaneously, but excitation transfer occurs unless other factors distract the viewer or otherwise prevent the process from occurring (Girodo & Pellegrini, 1976; Schachter & Singer, 1962).

A good example of excitation transfer in action can be found in the techniques that movie producers and directors use to enhance suspense. Sound effects, for example, are very important. Different types of music can create different moods and different degrees of arousal, thus affecting the emotional impact of a film (Thayer & Levenson, 1983). Another important device to enhance the effects of a movie is that of foreshadowing or forewarning of impending threats. Studies showed that adults become more upset when a distressing event occurs if the movie forewarned them of it (Cantor, Ziemke, & Sparks, 1984; Nomikos, Opton, Averill, & Lazarus, 1968), and children experience more fear in anticipation of a forewarned scene (Hoffner & Cantor, 1990).

Age and Gender Differences

Two of the most important factors that affect a viewer's reactions to frightening media fare are chronological age and gender. A meta-analysis of studies that examined media-induced fear, conducted between 1987 and 1996, underscored the importance of gender and age differences, as females were found to exhibit more fear than men, and the extent of the effect increased with age (Peck, 1999). As noted previously, gender differences may have resulted from social pressures to conform to gender-specific behavior (e.g., girls who scream at horror shows, boys who demonstrate self-controlled mastery of the disturbing content).

The significance of gender differences among adults in differing responses to frightful media content has already been discussed in the section on explanations for the appeal of fright, so we focus this section on the importance of age and gender differences among children. The most important determining factor of fright reactions in children is that of age, due to the great developmental differences that occur during childhood, especially as children learn to distinguish fantasy from reality. Gender differences among children have been less pronounced, despite the stereotypical images of girls being more easily frightened than boys (Birnbaum & Croll, 1984) and more emotional (Fabes & Martin, 1991; Grossman & Wood, 1993).

Cantor and her associates have identified various types of stimuli that frighten children at different ages, as well as strategies that help reduce fear responses in children. Monsters, ghosts, supernatural creatures, the dark, animals, strange-looking creatures, and fast-moving creatures tend to scare young children from ages three to eight. Slightly older children (9 to 12 years) are more frightened by threats of injury or destruction to themselves or their loved ones. Children older than 12 also are afraid of personal injury, but in addition they face social and peer pressures and accompanying fears, as well as global concerns such as politics, the economy, or the environment (Cantor, 2009; Cantor, 1994; Cantor et al., 1986).

The difference between the fears of very young children and those of older children can be stated plainly. Younger children fear the stimulus itself, no matter how unreal or fantastic it is. Older children are more afraid of what might occur to them, rather than simply the danger itself. Even older children fear more abstract concepts and issues that threaten *psychological* harm in addition to or instead of *physical* harm. See the sidebar "What Frightens Children" for a summary of fear reactions at different ages.

The reason for these differences has to do with cognitive development of the children. Until about age seven, children remember and sort items in terms of salient attributes they perceive. After age seven, this type of organization is replaced by one based upon *concepts or functions* of the items involved rather than physical characteristics alone (Birch & Bortner, 1966; Melkman, Tversky, & Baratz, 1981). Thus, as a child grows older, he or she responds more intensely to media depictions that are based more on reality than fantasy or the unrealistic (Flavell, 1963; Kelly, 1981; Morison & Gardner, 1978; Cantor & Sparks, 1984).

What Frightens Children?

At different ages, children experience different types of fear reactions to what they see on the screen. The reason for this has to do with their different levels of cognitive development. Younger children tend to fear stimuli themselves, no matter how unrealistic or fanciful they may be. Older children are more afraid of what might occur to them, rather than simply the danger itself. Still older children fear more abstract issues that threaten psychological harm in addition to or instead of physical harm.

Age: 3 to 8 Years

Frightening images on the screen such as monsters, ghosts, supernatural creatures, the dark, animals, strange-looking creatures, and fast-moving creatures tend to scare young children.

Age: 9 to 12 Years

Threats of injury or destruction to the self or loved ones most frighten children in this age group.

Age: Older than 12

Personal injury is also a fear for adolescents, but they also face social and peer pressures and accompanying fears, and global concerns such as politics, the economy, or the environment.

Sources: Cantor, J. (1994). Fright reactions to mass media. In J. Bryant & D. Zillmann (Eds.), Media effects: Advances in theory and research. Hillsdale, NJ: Erlbaum, p. 231; Cantor, J., Wilson, B. J. & Hoffner, C. (1986). Emotional responses to a televised nuclear holocaust film. Communication Research, 13, 257–277.

A good example of the differences in cognitive development and the fear responses they produce can be shown through a study that involved *The Incredible Hulk* television program. Sparks and Cantor (1986) found that preschoolers became intensely frightened whenever the normal-looking hero turned into the monster Hulk. Older children did not fear the transformation because they understood that the creature used his powers for the forces of good.

Another excellent example is that of a study conducted after a showing of the televised movie *The Day After* in the 1980s. The movie showed a community in Kansas under nuclear attack and the devastating aftermath, though depictions of injuries were rather mild in comparison to other television programs. Cantor et al. (1986) surveyed viewers by telephone the night after the movie played. They found that young children were least affected by the film, while children older than 12 (due to cognitive development) were highly disturbed, and their parents were even more disturbed.

Strategies for Coping with Fear

As would be expected, the same developmental and gender differences that cause children of different ages to fear different media portrayals also affect the different types of coping strategies, though gender differences play a much smaller role in determining effective coping mechanisms. At various ages, coping strategies have been shown to be effective in reducing or even preventing fears that are induced by mass media content.

Coping strategies fall into one of two categories: noncognitive and cognitive (Cantor, 2009). **Noncognitive strategies**, those that do not require the viewer to process verbal information, have been shown to work well among young children. **Cognitive strategies**, those that require the activation of cognitive processes (e.g., talking about the fear), tend to work well with children of elementary school age and older, though noncognitive strategies have also been shown to be useful. Research has shown that adolescent girls report using more noncognitive coping strategies than boys, but gender differences could not be measured in the use of cognitive coping strategies (Hoffner, 1995; Valkenburg, Cantor, & Peeters, 2000).

Types of Noncognitive Strategies

Several types of noncognitive strategies have been used to help young children cope with media-induced fear. *Visual desensitization* allows children to be gradually exposed to disturbing content. In one study, the children were shown a rubber tarantula in order to prepare them for a scene that featured the large spiders (Wilson, 1987). The backstage view of the application of makeup to the actor in *The Incredible Hulk* served as a visual desensitization (Sparks & Cantor, 1986).

Physical activity serves as another type of noncognitive coping strategy. Clinging to an object of attachment is an example of this strategy. Eating or drinking while viewing a scene has been shown to reduce fears, but some researchers argued that this takes place only because the child has been distracted from the program (Manis, Keating, & Morison, 1980). Covering the eyes is another example (Wilson, 1989), but research showed that only younger children used this as a means of reducing fear; older children actually became more frightened by doing it, mainly because they could still hear what was going on and understood it.

Types of Cognitive Strategies

As mentioned previously, cognitive strategies are typically more appropriate for older children because of their level of development. When children are told to remember that a program is not real, they are less likely to be frightened by it. When the media presentations depict highly realistic threats, one of the most effective cognitive coping strategies is that of offering reassuring information about the minimal danger of the depicted threat.

Studies have revealed that cognitive strategies can be modified for younger children to improve their effectiveness in helping the children cope with media-induced fears. Information can be provided verbally and visually (Cantor, Sparks, & Hoffner, 1988), and simple reassuring words can be repeated to calm the children (Wilson, 1987).

Summary

Fright reactions to media content among adults and especially among children have been the focus of one branch of media effects research. Self-reporting measures and measures of physiological responses have been most useful in these studies.

Research has revealed several important findings. Most fright reactions are usually transitory, but some may endure for an extended period of time. Fright reactions are debilitating in only a few cases. Parents are usually unaware of the intensity of their children's fright reactions. Finally, research has shown that, to an extent, people enjoy being frightened by films or television programs.

In the early 1930s and 1940s, the Payne Fund studies and the *War of the Worlds* study examined fright reactions among movie and radio audiences. In the 1950s and 1960s, studies focused upon the content of motion pictures and television and their long-term effects upon viewers. Research in the 1970s and 1980s identified the prevalence of media fright reactions among children. Recent research has continued to examine fright reactions among children and adults, and attempted to determine ways of reducing or eliminating fright reactions among young audiences.

Viewers' attraction to disturbing content can be explained by the mechanism of excitation transfer. This is a process of physiological arousal transference that allows greater enjoyment of media presentations.

Fright occurs despite viewers' understanding that they are not in danger. According to classical conditioning, certain stimuli cause certain responses, and similar stimuli evoke similar, albeit less intense, responses.

Three categories of stimuli that recur in media content usually result in fear responses in real life: (1) dangers and injuries, (2) distortions of natural forms, and (3) the experience of endangerment and fear by others.

The type of fright reaction experienced depends heavily upon the chronological age of the viewer. This is due to differences in the cognitive development of children at various ages. These differences affect a child's ability to distinguish fantasy from reality. Very young children (ages 3 to 8) fear the stimulus itself, no matter how unreal or fantastic it may be. Older children (ages 9 to 12) are more afraid of what might occur to them, rather than simply the danger itself. Children older than 12 fear more abstract concepts and issues that threaten psychological harm in addition to or instead of physical harm.

A number of different fright stimuli have been identified for children at different ages. Monsters, ghosts, supernatural creatures, the dark, animals, strange-looking creatures, and fast-moving creatures tend to scare young children from the ages of 3 to 8; children 9 to 12 years old are more frightened by threats of injury or destruction to themselves or their loved ones. Adolescents also fear personal injury, but in addition they face social and peer pressures and accompanying fears, as well as global concerns such as politics, the economy, or the environment.

Three factors cause viewers to react emotionally whenever they see fearful situations on the screen: (1) realism of the depiction, (2) motivations of the viewer, and (3) other factors that affect a viewer's emotionality.

Strategies for coping with media-induced fears include cognitive and noncognitive techniques. Cognitive strategies require the activation of cognitive processes such as talking about the fear. These strategies tend to work well with children in elementary school or beyond, though noncognitive strategies have also been shown to be useful. Visual desensitization and physical activity are types of noncognitive strategies. These usually work well with younger children.

fourteen

Political Communication Effects

The study of the effects on audiences from mass-mediated messages or symbols that are political in nature or have political consequences is but one division in the broad research domain of political communication effects. Within this particular area of inquiry, different levels of effects may occur—effects on individuals in society (called micro effects) or on the political system, institutions, or society as a whole (called macro effects). Effects may be periodic in nature, such as those produced by elections, or they may be continuous, such as the watchdog function the press performs in the United States, with the president and other elected officials under constant scrutiny. This chapter will discuss important findings in these various arenas.

Throughout the history of the study of media effects, researchers have been interested in the effects of political communication. As you have learned in earlier chapters, findings on the power of mass-mediated effects have varied through the years, and political communication effects are no exception. Studies of voting behavior in the 1940s and 1950s indicated that mass-mediated political communication effects were rather *limited* (Berelson, Lazarsfeld, & McPhee, 1954; Lazarsfeld, Berelson, & Gaudet, 1948). In these well-known studies, mass media were found to influence opinion leaders, who in turn influenced others through interpersonal communication. Later studies have put into question the integrity of the limited effects model by presenting findings of more direct and powerful media influence on voters from political campaign messages (Blumler & McLeod, 1974; Chaffee & Hochheimer, 1985; Gitlin, 1978; Iyengar & Simon, 2000; Noelle-Neumann, 1984). For example, Noelle-Neumann's Spiral of

Silence theory suggests powerful effects result whenever people fear social alienation or isolation enough to keep quiet and not speak their views.

After the 1970s, an increasing number of researchers became interested in political communication, and the number of studies mushroomed. McLeod, Kosicki, and Rucinski (1988) identified four major reasons for this increased interest:

1. Voting behaviors became increasingly unpredictable due to various socio-political changes.

2. The societal concern for the negative effects of television increased.

3. Studies by European scholars (e.g., Spiral of Silence theory by Noelle-Neumann, and the Marxist and radical views of the Frankfurt and Birmingham critical schools) attracted attention and stimulated additional research.

4. An emphasis on cognitive dimensions expanded the focus of political communication research.

In addition to their list, we might also add that researcher interest began to grow in the areas of negative political advertising (Johnson-Cartee & Copeland, 1991) and negative campaigning, and on the topic of decreasing voter turnout (Miron, 1999).

In this chapter we will examine some of the recent research findings in political communication. We will also discuss aspects of mass media and society that affect the nature of political communications, the various goals of mass media in a democratic society, the content of mediated political messages, and various types of effects at the micro and macro levels.

Influences on Political Communication

Several dynamic influences affect the nature of political communication in a society: the social scene, the political landscape, the media environment, and media content. We describe these influences as dynamic because they change, often considerably, over time with the introduction of new technologies, shifts in public opinion, fluctuations in the political climate, and other changes at the societal level.

Functions of Mass Media in a Democracy

Mass media attempt to provide a number of special functions for the body politic in democratic societies of the world. Gurevitch and Blumler (1990) identified eight such functions and McLeod, Kosicki, and McLeod (1994) paraphrased them in the following convenient way:

1. Surveillance of contemporary events that are likely to impinge, positively or negatively, upon the welfare of citizens.

2. Identification of key sociopolitical issues including their origins and possibilities for resolution.

3. Provision of platforms for advocacy by spokespersons for causes and interests.

4. Transmission of diverse content across the various dimensions and factions of political discourse, as well as bidirectionally between potential power holders and mass publics.

5. Scrutiny of government officials, their institutions, and other agencies of power by holding them accountable for their actions and policies.

6. Incentives and information to allow citizens to become active, informed participants rather than spectators in the political process.

7. Principled resistance to external forces attempting to subvert media autonomy.

8. Respectful consideration of the audience as potentially concerned, sense-making, and efficacious citizens. (p. 126)

According to Gurevitch and Blumler (1990), these special functions are actually *goals* or *standards* that mass media should try to attain in a democratic society. In reality, because of the fundamental nature of mass media as money-making, profits-dominated entities or any number of constraints, news media sometimes fall measurably short of the standards. For example, news media sometimes cover pseudo-events or other irrelevant but entertaining stories in their quest to attract the highest audience numbers. The tendency of the news media to cover *events* rather than *issues* represents another stumbling block in the path of the designated goals. When issues are addressed, they are often presented from the standpoint of the news network's institutional agenda (McLeod et al., 1994). Additionally, the media frequently dramatize their coverage of political campaigns and present the event as they would a horse race, with candidates neck and neck in the polls, or a dark horse candidate gaining ground, or a front-runner pulling away (see Figure 14.1).

Media Content

Studies have focused primarily on two types of media content related to political communication: political advertising and news stories. The first of these, political advertising, constitutes the primary form of communication between political candidates and the voting public (Kaid, 1996). In major political campaigns, television advertising usually consumes much of the campaign budget.

Studies have shown that political ads on television have been effective in presenting particular candidate images to the voting public, providing information about key issues, and sometimes influencing voting decisions (Kaid, 1981). Content analyses have revealed that political ads often provide more information about campaign issues than about candidate images (Joslyn, 1980; Kaid & Johnston, 1991).

In the area of news stories, several aspects of media content may influence political communication. Two common types of media content include framing and news flaws (see Chapter 7 on Framing).

Frames are abstract notions that media professionals use to present news stories in a particular way. Gamson and Lasch (1983) defined a frame as a "central organizing idea for understanding events related to the issue in question"

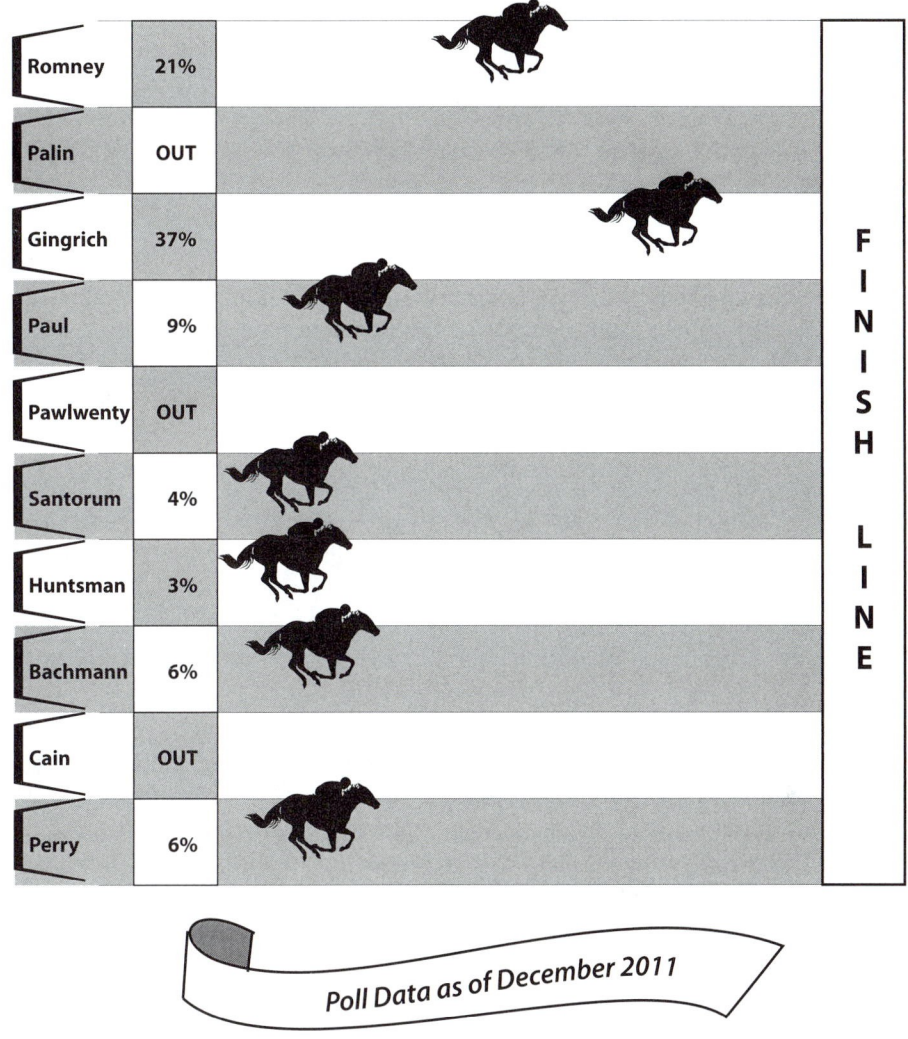

Figure 14.1   Example of media dramatization of political campaigns.

(p. 398). In terms of political media messages, campaigns are often framed using metaphors or catchphrases. Such framing devices often influence audience perceptions and interpretations (McLeod & Detenber, 1999; Valkenburg, Semetko, & de Vreese, 1999; Nelson, Oxley, & Clawson, 1997).

Bennett (1988) identified four *news flaws* common in news coverage: personalization, fragmentation, dramatization, and normalization. *Personalization* refers to the tendency for news stories to concentrate on individuals when reporting on large-scale social concerns. *Fragmentation* involves the delivery of news in disconnected, brief capsule summaries. Hart (1996) referred to the fragmentary presentations as resulting in "cameo politics" (p. 109). *Dramatization* occurs whenever news is selected on the basis of its dramatic or entertaining value rather than its importance as an issue. *Normalization* takes place whenever news stories show how particular problems can be solved within the existing political system. Each of these flaws may affect the nature of a political communication.

Micro-Level Political Communication Effects

Most research on effects from political communication has concentrated on the individual rather than society at large; in other words, micro-level effects studies rather than macro-level studies dominate the literature. At the micro level are four major areas: (1) formation and change of opinion; (2) cognitive effects, including agenda-setting research, priming, knowledge gain, and framing; (3) effects on individual perceptions of the political system; and (4) effects on political behavior or participation. Macro-level studies seek to examine effects on systems, or effects on individuals that affect systems.

At either level, the nature and strength of effects from mediated political communication depend on a number of different factors. These factors have to do with certain characteristics or orientations of individual audience members and their processing of media messages.

Formation and Change of Opinion

A number of studies have explored the power of media messages to produce or change the political opinions of audience members. The voting studies of Lazarsfeld and his colleagues (1948) found only a limited amount of influence from mass media on the political opinions of audiences. Later studies indicated that political media messages produced much stronger effects than previously thought (Blumler & McLeod, 1974; Ranney, 1983; McLeod & McDonald, 1985; Iyengar & Simon, 2000).

Models of persuasion, such as Petty and Cacioppo's elaboration likelihood model (1986a) and Fishbein and Ajzen's reasoned action model (1975) have been applied to the study of political communication effects. Several research studies have used these persuasion models as a basis for understanding campaign effects (Fazio & Williams, 1986; Granberg & Brown, 1989; Krosnick, 1988; O'Keefe, 1985; Rice & Atkin, 2000). The study of political advertising effects has also drawn from models of persuasion (Shah et al., 2007).

Effects of Cognitive Processes

In recent decades, five different types of research have examined cognitive effects from mediated political messages. These include agenda-setting research, priming research, knowledge gain, framing, and cognitive complexity (McLeod, Kosicki, & McLeod, 2009).

You will recall that **agenda-setting** theory states that the news media determine prominent issues through their expanded coverage of particular issues, and these issues are considered important by the public (McCombs & Shaw,

Politicians can never stop "campaigning" in today's communication environment. Here President Barack Obama attempts to rally support for his jobs bill. *AP Photo/Richmond Times-Dispatch, Eva Russo*

1972). Research supports the notion that the issues that receive the most coverage are the very issues that the public perceives as important (Funkhouser, 1973; Iyengar & Kinder, 1987; MacKuen, 1981; McCombs, 2004). In recent years, researchers have begun to study a second level of agenda setting, called *attribute agenda setting*, similar in some ways to framing studies, in which researchers are concerned with the way the news media present particular stories. The attributes of these stories have a cognitive component and an affective (emotional) component—people learn information from stories, and sometimes the presentation of the story in positive, negative, or neutral tones determines how audiences think and feel about the content of the stories (Ghanem, 1997; McCombs, 2004).

Priming, you may recall, occurs when exposure to a mediated message activates related thoughts in the mind of the audience member for a limited time period. Priming has been shown to affect political opinions and voting decisions. Iyengar and Kinder (1987) found that issues that received prominent media coverage primed audiences in their evaluations of presidential performance. Studies show that the way that a U.S. president handles high-coverage issues disproportionately influences the overall performance rating for that president in the eyes of an audience member (McGraw & Ling, 2003; Pan & Kosicki, 1997).

Other studies have found that although audiences may or may not be persuaded by mediated political communication, they often *learn* from such messages. News reports about campaign issues and candidates, political debates,

Research Spotlight

Priming Effects of Late-Night Comedy
Patricia Moy, Michael A. Xenos, and Verena K. Hess (2006)
International Journal of Public Opinion Research, 18(2), 198–210

In this study, researchers investigated the influence of a candidate's appearance on a late-night comedy show on voter perceptions of the candidate. They focused on priming effects on the viewers.

Methods

The researchers used data from the 2000 National Annenberg Election Survey from November 1999 through mid-January 2001. The presidential candidates, George W. Bush and Al Gore, appeared on the *Late Show with David Letterman* and *The Tonight Show with Jay Leno* during the weeks leading up to the election. Bush appeared on the Letterman show October 19, and on the Leno show October 30. Gore appeared on the Leno show October 31. During the period, 11,482 people were interviewed.

Variables

People were asked to rate Bush and Gore on a 0–100 point favorability/thermometer scale. They asked them also to rate which man would do a better job strengthening Social Security, protecting Medicare, keeping the economy strong, providing for a strong military defense, and improving education. Also, the researchers gave them phrases related to character such as "really cares about people like me," "honest," "inspiring," "knowledgeable," and so forth and asked them to respond on a scale from 1 to 4, with 1 being "extremely well" to 4 being "not well." In addition, people were asked how many nights per week they watched late-night comedy shows such as the *Late Show* or *The Tonight Show*. Researchers recorded the respondents' gender, education, income, race, and affiliation with a political party.

Analytic Procedures

The researchers divided the rolling cross-sectional data into six week-long increments to test for priming effects. Using ordinary least squares regressions, summary evaluations of each candidate were a result of demographics, issue and trait evaluations, exposure to late-night comedy, and interaction terms capturing the differences in evaluation strategies between viewers and nonviewers before and after the candidate's appearance. A significant difference in the interaction terms from one time period to another suggested evidence of a priming effect.

Results

Statistically significant differences were found in respondents' assessments of character evaluations. Bush was perceived to be more honest, inspiring, and a leader. He was rated slightly warmer on the thermometer scale. Gore was thought to be more knowledgeable and caring. In the week immediately following Bush's *Late Show* appearance, viewers rated him significantly higher than nonviewers. Throughout the survey period, late-night comedy viewers' assessments of Gore were significantly higher than those held by nonviewers. By comparing survey data collected prior to the candidates' appearances on the late-night shows with data collected after their appearances, researchers found that favorability ratings of Bush, both before and after his appearance, were a function of respondents' sociodemographic location (being male and white), their political affiliation (being Republican), their beliefs that he would do a better job than Gore on various issues, and their perceptions of his character. No priming effects were found in the aftermath of Gore's appearance. The researchers accounted for this by pointing out that Gore was the sitting Vice President, and more recognizable to viewers than the challenger Bush.

and conventions have all been shown to be responsible for various amounts of knowledge gain among audiences (Eveland, Hayes, Shah, & Kwak, 2005; Jerit, Barabas, & Bolsen, 2006; McLeod, Bybee, & Durall, 1979).

Several caveats must accompany these indications of political **knowledge gain**. First, other studies have revealed that Americans are not particularly knowledgeable about political affairs. Delli Carpini and Keeter (1991) found that the U.S. public's knowledge of politics increased only minimally in the decades following the 1960s, despite great increases in the number of Americans attending college. When the researchers controlled for education, they found that factual knowledge about politics had actually declined through the years. Most recently, however, Sotirovic and McLeod (2008) discovered that use of mass media and the information learned increased during the 2004 campaigns. Other recent studies have found that people learn from news content (Drew & Weaver, 2006).

You may recall that the knowledge gap hypothesis (Tichenor, Donohue, & Olien, 1970) posits that the "information rich" keep getting richer and the "information poor" never catch up. This has become a growing concern in this digital age of technological expansion. Studies have examined how new technologies are accessed and used, and how this affects political knowledge (Mossberger, Tolbert, & Stansbury, 2003; Shane, 2004).

In recent years, researchers have attempted to show the similarities and differences in agenda setting, priming, and **framing** approaches (Entman, 2007; Hwang, Gotlieb, Nah, & McLeod, 2007; Price & Tewksbury, 1997; Scheufele & Tewksbury, 2007). The way a story is framed by a journalist can affect the way audiences process and interpret the information. For example, if a journalist uses a human interest approach to a particular issue, audiences are more likely to react emotionally to the messages. As usual, individual differences in knowledge, values, and other factors can mediate the strength of the frame's effect.

Framing studies examine the manner in which journalists present particular issues, and they also focus on reactions of audience members to those stories. Framing theorists say that a person's individual mental schema determine which messages will be applicable to that person and accessible in memory in the future (see Chapter 7).

Some researchers have not focused on the mere retention of facts, but have tried to measure audiences' broader understanding of political information conveyed in news stories. Audience members are asked open-ended questions about news stories and they participate in group discussions. Using these techniques, researchers gain insights into the **cognitive complexity** of the audience members' understanding of the news stories (McLeod, Pan, & Rucinski, 1989; Shah et al., 2004; Sotirovic, 2001a, 2001b).

Voter Perceptions

What influences a person's voting decision? Is a voter motivated to select a particular candidate based on self-interest or on broader perceptions about the system? In other words, does a voter select a particular candidate because promised tax cuts or other measures will provide personal economic advantages to the voter, or does the voter base the decision upon less selfish motives, such as perceived economic benefits to the country at large?

Some evidence suggests that voters are persuaded less by personal "pocket-book" matters than by their perceptions about the economic health of the country (Fiorina, 1981; Kinder & Kiewiet, 1983). Such findings are important when one considers that news media coverage usually shapes those perceptions. The press plays an essential role in providing the public with information about governmental operations, the economy, and other aspects of the system. Often, however, the press does not fulfill this role satisfactorily (Popkin, 1991).

Studies have shown that media coverage, especially television coverage, may cause voters to perceive that individuals, rather than society at large, are responsible for particular social problems such as poverty or crime (Sotirovic, 2003). Many do not associate social problems with societal responsibility but prefer to blame individuals such as the poor, the homeless, or victims (Iyengar, 1989). Iyengar (1991) identified two types of frames for political news stories on television: *episodic,* using case study examples or reports of concrete events, and *thematic,* approaching an issue from a more abstract or general perspective. About 80 percent of the CBS news stories in his sample were episodic. A controlled experiment revealed that thematic framing caused audiences to associate social problems with societal and governmental responsibility rather than individuals. With episodic framing, however, the perceptions of system-level responsibility decreased. Results have been different in studies that involve political stories in newspapers, which tend to be more thematic than episodic (McLeod, Sun, Chi, & Pan, 1990).

Other recent studies (Ho & McLeod, 2008; Neuwirth, Frederick, & Mayo, 2007) have explored Noelle-Neumann's (1984) Spiral of Silence theory. You may recall that as society perceives a majority view to be dominant, those who do not agree with that view fear isolation and ultimately refuse to speak up, preferring instead to spiral into silence.

Political Behavior

Political communication researchers have long been interested in media effects on voting behavior. Through the years, studies have revealed that media effects may be direct or indirect, and that interpersonal communication sometimes has a place in the mix. For the most part, studies have shown that voting is a complex behavior influenced by a number of factors, with media presentations being one of those factors.

Political advertisements have proven effective in influencing voting decisions (Kaid, 1981). For this reason, candidates spend millions of dollars on television ads alone. During the past four decades, the length of televised political ads has decreased considerably, from 30-minute biographical ads in the 1950s and 1960s to 4-minute spots in the 1970s to the 60-second, 30-second, and 15-second spots of the 1980s and 1990s (Devlin, 1995; Kern, 1989). The most popular time length for political ads today is 30 seconds, leading one scholar to call this the "age of the 30-second spot" (Perloff, 1998, p. 348).

Research shows that many people learn from political advertisements (Brians & Wattenberg, 1996; Just, Crigler, & Wallach, 1990), and evidence shows that people may be influenced by both positive and negative ads (Houston & Doan, 1999). Studies reveal that weak partisans—for example, those who are not staunch Democrats or Republicans—and those with little interest in politics are more affected by political ads than staunch partisans and high-interest voters (Ansolabehere & Iyengar, 1995). Yet, as Perloff (1998) pointed out, such findings must be qualified:

> It is difficult to parcel out the influence of commercials from all the other forces impinging on voters during the election campaign. Clearly, political spots can affect voters' evaluations of candidates and their interpretations of political events. Ads also contribute to voters' storehouse of campaign knowledge, although even advertising consultants would agree that a campaign diet based exclusively on commercials would be an intellectually meager one. (p. 374)

Negative political ads have proven effective in influencing voters when voters perceive them to be fair, and when they focus on issues that are important to voters (Perloff, 1998). Studies show that people tend to remember negative ads more and recognize them more than they do positive ads (Shapiro & Rieger, 1992; Newhagen & Reeves, 1991). Research has also shown that failure to answer negative ads can be disastrous for a candidate because such silence allows the opposition to define the persona of the candidate (Johnson-Cartee & Copeland, 1991). For example, George H. W. Bush's attacks on the social policies of Governor Michael Dukakis in the 1988 presidential election proved highly effective when Dukakis failed to answer the charges. One political consultant explained the situation in this way: "There's one thing the American people dislike more than someone who fights dirty. And that's someone who climbs into the ring and won't fight" (Johnson-Cartee & Copeland, 1991, p. 224).

The presence of negative political ads seems to increase voter turnout, studies have shown (Freedman & Goldstein, 1999; Jackson & Carsey, 2007; Kahn & Kenney, 1999). Other studies suggest that negative ads alienate voters and suppress voter turnout (Ansolabehere, Iyengar, & Simon, 1999; Overton, 2006).

In recent years, political advertising campaigns have become so conspicuous that print and broadcast media have begun to report on them. Such "adwatches" provide analyses, interpretations, and evaluations of the ads (Kaid, 1996, p. 451). These adwatches have become important dimensions in political advertising (West, 1993; Kaid et al., 1993), and may influence voters' reactions to the candidates and the ads themselves (Cappella & Jamieson, 1994; Pfau & Louden, 1994).

Traditionally, a number of personal factors not related to media influence have predicted voter turnout. These factors include educational level, age, marital status, church attendance, and so forth (Strate, Parrish, Elder, & Ford, 1989; Wolfinger & Rosenstone, 1980). Yet some studies have revealed instances of abstention from voting that can be attributed to mass media (Ranney, 1983; Blumler & McLeod, 1974). In a study of the 1970 election in Great Britain, panel participants revealed that they abstained from voting because they did not like the image presented by the candidates on television.

One study examined voter knowledge and participation at the individual and community levels. The researchers extended the concept of the knowledge gap to what they called the "participation gap." Their work showed that people who lived in "denser, cohesive, and more educated" communities revealed more political knowledge, and that knowledge was a significant predictor on participation scales (Cho & McLeod, 2007, p. 223).

The strength of influence on voting behavior attributed to *interpersonal communication* rather than, or in addition to, *mass communication* has varied through the years. Lazarsfeld and his colleagues (1948) were the first to identify the influence of interpersonal communication on voters. They found that many people received information about the candidates or the election from other people rather than from news media reports. Later studies showed that conversations with others tend to work in conjunction with or complement news reports (Chaffee, 1982), and that media reports arouse interest in a campaign that leads to more interpersonal discussions (McLeod et al., 1979).

With the rise of the Internet, political communication researchers have found the basis for many additional studies, including the role of Internet communications in voter participation (Matei & Ball-Rokeach, 2003; Shah et al., 2002; Shah et al., 2005). One study found that Internet use directly affected the amount of information users acquired, and it predicted voter participation among individuals contingent upon their level of political interest (Xenos & Moy, 2007).

Macro-Level Political Communication Effects

Analytical macro-level effects studies that complement individual-level effects to explore consequences for society or the political system are few in number due to the difficulties encountered in measurement; however, purely *descriptive* macro-level studies abound. These studies provide much descriptive information about the American political system and its body of voters.

Descriptive Macro Studies

Descriptive macro studies suggest, for example, that only a small group of people in the United States is politically knowledgeable and active. The great numbers that constitute the remainder of the population are apathetic and politically uninformed (Neuman, 1986). People with high levels of education tend to vote more often, know more about politics, participate in politics, and know and discuss political news more than less-educated citizens (Burnham, 1982; Powell, 1986; Popkin, 1991).

Television has been blamed for many problems with the American political system. Ranney (1983) pointed out a few of these problems. The expense of television commercials has made fund-raising an increasingly important aspect in political campaigns. Also, the brevity of the TV commercial spot encourages less focus on discussion of issues and more emphasis on superficial factors such as the candidate's appearance and image.

Despite the rise of the Internet, the availability of online news, and the decline in newspaper readership, research has shown that traditional mass media continue to command large audiences (Ahlers, 2006). Several researchers have addressed the issues present with the changing technological news environment (Harrison & Falvey, 2001; Sunstein, 2006; Benkler, 2006).

Research has shown that the "discussion network" of people surrounding a person can have an effect on civic participation (Huckfeldt & Sprague, 1995; McLeod et al., 1996; Scheufele et al., 2006) and that the frequency of the discussions is an important consideration (Kwak et al., 2005).

Effects on Policy Making

When the mass media influence politicians and policy makers, influences at the system level may also occur. One study (Protess et al., 1991) found that the use of investigative reporting contributed to civic reforms in a number of areas. Such reports did not arouse readers to contact their elected officials and insist on reforms; rather, effects occurred because of interactions between the journalists, special interest groups, and public policy makers.

The effects of mass media on policy making are apparent in other ways as well. Local media usually support civic or other local "improvement" projects, some of which may be rather costly (Kaniss, 1991; Logan & Molotch, 1987). Also, media publicity has been shown to help lawmakers achieve their goals and raise money toward reelection campaigns (Smith, 1988; Etzioni, 1988; Goldenberg & Traugott, 1984).

Factors Influencing Media Effects

The impact from mass media political messages depends on a number of characteristics of the individual audience member and the way he or she processes the mediated information.

Individual Characteristics

Generally, the most politically active citizens are those with high educational levels. These politically sophisticated individuals are not only the most politically informed, but the most likely to learn new political information (Star & Hughes, 1950; Tichenor et al., 1970). Conversely, such informed people are less likely to exhibit agenda-setting effects from either print or broadcast media, probably due to the strength of their personal issues agendas (McLeod et al., 1974; Weaver et al., 1981; Iyengar & Kinder, 1987). Framing effects are also moderated by political sophistication (Valentino, Beckmann, & Buhr, 2001).

Other individual factors that influence the strength of political communication effects include political partisanship or party preference (Katz, 1987; Iyengar & Kinder, 1987; McLeod et al., 1974; Young, 2004; Gunther & Schmitt,

2004), personal images or evaluations of the news media (Kosicki & McLeod, 1990; McLeod et al., 1986), and personal motivations for particular gratifications (Blumler & McQuail, 1969; McLeod & Becker, 1974; McLeod et al., 1974). Those with strong political partisanship are less likely to be influenced by political messages that are counter to their political predispositions. Also, a person's image toward the news media has a marked effect on how much that person learns from the news. Research has shown that people who give high ratings to news quality usually learn *less* from the media, as do people who are highly critical of or skeptical about the accuracy of news content. People who are moderately skeptical about news content tend to think about it more carefully and therefore learn more from it (McLeod et al., 1986). Finally, people with the strongest interest in political communications are usually those who attend to the messages most carefully and learn the most from them; in this way, personal gratifications sought from political communications mediate media effects.

Information Processing

The effects of political communication are also modified by factors related to the *processing* of the messages. The more attention a person gives to a broadcast or print news story, the more the person learns from the story (Chaffee & Choe, 1980; Chaffee & Schleuder, 1986). Studies have identified three levels of information processing among news audiences (Kosicki & McLeod, 1990; Kosicki, McLeod, & Armor, 1987). These range from skimming or scanning the story (level one) to reading through the story (level two) to reading and then thinking about the story and possibly discussing it with others (level three).

Lower measures of political learning, interest, and participation are associated with processing at level one; higher measures occur when processing occurs at the third level. When information processing occurs at level two, interest and participation are enhanced but learning is not.

Summary

Findings on the power of mass-mediated political effects have varied through the years. Studies of voting behavior in the 1940s and 1950s indicated limited effects from mass media, but later studies found more direct and powerful media influences on voters.

Since the 1970s the number of studies of political communication effects has increased considerably. These studies have examined micro-level (affecting individuals) and macro-level (affecting society or the system) effects from political communications.

Several dynamic influences affect the nature of political communications in a society: the social scene, the political landscape, the media environment, and media content. Media influence on the political communication process is considerable in the United States; therefore, the media have a responsibility to provide a number of special functions.

Political advertising constitutes the primary form of communication between political candidates and the voting public. Political ads on television have been effective in presenting particular candidate images to the voting public, providing information about key issues, and sometimes influencing voting decisions.

Political communication is also influenced by the content of news stories and, specifically, their frames and news flaws. Frames are abstract notions that media professionals use to present news stories in a particular way. Framing devices often influence audiences' perceptions and interpretations. The four common flaws in news coverage are personalization, fragmentation, dramatization, and normalization.

Media effects research at the micro level usually falls into four divisions: formation and change of opinion; cognitive effects (including agenda-setting research, priming, knowledge gain, and framing); effects on individual perceptions of the political system; and effects on political behavior or participation. Macro-level studies, though problematic, seek to examine effects on systems, or effects on individuals that affect systems.

At either level, the nature and strength of effects from mediated political communication depend on a number of different factors, which have to do with certain characteristics or orientations of individual audience members and their processing of media messages.

fifteen

Media Effects on Health

> *Just say no.*
> —Drug Abuse Resistance Education (DARE) Program slogan

- A health communication campaign for AIDS awareness results in an increase in the use of condoms.
- After seeing a program about Farrah Fawcett's battle with anal cancer, a woman phones her doctor to make an appointment for a check-up.
- In the grocery store, a child begs his mother for a box of sweetened cereal that he has seen advertised during cartoon programming.
- After watching *Bridget Jones's Diary*, a teenage girl decides to start smoking and drinking like the character in the movie.

Mass media messages often have considerable impact on personal and public health. Mass media have served as essential components in a number of important health communication campaigns in recent years (Rice & Atkin, 2009). Communication campaigns attempt (often with successful results) to change or initiate attitudes and behaviors. The goal of the media health communication campaign is to present specific messages, designed by health and communication experts, which have intentional, positive, health-related effects on audiences.

Media campaigns are but one type of health communication presented via media. Every day audiences are inundated with a wide variety of health-related messages from the Internet, news reports, prime-time entertainment programs, daytime soaps, countless advertisements, and the effects from such messages are not always positive in nature. Studies have shown that Americans have long obtained much of their health-related information from mass media (Sandman, 1976), and this creates a problem when one considers that much of that health information, and many of the health behaviors presented to audiences, result in negative (albeit many times unintended) effects on their health.

> If we step back and look at the general picture of health provided in these most pervasive of media, we find a world in which people eat, drink, and have sex with abandonment but seldom suffer the consequences. Research shows that the audience does learn from these images and that, in general, what they learn is not good for their health. (Brown & Walsh-Childers, 1994, p. 409)

As with other types of media content, research has shown that effects from health-related messages may be positive or negative and intended or unintended in nature. This chapter will examine some of the research findings for effects from cigarette, alcohol, prescription drug, and food advertisements, and also explore the effects of entertainment portrayals, the nature of health news coverage, and the importance of the Internet in providing health-related information to millions. We will also discuss the use of health campaigns and other educational strategies designed to bring about individual health improvements or prompt positive changes at the policy level.

It should be remembered that the study of effects of health communication is a relatively young domain; many of the most important studies have been conducted since the 1970s. Much has been learned from research in recent years, especially the vast evidence that media can significantly affect health beliefs and behaviors on the individual level and public health level, for better or for worse (Walsh-Childers & Brown, 2009).

Research Findings

Many of the studies that have examined the effects of media messages on health have concentrated on advertisements, entertainment portrayals, news reports, and in recent years, the Internet. These messages have had either unintentional positive impacts or negative impacts on viewers, or they have been intentionally designed to promote healthier lifestyles.

Effects of Advertisements, Media Usage, and Entertainment Portrayals on Health

Research on the effects of commercial product advertising, media usage, and entertainment portrayals has focused primarily upon the health of individuals who use the products. Walsh-Childers and Brown (2009) reviewed the literature on the mediated health effects from four types of products: tobacco, alcoholic beverages, prescription drugs, and foods.

Tobacco

More than 20 million Americans smoke cigarettes. Cigarette advertisements have been banned from broadcast media in the United States since 1971, but the ban has not stopped tobacco companies from using other means to advertise their products. Print media, billboards, sponsorship of sporting events—such forums have kept cigarette ads in clear view of the public despite the broadcast ban.

One recent study found that exposure to characters in movies smoking and exposure to and receptivity of tobacco ads were associated with smoking among

Although cigarette advertisements have been banned from broadcast media in the U.S. since 1971, tobacco companies have found other ways—like sponsorship of sporting events—to keep their products in public view.

10- to 14-year-olds (Sargent, 2009). Nunez-Smith et al. (2010) reviewed dozens of quantitative studies on the connection between media usage and abuse of tobacco, alcohol, and drugs. They found that 83 percent of the studies found a causal relationship between media exposure and smoking initiation and use of alcohol and illicit drugs, and the evidence was strongest for the association between media use and tobacco use.

Sargent et al. (2005) surveyed adolescents aged 10 to 14 years and used statistical methods to identify a causal link between exposure to movie smoking and the onset of smoking among adolescents, and these researchers found that exposure to movie smoking is the greatest single risk factor determining smoking initiation among American youths.

Through the years, numerous studies have examined the effects of various cigarette advertising or promotional appeals. Research has shown that 90 percent of the people who smoke started smoking during adolescence (U.S. Dept.

of Health and Human Services, 1994). With the decline in smoking among White, middle-class males, tobacco companies have targeted cigarette ads to entice other segments of the population, such as women, minorities, and, arguably, children (Davis, 1987; Basil et al., 1991), and they have increased their level of advertising in other countries, many of which have fewer restrictions on cigarette advertising than does the United States. Even though tobacco company executives say they do not direct their ads to children or adolescents, research has shown that youngsters recognize the symbols and slogans of various cigarettes (Aitken, Leathar, & O'Hagan, 1985; Aitken, Leathar, & Squair, 1986). After Joe Camel ("Old Joe") appeared as the trademark for Camel cigarettes, the desire for Camel cigarettes increased from .5 percent to 32 percent among young smokers in a three-year period (DiFranza et al., 1991). The higher the ad recognition, the more likely one is to smoke (Goldstein, Fischer, Richards, & Creten, 1987). Bloom and his colleagues (1997) found an association between cigarette use among adolescents and watching stock car racing (where tobacco products are heavily advertised).

Studies in Australia revealed that adolescents are particularly attracted to brands of cigarettes that use "lifestyle" appeals in advertising. More than 75 percent of the adolescent smokers used brands that advertised in this way (Chapman & Egger, 1980; Chapman & Fitzgerald, 1982). Another study of Australian children revealed that approval of cigarette ads was second only to the smoking behavior of peers as a predictor of a child's smoking behavior (O'Connell et al., 1981).

Other studies have explored various issues related to the warning labels on tobacco product advertisements. One study tracked the eye movements of adolescents who were shown tobacco ads in magazines, and it found that almost half the children did not read the warning at all. Those who did look at the warning did so only briefly (Fischer, Richards, Berman, & Krugman, 1989). In another study, Davis and Kendrick (1989) found that the warning notices for tobacco ads on billboards and on taxis were very hard to read—yet the brand name of the cigarette could be clearly seen.

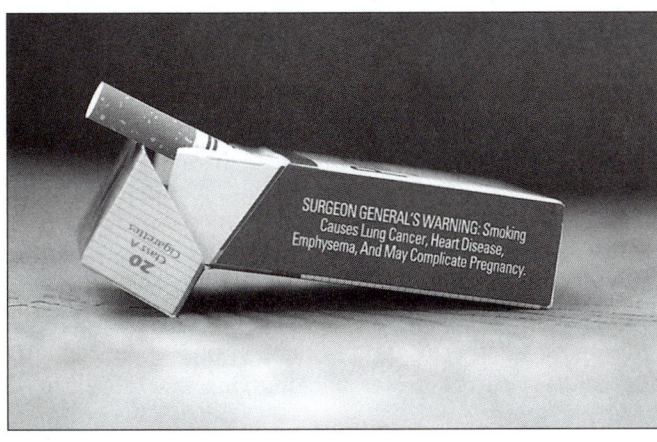

Cigarette warnings on package labels are somewhat more noticeable than warning notices that appear in print advertisements for tobacco products. © *Heather Swolsky*

Biener & Siegel (2000) found that exposure to cigarette ads in print media, on the Internet, and via radio, and also ownership of caps or lighters that have cigarette brand logos on them, were all related to an increase in tobacco use among the young.

Tobacco companies now spend more advertising dollars at the point of purchase than on all other advertising outlets (including billboards and the Internet) combined (Rabin, 2007). They tend to advertise in convenience stores that are near schools and in neighborhoods that have high numbers of teens and younger children (Woodruff, Agro, Wildey, & Conway, 1995; Pucci, Joseph, & Siegel, 1998). Henriksen and Flora (2001) found through experimental methods that ads inside convenience stores make youngsters more aware that tobacco is available and make them perceive that it is popular, and these perceptions make them more likely to start smoking. Internet advertising of tobacco products and Internet vendors of tobacco products cause concern for researchers and policy makers (Ribisl, Kim, & Williams, 2007).

Alcohol

Alcohol consumption has been known to result in battered spouses and children, rapes, and even murders (Fals-Stewart, 2003; Grant, 2000). More young people use and abuse alcohol than they do any other drug, including cigarettes and marijuana (Johnston et al., 2004).

One recent study determined that watching movie characters use alcohol is associated with early-onset of drinking among 10- to 14-year-olds (Sargent et al., 2006). A number of other studies have focused on the effects of alcohol use on the young. Grube (2004) found that the earlier a person starts drinking, the more dire the effects on health, both short-term and long-term. Binge drinking (usually defined as having five or more drinks at a time) is a serious problem in Europe, even more than in the United States (Kantrowitz & Underwood, 2007).

Research on the effects of alcohol advertising on personal and public health has generally focused on (1) whether such ads entice adolescents to start drinking, or (2) whether such ads cause increased alcohol consumption and, perhaps, drunk driving among established drinkers. With regard to the first of these issues, Atkin and his associates (1984) surveyed a group of adolescents and found that their likelihood to drink either beer or liquor was directly related to their exposure to TV alcohol ads. Moreover, other factors such as age, sex, social status, or parental influence were not as strong predictors of drinking behavior as was exposure to the TV ads. Rather than rely on evidence from this one survey, Atkin (1990) reviewed the body of research related to this issue and determined that alcohol ads on television *do seem to encourage* drinking among adolescents. Another study showed that the exposure of adolescents to football and basketball events where alcohol was promoted was linked to subsequent use of beer (Bloom, Hogan, & Blazing, 1997). Some alcohol brands associate alcohol use with fun, feature outdoor activities in their ads, and use animals like the Budweiser Clydesdales; all these features have strong appeal among youngsters (Collins, Ellickson, McCaffrey, & Hambarsoomians, 2007; Zwarun & Farrar, 2005).

Some alcohol brands associate their products with animals and other appealing features with which young people identify. *Christopher Halloran/Shutterstock.com*

When young people see desirable models in alcohol ads and identify with them, they are more likely to think that drinking is going to be a positive experience and are therefore more likely to engage in drinking (Austin & Knaus, 2000). Austin, Chen, and Grube (2006) found that parents can lessen the harmful effects of alcohol ads on their children by talking to their children and using proper guidance.

Prescription Drugs

In 1997, the Food and Drug Administration decided to allow prescription drug manufacturers to advertise their drugs directly to consumers via mass media, including magazines (Curry, Jarosch, & Pacholok, 2005) and television (Brownfield et al., 2004; Frosch et al., 2007).

Research has shown that these advertisements influence many people's behaviors. One survey (Murray et al., 2004) found that 6 percent of those surveyed talked to their doctor about the advertised drug, and about 30 percent of the people who discussed the drug with their doctors were prescribed the medication. Another 11.5 percent were prescribed the drug, even though their doctors did not think it would help them.

Food

A large amount of research on the effects of food advertisements on consumer health has focused on children. Studies have shown that food commercials may have positive or negative effects, depending upon the nutritional value of the food advertised.

Obesity in children and teens has been a primary concern for researchers (James et al., 2001; Ogden et al., 2002; Wang, Monteiro, & Popkin, 2002) and many research findings suggest that watching food ads on television is strongly related to childhood obesity (Committee on Food Marketing, 2006). Goldberg, Gorn, and Gibson (1978) found that TV food ads did influence the short-term and long-term food preferences of children, yet parental eating habits were much more influential than the commercials in determining a child's diet. When one considers the vast number of ads for food items that have low nutritional value, such a finding suggests negative health consequences.

On the positive side, Kellogg's campaign for All-Bran cereal during the 1980s used information from the National Cancer Institute to stress the healthy (anticancer) benefits of a diet high in fiber and low in fat. Studies found that as a result of this campaign, more people started eating high-fiber, low-fat foods (such as All-Bran) and more people became aware of the importance of nutrition in preventing particular types of cancer (Freimuth, Hammond, & Stein, 1988; Levy & Stokes, 1987).

Television and Health

Smoking and drinking or references to drinking are common on today's television programs. Roberts and Christenson (2000) found that approximately 20 percent of prime-time television episodes depicted characters who smoked. Alcohol use and references were not only found in adult programming, but also on teen shows (Christenson, Henriksen, & Roberts, 2000).

Another issue studied is the link between viewing television programs with predominantly thin characters and the effects on viewers' body image. In fact, the "slim standard" in America and its resulting health problems have spread to remote corners of the globe. An article in *Newsweek* (May 31, 1999) noted that teenage girls in the South Pacific island of Fiji (traditionally a culture with a full-figure ideal body type) began showing signs of serious eating disorders after Western programs with their pencil-thin actresses arrived in 1995. Researchers were reluctant to attribute all the blame to television alone, but it seemed to be a central factor in the mix. Becker (2004) and Becker et al. (2003) found that Fiji girls who watched the most television were precisely the ones who considered themselves too fat, and of those, two of three had resorted to dieting to lose the unwanted pounds. Moreover, 15 percent of those studied said they had used vomiting as a way of controlling their weight.

Other studies of the link between television viewing and nutrition have found that time spent watching television is a good predictor of weight problems in adolescents (Berkey et al., 2000; Dennison, Erb, & Jenkins, 2002; Dietz, 1990; Dietz & Gortmaker, 1985; Saelens et al., 2002). A study in the 1970s had already established that children who are heavy TV watchers also eat more snacks between meals than do light viewers (Clancy-Hepburn, Hickey, & Neville, 1974). More current studies have confirmed this (Coon et al., 2001; Matheson et al., 2004).

Sexual activity on television has become increasingly abundant and explicit in recent years, but few references are made to safe sex practices or commitments

(Escobar-Chaves et al., 2005; Kunkel et al., 2007). The number of references to and portrayals of homosexuality on television has increased considerably in recent years (see Chapter 12). Studies continue to show that exposure to sexual activity on television results in adolescents having sex earlier in life (Ashby, Arcari, & Edmonson, 2006; Collins et al., 2004).

Films and Health

As for cigarettes, alcohol, and illegal drugs, studies have shown that most movies regularly feature characters using alcohol and tobacco products (Roberts & Christensen, 2000). One study showed that actors in current films smoke about as much as actors on the screens of the 1950s (Glantz, Kacirk, & McCulloch, 2004). Even G-rated movies and three out of four Disney animated classics are not alcohol and tobacco-free (Thompson & Yokota, 2001; Ryan & Hoerrner, 2004).

Studies show that good characters as well as bad characters can be found smoking and/or drinking on the screen (Goldstein, Sobel, & Newman, 1999). In 2000, a study showed that the use of illegal drugs in movies did not occur so often as smoking and drinking, the ill effects of drug use were often portrayed, and drug addicts were usually portrayed as evil (Roberts & Christenson, 2000).

The images of sexual activities in film have been demonstrated to have various potential ill effects on the health of audience members. Studies in the 1980s on the effects of sexually explicit films revealed that male college students tended to trivialize rape as a crime and showed more sexually callous attitudes toward women after viewing such films (Zillmann & Bryant, 1982). Others found similar effects, but only in sexually explicit films that also contained violence (Linz, Donnerstein, & Penrod, 1988). Zillmann and Bryant (1988a) later determined that viewers (college students and nonstudent adults) of nonviolent but sexually explicit films were more likely than nonviewers to accept sexual infidelity or promiscuous behavior.

Music Lyrics, Music Videos, and Health

Since the 1980s, many contemporary rock music lyrics and music videos have emphasized physical (rather than romantic) sex, violence, and sometimes, violent sexual encounters (Fedler, Hall, & Tanzi, 1982; Sherman & Etling, 1991). The preponderance of such lyrics and depictions in rock and rap music today has led some researchers to suspect a negative effect on teen health, including teenage pregnancy, suicide, substance abuse, and sexual assault (Brown & Hendee, 1989; Gore, 1987). One study found that adolescents who watched a large number of rock music videos were more likely than other children to feel that premarital sex was okay (Greeson & Williams, 1986). Other studies revealed similar negative effects from heavy viewing of music videos and frequent listening to music with negative lyrics (Klein et al., 1993).

Roberts and Christenson (2000) found that drinking was mentioned in about 10 percent of country music songs. Rap/hip-hop and rock music videos often portray people drinking and using illicit drugs (Durant et al., 1997; Gruber et al., 2005). In the late 1990s, researchers found that three out of four music videos portrayed people smoking (Durant et al., 1997).

Effects of Health News

Research on the effects of health-related news has shown that people pay most attention to stories about public health issues among all health-related stories, but they also pay attention to public health policy stories and stories about specific diseases (Brodie et al., 2003).

Many studies of health-related news include measures of behavioral effects experienced after seeing certain news stories. For example, studies have shown that news coverage of the dangers of smoking can have a significant effect on the number of people who decide to kick the habit (Pierce & Gilpin, 2001). The use of marijuana among teens, as well as their attitudes about marijuana, can be affected by news coverage (Stryker, 2003). News stories about suicides can result in copycat suicides, but news outlets can mitigate negative effects by not revealing all the details of the death (Stack, 2005).

News stories can also have effects on public health policy. The way a health story is framed can have an impact on how the public and policy makers view the problem (Dorfman & Wallack, 2007). Intense media scrutiny on a particular health problem (Reese & Danielian, 1989; Shoemaker, Wanta, & Leggett, 1989) or controversial treatment (Benelli, 2003) can also cause governing officials to act, sometimes prematurely.

Walsh-Childers (1994a, 1994b) found that health-related news has its greatest impact on public policy when health experts are in agreement on how to solve health problems, when the change comes at the state or local level, and when news coverage supports the efforts of either private groups or public officials who are trying to bring about change.

Health and the Internet

The majority of Internet users—70 to 80 percent of them—search online for health-related information, and such searches are among the most common personal uses of the Internet (Greenberg, D'Andrea, & Lorence, 2003). Research has shown that females, people younger than 65, those experienced in using the Internet, and those with high-speed Internet connections (Fox, 2006) are more likely to go online to search for health-related information.

Even though many people are seeking out health topics on the Internet, the amount of information can overwhelm and confuse them (Fox, 2006). One study showed that people who seek information about their illnesses on the Internet are more likely to use the information to formulate questions for their physicians during doctor visits (Bass et al., 2006). Other studies have found that websites can contain inaccuracies and the quality of information is sometimes substandard (Eysenbach et al., 2002; Powell et al., 2005). Most people who get health information from Internet websites do not check on the validity of the information or other measures of information quality, such as the date of the material (Eysenbach & Köhler, 2002; Fox, 2006).

Research Spotlight

Let Your Conscience Be Your Guide: Smoking and Drinking in Disney's Animated Classics
Erin L. Ryan and Keisha L. Hoerrner (2004)
Mass Communication & Society, 7(3), 261–278

These researchers content analyzed 24 Disney G-rated, animated, feature-length motion pictures from 1937 to 2000, looking for instances of tobacco and alcohol use. They found 381 instances of substance use with no antiuse messages in the films.

Research Questions

RQ1: Are tobacco and alcohol products present in G-rated, feature-length, animated Disney films released between 1937 and 2000?

RQ2: If so, what is the context surrounding the use of such products?

RQ3: Do such occurrences decrease over time?

Operational Definitions

An incident of exposure to tobacco and alcohol products was defined as each instance of continuous display of a tobacco or alcohol product on the screen (Thompson & Yokota, 2001). Whenever a character was shown holding or using an alcohol or tobacco product, the elapsed time of the incident was recorded and timed with a stopwatch. Personified alcohol or tobacco products were also included in the analysis.

Researchers also coded the context surrounding the presence of tobacco and alcohol in the films, whether "shown only on screen," or if the character responded to the product by accepting or rejecting it. Also, if characters reacted positively to the use of the product, or encouraged the use of it, or were attempting to make the viewers laugh, it was coded as accepted. Negative reactions were coded as rejected.

Characters were classified as adult, teenager, or child. Protagonists, antagonists, and supporting characters were also coded. Personified products were coded as supporting characters.

Sample

The animated Disney classics included the following:

Snow White and the Seven Dwarfs (1937)	*Beauty and the Beast* (1991)
Pinocchio (1940)	*Aladdin* (1992)
Dumbo (1941)	*Pocahontas* (1995)
Cinderella (1950)	*The Hunchback of Notre Dame* (1996)
Alice in Wonderland (1951)	*The Rescuers* (1977)
Peter Pan (1953)	*The Fox and the Hound* (1981)
Lady and the Tramp (1955)	*Oliver and Company* (1988)
Sleeping Beauty (1959)	*The Little Mermaid* (1989)
101 Dalmatians (1961)	*Hercules* (1997)
The Sword in the Stone (1963)	*Mulan* (1998)
The Jungle Book (1967)	*Tarzan* (1999)
The Aristocats (1970)	*The Emperor's New Groove* (2000)

Results

The researchers coded 381 incidents of alcohol and tobacco exposure (106 tobacco and 275 alcohol) within the 24 films. The answer to RQ1 was yes. Only three of the films contained no alcohol or tobacco: *The Jungle Book*, *The Fox and the Hound*, and *Mulan*.

(continued)

Eighteen films contained at least one tobacco exposure; and 18 contained at least one alcohol exposure. The pipe was the most frequently shown tobacco product, then the cigar and the cigarette. Beer, followed by wine, champagne, and spirits were most frequently shown. Only 9 of the films did not have any cigar exposure, 10 did not have pipe exposure, and only six did not contain wine exposure.

Films were divided into decades (the 1937 film was included in the 1940s group) and a chi square was performed between release date by decade and type of exposure. The results showed that throughout time, tobacco exposure declined but alcohol exposure increased.

In terms of context and RQ2, 91 percent of exposures to the products were accepted, and only 4 percent were rejected. Only four films contained rejections: *Pinocchio, Peter Pan, 101 Dalmatians*, and *The Sword in the Stone*. Only one film, *Pinocchio*, depicted rejection of alcohol products.

Three films had scenes with children using alcohol or tobacco products: *Pinocchio, Peter Pan*, and *Oliver and Company*. Teen consumption of either alcohol or tobacco was present in *Peter Pan, The Little Mermaid*, and *Aladdin*. Of all instances of cigar use in the films, children accounted for 22 percent. Anti-use sentiment was almost completely absent from all the films.

RQ3 could be answered in the affirmative for tobacco but not for alcohol.

Reference

Thompson, K. M., & Yokota, F. (2001). Depiction of alcohol, tobacco, and other substances in G-rated animated feature films. *Pediatrics, 107*(6), 1369–1374.

Health Communication Campaign Effects

Health campaigns involve the purposive use of mass media for health education and behavioral change. Such campaigns have been used worldwide with varying levels of success (Brown & Walsh-Childers, 1994).

For whatever reason, some media health campaigns have not produced long-term behavioral changes whereas others have; some have produced positive, intended effects whereas others have produced negative, unintended effects; and some have produced a variety of effects. For an example of the latter, a North Dakota media campaign to promote mammography screening found that although the campaign seemed to encourage women who had already been screened to have another screening, it seemed to adversely affect women who had never had a mammogram (McCaul, Jacobson, & Martinson, 1998).

The public health campaigns in the 1980s that were designed to raise AIDS awareness and change at-risk behaviors succeeded in raising the awareness of the general public, but they also increased *anxieties* about the disease. Moreover, these campaigns, both in Great Britain and the United States, failed to reach high-risk audiences such as drug users (Department of Health and Social Security and the Welsh Office, 1987; Snyder, Anderson, & Young, 1989). Subsequent research revealed that sometimes media interventions *are* consumed by at-risk audiences and *do* result in the desired effects—in this case more positive behavioral change (Elwood & Ataabadi, 1996; Guenther-Grey, Schnell, & Fishbein, 1995). The sidebar "Risk Learning and Stereotype Priming Models" offers two models aimed at persuading people to engage in healthy and risk-free behaviors.

Risk Learning and Stereotype Priming Models

Pechmann (2001) offered descriptions of two different types of complementary models aimed at persuading people to engage in more healthy behaviors and avoid health risks. **Risk-learning models** operate with the goal of relating "new information about health risks and the behaviors that will minimize those risks," while **stereotype priming models** attempt to use "salient preexisting social stereotypes about people who do or do not behave as advocated" (p. 189) for the purpose of persuading people to avoid behaviors that cause health risks. Risk-learning models are based on protection motivation theory, which means they work to motivate behaviors that promote and protect good health. Four types of messages have been shown to increase a person's likelihood to engage in protective behavior. These include messages that

- show the severe disease consequences of engaging in risky behavior (risk severity)
- show how easy it is to contract the disease (risk vulnerability)
- show how protective behaviors reduce chances for or prevent or cure the disease (response efficacy)
- show effectiveness when engaging in protective behavior (self-efficacy)

The stereotype priming model depends upon a priming stimulus and preexisting links between a particular social group and particular behavior traits. For example, in a campaign that discourages smoking, cigarette smokers might be presented using negative stereotypical traits (e.g., having yellow teeth or smelling like tobacco), while nonsmokers would be shown with positive stereotypical traits (e.g., enjoying good health). According to Pechmann:

> Risk-learning models do not require message recipients to have any prior knowledge of the substantive message content. The main goal is, in fact, to impart knowledge where it is lacking. By comparison, the stereotype priming model requires the use of messages that reflect people's prior stereotypes. In other words, the prime must mirror or correspond to a belief that already resides in long-term memory. Priming merely serves to bring a preexisting stereotype to the forefront of memory. (p. 195)

Source: Pechmann, C. (2001). A comparison of health communication models: Risk learning versus stereotype priming, *Media Psychology, 3,* 189–210.

The use of different communication channels has also produced inconsistent findings across studies. Some studies have indicated that a campaign featuring a combination of mass media messages and interpersonal communications may be the most effective in producing desired attitudinal or behavioral changes (Flynn et al., 1994; Guenther-Grey et al., 1995; Svenkerud, Rao, & Rogers, 1999). Others, however, have shown that exposure to mass media messages alone was responsible for the changes in behaviors or attitudes (McDivitt, Zimicki, & Hornick, 1997). The differences in results may be attributable to fundamental differences in the campaigns themselves or to the degree of their adherence to the key principles for campaign success.

Different antitobacco campaigns also serve as good examples of campaigns that produced different results. A five-year antitobacco campaign in Minnesota resulted in teens reporting increased exposure to antismoking messages from the mass media, but these exposures had little effect on their beliefs about the health dangers of tobacco or on their smoking behaviors (Murray, Prokhorov, & Harty, 1994). On the other hand, a study by Flynn and his colleagues (1994), also conducted over several years, revealed that media interventions *in addition to* school smoking prevention programs resulted in rather positive behavioral effects. Students from two communities participated in smoking prevention programs at their schools. One group received mass media interventions in addition to the school program, and over time, the behavior of this group showed more positive results than did those who did not receive the interventions (Flynn et al., 1994).

Another study revealed that a different type of combination approach—in this case, a media antismoking campaign together with a cigarette sales tax—proved most effective in reducing cigarette consumption. The researchers examined cigarette sales from 1980 to 1992 and found that both tactics resulted in several million packs fewer being sold. The level of the effects varied, depending on the amount of the tax and the amount spent on the media campaign (Hu, Sung, & Keeler, 1995).

One health campaign approach that has regained attention in recent years is the scare tactic or fear appeal. Such campaigns targeted toward smokers in Massachusetts and in Australia have resulted in much public attention (measured by phone calls to antismoking counseling services and phone interviews with those who saw the ads), but overall effects from these campaigns are not yet known. In Massachusetts, the campaign featured commercials showing a 29-year-old mother battling emphysema and awaiting a second lung transplant (Worden & Flynn, 1999).

Other findings suggest that the use of fear appeals in health communication campaigns has been rather successful (Hale & Dillard, 1995). Quantitative reviews of fear-appeal research have shown that such appeals are persuasive (Mongeau, 1998; Sutton, 1982). According to Hale and Dillard (1995):

> The most recent of the meta-analyses, and by virtue of including several newer studies perhaps the best of the lot, concluded that perceived fear and the attitude of the target were positively correlated, as were perceived fear and behavior. It is clear from these findings that fear-arousing message content is persuasive and that abandoning the use of fear would be to abandon an effective persuasive strategy. . . . [T]he quantitative reviews also demonstrate that the relationship between fear and persuasion is a complex one. (p. 70)

Media health campaigns have sometimes been criticized for their "victim blaming" approaches. These campaigns offer individuals information that will allow them to take responsibility for their health by changing their lifestyles or going for health screenings. Critics argue that victims cannot take full blame for their actions when they have been bombarded since childhood with advertisements or media portrayals that feature the use of unhealthy products such as cigarettes or alcoholic beverages (Wallack, 1989).

Summary

Mass media messages often have considerable impact on personal and public health. As with other types of media content, effects from health-related messages may be positive or negative, and they can be intended or unintended in nature.

The goal of the media health communication campaign is to present specific messages, designed by health and communication experts, which have intentional, positive, health-related effects on audiences. Other sources of health-related messages in mass media—news reports, entertainment programs, and advertisements—do not always produce positive results.

Research on the effects of commercial product advertising has focused primarily upon the health of individuals who use the products. Health effects from cigarette, liquor, prescription drug, and food ads have been the focus of numerous studies; most have found that such ads result in negative effects on individual and public health.

Entertainment portrayals sometimes have rather powerful effects upon the health of audience members. Most studies in this area have concentrated on television programs, films, music videos, and musical lyrics, establishing links between entertainment portrayals and nutrition, smoking, alcohol consumption, drug abuse, and sexual activity.

People, including policy makers, obtain much of their health-related information from news media. In this respect, news coverage of health matters takes on much significance, because it has the potential to shape the impressions of average citizens and powerful policy makers alike. Some news coverage adopts a "victim-blaming" attitude which places most responsibility for the health problem on the shoulders of the victim or patient. Most of the news reports on health issues focus on concerns that affect mainstream America.

Health campaigns involve the purposive use of mass media for health education and behavioral change. For whatever reason, some media health campaigns have not produced long-term behavioral changes whereas others have; some have produced positive, intended effects while others have produced negative, unintended effects; and some have produced a mixed bag of effects.

The appeal to fear has persuasive power in communication campaigns. Some media campaigns have been criticized for using victim-blaming approaches. Certain media channels used in campaigns have characteristic benefits over other media channels. Health communication planners must assess the advantages and disadvantages of the different media when selecting channels for the delivery of their messages.

sixteen

The Effects of Stereotyping

In a lot of films, they're showing more complete, developed characters of diverse ethnic backgrounds. The larger concern is to be able to tastefully explore the stereotypes, and still move past them to see the core of people.
—Forest Whitaker, 2007 Academy Award winner for Best Actor

During the turbulent 1960s, African Americans in the United States fought for and gained their civil rights. Since then, other minority groups have stepped forward and demanded not only equal rights, but also social acceptance and recognition. These other groups include those different from others due to race, gender, religion, sexual orientation, physical challenges, or other factors.

In the past few decades, people of all colors and differences have begun to show more respect and tolerance for one another. But our society still has many miles to cover on the road to harmonious relations among the various races, creeds, and orientations. Many people still hold prejudices. Many are oblivious to the needs and feelings of others. Many wrongs remain to be righted.

Since the 1960s, portrayals of minority characters in mass media, particularly on television and in film, have reflected some of these societal changes. These changes in portrayals and, especially, their effects upon audiences' attitudes, values, and behaviors, are of particular interest to communication researchers. Many studies of stereotyping from the 1970s and 1980s offer useful information about those years.

Studies of the 1990s showed that Blacks achieved very positive gains in both the number and the nature of their portrayals in entertainment programs, but other minorities did not fare so well. Latinos, Asian Americans, Native Americans, and women continued to be underrepresented in mass media, sometimes to the point of exclusion. When members of these groups were depicted, it was sometimes in stereotypical or demeaning ways (Greenberg, Mastro, & Brand, 2002; Mastro, 2009; Smith & Granados, 2009).

Previous chapters have revealed the power of mass media to affect the cognitions or mental processes of media users. We learned that media messages are sometimes responsible for changing a person's attitudes and values. For better or worse, these changes may also alter a person's behavior.

This chapter explores the nature of media portrayals of race, ethnic minorities, and gender and their effects upon audiences. You will recall from Chapter 8 on cultivation research that the real world is often very different from the world portrayed on television and in the movies. Research analyses of media content have examined whether or not minority characters are present, how they compare to other characters, the significance of the minority characters, and the interaction of minority characters with others. Other studies have explored the differences of minority and majority viewers in terms of their preferences for content and characters.

First, we take a look back at how media have portrayed minorities in the past, then at how the media convey social information to audiences today through minority portrayals in entertainment programs, news reports, and advertisements. We examine the current state of minority portrayals in the media, the characteristics of minorities who use mass media, then look at the effects of media on racial, ethnic, and gender stereotyping.

Minority Portrayals in Entertainment: A Look Back

Television

Some of the first head count studies were conducted in the 1970s, when the proportion of minority characters on television fell far below their societal percentages. Two major head count studies examined television portrayals throughout the entire decade of the 1970s (Seggar, Hafen, & Hannonen-Gladden, 1981; Gerbner & Signorielli, 1979). These found that the percentage of White characters increased even beyond their actual percentage in the population, the percentage of Black characters increased slightly but remained below their societal percentages, and non-Black minority characters were practically nonexistent on television. The programs assessed included comedies, dramas, and movies (Seggar et al., 1981).

Another study also focused on television programs during the 1970s and reported somewhat similar findings. Communication scholars Gerbner and Signorielli (1979) analyzed the minority representation in television programs as a part of their Cultural Indicators Project. They found that the number of non-White characters accounted for an average of 11 percent of all characters per year. The year of greatest representation was 1977, when 14 percent of characters in prime-time dramatic programs were non-White, a percentage point above their societal percentages. (Whites accounted for slightly more than 87 percent of the U.S. population during the 1970s.)

In the late 1990s, the television networks responded to demands from minority activist groups by featuring more Black characters on prime time, but

During a time when non-Black minority characters were rare on prime-time television, "Hop Sing" (actor Victor Sen Yung) was a regular on the popular *Bonanza* series. *Photo courtesy of Bonanza Ventures/Andrew J. Klyde Collection. Copyright © 1959. All rights reserved.*

similar increases were not experienced by other minorities, such as Asian Americans, Hispanic Americans, or Native Americans (Greenberg et al., 2002). One study revealed that the number of Black characters on prime-time television was in excess of their actual percentage in society at that time (12 percent), with Blacks appearing in 16 percent of major and lesser prime-time roles (Mastro & Greenberg, 2000). Still, television does not reflect America's colors accurately, as other minority groups remain as underrepresented in major network programming today as they were 20 years ago (Mastro & Greenberg, 2000; Greenberg et al., 2002). In the early 1990s, only 1.1 to 1.6 percent of characters on television were Hispanic, despite actual population figures of 11 percent. One study showed that Hispanics made up 3 percent of the roles in prime-time fictional programming, Asian Americans only 1 percent, and Native Americans, less than 1 percent (Mastro & Greenberg, 2000; Greenberg et al., 2002).

Motion Pictures

In cinema, historically, Blacks and other minorities have been cast in roles that specifically call for a minority character; however, this began to change in the 1990s. Film star Halle Berry felt that her supporting role in the 1994 live-action version of *The Flintstones* was a breakthrough because "it was a part that could've gone to anybody. It could've gone to a White actress. But it went to me" (Ivry, 1998, p. 3G). In another example, Will Smith's portrayal of James West in the action adventure movie *Wild Wild West* represented another instance when a leading role could have gone to anyone, but happened to go to a Black actor. Denzel Washington's role in *The Pelican Brief* and Morgan Freeman's role as the President of the United States in *Deep Impact* are other examples of this. More recently, Danny Glover portrayed the President of the United States in the global disaster film *2012*.

Many films in the 1990s broke new ground by featuring Blacks in starring roles. Moreover, many of the more recent films do not portray the minority characters in stereotypical ways; that is, as criminals or inner-city residents. Stars such as Cuba Gooding, Jr., Denzel Washington, Samuel L. Jackson, Morgan Freeman, Halle Berry, Vanessa Williams, Vivica A. Fox, and the late Whitney Houston have landed roles that "could've gone to anybody," as Berry put it.

These stars have also proven that they can attract audiences of different races to a variety of different film genres. As Zhou, Greer, and Finklea (2010) noted:

> Some [actors] are known for their big-budget, action-packed summer films, others for their comedic talents, and some are known for the interesting character pieces they choose. For many of Hollywood's most famous actors and actresses, the brightness of their star power outshines the color of their skin. (p. 11)

Will Smith, for example, has proven to have broad box office appeal with a string of blockbusters, such as *Hitch, Pursuit of Happyness, Hancock, I Am Legend*, and *I, Robot.*

Advertising

Like entertainment portrayals of minorities, advertising images historically have been mostly White (Coltrane & Messineo, 2000; Wilson & Gutierrez, 1995). Blacks and Asian Americans have made significant gains in some media in the past few decades although other minorities remain underrepresented. The nature of the portrayals of Blacks, however, has been a cause for concern in the past (Greenberg & Brand, 1994).

From the 1940s to the 1960s, Blacks appeared in only about 3 percent of the ads in national magazines. Those that appeared usually fell into one of three categories: well-known entertainers, famous athletes, or unknowns depicted as servants (Colfax & Steinberg, 1972; Kassarjian, 1969; Stempel, 1971).

Two studies in the late 1970s found that the situation for Blacks in advertisements had not improved, and had actually deteriorated. One found a mere 2 percent presence of Blacks in magazine ads (Bush, Resnick, & Stern, 1980). A second study reviewed 8,700 advertisements for new products or services in issues of *Time, Cosmopolitan, Reader's Digest,* and *Ladies' Home Journal* from 1968 to 1977. Of this total, fewer than 1 percent featured Black models or characters (Reid & Vanden Bergh, 1980).

The situation did not change significantly in the 1980s. Jackson and Ervin (1991) examined almost a thousand ads from 1986 to 1988 that appeared in *Cosmopolitan, Glamour,* and *Vogue.* Only 2.4 percent of the ads featured Black women models, and of those 83 percent portrayed the Black woman from a distance. At that time, Blacks accounted for more than 12 percent of the female population of the United States and 15 percent of the subscribers to the magazines examined.

Several studies in the 1970s and 1980s found that White magazine readers did not respond negatively to the use of Black models in ads (Block, 1972; Schlinger & Plummer, 1972; Soley, 1983). One of these studies measured the actual readership of ads featuring Black models. It found that the race of the model did not affect ad readership (Soley, 1983).

Beginning in the 1990s, more and more Black and Asian faces have appeared in television ads. In fact, they have gone from virtual nonexistence to more representative numbers, to *overrepresentation* by more than double the numbers of African Americans and Asian Americans in society. By 1994, Blacks appeared in more than 31 percent of all commercial advertisements featuring models (Taylor & Stern, 1997), far higher than their societal percentage. Asian Americans appeared in more than 8 percent of all commercial ads featuring models. This compares rather favorably to their societal percentage of only 3.6 percent (Greenberg et al., 2002). The years have not been so kind to Native Americans and the disabled, who largely have been avoided in media portrayals (Wilson & Gutierrez, 1995; Greenberg et al., 2002).

Character Role Comparisons

The significance of roles for minority characters is another area of study that received a great amount of scrutiny in the 1970s and 1980s, but relatively few studies have been conducted since then (Greenberg & Brand, 1994). Researchers have examined the roles played by Whites and non-Whites to discover how television is portraying them in terms of characterization, violence, occupations, age, and other factors. Most of these studies have focused on television programs, but a few have investigated print media and movies as well.

From 1975 to 1980, Black men enjoyed more minor roles and bit parts on television, but they were featured in fewer leading and supporting roles. Blacks accounted for 9 percent of the men in major roles in 1975, although in 1980 their number dropped to 4.5 percent. In 1975, Black males were featured in 12 percent of the supporting roles, and in 1980 only 4.5 percent. Black female appearances also declined between 1975 and 1980: in major roles to 2.4 percent, and in supporting roles to 2.7 percent (Seggar et al., 1981).

Another study of minorities in major and supporting roles during the 1970s offered similar findings (Gerbner & Signorielli, 1979). Blacks appeared in 8.5 percent of the major roles in the programs examined, whereas Hispanics accounted for only 2.5 percent of the major roles. The numbers showed a decline toward the end of the decade.

Interactions between Blacks and Whites on television programs in the 1970s were found to be friendly in nature or to exhibit mutual respect only about 13 percent of the time. The Black and White characters were rather equal in status in 7 of 10 episodes examined (Weigel, Loomis, & Soja, 1980).

Several studies have examined television characters in terms of their aggressiveness, heroism, and villainy. In 1970, Gerbner attempted to determine which television characters were committing acts of violence. He found that 66 percent of the non-Whites, 60 percent of the White foreigners, and 50 percent of the White Americans were responsible for acts of TV violence. Gerbner also found that non-White characters were usually victims. Nearly 10 years later, Gerbner and Signorielli (1979) found that two groups of non-Whites—Blacks and Native Americans—usually portrayed killers rather than victims, and that Whites, Asians, and Hispanics usually played characters that were killed by others. Non-Whites were not always depicted as the bad guys; they were about as likely as White characters to appear as either good guys or bad guys.

Characters of color usually appeared in blue-collar or service jobs rather than in prestigious positions during the 1970s and 1980s, yet the percentage of minority characters depicted in professional or white-collar jobs, although small, actually exceeded their numbers in society. In terms of age, three of five non-Whites were under 35. Two of three White males were over the age of 35 (Gerbner, Gross, & Signorielli, 1985).

During the 1970s and 1980s, disabled characters on TV rarely appeared in a positive light. They were usually portrayed as poor, out-of-work, or abused (Elliot & Byrd, 1982; Donaldson, 1981). Most were physically challenged (68 percent) rather than mentally challenged (22 percent), and only one in three of all disabled characters was portrayed as an independent, productive individual. Also, about one in five exhibited some type of abusive or socially deviant behavior (Gardner & Radel, 1978).

Movies in the 1980s were even more negative in their presentations of disabled characters. A 1989 study that examined 67 disabled characters in movies from 1986 to 1988 found that about three of four exhibited abnormal or deviant personality traits. One in two was victimized at some point in the film (Byrd, 1989).

Portrayals of Interracial Interactions

How does television portray Whites, Blacks, and those of other races in their interactions with one another? One method of analysis used to answer this question involves studying the characters of different races in the same program and examining how those characters behave.

In one study from the 1970s, Black and White characters on sitcoms were examined for certain behavioral characteristics (Reid, 1979). Both Black and White male characters exhibited similar behaviors, but the female Black characters were found to behave in stereotypical ways. Black females were usually boastful and domineering, and they usually appeared on the Black-dominated comedies. Reid also found that Whites appearing on Black-dominated comedies behaved differently from the Whites on White-dominated comedies. Overall, Whites on the Black-dominated shows exhibited more aggressiveness and dependent behavior, and they were generally more negative toward others.

Another study of 1970s-era shows that featured either predominantly Black casts or mixed casts revealed that Black characters who were part of the mixed casts exhibited more competence, more cooperation, and higher social standing. Their counterparts on predominantly Black shows were generally less educated and troubled by more personal problems (Banks, 1977).

A 1980 study of Black and White characters selected from the same shows found the Black characters to be younger and funnier than the White characters, but more likely to be unemployed. One in two of the Black characters and one in three of the Whites appeared in comedies. White characters had eight times as many conversations with one another than with Black characters, but the ratio of Whites to Blacks was five to one (Baptista-Fernandez & Greenberg, 1980).

Boldly Going Where No Black Woman Had Gone Before

In the 1960s, Gene Roddenberry had an idea for a television show set in outer space: *Star Trek*. He wanted *Star Trek* to portray a future where people of all human races (and even some aliens) coexist peacefully. The bridge of the *U.S.S. Enterprise* was truly a racial melting pot. As the Asian Mr. Sulu and Russian Ensign Chekov piloted the ship to uncharted expanses of the galaxy, Montgomery Scott, the Scottish engineer, was working hard to ensure the warp core and transporters worked. The alien Mr. Spock was busy checking readouts and offering counsel to the Caucasian Captain Kirk and Dr. McCoy. But the *Enterprise* crew was not an all-boys club. Lieutenant Uhura, the ship's Black communications officer, was busy making sure the *Enterprise* was in contact with Earth and with aliens from unknown worlds.

During the late 1960s, Uhura (played by Nichelle Nichols) broke many racial barriers on television. Uhura was one of the first Black women on television who was not shown as a maid or nanny. She was seen as an equal among her male peers. However, her time on *Star Trek* almost came to an abrupt end when Nichols planned to leave the show in order to pursue other career options after the show's first season ended.

After telling Roddenberry that she wanted to leave the show, Nichols attended an NAACP dinner, where she happened to have a chance encounter with a man who admitted that he was one of her biggest fans: Reverend Martin Luther King, Jr. When Nichols told Dr. King that she was leaving the show, he told her that she could not beam off the *Enterprise*. "For the first time, we [African Americans] are being seen the world over . . . as we should be seen," King said to her, adding that Uhura was a crucial character in breaking down the racial stereotypes that prevailed at the time. King also told her that *Star Trek* was the only show that he and his wife Coretta allowed their children to stay up to watch. At Dr. King's urging, Nichols asked Roddenberry for her job back, and Lieutenant Uhura continued to warp around the galaxy for the rest of the show's run and the subsequent series of movies.

Not only was Nichols's character instrumental for showing Blacks in non-stereotypic roles, Nichols also had the first interracial kiss on American television. In the episode titled "Plato's Stepchildren," Lieutenant Uhura shared a kiss with William Shatner's Captain Kirk.

While Uhura and Kirk's lip lock was controversial at the time, interracial relationships have now become more commonplace on television (e.g., NBC's *Parenthood*, which at one

Interracial relationships, romantic and otherwise, have become rather commonplace on many daytime soap operas and in films, but unfortunately no recent studies have examined the phenomenon or its possible influence on majority and minority audiences. In the 1970s interactions between people of color on television programs were rare. In a study that examined one week of prime-time programming in 1978, most Whites interacted with other Whites and most Blacks interacted with other Blacks (Weigel et al., 1980).

Two studies in the 1970s approached the study of TV race relations by focusing on the behaviors of Black family members and White family members. One of these studies found that the Black family was usually made up of a single parent (usually the mother) with children, whereas the White family normally

time featured two interracial romances). Meanwhile, the *Star Trek* franchise has continued to show a future where racial (and alien) equality prevails. On the numerous *Star Trek* series, we have seen interracial and interspecies romances. On *Star Trek: Deep Space Nine*, the Klingon warrior Worf (played by Black actor Michael Dorn) married the Trill scientist Dax (played by White actress Terry Farrell). Moreover, *Star Trek: Deep Space Nine* and *Star Trek: Voyager* featured a Black man and a White woman as commanding officers, respectively, further shattering predominant racial and gender stereotypes seen on television.

Star Trek's Lt. Uhura was a breakthrough minority character whose role was not dictated by race.
© *Bettmann/CORBIS*

consisted of two parents and children. The most notable difference between portrayals of the different families was in their propensity for conflicts. One in six interactions among Black family members involved conflicts, compared to only one in ten interactions among White family members (Greenberg & Neuendorf, 1980).

Another study examined more than 90 episodes of 12 shows depicting the family unit, six featuring Whites and six featuring Blacks. This was another decade-long (1970–1980) study. It found that Black families were portrayed in negative and stereotypical ways. Females usually headed Black households, and Black family members were generally portrayed with lower levels of education and lower occupational standings than their White counterparts. Also, interactions among Black family members featured more conflicts than interactions among the White family members (Sweeper, 1983).

Media as Conveyors of Social Information: The Current Picture

Studies on minorities in mass media now generally focus on stereotypical portrayals of minorities and the effects those portrayals have on minority and majority audiences. These studies have been important in determining what messages about minorities various media have been sending the public, or what social information has been conveyed. This research recognizes that television, film, videos, and other media—through entertainment, advertisements, news reports, and children's programming—are influential in providing information about minorities, especially for young people.

Television

African Americans represent about 14 to 17 percent of the characters on prime-time television, higher than their actual numbers in society (12–13 percent) (Children Now, 2001; Children Now, 2004; Mastro & Behm-Morawitz, 2005; Mastro & Greenberg, 2000). Whites represent about 73 to 80 percent of prime-time characters (Mastro, 2009), higher than 2010 census numbers. Blacks are usually portrayed in sitcoms (that usually feature an all-Black cast) or crime dramas (Mastro & Behm-Morawitz, 2005; Mastro & Greenberg, 2000). Recent examples of these trends include *Tyler Perry's House of Payne*, a sitcom that features an all-Black cast, and Shemar Moore's role as an FBI agent on *Criminal Minds*.

The typical African American on prime-time television programs is a male in his thirties and a middle-class professional (Children Now, 2001; Children Now, 2004; Mastro & Behm-Morawitz, 2005; Mastro & Greenberg, 2000). He is usually one of the least aggressive characters on television, and usually dresses more provocatively than the White characters (Mastro & Greenberg, 2000).

In news stories, especially about crime, Blacks are far more likely to be depicted than Whites (Dixon & Linz, 2000a). Information on prior arrests is more likely to be reported in a story featuring a Black perpetrator than a White one. Black juvenile offenders are shown more frequently on television news than White offenders. Dixon and Azocar (2006) found that 39 percent of juvenile offenders on television news programs were Black, whereas 24 percent were White. Real-world crime statistics show a different picture. Department of Justice statistics show that of juvenile offenders, 18 percent are Black and 22 percent are White (Mastro, 2009). Other studies have shown that Black officers are shown on newscasts and reality police shows at rates far below their actual numbers in society (Dixon, Azocar, & Casas, 2003; Oliver, 1994).

Hispanics represent about 27 percent of the population in the United States, but on prime-time television their numbers are somewhere between 2 and 6 percent (Children Now, 2001; Children Now, 2004; Mastro & Behm-Morawitz, 2005; Mastro & Greenberg, 2000). Most of them appear, like African Americans, in crime dramas or sitcoms. They are generally represented as less intelligent, less articulate, and lazier than other characters (Mastro & Behm-Morawitz, 2005).

As far as television news is concerned, Hispanics are depicted as perpetrators of crimes more frequently than are Whites (Dixon & Linz, 2000a). The percentage of depictions on crime news for Hispanics falls below real-world crime reports for them (Dixon & Linz, 2000b).

Among television characters in prime time, Asian Americans represent 1 to 3 percent of the population (Children Now, 2001; Children Now, 2004; Mastro

The hit Fox series *Glee* features a racially diverse cast but still relies heavily on stereotyping in its characters, which include a dumb blond, fashion-loving gay men, and tech-savvy Asians. *Rex Features via AP Images*

& Behm-Morawitz, 2005; Mastro & Greenberg, 2000). In reality, Asian Americans constitute about 5 percent of the population in the United States. When they are shown on television, Asian Americans are usually in important professional jobs (Children Now, 2004).

Fewer than .5 percent of the characters on prime-time television are Native Americans (Children Now, 2001; Children Now, 2004; Mastro & Behm-Morawitz, 2005; Mastro & Greenberg, 2000). About 1 percent of the U.S. population is Native American.

Films

White Americans make up about 80 percent of the lead characters in films, while Black Americans comprise 19 percent (Eschholz, Bufkin, & Long, 2002). Hispanics represent about 1 percent of characters in blockbuster motion pictures in the United States (Eschholz et al., 2002). Hispanics, Asian Americans, and Latinos are rarely seen in motion pictures (Mastro, 2009).

Advertising

Men are more often shown in commercials as professionals than are females, and they usually promote products such as electronics, appliances, or other nondomestic items (Craig, 1992; Bartsch, Burnett, Diller, & Rankin-Williams, 2000; Stern & Mastro, 2004).

The 1990s witnessed a few breakthroughs for African Americans. A number of Black women achieved the status of "supermodel" and now enjoy enormous visibility in the press. Tyra Banks broke the *Sports Illustrated* color barrier by being the first Black woman to make the cover of the famed Swimsuit Edition in 1996; however, she did share the cover with a white model. The following year, Tyra was the solo model on the cover, marking the first time that a Black woman was featured on the swimsuit cover by herself. It would take another decade for the next Black woman to be featured on the cover of the Swimsuit Edition when Beyoncé was featured in 2007. In terms of quantitative evidence, Bowen and Schmid (1997) found that the use of Black models increased in major magazines in recent years; however, Hispanic and Asian models still rarely appear. Blacks were usually depicted as athletes or musicians. They appeared mostly in ads sponsored by the government and in public service messages.

In advertising, only 1 percent of characters are Hispanic (Coltrane & Messineo, 2000; Mastro & Stern, 2003). When Hispanics do appear in advertisements, they are more likely than other characters to be provocatively dressed and sexualized (Mastro & Stern, 2003).

Asian Americans represent about 2 percent of the characters shown in advertisements (Coltrane & Messineo, 2000; Mastro & Stern, 2003). They are usually depicted as passive in nature, and they are found most often in ads for technology products and services (Mastro & Stern, 2003).

Racial minority models, like Beyoncé, increasingly appear in advertising and on magazine covers. *Jon Kopaloff/ Getty Images*

Characteristics of Audiences

The studies that describe television content provide interesting data and take a step toward answering the questions: "Are minority portrayals sending accurate and fair pictures to the American public? Are interactions among minority and majority characters promoting pictures of racial harmony or of racial conflict?" Such studies, however, do very little to answer other important questions. For example, "What effects do stereotypical minority portrayals have on minority and majority audiences? What effects do such portrayals have on children of all colors?"

Media effects research attempts to provide answers to these difficult questions. You will recall that in previous chapters we discussed social cognitive theory, priming, and cultivation and their underlying importance in understanding much of the research on media effects. These theories lie at the heart of research that examines the effects of minority portrayals in mass media. Social

---

Research Spotlight

Television Viewing and Ethnic Stereotypes: Do College Students Form Stereotypical Perceptions of Ethnic Groups as a Result of Heavy Television Consumption?

Moon J. Lee, Shannon L. Bichard, Meagan S. Irey,
Heather M. Walt, and Alana J. Carlson (2009)
The Howard Journal of Communication, 20, 95–110

In this study, the researchers examined the relationship between television viewing and whether a viewer held stereotypical beliefs about different ethnic groups, particularly Caucasians, African Americans, Asians, Latino/Hispanics, and Native Americans. Previous research had found common stereotypes associated with each of those ethnic groups, with Caucasians perceived as being intelligent, pleasant, and friendly, whereas African Americans were perceived as inferior, dishonest, and lazy. Additionally, Asians were believed to be highly educated and soft-spoken while Latinos were thought of as hard workers, antagonistic, and unlikely to go to college. Lastly, previous research found that Native Americans were generally thought to be lazy, uneducated, out of work, and on welfare.

Based on social cognitive and cultivation theories that explain how people's thoughts and perceptions can be influenced by the images they see, the researchers formulated several questions to explore in relation to television viewing.

Research Questions

RQ1: Do heavy viewers of television hold primarily positive or negative perceptions (stereotypes) of Caucasians?

RQ2: Do heavy viewers of television hold primarily positive or negative perceptions (stereotypes) of Asians?

RQ3: Do heavy viewers of television hold primarily positive or negative perceptions (stereotypes) of African Americans?

RQ4: Do heavy viewers of television hold primarily positive or negative perceptions (stereotypes) of Latino/Hispanics?

RQ5: Do heavy viewers of television hold primarily positive or negative perceptions (stereotypes) of Native Americans?

Method

Participants were recruited from two universities, one in the Northwest and one in the Southwest. A total of 450 participants successfully took part in the study. Each participant completed a survey that assessed television consumption (independent variable) and its effect on ethnic stereotyping (dependent variable). Participants responded to questions about what type of television shows they watched (i.e., entertainment, drama, educational, informational, sports, reality, and soap operas) in addition to indicating how many hours of television they watched. Based on viewing hours per week, participants were divided into light viewer (14 or less hours a week) or heavy viewer (15 or more hours a week) categories.

To measure participants' stereotypes, they rated their personal beliefs about different ethnic groups on a bi-polar adjectives scale. This scale featured 10 pairs of descriptors—shy and outgoing, lazy and hard working, vengeful and forgiving, and so forth. Participants rated members of each ethnic group on a seven-point scale, aligning them closer to one of the adjectives in each pairing.

Results

The study found that viewers overwhelmingly reported positive perceptions of Caucasians. Heavy viewers viewed Caucasians as more dependable, stable, and less angry.

When examining stereotypes about Asians, heavy television viewers appeared to hold more negative perceptions of Asians than did light viewers. Overall, heavy viewers rated Asians as being less warm, less responsible, and more nervous than did light viewers. (The researchers noted that perhaps Asians' quiet demeanor conveys a lack of warmth and cooperation.)

Heavy television viewers, especially of entertainment shows, rated African Americans as less agreeable and less extroverted than did light viewers. However, heavy viewers of informational programming and reality television rated African Americans as more open and less neurotic, respectively. The researchers said these findings indicate that entertainment programs may present African Americans more negatively, whereas more realistic or informational programs may try to portray them more positively.

Little difference was found between heavy and light viewers when asked about Latinos. The only significant difference was that heavy viewers of sports programs rated Latinos as more agreeable (i.e., cooperative and fair) but less extroverted and less assertive than did light viewers.

For Native American stereotypes, heavy television viewers reported a significant increase in negative characteristics (i.e., less open, less contentious, and less extroverted) than did light viewers. Ultimately, heavy viewers held mainly negative stereotypes of Native Americans.

Discussion

Overall, heavy viewers of television reported holding more negative stereotypes for every ethnicity. Asians and Native Americans were perceived the most negatively, with heavy viewers associating them with only negative stereotypes.

Results showed that heavy viewers of entertainment, educational, and sports programming held more negative stereotypes overall, while heavy viewers of information programming tended to have more positive perceptions.

Although this study does not establish a causal link between television viewing and whether an individual holds ethnic stereotypes, it does show a relationship between the amount of television watched (both in terms of hours and programming type) and whether a viewer holds stereotypical ethnic views.

Some of the findings (e.g., Caucasians were rated most positively) were not surprising; however, this study did produce some unexpected results in that not all minorities were associated solely with negative qualities (i.e., positive characteristics were associated with African Americans and Latinos).

In line with social cognitive theory and cultivation, heavy television viewing does appear to relate directly to holding prejudicial stereotypes.

learning theory posits that individuals learn from what they see in the media. Children especially are likely to pick up attitudes and behaviors by simply viewing situations, actions, and interactions on television and in other media. For this reason, minority portrayals have the potential to educate children about race relations, for better or for worse.

The evidence for the effects of minority portrayals on majority and minority audiences reveals that some audience members might be more vulnerable to media effects than others. Individuals who identify highly with their race or ethnic group tend to form more stereotypical attitudes toward those outside of their group, and feel more favorably toward those in their group (Mastro, 2003).

African Americans

Nielsen data reveal that Blacks are among the heaviest viewers of television (Nielsen, 1998, 2007). The television is on in a Black household about three hours per day longer than in a White household, with implications for effects on children and adolescents (Brown, Campbell, & Fischer, 1986; Greenberg & Linsangan, 1993; Botta, 2000). For example, Black children would be more vulnerable to negative effects from mass media in many ways if not properly supervised while viewing.

Studies through the years have shown that Blacks enjoy watching Black characters on television (Eastman & Liss, 1980; Nielsen, 1998; Poindexter & Stroman, 1981). A recent study (Abrams & Giles, 2007) found that Blacks tend to select programs or avoid them based on the ethnicity of characters and to fulfill their needs for racial identity.

Hispanic Americans

This group is close behind Blacks in the number of hours spent viewing television (Kaiser Family Foundation, 2010; Nielsen, 2007). It should be noted that

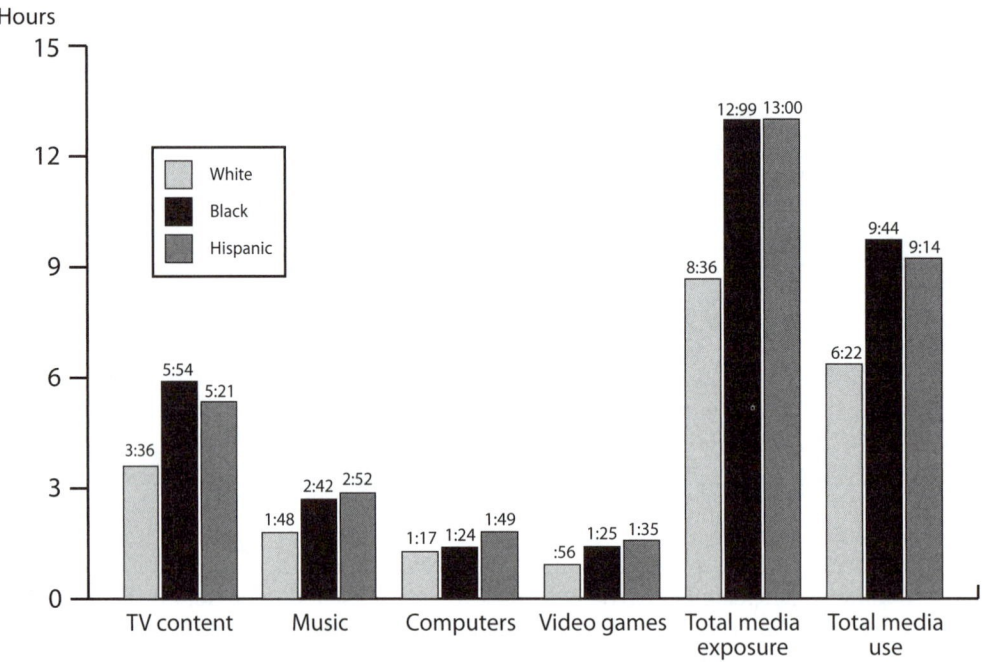

Figure 16.1   Media use by race/ethnicity: Average amount of time spent with each medium in a typical day.

Source: This information was reprinted with permission from the Henry J. Kaiser Family Foundation. The Kaiser Family Foundation, a leader in health policy analysis, health journalism and communication, is dedicated to filling the need for trusted, independent information on the biggest health issues facing the nation and its people. The Foundation is a nonprofit private operating foundation based in Menlo Park, California.

among Black and Hispanic children and adolescents, overall time of daily media exposure is virtually equal (Kaiser Family Foundation, 2010). Research shows that most Hispanics prefer Spanish-language networks such as Telemundo or Univision (Nielsen, 1998; Univision, 2005). Studies on advertisements have shown that ads in Spanish are more persuasive among Hispanics (those who are bilingual and those who predominantly speak Spanish) than are ads in English (Roslow & Nicholls, 1996).

Many Hispanics use television to learn about the culture in the United States and improve their English skills (Johnson, 1996; Stilling, 1997). Hispanics in the U.S. who wish to maintain their ethnicity tend to prefer Spanish-speaking television (Jeffres, 2000; Rios & Gaines, 1999).

Other Minorities

Very limited research has been done on the characteristics of other minority viewers. One exception is a study by Merskin (1998) that found that among Native American university students, 82 percent owned television sets but only watched 1 to 2 hours each day. Almost 70 percent of the students in the study indicated that they felt Native Americans were portrayed on television in ways that were incorrect and mostly negative.

Gender Stereotyping

Where gender is concerned, gender schema theory is used (in addition to social cognitive theory and social identity theory) to explain media content effects. Fiske and Taylor (1991) defined a schema as "a cognitive structure that represents knowledge about a concept or type of stimulus, including its attributes and the relations among those attributes" (p. 98). Schemata about gender can affect the way people (especially children) process information in the real world and from the world of mass media.

In terms of gender, one study (Gerbner, 1997) examined 20 years of prime-time television portrayals and found that women made up only 31.5 percent of all characters. These females were generally younger than males in prime time, and usually portrayed as wives and mothers rather than workers or professionals in positions of importance (Gerbner, 1997; Glascock, 2001; Lauzen & Dozier, 1999; Signorielli & Bacue, 1999).

Women have historically been underrepresented in films, and this trend continues in recent years. In one study that examined characters in movies released between 1990 and 2006, 73 percent of all characters were male (Smith, Granados, Choueiti, & Pieper, 2007).

When women do appear in films, even G-rated ones, they are usually portrayed as young and hypersexual (Bazzini et al., 1997; Herbozo, Tantleff-Dunn, Gokee-Larose, & Thompson, 2004). When they are shown, they are usually scantily clad and often are featured as sex objects (Smith & Granados, 2009).

Studies on gender issues reveal that females are both underrepresented and misrepresented in stereotypical ways in mass media (Smith & Granados,

The many different "James Bond Girls," like Halle Berry, are always sexy and typically succumb to the hero's sexual wiles. © *Greg Williams/CORBIS OUTLINE*

2009). Women are underrepresented on television in prime time, with about 60 percent of the characters being male (Glascock, 2001; Lauzen & Dozier, 1999, 2002, 2004; Lauzen, Dozier, & Cleveland, 2006; Signorielli & Bacue, 1999; Signorielli & Kahlenberg, 2001). Males are more likely to be shown in positions of power and authority (Lauzen & Dozier, 2004). Males were also shown as perpetrators of sexual harassment on women in about 84 percent of the prime-time shows examined in one study (Grauerholz & King, 1997).

Women represent about 45 to 49 percent of the people seen in commercials (Coltrane & Messineo, 2000; Ganahl, Prinsen, & Netzley, 2003), but they are more likely to be sexualized (Ganahl et al., 2003; Stern & Mastro, 2004).

Studies have found that when characters are shown in counter-stereotypic ways, gender effects are diminished (Davidson, Yasuna, & Tower, 1979; Davies, Spencer, Quinn, & Gerhardstein, 2002; Flerx, Fidler, & Rogers, 1976; Geis, Brown, Jennings-Walstedt, & Porter, 1984; Johnston & Ettema, 1982; Wroblewski & Huston, 1987). Children may be the most vulnerable to learning about sex role stereotypes, but negative effects can be mitigated by parental or caregiver supervision (Smith & Granados, 2009).

Sex role research has revealed that viewing stereotypical portrayals based on gender can have an effect on choice of occupation and attitudes toward particular occupations. Movies that expose children to "happily ever after" romantic scenarios may affect their relationships and expectations in life, and the "thin ideal" that is usually depicted in mass media can cause eating disorders, especially among females (Smith & Granados, 2009).

Disney and Pixar Animating Gender

Many of the concerns about gender stereotyping involve children's media, and much of the scholarly attention is focused on Disney. Due to its global dominance, Disney has been the cornerstone of children's entertainment for decades. Gender stereotypes concern many researchers because "much of what children learn about the world outside of their immediate family and community comes from the media" (Bryant & Bryant, 2003, p. 204). In a review of the impact of entertainment media on children, Bryant and Bryant (2003) stated that media function as "potent agents of socialization" (p. 204), meaning that children tend to view reality according to what they see on television and movie screens.

Most of the research has focused on the types of stereotypes presented in Disney's classic animated films, and the presence of these stereotypes is not a coincidence. Bell (1995) drew attention to this fact, saying that "Disney animation is not an innocent art form: nothing accidental or serendipitous occurs in animation as each *second* of action on screen is rendered in twenty-four different still paintings" (p. 108).

Wiersma (2001) conducted one of the most comprehensive stereotyping studies of the Disney classics. In a content analysis of 16 films, Wiersma found that male characters outnumbered female characters (199 to 83), females performed more in-home labor than males, and males performed a much wider range of out-of-home jobs and held more positions of power than women. Characters also tended to align with commonly held ideas about femininity (i.e., women are passive, dependent, romantic, and emotional) and masculinity (i.e., men are aggressive, independent, unromantic, and unemotional).

Towbin, Haddock, Zimmerman, Lund, and Tanner (2003) conducted a thematic analysis of 26 feature-length Disney films that revealed the following themes about what it means to be a boy/man or girl/woman:

> (a) Men primarily use physical means to express their emotions or show no emotions; (b) men are not in control of their sexuality; (c) men are naturally strong and heroic; (d) men have nondomestic jobs; and (e) overweight men have negative characteristics. (p. 28)

> (a) A woman's appearance is valued more than her intellect; (b) women are helpless and in need of protection; (c) women are domestic and likely to marry; (d) overweight women are ugly, unpleasant, and unmarried. (p. 30)

Disney's role as a "cultural narrator" (Brydon, 2009, p. 143) expands beyond its own film catalog. Disney's prominence and dominance in the entertainment industry sets the standard for other animation studios. Abel (1995) noted that "the work of the Disney studios defines the gender norm for the rest of the cartoon world" (p. 185).

Despite the prevalence of gender stereotypes in classic Disney films, recent studies are finding evidence that some stereotypes are changing. In a content analysis of recent Disney and Pixar films, Finklea (2010) found that men are seen performing more housework (e.g., Carl Fredricksen in *Up*) than women. Moreover, female characters were shown in more varied careers, including an actress, astrophysicist, botanist, and hotel chain owner. Although male characters still wielded the most power, they were also shown as more dependent on female characters. Males were also shown to be more romantic and emotional, especially compared with males in previous Disney films. This "softer" male is particularly noticeable in Pixar films.

After partnering with Disney in 1991 (Disney later bought Pixar in 2006), Pixar was essentially able to use the Disney brand as a "stamp of approval, signifying that this new

(continued)

form of animation met the same standards of excellence and wholesomeness in family entertainment associated with Disney" (Brookey & Westerfelhaus, 2005).

Pixar has now become the leader in children's animation, unseating Disney proper from its long-held position (Booker, 2010). Despite its dominance in the industry, little research has focused on Pixar and the possible gender stereotypes found in its films. The research that has been done has examined male characters in the films, because until 2012's *Brave*, all of Pixar's films were centered around male protagonists. Gillam and Wooden (2008) noted a common narrative thread for male protagonists in Pixar's *Toy Story*, *The Incredibles*, and *Cars*, where alpha-male characters are emasculated, giving them the opportunity to learn what it means to be a kinder, gentler man. Gillam and Wooden said these characters (e.g., Woody, Buzz Lightyear, Mr. Incredible, and Lightning McQueen) are examples of the "new man."

Finklea (2011) examined themes of masculinity in the *Toy Story* trilogy and found that Pixar's "new man" narrative had crossed over into the *Toy Story* sequels. However, some older stereotypes (for both males and females) were still present. Here is a list of the major themes that emerged from the study:

> (a) alpha male characters have trouble expressing nonviolent emotions to others until transforming into the "new man" after emasculation; (b) the emotions males express most often are anger and frustration, and they are often expressed through physical or derogatory verbal means; (c) males ask others for help and benefit from teamwork and cooperation; (d) males are natural leaders, brave, loyal, and willing to sacrifice themselves for the good of others; (e) males feel the desire to be loved and needed; (f) the characteristics females value most in males are strength and physical prowess, and males are concerned about their physical appearance; (g) males are not able to control their sexuality, and (h) males displaying effeminate qualities are ridiculed by other males, but not by females. (Finklea, 2011, p. 11)

Ultimately, these films are slowly moving away from traditional gender stereotypes; however, there is still much room for improvement. Alternate portrayals of masculinity (e.g., Ken in *Toy Story 3*) still pose interesting questions about gender. Because of Pixar's position atop the animation empire, research into these issues will continue for years to come.

Media Effects of Racial, Ethnic, and Gender Stereotyping

Media images of minorities have been shown to have a considerable impact on White audiences. The portrayal of a lazy, incompetent, rebellious, or violent person of color can be an enduring mental image. Subsequent stereotypes held by White viewers have been found to occur.

Priming Studies

Many priming studies have examined how exposure to minority stereotypes (such as thinking that Blacks are criminals and Hispanics are sensual) can have a short-term effect on audiences, especially majority audiences, and their evaluations of minorities in the real world (Dixon, 2006, 2007; Givens & Monahan, 2005). Other priming studies have found that stereotypical portrayals in mass media cause White audience members to respond to those stereotypes in their evaluations of minorities (Gilliam & Iyengar, 2000; Mendelberg, 1997).

Whenever stereotypes are primed in depictions of crime, majority audiences blamed dispositional factors, such as simply being more prone to criminality, as the reason that Black perpetrators committed a crime, but for White perpetrators, they blamed situational aspects (Johnson, Adams, Hall, & Ashburn, 1997). Whenever racial cues are implied in news stories visually, White audiences are reminded of racial stereotypes (Abraham & Appiah, 2006).

In one study, when White audiences were presented with a dark-skinned Black perpetrator they expressed more sympathy for the victim of the crime (Dixon & Maddox, 2005). Another study indicated that news stories about crime and welfare are expected to involve race, and coverage of these areas causes stereotypes to be activated in the mind of the viewer (Valentino, 1999).

Other studies reveal that whenever mass media news stories contain positive information about minorities and present counter-stereotypical behavior, Whites respond with more positive judgments about race and more sympathy toward discriminatory practices (Bodenhausen, Schwarz, Bless, & Wanke, 1995; Power, Murphy, & Coover, 1996).

Priming studies, you will recall, tell us much about what thoughts are prompted in the short term. Media effects researchers interested in stereotyping are also interested in long-term implications. Long-term exposure to stereotypical portrayals of Blacks has been shown to result in subtle discriminatory thoughts among Whites (Gorham, 2006). In other words, when Blacks are repeatedly depicted as criminals on news reports, Whites are repeatedly primed to think of "them" as criminals. The accessibility of these constructs in memory results in strengthening the view in the mind that Blacks are criminals (Dixon & Azocar, 2007).

Cultivation Studies

Cultivation studies have been conducted in the area of stereotyping among White audiences. Several studies have shown that Whites who are heavy consumers of television news tend to stereotype Blacks as being lower in socioeconomic status because of lack of initiative rather than lack of opportunity (Armstrong, Neuendorf, & Brentar, 1992; Busselle & Crandall, 2002). One cultivation study that made use of the mental models perspective found that White audiences who were heavy viewers of television cultivated attitudes in line with stereotypical portrayals of Hispanics (Mastro, Behm-Morawitz, & Ortiz, 2007). Interestingly, the study showed evidence that real-world contact with Hispanics tended to lessen the cultivation effects; in other words, those who had contact with Hispanics in the real world were more likely to have less stereotypical views of Hispanics than those who were simply exposed to portrayals of Hispanics on television.

Additional research has shown that heavy viewing of stereotypical portrayals of minorities on television can influence White viewers' voting and public policy decisions (Mendelberg, 1997; Valentino, 1999). More recent studies

(Mastro & Kopacz, 2006; Ramasubramanian, 2011; Tan, Fujioka, & Tan, 2000) revealed not only that Whites who were heavy viewers of stereotypical televised portrayals of minorities were impacted negatively, but that their views caused them to be less supportive of affirmative action or other race-based policies.

Minority Reactions to Stereotyped Portrayals

Most of the research on stereotyping has studied how Whites react to minority portrayals, but a few studies have delved into the question of how minorities themselves react to stereotypic portrayals of their own groups. Researchers have theorized that exposure to stereotypic portrayals would cause lessening of self-esteem among minority audiences, but the research has shown mixed results. Fryberg (2003) did find that Native Americans reacted to stereotypical portrayals of Native Americans on television with negative effects on their self-esteem. Rivadeneyra, Ward, and Gordon (2007) studied Hispanic high school students who watched stereotypical portrayals on television and found that certain aspects of self-esteem were influenced negatively, but overall these adolescents' self-esteem was not impacted by viewing. Subervi-Velez and Neco-chea (1990) studied Hispanic elementary children and found that their self-esteem measures were not affected by viewing either English-speaking or Spanish-speaking television.

Several studies have found that viewers enjoy seeing people of their own race in the media, particularly on television. They like these characters more, they trust them more, and they identify with them more. Black high school students have indicated a stronger liking than White students for shows featuring Black characters (Dates, 1980). White high school students have rated White newscasters higher than Black newscasters in terms of competency and the likelihood that those newscasters might someday be neighbors or relatives (Kaner, 1982). Grade school children tend to select their favorite characters on the basis of race. During a season when 85 percent of the characters on television were White, 96 percent of the White children selected a White character as their favorite, whereas only 75 percent of the Black children and 80 percent of the Hispanic children chose a White character (Eastman & Liss, 1980). When programs featuring minority characters are available, minority audiences tend to prefer these shows to others that feature White characters (Liss, 1981; Eastman & Liss, 1980; Greenberg et al., 1983).

Studies that compare the perceptions of young minority and majority audiences have produced interesting findings. One such study has indicated that Black youngsters may be more prone to the effects of cultivation. Black children are more likely than White children to believe that television portrayals of Blacks and non-Blacks are realistic. Greenberg and Atkin (1982) found that approximately 40 percent of Black children, compared to about 30 percent of White children, agreed that the portrayals they witnessed reflected the true state of affairs as they exist in the real world.

Summary

Since the 1960s, portrayals of minority characters in mass media, particularly on television and in film, have reflected societal changes. These changes in portrayals and, especially, their effects upon audiences' attitudes, values, and behaviors, are of particular interest to communication researchers. Many of the studies in this area from the 1970s and 1980s offer a large amount of informative data regarding those years.

Studies of the 1990s showed that Blacks achieved very positive gains in both the number and the nature of their portrayals in entertainment programs, but other minorities did not fare so well. Latinos, Asian Americans, Native Americans, and women continue to be underrepresented in mass media, sometimes to the point of exclusion. When these groups are depicted, it is sometimes in stereotypical or demeaning ways.

Some of the first head count studies were conducted in the 1970s, when the number of minority characters on television fell far below their societal numbers. In the late 1990s, the networks responded to demands from minority activist groups by featuring more Black characters on prime time, but not other minorities such as Asian Americans, Hispanic Americans, or Native Americans. One study revealed that the number of Black characters on prime-time television was in excess of their actual percentage in society at that time (12 percent), with Blacks appearing in 14 to 17 percent of major and lesser prime-time roles. Whites represent about 73 to 80 percent of prime-time characters. Blacks are usually portrayed in sitcoms (that usually feature an all-Black cast) or crime dramas. Still, television does not reflect America's colors accurately, as other minority groups remain as underrepresented in major network programming today as they were 20 years ago.

In terms of gender, one study examined 20 years of prime-time portrayals and found that women made up 31.5 percent of all characters. These females were generally younger than males in prime time, and usually portrayed as wives and mothers.

In cinema, historically, Blacks and other minorities were cast in roles that specifically called for a minority character; however, this began to change in the 1990s, when many Blacks enjoyed starring roles in major motion pictures. Women have historically been underrepresented in films, with 73 percent of all characters being male in movies examined between 1990 and 2006.

Like entertainment portrayals of minorities, advertising images historically have been mostly White until the 1990s. Blacks and Asian Americans have made significant gains in some media in the past few decades although other minorities remain underrepresented. The significance of roles for minority characters is another area of study that received a great amount of scrutiny in the 1970s and 1980s, but relatively few studies have been conducted since then.

Studies on minorities in mass media now generally fall under two main categories: descriptions of minority portrayals or their effects on audiences. Studies on gender issues reveal that females are both underrepresented and misrepresented in stereotypical ways in mass media. African Americans represent about 14 to 17 percent of the characters on prime-time television, higher than their actual numbers in society (12–13 percent).

In news stories, especially about crime, Blacks are far more likely to be depicted than Whites. Hispanics represent about 27 percent of the population in the United States, but on prime-time television their numbers are somewhere between 2–6 percent. Most of them appear, like African Americans, in crime dramas or sitcoms. They are generally represented as less intelligent, less articulate, and lazier than other characters.

Among television characters in prime time, Asian Americans represent 1–3 percent of roles. In reality, Asian Americans constitute about 5 percent of the population in the United States. When they are shown on television, Asian Americans are usually in important professional jobs.

Fewer than .5 percent of the characters on prime-time television are Native Americans. About 1 percent of the U.S. population is Native American.

Women continue to be underrepresented in films, and when they are shown, they are usually scantily clad and hypersexualized. White Americans constitute about 80 percent of the lead characters and Black Americans, 19 percent. Hispanics represent about 1 percent of characters in blockbuster motion pictures in the United States. Hispanics, Asian Americans, and Latinos are rarely seen in motion pictures.

Men are usually shown in commercials as professionals more than females, and they usually promote products such as electronics, appliances, or other non-domestic items. Women represent about 45 to 49 percent of the people seen in commercials, but they are more likely to be sexualized.

The 1990s saw a few breakthroughs for African Americans. A number of Black women achieved the status of "supermodel" and now enjoy enormous visibility in the press. Tyra Banks broke the *Sports Illustrated* color barrier by being the first Black woman to make the cover of the Swimsuit Edition. Blacks were usually depicted as athletes or musicians. They appeared mostly in ads sponsored by the government and in public service messages.

In advertising, 86 percent of characters are White and 11 percent are Black in commercials. Only 1 percent of characters are Hispanic. When Hispanics do appear in advertisements, they are more likely than other characters to be provocatively dressed and sexualized. Asian Americans represent about 2 percent of the characters shown in advertisements. They are usually depicted as passive in nature and they are found most often in ads that have to do with technology.

The evidence for the effects of minority portrayals on majority and minority audiences reveals that some audience members might be more vulnerable to media effects than others. Individuals who identify highly with their race or ethnic group tend to form more stereotypical attitudes toward those outside of their group, and feel more favorably toward those in their group.

Media images of minorities have been shown to have a considerable impact on White audiences. The portrayal of a lazy, incompetent, rebellious, or violent person of color is an enduring mental image. Subsequent stereotypes on the part of the White viewer have been found to occur.

Other studies reveal that whenever mass media news stories contain positive information about minorities and present counter-stereotypical behavior, Whites respond with more positive judgments about race and more sympathy toward discriminatory practices.

Several studies have found that viewers enjoy seeing people of their own color in the media, particularly on television. They like these characters more, they trust them more, and they identify with them more. Sex role research has revealed that viewing stereotypical portrayals based on gender can have an effect on choice of occupation and attitudes toward particular occupations. Movies that expose children to "happily ever after" romantic scenarios may affect their relationships and expectations in life, and the "thin ideal" that is usually depicted in mass media can cause eating disorders, especially among females.

seventeen

Effects of Children's Educational Television and Infant/Toddler Edutainment

Phil began laying out his vision for what television could become.
Above all else . . . television would become the world's greatest teaching tool.
—Evan I. Schwartz, on Philo Farnsworth, the inventor of television,
in *The Last Lone Inventor* (2002, p. 112)

Many of you, no doubt, grew up watching countless hours of *Sesame Street, The Magic School Bus, Blue's Clues, Barney & Friends*, and any of the other numerous shows marketed to children and their parents as "educational television" or "edutainment." Often when discussing the effects of television on children, critics and parenting groups focus on the negative effects of viewing; however, many of these so-called effects, such as shorter attention spans, apathy toward school, and the fear of children becoming mindless "zombie viewers" (e.g., Healy, 1990; Postman, 1985; Winn, 1977), are seldom backed by scientific evidence (Fisch, 2009). In an examination of attention and television watching, Newman (2010) highlighted the paradox that many technophobic writers and critics fall into: Television "holds attention so well that it destroys the ability to pay attention," and although many fear that edutainment will turn children into zombie viewers, Newman said that at least they will be "zombies who count and spell" (p. 589). In fact, research has shown that children are actually engaged, active viewers (Anderson & Lorch, 1983). Whereas many of our parents may have plopped us down in front of the television so they could enjoy a few moments of free time (Krcmar, 2010), you most likely benefited in some way from this time with Big Bird, Elmo, and Ms. Frizzle riding around in her magical school bus—and there is a large body of research that highlights the positive effects of children's educational media, which we will explore in this chapter. Additionally, we will examine the booming business of infant-targeted media, such as *Baby Einstein* and *Teletubbies,* and we will also look at research that tries to determine what, if anything, these young children are able to learn from them.

Educational Television

Research examining educational television has primarily focused on two key areas: preschool programming's impact on school readiness, and school-age programming's effects on literacy, math and problem solving, science, and social studies.

School Readiness

When talking about school readiness, we need to keep in mind that the term is not limited solely to knowledge and learning skills (Fisch, 2009). It also includes interpersonal skills and attitudes, such as cooperating with others and being self-confident (Zero to Three/National Center for Clinical Infant Programs, 1992). One of the most influential shows that promotes both academic and interpersonal skills is *Sesame Street*.

Over the years, *Sesame Street* has found many innovative ways to educate young audiences. Here, selected Muppet characters help children deal with the challenges of military life.

A lot of research and planning went into the creation of *Sesame Street*. Both academic researchers and television producers worked together to create a curriculum that would emphasize cognitive development through short segments and skits, songs, and "Muppet-filled fun" (Akerman, Bryant, & Diaz-Wionczek, 2011, p. 208). Shortly after its debut in 1969, researchers began to investigate Big Bird, Mr. Snuffleupagus, and Count von Count's ability to teach young children between the ages of three and five. A pair of studies (Ball & Bogatz, 1970; Bogatz & Ball, 1971) conducted in the early 1970s tested children's knowledge before watching *Sesame Street*, also known as a **pretest**, and then again after watching the show, which is known as a **posttest**. Another group of children did not watch the show at all; these children were a part of the **control group**. The researchers found that children who watched more *Sesame Street* exhibited significantly higher knowledge gains for several academic skills, such as identifying numbers, letters, shapes, and body parts. Fisch (2009) noted these same effects have also been seen in children watching international versions of *Sesame Street* in countries like Mexico (Diaz-Guerrero & Holtzman, 1974; UNICEF, 1996), Russia (*Ulitsa Sezam* Department of Research and Content, 1998), Portugal (Brederode-Santos, 1993), and Turkey (Sahin, 1990).

Whereas these studies show knowledge gains over a relatively short time period, what about the long-term effects of *Sesame Street* viewing? Part of Bogatz and Ball's 1971 study was to perform a follow-up on some of the children from their first *Sesame Street* study (Ball & Bogatz, 1970). The researchers had teachers rate their students on several school readiness skills, including language and math, attitude about school, and how they interacted with their classmates. The teachers, who did not know which children had watched a lot of *Sesame Street* during the 1970 study, rated the heavier viewers as more prepared for school compared to the lighter viewers. Studies conducted in the 1990s and early 2000s also found similar results, with teachers rating *Sesame Street* viewers as better prepared for school (Wright & Huston, 1995; Wright, Huston, Scantlin, & Kotler, 2001). A **correlational analysis** of data collected from approximately 10,000 children by the U.S. Department of Education's National Household Survey found that preschool-aged *Sesame Street* viewers performed better in recognizing letters of the alphabet and telling coherent stories while pretending to read; meanwhile, first and second graders who viewed *Sesame Street* as preschoolers were more apt to read books on their own and less likely to need remedial reading help (Zill, 2001; Zill, Davies, & Daly, 1994).

But the effects of *Sesame Street* go far beyond the first years of grade school. In fact, *Sesame Street* viewing as a preschooler has been shown to impact a student's performance in high school! Students in grades 9 through 12 who watched more *Sesame Street* as a child had higher grades and academic self-esteem, exhibited a higher drive to perform well in class, and read more books than did nonviewers (Anderson, Huston, Wright, & Collins, 1998; Huston, Anderson, Wright, Linebarger, & Schmitt, 2001).

Of course, *Sesame Street* is not the only show that helps promote school readiness in preschoolers. Shows like *Barney & Friends*, *Dragon Tales*, and *Blue's Clues* have also been shown to improve other important aspects of school readiness: knowledge, flexible thinking, willingness to pursue challenges and initiating play with others, and problem-solving skills (Fisch, 2009).

Although many of you may cringe when you think of Barney singing the theme song to the show ("I love you. You love me. We're a happy family . . ."), researchers Jerome and Dorothy Singer found that the big purple dinosaur's sing-song approach to teaching did help some children (mostly White, middle-class 3- and 4-year-olds) improve their ability to count and identify colors, while also improving their vocabulary knowledge about places in their neighborhood. However, it did not improve scores for identifying shapes or understanding emotions (Singer & Singer, 1994). When the Singers replicated this study with a more diverse sample, which included more minorities and working-class children, they observed only a very small benefit to watching *Barney* (Singer & Singer, 1995). However, if the children were presented with follow-up lessons about the material seen in the 10 episodes that were part of the study, additional benefits resulted (Singer & Singer, 1995).

PBS's *Dragon Tales*, an animated series about two Latino siblings that help a group of dragons, has been shown to improve children's interpersonal skills, making viewers more likely to ask others to engage in organized play and choose challenging tasks (Rust, 2001). Viewers of the show also exhibited more spontaneity and goal-oriented play (Rust, 2001).

Other shows, especially older series that were once staples in Nickelodeon's "Nick Jr." program schedule, have been shown to improve children's problem-solving skills, allowing them to better "think outside the box." Children who watched *Allegra's Window* and *Gullah Gullah Island* performed significantly better on hands-on problem-solving tasks than did nonviewers (Mulliken & Bryant, 1999), and caregivers rated children who watched the show as having greater flexible thinking skills (e.g., looking at a problem from different points of view, being curious) and problem-solving abilities (e.g., using different methods to solve a problem, focusing on the task at hand, not giving up) (Bryant et al., 1997).

One of the most enduring Nick Jr. shows that has been shown to have a positive impact on children is *Blue's Clues*. The show features an animated female dog, Blue, and her human companion, Steve (and later Steve's brother, Joe). In each episode, Blue and her owner solve a simple three-part puzzle by finding clues marked with Blue's paw print and writing the clues down in their "handy, dandy notebook." Along the way, the child viewers are directly asked to participate by helping to spot Blue's clues and trying to solve the puzzle. Akerman et al.'s (2011) discussion of *Blue's Clues*'s development described how the show's

> "think along, play along style" encouraged preschoolers to use higher order cognitive skills . . . [such as] sorting; categorizing and classifying; differentiating and discriminating; predicting and anticipating; what happened and why; ordering and sequencing; patterning; matching; inferential problem solving; associating; analogies; and relational concepts. (p. 212)

In addition to the focus on cognitive skills, *Blue's Clues*'s inclusion of catchy sing-along segments and audience interaction also sought to entertain children and build their self-esteem (Akerman et al., 2011).

Steve Burns and Blue launched the highly successful, curriculum-based *Blue's Clues* for Nickelodeon. *AP Photo/Suzanne Mapes*

Research into *Blue's Clues*'s effectiveness conducted by Anderson et al. (2000) and Bryant et al. (1999) found that, when presented with puzzles identical to the ones in specific episodes of the show, children who watched *Blue's Clues* gave a significantly higher number of correct answers compared to children who did not watch the show. This finding suggests that children were able to recall the information they saw on TV. In addition to solving show-specific puzzles, *Blue's Clues* viewers were able to correctly solve simple riddles not related to the show at a significantly higher rate than were nonviewers, suggesting an improvement in problem-solving skills.

Dora the Explorer is yet another mainstay in the children's educational television world, featuring the first Latina lead character in preschool programming (Ryan, 2010). *Dora*'s format differs from that of *Sesame Street* and *Blue's Clues* by using a structured linear narrative to present "high-stakes adventure wherein the solution of problems *requires* the participation of viewers—Dora could not do it without them" (Akerman et al., 2011, p. 210). Ryan (2010) suggested that Dora's repeated use of the word "we" throughout her adventures, which implies that the audience is a part of the story, could help preschoolers to believe that they are, in fact, instrumental in helping Dora solve the problems she faces in each episode. Thus, "the interactive style which *Sesame Street* utilized and *Blue's Clues* revolutionized, *Dora the Explorer* formalized" (Akerman et al., 2011, p. 211). Similar to *Blue's Clues*, *Dora the Explorer* also has the potential to boost the self-esteem and self-confidence of the children watching (Ryan, 2010). One unique feature of *Dora the Explorer* is the focus on bilingualism and language development.

Dora the Explorer champions school readiness and is a highly successful ethnic-minority character.
PRNewsFoto/Nickelodeon

Language and Vocabulary Development

Many children's shows place a heavy emphasis on vocabulary acquisition. Television is a unique medium for learning vocabulary because it can present words and concepts using images, speech, and sound effects (Linebarger & Piotrowski, 2010). In the mid-1980s, researchers examined the language used in *Sesame Street*, *Mister Rogers' Neighborhood*, and *The Electric Company* and compared it to the language patterns parents use when interacting with their young children (Rice, 1984; Rice & Haight, 1986). Rice and colleagues found that educational programming utilized many of the same verbal features that are believed to help children acquire language skills. Some of these features include short, simplified segments of speech, frequent use of repetition, and language that is based on things children see on the screen. The presence of these elements suggested that "the potential existed for such television series to contribute to language development" (Fisch, 2009, p. 406).

Many studies, though not all (e.g., Bryant et al., 1999), have found evidence that children do learn new vocabulary words from television (e.g., Linebarger & Piotrowski, 2010; Rice, Huston, Truglio, & Write, 1990; Rice & Woodsmall, 1988; Singer & Singer, 1994). In addition to learning vocabulary from television, some research has indicated that the more children watch the more they learn. Rice and colleagues (1990) observed that children between the ages of three and five who watched more hours of *Sesame Street* had higher vocabulary gains than did those that watched fewer hours. (It should be noted that Rice and colleagues noticed that vocabulary gains from watching *Sesame Street* essentially stopped after the age of five. They suggested that by that age, children have acquired all of the new words from *Sesame Street*, which is, after all, targeted at 3- to 5-year-old preschoolers.)

Vocabulary gains have also been observed with *Dora the Explorer*, which incorporates Spanish words as part of its vocabulary curriculum. Linebarger (2001) found that 4-year-old English-speaking children learned one new Spanish word for every 14 episodes they watched. Three-year-olds picked up one Spanish word for every 58 episodes watched.

While children can learn new words from television, research shows they learn little about correct usage and grammar (see Naigles & Mayeux, 2001 for a review). This could be due to the fact that televised communication is one-way, from the screen to the viewer, and children most likely learn grammar from social interactions involving two-way communication with parents and other caregivers (Naigles & Mayeux, 2001).

Literacy Development and Reading Comprehension

One of the most prominent children's programs focused on literacy is PBS's *Between the Lions*, which is targeted to children between the ages of three and seven (Jennings, Hooker, & Linebarger, 2009). *Between the Lions* shares several characteristics with *Sesame Street*, including its magazine format, animation, and combination of puppetry and live-action. The show takes place in a library, and the main characters are two lion librarians, Theo and Cleo, and their two children.

Prince and colleagues (2001) found that preschool children who watched *Between the Lions* learned to recognize the sounds of words more quickly than their nonwatching peers. Further research conducted by Linebarger (2006) showed that viewers also showed significant advances in sound awareness and sound blending, both of which are key elements used to predict reading achievement later in childhood. A large body of research also shows that watching *Between the Lions* results in advances in phonics skills and phonemic awareness (see Jennings et al., 2009, for a review), and is especially beneficial to kindergarten students learning about the alphabet and how to read (both identifying words and reading left to right) (Linebarger, 2000). A small qualitative study found that watching the show can increase correct verb usage and help children with developmental delays acquire age-appropriate literacy skills; however, the findings of this study should be viewed with caution because of a very small sample size (Jennings et al., 2009).

Targeted at 5- to 8-year-old children, *Reading Rainbow* presented audiences with specific books read on air and accompanied by the illustrations from the book pages (Fisch, 2009). Hosted by LeVar Burton, *Reading Rainbow* also incorporated segments related to that episode's featured book, such as songs, interviews with children, and documentaries (Fisch, 2009). Leitner (1991) investigated *Reading Rainbow*'s impact on reading comprehension by studying three groups of fourth graders who read a book about desert cacti. One group watched an episode of *Reading Rainbow* that featured the book and related segments about desert life. The second group was allowed to study a real cactus, while the third group of students was asked to think about the types of things that they might read about in a book about the desert. After the groups watched the show, examined the live cactus, or imagined what they would see in a book, all of the children read the book about desert cacti. Leitner found that the children who watched *Reading Rainbow* exhibited significantly higher reading comprehension compared to the other two groups. Leitner's main explanation of the effect was that the varied methods of presenting information about the desert impacted the students' comprehension; however, the author offered an alternative explanation: reading comprehension was improved for the *Reading Rainbow* group because they were exposed to the book twice (once on the show and again when they read it on their own). Although Leitner's findings may not present a clear answer as to why the *Reading Rainbow* group had higher comprehension scores, it does highlight part of the philosophy behind the show, which is to expose children to books in hopes that they will then read them on their own (Fisch, 2009).

Although *Reading Rainbow* is no longer being produced for television, LeVar Burton recently announced the launch of RRKidz, a free app for iPad and Android devices that will allow children to read books via an interactive platform (RRKidz.com, 2011).

Mathematics

Although many children's shows incorporate some type of math skills (e.g., *Sesame Street*'s Count von Count), a few series aimed at older children and preteens have focused solely on mathematics. The series that received the most attention from researchers was *Square One TV*, which aired on PBS in the late 1980s and early 1990s. The show's target audience was 8- to 12-year-olds and featured comedy sketches, music videos, a recurring detective-type segment, "Mathnet," all of which aimed to improve viewers' mathematical problem-solving skills (Fisch, 2009).

Studies of fifth graders who viewed *Square One TV* showed significantly higher gains in problem-solving skills (working a problem backward, finding patterns and sequences) as well as more complex and complete solutions compared to nonviewers (Hall, Esty, & Fisch, 1990; Hall, Fisch et al., 1990). *Square One TV* was also found to expand students' concept of what "math" was, increase the number of times students talked about enjoying math, and foster a desire to try more challenging math problems (Hall, Fisch et al., 1990).

Cyberchase, a math-based animated series about three preteens who use mathematics to defeat an online villain, aims to teach children that "math is everywhere and [is] a useful tool for solving problems" (PBS.org, 2011). Fisch (2003, 2005) found that watching the series significantly impacted students' math skills in three areas: direct learning (i.e., solving the same problems featured on the show), near transfer (solving problems similar to those shown on the program), and far transfer (solving problems different than those on the show, but using similar mathematic skills).

Science

Children's science programming began in 1951 with the premiere of *Mr. Wizard*, and the tradition continues with recent shows such as *Bill Nye the Science Guy, Beakman's World,* and *The Magic School Bus* (Fisch, 2009).

Many researchers have examined *3-2-1 Contact*, a 1980s daily science-based series that featured various segments and was targeted to 8- to 12-year-olds (Fisch, 2009). Children and preteens who watched the series showed greater comprehension compared to nonviewers (Cambre & Fernie, 1985; Johnston, 1980; Johnston & Luker, 1983; Wagner, 1985). Interestingly, female participants showed the greatest benefits from watching the show, despite other research showing that girls often struggle with learning science (see Gray, 2005, for a review). By the mid-1990s, many parents and teachers were concerned that girls and minority students were losing interest in science by the time they entered middle school (Clarke, 2005). As a result, Scholastic developed its popular book series about an eccentric teacher and her shape-shifting bus into a television series, giving birth to Ms. Frizzle (voiced by Lily Tomlin) and her fantastic field trips on *The Magic School Bus*, which originally aired on PBS (Clarke, 2005). Although it received little scholarly research attention, the show proved to be a hit with audiences, easily becoming one of PBS's highest-rated series for school-age children ("Scholastic Productions," 1997).

Another extremely popular series is *Bill Nye the Science Guy*, which featured scientist/comedian Bill Nye (in his signature bow tie and lab coat) as he performed a variety of demonstrations and experiments. Rockman et al (1996) found that watching the show not only encouraged children's scientific exploration—resulting in more complex thinking processes and solutions—but also

The Magic School Bus fosters children's imagination and love of fantasy. *THE MAGIC SCHOOL BUS materials courtesy of Scholastic Entertainment Inc.*

increased the rate at which children were able to successfully identify and explain scientific phenomena (Rockman et al 1996).

Civics and Social Studies

When most of you hear the words *Schoolhouse Rock*, you probably start thinking of some of the show's most famous segments, like "Conjunction Junction, What's Your Function?" or "I'm Just a Bill." The latter example, which described the steps through which a bill must go to become a law, and "The Shot Heard Round the World," which tells the story of the American Revolution, were the subjects of a series of studies testing children's comprehension (Calvert, 1995; Calvert & Pfordresher, 1994; Calvert, Rigaud, & Mazella, 1991; Calvert & Tart, 1993). These studies found that although the songs improved verbatim recall of the lyrics, they did not improve comprehension of the subject matter.

Although history-based programs for children are few and far between, PBS aired *Liberty's Kids*, which chronicled the Revolutionary War, from 2002 to 2004 (Schocket, 2011). The show featured a star-studded cast of celebrities who lent their voices to the animated series, including Whoopi Goldberg, Billy Crystal, Liam Neeson, and Arnold Schwarzenegger (Schocket, 2011). Although no quantitative research has been conducted about the effects that *Liberty's Kids* had on viewers, Schocket (2011) obtained anecdotal qualitative evidence that some college students credit the show for sparking their interest in the American Revolution. This evidence should be viewed with extreme caution because Schocket's primary research interest was the development of the show, not its educational impact.

In addition to examining children's comprehension of historical events, many researchers have examined the impact that news broadcasts and current events shows have on middle school and high school audiences. One of the most-studied news shows for preteens and teenagers is *Channel One*, which provides schools that air the program with free televisions and other audiovisual equipment (Fisch, 2009). *Channel One*, which is often viewed during homeroom or first period, helped launch the journalism careers of Lisa Ling and Anderson Cooper. Viewing the 10-minute news program has been shown to improve knowledge of current events that are covered on the show when compared to nonviewing students (Greenberg & Brand, 1993; Johnston & Brzezinski, 1994). The show's impact, however, is not equal for all viewers. Little effect was seen for students with "C" or "D" GPAs, whereas students whose teachers encouraged classroom discussions of news events showed much stronger effects (Johnston & Brzezinski, 1994).

Infant and Toddler Edutainment

Despite repeated suggestions from the American Academy of Pediatrics (1999, 2001) discouraging parents from letting children under the age of two watch television, in recent years the market for infant and toddler-targeted programming has grown exponentially. In addition to the plethora of DVDs targeted at babies, such as *Baby Einstein*, *Brainy Baby*, and *Baby Genius*, there are also entire channels dedicated to infants and toddlers, such as BabyTV and BabyFirstTV, providing round-the-clock programs for children who aren't even old enough to use the TV remote control. Nearly all media for children under two is promoted as educational or as "stimulating brain development" (Anderson & Pempek, 2005). Many parents hoping to give their little ones a head start on learning spend millions of dollars on these products. According to Barr, Lally, Hilliard, Andolina, and Ruskis (as cited in Linebarger & Vaala, 2010), the average 6-month-old U.S. infant has at least four "baby videos," and by 18 months, that number is more than seven. Linebarger and Walker (2005) found that parents noticed infants showing interest in television at around 9 months of age.

Two areas on which researchers have focused when studying infants, toddlers, and television are if babies (1) imitate what they see on television and (2) learn new words from television (Krcmar, 2011).

Mimicry

Several studies have shown that children are able to mimic what they see on television. Children as young as 14 months have imitated a video that showed a person taking apart and reassembling a simple toy (Meltzoff, 1988). However, other studies have shown that children do not relate what they see on television to real life. A popular type of imitation research involves a child watching an adult on television or in person hide a toy in another room; then the child is put in the room and told to find the toy (Schmitt & Anderson, 2002; Troseth, 2003; Troseth & DeLoache, 1998). Children between the ages of 24 and 30 months performed worse at finding the toy if they had watched the video. Children aged 36 months performed equally well despite being in either the television or live condition; however, the ones who watched it live found the toy faster.

These find-the-toy studies indicate a phenomenon that researchers have dubbed the **video deficit**, meaning that younger children appear not to be able to readily connect what they see on television and the real world (see Krcmar, 2010, for a review). Although children are bombarded with media from the moment they enter the world, there is some evidence that this video deficit emerges around 15 months of age. Barr, Muentener, and Garcia (2007) observed 6-month-old children imitating an action seen on video or live equally well; however, 15-month-olds imitated the video less readily when compared to peers who saw a live demonstration. Recall that Meltzoff (1988) observed 14-month-olds imitating on-screen actions. So what happens between 14 and 15 months of age to cause the video deficit to emerge? Right now, researchers are not entirely sure, but more studies are being conducted to better understand the deficit's emergence.

Word Learning

Although we have seen earlier in this chapter that preschoolers can learn words from television, research into infants and toddlers has shown quite different (and mixed) results. Pempek et al. (2010) found that infants do not appear to begin comprehending video until they are 18 months old. Pempek and colleagues manipulated episodes of *Teletubbies* so that shots were out of order and the dialog was played in reverse. They found that babies did not begin to show increased attention (i.e., longer looks at the screen) until the 18-month mark, whereas 6- to 12-month-olds did not react differently toward the manipulated stimuli. This finding suggests that young children may not be able to comprehend what they are watching on television until they are approximately a year and a half old.

Krcmar, Grela, and Lin (2007) discovered that children do not begin **fast-mapping** words from television until they are approximately two years old; however, children as young as 15 months were able to learn the same words if taught by a live adult. Krcmar (2011) found that 6- to 24-month-olds did not learn words from television, even if the person on the television was the infant's own mother! Robb, Richert, and Wartella (2009) found that 12- to 15-month-olds did not learn words after repeated exposure to a *Baby Wordsworth* DVD. Zimmerman, Christakis, and Meltzoff (2007) found that watching one hour of *Baby Einstein* a day was linked to a 17-point *drop* in language scores for 8- to 16-month-olds! However, the negative effect was not found in toddlers from 17 months to 24 months old.

Other Linguistic Learning

Vandewater, Barr, Park, and Lee (2010) discovered that repeated daily exposure to *Brainy Baby's Baby, Shapes, and Colors* DVD did teach older toddlers (18 to 33 months) to be able to correctly identify the crescent shape. Toddlers watched the 10-minute video at least once a day for 15 days, and were tested against nonviewers. Although the viewers performed significantly better, Vandewater and her colleagues acknowledged that the success of the video was likely due to the participants' age, the fact that the stimulus (the video) and post-test (a picture book that the children pointed to) were visually similar, and the toddlers being repeatedly exposed to the *Baby Genius* DVD.

Linebarger and Walker (2005) found that infants and toddlers who watched children's shows not targeted to their age range also showed linguistic improvements. In a 27-month-long study, Linebarger and Walker found that watching *Dora the Explorer*, *Blue's Clues*, *Arthur*, *Clifford the Big Red Dog*, and *Dragon Tales* resulted in greater vocabularies for children who began watching at six months of age until 30 months of age. The study also found that *Sesame Street* and *Teletubbies* were related to negative expressive language (i.e., talking during the show) outcomes. Linebarger and Walker posited that perhaps *Sesame Street* tested negatively because the changing vignettes did not provide the support necessary for comprehension and language learning. According to Linebarger and Walker, *Sesame Street* has since made changes to its format, promoting more cohesive story lines and an integrated narrative structure, which has been shown to improve comprehension (e.g., Linebarger & Piotrowski, 2009). The study also found mixed results for *Barney & Friends:* viewers used fewer vocabulary words, but showed increases in expressive communication.

Overall, we see that younger children are able to mimic actions seen on TV, and, when certain conditions are met (e.g., novel content, presentation style,

Just a Talking Book? Word Learning from Watching Baby Videos
Michael B. Robb, Rebekah A. Richert, and Ellen A. Wartella (2009)
British Journal of Developmental Psychology, 27, 27–45

Baby-targeted videos continue to be a booming business, and makers of the videos target children as young as one month old. Previous research has shown that babies are capable of mimicking actions they see on television, but are young children between 12 and 15 months of age capable of learning words from repeated exposure to these videos? Answering that question was the purpose of this study.

Method

The participants were recruited through a variety of means, including local ads, direct mailings, and referrals from local pediatricians in southern California. The final sample consisted of 45 babies (26 male, 19 female; mean age: 59.38 weeks at first visit) and their parents.

Parents completed surveys about general demographics and their household's media consumption. The media consumption survey included questions about a "typical day" of media use, including how long the television was on in the background, how long children watched television or DVDs, and how much time was spent reading to their child.

After splitting their sample into experimental and control groups, the parents of children in the experimental condition were given a viewing diary and a copy of a *Baby Wordsworth* DVD to take home. Parents were instructed to show the DVD to their children five times every two weeks for a total of six weeks. To increase the external validity of this study, all viewings occurred in the children's homes.

Baby Wordsworth: First Words Around the House, which is part of the *Baby Einstein* series, is a 39-minute video targeted at children 12 months and older. During the video, 30 words about household items are presented on the screen, which is divided into three sections. Two side-by-side sections show a visual representation of the object (e.g., flower, table, bowl, cup) and either a woman or child performing the American Sign Language gesture for the word. Across the bottom of the screen, the word matching the object and Sign Language gesture is shown.

Parents and their children returned to the lab every two weeks for follow up testing. During each visit, parents also filled out a vocabulary questionnaire, rating their children's ability to understand and say the word. (Close pronunciations were accepted, such as "dah" for "dog." However, "woof-woof" was not accepted.)

Results

Statistical analyses showed no significant differences between the DVD viewers and the control group. However, a significant relationship existed between words spoken (WS) and words understood (WU) by the children and the amount of time their parents read to them each day. Results indicated that for every 15 minutes of daily reading time, a child's WS score rose by 0.61 words, and WU scores increased by 3.01 words. A very small significant relationship was also observed between WS and WU scores and the amount of background television, where every 30 minutes of background TV was shown to increase WS scores by 0.069 words and WU scores by 0.40 words.

The researchers concluded that the DVD may have been unsuccessful for a variety of reasons: the DVD may not present the words in a context that children can comprehend, the inclusion of written text and the sign language demonstration may have been too distracting, or the DVD is simply too difficult for 12- to 15-month-olds to follow.

Reading was shown to have significant effects on language development, and although background television was shown to have a very small positive effect on vocabulary, the authors warned that "it would be irresponsible to recommend leaving the television on as a useful strategy for developing language" (p. 40).

and amount of repetition), they are also able to acquire some language knowledge. (For a more in-depth discussion about learning conditions for infants and toddlers, see Linebarger & Vaala, 2010.)

Although there is still much to discover about how infants and toddlers comprehend and learn from media, one factor has been shown to improve attention and learning: coviewing with an adult. Wright, St. Peters, and Huston (1990) found that a mother's mere presence in the room can improve a child's learning, although children learn the most when the adult actively engages them in conversations about what is happening on the screen. To help facilitate coviewing, *Sesame Street* includes content that adults will enjoy and find humorous (Strasburger, Wilson, & Jordan, 2009). Recent examples include spoofs of popular television commercials and shows, such as Old Spice's "The Man Your Man Could Smell Like" that becomes "Smell Like a Monster" to teach about the word *on,* or adult-themed shows such as HBO's *True Blood* becomes *True Mud* to teach kids about rhyming, and a Muppet-fied parody of TNT's *The Closer* that teaches kids about things that are opened and closed (e.g., doors, boxes, eyeglass cases). Coviewing has also been shown to be effective when on-screen prompts give parents specific talking points to discuss with their child about a program (Fisch et al., 2008).

Summary

Although many parents and critics fear that decades of children's programming have created generations of mindless zombie viewers, research has shown quite the opposite effect. The time you spent watching Big Bird and Elmo on *Sesame Street* or Blue and Steve try to figure out the puzzle of the day on *Blue's Clues* probably did teach you something.

Educational programming has been found to foster language development, particularly vocabulary acquisition, in preschoolers, as well as developing flexible thinking and problem-solving skills. One way that programs encourage children to learn is by giving them the chance to interact with characters on the screen (often via pauses during question-and-answer segments). Children's shows have also been shown to improve reading skills and comprehension.

Shows for older children focusing on math and science have a strong track record of improving problem-solving skills and encouraging exploration. However, programs that focus on civics and social studies have not shown improved comprehension of historical events, but they have been successful at creating catchy tunes that stick with us for many, many years.

Programs and DVDs targeted at very young children have shown mixed results. While infants and toddlers are able to imitate what they see on the TV screen, they often are not able to learn vocabulary words from watching these types of media; however, as they grow older, their ability to learn does improve.

Overall, researchers have concluded that children are not just a bunch of zombies watching television; they are most likely learning *something*. Even if children appear to zone out while watching, as we mentioned at the beginning of the chapter, at least they are zombies who can spell and count (Newman, 2010).

eighteen

Effects of Computer and Video Games

For the same reason we don't allow kids to buy pornography, for the same reason we don't allow kids to buy cigarettes, for the same reason we don't allow kids to buy alcohol, we shouldn't allow them to go to stores and buy violent and sexually explicit video games— games that teach them to do the very things we put people in jail for.
—Rod Blagojevich, former governor of Illinois (2005)

I think video games and that stuff should be as violent as possible, but age-appropriate. It should be realistic. When it's not realistic you run into kids running around shooting people and not realizing the consequences.
—Darren Aronofsky, Oscar-nominated film director (2009)

There is no doubt about the popularity of computer and video games. There is also little doubt about the whirlwind of controversy that surrounds them. Since the release of the first home television games, *Odyssey* and *Pong*, in the 1970s, the home video game market has boomed. In 2010, American consumers spent a whopping $25.1 billion on video games, consoles, and other game-related accessories (Entertainment Software Association [ESA], 2011). And gaming isn't just for teenagers. According to the ESA (2011), 72 percent of U.S. house-holds play some type of computer or video games (from now on we will use the term *video game* to refer to computer and video games in general), and the aver-age player is 37 years old. Women are also getting in on the gaming action. In fact, 42 percent of all game players are women, and women age 18 and older make up more of the total gaming population than teenage boys (37 percent vs. 13 percent, respectively) (ESA, 2011).

The Interactive Digital Software Association (cited in Lee, Peng, & Park, 2009) found that in the year 2000, video game play already ranked as the top entertaining media activity, pushing television to second place. Video gaming's dominance in the entertainment world is expected to continue as high-speed Internet access becomes more available and the prices for game consoles, computers, and mobile gaming systems continue to drop (Lee et al., 2009).

Much like the rise of television, video games have been and will continue to be the focus of many research studies, as well as a source of public debate about the effects that the games have on their players (as illustrated by the quotes at the beginning of this chapter). In this chapter, we will examine four of the main areas in video game research: the ongoing debate surrounding negative effects of violent video games; video game addiction; the positive effects of serious games and exercise games (exergames); and the uses and gratifications of video games (answering questions about who plays video games, how frequently they play, and why they play).

Negative Effects of Violent Video Games

As with any issue that may impact our society (especially children), there are opposing sides in the debate about the negative effects resulting from playing violent video games. Although much of the academic debate centers around methodological differences and the interpretation of data (see Anderson et al., 2010; Bushman, Rothstein, & Anderson, 2010; Ferguson & Kilburn, 2010) the controversy in the public forum is often about what is or is not appropriate for children to see.

An example of the public firestorm surrounding violent video games can be found with the recent debate about the online game *School Shooter: North American Tour 2012*, a first-person shooter game where players earn points by killing innocent students and teachers using the same weapons that real-life gunmen Eric Harris and Dylan Klebold used in their shooting rampage in Columbine High School in 1999, and that Seung-Hui Cho used to shoot and kill 32 people at Virginia Tech in 2007 (Rhen, 2011). In an interview with *The Escapist*, an online magazine devoted to video games, the creator of *School Shooter*, who would only identify himself as Pawnstick, said that the game was not harmful to the players nor disrespectful to the families of the Columbine or Virginia Tech victims (Tito, 2011a). In fact, Pawnstick said his game was designed so that players "can just shut off their brains and let their reflexes take over," and he went on to praise his game for its "preventative quality," which would "satisfy those with the idea to commit spree killings in their head enough to keep them from doing so" (Tito, 2011a, p. 3). Public outcry against the game, both for its lack of taste and sensitivity and the fear of what impact the game would have on players, caused it to be pulled from its host site within a matter of weeks (Tito, 2011b).

The main fear about violent video games like *School Shooter* is that they will cause increased aggression in players, which could in turn result in real-world violence. Despite a wide body of research, the debate about whether video games are harmful or not has yet to be solved. While some argue that the games do have a statistically significant, albeit small, impact on players' aggression (see Anderson et al., 2010; Bushman et al., 2010), others argue that there is no effect of violent games on players' aggression (see Ferguson, 2007; Ferguson & Kilburn, 2010).

Significant Effects of Violent Video Games on Aggression

Bushman and Anderson's (2002) general aggression model (GAM) is one of the most complete theoretical frameworks used to explain how violent video games affect players' levels of aggression. When looking at the short-term effects through the GAM, violent game play primes aggression-related mental scripts and schemata, which in turn result in an elevated state of aggression (Bushman & Anderson, 2002). When these mental pathways are primed, they are more readily available for us to act on. Repeated exposure to video game violence over time helps to hardwire these mental structures, which can ultimately result in creating a more aggressive personality (Bushman & Anderson, 2002).

Anderson et al.'s (2010) meta-analysis of violent-video-game research was finally able to include a missing piece of the puzzle of video game effects: longitudinal data. In their analysis of numerous studies, Anderson and his colleagues discovered that long-term repeated exposure to violent games can lead to an increase in aggression over time—and this was seen in gaming populations from around the world, not just the U.S.! In their review of video games and the "joy-

Studies have shown that playing violent video games can increase a person's aggressive thoughts, emotions, and behaviors. *Barone Firenze/Shutterstock.com*

stick generation," Barenthin and Puymbroeck (2006) concluded that "violent video games proved an environment for aggression, with simultaneous exposure to modeling, reinforcement and rehearsal of behaviors" (p. 25).

Many studies have investigated the effects of violent games on players' aggression. Overall, the research has focused on the areas of aggressive thoughts and behaviors, physical arousal, and pro-social activities (Lee et al., 2009). Multiple studies conducted by Anderson and his colleagues used meta-analytical research methods (synthesizing the statistical findings of multiple studies into one overall analysis) to show that playing violent video games resulted in higher levels of aggressive thoughts, emotions, and behavior, as well as decreases in empathy and helping behaviors, when compared to nonplayers (Anderson, 2004; Anderson et al., 2004, 2010). Rewarding violent behaviors during video game play has also been shown to increase hostile emotions and behaviors (Carnagey & Anderson, 2005).

Recently, Greitemeyer and McLatchie (2011) discovered that one mechanism that can increase aggressive behavior is dehumanization, the act of viewing others as less human. Game players also become desensitized to the violence seen on the screen (Anderson et al., 2010; Carnagey, Anderson, & Bushman, 2007; Engelhardt, Bartholow, Kerr, & Bushman, 2011). In fact, people who have little experience with video games show greater desensitization toward violent acts after playing a violent video game (such as *Call of Duty: Finest Hour* and *Grand Theft Auto: Vice City*), whereas long-time players showed little change (Engelhardt et al., 2011). This would seem to indicate that long-time players are already extremely desensitized to violence, and therefore do not react to it as readily (Engelhardt et al., 2011).

Many of us know the thrill of finally beating a challenging level of a video game. We may bask in the glory of our triumph for a few minutes or hours (of course, some of you probably bask in the glory all day and miss a few classes in the process), but if the game was violent, how long do the short-term effects last on our minds and in our bodies? Barlett, Branch, Rodeheffer, and Harris (2009) found that playing *Mortal Combat: Deadly Alliance* for 15 minutes resulted in significant increases in physical arousal (i.e., heart rate) and aggressive thoughts and behaviors. Their study found that the hostile thoughts and feelings lasted less than four minutes after the end of the game; however, aggressive behavior and elevated heart rate lasted at least four minutes, but returned to normal around the 10-minute mark. (It should be noted that Barlett et al. did caution that the study shows there is the possibility that aggressive behavior and increased arousal could last longer than 10 minutes.)

By this point, you may be wondering how increased aggression is measured in these studies. Do researchers see if a game player goes out and punches another person? Of course not! (Besides, the Institutional Review Board at any university would never approve such a study.) According to Anderson et al. (2010), most high-quality experiments measure a player's aggressive behavior via artificial means such as blasts of white noise (see Engelhardt et al., 2011) or giving hot sauce to a person who does not like spicy food, who in fact does not exist (see Barlett et al., 2009). Players with higher aggression will select louder

---

Research Spotlight

How Long Do the Short-Term Violent Video Game Effects Last?
Christopher Barlett, Omar Branch, Christopher Rodeheffer, and Richard Harris (2009)
Aggressive Behavior, 35, 225–236

Although many researchers are concerned about the violent effects of video games, less attention is devoted to studying how long the effects last. In this two-part study, Barlett, Branch, Rodeheffer, and Harris examined just how long our minds, bodies, and behaviors are affected by violent video game play.

Research Questions

In order to examine the short-term effects of violent video games, the researchers tested the following three research questions:

1. Will long-term exposure to violent video games increase aggressive behavior?

2. Does violent video game play increase aggressive behavior immediately after game play has concluded?

3. How long does this heightened aggression last?

Study 1

Although the main objective of this study was to answer the third research question, Barlett et al. had to first prove that their stimulus material fulfilled the requirements of the first two questions.

Method

To accomplish this task, 91 students (69 male, 22 female; mean age: 19.45 years) from a general psychology class were recruited in exchange for class credit. The participants, who came to the lab one at a time, were told they would be taking part in two unrelated studies, one for video games, the other for food preference. The participants were randomly assigned into experimental and control groups. The experimental group played a violent video game (i.e., *Mortal Combat: Deadly Alliance* on a PlayStation 2), while the control group played a nonviolent game (i.e., *Hard Hitter Tennis* for the PlayStation 2). The groups were subdivided into 4-minute and 9-minute conditions.

To begin, each participant filled out questionnaires about aggression and hostility and completed one-third of the Word Completion Task. This instrument provided participants with word fragments, such as K I _ _ . Participants were asked to quickly fill in the blanks to complete the word, which could be filled in as K I L L or K I S S.

Participants were then given a brief tutorial on how to play the game before the timed game play session began. While each participant was playing either the violent or nonviolent game, the experimenter set out materials for the Hot Sauce Paradigm, which is used to assess overt aggressive behavior based on how much hot sauce the participant would force someone who does not like spicy foods to eat. The materials included four bottles of hot sauce, a plastic spoon, four Popsicle sticks, and two plastic cups. The experimenter then told the participant that while they continued to play the game, the experimenter had to step out for a few minutes to assist another participant who was taking part in a food preference study. (In fact, this "other participant" and the food preference study did not exist.)

When the experimenter returned and game play ended, participants' heart rate was measured, and they were given questions to assess their hostility and another one-third of the Word Completion Task. Participants then answered questions about their preferences for sweet, savory, spicy, hot, bland, and salty foods.

After completing the assessments, participants were given a food preference questionnaire from the "other participant" down the hall. It clearly indicated that the other participant did not like spicy foods. The participants were told that the other person would have to eat all of whichever hot sauce they selected for them. After tasting each sauce with a Popsicle stick to see how spicy each one was, participants poured the sauce of their choice into a cup for the other person to eat. After pouring the desired amount of sauce into the cup, the experimenter took it and left the room to give it to the "other participant."

For those in the 4-minute condition, the researcher actually stepped into the hallway, set the cup on the floor, and then reentered the room, telling the participant that they had handed the cup to a research assistant to take to the other person. At this point, about four minutes had elapsed since the end of game play.

The participants' heart rate was measured, and the researcher gave the participant another set of hostility and word completion questionnaires and the final one-third of the Word Completion Task for the "second study" they were participating in (i.e., the fictitious food preference study). The participants were told that if the questionnaires seemed similar to the other sets, it was because both studies were examining similar variables.

After completion, the participants were thanked and debriefed.

Participants in the 9-minute condition underwent identical procedures, except that when the experimenter left to take the hot sauce to the other person, they did not reenter the room for five minutes.

Results

Analyses showed the violent games did result in significant increases in physical arousal and aggressive thoughts and feelings compared to those in the nonviolent game condition. Aggressive thoughts and feelings lasted less than four minutes, meaning that by the time they conducted the hot sauce test, aggressive thoughts and feelings had returned to baseline, no matter which delay condition participants were in. Meanwhile, the effects on physical arousal (i.e., heart rate) lasted more than four minutes but less than nine minutes.

Study 2

Whereas the first study focused on internal variables (i.e., feelings, thoughts, and heart rate) which have been shown to influence aggressive behavior, the researchers conducted a second experiment to determine how long the effects on overt aggressive behavior last after game play.

Method

Ninety-one participants (48 male, 43 female; mean age: 18.60 years) were recruited for this part of the study. Because the first study showed that the violent video game did lead to increases in aggression, no control group was used in the second study. These participants were randomly assigned to three time-delayed conditions: 0-minute delay, 5-minute delay, and 10-minute delay.

Similar to the first study, participants played the violent video game for 15 minutes. Depending on which condition each participant was assigned to, they completed the Hot Sauce Paradigm zero, five, or ten minutes after their gaming session had ended.

Results

After conducting several statistical analyses, the data revealed that aggressive behavior resulting from the violent video game lasted between five and 10 minutes.

Overall Findings

Combined, these two studies shed new light on the short-term effects of violent video game play. Whereas aggressive thoughts and feelings dissipate within four minutes of ending a violent game, the effects on arousal and behavior last slightly longer, between five and 10 minutes. This may seem like a small window for violent behavior, but the authors admitted that the effects could last much longer.

volumes and longer durations for the white noise blasts, or they choose to give a person a larger quantity of a spicier hot sauce. While these methods may seem silly to us when we read about them, researchers design their studies so that participants are not suspicious of their motives. The noise blasts and hot sauce tests typically provide a reliable means of determining what type of discomfort they are willing to subject another person to. High-quality nonexperimental studies usually use standardized questionnaires as their means of measurement (Anderson et al., 2010).

The Other Side of the Coin

Although a large body of research indicates linkages between violent video games, increases in aggression, and decreases in empathy, some researchers say this research is flawed. The crux of their argument is related to methodological issues (Ferguson, 2007, Ferguson & Kilburn, 2010; Freedman, 2002; Olson, 2004) and alleged publisher bias in academic journals (Ferguson, 2007). Lee et al. (2009) outlined the general arguments that researchers on this side of the issue cite as major flaws with video game effects studies:

1. Aggression often is not clearly defined, and the terms *aggression* and *violence* are often used interchangeably.

2. Most studies use only one particular game as the stimulus and it is played for a fixed amount of time.

3. The causal relationship between aggression in real life and playing video games is not straightforward. Variables such as age, gender, and personality come into play.

4. Many studies are conducted with small, nonrandom, nonrepresentative samples.

Ferguson (2007) also asked the reasonable question:

> Is it possible that a behavior with such a high base rate (i.e., video game playing) is useful in explaining a behavior with a very low base rate (i.e., school shootings)? Put another way, can an almost universal behavior truly predict a rate behavior? (p. 310)

Clearly, Ferguson and other like-minded critics argue that the answer is a firm "no," and some studies support this position (see Williams & Skoric, 2005; Baldaro et al., 2004). Obviously, the video game industry supports this side of the argument, although the weight of the evidence is on the other side.

Is There a Third Side of the Coin?

Although it is obvious that Anderson and colleagues and Ferguson and colleagues are not willing to back down, another group of researchers has proposed an alternative framework for examining the relationship between video games and aggression. Slater, Henry, Swaim, and (a different) Anderson (2003) have proposed that people with aggressive personalities may seek out violent games, thus creating a reinforcing and reciprocal cycle. Dubbed the "downward spiral model" (p. 714), the foundation for this model is that aggressive players seek out violent games to satisfy their needs, thus grounding the model in the uses and gratifications approach (which we will discuss later in this chapter) and Zillmann and Bryant's (1985) selective exposure theory.

Of course, the downward spiral model is often overshadowed by the major voices in the video game debate, and more studies need to be conducted before this model is seen as a viable alternative (or perhaps a complementary point of view) in the realm of video game effects research (Lee et al., 2009).

Video Game Addiction

Although video game addiction has not been deemed an "official" mental illness by the American Psychiatric Association (APA), the American Medical Association (AMA) released a report in 2007 on the "addictive potential" of video games. In this report, the AMA "strongly encouraged" the APA, which drafts diagnostic criteria for the *Diagnostic and Statistical Manual of Mental Disorders-IV,* to include Internet and video game addiction as part of a new category of "behavioral addictions" (2007a, p. 7). This new category currently lists gambling as the only behavioral addiction disorder. The APA is currently gathering data about both Internet and video game effects before making an official decision about their addictive potential. Meanwhile, the media are quick to report on any story that may be related to game addiction. For example, in 2010 a Korean couple was arrested after their three-month-old daughter died of starvation after the couple repeatedly spent up to 12 hours a day in an Internet café playing a video game (Cho, 2010). You may ask yourself, "What game could be so interesting that they would neglect their baby girl like that?" According to police, the couple was playing a game called *Prius Online*—where they were raising a "virtual daughter" (Cho, 2010).

Video game addiction seems to be a serious problem in South Korea, where 95 percent of all households have broadband Internet (Cho, 2010). In fact, the South Korean government has opened special hospitals and clinics to treat players suffering from addiction (Faiola, 2006). In 2005, 10 South Koreans died from game addiction-related causes (e.g., blocked blood circulation) (Faiola, 2006).

In general, researchers have found that younger male players are the most at risk for becoming video game addicts or problematic (i.e., heavy) users (Mentzoni et al., 2011). Although the percentage of gamers that could be considered addicts is inconsistent from nation to nation (e.g., one study found that 8.5 percent of U.S. gamers between the ages of 8–18 were addicts [Harris Interactive, 2007], whereas a study of Norwegian gamers found that only 0.6 percent could be considered addicts [Mentzoni et al., 2011]), the symptoms of game addiction appear to be global. Numerous studies have examined the negative consequences of video game addiction. Research has shown that scans of video game addicts' brains are very similar to scans of people suffering from substance abuse (Han et al., 2010; Weinstein, 2010).

One area of great concern about video game addiction is with players of MMORPGs (massively multiplayer online role-playing games) (Lee et al., 2009). These games feature interactive, real-time game-play features that are likely to lead to "overuse" (AMA, 2007a, 2007b). One of the most popular MMORPGs is *World of Warcraft* (*WoW*). *WoW* players have reported that part of their motivations for playing are the social aspects of the game, especially communicating with people from different areas (Frostling-Henningsson, 2009), thus building high levels of online social support, particularly for heavy users (Longman, O'Connor, & Obst, 2009). However, the heavy users were found to have lower real-world social support and higher rates of depression, stress, and anxiety (Longman et al., 2009). Those findings backed the AMA's (2007a, 2007b) fears about players becoming socially marginalized in the real world, leading to loneliness and difficulty dealing with social situations. *WoW* players often play at various times of day (and night). Lemola and colleagues (2011) found that users who play between 10 p.m. and 6 a.m. showed higher levels of depression.

Whereas a substantial amount of research has been conducted into the effects of video game addiction, little work has been targeted at how to prevent or ameliorate its effects. One group of researchers suggested a two-pronged approach to combating alleged video game addiction, particularly with online gamers: (1) game makers should increase efforts to make players aware of the risks related to gaming addiction, and (2) the video game industry should become proactive and socially responsible by contacting heavy users and referring them to specialists to receive help with their addiction (Van Rooij et al., 2010).

Positive Effects of Video Games

Not all of the effects of video games are bad. In fact, video games have been found to be useful tools for education. In Chapter 17, we saw how television can be used for educational purposes, and luckily for the joystick generation, the same can be said about some video games. In fact, you may remember playing some computer games in elementary school—games like *The Oregon Trail* or *Where in the World Is Carmen Sandiego?*—to learn about life on the American frontier or global geography, respectively. Games such as these that have a purpose other than just entertainment are known as "serious games" (Lee et al., 2009; Ritterfeld, Cody, & Vorderer, 2009).

According to educational theories, teaching is more effective if students are motivated to learn, receive instantaneous feedback, and can apply their knowledge in a variety of different contexts (Lee et al., 2009; see also the education chapters in Ritterfeld et al., 2009, for further review). Video games can accomplish all of these things by challenging students to complete a task or level, and the difficulty of a game can be adjusted to match a player's growing knowledge (Fisch, 2009). Serious games have been used in an educational capacity to facilitate learning, healthy behaviors, and social change, and we will examine each of those areas in this section.

Educational Games

Some of you probably think back to your middle school and high school history classes and remember them as extremely boring—just a bunch of dates and names. Video games, such as *Making History*, can allow students to get "hands-on" experience with the past, so to speak. McDivitt (2006) realized that his high school history students were not really interested in learning about European history leading up to World War II. In a semi-experimental study, McDivitt divided his classes into two groups: the control group continued to receive standard lectures, while the experimental group played *Making History*, a game that allows players to take control of a country between 1938 and 1945. Although McDivitt did not analyze his data with standard statistical methods, the results showed that students who played the game showed a better understanding of historical events leading up to WWII when compared with students who just listened to normal lectures.

Bellotti, Berta, De Gloria, and Primavera (2009) found that educational games can be enjoyed as much as commercial off-the-shelf (COTS) games. In their experiment, the researchers developed a MMORPG called *SeaGame* to teach proper behaviors about water-related activities (e.g., boating, jet skiing, scuba diving).

Vogel et al. (2006) conducted a meta-analysis of serious games and interactive simulations and found that when used as teaching tools, they have advantages over traditional teaching methods. Gaskin and Berente (2011) found that allowing students to create their own video games is also an effective teaching method, because it encourages students to be creative and develop their own solutions to problems they create. Although serious games are primarily looked at as 21st-century teaching tools, some researchers report that games may also be a good assessment tool (e.g., tests and quizzes). Whereas conventional paper-and-pencil tests may show teachers *what* a student knows, they tell us little about what students can *do* with that knowledge (Rothman, 2011). Researchers predict that game-based testing will become more mainstream in the coming years (Rothman, 2011). Maybe one day in the future, there will be a video game to assess whether you learned anything from this chapter about video games!

Exergames and Games for Health-Based Knowledge

Of course one of the major fears about gaming is that it is turning millions of youth and adults into inactive, unhealthy couch potatoes. In fact, Chaput et al. (2011) found that just one hour of video game play resulted in an increase in what is generally known as "mindless eating," which is eating without feeling hungry. Instead of trying to figure out how to lure players away from their consoles and flat-screen televisions, game producers have designed games to promote exercise and other healthy activities. These games are known as **exergames**, and they have shown a lot of promise in the fight against childhood obesity. Maddison et al. (2011) found that playing exergames with the Sony PlayStation EyeToy for six months resulted in reductions in body-mass index (BMI) and total fat percentages, although the results were small.

The most well-known console for exergames is the Nintendo Wii. Utilizing motion-sensing technology, players must move their bodies to play various games like *Wii Tennis* and *Wii Bowling*. The *Wii Fit* game also includes exercises for balance, muscle toning, aerobic activity, and yoga (Cummings & Duncan, 2010). Research into the Wii's effectiveness as a tool for improving healthy behaviors has found that players rate exercising with the Wii higher than traditional exercise activities like walking and jogging (Graves et al., 2010); and the hula and step games produce equivalent energy expenditures to speed walking (Worley, Rogers, & Kraemer, 2011). As entertaining as the Wii can be, Lyons et al. (2011) found that game players aged 18–35 rated band simulation games (e.g., *Rock Band* and *Guitar Hero*) more entertaining. Another finding of their study was that overweight players rated all types of video games as more enjoyable when compared to normal weight players. This finding hints at the continued possibility that video games may be able to change behaviors for overweight players (Lyons et al., 2011). After all, if people enjoy these types of games, over time they may ultimately engage in more physical activity (Graves et al., 2010). *Dance Dance Revolution*, which can be played on a variety of game consoles, has also been shown to engage gamers in moderate levels of physical activity (see Anderson, Gentile, & Dill, 2011, for a review).

Wii gaming was the primary catalyst for the current exergaming craze. © *Heather Swolsky*

Another burgeoning area of effects research involves using the Wii with older populations. In fact, you've probably see a story on the news or online about seniors playing the Wii in retirement homes or hospitals. Research has shown that using the Wii can be very beneficial to older players. Due to the Wii's low cost (compared to expensive equipment), therapists have used it to improve balance in adults over 65 (Bainbridge, Bevans, Keley, & Oriel, 2011). (It should be noted that although Bainbridge et al.'s findings were not statistically significant, participants did show *clinically* significant improvements in balance.) Wii usage has also been shown to improve balance and leg strength in women 30 to 58 years old (Nitz, Kuys, Isles, & Fu, 2010).

Additionally, the Wii has been shown to have positive effects for those with special needs. Wuang, Chiang, Su, and Wang (2011) found that children with Down syndrome who played with Wii showed improvement in sensorimotor functions. Shih (2011) found that using the Wii helped mentally disabled people to engage in daily physical activities.

Although video games may be a convenient form of exercise for many armchair athletes, playing exergames is not without its risks. Patients have developed what is known as "Wii-itis" from playing too much *Wii Tennis* (Bonis, 2007), Wii knee (i.e., dislocating the knee) during bowling, and even Achilles Wii-itis where the Achilles tendon ruptures during running or stretching games (see Sparks, Coughlin, & Chase, 2011, for a more thorough review of Wii-related injuries).

Health-related games have also been used to help patients learn to cope with diseases, such as cancer (Cole et al., 2006), diabetes (Brown et al., 1997; Lieberman, 2001) and asthma (Homer et al., 2000; Lieberman, 2001). The benefits to using video games in these situations is that it allows patients to safely experiment with behavior change in a virtual world (Lee et al., 2009). In a game, patients can learn ways to correctly manage their disease (e.g., checking blood pressure, taking insulin), or they can experience the negative outcomes of mismanagement without ever being in real danger (Lee et al., 2009).

Games for Social Change

In addition to education and health, games can be used to increase awareness about political, religious, and social issues. A recent example of a game that fits into this category is *Crisis in the Gulf*, which was created in response to the 2010 BP oil spill in the Gulf of Mexico. *Darfur Is Dying* is perhaps one of the most viral social video games. The game allows players to experience life as one of the 2.5 million refugees in the Sudan's Darfur region, keeping their refugee camp operational while facing attacks by militias (DarfurIsDying.com, 2008). Researchers have also allowed inner-city children to design their own video games as a way for them to express and explore social issues in their neighborhoods (Ross & Tomlinson, 2010).

Uses and Gratifications of Video Games

While we have discussed the potential effects that video game play can have on people, researchers are also interested in learning what type of people play games and why they play them. One way to try to answer these questions is with the uses and gratifications (U&G) approach (see Chapter 9). In short, U&G can be used to explain why people from diverse backgrounds choose a certain video game to play and what satisfactions they get from playing. Three of the key areas in this body of research examine gender, age, and personality.

Gender

As we mentioned earlier, gaming is not just for nerdy guys living in their parents' basement. Forty-two percent of all gamers are female (ESA, 2011). Despite women's growing presence in the gaming world, boys are still more likely to play games and play them more often (Griffiths, Davies, Chappel, 2004; Terlecki et al., 2011). Girls are also less likely to play video games if they have a real-world opportunity to engage in other social activities (Lucas & Sherry, 2004).

Age

Although games were once solely targeted to kids and teens, the gaming industry is now appealing to gamers of all ages. In fact, the average gamer is 37 years old and has been playing for 12 years (ESA, 2011). The average age of video game purchasers is 41 (ESA, 2011). As we previously discussed, the Nintendo Wii is marketed to gamers of all ages, and is catching on with older generations. In 2011, 29 percent of Americans 50 and older played games, which is up from only 9 percent in 1999 (ESA, 2011). Whereas older players often enjoy the physical and mental challenges video games present, younger players also cited violence as their favorite aspect of video games (Griffiths et al., 2004). This preference only fuels the cycle of research into video game violence and its effects on youth.

Personality

While many older studies from the 1980s and 1990s examine personality factors related to video game play (see Lee et al., 2009, for a review), recent research has found that people with high levels of openness (toward fantasy, feelings, actions, aesthetics, values, and ideas) but lower levels of agreeableness (defined as altruism, empathy, nurturance, nonaggression, and trusting) prefer to play violent video games (Chory & Goodboy, 2011). Additionally, players who were more open, extroverted, and neurotic (defined as anxious, shy, emotionally unstable, with low self-esteem) but were less agreeable preferred games with stronger violence (Chory & Goodboy, 2011). Moreover, players with a highly aggressive personality have been found to play video games in more violent ways than nonviolent players (Peng, Liu, & Mou, 2008).

Future Research

Although researchers have made great strides in understanding video game effects, many aspects of gaming still are being explored. One of the popular areas now is the concept of **flow**. Flow is a mental state where a person is fully absorbed in an activity that requires complete focus, attention, and involvement (Csikszentmihalyi, 1988). All of us have experienced flow at some point in our lives. Perhaps you were reading a good book or watching television and didn't hear your cell phone ring or notice another person enter the room. Although flow has been examined in terms of book reading and television watching, video games present a unique opportunity to study flow because it is such an active medium. Jin (2011) explored the concept of flow in video games. She found that greater flow was achieved when there is an optimal balance between a game's level of difficulty and the player's level of skill. As companies seek to produce the most entertaining games on the market, Jin (2011) said that the ability for a game to induce a flow experience could be the key to maintaining a repeat-buyer consumer base.

Summary

In this chapter, we have examined the major debate surrounding violent video games: do they result in an increase in aggression? And the answer is . . . perhaps. Whereas a large body of research seems to indicate a negative effect, some critics of this research have argued that these studies contain methodological flaws, rendering their results invalid. Moreover, it is also possible that aggressive people seek out violent video games. Ultimately, more high-quality studies and meta-analyses are needed in order to develop a more definitive answer.

We also examined video game addiction. Although it has not been classified as a mental illness by the American Psychiatric Association, research has found that the brain responds to video game addiction in much the same way as a drug addict's brain to illegal substances. Many of the concerns about gaming addiction are centered around MMORPGs like *World of Warcraft*, which have been shown to result in a lack of social support in the real world and can be related to symptoms of depression.

All of the findings about video games are not negative. Serious games have been effective tools for teaching students. This is often credited to the adaptive nature of video games that allow for player input and the constant feedback supplied in an engaging mediated environment. In addition to school use, many serious games have proven to be an effective means of health education. The Nintendo Wii is paving the way for the development of new exergames that are both fun and engage players in physical activity. Games are also a means by which people can learn about social issues happening around the world, like *Darfur Is Dying*.

Lastly, we examined gamer demographics with the uses and gratifications approach. Gamers are more likely to be male, although there is a growing population of female gamers. Males are also more interested in video games and play them more often. Gaming is not just for kids, either. The average U.S. gamer is 37 years old, and many older Americans are starting to play video games. Personality traits like openness, agreeableness, and neuroticism can also be used to predict game play.

Of course, video games change rapidly, therefore research in this field will be ongoing. Much like a video game, researchers will encounter new challenges and levels of difficulty. With video games dominance in the entertainment market, it is unlikely that they will fade away any time soon. Therefore, researchers will need to continue to investigate the effects that video games have on our society. Alas, for the researcher the words GAME OVER will probably never be seen.

nineteen

Effects of the Internet

> *The explosion of information has changed everyone's life, nowhere more than on the Internet. Now, think about the Internet, how rapidly it's become part of our lives. In 1969 the government invested in a small computer network that eventually became the Internet. When I took office [in 1993], only high energy physicists had ever heard of what is called the World Wide Web. . . . Now even my cat has its own Web page.*
> —Bill Clinton, former President of the United States
> (White House, 1996)

When President Clinton made the above remarks about the Internet and the World Wide Web in 1996, he highlighted the fact that almost *everything* is on the Internet these days. Even after the cat's death in 2009 (Cotliar, 2009), "Socks" continues to have an online presence. A Facebook page dedicated to the former First Cat has been "liked" by more than 9,600 people.

The Internet is easily the most pervasive form of mediated communication that we encounter in our lives. Even traditional forms of mass communication drive us toward the Internet. Radio shows and newspapers promote exclusive content on their websites, and television shows often have Twitter hashtags (e.g., #CriminalMinds, #CovertAffairs, #Glee) displayed in the corner of the screen encouraging viewers to talk about the show online and engage with fellow viewers on the microblogging site. Internet-based terminology has even become a staple of everyday vocabulary. Google and Facebook are not just websites we visit, they are verbs that we use in regular conversations (e.g., "I Googled how to make mac and cheese" and "I'll Facebook Jackie about going to the movies this Friday").

As of June 2010, there were 1.97 billion Internet users worldwide (pingdom.com, 2011). As technology continues to develop, making the Internet faster and more available, we find new ways to incorporate online activities into

NEWS ROOM | MISS. HIGH COURT UPHOLDS PARDONS | LIVE CNN
Victims & families express shock at court ruling
Follow CNN on twitter.com/CNN and twitter.com/CNNbrk   9:17 AM ET

VIZIO

Twitter references and hashtags are utilized to encourage media users to talk about show content online. © *Heather Swolsky*

our daily lives. We have the ability to access the Internet from anywhere at any time via smart phones. Automobile manufacturers now promote cars that can read your Facebook news feed to you as you drive! Needless to say, the Internet not only covers nearly everything (including President Clinton's cat), it is our constant companion—our lifeline to the world, so to speak.

In this chapter, we will examine a brief history of the Internet, explore how and why hundreds of millions of people worldwide are flocking to social network sites (SNSs), and investigate how people are using the Internet for surveillance and interaction with their governments. We will also discuss the concerns about privacy and the debate about Internet addiction versus problematic Internet use.

Evolution of the Internet and Birth of the World Wide Web

Many of you probably do not remember a time without a computer in your home, much less what life was like before the widespread adoption of the Internet and World Wide Web. However, the Internet that we know today is a far cry from its 1960s roots. The Internet was originally developed in the late 1960s as a means of sharing computer processing time for military and academic researchers. Developed by the Defense Department's Advanced Research Projects Agency (ARPA), the original Internet was called ARPAnet and was nicknamed simply "the Net" (Campbell, Martin, & Fabos, 2011). Of course, once researchers had access to the Net, they needed a new method of communicating with other users in distant locations. In 1971, Ray Tomlinson developed software that allowed users to send electronic messages to each other, and e-mail was born.

Technological advances over the next two decades made computers smaller, faster, and more affordable; meanwhile, the Internet also became much faster and more accessible. In the late 1980s, software engineer Tim Berners-Lee realized engineers needed a better way to collaborate on the Internet. Berners-Lee developed the World Wide Web, which allowed users to link text to other information on the Web via HyperText Markup Language (HTML). With the advent of early Web browsers (i.e., Mosaic and Netscape) that helped people easily navigate the Web, the Internet became a mass medium that has grown into the Internet that we all know and use today.

What Do We Do When We Log On?

Lin (2009) suggested that to examine the effects of Internet use, we must first look at what people do when they log on to the Internet. Nielsen (2011a) found that when Americans go online, they spend nearly a quarter of their time (22.5 percent) on social networks and blogs. Coming in a distant second place, online games accounted for only 9.8 percent of time spent online (for more about online games, see Chapter 18), and third was e-mail with 7.6 percent. Other main uses for the Internet included using portals (4.5 percent), watching videos and movies (4.4 percent), searching for information (4 percent), instant messaging (3.3. percent), looking at software manufacturers (3.2 percent), viewing classified ads or auctions (2.9 percent), and finding out about the current events and global news (2.6 percent) (Nielsen, 2011). Seventy-five remaining categories (e.g., pornography, sports, music, shopping, etc.) were grouped in the "Other" category, collectively representing only 35 percent of online time.

Obviously, social network sites (e.g., Facebook, MySpace, LinkedIn) and blogging sites (e.g., Blogger, Twitter, and Tumblr) are the main things people look at when they log on. In fact, U.S. Internet users collectively spend more time on Facebook each month than on any other site—53.4 *billion* minutes a month (Nielsen, 2011a)! That is roughly 20,300 years' worth of time!

Effects of Internet Use

Part of what makes the Internet such a unique medium for communication is its technological fluidity (Lin, 2009). With the Internet, we can send and receive information in various ways (e.g., text, pictures, videos, music)—all of which allow us to multitask in an online environment (Lin, 2003). For example, you can Facebook chat with your brother while uploading pictures from your roommate's birthday party, e-mailing your journalism professor about tomorrow's looming deadline, listening to Adele's latest album on Pandora (and then buying it on iTunes), and watching the latest viral YouTube video all at the same time! Media scholars refer to this type of behavior as **media multitasking** (Roberts, Foehr, & Rideout, 2005; Zhong, Hardin, & Sun, 2011).

As Lin (2009) lamented, despite the prevalence of the Internet in our daily lives, the amount of research examining the long-term effects is minimal; however, the research examining how people use the Internet and short-term behavior outcomes is widely available. We will begin our look at Internet effects by focusing on the most popular Internet activity: social networks and blogs.

Social Network Sites

The terms "social network sites" and "social media" are often used interchangeably in conversations about sites like Facebook and Twitter. Before we proceed with our discussion, we feel that it is important to put forth a more definitive definition of a social network site:

> We define social network sites as web-based services that allow individuals to (1) construct a public or semi-public profile within a bounded system, (2) articulate a list of other users with whom they share a connection, and (3) view and traverse their list of connections and those made by others in the system. (boyd & Ellison, 2008)

Due to Facebook's dominance online, both in terms of total Internet use and being the top SNS, a great deal of research has been conducted on the site and the type of people who use it. Although much of the research focuses on reasons why people visit the site and what type of people are likely to share certain

Facebook provides both entertainment and information to communities of networked users.

types of information, some research has examined the effects of using Facebook. We will primarily focus our discussion of SNSs on Facebook, but we will note when research has looked at more general SNS use. Some of the areas of interest in SNS research that we will explore include what factors lead to SNS use, the uses and gratifications (U&G) people seek from their use (see Chapter 9 for more about U&G), the effects of profile pictures and number of friends on SNS users, and concerns about privacy. We'll also discuss the notion of building and maintaining social capital via SNSs.

Personality Factors and Uses and Gratifications

Facebook currently has more than 800 million active users (i.e., users that log in at least once a month) (Facebook, 2011a), and more than 50 percent of those users go to the site on any given day (Facebook, 2011b). When examining the type of personality factors that affect Facebook use, Amichai-Hamburger and Vinitzky (2010) discovered that users who scored higher on measures of openness were more likely to use Facebook as a communication tool and were more likely to use more of Facebook's features, whereas those scoring higher on measures of neuroticism and introversion were more likely to post personal information and photos than less neurotic and more extroverted users. (Facebook, 2011b, reported that 250 million photos are uploaded to the site daily.) Additionally, those with a lower score on need for cognition (NFC) were more likely to use SNSs in general compared to those with a higher NFC score (Zhong, Hardin, Sun, 2011). The higher people score on a need for cognition scale, the greater their "propensity to engage in and enjoy cognitively demanding tasks" (B. Zhong et al., 2011, p. 1265). Moreover, B. Zhong et al. found that media multitaskers are more likely to use SNSs and stay on the Internet for longer periods of time than non-multitaskers.

One of the main reasons people use Facebook is to keep up with friends (Brandtzæg, Lüders, & Skjetne, 2010; Coyle & Vaughn, 2008; Joinson, 2008; Lenhart, Purcell, Smith, & Zickuhr, 2010). That leads to the question, who exactly are our so-called online friends? Debatin, Lovejoy, Horn, and Hughes (2009) highlighted the fact that "the category 'friend' is very broad and ambiguous in the online world; it may include anyone from an intimate to casual acquaintance or a complete stranger of whom only their online identity is known" (p. 87). Although Debatin et al. acknowledge that some online "friends" may be complete strangers, several studies (e.g., boyd & Ellison, 2008; Coyle & Vaughn, 2008) have found that SNS users generally do not seek out new people online, but rather focus on the relationships with people they already know. However, Facebook has been shown to be an effective means for new friends to become better acquainted (Hsu, Wang, & Tai, 2011).

Other uses and gratifications for SNS use include not only networking with friends and family, but also collecting information, relieving stress, and recording daily events (Kim, Shim, & Ahn, 2011). Coyle and Vaughn (2008) referred to this recording of daily events as "publish[ing] one's own life" (p. 16). Joinson (2008) found that additional U&Gs for using Facebook included social investigation, social network surfing, and status updating.

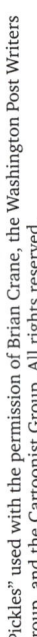

Effects on Well-Being

Most SNS research is conducted using college-age participants. This is done for two reasons: (1) they are convenient for researchers, who are largely college professors, and (2) they are more likely than the average citizen to be using SNSs. Kalpidou, Costlin, and Morris (2011) studied college students and the effects of Facebook use and found that first-year college students spent more time on the site when compared to upperclassmen. Additionally, their heavy use of Facebook was connected to lower self-esteem and academic performance. Moreover, the number of friends a user has on Facebook was negatively linked to emotional and academic adjustment. Kalpidou et al. posited that first-year students turn to Facebook as a coping strategy to alleviate the stresses of college life. It is possible that a first-year college student with a high number of friends is keeping up with old high school friends rather than seeking new friends on campus. Conversely, upperclassmen with more Facebook friends showed more positive relationships for emotional and academic adjustment. Kalpidou et al. suggested this relationship exists because by the time a student is an upperclassman, he or she has made more friends on campus than have lowerclassmen and is engaged in campus activities. When considering overall Internet use, research has shown that the Web can be very beneficial to foreign students as they create new social networks (Lee, Lee, & Jang, 2011). Additionally, students who are more confident in their social skills tend to be more extroverted online, build more online social support, and are more satisfied with their school lives (Liu & LaRose, 2008).

Kim and Lee (2011) discovered that positive self-presentation strategies (i.e., framing yourself with socially desirable qualities, or put simply, selectively representing yourself in a positive light) and the number of Facebook friends were positively associated with well-being. Additionally, Kim and Lee found that honest self-presentation (i.e., showing your true self, "warts and all") resulted in greater happiness derived from Facebook friends. Generally, a greater amount of self-disclosure on SNSs was also found to result in higher levels of well-being (Lee, Lee, & Kwon, 2011). The results of these studies mirror the findings of earlier research (e.g., McKenna, Green, & Gleason, 2002) that suggested the foundation of a successful online relationship was honestly revealing one's true self.

Negative Effects of SNS Use

Although many studies have found positive links to well-being related to SNS use, some studies have shown negative effects. Haferkamp and Krämer (2011) found that SNS users were more dissatisfied with their own bodies after viewing the profiles of attractive users than when shown profiles of unattractive users. It turns out that this dissatisfaction arose from beliefs that the users could never attain the level of physical beauty seen on attractive users' profiles. Additionally, male participants were more dissatisfied with their own careers after viewing the profiles of successful users (Haferkamp & Krämer, 2011). Such findings are as would be predicted by social comparison theory (Festinger, 1954).

Another negative effect of SNS use has been fears of privacy invasion. For college students, one of their most-cited concerns about invasions of privacy is that potential employers will look at their SNS profiles; however, this does not stop them from posting questionable content (Miller, Parsons, & Lifer, 2010). Brandtzæg et al. (2010) found that older Facebook users are afraid that burglars will monitor their posts to determine if they are at home. These fears are not unwarranted. In 2009, police in Hoover, Alabama, arrested two young men who had used Facebook to check the pages of their friends and friends of friends to see when people were out of town and then broke into their homes (Hoover Police, 2009).

Blogs

Although many blogs are associated with amateur right- or left-wing political "analysts" or muckraking novice journalists, the vast majority of blogs are written by ordinary people for a variety of purposes (Nardi, Schiano, Gumbrecht, & Swartz, 2004). Blogs can also take many forms other than their traditional written form, such as video blogs on YouTube and audio blogs available as downloadable podcasts (Lin, 2009).

When looking at traditional blogging sites, such as Blogger or WordPress, Nardi et al. (2004) found five major uses for blog authors: "documenting one's life, providing commentary and opinions, expressing deeply felt emotions, articulating ideas through writing, and forming and maintaining community forums" (p. 43). Generally, personal blogs reflect a mixture of all of these uses. Many Internet users like writing blogs because it allows them to voice their ideas and thoughts without forcing them on their audience; the audience responds only if members desire to (Nardi et al., 2004). Most bloggers write a new post every couple of days; on the other hand, microbloggers generally post multiple updates several times a day (Java, Song, Finin, & Tseng, 2007).

When compared to traditional blogging, microblogging focuses much more on interactivity, engagement, and conversations, similar to SNSs like Facebook. Twitter, the top microblogging site in the world, has 100 million active users ("One Hundred," 2011). Microbloggers use short, 140-character posts, called "tweets," rather than longer posts seen on traditional blogs.

Research into Twitter usage has revealed three main user motivations: information seeking, information sharing, and communicating with friends (Java et al., 2007). These motivations also mirror the main categories users fall into (Java et al., 2007):

1. Information Source: This type of user has a large group of followers. Examples of information sources include celebrities (e.g., @justinbeiber, @ladygaga, @Oprah), politicians (e.g., @BarackObama, @SenJohnMc-Cain), and news organizations and prominent anchors (e.g., @nytimes, @cnnbrk, @andersoncooper, @AnnCurry).

2. Information Seeker: According to Java et al. (2007), these are people who log on regularly, but rarely post. In fact, 40 percent of Twitter users fall into this category ("One Hundred," 2011).

3. Friends: Most Twitter relationships fall into this category (Java et al., 2007). These are connections with people that you actually know in reality.

Many news organizations have jumped on the Twitter bandwagon, and now the site is used by many as a primary news source, due to the fact that users can selectively follow accounts that will provide them with news in which they are interested (e.g., everything from global to local news, entertainment news). During the 2008 elections, 49 percent of young voters reported that they used the Internet as their primary source of political news, whereas only 17 percent cited newspapers as their main news source ("Internet Now Major," 2008). However, television was still the overall dominant news source, with 61 percent ("Internet Now Major," 2008). In general, Tedesco (2011) found Internet use increased young voters' sense of political efficacy, which Campbell, Gurin, and Miller (cited in Tedesco, 2011) defined as a person's beliefs about his or her power to influence the political system.

Not only does Twitter give users more direct communication access to their favorite celebrities (who often "retweet," or repost) fans' comments as part of their response, Twitter also empowers users to communicate with government officials like never before. According to Twitter, 35 global heads of state use the site to communicate with the public ("One Hundred," 2011). A content analysis of Twitter usage by members of the United States Congress found that Twitter does facilitate direct communication between constituents and their representatives (Golbeck, Grimes, & Rogers, 2010). Even the White House has an official Twitter account (@whitehouse). On a state level, 84 percent of governors have an account ("One Hundred," 2011). Although the effects of Twitter accessibility to government officials have yet to be explored, one can hope that it will increase communication between representatives and constituents. This is likely

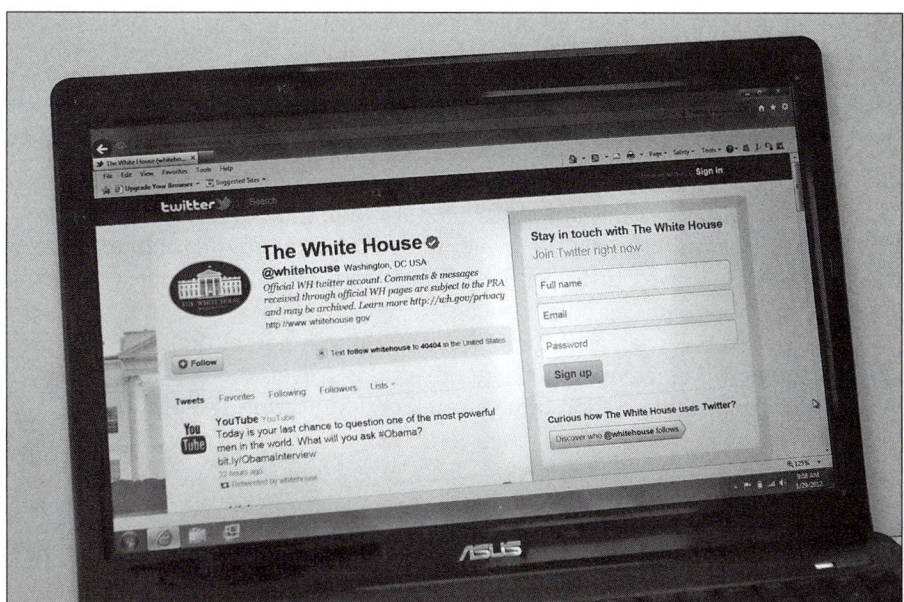

Even the White House utilizes Twitter. © *Heather Swolsky*

to happen because it is easier to send a tweet than it is to write a letter or even send an e-mail; however, only time will tell.

Due to Twitter's ability to be an information source that covers an extremely wide range of topics, it is likely that users will continue to use the site because of its perceived usefulness in their daily lives. This usefulness has been shown to be a key factor in continued Twitter usage (Barnes & Böhringer, 2010).

Computer-Mediated Communication

As we mentioned previously, e-mail use accounts for the third-highest amount of time spent online (7.6 percent). While SNSs may serve our computer-mediated communication (CMC) needs (e.g., you can send a Facebook message or a direct message on Twitter instead of an e-mail), e-mail is still used for communication for a variety of reasons between diverse groups, including family and friends, social groups and clubs, and work colleagues. In fact, 107 trillion e-mails were sent in 2010, and 2.9 billion e-mail accounts exist worldwide (pingdom.com, 2011). A key factor in this type of CMC is that the messages are asynchronous (Lin, 2009). Users are not communicating in real time, as with synchronous communication (e.g., instant messaging). You can send and receive messages at your convenience.

Another aspect that we must consider when communicating online is that CMC has a drastically reduced number of verbal and nonverbal cues (Lin, 2009). How many times have you received an e-mail and you could not tell if the person was joking or being serious? When verbal and nonverbal cues are reduced, it can become much more difficult for us to understand the sender's true meaning. To help provide some context clues, users and texters often use emoticons, such as winking, happy, or sad faces, to help convey emotional cues to the receiver (see Figure 19.1).

Some scholars (e.g., Burgoon et al., 2002; Cummings, Butler, & Kraut, 2002) have said that the lack of cues prevents meaningful interpersonal communication; however, others (e.g., Walther, Loh, & Granka, 2005) do not think the lack of cues will prevent effective, meaningful online communication. Regardless, we must take these considerations into account when communicating online, and as communicators, we must make sure that our messages are clear and will be easily understood. Despite inherent drawbacks of CMC, people continue to increase their amounts of CMC, even though they acknowledge that it is less fulfilling than face-to-face communication (Schiffrin, Edelman, Falkenstern, & Stewart, 2010).

The Internet Paradox

The first major study to examine the impact of Internet use on communication was conducted by Kraut et al. (1998). They collected data during the mid-1990s, when the Internet was still a relatively new form of communication for the public. Kraut et al. determined that participants used the Internet largely for

To send this:		Type this:	To send this:		Type this:
	Smile	**:-) or :)**		Open-mouthed	**:-D or :d**
	Surprised	**:-O or :o**		Tongue out	**:-P or :p**
	Wink	**;-) or ;)**		Sad	**:-(or :(**
	confused	**:-S or :s**		Disappointed	**:-| or :|**
	Crying	**:'(**		Embarrassed	**:-$ or :$**
	Hot	**(H) or (h)**		Angry	**:-@ or :@**
	Angel	**(A) or (a)**		Devil	**(6)**
	Don't tell anyone	**:-#**		Baring teeth	**8o|**
	Nerd	**8-|**		Sarcastic	**^o)**
	Secret telling	**:-***		Sick	**+o(**
	I don't know	**:^)**		Thinking	***-)**
	Party	**<:o)**		Eye-rolling	**8-)**

Figure 19.1   Sample emoticons.

communication; however, the heavier users were found to be more lonely, depressed, and socially isolated than peers who utilized the Internet less. The paradox, according to Kraut and colleagues, was that despite high levels of communication with others via the Internet, those that communicated the most were found to be lonely and isolated.

The study was criticized for a variety of methodological flaws (see Gross, Juvonen, & Gable, 2002; Shapiro, 1999, for a review). As a result, Kraut et al. (2002) conducted a follow-up study, where they found that users who were more extroverted actually benefited from online socialization more than their less social counterparts in a variety of outcomes, including psychological well-being, trust in people, face-to-face communication, and social involvement.

Of course with the rise of SNSs, it is easy to maintain contact with friends and family around the world, which mirrors findings from earlier research that has shown that Internet use can expand social networks (Dimaggio, Hargittai, Neuman, & Robinson, 2001) and help us keep in touch with those we know across great distances (Howard, Raine, & Jones, 2001).

Social Capital: Bridging and Bonding

The effect that CMC has on social capital has been of particular interest to researchers. Put broadly, **social capital** is defined as the resources accrued from individuals in a network (Coleman, 1988). On an individual level, "social capital allows for a person to draw on resources from other members of the networks to which he or she belongs" (Ellison, Steinfield, & Lampe, 2007, p. 1145). Of course, within our own social networks, there are varying levels of closeness to certain individuals. These variations divide social capital into two types: bridging and bonding (Putnam, 2000). *Bridging* social capital refers to those we are acquainted with, but to whom we are not especially close. These relationships are generally known as "weak ties." These ties provide us with access to useful information and services, but typically do not provide emotional support (Granovetter, 1982). On the other hand, *bonding* social capital is found in close-knit relationships that provide emotional support (Ellison et al., 2007).

Social capital is of particular salience to college students, who are often removed from old social networks when they head off to college. Ellison et al. (2007) claimed that a third type of social capital exists: *maintained* social capital, which is related to one's ability to stay connected with old social networks despite not being physically connected anymore. They found that people are able to maintain levels of all three types of social capital, but the largest gains were with bridging social capital.

Choi, Kim, Sung, and Sohn (2011) conducted an international study of SNS use and social capital between American and Korean college students. Their results showed that American students had larger networks of friends that consisted of many weak ties. According to Choi et al., the average American student had 392 friends. According to Facebook (2011b) the average user has 130 friends. Conversely, Korean students had smaller networks, with an average friend count of 79, but their networks consisted of a balance between strong

Research Spotlight

The Benefits of Facebook "Friends": Social Capital and College Students' Use of Online Social Network Sites
Nicole B. Ellison, Charles Steinfield, and Cliff Lampe (2007)
Journal of Computer-Mediated Communication, 12, 1142–1168

In this 2007 study, the researchers examined the relationship between using Facebook and the formation and maintenance of social capital for college students. They chose to examine Facebook use because it is the most popular SNS. The researchers also chose to include self-esteem measures, which can be linked to poor social skills, to see if Facebook enabled them to reach out to people. Additionally, because many college students are no longer physically near their high school friends, the researchers wanted to investigate whether social capital from older social networks could be maintained.

Hypotheses

H1: Intensity of Facebook use will be positively associated with individuals' perceived bridging social capital.

H2: Intensity of Facebook use will be positively associated with individuals' perceived bonding social capital.

H3a: The relationship between intensity of Facebook use and bridging social capital will vary depending on the degree of a person's self-esteem.

H3b: The relationship between intensity of Facebook use and bridging social capital will vary depending on the degree of a person's satisfaction with life.

H4a: The relationship between intensity of Facebook use and bonding social capital will vary depending on the degree of a person's self-esteem.

H4b: The relationship between intensity of Facebook use and bonding social capital will vary depending on the degree of a person's satisfaction with life.

H5: Intensity of Facebook use will be positively associated with individual's perceived maintained social capital.

Method

The researchers sent an online survey to a random sample of 800 Michigan State University undergraduate students. After sending two reminder e-mails to the participants, a total of 286 students (a response rate of 35.8 percent) took the online survey. Of those students, 188 (66 percent) were female, 247 (87 percent) were White, 259 (91 percent) were in-state, and 157 (55 percent) lived on campus. The average age was 20, and the average time spent online each day was two hours and 56 minutes.

Participants answered questions about their Facebook usage, psychological well-being, and social capital. The following are a few of the questions students responded to, using a five-point Likert-type scale:

Facebook is a part of my everyday activity.

I feel out of touch when I haven't logged onto Facebook for a while.

I feel I am a part of the Facebook community.

I use Facebook to keep in touch with my old friends.

I use Facebook to learn more about other people in my classes.

I feel that I have a number of good qualities.

I feel I do not have much to be proud of.

I am satisfied with my life at MSU.

Findings

After performing statistical analyses, the data showed that participants "reported significantly more Facebook use involving people with whom they share an offline connection—either an existing friend, a classmate, someone living near them, or someone they met socially . . . than use involving meeting new people" (p. 153). These results suggested that Facebook users mainly use the site to maintain existing offline relationships and to become more acquainted with those that they had met only briefly.

Data supported Hypothesis 1, showing that the intensity of Facebook use contributed significantly toward perceived bridging social capital.

Hypotheses 3a and 3b were also supported. Students who reported low satisfaction and low self-esteem showed higher levels of bridging social capital if they had higher Facebook intensity scores. The researchers concluded that Facebook's features may be especially useful for these types of students to build social capital.

Hypotheses 2, 4a, and 4b were supported. Bonding social capital was significantly predicted by Facebook intensity, and self-esteem and satisfaction were related to bonding social capital. However, these factors only accounted for almost a quarter of students' reported bonding social capital. Therefore, the researchers concluded that Facebook is much less effective for creating bonding social capital. Whereas Facebook is useful for creating weak ties, it lacks the ability to create close-knit relations associated with bonding social capital. However, because Facebook intensity was linked to bonding social capital, perhaps Facebook does allow people to *maintain* the close relationships they already have.

Hypothesis 5 was also supported; however, general Internet use was also a significant predictor of maintained social capital, suggesting that other websites play a large role in maintaining social capital.

Overall, Facebook is most useful for creating bridging social capital, especially for users with low self-esteem and low satisfaction with life.

and weak ties. The American students reported more bridging social capital from their networks, but both American and Korean students reported roughly equal levels of bonding social capital. Choi et al. concluded that SNS use reflected dominate cultural values of each country.

Facebook has been found to have the greatest social capital gains for users with low self-esteem (Ellison, Steinfield, & Lampe, 2007; Steinfield, Ellison, & Lampe, 2008). Researchers suggest this is because users with lower self-esteem are usually shyer, and using online communication enables them to form connections more easily than in person. One study participant noted that Facebook "breaks the ice for certain people . . . people that you don't necessarily know really, really well, and you might not want to call them up because a phone call could be awkward, but it's really easy to send them a two sentence message" (Steinfield et al., 2008, p. 443).

Internet Addiction versus Problematic Internet Use

Although video game addiction is a concern in the study of Internet use (see Chapter 18), a large body of research focuses on addiction-like qualities related to Internet use in general. Of course, determining if someone is truly addicted to the Internet has led to a debate among scholars. In the United States, there currently is no approved medical diagnosis for Internet addiction. However, the American Medical Association (AMA) released a report in 2007 on the "addictive potential" of the Internet and video games. In this report, the AMA "strongly encouraged" the American Psychiatric Association, which drafts diagnostic criteria for the *Diagnostic and Statistical Manual of Mental Disorders-IV*, to include Internet and video game addiction as part of a new category of "behavioral addictions" (AMA, 2007a, p. 7). The American Psychiatric Association is currently gathering data in order to make their determination in this regard.

Some researchers (e.g., Brenner, 1997; Griffiths, 2000; Young, 1996) adopted the term "Internet addict" anyway, which, as Lin (2009) highlighted, implies that the user is dependent on Internet usage. Conversely, many researchers have claimed that excessive Internet use is not a sign of addiction, but rather a form of deficient impulse control (e.g., LaRose & Eastin, 2002; LaRose, Lin, & Eastin, 2003). One possible reason that excessive users are unable to self-regulate their online usage is that they are unaware of their behavior, thus making it harder to control (LaRose et al., 2003). After all, how can you control a habit that you do not even realize you have? Caplan (2005) offered another possible explanation: users who have lower social skills prefer CMC and therefore use the Internet more often, which can lead to negative symptoms linked to problematic Internet usage. Ceyhan (2011) found that, in addition to social interaction, using the Internet for entertainment was another important risk factor for problematic Internet use.

Some studies have proposed methods of battling excessive Internet use, particularly in children and adolescents. Lin, Lin, and Wu (2009) reported that children who are often bored during free time were more likely to become excessive Internet users; however, they found that increased participation in family activities and parental monitoring of Internet use could greatly decrease the likelihood of problematic use. Additionally, X. Zhong et al. (2011) found that for Chinese adolescents diagnosed with Internet addiction, family-based group interventions were far more effective than conventional intervention methods.

Internet in the Workplace

Companies and organizations use the Internet both to communicate externally with their customers and internally to communicate with employees. When used for internal purposes, the Internet is known as the Intranet. While every company has different internal communication needs, Holtz (2006) proposed some various Intranet-based communication channels that companies could utilize. Some of Holtz's ideas included RSS (Really Simple Syndication) feeds to ensure that people receive corporate content, blogs that could open a dialogue between CEOs and employees, wikis that people could use for research and project management, podcasts of internal discussions, and social tags to easily share information between coworkers.

One well-known method of integrating the Intranet into the work environment is telework, also known as telecommuting, where technology allows for an employee to work from home rather than having to come to the office (Sullivan, 2003). Video conferencing technologies, such as Skype or Apple's Facetime, are one way that people are able to telework, allowing them to still participate in work-related activities via audiovisual means.

Telework has been shown to help employees balance the demands of their job and home life (Britton, Halfpenny, Devine, & Mellor, 2004), although some research has found that those who telecommute can feel lonely, isolated, and stressed (Mann & Holdsworth, 2003). One reason that companies allow employees to telework is that it can be a cost-saving measure (Harris, 2003; Peters & den Dulk, 2003). Of course, for any telework arrangement to be successful, both the company and the employee must be committed to it (Atkin & Lau, 2007).

Lastly, one other aspect of the Internet in the workplace that nearly every employee with a computer will face is surfing the Web for pleasure. Although most employers would frown on their employees using company time to check Facebook, send a couple of tweets, or watch a video clip on YouTube, Coker (2011) found that taking short breaks to surf the Web actually improved worker productivity by as much as 9 percent.

Skype has been a boon to business and social users alike. © *Heather Swolsky*

Summary

As we have seen, the Internet is incorporated into our lives like any other type of mass medium. The Internet is also one of the most pervasive mediated communication media.

SNSs dominate our time online, providing us with ways to keep in touch with friends and family, build social capital with those we know, and allowing us to draw on the resources of those in our networks. Blogs have also revolutionized some aspects of Internet use, especially with the advent of microblogs, such as Twitter. Sites like Twitter and Tumblr that allow for brief messages but grant access to extremely wide ranges of people are beginning to show signs of impact, such as direct contact with congressional representatives on Twitter. However, more research will need to be conducted in this area.

CMC is also fundamentally different than other types of communication. Lacking most of the verbal and nonverbal cues that we are accustomed to during face-to-face interaction, users have reported CMC to be less fulfilling, yet they are increasing their use of online communication.

We examined the opposing views of Internet addiction and problematic Internet use. The issue of whether to include Internet addiction as a mental health disorder is currently being considered by the American Psychiatric Association, and the American Medical Association has urged them to consider Internet addiction as a category of behavioral addiction. An alternative mind-set is that excessive use is not a sign of addiction, but rather a lack of sufficient self-regulation of behavior.

Lastly, we discussed implications of the Internet and Intranet in the workplace. Research has shown that communication technology that allows employees to work from home helps them maintain a better balance between their job and personal responsibilities. Also, research indicates that surfing the web for pleasure for a few minutes throughout the workday can increase worker productivity.

In the coming years, we will likely see an increase in longitudinal studies concerning Internet use, which will shed more light on the long-term effects of Internet usage. Until then, a growing body of research continues to point to some specific effects of Internet use (e.g., psychological well-being). With each Facebook status update, tweet, and YouTube video, researchers grow closer to understanding more about the Internet's impact on our lives.

Effects of
Mobile Communication

---

*It's getting harder and harder to differentiate between schizophrenics
and people talking on a cell phone. It still brings me up short to
walk by somebody who appears to be talking to themselves.*
—Bob Newhart, comedian

You have probably experienced a similar situation to that described in Bob
Newhart's quote above. (A common part of Newhart's comedy routines involved
skits where the audience is only privy to one side of a phone conversation.) How
many times have you responded to someone who said "Hello" only to realize
that they were talking on their cell phone and not to you?

Cell phones are everywhere, and they have become an integral part of
everyday communication. You probably have your cell phone either in your
pocket or in your hand while you read this (or it is at least within arm's reach).

Wireless communication technology has become one of the defining media
of our time (Campbell & Ling, 2009). In fact, mobile technology is the fastest
growing communication medium of all time (Castells, 2009; Castells, Fernandez-Ardevol, Qui, & Sey, 2007). We use mobile technology to stay in touch with
friends and family members on a daily basis. For most of you, life without a cell
phone would, no doubt, seem impossible.

In the previous chapters of this book, we've discussed how mass media can
impact people. However, when we examine cell phones, we are not dealing with
a medium that seems to fit in the traditional media effects paradigm. After all,
we have seen in the other chapters that mass media involve a one-to-many
model of communication; however, with cell phones, we are dealing with "per-
son-to-person mediated interaction" (Campbell & Ling, 2009, p. 592). Moreover,
smart phones combine many forms of media (e.g., music, movies, Internet,

video games) into a device that can fit in your pocket. Not only do we have more types of media to engage with than ever before, mobile technology gives us the ability to take them with us anywhere . . . at least anywhere with good service.

Castells (2000) noted that, since the 1980s, our culture has morphed into a network-based society in which people interact with those with whom they share interests, not with whom they share physical space. Perhaps Campbell and Ling (2009) explained it best:

> The relationship between communication technologies and their users changed from that of receiving broadcast messages to actively seeking, producing, and distributing content while using the same media for point-to-point networking. (p. 593)

Thus, we must expand the media effects paradigm to reflect this change in society (for further discussion about the impact mobile communication has had on society, see Campbell & Ling, 2009). Mobile technology has changed the way we live. In this chapter, we will explore those changes, including how we coordinate our lives with others, how we relate to other people, the role and effects that cell phones have on youth culture, and the transformation of public spaces into private realms. However, we will begin with a brief look at the call that changed it all.

The Birth of the "Brick"

Although wireless communication (e.g., radios, bulky car phones) had been in existence for several decades before Martin Cooper made the world's first public cell phone call on April 3, 1973, the technology was not suitable for everyday personal use (Greene, 2011). Even the early wireless technology restricted users to a physical location. Early car phones were so large, that the equipment used to power them had to be stored in the car's trunk (Greene, 2011).

Martin Cooper demonstrating an early brick-style cell phone. *Rico Shen*

One day in the late 1960s, Martin Cooper, who was the general manager of Motorola's division of communication systems, happened upon an episode of the sci-fi show *Star Trek*. He saw Captain Kirk walking on some alien planet, while talking to his crew aboard the *Enterprise* via his small, hand-held communicator. "Suddenly, there was Captain Kirk talking on his communicator. Talking! With no wires!" Cooper later recalled (quoted in Laytner, 2009). Unsatisfied with the limited abilities of wireless technology at the time, Cooper set out to make wireless communication as easy as it looked on *Star Trek*. "To the rest of the world it was a fantasy. To me it was an objective," Cooper said (quoted in Laytner, 2009).

A few years later, as Cooper was walking down a busy Manhattan sidewalk on his way to a press conference to unveil Motorola's first cell phone, he used the phone, which was so large and bulky that it was nicknamed the "brick," to call his chief competitor, Bell Labs, to tell them that he had beaten them to the punch (Greene, 2011).

Effects on Social Coordination

Mobile communication fundamentally changes how we perceive space and time (Ling & Campbell, 2008). As a result, it impacts how we coordinate our lives with others. Ling and Yttri (1999, 2002) outlined several aspects of social coordination that cell phone use has transformed, including logistics, scheduling, and ongoing refinement. We will explain each aspect in turn.

Logistics

Mobile phones give us the power to change plans or give new instructions to someone on the fly. For example, imagine you are preparing to head to class to take your midterm, but just before leave your dorm room, you get a call from your friend, who is also in the class. Your professor is sick, and class is canceled. Now instead of walking across campus to discover this for yourself, you and your friend are able to make impromptu plans to go to the library and study together.

Scheduling

Cell phones give us the ability to soften our schedules when making arrangements with other people. In other words, they give us more flexibility. For example, when you are running late to meet your friends for dinner, you can simply call them to let them know, allowing them to adjust their schedule so that they will not have to sit around waiting for you to show up. Improvements in cell phone technology even allow for some devices to manage and adapt your schedule for you. For instance, Apple's iPhone now comes equipped with software that allows you to create and change your schedule through voice commands.

Ongoing Refinement

Because cell phones enable us to call anyone at any place at any time, we are able to coordinate with other people on an as-needed basis. Imagine that you go with your friends to the mall. While in the car, the group discusses what the plans for the evening will include: shopping, dinner, and a movie. However, you do not plan where to eat or what movie to see. Once at the mall, some of your friends split off from the group to go to certain stores. Everyone is confident that they can later use their cell phones to sort out details about where to meet for dinner and to find out what movie the group will see.

As you can see, there are many conveniences of mobile technology that we take for granted. Without them, the people in our examples would have walked across campus only to discover class was canceled, waited on a friend to show up for dinner, and would have no clue about when or where to meet up with their friends.

Another aspect of coordination affected by cell phones is face-to-face (FtF) encounters. Although some researchers fear that mediated communication can be detrimental to FtF sociability (see Kraut et al., 1998), studies have shown that mobile communication can actually result in more real-life encounters with those we know (Hashimoto et al., 2000; Ishii, 2006). For example, talking to your friend on the phone about working out may result in the two of you actually meeting at the gym to work out together.

Most of you have experienced the ways that mobile technology impacts family life. It allows parents to coordinate daily routines and errands (Ling, 2004), and is especially useful when both parents are busy or work outside the home (Frissen, 2000).

In addition to family use, mobile technology is also affecting the way people work, presenting both benefits and challenges (Andriessen & Vartiainen, 2006; Julsrud, 2005; Julsrud & Bakke, 2008). Although many of you may be familiar with the concept of telework, or working from home via the Internet (see Chapter 19), cell phones have given rise to mobile work (Campbell & Ling, 2009). Similar to teleworkers, mobile workers primarily work away from an office; however, mobile workers tend to be on the go, whether it's working from various sites within a given location or constantly moving from one new place to the next in a more nomadic fashion (Lilischkis, 2003). The benefits of mobile work include increased adaptability, flexibility, and access to resources (Campbell & Ling, 2009).

No doubt, mobile work sounds pretty appealing to some of you who dread being stuck in an office or cubicle all day, but it is not without its pitfalls. Mobile communication lowers the boundaries between work and home, allowing work matters to spill into family time, which can cause increased stress for both men and women (Chesley, 2005). Of course, the spillover can go both ways. Chesley (2005) found that women particularly felt the stressful effects of mobile communication due to the fact that family issues often seep into their workplace.

Effects on Relational Communication

By nature, the cell phone is a very personal piece of technology. Not only do we carry it with us most of the time, it often is viewed as an extension of ourselves. Many of us customize our phones with colored cases, download custom ringtones, and use personal photographs as screen backgrounds. Often phones are viewed as a type of fashion accessory (Fortunati, 2005a; Ling, 2004).

One of the biggest impacts cell phones have had in terms of relational communication is the notion of "perpetual contact" (Katz & Aakhus, 2002). Even when we are not communicating with another person, just knowing that communication is *possible* changes how we relate to each other and to technology (Campbell, 2008). Ultimately, this heightened sense of connection results in the strengthening of our social bonds (Campbell & Ling, 2009).

Of course, text messages also play a large part in communicating via cell phone. Although many of you, no doubt, do not give a second thought about sending text messages, scholars have found that "in actuality they are symbolic gestures of companionship, even intimacy" (Campbell & Ling, 2009). In a sense, they are similar to passing notes (Ling, 2004), and can be regarded as "digital gifts" (Johnsen, 2003) that play a critical role in connecting us to others. Ling and Yttri (2002) explained how this idea of connectedness works:

> The receiver is in the thoughts of the sender and when they meet they will be able to base a certain portion of their further interaction on the exchange of messages. The messages serve to tie the group together through the development of a common history or narrative. (pp. 158–159)

Put another way, text messages can function as building blocks for future FtF interactions by laying a common groundwork for all those involved. This shared history can help us feel more connected.

Of course, some scholars fear that too much connectedness among members of a tight-knit group could actually prove harmful to forming new relations outside of close networks. Some research has shown that heavy cell phone use has a cocooning effect, in which we are insulated inside our close-knit social group (Habuchi, 2005; Ito, Okabe, & Anderson, 2008). Campbell and Ling (2008) and Ling (2008) have said that one possible result of social cocooning is that those who are cocooned could feel less connected to the "outside" world and are kept from hearing alternative ideas and voices.

Effects on Youth Culture

The widespread adoption of mobile communication has reshaped many traditional issues of how teens transition into adulthood (Campbell & Ling, 2009). In years past, many teens were brought up to follow in the same footsteps as their parents; however, in today's modern society, cultural change occurs so quickly that children's experiences are drastically different from those of their parents. In fact, a *New York Times* article entitled "The Children of Cyberspace: Old Fogies by Their 20s" (Stone, 2010) argued that today's children change so rapidly, especially in terms of their media use, that they will not even be like their siblings in terms of mobile media use and the way these media affect their lives. Such rapid changes in technology purportedly will create a series of "mini generation gaps" among siblings of the iGeneration. For example, you may remember what it was like to have to use a numeric keypad to send a text (e.g., pressing the "2" key three times to type the letter *c*), but your younger siblings or cousins cannot imagine a phone that did not have a full QWERTY keyboard or touch screen.

In addition to formal education, adolescents must also learn how to function in society. Many of the ways that they learn how to live in today's world is through interaction with their peers, and cell phones are the perfect tool for teens to interact. Cell phones give teens the ability to have constant contact with their friends, which has been shown to strengthen feelings of in-group belonging (Ling, 2004, 2008; Ling & Yttri, 2002; Taylor & Harper, 2001). In fact, 22 percent of teens said that the desire to "always be available" was the main reason they got a cell phone (Nielsen, 2010).

Moreover, features such as caller ID and voice mail also help adolescents manage their relationships with their parents (Campbell & Ling, 2009). They can choose to answer their parents' call or simply send it to voice mail.

Of course, there have been some negative effects to adolescents' use of cell phones. Ling (2005b) and Pedersen and Samuelsen (2003) found that teens who report heavier cell phone use—particularly to make voice calls, not texts— were more likely to also be involved in a variety of unwanted behaviors (e.g., stealing, fighting, alcohol and narcotics use). These findings did not point to a linear relationship between phone use and deviant activity; rather, heavy cell phone users are simply the most likely to also engage in those types of behaviors. However, their data did indicate a more linear relationship between cell phone use and sexuality; increases in phone use were accompanied by increases in sexual activity. The exact reason for the correlation is not fully understood. Campbell and Ling (2009) posited that cell phones increase the ability to set up trysts between "all too willing teens" (p. 599). Another possible explanation is the increase in sexting that has occurred in recent years. **Sexting** is defined as sending sexually explicit (often nude or semi-nude) photos or videos of oneself via text message or online (O'Donovan, 2010). One recent study found that 65.5 percent of teenagers and 73.5 percent of young adults (20–26) had engaged in sexting (Lipkins, Levy, & Jerabkova, 2011).

Additional negative effects of cell phone use have been related to academic performance. One study found that heavy cell phone use among high school students was linked to higher failure rates in class, causing them to have to repeat a grade (Sánchez-Martínez & Otero, 2009).

At the collegiate level, students who are engaged in cell phone use in class are less likely to be able to identify lecture material (End, Worthman, Mathews, & Wetterau, 2010). Text messaging during class has also been shown to result in lower test scores (Ellis, Daniels, & Jauregui, 2010). Additionally, students with higher rates of text messaging in class were also found to have lower overall GPAs (Harman & Sato, 2011). You have been warned . . .

Effects of Texting

Texting has become an important form of mobile communication, especially for teens. Forty-three percent of teens cite the desire to text as their primary reason for getting a cell phone (Nielsen, 2010). On average, teen girls send and receive 4,050 texts a month, whereas teen boys exchange an average of 2,539 (Nielsen, 2010). Despite messages often being short (Ling, 2006), they often cover a wide range of topics, ranging from social coordination to emotional expression (Ling, 2005a).

Of course many texters have developed their own shorthand that they use when communicating with their friends. Texts like "where u @?," "call me l8r," and "i luv u <3" can become a "badge of membership" signifying one's belonging in certain social networks (Campbell & Ling, 2009). Moreover, texting shorthand codes like LOL, ROFLMFAO, and TTYL are often found in various forms of online communication (e.g., instant messages, e-mails, Facebook posts, and tweets). Whereas this style of communication may come naturally to younger generations, parents and grandparents often struggle to decipher the meanings behind this "alphabet soup."

When it comes to texting versus calling, the number of texts exchanged has risen while the number of voice minutes has dropped (Nielsen, 2010). Additionally, 78 percent of teens said that texting was functional and convenient, and when compared to voice calls, 22 percent said texting was easier and 20 percent said texting was faster (Nielsen, 2010). The rise in texting's popularity could be attributed to the continuing adoption of smart phones, which come equipped with touch screens or full QWERTY keyboards making texting less cumbersome than on older phones. Obviously, teens are demonstrating that texting is and will remain a key tool for communication. Only time and more research will tell what further effects texting will have on communication.

Private Use in Public Space

The rapid adoption of cell phone use has transformed our social landscape into a place where individuals are privately using public spaces. Because societal rules for public behavior and phone conversations often conflict with each other (Love & Kewley, 2005; Palen, Salzman, & Youngs, 2001), the lines between public and privates spaces are often blurred (Campbell & Ling, 2009).

We have seen that mobile phone use makes it easier for us to communicate with friends and family; however, Campbell and Ling (2009) pointed out that it often does so at the expense of those around us in public, who must listen to our ringtones, text message alerts, and half-conversations. Some studies have shown that some people find it entertaining to be able to overhear someone's cell phone conversation (Fortunati, 2005b; Paragas, 2003); however, most post people do not like having to hear a person talking on their phone (Monk, Carroll, Parker, & Blythe, 2004). In fact, Emberson, Lupyan, Goldstein, and Spivey (2010) found that listening to one side of a cell phone conversation, called a "halfalogue," is more distracting than if the person could hear both sides of the conversation!

Research Spotlight

Overheard Cell-Phone Conversations: When Less Speech Is More Distracting

Lauren L. Emberson, Gary Lupyan, Michael H. Goldstein, and Michael J. Spivey (2010)
Psychological Science, 21, 1383–1388

One of the more annoying side effects of cell phone use in a public space is that we are often forced to overhear one half of a cell phone conversation, or a "halfalogue," as opposed to a true two-way dialogue. These snippets of conversation are often unpredictable in nature.

Experiment 1

Research has shown that unpredictable events generate internal errors and result in disrupting our attention. Therefore, Emberson et al. (2010) developed the following hypothesis:

> The relative unpredictability of a halfalogue will draw on limited attentional resources, resulting in poorer performance in concurrent tasks. (p. 1384)

Method

To create the stimulus for the experiment, the researchers recorded two pairs of roommates having phone conversations in separate soundproof rooms. This allowed them to record each half of the conversation separately.

Twenty-four Cornell University undergraduates (18 female, 6 male; mean age: 19.45 years) agreed to participate in the experiment. To test the disruptive effects on attention, participants were given two attentionally demanding tasks to complete during the experiment: the first involved tracking a moving dot on a computer with a circular mouse cursor in an effort to keep the dot in the center of the circle, and the second involved responding to a series of letters displayed on the screen. The participants were shown the four letters they were supposed to respond to before the experiment started. They were instructed to ignore any other letters that appeared on the screen.

The experiment consisted of 32 one-minute segments. During the segments, participants either heard a halfalogue, dialogue, monologue (where one "caller" gave a summary of the conversation), or silence. The dot-tracking and letter recognition tasks alternated between each segment. Participants' performance during the silent condition was used as a baseline measure of their ability to pay attention.

Results

Statistical analyses supported the hypothesis that hearing only one side of a conversation will significantly disrupt attention. Participants performed significantly worse on the dot-tracking and letter recognition tasks during the halfalogue conditions, whereas performance during the silent, dialogue, and monologue conditions were the same.

Experiment 2

After finding that halfalogues are distracting to those who hear them, Emberson et al. wanted to rule out the possibility that the effects were due to the sudden changes in sound levels. Put simply, they wanted to see if the sudden change from silence to the sound of someone speaking is what caused the lapse in attention.

Method

To explore this possibility, the researchers filtered the phone conversations, rendering them incomprehensible, but maintaining the same volume. The filtered speech sounded similar to hearing someone talk underwater.

Seventeen additional participants were recruited (16 female, 1 male; mean age: 19.81 years). These participants underwent the identical procedures as in the first experiment, except they heard the filtered versions of halfalogues, dialogues, and monologues.

Results

No attentional deficits were found for this group of participants, indicating that it is indeed the words in the conversation, not the sound, that proved to be distracting. Emberson et al. said these findings are especially applicable to situations where automobile drivers overhear a passenger's cell phone call and may become distracted, pointing out that the attentional tasks in this experiment (dot-tracking and letter recognition) require similar attentional behaviors as staying in one's lane and responding to traffic lights.

Earlier in this chapter, we discussed the idea of social cocooning caused by cell phone use. In a public space, we may be further cocooning ourselves due to the nature of cell phone use. Ling (2008) said:

> While generally we must be open to both intimates and strangers when we interact in daily life, the mobile phone tips the balance in the favor of the intimate sphere of friends and family. In a situation where there otherwise might have been the opportunity for talking with a stranger (e.g., waiting for a bus or standing in the checkout line), we can instead gossip, flirt, or joke with friends, intimates, or family members. (pp. 159–160)

In these situations that Ling described, we are exhibiting what Gergen (2002) called *absent presence*. This is when our bodies are physically present, but our minds are elsewhere engaged in conversation via mobile technology. Campbell and Kwak (2011) recently investigated how people using mobile technology engaged with others in public. Interestingly, they found that when people used mobile technology for informational purposes (i.e., coordination and to check up on the news), they were significantly more likely to engage in a conversation with a stranger. Conversely, they found that when people used mobile technology for relational purposes (i.e., more intimate conversations with friends and family), they were less likely to talk to strangers. Campbell and Kwak suggested that the link between informational use of mobile technology and the increase in talking to strangers is that information use gives people something to talk about (e.g., current events, sports, weather).

Katz and Acord (2008) noted the increasing popularity of mobile gaming, which Campbell and Kwak (2011) said can have significant implications on patterns of mobile technology use and talking to strangers in public. In fact, improvements in wireless technology (e.g., faster speeds, greater bandwidth) have improved cell phones' data transfer capabilities, allowing million of people to play mobile games (Soh & Tan, 2008). Games like Words with Friends and Angry Birds have proven to be very popular—and very profitable. Angry Birds, which cost $100,000 to develop, has already earned more than $8 million dollars in revenue (Wortham, 2010). Mobile gaming revenue is projected to reach roughly $11.4 billion by 2014 (Juergen, 2010).

Mobile gaming like Words with Friends is both popular and profitable. © *Heather Swolsky*

Because many of the levels on Angry Birds take less than a minute to complete, Richmond (2010) said they are ideal for playing in a "spare moment." These moments often tend to be in public. The average person has 35 apps installed on his or her phone, and smart-phone users spend two-thirds of their time on the phone using apps (Nielsen, 2011b). This can result in a lot of time playing mobile games. According to Rovio, the company that created Angry Birds, global users collectively play for 200 million minutes each day, or, put another way, people around the world catapult birds at pigs for 16 years' worth of time every hour (Wortham, 2010).

In conjunction with mobile gaming, more mobile phone users are increasingly using their devices to access their social media accounts, and 60 percent of smart-phone users have social media apps on their phones (Neilsen, 2011a). (For a discussion of the effects of social media, see Chapter 19.) Of course, social media apps make up only a small fraction of the apps available for smart-phone users. Apps for almost every purpose under the sun are available, a fact that Apple's "There's an app for that" slogan so perfectly illustrates. As of July 2011, Apple reported that 15 billion apps have been downloaded from its App Store, which has more than 425,000 apps available for iPhones, iPods, and iPads (Apple, 2011).

Summary

It is easy for us to overlook many of the effects of mobile communication in our daily lives because we often do not give our cell phone a second thought—unless we forget it or lose it! Then we are painfully aware of how dependent we have become on it.

Cell phones give us much greater control and flexibility when it comes to social coordination. We can tackle logistical issues, shuffle our schedule around, or firm up plans with a single cell phone call.

Mobile technology has been shown to impact the daily lives of busy families and of mobile workers. However, we must remain aware that mobile work has some potentially negative effects on our home life and vice versa.

Cell phones are a very personal technology, and with them, we are able to not only communicate with friends and family, but we are able to coordinate actual FtF meetings. However, some research has shown that cell phone use can insulate us from contact with those outside of our close-knit groups.

Youth culture has been transformed by the wide-spread adoption of the cell phone. Now teens have the ability to stay in constant contact with their friends, often via text messages. Cell phones also give teens some measure of control over the ways that they interact with their parents.

Although texting may be beneficial for teens to build relationships, heavy cell phone use has been linked to increased promiscuity, and teen sexting continues to be a problem for both girls and boys. College students are not immune to the negative consequences of cell phone use. Generally, cell phones in the classroom lead to poor performance and low grades.

Lastly, cell phones blur the line between public and private space. When cell phone calls, which are generally considered to be private, are made in public, there are many unintended consequences on those around the caller. However, some types of cell phone use has been shown to help callers strike up conversations with strangers they encounter in the public world.

Overall, mobile communication has fundamentally changed the way we think about people, space, and time; therefore, we cannot underestimate the impact that it has made on our society.

References

Abel, G. G., Barlow, D. H., Blanchard, E. B., & Guild, D. (1977). The components of rapists' sexual arousal. *Archives of General Psychiatry, 34,* 895–903.

Abel, S. (1995). The rabbit in drag: Camp and gender construction in the American animated cartoon. *Journal of Popular Culture, 29,* 183–202.

Abraham, L., & Appiah, O. (2006). Framing news stories: The role of visual imagery in priming racial stereotypes. *The Howard Journal of Communications, 17,* 183–203.

Abrams, J., & Giles, H. (2007). Ethnic identity gratifications selection and avoidance by African Americans: A group vitality and social identity perspective. *Media Psychology, 9,* 115–134.

Abramson, P. R., Perry, L., Seeley, T., Seeley, D., & Rothblatt, A. (1981). Thermographic measurement of sexual arousal: A discriminant validity analysis. *Archives of Sexual Behavior, 10*(2), 175–176.

Ahlers, D. (2006). News consumption and the new electronic media. *Harvard International Journal of Press/Politics, 11*(1), 29–52.

Aitken, P. P., Leathar, D. S., & O'Hagan, F. J. (1985). Children's perceptions of advertisements for cigarettes. *Social Science Medicine, 2,* 785–797.

Aitken, P. P., Leathar, D. S., & Squair, S. I. (1986). Children's awareness of cigarette brand sponsorship of sports and games in the UK. *Health Education Research, 1,* 203–211.

Ajzen, I. (1988). *Attitudes, personality, and behavior.* Homewood, IL: Dorsey.

Ajzen, I. (1991). The theory of planned behavior. *Organizational Behavior and Human Decision Processes, 50*(2), 179–211.

Akerman, A., Bryant, J. A., & Diaz-Wionczek, M. (2011). Educational preschool programming in the US: An ecological and evolutionary story. *Journal of Children and Media, 5,* 204–220. doi: 10.1080/17482798.2011.558284

Alba, J. W., & Marmorstein, H. (1987). The effects of frequency knowledge on consumer decision making. *Journal of Consumer Research, 14*(1), 14–25.

Allen, M., D'Alessio, D., & Emmers-Sommer, T. M. (1999). Reactions of criminal sexual offenders to pornography: A meta-analytic summary. In M. Roloff (Ed.), *Communication Yearbook 22* (pp. 139–169). Thousand Oaks, CA: Sage.

Althaus, S. L., & Kim, Y. M. (2006). Priming effects in complex information environments: Reassessing the impact of news discourse on presidential approval. *Journal of Politics, 68,* 960–976.

Althaus, S. L., & Tewksbury, D. (2002). Agenda setting and the "new" news: Patterns of issue importance among readers of the paper and online versions of *The New York Times*. *Communication Research, 29,* 180–207.

American Academy of Pediatrics. (1999). Media education. *Pediatrics, 104*, 341–343.

American Academy of Pediatrics. (2001). Children, Adolescents, and Television. *Pediatrics, 107*, 423–426.

American Medical Association. (2007a). *Emotional and behavioral effects, including addictive potential, of video games* (CSAPH Report 12-A-07). Retrieved from http://www.ama-assn.org/ama1/pub/upload/mm/467/csaph12a07.doc

American Medical Association. (2007b). Featured report: Emotional and behavioral effects of computer games and Internet overuse. Retrieved from http://www.ama-assn.org/ama/pub/category/17694.html

Amichai-Hamburger, Y., & Vinitzky, G. (2010). Social network use and personality. *Computers in Human Behavior, 26*, 1289–1295.

Anastasio, P. A. (2005). Does viewing "justified" violence lead to devaluing others? *Current Psychology, 23*, 259–266.

Ancu, M., & Cozma, R. (2009). MySpace politics: Uses and gratifications of befriending candidates. *Journal of Broadcasting & Electronic Media, 53*(4), 567–583.

Anderson, C. A. (1997). Effects of violent movies and trait hostility on hostile feelings and aggressive thoughts. *Aggressive Behavior, 23*, 161–178.

Anderson, C. A. (2004). An update on the effects of playing violent video games. *Journal of Adolescence, 27,* 113–122.

Anderson, C. A., Berkowitz, L., Donnerstein, E., Huesmann, L. R., Johnson, J. D., Linz, D., Malamuth, N. M., & Wartella, E. (2003). The influence of media violence on youth. *Psychological Science in the Public Interest, 4*(3).

Anderson, C. A., & Bushman, B. J. (2001). Effects of violent video games on aggressive behavior, aggressive cognition, aggressive affect, physiological arousal, and prosocial behavior: A meta-analytic review of the scientific literature. *Psychological Science, 12,* 353–359.

Anderson, C. A., Carnagey, N. L., Flanagan, M., Benjamin, A. J., Eubanks, J., & Valentine, J. C. (2004). Violent video games: Specific effects of violent content on aggressive thoughts and behavior. In M. Zanna (Ed.), *Advances in experimental social psychology* (Vol. 36, pp. 199–249). New York: Elsevier.

Anderson, C. A., & Dill, K. E. (2000). Video games and aggressive thoughts, feelings, and behavior in the laboratory and in life. *Journal of Personality and Social Psychology, 78,* 772–790.

Anderson, C. A., Gentile, D. A., & Buckley, K. E. (2007). *Violent video game effects on children and adolescents: Theory, research, and public policy.* New York: Oxford University Press.

Anderson, C. A., Gentile, D. A., & Dill, K. E. (2011). Prosocial, antisocial, and other effects of recreational video games. In D. G. Singer & J. L. Singer (Eds.), *Handbook of children and the media* (2nd ed., pp. 249–272). Thousand Oaks, CA: Sage.

Anderson, C. A., & Murphy, C. R. (2003). Violent video games and aggressive behavior in young women. *Aggressive Behavior, 29,* 423–429.

Anderson, C. A., Shibuya, A., Ihori, N., Swing, E. L., Bushman, B. J., Sakamoto, A., Rothstein, H. R., & Saleem, M. (2010). Violent video game effects on aggression, empathy, and prosocial behavior in eastern and western countries: A meta-analytic review. *Psychological Bulletin, 136*(2), 151–173.

Anderson, D. R., Bryant, J., Wilder, A., Santomero, A., Williams, M., & Crawley, A. M. (2000). Researching *Blue's Clues:* Viewing behavior and impact. *Media Psychology, 2,* 179–194.

Anderson, D. R., Huston, A. C., Wright, J. C., & Collins, P. A. (1998). *Sesame Street* and educational television for children. In R. G. Noll & M. E. Price (Eds.), *A communica-*

tions cornucopia: Markle Foundation essays on information policy (pp. 279–296). Washington, DC: Brookings Institution Press.

Anderson, D. R., & Lorch, E. P. (1983). Looking at television: Action or reaction. In J. Bryant & D. R. Anderson (Eds.), *Children's understanding of television: Research on attention and comprehension* (pp. 1–33). New York: Academic Press.

Anderson, D. R., & Pempek, T. A. (2005). Television and very young children. *The American Behavioral Scientist, 48*, 505–522. doi: 10/1177/0002764204271506

Anderson, I. K. (2011). The uses and gratifications of online care pages: A study of CaringBridge. *Health Communication, 26*, 546–559. doi: 10.1080/10410236.2011.558335

Anderson, J., & Bower, G. (1973). *Human associative memory.* Washington, DC: Winston.

Anderson, J. A., & Meyer, T. P. (1975). Functionalism and the mass media. *Journal of Broadcasting, 19,* 11–22.

Andison, F. (1977). TV violence and viewer aggression: A cumulation of study results 1956–1976. *Public Opinion Quarterly, 41,* 314–331.

Andriessen, J. H., & Vartiainen, M. (2006). *Mobile virtual work: A new paradigm?* Berlin: Springer.

Andsager, J. L. (2000). How interest groups attempt to shape public opinion with competing news frames. *Journalism & Mass Communication Quarterly, 77,* 577–592.

Angell, J. R. (1941). Radio and national morale. *The American Journal of Sociology, 47,* 352–359.

Ansolabehere, S., & Iyengar, S. (1995). *Going negative: How political advertisements shrink and polarize the electorate.* New York: Free Press.

Ansolabehere, S., Iyengar, S., & Simon, A. (1999). Replicating experiments using aggregate and survey data: The case of negative advertising and turnout. *American Political Science Review, 93,* 901–909.

Appel, M. (2008). Fictional narratives cultivate just-world beliefs. *Journal of Communication, 58*, 62–83.

Apple. (2011). Apple's app store downloads top 15 billion. Retrieved from http://www.apple.com/pr/library/2011/07/07Apples-App-Store-Downloads-Top-15-Billion.html

Applegate, E. (1998). *Personalities and products: A historical perspective on advertising in America.* Westport, CT: Greenwood.

Armstrong, G., Neuendorf, K., & Brentar, J. (1992). TV entertainment, news, and racial perceptions of college students. *Journal of Communication, 42*, 153–176.

Ashby, S. L., Arcari, C. M., & Edmonson, M. B. (2006). Television viewing and risk of sexual initiation by young adolescents. *Archives of Pediatric Adolescent Medicine, 160*(4), 375–380.

Atkin, C. (1983). Effects of realistic TV violence vs. fictional violence on aggression. *Journalism Quarterly, 60,* 615–621.

Atkin, C. (1990). Effects of televised alcohol messages on teenage drinking patterns. *Journal of Adolescent Health Care, 1,* 10–24.

Atkin, C., Hocking, J., & Block, M. (1984). Teenage drinking: Does advertising make a difference? *Journal of Communication, 34*(2), 157–167.

Atkin, D. J., & Lau, T. Y. (2007). Information technology and organizational telework. In C. A. Lin & D. J. Atkin (Eds.), *Communication technology and social change: Theory and implications* (pp. 79–100), Mahwah, NJ: Erlbaum.

Austin, E. W., Chen, M.-J., & Grube, J. W. (2006). How does alcohol advertising influence underage drinking? The role of desirability, identifixation and skepticism. *Journal of Adolescent Health, 38*(4), 376–384.

Austin, E. W., & Knaus, C. (2000). Predicting the potential for risky behavior among those "too young" to drink, as the result of appealing advertising. *Journal of Health Communication, 5*(1), 13–27.

Axsom, D., Yates, S., & Chaiken, S. (1987). Audience response as a heuristic cue in persuasion. *Journal of Personality and Social Psychology, 53,* 30–40.

Babrow, A. S. (1988). Theory and method in research on audience motives. *Journal of Broadcasting & Electronic Media, 32,* 471–487.

Bainbridge, E., Bevans, S., Keeley, B., & Oriel, K. (2011). The effects of Nintendo Wii Fit on community-dwelling older adults with perceived balance deficits: A pilot study. *Physical & Occupational Therapy in Geriatrics, 29,* 126–135. doi: 10.3109/02703181.2011.569053

Baldaro, B., Tuozzi, G., Codispoti, M., Montebarocci, O., Barbagli, F., Trombini, E., & Rossi, N. (2004). Aggressive and nonviolent video games: Short-term psychological and cardiovascular effects on habitual players. *Stress and Health, 20,* 203–208.

Ball, S., & Bogatz, G. A. (1970). *The first year of* Sesame Street: *An evaluation.* Princeton, NJ: Educational Testing Service.

Ball, S., & Bogatz, G. A. (1973). *Reading with television: An evaluation of* The Electric Company. Princeton, NJ: Educational Testing Service.

Ball, S., Bogatz, G. A., Karazow, K. M., & Rubin, D. B. (1974). *Reading with television: A follow-up evaluation of* The Electric Company. Princeton, NJ: Educational Testing Service.

Ball-Rokeach, S. J., & DeFleur, M. L. (1976). A dependency model of mass-media effects. *Communication Research, 3,* 3–21.

Ball-Rokeach, S. J., Rokeach, M., & Grube, J. W. (1984a, November). The great American values test. *Psychology Today, 34,* 41.

Ball-Rokeach, S. J., Rokeach, M., & Grube, J. W. (1984b). *The great American values test: Influencing behavior and belief through television.* New York: Free Press.

Bancroft, J., & Mathews, A. (1971). Autonomic correlates of penile erection. *Journal of Psychosomatic Research, 15,* 159–167.

Bandura, A. (1965a). Influence of models' reinforcement contingencies on the acquisition of imitative responses. *Journal of Personality and Social Psychology, 1,* 589–595.

Bandura, A. (1965b). Vicarious processes: A case of no-trial learning. In L. Berkowitz (Ed.), *Advances in experimental social psychology* (Vol. 2, pp. 1–55). New York: Academic.

Bandura, A. (1973). *Aggression: A social learning analysis.* Englewood Cliffs, NJ: Prentice-Hall.

Bandura, A. (1977). *Social learning theory.* Englewood Cliffs, NJ: Prentice-Hall.

Bandura, A. (1978). A social learning theory of aggression. *Journal of Communication, 28*(3), 12–29.

Bandura, A. (1979). Psychological mechanisms of aggression. In M. von Cranach, K. Foppa, W. Lepenies, & D. Ploog (Eds.), *Human ethology: Claims and limits of a new discipline* (pp. 316–356). Cambridge, UK: Cambridge University Press.

Bandura, A. (1982). Self-efficacy mechanism in human agency. *American Psychologist, 37*(2), 122–147.

Bandura, A. (1986). *Social foundations of thought and action: A social cognitive theory.* Englewood Cliffs, NJ: Prentice-Hall.

Bandura, A. (1989). Self-regulation of motivation and action through internal standards and goal systems. In L. A. Pervin (Ed.), *Goal concepts in personality and social psychology* (pp. 19–85). Hillsdale, NJ: Erlbaum.

Bandura, A. (1991). Social cognitive theory of moral thought and action. In W. M. Kurtines & J. L. Gerwitz (Eds.), *Handbook of moral behavior and development* (Vol. 1, pp. 45–103). Hillsdale, NJ: Erlbaum.

Bandura, A. (1992). Self-efficacy mechanism in psychobiological functioning. In R. Schwarzer (Ed.), *Self-efficacy: Thought control of action* (pp. 355–394). Washington, DC: Hemisphere.

Bandura, A. (1994). Social cognitive theory of mass communication. In J. Bryant & D. Zillmann (Eds.), *Media effects: Advances in theory and research* (pp. 61–90). Mahwah, NJ: Erlbaum.

Bandura, A. (2002). Social cognitive theory of mass communication. In J. Bryant & D. Zillmann (Eds.), *Media effects: Advances in theory and research* (2nd ed., pp. 121–153). Mahwah, NJ: Erlbaum.

Bandura, A. (2004). Health promotion by social cognitive means. *Health Education & Behavior, 31,* 143–164.

Bandura, A. (2006). On integrating social cognitive and social diffusion theories. In A. Singhal & J. Dearing (Eds.), *Communication of innovations: A journey with Ev Rogers* (pp. 111–135). Beverly Hills, CA: Sage.

Bandura, A. (2009). Social cognitive theory of mass communication. In J. Bryant & M. B. Oliver (Eds.), *Media effects: Advances in theory and research* (3rd ed., pp. 94–124). New York: Routledge.

Bandura, A., Ross, D., & Ross, S. A. (1963a). Imitation of film-mediated aggressive models. *Journal of Abnormal and Social Psychology, 66,* 3–11.

Bandura, A., Ross, D., & Ross, S. A. (1963b). Vicarious reinforcement and imitative learning. *Journal of Abnormal and Social Psychology, 67,* 601–607.

Bandura, A., Underwood, B., & Fromson, M. E. (1975). Disinhibition of aggression though diffusion of responsibility and dehumanization of victims. *Journal of Research in Personality, 9,* 253–269.

Bandura, A., & Walters, R. H. (1963). *Social learning and personality development.* New York: Holt, Rinehart and Winston.

Banks, C. M. (1977). A content analysis of the treatment of black Americans on television. *Social Education, 41*(4), 336–339.

Banning, S. A. (2007). Factors affecting the marketing of a public safety message: The third-person effect and uses of gratifications theory in public reaction to a crime reduction program. *Atlantic Journal of Communication, 15*(1), 1–18.

Baptista-Fernandez, P., & Greenberg, B. (1980). The context, characteristics and communication behavior of blacks on television. In B. Greenberg (Ed.), *Life on television* (pp. 13–21). Norwood, NJ: Ablex.

Barbaree, H. E., Marshall, W. L., & Lanthier, R. D. (1979). Deviant sexual arousal in rapists. *Behavior Research and Therapy, 17,* 215–222.

Barenthin, J., & Puymbroeck, M. V. (2006, August). Research update: The joystick generation. *Parks & Recreation, 48*(8), 24–29.

Bargh, J., & Chartrand, T. (2000). The mind in the middle: A practical guide to priming and automaticity research. In H. Reis & C. Judd (Eds.), *Handbook of research methods in social and personality psychology* (pp. 253–285). Cambridge, UK: Cambridge University Press.

Bargh, J., & Pietromonaco, P. (1982). Automatic information processing and social perception: The influence of trait information presented outside of conscious awareness on impression formation. *Journal of Personality and Social Psychology, 43,* 437–449.

Barlett, C., Branch, O., Rodeheffer, C., & Harris, R. (2009). How long do the short-term violent video game effects last? *Aggressive Behavior, 35,* 225–236.

Barnes, S. J., & Böhringer, M. (2011). Modeling use continuance behavior in microblogging services: The case of Twitter. *Journal of Computer Information Systems, 51,* 1–10.

Baron, L., & Straus, M. A. (1987). Four theories of rape: A macrosociological analysis. *Social Problems, 34,* 467–490.

Baron, R. A. (1974a). The aggression-inhibiting influence of heightened sexual arousal. *Journal of Personality and Social Psychology, 30,* 318–322.

Baron, R. A. (1974b). Sexual arousal and physical aggression: The inhibiting influence of "cheesecake" and nudes. *Bulletin of the Psychonomic Society, 3,* 337–339.

Baron, R. A. (1979). Heightened sexual arousal and physical aggression: An extension to females. *Journal of Research in Personality, 13,* 91–102.

Baron, R. A., & Bell, P. A. (1973). Effects of heightened sexual arousal on physical aggression. *Proceedings of the 81st Annual Convention of the American Psychological Association, 8,* 171–172.

Barr, R., Muentener, P., & Garcia, A. (2007). Age related changes in deferred imitation from television by 6- to 18-month-olds. *Developmental Science, 10*(6), 910–921.

Bartholow, B. D., & Anderson, C. A. (2002). Effects of violent video games on aggressive behavior: Potential sex differences. *Journal of Experimental Social Psychology, 38,* 283–290.

Bartholow, B. D., Bushman, B. J., & Sestir, M. A. (2006). Chronic violent video game exposure and desensitization to violence: Behavioral and event-related brain potential data. *Journal of Experimental Social Psychology, 42,* 532–539.

Barton, K. M. (2009). Reality television programming and diverging gratifications: The influence of content on gratifications obtained. *Journal of Broadcasting & Electronic Media, 53*(3), 460–476.

Bartsch, R. A., Burnett, T., Diller, T. R., & Rankin-Williams, E. (2000). Gender representation in television commercials: Updating the update. *Sex Roles, 43,* 735–743.

Basil, M. D., Schooler, C., Altman, D. G., Slater, M., Albright, C. L., & Maccoby, N. (1991). How cigarettes are advertised in magazines: Special messages for special markets. *Health Communication, 3,* 75–91.

Bass, S. B., Ruzek, S. B., Gordon, T. F., Fleisher, L., McKeown, N., & Moore, D. (2006). Relationship of Internet health information use with patient behavior and self-efficacy: Experiences of newly diagnosed cancer patients who contact the national Cancer Institute's Cancer Information Service. *Journal of Health Communication, 11*(2), 219–236.

Bauserman, R. (1996). Sexual aggression and pornography: A review of correlational research. *Basic and Applied Social Psychology, 18*(4), 405–427.

Baxter, R. L., Deriemer, C., Landini, A., Leslie, L., & Singletary, M. W. (1985). A content analysis of music videos. *Journal of Broadcasting & Electronic Media, 29,* 333–340.

Bazzini, D. G., McIntosh, W. D., Smith, S. M., Cook, S., & Harris, C. (1997). The aging woman in popular film: Underrepresented, unattractive, unfriendly, and unintelligent. *Sex Roles, 36,* 531–543.

Becker, A. E. (2004). Television, disordered eating, and young women in Fiji: Negotiating body image and identity during rapid social change. *Culture, Medicine & Psychiatry, 28*(4), 533–559.

Becker, A. E., Burwell, R. A., Navara, K., & Gilman, S. E. (2003). Binge eating and binge eating disorder in a small-scale, indigenous society: The view from Fiji. *International Journal of Eating Disorders, 34*(4), 423–431.

Becker, L. B., & Kosicki, G. M. (1991). Einege historische und aktuelle Anmerkungen zur amerikanischen Wirkungforschung und der Versuch einer transaktionalen analyse [Some historical notes and contemporary comments on American message-producer/message-receiver transaction]. In W. Fruh (Ed.), *Medienwirkungen: Das dynamisch-transaktionale Modell: Theorie und emirische forschung* (pp. 193–213). Opladen: Westdeutscher Verlag.

Becker, L., & McCombs, M. E. (1978). The role of the press in determining voter reaction to presidential primaries. *Human Communication Research, 4,* 301–307.

Becker, L. B., McCombs, M. E., & McLeod, J. M. (1975). The development of political cognitions. In S. H. Chaffee (Ed.), *Political communication* (pp. 21–64). Newbury Park, CA: Sage.

Bell, E. (1995). Somatexts at the Disney shop: Constructing the pentimentos of women's animated bodies. In E. Bell, L. Haas, & L. Sells (Eds.), *From mouse to mermaid: The politics of film, gender, and culture* (pp. 107–124). Bloomington: Indiana University Press.

Bell, S. B., Ford, S. G., & Ozley, R. R. (2010). *Guide to communication at the University of Montevallo* (3rd ed.). Southlake, TX: Fountainhead Press.

Bellotti, F., Berta, R., De Gloria, A., & Primavera, L. (2009). Enhancing the educational value of video games. *Computers in Entertainment, 7*(2), article 23. doi: 10.1145/1541895.1541903

Benelli, E. (2003). The role of the media in steering public opinion on health care issues. *Health Policy, 63*(2), 179–186.

Benkler, Y. (2006). *The wealth of networks: How social production transforms markets and freedom.* New Haven, CT: Yale University Press.

Bennett, W. L. (1988). *News: The politics of illusion* (2nd ed.). New York: Longman.

Bennett, W. L., Lawrence, R. G., & Livingston, S. (2006). None dare call it torture: Indexing and the limits of press independence in the Abu Ghraib scandal. *Journal of Communication, 56* (3), 467–485.

Bennett, W. L., Lawrence, R. G., & Livingston, S. (2007). *When the press fails: Political power and the news media from Iraq to Katrina.* Chicago: University of Chicago Press.

Ben-Porath, E. N., & Shaker, L. K. (2010). News images, race, and attribution in the wake of Hurricane Katrina. *Journal of Communication, 60*(3), 466–490.

Bent, S. (1969). *Newspaper crusaders: A neglected story.* Freeport, NY: Books for Libraries Press.

Berelson, B. (1948). Communications and public opinion. In W. Schramm (Ed.), *Communications in modern society* (pp. 168–185). Urbana: University of Illinois Press.

Berelson, B. (1949). What "missing the newspaper" means. In P. F. Lazarsfeld & F. N. Stanton (Eds.), *Communications research 1948–1949* (pp. 111–129). New York: Harper.

Berelson, B., & Janowitz, M. (1950). (Eds.). *Reader in public opinion and communication.* Glencoe, IL: Free Press.

Berelson, B. R., Lazarsfeld, P. F., & McPhee, W. N. (1954). *Voting: A study of opinion formation in a presidential campaign.* Chicago: University of Chicago Press.

Berkey, C. S., Rockett, H. R., Field, A. E., Gillman, M. W., Frazier, A. L., Camargo, C. A., Jr., & Colditz, G. A. (2000). Activity, dietary intake, and weight changes in a longitudinal study on preadolescent and adolescent boys and girls. *Pediatrics, 105*(4), 446–452.

Berkowitz, L. (1962). Violence in the mass media. In L. Berkowitz (Ed.), *Aggression: A social psychological analysis* (pp. 229–255). New York: McGraw-Hill.

Berkowitz, L. (1965). Some aspects of observed aggression. *Journal of Personality and Social Psychology, 2*(3), 359–369.

Berkowitz, L. (1970). Aggressive humors as a stimulus to aggressive responses. *Journal of Personality and Social Psychology, 16,* 710–717.

Berkowitz, L. (1973). Words and symbols as stimuli to aggressive responses. In J. Knutson (Ed.), *Control of aggression: Implications from basic research* (pp. 113–143). Chicago: Aldine-Atherton.

Berkowitz, L. (1974). Some determinants of impulsive aggression: The role of mediated associations with reinforcements for aggression. *Psychological Review, 81*(2), 165–176.

Berkowitz, L. (1984). Some effects of thoughts on anti- and prosocial influences of media events: A cognitive-neoassociation analysis. *Psychological Bulletin, 95,* 410–427.

Berkowitz, L. (1990). On the formation and regulation of anger and aggression: A cognitive neoassociationistic analysis. *American Psychologist, 45,* 494–503.

Berkowitz, L. (1994). Is something missing? Some observations prompted by the cognitive-neoassociationist view of anger and emotional aggression. In L. R. Huesmann (Ed.), *Aggressive behavior: Current perspectives* (pp. 35–57). New York: Plenum Press.

Berkowitz, L. (1997). Some thoughts extending Bargh's argument. In R. S. Wyer (Ed.), *The automaticity of everyday life: Advances in social cognition* (Vol. 10, pp. 83–92). Mahwah, NJ: Erlbaum.

Berkowitz, L., & Alioto, J. T. (1973). The meaning of an observed event as a determinant of its aggressive consequences. *Journal of Personality and Social Psychology, 28*(2), 206–217.

Berkowitz, L., Corwin, R., & Heironimus, M. (1963). Film violence and subsequent aggressive tendencies. *Public Opinion Quarterly, 27*(2), 217–229.

Berkowitz, L., & Geen, R. G. (1966). Film violence and the cue properties of available targets. *Journal of Personality and Social Psychology, 3*(5), 525–530.

Berkowitz, L., & Heimer, K. (1989). On the construction of the anger experience: Aversive events and negative priming in the formation of feelings. In L. Berkowitz (Ed.), *Advances in experimental social psychology* (Vol. 22, pp. 1–37). New York: Academic.

Berkowitz, L., & Rawlings, E. (1963). Effects of film violence on inhibitions against subsequent aggression. *Journal of Abnormal and Social Psychology, 66*(3), 405–412.

Berlyne, D. E. (1967). Arousal and reinforcement. In D. Levine (Ed.), *Nebraska Symposium on Motivation* (Vol. 15, pp. 1–110). Lincoln: University of Nebraska Press.

Berlyne, D. E. (1971). *Aesthetics and psychobiology.* Englewood Cliffs, NJ: Prentice-Hall.

Biblow, F. (1973). Imaginative play and the world of aggressive behaviour. In J. L. Ian (Ed.), *The child's world of make-believe. Experimental studies of imagination play* (pp. 104–128). New York: Academic Press.

Biener, L., & Siegel, M. (2000). Tobacco marketing and adolescent smoking: More support for a causal inference. *American Journal of Public health, 90*(3), 407–411.

Bilandzic, H., & Rossler, P. (2004). Life according to television: Implications of genre-specific cultivation effects. The gratification/cultivation model. *Communications: The European Journal of Communication Research, 29,* 295–326.

Birch, H. B., & Bortner, M. (1966). Stimulus competition and category usage in normal children. *Journal of Genetic Psychology, 109,* 195–204.

Birnbaum, D. W., & Croll, W. L. (1984). The etiology of children's stereotypes about sex differences in emotionality. *Sex Roles, 10,* 677–691.

Blank, D. M. (1977a). Final comments on the violence profile. *Journal of Broadcasting, 21,* 287–296.

Blank, D. M. (1977b). The Gerbner violence profile. *Journal of Broadcasting, 21,* 273–279.

Bleakley, A., Hennessy, M., Fishbein, M., & Jordan, A. (2008). It works both ways: The relationship between exposure to sexual content in the media and adolescent sexual behavior. *Media Psychology, 11,* 443–461.

Block, C. (1972). White backlash to Negro ads: Fact or fantasy. *Journalism Quarterly, 49*(2), 253–262.

Bloom, P. N., Hogan, J. E., & Blazing, J. (1997). Sports promotion and teen smoking and drinking: An exploratory study. *American Journal of Health Behavior, 2,* 100–109.

Blumer, H. G. (1933). *Movies and conduct.* New York: Macmillan.

Blumer, H. G. (1951). The mass, the public, and public opinion. In A. M. Lee (Ed.), *New outlines of the principles of sociology* (2nd rev. ed.). New York: Barnes & Noble.

Blumer, H. G., & Hauser, P. M. (1933). *Movies, delinquency and crime.* New York: Macmillan.

Blumler, J. G. (1979). The role of theory in uses and gratifications studies. *Communication Research, 6,* 9–36.

Blumler, J. G., & McLeod, J. M. (1974). Communication and voter turnout in Britain. In T. Legatt (Eds.), *Sociological theory and social research* (pp. 265–312). Beverly Hills, CA: Sage.

Blumler, J. G., & McQuail, D. (1969). *Television in politics: Its uses and influence*. Chicago: University of Chicago Press.

Bodenhausen, G., Schwarz, N., Bless, H., & Wanke, M. (1995). Effects of atypical exemplars on racial beliefs: Enlightened racism or generalized appraisals? *Journal of Experimental Social Psychology, 31,* 48–63.

Bogatz, G. A., & Ball, S. (1971). *The second year of* Sesame Street: *A continuing evaluation*. Princeton, NJ: Educational Testing Service.

Bolsen, T. (2011). The construction of news: Energy crises, advocacy messages, and frames toward conservation. *International Journal of Press/Politics, 16*(2), 143–162.

Bond, B., & Harrison, K. (2008). *Media-induced fright during a national tragedy: The case of the Virginia Tech massacre.* National Communication Association conference paper.

Bonis, J. (2007). Acute Wiiitis. *The New England Journal of Medicine, 356,* 2431–2432. doi: 10.1056/NEJMc070670

Booker, M. K. (2010). *Disney, Pixar, and the hidden messages of children's films.* Santa Barbara, CA: Praeger.

Born, M. (1949). *Natural philosophy of cause and chance.* Oxford: Clarendon Press.

Botta, R. (2000). The mirror of television: A comparison of Black and White adolescents' body image. *Journal of Communication, 50,* 144–159.

Bowen, L., & Schmid, J. (1997). Minority presence and portrayal in mainstream magazine advertising: An update. *Journalism & Mass Communication Quarterly, 74*(1), 134–146.

boyd, d. m., & Ellison, N. B. (2008). Social network sites: Definition, history, and scholarship. *Journal of Computer-Mediated Communication, 13,* 210–230.

Boyle, M. P., Schmierbach, M., Armstrong, C. L., Cho, J., McCluskey, M., McLeod, D. M., & Shah, D. V. (2006). Expressive responses to news stories about extremist groups: A framing experiment. *Journal of Communication, 56,* 271–288.

Boyle, T. P. (2001). Intermedia agenda setting in the 1996 presidential election. *Journalism & Mass Communication Quarterly, 78,* 26–44.

Bradley, S. D. (2007). Neural network simulations support heuristic processing model of cultivation effects. *Media Psychology, 10,* 449–469.

Bradtzæg, P. B., Lüders, M., & Skjetne, J. H. (2010). Too many Facebook "friends"? Content sharing and sociability versus the need for privacy in social network sites. *International Journal of Human-Computer Interaction, 26,* 1006–1030. doi: 10.1080/10447318.2010.516719

BrainyQuote.com. (2011). Cell phone quotes. Retrieved from http://www.brainyquote.com/quotes/keywords/cell_phone.html

Brederode-Santos, M. E. (1993). *Learning with television: The secret of* Rua Sésamo. [English translation of Portuguese, Brederode-Santos, M. E. (1991). *Com a Televiso o Segredo da* Rua Sésamo. Lisbon: TV Guia Editora.] Unpublished research report.

Brenner, V. (1997). Psychology of computer use. XLVII. Parameters of Internet use, abuse, and addiction. *Psychological Reports, 80,* 879–882.

Brewer, P. R. (2002). Framing, value words, and citizens' explanations of their issue opinions. *Political Communication, 19,* 303–316.

Brians, C. L., & Wattenberg, M. P. (1996). Campaign issue knowledge and salience: Comparing reception from TV commercials, TV news, and newspapers. *American Journal of Political Science, 40,* 172–193.

Brickner, M. A., Harkins, S. G., & Ostrom, T. M. (1986). Effects of personal involvement: Thought provoking implications for social loafing. *Journal of Personality and Social Psychology, 51,* 763–769.

Bridges, A. J., Wosnitzer, R., Scharrer, E., Sun, C., & Liberman, R. (2010). Aggression and sexual behavior in best-selling pornography videos: A content analysis update. *Violence Against Women, 16*(10), 1065–1085.

Briñol, P., & Petty, R. E. (2004). Self-validation processes: The role of thought confidence in persuasion. In G. Haddock and G. Maio (Eds.), *Contemporary perspectives in the psychology of attitudes* (pp. 205–226). Philadelphia: Psychology Press.

Briñol, P., Petty, R. E., & Barden, J. (2007). Happiness versus sadness as a determinant of thought confidence in persuasion: A self-validation analysis. *Journal of Personality and Social Psychology, 93*(5), 711–727.

Briñol, P., Petty, R. E., & McCaslin, M. J. (2008). Automatic and deliberative attitude change from thoughtful and non-thoughtful processes. In R. E. Petty, R. H. Fazio, & P. Briñol (Eds.), *Attitudes: Insights from the new implicit measures* (pp. 285–326). New York: Psychology Press.

Britton, J., Halfpenny, P., Devine, F., & Mellor, R. (2004). The future of regional cities in the information age: The impact of information technology on Manchester's financial and business service sector. *Sociology, 38,* 795–814.

Brock, T. C., & Buss, A. H. (1962). Dissonance, aggression, and evaluation of pain. *Journal of Abnormal and Social Psychology, 65,* 197–202.

Brock, T. C., & Buss, A. H. (1964). Effects of justification for aggression and communication with the victim on postaggression dissonance. *Journal of Abnormal and Social Psychology, 68,* 404–412.

Brodie, M., Hamel, E. C., Altman, D. E., Blendon, R. J., & Benson, J. M. (2003). Health news and the American public, 1996–2002. *Journal of Health Politics, Policy and Law, 28*(5), 927–950.

Brookey, R. A., & Westerfelhaus, R. (2005). The digital auteur: Branding identity on the *Monsters, Inc.* dvd. *Western Journal of Communication, 69*(2), 109–128.

Brown, J. D., Campbell, K., & Fischer, L. (1986). American adolescents and music videos—Why do they watch? *Gazette, 37*(1–2), 19–32.

Brown, J. D., & Hendee, W. R. (1989). Adolescents and their music: Insights into the health of adolescents. *Journal of the American Medical Association, 62,* 1659–1663.

Brown, J. D., & Walsh-Childers, K. (1994). Effects of media on personal and public health. In J. Bryant & D. Zillmann (Eds.), *Media effects: Advances in theory and research.* Hillsdale, NJ: Erlbaum.

Brown, S. J., Lieberman, D. A., Gemeny, B. A., Fan, Y. C., Wilson, D. M., & Pasta, D. J. (1997). Educational computer game for juvenile diabetes: Results of a controlled trial. *Medical Informatics, 22,* 77–89.

Brownfield, E. D., Bernhardt, J. M., Phan, J. L., Williams, M. V., & Parker, R. M. (2004). Direct-to-consumer drug advertisements on network television: An exploration of quantity, frequency, and placement. *Journal of Health Communication, 9*(6), 491–497.

Brummert Lennings, H. I., & Warburton, W. A. (2011). The effect of auditory versus visual violent media exposure on aggressive behavior: The role of song lyrics, video clips and musical tone. *Journal of Experimental Social Psychology, 47*(4), 794–799.

Bruntz, G. G. (1938). *Allied propaganda and the collapse of the German empire in 1918.* Stanford, CA: Stanford University Press.

Bruselle, R., & Crandall, H. (2002). Television viewing and perceptions about race differences in socioeconomic success. *Journal of Broadcasting & Electronic Media, 46,* 256–282.

Bryant, J. (1986). The road most traveled: Yet another cultivation critique. *Journal of Broadcasting & Electronic Media, 30,* 231–235.

Bryant, J., McCollum, J., Ralston, L., Raney, A., McGavin, L., Miron, D., Maxwell, M., Venugopalan, G., Thompson, S., Dewitt, D., Lewis, K., Mundorf, N., & Smith, S. (1997). Report 8: Effects of two years' viewing of *Allegra's Window* and *Gullah Gullah Island.* Report to Nick, Jr. Tuscaloosa: University of Alabama, Institute for Communication Research.

Bryant, J., Mulliken, L., Maxwell, M., Mundorf, N., Mundorf, J., Wilson, B., Smith, S., McCollum, J., & Owens, J. W. (1999). *Effects of two years' viewing of* Blue's Clues. Tuscaloosa: University of Alabama, Institute for Communication Research.

Bryant, J., & Rockwell, S. C. (1994). Effects of massive exposure to sexually oriented prime-time television programming on adolescents' moral judgment. In D. Zillmann, J. Bryant, & A. Huston (Eds.), *Media, children, and the family: Social scientific, psychodynamic, and clinical perspectives.* Hillsdale, NJ: Erlbaum.

Bryant, J., & Zillmann, D. (1984). Using television to alleviate boredom and stress: Selective exposure as a function of induced excitational states. *Journal of Broadcasting, 28,* 1–20.

Bryant, J., & Zillmann, D. (1994). (Eds.). *Media effects: Advances in theory and research.* Mahwah, NJ: Erlbaum.

Bryant, J. A., & Bryant, J. (2003). Effects of entertainment televisual media on children. In E. L. Palmer & B. M. Young (Eds.), *The faces of televisual media: Teaching, violence, selling to children* (2nd ed., pp. 195–217). Mahwah, NJ: Erlbaum.

Brydon, S. G. (2009). Men at the heart of mothering: Finding mother in *Finding Nemo. Journal of Gender Studies, 18,* 131–146. doi: 10.1080/09589230902812448

Buchwald, E., Fletcher, P., & Roth, M. (Eds.) (1993). *Transforming a rape culture.* Minneapolis: Milkweed Eds.

Buerkel-Rothfuss, N. L., & Mayes, S. (1981). Soap opera viewing: The cultivation effect. *Journal of Communication, 31,* 108–115.

Burgoon, J. K., Bonito, J. A., Ramierez, A., Dunbar, N. E., Kam, K., & Fischer, J. (2002). Testing the interactivity principle: Effects of mediation, propinquity, and verbal and nonverbal modalities in interpersonal interaction. *Journal of Communication, 52,* 657–677.

Burgoon, M., & Klingle, R. S. (1998). Gender differences in being influential and/or influenced: A challenge to prior explanations. In D. J. Canary & K. Dindia (Eds.), *Sex differences and similarities in communication: Critical essays and empirical investigations of sex and gender in interaction* (pp. 257–285). Mahwah, NJ: Erlbaum.

Burnham, W. D. (1982). *The current crisis in American politics.* New York: Oxford University Press.

Burnkrant, R., & Unnava, R. (1989). Self-referencing: A strategy for increasing processing of message content. *Personality and Social Psychology Bulletin, 15,* 628–638.

Bush, R., Resnick, A., & Stern, B. (1980). A content analysis of the portrayal of black models in magazine advertising. In R. Bagozzi et al. (Eds.), *Marketing in the 80's: Changes and challenges* (pp. 484–487). Chicago: American Marketing Association.

Bushman, B. J. (1998). Priming effects of media violence on the accessibility of aggressive constructs in memory. *Personality & Social Psychology Bulletin, 24,* 537–546.

Bushman, B. J., & Anderson, C. A. (2002). Violent video games and hostile expectations: A test of the general aggression model. *Personality & Social Psychology Bulletin, 28,* 1679–1686. doi: 10.1177/014616702237649

Bushman, B. J., & Anderson, C. A. (2009). Comfortably numb: Desensitizing effects of violent media on helping others. *Psychological Science, 21*(3), 273–277.

Bushman, B. J., Rothstein, H. R., & Anderson, C. A. (2010). Much ado about something: Violent video game effects and a school of red herring: Reply to Ferguson and Kilburn (2010). *Psychological Bulletin, 136,* 182–187.

Busselle, R. (2003). Television exposure, parents' precautionary warnings and young adults' perceptions of crime. *Communication Research, 30,* 530–556.

Buzzuto, J. C. (1975). Cinematic neurosis following *The Exorcist. Journal of Nervous and Mental Disease, 161,* 43–48.

Byrd, E. K. (1989). A study of depiction of specific characteristics of characters with disability in film. *Journal of Applied Rehabilitation Counseling, 20*(2), 43–45.

Calvert, S. L. (1995). *Impact of televised songs on children's and young adults' memory of verbally-presented content.* Unpublished manuscript, Department of Psychology, Georgetown University, Washington, DC.

Calvert, S. L., & Pfordresher, P. Q. (1994, August). *Impact of a televised song on students' memory of information.* Poster presented at the annual meeting of the American Psychological Association, Los Angeles, CA.

Calvert, S. L., Rigaud, E., & Mazella, J. (1991). *Presentational features for students' recall of televised educational content.* Poster presented at the biennial meeting of the Society for Research in Child Development, Seattle, WA.

Calvert, S. L., & Tart, M. (1993). Song versus verbal forms for very-long-term, long-term, and short-term verbatim recall. *Journal of Applied Developmental Psychology, 14,* 245–260.

Cambre, M. A., & Fernie, D. (1985). *Formative evaluation of Season IV, 3-2-1 Contact: Assessing the appeal of four weeks of educational television programs and their influence on children's science comprehension and science interest.* New York: Children's Television Workshop.

Campbell, R., Martin, C. R., & Fabos, B. (2011). *Media & culture: An introduction to mass communication.* (7th ed.). Boston: Bedford/St. Martin's.

Campbell, S. W. (2008). Mobile technology and the body: Apparatgeist, fashion, and function. In J. Katz (Ed.), *Handbook of mobile communication studies* (pp. 153–164). Cambridge, MA: MIT Press.

Campbell, S. W., & Kwak, N. (2011). Mobile communication and civil society: Linking patterns and places of use to engagement with others in public. *Human Communication Research, 37,* 207–222.

Campbell, S. W., & Ling, R. (2008). Conclusion: Mobile communication in space and time—Furthering the theoretical dialogue. In R. Ling and S. Campbell (Eds.), *The mobile communication research series: Reconstruction of space and time through mobile communication practices* (pp. 251–260). New Brunswick, NJ: Transaction.

Campbell, S. W., & Ling, R. (2009). Effects of mobile communication. In J. Bryant & M. B. Oliver (Eds.), *Media effects: Advances in theory and research* (3rd ed., pp. 592–606). New York: Routledge.

Cantor, J. (1994). Fright reactions to mass media. In J. Bryant & D. Zillmann (Eds.), *Media effects: Advances in theory and research* (pp. 213–245). Hillsdale, NJ: Erlbaum.

Cantor, J. (1998). *"Mommy, I'm scared": How TV and movies frighten children and what we can do to protect them.* San Diego, CA: Harcourt Brace.

Cantor, J. (1999). Comments on the coincidence: Comparing the findings on retrospective reports of fear. *Media Psychology, 1,* 141–143.

Cantor, J. (2009). Fright reactions to mass media. In J. Bryant and M. B. Oliver (Eds.), *Media effects: Advances in theory and research* (3rd ed.). New York: Routledge.

Cantor, J., Byrne, S., Moyer-Guse, E., & Riddle, K. (2010). Descriptions of media-induced fright reactions in a sample of US elementary school children. *Journal of Children and Media, 4*(1), 1–17.

Cantor, J., & Hoffner, C. (1987, April). *Children's fear reactions to a televised film as a function of perceived immediacy of depicted threat.* Paper presented at the Convention of the Society for Research in Child Development, Baltimore.

Cantor, J., & Hoffner, C. (1990). Children's fear reactions to a televised film as a function of perceived immediacy of depicted threat. *Journal of Broadcasting & Electronic Media, 34,* 421–442.

Cantor, J., Mares, M. L., & Oliver, M. B. (1993). Parents' and children's emotional reactions to televised coverage of the Gulf War. In B. Greenberg & W. Gantz (Eds.), *Desert Storm and the mass media* (pp. 325–340). Cresskill, NJ: Hampton Press.

Cantor, J., & Nathanson, A. (1996). Children's fright reactions to television news. *Journal of Communication, 46*(4), 139–152.

Cantor, J., & Omdahl, B. (1991). Effects of fictional media depictions of realistic threats on children's emotional responses, expectations, worries, and liking for related activities. *Communication Monographs, 58,* 384–401.

Cantor, J., & Omdahl, B. (1999). Children's acceptance of safety guidelines after exposure to televised dramas depicting accidents. *Western Journal of Communication, 63*(1), 57–71.

Cantor, J., & Reilly, S. (1982). Adolescents' fright reactions to television and films. *Journal of Communication, 32*(1), 87–99.

Cantor, J., & Sparks, G. G. (1984). Children's fear responses to mass media: Testing some Piagetian predictions. *Journal of Communication, 34*(2), 90–103.

Cantor, J., Sparks, G. G., & Hoffner, C. (1988). Calming children's television fears: Mr. Rogers vs. the Incredible Hulk. *Journal of Broadcasting & Electronic Media, 32,* 271–288.

Cantor, J., & Wilson, B. J. (1984). Modifying fear responses to mass media in preschool and elementary school children. *Journal of Broadcasting, 28,* 431–443.

Cantor, J., Wilson, B. J., & Hoffner, C. (1986). Emotional responses to a televised nuclear holocaust film. *Communication Research, 13,* 257–277.

Cantor, J., Ziemke, D., & Sparks, G. G. (1984). Effect of forewarning on emotional responses to a horror film. *Journal of Broadcasting, 28,* 21–31.

Cantor, J., Zillmann, D., & Bryant, J. (1975). Enhancement of experienced sexual arousal in response to erotic stimuli through misattribution of unrelated residual excitation. *Journal of Personality and Social Psychology, 32,* 69–75.

Cantor, J. R., Zillmann, D., & Einsiedel, E. F. (1978). Female responses to provocation after exposure to aggressive and erotic films. *Communication Research, 5,* 395–411.

Cantril, H. (1940). *The invasion from Mars: A study in the psychology of panic.* Princeton, NJ: Princeton University Press.

Cantril, H., Gaudet, H., & Herzog, H. (1940). *The invasion from Mars: A study in the psychology of panic.* Princeton, NJ: Princeton University Press.

Caplan, S. E. (2005). A social skill account of problematic Internet use. *Journal of Communication, 55,* 721–736.

Cappella, J. N., & Jamieson, K. H. (1994). Broadcast adwatch effects: A field experiment. *Communication Research, 21,* 342–365.

Cappella, J. N., & Jamieson, K. H. (1997). *Spiral of cynicism: The press and the public good.* New York: Oxford University Press.

Carey, J. W. (1996). The Chicago School and mass communication research. In E. E. Dennis & E. Wartella (Eds.), *American communication research: The remembered history* (pp. 21–38). Mahwah, NJ: Erlbaum.

Carey, J. W., & Kreiling, A. L. (1974). Popular culture and uses and gratifications: Notes toward an accommodation. In J. G. Blumler & E. Katz (Eds.), *The uses of mass communications: Current perspectives on gratifications research* (pp. 225–248). Beverly Hills, CA: Sage.

Carnagey, N. L., & Anderson, C. A. (2005). The effects of reward and punishment in violent video games on aggressive affect, cognition, and behavior. *Psychological Science, 16,* 882–889.

Carnagey, N. L., Anderson, C. A., & Bartholow, B. D. (2007). Media violence and social neuroscience: New questions and new opportunities. *Current Directions in Psychological Science 16*(4), 178–182.

Carnagey, N. L., Anderson, C. A., & Bushman, B. J. (2007). The effect of computer game violence on physiological desensitization to real-life violence. *Journal of Experimental Psychology, 43,* 489–496.

Cassino, D., & Erisen, C. (2010). Priming Bush and Iraq in 2008: A survey experiment. *American Politics Research, 38*(2), 372–394.

Castells, M. (2000). *The rise of the network society* (2nd ed.). Oxford: Blackwell.

Castells, M. (2009). *Communication power.* New York: Oxford University Press.

Castells, M., Fernandez-Ardevol, M., Qiu, J., & Sey, A. (2007). *Mobile communication and society: A global perspective.* Cambridge, MA: MIT Press.

Centerwall, B. S. (1989). Exposure to television as a cause of violence. *Public Communication and Behavior, 2,* 1–58.

Ceyhan, A. A. (2011). University students' problematic Internet use and communication skills according to the Internet use purposes. *Educational Sciences: Theory & Practice, 11,* 69–77.

Chaffee, S. H. (1977). Mass media effects. In D. Lerner & L. Nelson (Eds.), *Communication research* (pp. 210–241). Honolulu: University of Hawaii Press.

Chaffee, S. H. (1982). Mass media and interpersonal channels: Competitive, convergent or complementary? In G. Gumpert & R. Cathcart (Eds.), *Inter /media: Interpersonal communication in a media world* (pp. 57–77). New York: Oxford University Press.

Chaffee, S. H., & Choe, S. Y. (1980). Time of decision and media use during the Ford-Carter campaign. *Public Opinion Quarterly, 44,* 53–59.

Chaffee, S. H., & Hochheimer, J. L. (1985). The beginnings of political communication research in the United States: Origins of the "limited effects" model. In E. M. Rogers & F. Balle (Eds.), *The media revolution in America and Western Europe* (pp. 60–95). Norwood, NJ: Ablex.

Chaffee, S. H., & Schleuder, J. (1986). Measurement and effects of attention to media news. *Human Communication Research, 13,* 76–107.

Chaiken, S. (1987). The heuristic model of persuasion. In M. P. Zanna, J. Olson, & C. P. Herman (Eds.), *Social influence: The Ontario symposium, 5* (pp. 3–39). Hillsdale, NJ: Erlbaum.

Chaiken, S., Wood, W., & Eagly, A. H. (1996). Principles of persuasion. In E. T. Higgins & A. W. Kruglanski (Eds.), *Social psychology: Handbook of basic principles.* New York: Guilford Press.

Chapman, S., & Egger, G. (1980). Forging an identity for the non-smoker: The use of myth in promotion. *International Journal of Health Education, 23,* 2–16.

Chapman, S., & Fitzgerald, B. (1982). Brand preference and advertising recall in adolescent smokers: Some implications for health promotion. *American Journal of Public Health, 72,* 491–494.

Chaput, J.-P., Visby, T., Nyby, S., Klingenberg, L., Gregersen, N. T., Tremblay, A., . . . & Sjodin, A. (2011). Video game playing increases food intake in adolescents: A randomized crossover study. *The American Journal of Clinical Nutrition, 93,* 1196–1203.

Charters, W. W. (1950). Motion pictures and youth. In B. Berelson & M. Janowitz (Eds.), *Reader in public opinion and communication* (pp. 397–406). Glencoe, IL: Free Press.

Check, J. V. P. (1995). Teenage training: The effects of pornography on adolescent males. In L. Lederer & R. Delgado (Eds.), *The price we pay: The case against racist speech, hate propaganda, and pornography* (pp. 89–91). New York: Hill and Wang.

Chesley, N. (2005). Blurring boundaries? Linking technology use, spillover, individual distress, and family satisfaction. *Journal of Marriage and Family, 67,* 1237–1248.

Children Now. (2001). *Fall colors, 2000–2001: Primetime diversity report.* Oakland, CA: Author.

Children Now. (2004). *Fall colors, 2003–2004: Primetime diversity report.* Oakland, CA: Author.

Cho, J. (2010). Game addicts arrested for starving baby to death. Retrieved from http://abcnews.go.com/international/thelaw/baby-death-alleged-result-parents-online-games-addiction/story?id=10007040

Cho, J., & McLeod, D. M. (2007). Structural antecedents to knowledge and participation: Extending the knowledge gap concept to participation. *Journal of Communication, 57,* 205–228.

Choi, S. M., Kim, Y., Sung, Y., & Sohn, D. (2011). Bridging or bonding? A cross-cultural study of social relationships in social networking sites. *Information, Communication & Society, 14,* 107–129. doi: 10.1080/13691181003792624

Chory, R. M., & Goodboy, A. K. (2011). Is basic personality related to violent and non-violent video game play and preferences? *Cyberpsychology, Behavior, and Social Networking, 14,* 191–198. doi: 10.1089/cyber.2010.0076

Christensen, P., & Wood, W. (2007). Effects of media violence on viewers' aggression in unconstrained social interaction. In R. W. Preiss, B. M. Gayle, N. Burrell, M. Allen, & J. Bryant (Eds.), *Mass media effects research: Advances through meta-analysis* (pp. 145–168). Mahwah, NJ: Erlbaum.

Christenson, P. G. (1992). The effects of parental advisory labels on adolescent music preferences. *Journal of Communication, 42*(1), 106–113.

Christenson, P. G., Henriksen, L., & Roberts, D. F. (2000). *Substance use in popular prime time television.* Washington, DC: Office of National Drug Control Policy.

Clancy-Hepburn, K., Hickey, A. A., & Neville, G. (1974). Children's behavior responses to TV food advertisements. *Journal of Nutrition Education, 7,* 93–96.

Clarens, C. (1967). *An illustrated history of the horror film.* New York: Putnam.

Clark, N. M., & Gong, M. (1997). A scale for assessing health care providers' teaching and communication behavior regarding asthma. *Health Education & Behavior, 24,* 245–257.

Clarke, M. M. (2005, June). A scholastic achievement: Building an entertainment division? Forte aced the test. *Broadcasting & Cable, 135*(25), 30.

Clarke, P., & Kline, F. G. (1974). Media effects reconsidered. *Communication Research, 1,* 224–240.

Cline, V. B. (1994). Pornography effects: Empirical and clinical evidence. In D. Zillmann, J. Bryant, & A. Huston (Eds.), *Media, children, and the family: Social scientific, psychodynamic, and clinical perspectives.* Hillsdale, NJ: Erlbaum.

Cline, V. B., Croft, R. G., & Courrier, S. (1973). Desensitization of children to television violence. *Journal of Personality and Social Psychology, 27*(3), 360–365.

Coffin, T. E., & Tuchman, S. (1973). Rating television programmes for violence: A comparison of five surveys. *Journal of Broadcasting, 17,* 3–22.

Cohen, B. C. (1963). *The press and foreign policy.* Princeton, NJ: Princeton University Press.

Coker, B. L. S. (2011). Freedom to surf: The positive effects of workplace Internet leisure browsing. *New Technology, Work and Employment, 26,* 238–247.

Cole, S. W., Kato, P. M., Marin-Bowling, V. M., Dahl, G. V., & Pollock, B. H. (2006). Clinical trial of *Re-Mission:* A computer game for young people with cancer. *Cyberpsychology & Behavior, 9,* 665–666.

Coleman, J. S. (1988). Social capital in the creation of human capital. *American Journal of Sociology, 94*(Supplement), S95–S120.

Colfax, D., & Steinberg, S. (1972). The perpetuation of racial stereotypes: Blacks in mass circulation magazine advertisements. *Public Opinion Quarterly, 35,* 8–18.

Collins, A., & Loftus, E. (1975). A spreading-activation theory of semantic memory. *Psychological Review, 82,* 407–428.

Collins, R. L., Ellickson, P. L., McCaffrey, D., & Hambarsoomians, K. (2007). Early adolescent exposure to alcohol advertising and its relationship to underage drinking. *Journal of Adolescent Health, 40*(6), 527–534.

Collins, R. L., Elliot, M. N., Berry, S. H., Kanouse, D. E., Kunkel, D. K., Hunter, S. B., & Miu, A. (2004). Watching sex on TV predicts adolescent initiation of sexual behavior. *Pediatrics, 114,* e280–e289.

Collins, W. A. (1973). Effect of temporal separation between motivation, aggression and consequences: A developmental study. *Developmental Psychology, 8,* 215–221.

Coltrane, S., & Messineo, M. (2000). The perpetuation of subtle prejudice: Race and gender imagery in 1990s television advertising. *Sex Roles, 42,* 363–389.

Committee on Food Marketing and the Diets of Children and Youth. (2006). *Food marketing to children and youth: Threat or opportunity?* Washington, DC: National Academy Press.

Comstock, G. (1980). New emphasis in research on the effects of television and film violence. In E. Palmer & A. Dorr (Eds.), *Children and the faces of television* (pp. 129–148). New York: Academic.

Comstock, G., Chaffee, S., Katzman, N., McCombs, M., & Roberts, D. (1978). *Television and human behavior.* New York: Columbia University Press.

Coon, K. A., Goldberg, J., Rogers, B. L., & Tucker, K. (2001). Relationships between use of television during meals and children's food consumption patterns. *Pediatrics, 107*(1), e7.

Cooper, C. A. (1996). *Violence on television, congressional inquiry, public criticism and industry response: A policy analysis.* Lanham, MD: University Press of America.

Cooper, J., & Mackie, D. (1986). Video games and aggression in children. *Journal of Applied Social Psychology, 16,* 726–744.

Cooper, R., & Tang, T. (2009). Predicting audience exposure to television in today's media environment: An empirical integration of active-audience and structural theories. *Journal of Broadcasting & Electronic Media, 53*(3), 400–418.

Cotliar, S. (2009, February 20). Clintons bid farewell to Socks the cat. Retrieved from http://www.people.com/people/article/0,20260477,00.html

Court, J. H. (1984). Sex and violence: A ripple effect. In N. M. Malamuth & E. Donnerstein (Eds.), *Pornography and sexual aggression* (pp. 143–172). Orlando, FL: Academic Press.

Cowan, G., & Campbell, R. R. (1994). Racism and sexism in interracial pornography: A content analysis. *Psychology of Women Quarterly, 18,* 323–338.

Cowan, G., Lee, C., Levy, D., & Snyder, D. (1988). Dominance and inequality in X-rated videocassettes. *Psychology of Women Quarterly, 12,* 299–311.

Cowley, M., & Smith, B. (1939). *Books that changed our minds.* New York: Doubleday, Doran & Company.

Coyle, C. L., & Vaughn, H. (2008). Social networking: Communication revolution or evolution? *Bell Labs Technical Journal, 13*(2), 13–18. doi: 10.1002/bltj.20298

Craig, R. S. (1992). The effect of television day part on gender portrayals in television commercials: A content analysis. *Sex Roles, 26,* 197–211.

Csikszentmihalyi, M. (1988). The flow experience and its significance for human psychology. In M. Csikszentmihalyi and I. S. Csikszentmihalyi (Eds.), *Optimal experience: Psychological studies of flow in consciousness* (pp. 15–35). New York: Cambridge University Press.

Cummings, J., Butler, B., & Kraut, R. (2002). The quality of online social relationships. *Communications of the ACM, 45,* 103–108.

Cummings, J., & Duncan, E. (2010). Changes in affect and future exercise intentions as a result of exposure to a regular exercise programme using Wii Fit. *Sport & Exercise Psychology Review, 6*(2), 31–41.

Curry, T. J., Jarosch, J., & Pacholok, S. (2005). Are direct to consumer advertisements of prescription drugs educational? Comparing 1992 to 2002. *Journal of Drug Education, 35*(3), 217–232.

Czyzewska, M., & Ginsburg, H. J. (2007). Explicit and implicit effects of anti-marijuana and anti-tobacco TV advertisements. *Addictive Behaviors, 32,* 114–127.

Dahlstrom, M. F., & Scheufele, D. A. (2010). Diversity of television exposure and its association with the cultivation of concern for environmental risks. *Environmental Communication, 4*(1), 54–65.

Dalisay, F., & Tan, A. (2009). Assimilation and contrast effects in the priming of Asian American and African American stereotypes through TV exposure. *Journalism & Mass Communication Quarterly, 86*(1), 7–22.

Damned Old Crank: A Self-Portrait of E. W. Scripps. (1951). Edited by C. R. McCabe. New York: Harper & Brothers.

DarfurIsDying.com (2008). About the game. Retrieved from http://www.darfurisdying.com/aboutgame.html

Dates, J. (1980). Race, racial attitudes and adolescent perceptions of black television characters. *Journal of Broadcasting, 24*(4), 549–560.

Davidson, E. S., Yasuna, A., & Tower, A. (1979). The effects of television cartoons on sex-role stereotyping in young girls. *Child Development, 50,* 597–600.

Davies, D. R. (1998). The contemporary newspaper, 1945–present. In W. D. Sloan (Ed.), *The age of mass communication* (pp. 453–469). Northport, AL: Vision Press.

Davies, P. G., Spencer, S. J., Quinn, D. M., & Gerhardstein, R. (2002). Consuming images: How television commercials that elicit stereotype threat can restrain women academically and professionally. *Personality & Social Psychology Bulletin, 28,* 1615–1628.

Davis, R. M. (1987). Current trend in cigarette advertising and marketing. *New England Journal of Medicine, 316,* 725–732.

Davis, R. M., & Kendrick, J. S. (1989). The Surgeon General's warning in outdoor cigarette advertising. *Journal of the American Medical Association, 61*(1), 90–94.

Davison, W. P. (1983). The third-person effect in communication. *Public Opinion Quarterly 47,* 1–15.

De Vreese, C. H., Boomgaarden, H. G., & Semetko, H. A. (2011). (In)direct framing effects: The effects of news media framing on public support for Turkish membership in the European Union. *Communication Research, 38*(2), 179–205.

DeAngelis, T. (2007, November). Web pornography's effect on children. American Psychological Association. Retrieved from http//www.apa.org/monitor/nov07/webporn.aspx.

Debatin, B., Lovejoy, J. P., Horn, A., & Hughes, B. N. (2009). Facebook and online privacy: Attitudes, behaviors, and unintended consequences. *Journal of Computer-Mediated Communication, 15,* 83–108.

Delli Carpini, M. X., & Keeter, S. (1991). U.S. public's knowledge of politics. *Public Opinion Quarterly, 55,* 583–612.

Dennis, E. E., & Wartella, E. (Eds.) (1996). *American communication research: The remembered history.* Mahwah, NJ: Erlbaum.

Dennison, B. A., Erb, T. A., & Jenkins, P. l. (2002). Television viewing and television in bedroom associated with overweight risk among low-income preschool children. *Pediatrics, 109*(6), 1028–1035.

Department of Health and Social Security and the Welsh Office. (1987). *AIDS: Monitoring response to the public education campaign, Feb. 1986–Feb. 1987.* London: H. M. Stationery Office.

Derry, C. (1987). More dark dreams: Some notes on the recent horror film. In G. A. Waller (Ed.), *American horrors: Essays on the modern American horror film* (pp. 162–174). Urbana: University of Illinois Press.

DeSteno, D., Petty, R. E., Rucker, D. D., Wegener, D. T., & Braverman, J. (2004). Discrete emotions and persuasion: The role of emotion-induced expectancies. *Journal of Personality and Social Psychology, 86,* 43–56.

DeSteno, D., Petty, R. E., Wegener, D. T., & Rucker, D. D. (2000). Beyond valence in the perception of likelihood: The role of emotion specificity. *Journal of Personality and Social Psychology, 78,* 397–416.

Deutsch, K. (1966). *The nerves of government.* New York: Free Press.

Devlin, L. P. (1995). Political commercials in American presidential elections. In L. L. Kaid & C. Holtz-Bacha (Eds.), *Political advertising in western democracies: Parties and candidates on television* (pp. 186–205). Thousand Oaks, CA: Sage.

Diaz-Guerrero, R., & Holtzman, W. H. (1974). Learning by televised *Plaza Sésamo* in Mexico. *Journal of Educational Psychology, 66*(5), 632–643.

Dicken-Garcia, H. (1998). The popular press, 1833–1865. In W. D. Sloan (Ed.), *The age of mass communication* (pp. 147–170). Northport, AL: Vision Press.

Diefenbach, D., & West, M. (2007). Television and attitudes toward mental health issues: Cultivation analysis and third person effect. *Journal of Community Psychology, 35,* 181–195.

Dietz, W. H. (1990). You are what you eat—What you eat is what you are. *Journal of Adolescent Health Care, 11,* 76–81.

Dietz, W. H., & Gortmaker, S. L. (1985). Do we fatten our children at the TV set? Television viewing and obesity in children and adolescents. *Pediatrics, 75*(5), 807–812.

DiFranza, J. R., Richards, J. W., Paulman, P. M., Wolf-Gillespie, N., Fletcher, C., Jaffe, R. D., & Murray, D. (1991). RJR Nabisco's cartoon camel promotes Camel cigarettes to children. *Journal of the American Medical Association, 266*(22), 3149–3153.

Dill, K. E., & Dill, J. G. (1998). Video game violence: A review of the empirical literature. *Aggression and Violent Behavior, 3,* 407–428.

Dimaggio, P., Hargittai, E., Neuman, W. R., & Robinson, J. P. (2001). Social implications of the Internet. *Annual Review of Sociology, 27,* 307–336.

Dixon, T. (2006). Psychological reactions to crime news portrayals of black criminals: Understanding the moderating roles of prior news viewing and stereotype endorsement. *Communication Monographs, 73,* 162–187.

Dixon, T. (2007). Black criminals and white officers: The effects of racially misrepresenting law breakers and law defenders on television news. *Media Psychology, 10,* 270–291.

Dixon, T., & Azocar, C. (2006). The representation of juvenile offenders by race on Los Angeles area television news. *The Howard Journal of Communications, 17,* 143–161.

Dixon, T., & Azocar, C. (2007). Priming crime and activating blackness: Understanding the psychological impact of the overrepresentation of blacks as lawbreakers on television news. *Journal of Communication, 57,* 229–253.

Dixon, T., Azocar, C., & Casas, M. (2003). The portrayal of race and crime on television network news. *Journal of Broadcasting & Electronic Media, 47,* 498–523.

Dixon, T., & Linz, D. (2000a). Overrepresentation and underrepresentation of African Americans and Latinos as lawbreakers on television news. *Journal of Communication, 50,* 131–154.

Dixon, T., & Linz, D. (2000b). Race and the misrepresentation of victimization on local television news. *Communication Research, 27,* 547–573.

Dixon, T., & Maddox, K. (2005). Skin tone, crime news, and social reality judgments: Priming the stereotype of the dark and dangerous black criminal. *Journal of Applied Social Psychology, 35,* 1555–1570.

Donaldson, J. (1981). The visibility and image of handicapped people on television. *Exceptional Children, 47*(6), 413–416.

Donaldson-Evans, C. (n.d.). Study: 1 in 10 sexually active teens has had same sex partner. Retrieved from http//www.aolhealth.com/2010/10/25/10-percent-teens-have-same-sex-partner/

Donnerstein, E. (1980). Aggressive erotica and violence against women. *Journal of Personality and Social Psychology, 39,* 269–277.

Donnerstein, E., & Berkowitz, L. (1981). Victim reactions in aggressive erotic films as a factor in violence against women. *Journal of Personality and Social Psychology, 41,* 710–724.

Donnerstein, E., Donnerstein, M., and Evans, R. (1975, August). Erotic stimuli and aggression: Facilitation or inhibition. *Journal of Personality and Social Psychology, 32*(2), 237–244.

Donnerstein, E., & Hallam, J. (1978). Facilitating effects of erotica on aggression against women. *Journal of Personality and Social Psychology, 36,* 1270–1277.

Doob, A. N., & MacDonald, G. E. (1979). Television viewing and fear of victimization: Is the relationship causal? *Journal of Personality and Social Psychology, 37,* 170–179.

Door, A. (1980). When I was a child I thought as a child. In S. B. Withey & R. P. Abeles (Eds.), *Television and social behavior: Beyond violence and children* (pp. 191–230). Hillsdale, NJ: Erlbaum.

Dorfman, L., & Wallack, L. (2007). Moving nutrition upstream: The case for reframing obesity. *Journal of Nutrition Education and Behavior, 39*(2), S45–S50.

Douglas, D. (1966). *Horror!* New York: Macmillan.

Drabman, R. S., & Thomas, M. H. (1974). Does media violence increase children's toleration of real life aggression? *Developmental Psychology, 10,* 418–421.

Drew, D., & Weaver, D. (2006). Voter learning in the 2004 presidential election: Did the media matter? *Journalism and Mass Communication Quarterly, 83,* 25–42.

Duncker, K. (1938). Experimental modification of children's food preferences through social suggestion. *Journal of Abnormal Social Psychology, 33,* 489–507.

Durant, R. H., Rome, E. S., Rich, M., Allred, E., Emans, S. J., & Woods, E. R. (1997). Tobacco and alcohol use behaviors portrayed in music videos: A content analysis. *American Journal of Public Health, 87*(7), 1131–1135.

Dysinger, W. S., & Ruckmick, C. A. (1933). *The emotional responses of children to the motion picture situation.* New York: Macmillan.

Eastman, H., & Liss, M. (1980). Ethnicity and children's preferences. *Journalism Quarterly, 57*(2), 277–280.

Eccles, A., Marshall, W. L., & Barbaree, H. E. (1988). The vulnerability of erectile measures to repeated assessments. *Behavior Research and Therapy, 26,* 179–183.

Eisenberg, A. L. (1936). *Children and radio programs.* New York: Columbia University Press.

Eisenstein, E. L. (1979). *The printing press as an agent of change: Communications and cultural transformations in early modern Europe.* Cambridge, England: Cambridge University Press.

Eisenstein, E. L. (1983). *The printing revolution in early modern Europe*. Cambridge, England: Cambridge University Press.

Elliott, P. (1974). Uses and gratifications research: A critique and a sociological alternative. In J. G. Blumler & E. Katz (Eds.), *The uses of mass communications: Current perspectives on gratifications research* (pp. 249–268). Beverly Hills, CA: Sage.

Elliott, T. R., & Byrd, E. K. (1982). Media and disability. *Rehabilitation Literature, 43*(11–12), 348–355.

Ellis, Y., Daniels, B., & Jauregui, A. (2010). The effect of multitasking on the grade performance of business students. *Research in Higher Education Journal, 8,* 1–10.

Ellison, N. B., Steinfield, C., & Lampe, C. (2007). The benefits of Facebook "friends": Social capital and college students' use of online social network sites. *Journal of Computer-Mediated Communication, 12,* 1142–1168.

Elwood, W. N., & Ataabadi, A. N. (1996). Tuned in and turned off: Out-of-treatment injection drug and crack users' response to media intervention campaigns. *Communication Reports, 9,* 49–59.

Emberson, L. L., Lupyan, G., Goldstein, M. H., & Spivey, M. J. (2010). Overheard cell-phone conversations: When less speech is more distracting. *Psychological Science, 21,* 1383–1388. doi: 10.1177/0956797610382126

End, C. M., Worthman, S., & Mathews, M. B. (2010). Costly cell phones: The impact of cell phone rings on academic performance. *Teaching of Psychology, 37,* 55–57.

Engelhardt, C. R., Bartholow, B. D., Kerr, G. T., & Bushman, B. J. (2011). This is our brain on violent video games: Neural desensitization to violence predicts increased aggression following violent video game exposure. *Journal of Experimental Psychology, 47,* 1033–1036. doi: 10.10/j.jesp.2011.03.027

Entertainment Software Association (ESA). (2011). Industry facts. Retrieved from http://www.theesa.com/facts/index.asp

Entman, R. M. (1993). Framing: Towards clarification of a fractured paradigm. *Journal of Communication, 43,* 51–58.

Entman, R. M. (2007). Framing bias: Media in the distribution of power. *Journal of Communication, 57,* 163–173.

Entman, R. M. (2010). Media framing biases and political power: Explaining slant in news of Campaign 2008. *Journalism, 11*(4), 389–408.

Eron, L. D., Huesmann, L. R., Lefkowitz, M. M., & Walder, L. O. (1972). Does television violence cause aggression? *American Psychologist, 27,* 253–263.

Eschholz, S., Bufkin, J., & Long, J. (2002). Symbolic reality bites: Women and racial/ethnic minorities in modern film. *Sociological Spectrum, 22,* 299–334.

Escobar-Chaves, S. L., Tortolero, S. R., Markham, C. M., Low, B. J., Eitel, P., & Thickstun, P. (2005). Impact of the media on adolescent sexual attitudes and behaviors. *Pediatrics, Supplement P, 116,* 303–326.

Etzioni, A. (1988). *Capital corruption: The new attack on American democracy*. New Brunswick, NJ: Transaction Books.

Evans, M. (2010). Framing international conflicts: Media coverage of fighting in the Middle East. *International Journal of Media and Cultural Politics, 6*(2), 209–233.

Evans, W. (1984). Monster movies: A sexual theory. In B. K. Grant (Ed.), *Planks of reason: Essays on the horror film* (pp. 53–64). Metuchen, NJ: Scarecrow Press.

Eveland, W. P. (2004). The effect of political discussion in producing informed citizens: The roles of information, motivation, and elaboration. *Political Communication, 21,* 177–193.

Eveland, W. P., Hayes, A. F., Shah, D. V., & Kwak, N. (2005). Understanding the relationship between communication and political knowledge: A model comparison approach using panel data. *Political Communication, 22,* 423–446.

Eysenbach, G., & Köhler, C. (2002). How do consumers search for and appraise health information on the World Wide Web? Qualitative study using focus groups, usability tests, and in-depth interviews. *British Medical Journal, 324,* 573–577.

Eysenbach, G., Powell, J., Kuss, O., & Sa, E. R. (2002). Empirical studies assessing the quality of health information for consumers on the World Wide Web: A systematic review. *Journal of the American Medical Association, 287*(20), 2691–2700.

Fabes, R. A., & Martin, C. L. (1991). Gender and age stereotypes of emotionality. *Personality and Social Psychology Bulletin, 17,* 532–540.

Facebook. (2011a). Factsheet. Retrieved from http://www.facebook.com/press/info.php?factsheet

Facebook. (2011b). Statistics. Retrieved from http://www.facebook.com/press/info.php?statistics

Faiola, A. (2006, May 27). When escape seems just a mouse-click away. *Washington Post.* Retrieved from http://www.washingtonpost.com/wp-dyn/content/article/2006/05/26/ar2006052601960_pf.html

Falkowski, J., & Steptoe, A. (1983). Biofeedback-assisted relaxation in the control of reactions to a challenging task and anxiety-provoking film. *Behavior Research and Therapy, 21,* 161–167.

Fals-Stewart, W. (2003). The occurrence of partner physical aggression on days of alcohol consumption: A longitudinal diary study. *Journal of Consulting and Clinical Psychology, 71,* 41–52.

Farrar, K., & Krcmar, M. (2006). Measuring state and trait aggression: A short, cautionary tale. *Media Psychology, 8,* 127–138.

Fazio, R. H. (1990). Multiple processes by which attitudes guide behavior: The MODE model as an integrative framework. *Advances in Experimental Social Psychology, 23,* 75–102.

Fazio, R. H., Jackson, J. R., Dunton, B. C., & Williams, C. J. (1995). Variability in automatic activation as an unobtrusive measure of racial attitudes: A bona fide pipeline? *Journal of Personality and Social Psychology, 69,* 1013–1027.

Fazio, R. H., & Olson, M. A. (2003). Implicit measures in social cognition research: Their meaning and use. *Annual Review of Psychology, 54,* 297–327.

Fazio, R. H., & Williams, C. J. (1986). Attitude accessibility as a moderator of the attitude-perception and attitude-behavior relations: An investigation of the 1984 presidential election. *Journal of Personality and Social Psychology, 51,* 505–514.

Febvre, L., & Martin, H-J. (1984). The *coming of the book: The impact of printing 1450–1800* (D. Gerard, trans.). London: Verso Editions.

Federman, J. (Ed.). (1998). *National television violence study: Vol. 3, Executive summary.* Santa Barbara: Center for communication and social policy, University of California.

Fedler, F., Hall, J., & Tanzi, L. A. (1982, Spring–Fall). Popular songs emphasize sex, de-emphasize romance. *Mass Communication Research,* 10–15.

Fenton, F. (1910). The influence of newspaper presentations upon the growth of crime and other anti-social activity. *The American Journal of Sociology, 16*(3), 342–371.

Fenton, F. (1911). The influence of newspaper presentations upon the growth of crime and other anti-social activity (cont.). *The American Journal of Sociology, 16*(4), 538–564.

Ferguson, C. J. (2007). The good, the bad and the ugly: A meta-analytic review of positive and negative effects of violent video games. *Psychiatric Quarterly, 78,* 309–316. doi: 10.1007/s11126-007-9056-9

Ferguson, C. J., & Kilburn, J. (2010). Much ado about nothing: The misestimation and overinterpretation of violent video game effects in Eastern and Western nations: Comment on Anderson et al. (2010). *Psychological Bulletin, 136,* 174–178. doi: 10.1037/a0018566

Feshbach, N. D. (1982). Sex differences in empathy and social behavior in children. In N. Eisenberg (Ed.), *The development of prosocial behavior* (pp. 315–338). New York: Academic Press.

Feshbach, S. (1955). The drive-reducing function of fantasy behaviour. *Journal of Abnormal and Social Psychology, 50,* 3–11.

Feshbach, S. (1961). The stimulating versus cathartic effects of vicarious aggressive activity. *Journal of Abnormal and Social Psychology, 63,* 381–385.

Feshbach, S., & Singer, R. D. (1971). *Television and aggression: An experimental field study.* San Francisco: Jossey-Bass.

Festinger, L. (1954). A theory of social comparison processes. *Human Relations, 7,* 117–140.

Festinger, L. (1957). *A theory of cognitive dissonance.* Evanston, IL: Row, Peterson.

Festinger, L., Schachter, S., & Bach, K. (Eds.). (1950). *Social pressures in informal groups: A study of human factors in housing.* Stanford, CA: Stanford University Press.

Film.com. (2009). Darren Aronofsky interview—*The Wrestler.* Retrieved from http://www.film.com/movies/darren-aronofsky-interview-the-wrestler

Final Report of the Attorney General's Commission on Pornography. (1986). Nashville, TN: Rutledge Hill Press.

Finklea, B. W. (2010, August). *Changing gender stereotypes in Disney films: A content analysis of animated and live-action movies.* Poster presented at the 94th annual meeting of the Association for Education of Journalism and Mass Communication, Denver, CO.

Finklea, B. W. (2011, August). *Pixar's "new man": A textual and thematic analysis of masculinity in the* Toy Story *trilogy.* Poster presented at the 95th annual meeting of the Association for Education of Journalism and Mass Communication, St. Louis, MO.

Finn, S. (1992). Television addiction? An evaluation of four competing media-use models. *Journalism Quarterly, 69,* 422–435.

Fiorina, M. P. (1981). *Retrospective voting in American national elections.* New Haven, CT: Yale University Press.

Fisch, S. M. (2002). Vast wasteland or vast opportunity?: Effects of educational television on children's academic knowledge, skills, and attitudes. In J. Bryant & D. Zillmann (Eds.), *Media effects: Advances in theory and research* (2nd ed.). Mahwah, NJ: Erlbaum.

Fisch, S. M. (2003). *The impact of Cyberchase on children's mathematical problem solving: Cyberchase season 2 summative study.* Teaneck, NJ: MediaKidz Research & Consulting.

Fisch, S. M. (2005, April). *Transfer of learning from educational television: Near and far transfer from Cyberspace.* Poster session presented at the biennial meeting of the Society for Research in Child Development, Atlanta, GA.

Fisch, S. M. (2009). Educational television and interactive media for children: Effects on academic knowledge, skills, and attitudes. In J. Bryant & M. B. Oliver (Eds.), *Media effects: Advances in theory and research* (3rd ed., pp. 402–435). New York: Routledge.

Fisch, S. M., Akerman, A., Morgenlander, M., McCann Brown, S. K., Fisch, S. R. D., Schwartz, B. B., & Tobin, P. (2008). Coviewing preschool television in the US: Eliciting parent-child interaction via onscreen prompts. *Journal of Children and Media, 2,* 163–173. doi: 10.1080/17482790802078680

Fisch, S. M., & Truglio, R. T. (Eds.). (2001). *"G" is for "growing": Thirty years of research on children and* Sesame Street. Mahwah, NJ: Erlbaum.

Fischer, P. M., Richards, J. W., Berman, E. J., & Krugman, D. M. (1989). Recall and eye tracking study of adolescents viewing tobacco advertisements. *Journal of the American Medical Association, 261*(1), 84–89.

Fischer, P., Kastenmüller, A., & Greitemeyer, T. (2010). Media violence and the self: The impact of personalized gaming characters in aggressive video games on aggressive behavior. *Journal of Experimental Social Psychology, 46*(1), 192–195.

Fishbein, M., & Ajzen, I. (1975). *Belief, attitude, intention and behavior: An introduction to theory and research*. Reading, MA: Addison-Wesley.

Fishbein, M., & Ajzen, I. (1976). Misconceptions about the Fishbein model: Reflections on a study by Songer-Nocks. *Journal of Experimental Social Psychology, 12,* 579–584.

Fisher, D. A., Hill, D. L., Grube, J. W., Bersamin, M. M., Walker, S., & Gruber, E. L. (2009). Televised sexual content and parental mediation: Influences on adolescent sexuality. *Media Psychology, 12,* 121–147.

Fiske, S. T., & Taylor, S. E. (1991). *Social cognition* (2nd ed.). New York: McGraw-Hill.

Flavell, J. (1963). *The developmental psychology of Jean Piaget.* New York: Van Nostrand.

Flerx, V. C., Fidler, D. S., & Rogers, R. W. (1976). Sex role stereotypes: Developmental aspects and early intervention. *Child Development, 47,* 998–1007.

Floyd, D. L., Prentice-Dunn, S., & Rogers, R. W. (2000). A meta-analysis of research on protection motivation theory. *Journal of Applied Social Psychology, 30,* 407–429.

Flynn, B. S., Worden, J. K., Secker-Walker, R. H., Pirie, P. L., & Badger, G. J. (1994). Mass media and school interventions for cigarette smoking prevention: Effects 2 years after completion. *American Journal of Public Health, 84,* 1148–1150.

Fortunati, L. (2005a). Mobile phones and fashion in post-modernity. *Telektronikk, 3/4,* 35–48.

Fortunati, L. (2005b). Mobile telephone and the presentation of self. In R. Ling and P. Pedersen (Eds.), *Mobile communications: Re-negotiation of the social sphere* (pp. 203–218). London: Springer.

Foster, E., & Gamble, E. A. (1906). The effect of music on thoracic breathing. *The American Journal of Psychology, 17,* 406–414.

Fox, S. (2006). *Online Health Search 2006.* Washington, DC: Pew Internet and American Life Project. Retrieved from http://www.pewinternet.org/pdfs/PIP_Online_health_2006.pdf

Freedman, J. (2002). *Media violence and its effects on aggression: Assessing the scientific evidence.* Toronto: University of Toronto Press.

Freedman, P., & Goldstein, K. (1999). Measuring media exposure and the effects of negative campaign ads. *American Journal of Political Science, 43,* 1189–1208.

Freimuth, V. S., Hammond, S. L., & Stein, J. A. (1988). Health advertising: Prevention for profit. *American Journal of Public Health, 78*(5), 557–561.

Fremont, W. P., Pataki, C., & Beresin, E. V. (2005). The impact of terrorism on children and adolescents: Terror in the skies, terror on television. *Child and Adolescent Psychiatric Clinics of North America, 14,* 429–451.

Frissen, B. (2000). ICT in the rush hours of life. *The Information Society, 16,* 65–75.

Frosch, D. L., Krueger, P. M., Hornik, R. C., Cronholm, P. F., & Barg, F. K. (2007). Creating demand for prescription drugs: A content analysis of television direct-to-consumer advertising. *Annals of Family Medicine, 5,* 6–13.

Frostling-Henningsson, M. (2009). First-person shooter games as a way of connecting to people: "Brothers in Blood." *Cyberpsychology & Behavior, 12,* 557–562. doi: 10.1089/cpb.2008.0345

Fryberg, S. (2003). Really? You don't look like an American Indian: Social representations and social group identities. *Dissertation Abstracts International* (Vol. 64).

Funk, J. B., Baldacci, H. B., Pasold, T., & Baumgardner, J. (2004). Violence exposure in real-life, video games, television, movies, and the Internet: Is there desensitization? *Journal of Adolescence, 27,* 23–39.

Funkhouser, G. R. (1973). The issues of the sixties: An exploratory study in the dynamics of public opinion. *Public Opinion Quarterly, 37,* 62–75.

Gamson, W. A., & Lasch, K. E. (1983). The political culture of social welfare policy. In S. Spiro & E. Yuchtman-Yaar (Eds.), *Evaluating the welfare state: Social and political perspectives* (pp. 397–415). New York: Academic Press.

Gamson, W. A., & Modigliani, A. (1987). The changing culture of affirmative action. *Research in Political Sociology, 3,* 137–177.

Ganahl, D. J., Prinsen, T. J., & Netzley, S. B. (2003). A content analysis of primetime commercials: A contextual framework of gender representation. *Sex Roles, 49,* 545–551.

Garcia, M. M. (2011). Perception is truth: How U.S. newspapers framed the "Go Green" conflict between BP and Greenpeace. *Public Relations Review, 37*(1), 57–59.

Gardner, J., & Radel, M. S. (1978). Portrait of the disabled in the media. *Journal of Community Psychology, 6,* 269–274.

Gaskin, J., & Berente, N. (2011). Video game design in the MBA curriculum: An experiential learning approach for teaching design thinking. *Communications of the Association for Information Systems, 29,* 103–122.

Gawronski, B., & Bodenhausen, G. V. (2006). Associative and prepositional processes in evaluation: An integrative review of implicit and explicit attitude change. *Psychological Bulletin, 132,* 692–731.

Geen, R. G. (1975). The meaning of observed violence: Real vs. fictional violence and consequent effects on aggression and emotional arousal. *Journal of Research in Personality, 9,* 270–281.

Geen, R. G., & Rakosky, J. J. (1973). Interpretations of observed violence and their effects on GSR. *Journal of Experimental Research in Personality, 6,* 289–292.

Geis, F. L., Brown, V., Jennings-Walstedt, J., & Porter, N. (1984). TV commercials as achievement scripts for women. *Sex Roles, 10,* 513–525.

Gentile, D. A., Coyne, S., & Walsh, D. A. (2011). Media violence, physical aggression, and relational aggression in school age children: A short-term longitudinal study. *Aggressive Behavior, 37*(2), 193–206.

Gerbner, G. (1970). Cultural indicators: The case of violence in television drama. *Annals of the American Academy of Political and Social Science, 388,* 69–81.

Gerbner, G. (1972). Violence in television drama: Trends and symbolic functions. In G. A. Comstock & E. Rubinstein (Eds.), *Television and social behaviour: Vol. 1. Media content and control* (pp. 28–187). Washington, DC: Government Printing Office.

Gerbner, G. (1997). Gender and age in primetime television. In S. Kirschner & D. A. Kirschner (Eds.), *Perspectives on psychology and the media* (pp. 69–94). Washington, DC: American Psychological Society.

Gerbner, G., & Gross, L. (1976). Living with television: The violence profile. *Journal of Communication, 26,* 173–199.

Gerbner, G., Gross, L., Eleey, M. F., Jackson-Beeck, M., Jeffries-Fox, S., & Signorielli, N. (1977). Television violence profile no. 8: The highlights. *Journal of Communication, 27,* 171–180.

Gerbner, G., Gross, L., Jackson-Beeck, M., Jeffries-Fox, S., & Signorielli, N. (1978). Cultural indicators: Violence profile no. 9. *Journal of Communication, 28,* 176–207.

Gerbner, G., Gross, L., Morgan, M., & Signorielli, N. (1980). The "mainstreaming" of America: Violence profile no. 11. *Journal of Communication, 30,* 10–29.

Gerbner, G., Gross, L., Morgan, M., & Signorielli, N. (1994). Growing up with television: The cultivation perspective. In J. Bryant & D. Zillmann (Eds.), *Media effects: Advances in theory and research* (pp. 17–41). Hillsdale, NJ: Erlbaum.

Gerbner, G., Gross, L., Morgan, M., Signorielli, N., & Shanahan, J. (2002). Growing up with television: Cultivation processes. In J. Bryant & D. Zillmann (Eds.), *Media effects: Advances in theory and research* (2nd ed.). Mahwah, NJ: Erlbaum.

Gerbner, G., Gross, L., & Signorielli, N. (1985). *The role of television entertainment in public education about science.* Philadelphia: Annenberg School of Communication, University of Pennsylvania.

Gerbner, G., & Signorielli, N. (1979). *Women and minorities in television drama 1969–1978.* Philadelphia: Annenberg School of Communication, University of Pennsylvania.

Gergen, K. J. (2002). The challenge of absent presence. In J. Katz & M. Aakhus (Eds.), *Perpetual contact: Mobile communication, private talk, public performance* (pp. 227–241). Cambridge, UK: Cambridge University Press.

Gettleman, J. (1999, 28 October). XXX=$$$. *Manhattan Mercury,* p. A6.

Ghanem, S. (1997). Filling in the tapestry: The second level of agenda setting. In M. E. McCombs, D. L. Shaw, & D. Weaver (Eds.), *Communication and democracy: Exploring the intellectual frontiers in agenda-setting theory* (pp. 3–14). Mahwah, NJ: Erlbaum.

Gillam, K., & Wooden, S. R. (2008). Post-princes models of gender: The new man in Disney/Pixar. *Journal of Popular Film and Television, 36,* 2–8.

Gilliam, F., & Iyengar, S. (2000). Prime suspects: The influence of local television news on the viewing public. *American Journal of Political Science, 44,* 560–573.

Girodo, M., & Pellegrini, W. (1976). Exercise-produced arousal, film-induced arousal and attribution of internal state. *Perceptual and Motor Skills, 42,* 931–935.

Gitlin, T. (1978). Media sociology: The dominant paradigm. *Theory and Society, 6,* 205–253.

Givins, S., & Monahan, J. (2005). Priming mammies, jezebels, and other controlling images: An examination of the influence of mediated stereotypes on perceptions of an African American woman. *Media Psychology, 7,* 87–106.

Glantz, S., Kacirk, K. W., & McCulloch, C. (2004). Back to the future: Smoking in movies in 2002 compared with 1950 levels. *American Journal of Public Health, 94*(2), 261–263.

Glascock, J. (2001). Gender roles on primetime network television: Demographics and behaviors. *Journal of Broadcasting & Electronic Media, 45,* 656–669.

Goffman, E. (1974). *Frame analysis: An essay on the organization of experience.* Cambridge, MA: Harvard University Press.

Goidel, R., Freeman, C., & Procopio, S. (2006). The impact of television on perceptions of juvenile crime. *Journal of Broadcasting & Electronic Media, 50,* 119–139.

Golbeck, J., Grimes, J. M., Rogers, A. (2010). Twitter use by the U.S. Congress. *Journal of the American Society for Information Science and Technology, 61,* 1612–1621.

Goldberg, M. E., Gorn, G. J., & Gibson, W. (1978). TV messages for snack and breakfast foods: Do they influence children's preferences? *Journal of Consumer Research, 5,* 73–81.

Goldenberg, E., & Traugott, M. (1984). *Campaigning for Congress.* Washington, DC: CQ Press.

Goldstein, A. O., Fischer, P. M., Richards, J. W., & Creten, D. (1987). Relationship between high school student smoking and recognition of cigarette advertisements. *Journal of Pediatrics, 110,* 488–491.

Goldstein, A. O., Sobel, R. A., & Newman, G. R. (1999). Medicine in the media: Tobacco and alcohol use in G-rated children's animated films. *Journal of the American Medical Association, 28,* 1131–1136.

Good, J. (2007). Shop 'til we drop? Television, materialism and attitudes about the natural environment. *Mass Communication & Society, 10*(3), 365–383.

Good, J. E. (2009). The cultivation, mainstreaming, and cognitive processing of environmentalists watching television. *Environmental Communication, 3*(3), 279–297.

Goranson, R. (1969). *Observed violence and aggressive behavior: The effects of negative outcomes to the observed violence* (Unpublished doctoral dissertation). University of Wisconsin-Madison.

Gore, T. (1987). *Raising PG kids in an X-rated society.* Nashville: Abingdon Press.

Gorham, B. (2006). News media's relationship with stereotyping: The linguistic intergroup bias in response to crime news. *Journal of Communication, 56,* 289–308.

Grabe, M. E., & Drew, D. G. (2007). Crime cultivation: Comparisons across media genres and channels. *Journal of Broadcasting & Electronic Media, 51*(1), 147–171.

Granberg, D., & Brown, T. A. (1989). On affect and cognition in politics. *Social Psychology Quarterly, 52,* 171–182.

Granovetter, M. S. (1982). The strength of weak ties: A network theory revisited. In P. V. Mardsen & N. Lin (Eds.), *Social structure and network analysis* (pp. 105–130). Thousand Oaks, CA: Sage.

Grant, B. F. (2000). Estimates of US children exposed to alcohol abuse and dependence in the family. *American Journal of Public Health, 90,* 112–115.

Grauerholz, E., & King, A. (1997). Primetime sexual harassment. *Violence against Women, 3,* 129–148.

Graves, L. E. F., Ridgers, N. D., Williams, K., Stratton, G., Atkinson, G., & Cable, N. T. (2010). The physiological cost of enjoyment of Wii Fit in adolescents, young adults, and older adults. *Journal of Physical Activity and Health, 7,* 393–401.

Gray, J. B. (2005). Sugar and spice and science: Encouraging girls through media mentoring. *Current Issues in Education, 8*(18). Retrieved from http://cie.ed.asu.edu/volume8/number18/

Graybill, D., Kirsch, J., & Esselman, E. (1985). Effects of playing violent verses nonviolent video games on the aggressive ideation of aggressive and nonaggressive children. *Child Study Journal, 15,* 199–205.

Greenberg, B. S. (1974). Gratifications of television viewing and their correlates for British children. In J. G. Blumler & E. Katz (Eds.), *The uses of mass communications: Current perspectives on gratifications research* (pp. 71–92). Beverly Hills, CA: Sage.

Greenberg, B. S. (1975). British children and televised violence. *Public Opinion Quarterly, 38,* 531–547.

Greenberg, B. S. (1994). Content trends in media sex. In D. Zillmann, J. Bryant, & A. C. Huston (Eds.), *Media, children, and the family: Social scientific, psychodynamic, and clinical perspectives.* Hillsdale, NJ: Erlbaum.

Greenberg, B. S., & Atkin, C. (1982). Learning about minorities from television: A research agenda. In G. Berry & C. Mitchell-Kernan (Eds.), *Television and the socialization of the minority child* (pp. 215–243). New York: Academic Press.

Greenberg, B. S., & Brand, J. E. (1993). Television news and advertising in school: The "Channel One" controversy. *Journal of Communication, 43,* 143–151.

Greenberg, B. S., & Brand, J. E. (1994). Minorities and the mass media: 1970s to 1990s. In D. Zillmann & J. Bryant (Eds.), *Media effects: Advances in theory and research* (pp. 273–314). Hillsdale, NJ: Erlbaum.

Greenberg, B. S., Brown, J. D., & Buerkel-Rothfuss, N. L. (1993). *Media, sex, and the adolescent.* Cresskill, NJ: Hampton Press.

Greenberg, B. S., Heeter, C., Burgoon, J., Burgoon, M., & Korzenny, F. (1983). Mass media use, preferences and attitudes among young people. In B. Greenberg, M. Burgoon, J. Burgoon, & F. Korzenny (Eds.), *Mexican Americans and the mass media* (pp. 147–201). Norwood, NJ: Ablex.

Greenberg, B. S., & Hofshire, L. (2000). Sex on entertainment television. In D. Zillmann and P. Vorderer (Eds.), *Media entertainment: The psychology of its appeal* (pp. 93–111). Mahwah, NJ: Erlbaum.

Greenberg, B. S., & Linsangan, R. (1993). Gender differences in adolescents' media use, exposure to sexual content, parental mediation and self-perceptions. In B. S. Greenberg, J. Brown, & N. Buerkel-Rothfuss (Eds.), *Media, sex and the adolescent* (pp. 134–144). Cresskill, NJ: Hamilton Press.

Greenberg, B. S., Mastro, D., & Brand, J. E. (2002). Minorities and the mass media: Television into the 21st century. In J. Bryant & D. Zillmann (Eds.), *Media effects: Advances in theory and research* (2nd ed., pp. 333–351). Hillsdale, NJ: Erlbaum.

Greenberg, B. S., & Neuendorf, K. (1980). Black family interactions on television. In B. S. Greenberg (Ed.), *Life on television* (pp. 173–182). Norwood, NJ: Ablex.

Greenberg, B. S., Stanley, C., Siemicki, M., Heeter, C., Soderman, A., & Linsangan, R. (1993a). Sex content on soaps and primetime television series most viewed by adolescents. In B. S. Greenberg, J. D. Brown, & N. L. Buerkel-Rothfuss (Eds.), *Media, sex and the adolescent*. Cresskill, NJ: Hampton Press.

Greenberg, B. S., Stanley, C., Siemicki, M., Heeter, C., Soderman, A., & Linsangan, R. (1993b). Sex content in R-rated films viewed by adolescents. In B. S. Greenberg, J. D. Brown, & N. L. Buerkel-Rothfuss (Eds.), *Media, sex and the adolescent*. Cresskill, NJ: Hampton Press.

Greenberg, L., D'Andrea, G., & Lorence, D. (2003). Setting the public agenda for online health search: A white paper and action agenda. Washington, DC: Utilization Review Accreditation Commission Inc (URAC). Retrieved September 16, 2006, from http://www.urac.org/documents/URAC_CWW_Health_%20Search_White_Paper1203.pdf7arch=%22%22Setting%20the%20Public%20Agenda%20for%Online%20Health%20Search%22%22

Greene, B. (2011). 38 years ago he made the first cell phone call. Retrieved from http://www.cnn.com/2011/opinion/04/01/greene.first.cellphone.call/index.html

Greenwald, A. G. (1968). Cognitive learning, cognitive response to persuasion, and attitude change. In A. Greenwald, T. Brock, & T. Ostrom (Eds.), *Psychological foundations of attitudes* (pp. 147–170). New York: Academic Press.

Greenwald, A. G., McGhee, D. E., & Schwartz, J. L. K. (1998). Measuring individual differences in implicit cognition: The implicit association task. *Journal of Personality and Social Psychology, 74,* 1464–1480.

Greeson, L. E., & Williams, R. A. (1986). Social implications of music videos for youth. *Youth & Society, 18*(2), 177–189.

Greitemeyer, T., & McLatchie, N. (2011). Denying humanness to others: A newly discovered mechanism by which violent video games increase aggressive behavior. *Psychological Science, 22,* 659–665. doi: 10.1177/0956797611403320

Griffiths, M. (2000). Does Internet and computer "addiction" exist? Some case study evidence. *Cyberpsychology & Behavior, 3,* 211–218.

Griffiths, M. D., Davies, M. N. O., & Chappell, D. (2004). Online computer gaming: A comparison of adolescent and adult gamers. *Journal of Adolescence, 27,* 87–96. doi: 10.1016/j.adolescence.2003.10.007

Grimes, T., & Bergen, L. (2008). The epistemological argument against a causal relationship between media violence and sociopathic behavior among psychologically well viewers. *American Behavioral Scientist, 51*(8), 1137–1154.

Grimes, T., Bergen, L., Nichols, K., Vernberg, E., & Fonagy, P. (2004). Is psychopathology the key to understanding why some children become aggressive when they are exposed to violent television programming? *Human Communication Research, 30,* 153–181.

Grimsted, D. (1998). *American mobbing, 1828–1861: Toward Civil War*. New York: Oxford University Press.

Gross, E. F., Juvonen, J., & Gable, S. L. (2002). Internet use and well-being in adolescence. *Journal of Social Issues, 58*(1), 75–90.

Grossman, M., & Wood, W. (1993). Sex differences in the intensity of emotional experience: A social role interpretation. *Journal of Personality and Social Psychology, 65,* 1010–1022.

Grube, J. W. (2004). Alcohol in the media: Drinking portrayals, alcohol advertising, and alcohol consumption among youth. In R. J. Bonnie & M. E. O'Connell (Eds.), *Reducing underage drinking: A collective responsibility* (pp. 597–622). Washington, DC: The National Academy of Sciences.

Gruber, E. L., Thau, H. M., Hill, D. L., Fisher, D. A., & Grube, J. W. (2005). Alcohol, tobacco and illicit substances in music videos: A content analysis of prevalence and genre. *Journal of Adolescent Health, 37,* 81–83.

Guenther-Grey, C. A., Schnell, D., & Fishbein, M. (1995). Sources of HIV/AIDS information among female sex traders. *Health Education Research, 10,* 385–390.

Gunter, B. (1980). The cathartic potential of television drama. *Bulletin of the British Psychological Society, 33,* 448–450.

Gunter, B. (1985). *Dimensions of television violence.* Aldershots, England: Gower.

Gunter, B. (1987). *Television and the fear of crime.* London: John Libbey.

Gunter, B. (1988). The perceptive audience. In J. A. Anderson (Ed.), *Communication yearbook II* (pp. 22–50). Newbury Park, CA: Sage.

Gunter, B. (1994). The question of media violence. In J. Bryant & D. Zillmann (Eds.), *Media effects: Advances in theory and research* (pp. 163–211). Hillsdale, NJ: Erlbaum.

Gunter, B. (2002). *Media sex: What are the issues?* Mahwah, NJ: Erlbaum.

Gunter, B. (2008). Media violence: Is there a case for causality? *American Behavioral Scientist, 51*(8), 1061–1122.

Gunter, B., & Furnham, A. (1984). Perceptions of television violence. Effects of programme genre and type of violence on viewers' judgements of violent portrayals. *British Journal of Social Psychology, 23,* 155–164.

Gunter, B., & Wober, M. (1988). *Violence on television: What the viewers think.* London: John Libbey.

Gunther, A. C., & Schmitt, K. (2004). Mapping boundaries of the hostile media effect. *Journal of Communication, 54,* 55–75.

Gurevitch, M., & Blumler, J. G. (1990). Political communication systems and democratic values. In J. Lichtenberg (Ed.), *Democracy and the mass media* (pp. 269–289). Cambridge, UK: Cambridge University Press.

Gutschoven, K., & Van Den Bulk, J. (2005). *Nicotine & Tobacco Research, 7*(3), 381–385.

Ha, S. (2011). Attribute priming effects and presidential candidate evaluation: The conditionality of political sophistication. *Mass Communication & Society, 14*(3), 315–342.

Habuchi, I. (2005). Accelerating reflexivity. In M. Ito, D. Okabe, & M. Matsuda (Eds.), *Personal portable, pedestrian: Mobile phones in Japanese life* (pp. 165–182). Cambridge, MA: MIT Press.

Haferkamp, N., & Krämer, N. C. (2011). Social comparison 2.0: Examining the effects of online profiles on social-networking sites. *Cyberpsychology, Behavior, and Social Networking, 14,* 209–314. doi: 10.1089/cyber.2010.0120

Hakluyt, R. (1582/1850). *Divers voyages touching the discovery of America and the islands adjacent.* New York: Burt Franklin, published by the Hakluyt Society.

Hale, J. L., & Dillard, J. P. (1995). Fear appeals in health promotion campaigns: Too much, too little, or just right? In E. Maibach & R. L. Parrott (Eds.), *Designing health messages: Approaches from communication theory and public health practice.* Thousand Oaks, CA: Sage.

Hall, C. C. (Ed.), & Jameson, J. F. (Gen. Ed.). (1910). *Original narratives of early American history: Narratives of early Maryland 1633–1684,* reproduced under the auspices of the American Historical Association. Reprint of *A relation of Maryland; together with a map of the countrey* (1635). New York: Charles Scribner's Sons.

Hall, E. R., Esty, E. T., & Fisch, S. M. (1990). Television and children's problem-solving behavior: A synopsis of an evaluation of the effects of *Square One TV. Journal of Mathematical Behavior, 9,* 161–174.

Hall, E. R., Fisch, S. M., Esty, E. T., Debold, E., Miller, B. A., Bennett, D. T., & Sloan, S. V. (1990). *Children's problem-solving behavior and their attitudes toward mathematics: A study of the effects of* Square One TV (Vols. 1–5). New York: Children's Television Workshop.

Han, D. H., Kim, Y. S., Lee, Y. S., Min, K. J., & Renshaw, P. F. (2010). Changes in cue-induced, prefrontal cortex activity with video-game play. *Cyberpsychology, Behavior, and Social Networking, 13,* 655–661. doi: 10.1089/cyber.2009.0327

Hare, R. D., & Blevings, G. (1975). Defensive responses to phobic stimuli. *Biological Psychology, 3,* 1–13.

Haridakis, P. M., & Rubin, A. M. (2005). Third-person effects in the aftermath of terrorism. *Mass Communication & Society, 8*(1), 39–59.

Hariot, T. (1590/1972*). A briefe and true report of the new found land of Virginia, by Thomas Hariot. The complete 1590 Theodor de Bry edition*. New York: Dover.

Harman, B. A., & Sato, T. (2011). Cell phone use and grade point average among undergraduate university students. *College Student Journal, 45,* 544–549.

Harris Interactive. (2007, April 2). Computer game addiction: Is it real? Retrieved from http://www.harrisinteractive.com/news/allnewsbydate.asp?newsid=1196

Harris, L. (2003). Home-based teleworking and the employment relationship: Managerial challenges and dilemmas. *Personnel Review, 32,* 422–439.

Harris, R. J. (1994). The impact of sexually explicit media. In J. Bryant and D. Zillmann (Eds.), *Media effects: Advances in theory and research* (pp. 247–272). Hillsdale, NJ: Erlbaum.

Harris, R. J., & Bartlett, C. P. (2009). Effects of sex in the media. In J. Bryant and M. B. Oliver (Eds.), *Media effects: Advances in theory and research* (3rd ed., pp. 304–324). New York: Routledge.

Harris, R. J., & Scott, C. L. (2002). Effects of sex in the media. In J. Bryant and D. Zillmann (Eds.), *Media effects: Advances in theory and research* (2nd ed., pp. 307–332). Hillsdale, NJ: Erlbaum.

Harrison, K., & Cantor, J. (1999). Tales from the screen: Enduring fright reactions to scary media. *Media Psychology, 1,* 97–116.

Harrison, T. M., & Falvey, L. (2001). Democracy and new communication technologies. *Communication Yearbook, 25,* 1–43.

Hart, R. P. (1996). Easy citizenship: Television's curious legacy. *Annals of the American Academy of Political and Social Science, 546,* 109–119.

Hashimoto, Y., Ishii, K., Nakamura, I., Korenaga, R., Tsuji, D., & Mori, Y. (2000). Keitai denwa wo chuushin to suru tsusin media riyo ni kansuru chosa kenkyu [A study on mobile phone and other communication media usage]. *Tokyo Daigaku Shyakai Joho Kenkyusyo Chosa Kenkyu, Kiyo, 14,* 180–192.

Hawkins, R. P, & Pingree, S. (1982). Television's influence on social reality. In D. Pearl, L. Bouthilet, & J. Lazar (Eds.), *Television and behavior: Ten years of scientific progress and implications for the eighties* (DHHS Publication No. ADM 82–1196, Vol. 2, pp. 224–247). Washington, DC: Government Printing Office.

Hawkins, R. P, & Pingree, S. (1990). Divergent psychological processes in constructing social reality from mass media content. In N. Signorielli & M. Morgan (Eds.), *Cultivation analysis: New directions in media effects research* (pp. 35–50). Newbury Park, CA: Sage.

Healy, J. M. (1990). *Endangered minds: Why our children don't think*. New York: Simon & Schuster.

Hearold, S. (1986). A synthesis of 1043 effects of television on social behavior. In G. Comstock (Ed.), *Public communication and behavior* (Vol. 1, pp. 65–133). Orlando, FL: Academic Press.

Heath, R. L., & Bryant, J. (2000). *Human communication theory and research: Concepts, contexts, and challenges.* Mahwah, NJ: Erlbaum.

Heesacker, M., Petty, R. E., & Cacioppo, J. T. (1983). Field dependence and attitude change: Source credibility can alter persuasion by affecting message-relevant thinking. *Journal of Personality, 51,* 653–666.

Heider, F. (1959). *The psychology of interpersonal relations* (2nd ed.). New York: Wiley.

Heider, F., & Simmel, M. (1944). An experimental study of apparent behavior. *American Journal of Psychology, 57,* 243–259.

Hennigan, K. M., Del Rosario, M. L., Heath, L., Cook, T. D., Wharton, J. D., & Calder, B. J. (1982). Impact of the introduction of television on crime in the United States: Empirical findings and theoretical implications. *Journal of Personality and Social Psychology, 42,* 461–477.

Henriksen, L., & Flora, J. A. (2001). *Effects of adolescents' exposure to retail tobacco advertising.* Paper presented at the annual conference of the International Communication Association, Washington, DC.

Herbozo, S., Tantleff-Dunn, S., Gokee-Larose, J., & Thompson, J. K. (2004). Beauty and thinness messages in children's media: A content analysis. *Eating Disorders, 12,* 21–34.

Herzog, H. (1940). Professor quiz: A gratification study. In P. F. Lazarsfeld (Ed.), *Radio and the printed page* (pp. 64–93). New York: Duell, Sloan, & Pearce.

Herzog, H. (1944). What do we really know about daytime serial listeners? In P. F. Lazarsfeld & F. N. Stanton (Eds.), *Radio research 1942–1943* (pp. 3–33). New York: Duell, Sloan, & Pearce.

Hess, R. D., & Goldman, H. (1962). Parents' views of the effects of television on their children. *Child Development, 33,* 411–426.

Hester, J. B., & Gibson, R. (2003). The economy and second-level agenda setting: A time-series analysis of economic news and public opinion about the economy. *Journalism & Mass Communication Quarterly, 80*(1), 73–90.

Hestroni, A. (2007). Three decades of sexual content on prime-time network programming: A longitudinal meta-analytic review. *Journal of Communication, 57,* 318–348.

Hestroni, A. (2008). Geo-cultural proximity, genre exposure, and cultivation. *Communications, 33,* 69–90.

Hestroni, A., Elphariach, H., Kapuza, R., & Tsfoni, B. (2007). Geographical proximity, cultural imperialism, and the cultivation effect. *Communication Monographs, 74*(2), 181–199.

Hill, C., Davis, H., Holman, R., & Nelson, G. (1984). *Video violence and children.* London: H. M. Stationery Office.

Himmelweit, H. T., Oppenheim, A. N., & Vince, P. (1958). *Television and the child.* London: Oxford University Press.

Hirsh, P. (1980). The "scary" world of the non-viewer and other anomalies: A reanalysis of Gerbner et al.'s findings on cultivation analysis: Part 1. *Communication Research, 7,* 403–456.

Ho, S., & McLeod, D. M. (2008). Social-psychological influences on opinion expression in face-to-face and computer-mediated communication. *Communication Research, 35*(2), 190–207.

Hoekstra, S. J., Harris, R. J., & Helmick, A. L. (1999). Autobiographical memories about the experience of seeing frightening movies in childhood. *Media Psychology, 1,* 127–140.

Hoff, E. E. (1998). The press and a new America, 1865–1900. In W. D. Sloan (Ed.), *The age of mass communication* (pp. 233–250). Northport, AL: Vision Press.

Hoffner, C. (1995). Adolescents' coping with frightening mass media. *Communication Research, 22,* 325–346.

Hoffner, C., & Cantor, J. (1985). Developmental differences in responses to a television character's appearance and behavior. *Developmental Psychology, 21,* 1065–1074.

Hoffner, C., & Cantor, J. (1990). Forewarning of a threat and prior knowledge of outcome: Effects on children's emotional responses to a film sequence. *Human Communication Research, 16,* 323–354.

Hoffner, C., & Levine, K. J. (2005). Enjoyment of mediated fright and violence: A meta-analysis. *Media Psychology, 7,* 207–237.

Holbert, L., Shah, D., & Kwak, N. (2004). Fear, authority, and justice: Crime-related TV viewing and endorsements of capital punishment and gun ownership. *Journalism & Mass Communication Quarterly, 81,* 343–363.

Holbert, R. L., & Hansen, G. J. (2006). *Fahrenheit 9–11,* need for closure, and the priming of affective ambivalence: An assessment of intra-affective structures by party identification. *Human Communication Research, 32,* 109–129.

Holbrook, R. A., & Hill, T. G. (2005). Agenda-setting and priming in prime time television: Crime dramas as political cues. *Political Communication, 22,* 277–295.

Holtz, S. (2006). The impact of new technologies on internal communication. *Strategic Communication Management, 10*(1), 22–25.

Homer, C., Susskind, O., Alpert, H. R., Owusu, C., Schneider, L., Rappaport, L. A., & Rubin, D. H. (2000). An evaluation of an innovative multimedia educational software program for asthma management: Report of a randomized, controlled trial. *Pediatrics, 106,* 210–215.

Hoover Police. (2009, July 31). Arrests made in "Facebook" burglaries. Retrieved from http://hooverpd.com/ftupload/ . . . facebookburglararrest073109.pdf

Horton, D., & Wohl, R. R. (1956). Mass communication and para-social interaction. *Psychiatry, 19,* 215–229.

Houston, D. A., & Doan, K. (1999). Can you back that up? Evidence (or lack thereof) for the effects of negative and positive political communication. *Media Psychology, 1,* 191–206.

Hovland, C. I. (1954). Effects of the mass media on communication. In G. Lindzey (Ed.), *Handbook of social psychology, 2,* 1062–1103. Cambridge, MA: Addison-Wesley.

Hovland, C. I. (1959). Reconciling conflicting results derived from experimental and survey studies of attitude change. *American Psychologist, 14,* 8–17.

Hovland, C. I., Lumsdaine, A., & Sheffield, F. (1949). *Experiments on mass communication.* Princeton, NJ: Princeton University Press.

Howard, D. J. (1990). Rhetorical question effects on message processing and persuasion: The role of information availability and the elicitation of judgment. *Journal of Experimental Social Psychology, 26,* 217–239.

Howard, P. E. N., Raine, L., & Jones, S. (2001). Days and nights on the Internet. *American Behavioral Scientist, 45,* 383–404.

Hsu, C.-W., Wan, C.-C., & Tai, Y.-T. (2011). The closer the relationship, the more interaction on Facebook? Investigating the case of Taiwan users. *Cyberpsychology, Behavior, and Social Networking, 14,* 473–476. doi: 10.1089/cyber.2010.0267

Hu, T-W., Sung, H-Y, & Keeler, T. E. (1995). Reducing cigarette consumption in California: Tobacco taxes vs. an anti-smoking media campaign. *American Journal of Public Health, 85,* 1218–1222.

Huckfeldt, R., & Sprague, J. (1995). *Citizens, politics, and social communication.* Cambridge, UK: Cambridge University Press.

Huesmann, L. R. (1982). Violence and aggression. In National Institute of Mental Health, *Television and behavior: Ten years of scientific progress* (Vol. 1, pp. 36–44). Washington, DC: Government Printing Office.

Huesmann, L. R., & Eron, L. D. (Eds.). (1986). *Television and the aggressive child: A cross-national comparison.* Hillsdale, NJ: Erlbaum.

Huesmann, L. R., Moise-Titus, J., Podolski, C. L., & Eron, L. D. (2003). Longitudinal relations between children's exposure to TV violence and their aggressive and violent behavior in young adulthood: 1977–1992. *Developmental Psychology, 39,* 201–221.

Huesmann, L. R., & Taylor, L. D. (2006). The role of media violence in violent behavior. *Annual Review of Public Health, 27*(1), 393–415.

Hughes, M. (1980). The fruits of cultivation analysis: A reexamination of some effects of television watching. *Public Opinion Quarterly, 44,* 287–302.

Hume, R. (1977, October). Selling the Swedish nightingale: Jenny Lind and P. T. Barnum. *American Heritage, 28,* 90–107.

Huntzicker, W. E. (1998). The pioneer press, 1800–1900. In W. D. Sloan (Ed.), *The age of mass communication* (pp. 187–211). Northport, AL: Vision Press.

Hurley, R. (2009). How gay porn undermines safe sex campaigns. *British Medical Journal 338*(7697), 775.

Huston, A. C., Anderson, D. R., Wright, J. C., Linebarger, D. L., & Schmitt, K. L. (2001). *Sesame Street* viewers as adolescents: The recontact study. In S. M. Fisch & R. T. Truglio (Eds.), *"G" is for "growing": Thirty years of research on children and Sesame Street* (pp. 131–144). Mahwah, NJ: Erlbaum.

Huston, A. C., Wartella, E., & Donnerstein, E. (1998). *Measuring the effects of sexual content in the media: A report to the Kaiser Family Foundation.* Menlo Park, CA: The Henry J. Kaiser Family Foundation.

Hwang, H., Gotlieb, M. R., Nah, S., & McLeod, D. M. (2007). Applying a cognitive-processing model to presidential debate effects: Postdebate news analysis and primed reflection. *Journal of Communication, 57,* 40–59.

Hyde, J. (1994). The media and the diffusion of innovation: The phonograph and radio broadcasting. In J. D. Startt & W. D. Sloan (Eds.), *The significance of the media in American history.* Northport, AL: Vision Press.

Hyman, H., & Sheatsley, P. (1947). Some reasons why information campaigns fail. *Public Opinion Quarterly, 11,* 412–423.

Illinois.gov. (2005). Gov. Blagojevich signs law making Illinois the only state in the nation to protect children from violent and sexually explicit video games. Retrieved from http://www.illinois.gov/pressreleases/ShowPressRelease.cfm?SubjectID=1&RecNum=4170

Internet now major source of campaign news. (2008). Pew Internet and American Life Project. Retrieved from http://pewresearch.org/pubs/1017/Internet-now-major-source-of-campaign-news

Intons-Peterson, M. J., & Roskos-Ewoldsen, B. (1989). Mitigating the effects of violent pornography. In S. Gubar & J. Hoff-Wilson (Eds.), *For adult users only.* Bloomington: Indiana University Press.

Intons-Peterson, M. J., Roskos-Ewoldsen, B., Thomas, L., Shirley, M., & Blut, D. (1989). Will educational materials reduce negative effects of exposure to sexual violence? *Journal of Social and Clinical Psychology, 8,* 256–275.

Irwin, A. R., & Gross, A. M. (1995). Cognitive tempo, violent video games, and aggressive behavior in young boys. *Journal of Family Violence, 10,* 337–350.

Ishii, K. (2006). Implications of mobility: The uses of personal communication media in everyday life. *Journal of Communication, 56*(2), 346–365.

Ito, M., Okabe, D., & Anderson, K. (2008). Portable objects in three global cities: The personalization of urban places. In R. Ling and S. Campbell (Eds.), *The mobile communication research series: Reconstruction of space and time through mobile communication practices* (pp. 67–88). New Brunswick, NJ: Transaction.

Ivry, B. (1998, September 25). In movies, a question of race. *Buffalo News,* p. 3G.

Iyengar, S. (1989). How citizens think about national issues. *American Journal of Political Science, 33,* 878–897.

Iyengar, S. (1991). *Is anyone responsible? How television frames political issues.* Chicago: University of Chicago Press.

Iyengar, S., & Kinder, D. R. (1987). *News that matters: Television and American opinion.* Chicago: University of Chicago Press.

Iyengar, S., Peters, M. D., & Kinder, D. R. (1982). Experimental demonstrations of the "not-so-minimal" consequences of television news programs. *American Political Science Review, 76,* 848–858.

Iyengar, S., & Simon, A. F. (2000). New perspectives and evidence on political communication and campaign effects. *Annual Review of Psychology, 51,* 149–169.

Izard, C. E. (1977). *Human emotions.* New York: Plenum Press.

Jackson, L. A., & Ervin, K. S. (1991). The frequency and portrayal of black families in fashion advertisements. *Journal of Black Psychology, 18*(1), 67–70.

Jackson, R. A., & Carsey, T. M. (2007). U.S. Senate campaigns, negative advertising, and voter mobilization in the 1998 midterm election. *Electoral Studies, 26,* 180–195.

James, P. T., Leach, R., Kalamara, E., & Shayeghi, M. (2001). The worldwide obesity epidemic. *Obesity Research, 9*(S4), 228S–233S.

James, T., Jr. (1982, May). World went mad when mighty Jumbo came to America. *Smithsonian, 13,* 134–152.

Jansz, J. (2005). The emotional appeal of violent video games for adolescent males. *Communication Theory, 15,* 219–241.

Java, A., Song, X., Finin, T., & Tseng, B. (2007). Why we Twitter: Understanding micro-blogging usages and communities. Proceedings of the 9th WebKDD and 1st SNA-KDD '07 (pp. 56–65). San Jose, CA: ACM Press.

Jeffres, L. W. (2000). Ethnicity and ethnic media use: A panel study. *Communication Research, 27,* 496–535.

Jenks, J. W. (1895). The guidance of public opinion. *The American Journal of Sociology, 1,* 158–169.

Jennings, N. A., Hooker, S. D., & Linebarger, D. L. (2009). Educational television as mediate literacy environments for preschoolers. *Learning, Media and Technology, 34,* 229–242.

Jerit, J., Barabas, J., & Bolsen, T. (2006). Citizens, knowledge, and the information environment. *American Journal of Political Science, 50,* 266–282.

Jin, B. & Jeong, S. (2010). The impact of Korean television drama viewership on the social perceptions of single life and having fewer children in married life. *Asian Journal of Communication, 20*(1), 17–32.

Jin, S.-A. (2011). "I feel present. Therefore I experience flow": A structural equation modeling approach to flow and presence in video games. *Journal of Broadcasting & Electronic Media, 55,* 114–136. doi: 10.1080/08838151.2011.546248

Jo, E., & Berkowitz, L. (1994). A priming effect analysis of media influences: An update. In J. Bryant & D. Zillmann (Eds.), *Media effects: Advances in theory and research* (pp. 43–60). Hillsdale, NJ: Erlbaum.

Johnsen, T. E. (2003). The social context of the mobile phone use of Norwegian teens. In J. Katz (Ed.), *Machines that become us: The social context of communication technology* (pp. 161–170). New Brunswick, NJ: Transaction.

Johnson, B. R. (1980). General occurrence of stressful reactions to commercial motion pictures and elements in films subjectively identified as stressors. *Psychological Reports, 47,* 775–786.

Johnson, J. D., Adams, M. S., Hall, W., & Ashburn, L. (1997). Race, media, and violence: Differential racial effects of exposure to violent news stories. *Basic and Applied Social Psychology, 19,* 81–90.

Johnson, J. G., Cohen, P., Kasen, S., First, M. B., & Brook, J. S. (2004). Association between television viewing and sleep problems during adolescence and early adulthood. *Archives of Pediatrics and Adolescent Medicine, 158,* 562–568.

Johnson, M. (1996). Latinas and television in the United States: Relationships among genre identification, acculturation, and acculturation stress. *The Howard Journal of Communications, 7,* 289–313.

Johnson, R. (1609). *Nova Britannia: Offering most excellent fruites by planting in Virginia: Exciting all such as be well affected to further the same.* London: Printed for Samuel Macham.

Johnson-Cartee, K. S., & Copeland, G. A. (1991). *Negative political advertising: Coming of age.* Hillsdale, NJ: Erlbaum.

Johnson-Laird, P. N. (1983). *Mental models.* Cambridge, MA: Harvard University Press.

Johnson-Laird, P. N. (1989). Mental models. In M. I. Posner (Ed.), *Foundations of cognitive science* (pp. 469–499). Cambridge, MA: MIT Press.

Johnston, J. (1980). *An exploratory study of the effects of viewing the first season of* 3-2-1 Contact. New York: Children's Television Workshop.

Johnston, J., & Brzezinski, E. (1994). *Executive summary, Channel One: A three year perspective.* Ann Arbor: Institute for Social Research, University of Michigan.

Johnston, J., & Ettema, J. S. (1982). *Positive images: Breaking stereotypes with children's television.* Beverly Hills, CA: Sage.

Johnston, J., & Luker, R. (1983). *The "Eriksson Study": An exploratory study of viewing two weeks of the second season of* 3-2-1 Contact. New York: Children's Television Workshop.

Johnston, L. D., O'Malley, P. M., Bachman, J. G., & Schulenberg, J. E. (2004). *Monitoring the future, national survey results on drug use, 1975–2004. Vol. 1: Secondary school students.* NIH Publication No. 05–5727. Bethesda, MD: National Institute on Drug Abuse.

Joinson, A. N. (2008). "Looking at," "looking up," or "keeping up with" people? Motives and uses for Facebook. *CHI 2008 Proceedings* (pp. 1027–1036). Florence, Italy: ACM.

Joint Statement. (2000). *Joint statement on the impact of entertainment violence on children.* Retrieved from http://www.aap.org/advocacy/releases/jstmtevc.htm

Jorgensen, P. F. (1998). Affect, persuasion, and communication processes. In P. A. Anderson & L. K. Guerrero (Eds.), *Handbook of communication and emotion: Research, theory, applications, and contexts* (pp. 403–422). San Diego, CA: Academic Press.

Josephson, W. L. (1987). Television violence and children's aggression: Testing the priming, social script, and disinhibition predictions. *Journal of Personality and Social Psychology, 53,* 882–890.

Joslyn, R. A. (1980). The content of political spot ads. *Journalism Quarterly, 57,* 92–98.

Juergen, M. (2010). A brief history of play. *Entrepreneur, 38*(11), 30–36.

Julsrud, T. E. (2005). Behavioral changes at the mobile workplace: A symbolic interactionist approach. In R. Ling & P. Pedersen (Eds.), *Mobile communications: Re-negotiation of the social sphere* (pp. 93–112). London: Springer-Verlag.

Julsrud, T. E., & Bakke, J. W. (2008). Trust, friendship and expertise: The use of e-mail, mobile dialogues, and SMS to develop and sustain social relations in a distributed work group. In R. Ling & S. W. Campbell (Eds.), *The mobile communication research series: Reconstruction of space and time through mobile communication practices* (pp. 159–190). New Brunswick, NJ: Transaction.

Just, M. R., Crigler, A. N., & Wallach, L. (1990). Thirty seconds or thirty minutes: What viewers learn from spot advertisements and candidate debates. *Journal of Communication, 40*(3), 120–133.

Kahn, K. F., & Kenney, P. J. (1999). Do negative campaigns mobilize or suppress turnout?: Clarifying the relationship between negativity and participation. *American Political Science Review, 93,* 877–889.

Kahneman, D. (2003). Maps of bounded rationality: A perspective on intuitive judgment and choice. In T. Frangsmyr (Ed.), *Les Prix Nobel: The Nobel Prizes 2002* (pp. 449–489). Stockholm, Sweden: Nobel Foundation.

Kahneman, D., & Tversky, A. (1979). Prospect theory—Analysis of decision under risk. *Econometrica, 47*(2), 263–291.

Kahneman, D., & Tversky, A. (1984). Choices, values, and frames. *American Psychologist, 39*(4), 341–350.

Kaid, L. L. (1981). Political advertising. In D. Nimmo & K. R. Sanders (Eds.), *Handbook of political communication* (pp. 249–271). Beverly Hills, CA: Sage.

Kaid, L. L. (1996). Political communication. In M. B. Salwen & D. W. Stacks (Eds.), *An integrated approach to communication theory and research* (pp. 443–457). Mahwah, NJ: Erlbaum.

Kaid, L. L., Gobetz, R., Garner, J., Leland, C. M., & Scott, D. (1993). Television news and presidential campaigns: The legitimization of televised political advertising. *Social Science Quarterly, 74,* 274–285.

Kaid, L. L., & Johnston, A. (1991). Negative versus positive television advertising in U.S. presidential campaigns. *Journal of Communication, 41,* 53–64.

Kaiser Family Foundation (1999). *Progress on the entertainment media & public health* [Brochure]. Menlo Park, CA: Author.

Kaiser Family Foundation. (2010). *Generation M2: Media in the lives of 8–18-year-olds.* Menlo Park, CA: Author.

Kalnin, A. J., Edwards, C. R., Want, Y., Kronenberger, W. G., Hummer, T. A., Mosier, K. M., Dunn, D. W., & Mathews, V. P. (2011). The interacting role of media violence exposure and aggressive-disruptive behavior in adolescent brain activation during an emotional Stroop task. *Psychiatry Research: Neuroimaging Section, 192*(1), 12–19.

Kalpidou, M., Costin, D., & Morris, J. (2011). The relationship between Facebook and the well-being of undergraduate college students. *Cyberpsychology, Behavior, and Social Networking, 14,* 183–189. doi: 10.1089/cyber.2010.0061

Kaner, G. (1982). *Adolescent reactions to race and sex of professional television newscasters* (Unpublished doctoral dissertation). New York University, New York.

Kang, J. G., & Morgan, M. (1988). Culture clash: US television programs in Korea. *Journalism Quarterly, 65,* 431–438.

Kaniss, P. (1991). *Making local news.* Chicago: University of Chicago Press.

Kantrowitz, B., & Underwood, A. (2007, June 25). The teen drinking dilemma. *Newsweek,* 36–37.

Kassarjian, H. (1969). The Negro and American advertising: 1946–1965. *Journal of Marketing Research, 6,* 29–39.

Katz, D., & Lazarsfeld, P. R. (1955). *Personal influence.* New York: The Free Press.

Katz, E. (1980). On conceptualizing media effects. In T. McCormack (Ed.), *Studies in communication* (Vol. 1, pp. 119–141). Greenwich, CT: JAI Press.

Katz, E. (1983). On conceptualizing media effects. In S. Oskamp (Ed.), *Television as a social issue (Applied Social Psychology Annual 8)*, 361–374. Newbury Park, CA: Sage.

Katz, E. (1987). On conceptualizing media effects: Another look. In S. Oskamp (Ed.), *Applied Social Psychology Annual* (Vol. 8, pp. 32–42). Beverly Hills, CA: Sage.

Katz, E., Gurevitch, M., & Haas, H. (1973). On the use of the mass media for important things. *American Sociological Review, 38,* 164–181.

Katz, J. E., & Aakhus, M. A. (Eds.). (2002). *Perpetual contact: Mobile communication, private talk, public performance.* Cambridge, UK: Cambridge University Press.

Katz, J. E., & Acord, S. K. (2008). Mobile games and entertainment. In J. Katz (Ed.), *Handbook of mobile communication studies* (pp. 403–418). Cambridge, MA: MIT Press.

Kelly, H. (1981). Reasoning about realities: Children's evaluations of television and books. In H. Kelly & H. Gardner (Eds.), *Viewing children through television* (pp. 59–71). San Francisco: Jossey-Bass.

Kern, M. (1989). *30-second politics: Political advertising in the eighties.* New York: Praeger.

Kim, J., & Lee, J.-E. R. (2011). The Facebook paths to happiness: Effects of the number of Facebook friends and self-presentation on subjective well-being. *Cyberpsychology, Behavior, and Social Networking, 14,* 359–365. doi: 10.1089/cyber.2010.0374

Kim, J. L., Collins, R. L., Kanouse, D. E., Elliott, M. N., Berry, S. H., Hunter, S. B., Miu, A., & Kunkel, D. (2006). Sexual readiness, household policies, and other predictors of adolescents' exposure to sexual content in mainstream entertainment television. *Media Psychology, 8,* 449–471.

Kim, J. Y., Shim, J. P., & Ahn, K. M. (2011). Social networking service: Motivation, pleasure, and behavioral intention to use. *Journal of Computer Information Systems, 51,* 92–101.

Kim, K., & McCombs, M. (2007). News story descriptions and the public's opinions of political candidates. *Journalism & Mass Communication Quarterly, 84*(2), 299–314.

Kim, S-H., Carvalho, J. P., Davis, A. G., & Mullins, A. M. (2011). The view of the border: News framing of the definition, causes, and solutions to illegal immigration. *Mass Communication & Society, 14*(3), 292–314.

Kim, S-H., Han, M., & Scheufele, D. A. (2010). Think about him this way: Priming, news media, and South Koreans' evaluation of the president. *International Journal of Public Opinion Research, 22*(3), 299–319.

Kinder, D. R., & Kiewiet, D. R. (1983). Sociotropic politics: The American case. *British Journal of Political Science, 11,* 129–161.

King, P. (1997). The press, candidate images and voter perceptions. In M. E. McCombs, D. L. Shaw, & D. Weaver (Eds.), *Communication and democracy: Exploring the intellectual frontiers in agenda setting* (pp. 29–40). Mahwah, NJ: Erlbaum.

King, S. (1981). *Danse macabre.* New York: Everest.

Klapper, J. T. (1949). *The effects of mass media: A report to the director of the public library inquiry.* New York: Columbia University Bureau of Applied Social Research.

Klapper, J. T. (1960). *The effects of mass communication.* New York: Free Press.

Klapper, J. T. (1963). Mass communication research: An old road resurveyed. *Public Opinion Quarterly, 27,* 515–527.

Klein, J. O., Brown, J. D., Walsh-Childers, K., Oliveri, J., Porter, C., & Dykers, C. (1993, July). Adolescents' risky behavior and mass media use. *Pediatrics, 92,* 24–32.

Kline, L. W. (1907). The psychology of humor. *The American Journal of Psychology, 18,* 421–441.

Ko, H., Cho, C., & Roberts, M. S. (2005). Internet uses and gratifications. *Journal of Advertising, 34*(2), 57–70.

Koriat, A., Melkman, R., Averill, J. R., & Lazarus, R. S. (1972). The self-control of emotional reactions to a stressful film. *Journal of Personality, 40,* 601–619.

Kosicki, G. M. (1993). Problems and opportunities in agenda-setting research. *Journal of Communication, 43*(2), 100–127.

Kosicki, G. M., & McLeod, J. M. (1990). Learning from political news: Effects of media images and information-processing strategies. In S. Kraus (Ed.), *Mass communication and political information processing* (pp. 69–83). Hillsdale, NJ: Erlbaum.

Kosicki, G. M., McLeod, J. M., & Armor, D. L. (1987, May). *Processing the news: Some individual strategies for selecting, sense-making and integrating.* Paper presented at the Annual meeting of the International Communication Association, Montreal, Quebec.

Krafka, C. L. (1985). *Sexually explicit, sexually violent, and violent media: Effects of multiple naturalistic exposures and debriefing on female viewers* (Unpublished doctoral dissertation). University of Wisconsin-Madison.

Krahé, B. & Möller, I. (2010). Longitudinal effects of media violence on aggression and empathy among German adolescents. *Journal of Applied Developmental Psychology, 31*(5), 401–409.

Kraut, R., Kiesler, S., Boneva, B., Cummings, J., Helgeson, V., & Crawford, A. (2002). Internet paradox revisited. *Journal of Social Issues, 58,* 49–74.

Kraut, R. E., Patterson, M., Lundmark, V., Kiesler, S., Mukhopadhyay, T., & Scherlis, W. (1998). Internet paradox: A social technology that reduces social involvement and psychological well-being? *American Psychologist, 53,* 1017–1032.

Krcmar, M. (2010). Assessing the research on media, cognitive development, and infants: Can infants really learn from television and videos? *Journal of Children and Media, 4*(2), 120–134. doi: 10.1080/17482791003629586

Krcmar, M. (2011). Can past experience with television help US infants learn from it? *Journal of Children and Media, 5,* 235–247. doi: 10.1080/17482798.2011.584373

Krcmar, M., Grela, B., & Lin, K. (2007). Can toddlers learn vocabulary from television? An experimental approach. *Media Psychology, 10,* 41–63. doi: 10.108/15213260701300931

Kreuter, M. W., Strecher, V. J., & Glassman, B. (1999). One size does not fit all: The case for tailoring print materials. *Annals of Behavioral Medicine, 21*(4), 276–283.

Krosnick, J. A. (1988). The role of attitude importance in social evaluation: A study of policy preference, presidential candidate evaluations, and voting behavior. *Journal of Personality and Social Psychology, 55,* 196–210.

Krosnick, J. A., & Kinder, D. R. (1990). Altering the foundations of support for the president though priming. *American Political Science Review, 84,* 497–512.

Ku, G., Kaid, L. L., & Pfau, M. (2003). The impact of web site campaigning on traditional news media and public information processing. *Journalism & Mass Communication Quarterly, 80*(3), 528–547.

Kunkel, D., Biely, E., Eyal, K., Cope-Farrar, K. M., Donnerstein, E., & Fandrich, R. (2003). *Sex on TV 3: Content and context.* Menlo Park, CA: Henry J. Kaiser Family Foundation.

Kunkel, D., Cope, K. M., Farinola, W. J. M., Biely, E., Rollin, E., & Donnerstein, E. (1999). *Sex on TV: A biennial report to the Kaiser Family Foundation.* Menlo Park, CA: Kaiser Family Foundation.

Kunkel, D., Eyal, K., Donnerstein, E., Farrar, K. M., Biely, E., & Rideout, V. (2007). Sexual socialization messages on entertainment television: Comparing content trends 1997–2002. *Media Psychology, 9*(3), 595–622.

Kwak, N., Williams, A. E., Wang, X. R., & Lee, H. (2005). Talking politics and engaging in politics: An examination of the interactive relationships between structural features of political talk and discussion engagement. *Communication Research, 32,* 87–111.

Landman, J., & Manis, M. (1983). Social cognition: Some historical and theoretical perspectives. In L. Berkowitz (Ed.), *Advances in experimental social psychology* (Vol. 16, pp. 49–123). New York: Academic.

Lang, K., & Lang, G. E. (1959). The mass media and voting. In E. Burdick & A. J. Brodbeck (Eds.), *American voting behavior* (pp. 217–235). Glencoe, IL: Free Press.

Lapinski, M. K., & Witte, K. (1998). Health communication campaigns. In L. D. Jackson & B. K. Duffy (Eds.), *Health communication research: A guide to developments and directions* (pp. 139–161). Westport, CT: Greenwood.

LaRose, R., & Eastin, M. S. (2002). Is online buying out of control? Electronic commerce and consumer self-regulation. *Journal of Broadcasting & Electronic Media, 46*, 549–564.

LaRose, R., Lin, C. A., & Eastin, M. S. (2003). Unregulated Internet usage: Addiction, habit, or deficient self-regulation? *Media Psychology, 5*(3), 225–253. doi: 10.1207/S1532785XME0503_01

Lasswell, H. D. (1927). *Propaganda technique in the World War.* New York: Knopf.

Lasswell, H. D. (1948). The structure and function of communication in society. In L. Bryson (Ed.), *The communication of ideas* (pp. 37–51). New York: Harper.

Lauzen, M. M., & Dozier, D. M. (1999). Making a difference in primetime: Women on screen and behind the scenes in the 1995–96 season. *Journal of Broadcasting & Electronic Media, 43,* 1–19.

Lauzen, M. M., & Dozier, D. M. (2002). You look mahvelous: An examination of gender and appearance comments in the 1999–2000 primetime season. *Sex Roles, 46,* 429–437.

Lauzen, M. M., & Dozier, D. M. (2004). Evening the score in primetime: The relationship between behind the scenes women and on-screen portrayals in the 2002–2003 season. *Journal of Broadcasting & Electronic Media, 48,* 484–500.

Lauzen, M. M., Dozier, D. M., & Cleveland, E. (2006). Genre matters: An examination of women working behind the scenes and on-screen portrayals in reality and scripted primetime programming. *Sex Roles, 55,* 445–455.

Laytner, L. (2009). *Star Trek tech.* Retrieved from http://editinternational.com/read.php?id=4810edf3a83f8

Lazarsfeld, P. F. (1940). *Radio and the printed page.* New York: Duell, Sloan, & Pearce.

Lazarsfeld, P. F. (1949). Forward. In J. T. Klapper, *The effects of mass media: A report to the director of the public library inquiry* (pp. 1–9). New York: Columbia University Bureau of Applied Social Research.

Lazarsfeld, P. F. (1962). Introduction. In S. A. Stouffer, *Social research to test ideas: Selected writings of Samuel A. Stouffer* (pp. xv–xxxi). New York: Free Press.

Lazarsfeld, P. F., Berelson, B. R., & Gaudet, H. (1944). *The people's choice.* New York: Columbia University Press.

Lazarsfeld, P. F., Berelson, B. R., & Gaudet, H. (1948). *The people's choice* (2nd ed.). New York: Columbia University Press.

Lazarus, R. S., Speisman, J. C., Mordkoff, A. M., & Davidson, L. A. (1962). A laboratory study of psychological stress produced by a motion picture film. *Psychological Monographs: General and Applied, 76*(34), 553.

Lee, A., & Lee, E. B. (1939). *The fine art of propaganda: A study of Father Coughlin's speeches.* New York: Harcourt, Brace.

Lee, E.-J., Lee, L., & Jang, J. (2011). Internet for the internationals: Effects of Internet use motivations on international students' college adjustment. *Cyberpsychology, Behavior, and Social Networking, 14,* 433–437. doi: 10.1089/cyber.2010.0406

Lee, G., Lee, J., & Kwon, S. (2011). Use of social-networking sites and subjective well-being: A study in South Korea. *Cyberpsychology, Behavior, and Social Networking, 14,* 151–155. doi: 10.1089/cyber.2009.0382

Lee, K. M., Peng, W., & Park, N. (2009). Effects of computer/video games and beyond. In J. Bryant & M. B. Oliver (Eds.), *Media effects: Advances in theory and research* (3rd ed., pp. 551–566). New York: Routledge.

Lee, M. J., Bichard, S. L., Irey, M. S., Walt, H. M., & Carlson, A. J. (2009). Television viewing and ethnic stereotypes: Do college students form stereotypical perceptions of ethnic groups as a result of heavy television consumption? *The Howard Journal of Communications, 20,* 95–110. doi: 10.1080/10646170802665281

Leippe, M. R., & Elkin, R. A. (1987). When motives clash: Issue involvement and response involvement as determinants of persuasion. *Journal of Personality and Social Psychology, 52,* 269–278.

Leitner, R. K. (1991). *Comparing the effects on reading comprehension of educational video, direct experience, and print* (Unpublished doctoral thesis). University of San Francisco, California.

Lemola, S., Brand, S., Vogler, N., Perkinson-Gloor, N., Allemand, M., & Grob, A. (2011). Habitual computer game playing at night is related to depressive symptoms. *Personality and Individual Differences, 51,* 117–122. doi: 10.1016/j.paid.2011.03.024

Lenhart, A., Purcell, K., Smith, A., & Zickuhr, K. (2010). *Social media and young adults: Social media and mobile Internet use among teens and adults.* Washington, DC: Pew Internet & American Life Project.

Lerner, D., & Nelson, L. M. (1977). *Communication research:-A half-century appraisal.* Honolulu: The University Press of Hawaii.

Levy, A., & Stokes, R. (1987). Effects of a health promotion advertising campaign on sales of ready to eat cereals. *Public Health Reports, 102*(4), 398–403.

Levy, M. R., & Windahl, S. (1984). Audience activity and gratifications: A conceptual clarification and exploration. *Communication Research, 11,* 51–78.

Lieberman, D. A. (2001). Management of chronic pediatric diseases with interactive health games: Theory and research findings. *Journal of Ambulatory Care Management, 24,* 26–38.

Liebert, R. M., & Schwartzberg, N. S. (1977). Effects of mass media. *Annual Review of Psychology, 28,* 141–183.

Liebert, R. M., Sprafkin, J. N., & Davidson, E. S. (1982). *The early window: Effects of television on children and youth.* Elmsford, NY: Pergamon.

Lilischkis, S. (2003). *More yo-yos, pendulums and nomads: Trends of mobile and multi-location work in the information society* (Issue report no. 36). Socioeconomic trends assessment for the digital revolution.

Lin, C. A. (2003). An interactive communication technology adoption model. *Communication Theory, 13*(4), 345–365.

Lin, C. A. (2009). Effects of the Internet. In J. Bryant & M. B. Oliver (Eds.), *Media effects: Advances in theory and research* (3rd ed., pp. 567–591). New York: Routledge.

Lin, C.-H., Lin, S.-L., & Wu, C.-P. (2009). The effects of parental monitoring and leisure boredom on adolescents' Internet addiction. *Adolescence, 44,* 993–1004.

Linebarger, D. L. (2000). *Summative evaluation of* Between the Lions: *A final report to WGBH Educational Foundation.* Kansas City: University of Kansas, Juniper Gardens Children's Project.

Linebarger, D. L. (2001). *Summative evaluation of* Dora the Explorer, *Part 1: Learning outcomes.* Kansas City, KS: Media & Technology Projects, ABCD Ventures.

Linebarger, D. L. (2006). *The* Between the Lions *American Indian literacy initiative research component: A report prepared for the United States Department of Education.* Philadelphia: Annenberg School for Communication, University of Pennsylvania.

Linebarger, D. L., & Piotrowski, J. T. (2009). TV as storyteller: How exposure to television narratives impacts at-risk preschoolers' story knowledge and narrative skills. *British Journal of Developmental Psychology, 27,* 47–69.

Linebarger, D. L., & Piotrowski, J. T. (2010). Structures and strategies in children's educational television: The roles of program type and learning strategies in children's learning. *Child Development, 81,* 1582–1597.

Linebarger, D. L., & Vaala, S. E. (2010). Screen media and language development in infants and toddlers: An ecological perspective. *Developmental Review, 30,* 176–202. doi: 10.1016/j.dr.2010.03.006

Linebarger, D. L., & Walker, D. (2005). Infants' and toddlers' television viewing and language outcomes. *The American Behavioral Scientist, 45,* 624–644. doi: 10.1177/0002764204271505

Ling, R. (2004). *The mobile connection: The cell phone's impact on society.* San Francisco: Morgan Kaufman.

Ling, R. (2005a). The sociolinguistics of SMS: An analysis of SMS use by a random sample of Norwegians. In R. Ling & P. Pedersen (Eds.), *Mobile communications: Re-negotiation of the social sphere* (pp. 335–350). London: Springer-Verlag.

Ling, R. (2005b). Mobile communications vis-á-vis teen emancipation, peer group interaction and deviance. In R. Harper, A. Taylor, & L. Palen (Eds.), *The inside text: Social perspectives on SMS in the mobile age* (pp. 175–192). London: Kluwer.

Ling, R. (2006, December). *The length of text messages and the use of predictive texting.* Paper presented at the annual meeting of the Association of Internet Researchers, Brisbane, Australia.

Ling, R. (2008). New tech, new ties: How mobile communication is reshaping social cohesion. Cambridge, MA: MIT Press.

Ling, R., & Campbell, S. W. (2008). *The mobile communication research series: Reconstruction of space and time through mobile communication practices.* New Brunswick, NJ: Transaction Publishers.

Ling, R., & Yttri, B. (1999). *Nobody sits at home and waits for the telephone to ring: Micro and hyper-coordination through the use of the mobile phone* (Report 30/99). Kjeller, Norway: Telenor Research and Development.

Ling, R., & Yttri, B. (2002). Hyper-coordination via mobile phones in Norway. In J. Katz & M. Aakhus (Eds.), *Perpetual contact: Mobile communication, private talk, public performance* (pp. 139–169). Cambridge, UK: Cambridge University Press.

Linz, D., Donnerstein, E., Bross, M., & Chapin, M. (1986). Mitigating the influence of violence on television and sexual violence in the media. In R. Blanchard (Ed.), *Advances in the study of aggression* (Vol. 2, pp. 165–194). Orlando, FL: Academic Press.

Linz, D., Donnerstein, E., & Penrod, S. (1984). The effects of multiple exposures to filmed violence against women. *Journal of Communication, 34*(3), 130–147.

Linz, D., Donnerstein, E., & Penrod, S. (1988). The effects of long-term exposure to violent and sexually degrading depictions of women. *Journal of Personality and Social Psychology, 55*(5), 758–768.

Linz, D., Fuson, I. A., & Donnerstein, E. (1990). Mitigating the negative effects of sexually violent mass communications through pre-exposure briefings. *Communication Research, 17,* 641–674.

Linz, D., & Malamuth, N. (1993). *Pornography.* Newbury Park, CA: Sage.

Lipkins, S., Levy, J. M., & Jerabkova, B. (2011). Sexting . . . is it all about power? Retrieved from http://www.realpsychology.com/content/tools-life/sextingis-it-all-about-power

Lippmann, W. (1922). *Public opinion.* New York: Harcourt Brace.

Liss, M. (1981). Children's television selections: A study of indicators of same-race preference. *Journal of Cross Cultural Psychology, 12*(1), 103–110.

Liu, X., & LaRose, R. (2008). Does using the Internet make people more satisfied with their lives? The effects of the Internet on college students' school life satisfaction. *Cyberpsychology & Behavior, 11*(3), 310–320. doi: 10.1089/cpb.2007.0040

Logan, J. R., & Molotch, H. L. (1987). *Urban fortunes: The political economy of place.* Berkeley: University of California Press.

Long, N. E. (1958). The local community as an ecology of games. *American Journal of Sociology, 64,* 251–261.

Longman, H., O'Connor, D., & Obst, P. (2009). The effect of social support derived from *World of Warcraft* on negative psychological symptoms. *Cyberpsychology & Behavior, 12,* 563–566. doi: 10.1089/cpb.2009.0001

Love, S., & Kewley, J. (2005). Does personality affect people's attitudes towards mobile phone use in public places? In R. Ling & P. Pedersen (Eds.), *Mobile communications: Re-negotiation of the social sphere* (pp. 273–284). London: Springer-Verlag.

Lowery, S. A., & DeFleur, M. L. (1995). *Milestones in mass communication research: Media effects*. White Plains, NY: Longman.

Lowry, D. T., & Towles, D. E. (1989). Soap opera portrayals of sex, contraception, and sexually transmitted diseases. *Journal of Communication, 39*(2), 76–83.

Lucas, K., & Sherry, J. L. (2004). Sex differences in video game play: A communication-based approach. *Communication Research, 31,* 499–523. doi: 10.1177/0093650204267930

Lundy, L. K., Ruth, A. M., & Park, T. D. (2008). Simply irresistible: Reality TV consumption patterns. *Communication Quarterly, 56*(2), 208–225.

Lyle, J., & Hoffman, H. R. (1972). Children's use of television and other media. In E. A. Rubinstein, G. A. Comstock, & J. P. Murray (Eds.), *Television and social behavior* (Vol. 4, pp. 129–256). Washington, DC: Government Printing Office.

Lyons, E. J., Tate, D. F., Ward, D. S., Bowling, J. M., Ribisl, K. M., & Kalyararaman, S. (2011). Energy expenditure and enjoyment during video game play: Differences by game type. *Medicine & Science in Sports & Exercise, 43,* 1987–1993. doi: 10.1249/MSS.0b013e318216ebf3

Maccoby, N., & Farquhar, J. W. (1975). Communication for health: Unselling heart disease. *Journal of Communication, 25,* 114–126.

MacKuen, M. (1981). Social communication and the mass policy agenda. In M. MacKuen & S. Coombs (Eds.), *More than news: Media power in public affairs* (pp. 19–144). Beverly Hills, CA: Sage.

Maddison, R., Foley, L., Mhurchu, C. N., Jiang, Y., Jull, A., Prapavessis, H., . . . & Rodgers, A. (2011). Effects of active video games on body composition: A randomized controlled trial. *The American Journal of Clinical Nutrition, 94,* 156–163.

Magliano, J. P., Dijkstra, K., & Swann, R. A. (1996). Generating predictive inferences while viewing a movie. *Discourse Processes, 22,* 199–224.

Maibach, E. W., Maxfieldd, A., Ladin, K., & Slater, M. (1996). Translating health psychology into effective health communication: The American Healthstyles Audience Segmentation Project. *Journal of Health Psychology, 1,* 261–277.

Maio, G., Haddock, G., Watt, S. E., & Hewstone, M. (2008). Implicit measures in applied contexts: An illustrative examination of anti-racism advertising. In R. E. Petty, R. H. Fazio, & P. Briñol (Eds.), *Attitudes: Insights from the new implicit measures* (pp. 327–357). New York: Psychology Press.

Malamuth, N. M. (1981). Rape fantasies as a function of exposure to violent sexual stimuli. *Archives of Sexual Behavior, 10,* 33–47.

Malamuth, N. M. (1993). Pornography's impact on male adolescents. *Adolescent Medicine: State of the Art Reviews, 4,* 563–576.

Malamuth, N. M. (1996). Sexually explicit media, gender differences, and evolutionary theory. *Journal of Communication, 46*(3), 8–31.

Malamuth, N. M., & Check, J. V. P. (1980a). Penile tumescence and perceptual responses to rape as a function of victim's perceived reactions. *Journal of Applied Social Psychology, 10,* 528–547.

Malamuth, N. M., & Check, J. V. P. (1980b). Sexual arousal to rape and consenting depictions: The importance of the woman's arousal. *Journal of Abnormal Psychology, 89,* 763–766.

Malamuth, N. M., & Check, J. V. P. (1983). Sexual arousal to rape depictions: Individual differences. *Journal of Abnormal Psychology, 92,* 55–67.

Malamuth, N. M., & Donnerstein, E. (Eds.). (1984). *Pornography and sexual aggression.* New York: Academic.

Malamuth, N. M., Heim, M., & Feshbach, S. (1980). Sexual responsiveness of college students to rape depictions: Inhibitory and disinhibitory effects. *Journal of Personality and Social Psychology, 38,* 399–408.

Malamuth, N. M., & Impett, E. A. (2001). Research on sex in the media: What do we know about effects on children and adolescents? In D. Singer & J. Singer (Eds.), *Handbook of children and the media* (pp. 269–278). Newbury Park, CA: Sage.

Malamuth, N. M., & Spinner, B. (1980). A longitudinal content analysis of sexual violence in the best-selling erotica magazines. *Journal of Sex Research, 16,* 226–237.

Manis, F. R., Keating, D. P., & Morison, F. J. (1980). Developmental differences in the allocation of processing capacity. *Journal of Experimental Child Psychology, 29,* 156–169.

Mann, S., & Holdsworth, L. (2003). The effects of home-based teleworking on work-family conflicts. *Human Resources Development Quarterly, 14,* 35–38.

Manusov, V., & Harvey, J. (2011). Bumps and tears on the road to the presidency: Media framing of key nonverbal events in the 2008 Democratic election. *Western Journal of Communication, 75*(3), 282–303.

Marcus, B. H., Owen, N., Forsyth, L. H., Cavill, N. A., & Fridinger, F. (1998). Physical activity interventions using mass media, print media, and information technology. *American Journal of Preventive Medicine, 15,* 362–378.

Mares, M. (1996). The role of source confusion in television's cultivation of social reality judgments. *Human Communication Research, 23,* 278–297.

Marshall, W. L. (1989). Pornography and sex offenders. In D. Zillmann & J. Bryant (Eds.), *Pornography: Research advances and policy considerations.* Hillsdale, NJ: Erlbaum.

Marvin, C. (1988). *When old technologies were new: Thinking about electric communication in the late nineteenth century.* New York: Oxford University Press.

Mastro, D. (2003). A social identity approach to understanding the impact of television messages. *Communication Monographs, 70,* 98–113.

Mastro, D. (2009). Effects of racial and ethnic stereotyping. In J. Bryant & M. B. Oliver (Eds.), *Media effects: Advances in theory and research* (3rd ed., pp. 325–341). New York: Routledge.

Mastro, D., & Behm-Morawitz, E. (2005). Latino representation on primetime television. *Journalism & Mass Communication Quarterly, 82,* 110–130.

Mastro, D., Behm-Morawitz, E., & Ortiz, M. (2007). The cultivation of social perceptions of Latinos: A mental models approach. *Media Psychology, 9,* 1–19.

Mastro, D., & Greenberg, B. S. (2000). The portrayal of racial minorities on primetime television. *Journal of Broadcasting & Electronic Media, 44,* 690–703.

Mastro, D., & Kopacz, M. (2006). Media representations of race, prototypicality, and policy reasoning: An application of self-categorization theory. *Journal of Broadcasting & Electronic Media, 50,* 305–322.

Mastro, D., & Stern, S. (2003). Representations of race in television commercials: A content analysis of primetime advertising. *Journal of Broadcasting & Electronic Media, 47,* 638–647.

Matei, S., & Ball-Rokeach, S. (2003). The Internet in the communication infrastructure of urban residential communities: Macro- or mesolinkage? *Journal of Communication, 53,* 642–657.

Mathai, J. (1983). An acute anxiety state in an adolescent precipitated by viewing a horror movie. *Journal of Adolescence, 6,* 197–200.

Matheson, D. M., Killen, J. D., Wang, Y., Varady, A., & Robinson, T. N. (2004). Children's food consumption during television viewing. *American Journal of Clinical Nutrition, 79*(6), 1088–1094.

Mazur, A. (1987). Putting radon on the public risk agenda. *Science, Technology and Human Values, 12,* 86–93.

McCaul, K. D., Jacobson, K., & Martinson, B. (1998). The effects of state-wide media campaign on mammography screening. *Journal of Applied Social Psychology, 28,* 504–515.

McCombs, M. E. (1992). Explorers and surveyors: Expanding strategies for agenda-setting research. *Journalism Quarterly, 69,* 813–824.

McCombs, M. E. (2004). *Setting the agenda: The mass media and public opinion.* Malden, MA: Blackwell.

McCombs, M., & Bell, T. (1996). The agenda-setting role of mass communication. In M. B. Salwen & D. W. Stacks (Eds.), *An integrated approach to communication theory and research* (pp. 93–110). Mahwah, NJ: Erlbaum.

McCombs, M. E., Lopez-Escobar, E., & Llamas, J. P. (2000). Setting the agenda of attributes in the 1996 Spanish general election. *Journal of Communication, 50,* 77–92.

McCombs, M. E., & Reynolds, A. (2009). How the news shapes our civic agenda. In J. Bryant & M. B. Oliver (Eds.), *Media effects: Advances in theory and research* (3rd ed., pp. 1–16). New York: Routledge.

McCombs, M. E., & Shaw, D. L. (1972). The agenda-setting function of the mass media. *Public Opinion Quarterly, 36,* 176–187.

McCombs, M. E., & Shaw, D. L. (1993). The evolution of agenda-setting research: Twenty-five years in the marketplace of ideas. *Journal of Communication, 43*(2), 58–67.

McDivitt, D. (2006). Do gamers score better in school? *Serious Game Source.* Retrieved from http://seriousgamesource.com/features/feature_051606.php

McDivitt, J. A., Zimicki, S., & Hornick, R. C. (1997). Explaining the impact of a communication campaign to change vaccination knowledge and coverage in the Philippines. *Health Communication, 9,* 95–118.

McGhee, P. E., & Frueh, T. (1980). Television viewing and the learning of sex-role stereotypes. *Sex Roles, 6,* 179–188.

McGraw, K. M., & Ling, C. (2003). Media priming of presidential and group evaluations. *Political Communication, 20,* 23–40.

McGuire, W. J. (1985). Attitudes and attitude change. In G. Lindzey & E. Aronson (Eds.), *Handbook of social psychology* (3rd ed., Vol. 2, pp. 43–65). Newbury Park, CA: Sage.

McGuire, W. J. (1986). The myth of massive media impact: Savagings and salvagings. *Public Communication and Behavior, 1,* 173–257.

McGuire, W. J. (1989). Theoretical foundations of campaigns. In R. E. Rice & C. K. Atkin (Eds.), *Public communication campaigns* (2nd ed., pp. 43–65). Newbury Park, CA: Sage.

McKenna, K. Y. A., Green, A. S., & Gleason, M. E. J. (2002). Relationship formation on the Internet: What's the big attraction? *Journal of Social Issues, 58,* 9–31.

McKinney, M. S., Rill, L. A., & Watson, R. G. (2011). Who framed Sarah Palin? Viewer reactions to the 2008 vice presidential debate. *American Behavioral Scientist, 55*(3), 212–231.

McLeod, J. M., & Becker, L. B. (1974). Testing the validity of gratification measures through political effects analysis. In J. G. Blumler & E. Katz (Eds.), *The uses of mass communications: Current perspectives on gratifications research* (pp. 137–164). Beverly Hills, CA: Sage.

McLeod, J. M., Becker, L. B., & Byrnes, J. E. (1974). Another look at the agenda-setting function of the press. *Communication Research, 1,* 131–165.

McLeod, J. M., Bybee, C. R., & Durall, J. A. (1979). The 1976 presidential debates and the equivalence of informed political participation. *Communication Research, 6,* 463–487.

McLeod, J. M., Daily, C., Guo, Z., Eveland, W. P., Bayer, J., Yang, S., & Wang, H. (1996). Community integration, local media use, and democratic processes. *Communication Research, 23,* 179–209.

McLeod, J. M., & Detenber, B. H. (1999). Framing effects of television news coverage of social protest. *Journal of Communication, 49*(3), 3–23.

McLeod, J. M., Kosicki, G. M., Armor, D. L., Allen, S. G., & Philps, D. M. (1986, August). *Public images of mass media news: What are they and does it matter?* Paper presented at the annual meeting of the Association for Education in Journalism and Mass Communication, Norman, OK.

McLeod, J. M., Kosicki, G. M., & McLeod, D. M. (1994). The expanding boundaries of political communication effects. In J. Bryant & D. Zillmann (Eds.), *Media effects: Advances in theory and research* (pp. 123–162). Hillsdale, NJ: Erlbaum.

McLeod, J. M., Kosicki, G. M., & McLeod, D. M. (2009). Political communication effects. In J. Bryant & M. B. Oliver (Eds.), *Media effects: Advances in theory and research* (3rd Ed.). New York: Routledge.

McLeod, J. M., Kosicki, G. M., & Rucinski, D. M. (1988). Political communication research: An assessment of the field. *Mass Communication Review, 15*(1), 8–15, 30.

McLeod, J. M., & McDonald, D. G. (1985). Beyond simple exposure: Media orientations and their impact on political processes. *Communication Research, 12,* 3–33.

McLeod, J. M., Pan, Z., & Rucinski, D. (1989, May). *Framing a complex issue: A case of social construction of meaning.* Paper presented at the annual meeting of the International Communication Association, San Francisco.

McLeod, J. M., Sun, S., Chi, A., & Pan, Z. (1990, August). *Metaphor and the media: What shapes public understanding of the "war" on drugs?* Paper presented at the annual meeting of the Association for Education in Journalism and Mass Communication, Minneapolis, MN.

McQuail, D. (1972). *Towards a sociology of mass communications.* London: Collier-Macmillan. (Original work published 1969).

McQuail, D., Blumler, J. G., & Brown, J. R. (1972). The television audience: A revised perspective. In D. McQuail (Ed.), *Sociology of mass communications* (pp. 135–165). Middlesex, England: Penguin.

McQuail, D., & Windahl, S. (1993). *Communication models for the study of mass communications* (2nd ed.). New York: Longman.

Melkman, R., Tversky, B., & Baratz, D. (1981). Developmental trends in the use of perpetual and conceptual attributes in grouping, clustering and retrieval. *Journal of Experimental Child Psychology, 31,* 470–486.

Meltzoff, A. N. (1988). Imitation of televised models by infants. *Child Development, 59,* 1221–1229.

Mendelberg, T. (1997). Executing Hortons. Racial crime in the 1988 presidential campaign. *Public Opinion Quarterly, 61,* 134–157.

Mendelsohn, H. (1963). Socio-psychological perspectives on the mass media and public anxiety. *Journalism Quarterly, 40,* 511–516.

Mendelsohn, H. (1973). Some reasons why information campaigns can succeed. *Public Opinion Quarterly, 37,* 50–61.

Mentzoni, R. A., Brunborg, G. S., Molde, H., Myrseth, H., Skouverøe, K. J. M., Hetland, J., & Pallesen, S. (2011). Problematic video game use: Estimated prevalence and associations with mental and physical health. *Cyberpsychology, Behavior, and Social Networking, 14,* 591–596. doi: 10.1089/cyber.2010.0260

Merskin, D. (1998). Sending up signals: A survey of Native American media use and representation in the mass media. *The Howard Journal of Communications, 9,* 333–345.

Meyer, T. P. (1972). The effects of sexually arousing and violent films on aggressive behavior. *Journal of Sex Research, 8,* 423–433.

Miller, M. M., Andsager, J. L., & Riechert, B. P. (1998). Framing the candidates in presidential primaries: Issues and images in press releases and news coverage. *Journalism & Mass Communication Quarterly, 75,* 312–324.

Miller, M. M., & Reese, S. D. (1982). Media dependency as interaction: Effects of exposure and reliance on political activity and efficacy. *Communication Research, 9,* 227–248.

Miller, R., Parsons, K., & Lifer, D. (2010). Students and social networking sites: The posting paradox. *Behaviour & Information Technology, 29,* 377–382.

Miron, D. (1999). Grabbing the nonvoter. In B. I. Newman (Ed.), *Handbook of political marketing* (pp. 321–343). Thousand Oaks, CA: Sage.

Möller, I. & Krahé, B. (2009). Exposure to violent video games and aggression in German adolescents: A longitudinal analysis. *Aggressive Behavior, 35* (1), 75–89.

Monahan, J. L., Shtrulis, I., & Givens, S. B. (2005). Priming welfare queens and other stereotypes: The transference of media images into interpersonal contexts. *Communication Research Reports, 22*(3), 199–205.

Mongeau, P. A. (1998). Fear-arousing persuasive messages: A meta-analysis revisited. In M. Allen & R. Preiss (Eds.), *Persuasion: Advances through meta-analysis.* Thousand Oaks, CA: Sage.

Monk, A., Carroll, J., Parker, S., & Blythe, M. (2004). Why are mobile phones annoying? *Behavior and Information Technology, 23,* 33–41.

Moore, D. L., Hausknecht, D., & Thamodaran, K. (1986). Time compression, response opportunity, and persuasion. *Journal of Consumer Research, 13,* 85–99.

Morais, R. C. (1999, June 14). Porn goes public. *Forbes,* p. 214.

Morgan, M. (1983). Symbolic victimization and real world fear. *Human Communication Research, 9,* 146–157.

Morgan, M. (1990). International cultivation analysis. In N. Signorielli & M. Morgan (Eds.), *Cultivation analysis: New directions in media effects research* (pp. 225–248). Newbury Park, CA: Sage.

Morgan, M., Leggett, S., & Shanahan, J. (1999). Television and "family values": Was Dan Quayle right? *Mass Communication and Society, 2*(1/2), 47–63.

Morgan, M., & Shanahan, J. (1995). *Democracy tango: Television, adolescents, and authoritarian tensions in Argentina.* Cresskill, NJ: Hampton Press.

Morgan, M., Shanahan, J., & Harris, C. (1990). VCRs and the effects of television: New diversity or more of the same? In J. Dobrow (Ed.), *Social and cultural aspects of VCR use* (pp. 107–123). Hillsdale, NJ: Erlbaum.

Morgan, M., Shanahan, J., & Signorielli, N. (2009). Growing up with television: Cultivation processes. In J. Bryant & M. B. Oliver (Eds.), *Media effects: Advances in theory and research* (3rd ed., pp. 34–49). New York: Routledge.

Morgan, M., & Signorielli, N. (1990). Cultivation analysis: Conceptualization and methodology. In N. Signorielli & M. Morgan (Eds.), *Cultivation analysis: New directions in media effects research* (pp. 13–34). Newbury Park, CA: Sage.

Morison, P., & Gardner, H. (1978). Dragons and dinosaurs: The child's capacity to differentiate fantasy from reality. *Child Development, 49,* 642–648.

Mosher, D. L., & Maclan, P. (1994). College men and women respond to X-rated videos intended for male or female audiences: Gender and sexual scripts. *The Journal of Sex Research, 31,* 99–113.

Mossberger, K., Tolbert, C. J., & Stansbury, M. (2003). *Virtual inequality: Beyond the digital divide*. Georgetown: Georgetown University Press.

Mott, F L. (1944). Newspapers in presidential campaigns. *Public Opinion Quarterly, 8,* 348–367.

Moy, P., Xenos, M. A., & Hess, V. K. (2006). Priming effect of late-night comedy. *International Journal of Public Opinion Research, 18*(2), 198–210.

Mulliken, L., & Bryant, J. A. (1999, May). *Effects of curriculum-based television programming on behavioral assessments of flexible thinking and structured and unstructured prosocial play behaviors*. Poster presented at the 49th annual conference of the International Communication Association, San Francisco, CA.

Mundorf, N., D'Alessio, D., Allen, M., & Emmers-Sommer, T. M. (2007). Effects of sexually explicit media. In R. W. Preiss, B. M. Gayle, N. Burrell, M. Allen, and J. Bryant (Eds.), *Mass media effects research: Advances through meta-analysis* (pp. 181–198). Mahwah, NJ: Erlbaum.

Munoz, R. F., Lenert, L. L., Delucchi, K., Stoddard, J., Perez, J. E., Penilla, C., & Perez-Stable, E. J. (2006). Toward evidence-based Internet interventions: A Spanish/English web site for international smoking cessation trials. *Nicotine & Tobacco Research, 8,* 77–87.

Murnen, S. K., & Stockton, M. (1997). Gender and self-reported sexual arousal in response to sexual stimuli: A meta-analytic review. *Sex Roles, 37,* 135–153.

Murray, D. M., Prokhorov, A. V., & Harty, K. C. (1994). Effects of a statewide antismoking campaign on mass media messages and smoking beliefs. *Preventive Medicine, 23,* 54–60.

Murray, E., Lo, B., Pollack, L., Donelan, K., & Lee, K. (2004). Direct-to-consumer advertising: Public perceptions of its effects on health behaviors, health care, and the doctor-patient relationship. *Journal of the American Board of Family Practice, 17,* 6–18.

Murray, J. P. (2008). Media violence: The effects are both real and strong. *American Behavioral Scientist, 51*(8), 1212–1230.

Murray, J. P., Liotti, M., Ingmundson, P. T., Mayberg, H. S., Pu, Y., Zamarripa, F., et al. (2006). Children's brain activations while viewing televised violence revealed by MRI. *Media Psychology, 8,* 25–37.

Mustonen, A., & Pulkkinen, L. (1997). Television violence: A development of a coding scheme. *Journal of Broadcasting & Electronic Media, 41,* 168–189.

Naigles, L. R., & Mayeux, L., (2001). Television as incidental language teacher. In D. G. Singer & J. L. Singer (Eds.), *Handbook of children and the media* (pp. 135–152). Thousand Oaks, CA: Sage.

Nardi, B. A., Schiano, D. J., Gumbrecht, M., & Swartz, L. (2004). Why we blog. *Communications of the ACM, 47*(12), 41–46.

Nathanson, A. I. (1999). Identifying and explaining the relationship between parental mediation and children's aggression. *Communication Research, 26,* 124–143.

National Commission on the Causes and Prevention of Violence. (1969). *Commission statement on violence in television entertainment programs*. Washington, DC: Government Printing Office.

National Institute of Mental Health. (1982a). *Television and behavior: Ten years of scientific progress and implications for the eighties. Vol. 1: Summary report* (DHHS Publication No. ADM 82–1195). Washington, DC: Government Printing Office.

National Institute of Mental Health. (1982b). Television and behavior: Ten years of scientific progress and implications for the eighties. In E. Wartella & D. C. Whitney (Eds.), *Mass communication review yearbook,* (Vol. 4, pp. 23–35). Beverly Hills, CA: Sage.

Nelson, T. E., Clawson, R. A., & Oxley, Z. M. (1997). Media framing of civil liberties conflict and its effects on tolerance. *American Political Science Review, 91,* 567–583.

Nelson, T. E., & Oxley, Z. M. (1999). Issue framing effects on belief importance and opinion. *The Journal of Politics, 61,* 1040–1067.

Nelson, T. E., Oxley, Z. M., & Clawson, R. A. (1997). Toward a psychology of framing effects. *Political Behavior, 19,* 221–246.

Nerone, J. (1994). *Violence against the press: Policing the public sphere in U.S. history.* New York: Oxford University Press.

Neuman, W. R. (1986). *The paradox of mass politics: Knowledge and opinion in the American electorate.* Cambridge, MA: Harvard University Press.

Neuwirth, K., Frederick, E., & Mayo, C. (2007). The spiral of silence and fear of isolation. *Journal of Communication, 57,* 450–468.

Newhagen, J. E., & Reeves, B. (1991). Emotion and memory responses for negative political advertising: A study of television commercials used in the 1988 presidential election. In F. Biocca (Ed.), *Television and political advertising, Volume 1: Psychological processes* (pp. 197–220). Hillsdale, NJ: Erlbaum.

Newman, M. Z. (2010). New media, young audiences and discourses of attention: From *Sesame Street* to "snack culture." *Media, Culture, & Society, 32*(4), 581–596.

Newsweek. (1999, 31 May). Fat-phobia in the Fijis: TV-thin is in. Article quotes Dr. Anne Becker, research director at the Harvard Eating Disorders Center, in her report to the American Psychiatric Association.

Nielsen Media Research. (1998). *1998 Report on Television.* New York: Author.

Nielsen Media Research. (2007). Retrieved from http://www.nielsenmedia.com/nc/portal/site/Public/menuitem.55dc65b4a7d5adff3f65936147a062a0//?vgnextoid=4156527aaccd010VgnVCM100000ac0a260aRCRD

Nielsen Media Research. (2010). U.S. teen mobile report card: Calling yesterday, texting today, using apps tomorrow. Retrieved from http://blog.nielsen.com/nielsenwire/online_mobile/u-s-teen-mobile-report-card-calling-yesterday-texting-today-using-apps-tomorrow

Nielsen Media Research. (2011a). State of the media: The social media report. Retrieved from http://blog.nielsen.com/nielsenwiare/social/

Nielsen Media Research. (2011b). The most valuable digital consumer. Retrieved from http://blog.nielsen.com/nielsenwire/online_mobile/infographic-the-most-valuable-digital-consumer

Nisbet, M. C., Brossard, D., & Kroepsch, A. (2003). Framing science—The stem cell controversy in an age of press/politics. *The Harvard International Journal of Press/Politics, 8*(2), 36–70.

Nisbet, M. C., & Huge, M. (2006). Attention cycles and frames in the plant biotechnology debate: Managing power and participation through the press/policy connection. *The Harvard International Journal of Press/Politics, 11*(2), 3–40.

Nitz, J. C., Kuys, S., Isles, R., & Fu, S. (2010). Is the Wii Fit™ a new-generation tool for improving balance, health and well-being? A pilot study. *Climacteric, 13,* 487–491. doi: 10.3109/13697130903395193

Noelle-Neumann, E. (1973). Return to the concept of powerful mass media. *Studies of Broadcasting, 9,* 67–112.

Noelle-Neumann, E. (1984). *Spiral of silence: Public opinion—Our social skin.* Chicago: University of Chicago Press.

Nomikos, M., Opton, E., Averill, J., & Lazarus, R. (1968). Surprise versus suspense in the production of stress reaction. *Journal of Personality and Social Psychology, 8,* 204–208.

Norman, D. A. (1983). Some observations on mental models. In D. Genter & A. L. Stevens (Eds.), *Mental models* (pp. 299–324). Mahwah, NJ: Erlbaum.

Nunez-Smith, M., Wolf, E., Huang, H. M., Chen, P. G., Lee, L., Emanuel, E. J., & Gross, C. P. (2010). Media exposure and tobacco, illicit drugs, and alcohol use among children and adolescents: A systematic review. *Substance Abuse, 31* (3), 174–192.

O'Brien, F. M. (1968). *The story of* The Sun. New York: Greenwood Press.

O'Connell, D. L., Alexander, H. M., Dobson, A. J., Lloyd, D. M., Hardes, G. R., Springthorpe, J. J., & Leeder, S. R. (1981). Cigarette smoking and drug use in schoolchildren: 11 factors associated with smoking. *International Journal of Epidemiology, 10,* 223–231.

O'Donovan, E. (2010). Sexting and student discipline. *District Administration, 46*(3), 60–64.

O'Keefe, D. J. (2009). Theories of persuasion. In R. L. Nabi & M. B. Oliver (Eds.), *The SAGE handbook of media processes and effects* (pp. 269–282). Thousand Oaks, CA: Sage.

O'Keefe, G. J. (1985). "Taking a bite out of crime": The impact of a public information campaign. *Communication Research, 12,* 147–178.

Oddone-Paolucci, E., Genuis, M., & Violato, C. (2000). A meta-analysis on the published research on the effects of pornography. In C. Violato, E. Oddone-Paolucci, & M. Genuis (Eds.), *The changing family and child development* (pp. 48–59). Aldershot, UK: Ashgate Publishing.

Ogden, C. L., Flegal, K. M., Carroll, M. D., & Johnson, C. L. (2002). Prevalence and trends of overweight among US children and adolescents, 1999–2000. *Journal of the American Medical Association, 288*(14), 1728–1732.

Oliver, M. B. (1994). Portrayals of crime, race, and aggression in reality-based police shows: A content analysis. *Journal of Broadcasting & Electronic Media, 38,* 179–192.

Olson, C. K. (2004). Media violence research and youth violence data: Why do they conflict? *Academic Psychiatry, 28,* 144–150.

One Hundred Million Voices. (2011, September 8). Retrieved from http://blog.twitter.com/2011/09one-hundred-million-voices.html

Orton, W. (1927). News and opinion. *The American Journal of Sociology, 33,* 80–93.

Osborn, D. K., & Endsley, R. C. (1971). Emotional reactions of young children to TV violence. *Child Development, 42,* 321–331.

Overton, S. (2006). *Stealing democracy: The new politics of voter suppression.* New York: W. W. Norton.

Owens, J., Maxim, R., McGuinn, M., Nobile, C., Msall, M., & Alario, A. (1999). Television viewing habits and sleep disturbance in school children. *Pediatrics, 104*(3), 552 (Abstract). [Online]. Retrieved from http://www.pediatrics.org/cgi/content/full/104/3/c27

Paavonen, E. J., Pennonen, M., Roine, M., Valkonen, S., & Lahikainen, A. R. (2006). TV exposure associated with sleep disturbances in 5- to 6-year-olds. *Journal of Sleep Research, 15,* 154–161.

Paik, H., & Comstock, G. (1994). The effects of television violence on antisocial behavior: A meta-analysis. *Communication Research, 21,* 516–546.

Palazzolo, K. E., & Roberto, A. J. (2011). Media representations of intimate partner violence and punishment preferences: Exploring the role of attributions and emotions. *Journal of Applied Communication Research, 39*(1), 1–18.

Palen, L., Salzman, M., & Youngs, E. (2001). Discovery and integration of mobile communications in everyday life. *Personal and Ubiquitous Computing, 5,* 108–122.

Palmer, E. L., Hockett, A. B., & Dean, W. W. (1983). The television family and children's fright reactions. *Journal of Family Issues, 4,* 279–292.

Palmgreen, P. (1984). Uses and gratifications: A theoretical perspective. *Communication Yearbook, 8,* 20–55.

Palmgreen, P., & Rayburn, J. D., II. (1982). Gratifications sought and media exposure: An expectancy value model. *Communication Research, 9,* 561–580.

Palmgreen, P., Wenner, L. A., & Rosengren, K. E. (1985). Uses and gratifications research: The past ten years. In K. E. Rosengren, L. A. Wenner, & P. Palmgreen (Eds.), *Media gratifications research: Current perspectives* (pp. 11–37). Beverly Hills, CA: Sage.

Palys, T. S. (1986). Testing the common wisdom: The social content of video pornography. *Canadian Psychology, 27*(1), 22–35.

Pan, Z., & Kosicki, G. M. (1997). Priming and media impact on the evaluations of the president's performance. *Communication Research, 24,* 3–30.

Paragas, F. (2003). *Being mobile with the mobile: Cellular telephony and renegotiations of public transport as public sphere.* Paper presented at the Front Stage/Back Stage: Mobile Communication and the Renegotiation of the Social Sphere Conference, Grimstad, Norway.

Park, J., Felix, K., & Lee, G. (2007). Implicit attitudes toward Arab-Muslims and the moderating effect of social information. *Basic and Applied Social Psychology, 29*(1), 35–45.

Park, R. E. (1941). News and the power of the press. *The American Journal of Sociology, 47,* 1–11.

Parke, R., Berkowitz, L., & Leyens, J. (1977). Some effects of violent and nonviolent movies on the behavior of juvenile delinquents. *Advances in Experimental Social Psychology, 16,* 135–172.

Pathela, P., & Schillinger, J. A. (2010) Sexual behaviors and sexual violence: Adolescents with opposite-, same-, or both-sex partners. *Pediatrics, 125*(5), 879–886.

Pavlov, I. P. (1927/1960). *Conditioned reflexes* (G. V. Anrep, Trans.). London: Oxford University Press.

PBS.org. (2011). Project summary. Retrieved from http://www.pbs.org/parents/cyberchase/show/index.html

Pearlin, L. I. (1959). Social and personal stress and escape television viewing. *Public Opinion Quarterly, 23,* 255–259.

Peck, E. Y. (1999). *Gender differences in film-induced fear as a function of type of emotion measure and stimulus content: A meta-analysis and a laboratory study* (Unpublished doctoral dissertation). University of Wisconsin-Madison.

Pedersen, W., & Samuelsen, S. O. (2003). Nye mønster av seksualatferd blant ungdom. *Tidsskrift for Den norske loegeforeningen, 21,* 3006–3009.

Pempek, T. A., Kirkorian, H. L., Anderson, D. R., Lund, A. F., Richards, J. E., & Stevens, M. (2010). Video comprehensibility and attention in very young children. *Developmental Psychology, 46,* 1283–1293. doi: 10.1037/a0020614

Pena, J., Hancock, J. T., & Merola, N. A. (2009). The priming effects of avatars in virtual settings. *Communication Research, 36*(6), 838–856.

Peng, W., Liu, M., & Mou, Y. (2008). Do aggressive people play violent computer games in a more aggressive way? Individual difference and idiosyncratic game playing experience. *Cyberpsychology & Behavior, 11,* 157–161. doi: 10.1089/cpb.2007.0026

Penn, W. (1681). *Some account of the province of Pennsylvania.* Reprinted in J. R. Soderlund (Ed.), (1938), *William Penn and the founding of Pennsylvania, 1680–1684: A documentary history* (pp. 58–66). Philadelphia: University of Pennsylvania Press.

Perloff, R. M. (1998). *Political communication: Politics, press, and public in America.* Mahwah, NJ: Erlbaum.

Pernicious Literature. (1847, January). *United States Catholic Magazine and Monthly Review, 4,* 46–48.

Perry, D. K. (1996). *Theory & research in mass communication: Contexts and consequences.* Mahwah, NJ: Erlbaum.

Perse, E. M., & Rubin, A. M. (1990). Chronic loneliness and television use. *Journal of Broadcasting & Electronic Media, 34,* 37–53.

Peter, J., & Valkenburg, P. M. (2006). Adolescents' exposure to sexually explicit online material and recreational attitudes toward sex. *Journal of Communication, 56,* 639–660.

Peter, J., & Valkenburg, P. M. (2009). Adolescents' exposure to sexually explicit Internet material and notions of women as sex objects: Assessing causality and underlying processes. *Journal of Communication, 59,* 407–433.

Peters, P., & den Dulk, L. (2003). Cross-cultural differences in managers' support for home-based telework: A theoretical elaboration. *International Journal of Cross-Cultural Management, 3,* 329–346.

Peterson, R. C., & Thurstone, L. L. (1933). *Motion pictures and the social attitudes of children.* New York: Macmillan.

Petty, R. E., Briñol, P., & Priester, J. R. (2009). Mass media attitude change: Implications of the elaboration likelihood model of persuasion. In J. Bryant & M. B. Oliver (Eds.), *Media effects: Advances in theory and research* (3rd ed., pp. 125–164). New York: Routledge.

Petty, R. E., Briñol, P., & Tormala, Z. L. (2002). Thought confidence as a determinant of persuasion: The self-validation hypothesis. *Journal of Personality and Social Psychology, 82,* 722–741.

Petty, R. E., & Cacioppo, J. T. (1979). Issue-involvement can increase or decrease persuasion by enhancing message-relevant cognitive responses. *Journal of Personality and Social Psychology, 37,* 1915–1926.

Petty, R. E., & Cacioppo, J. T. (1981). *Attitudes and persuasion: Classic and contemporary approaches.* Dubuque, IA: W. C. Brown.

Petty, R. E., & Cacioppo, J. T. (1986a). *Communication and persuasion: Central and peripheral routes to attitude change.* New York: Springer/Verlag.

Petty, R. E., & Cacioppo, J. T. (1986b). The elaboration likelihood model of persuasion. In L. Berkowitz (Ed.), *Advances in experimental social psychology, 19* (pp. 123–205). New York: Academic Press.

Petty, R. E., & Cacioppo, J. T. (1996). *Attitudes and persuasion: Classic and contemporary approaches.* Boulder, CO: Westview.

Petty, R. E., Cacioppo, J. T., & Goldman, R. (1981). Personal involvement as a determinant of argument-based persuasion. *Journal of Personality and Social Psychology, 41,* 847–855.

Petty, R. E., Cacioppo, J. T., & Haugtvedt, C. (1992). Involvement and persuasion: An appreciative look at the Sherifs' contribution to the study of self-relevance and attitude change. In D. Granberg & G. Sarup (Eds.), *Social judgment and intergroup relations: Essays in honor of Muzafer Sherif* (pp. 147–174). New York: Springer/Verlag.

Petty, R. E., Cacioppo, J. T., & Heesacker, M. (1981). The use of rhetorical questions in persuasion: A cognitive response analysis. *Journal of Personality and Social Psychology, 40,* 432–440.

Petty, R. E., Fazio, R. H., & Briñol, P. (Eds.). (2008). *Attitudes: Insights from the new implicit measures.* New York: Psychology Press.

Petty, R. E., Gleicher, F. H., & Jarvis, B. (1993). Persuasion theory and AIDS prevention. In J. B. Pryor & G. Reeder (Eds.), *The social psychology of HIV infection* (pp. 155–182). Hillsdale, NJ: Erlbaum.

Petty, R. E., Ostrom, T. M., & Brock, T. C. (Eds.). (1981). *Cognitive responses in persuasion.* Hillsdale, NJ: Erlbaum.

Petty, R. E., & Priester, J. R. (1994). Mass media attitude change: Implications of the elaboration likelihood model of persuasion. In J. Bryant & D. Zillmann (Eds.), *Media effects: Advances in theory and research* (pp. 91–122). Hillsdale, NJ: Erlbaum.

Petty, R. E., Schumann, D., Richman, S., & Strathman, A. (1993). Positive mood and persuasion: Different roles for affect under high and low elaboration conditions. *Journal of Personality and Social Psychology, 64,* 5–20.

Petty, R. E., & Wegener, D. T. (1998). Matching versus mismatching attitude functions: Implications for the scrutiny of persuasive messages. *Personality and Social Psychology Bulletin, 24,* 227–240.

Petty, R. E., & Wegener, D. T. (1999). The elaboration likelihood model: Current status and controversies. In S. Chaiken & Y. Trope (Eds.), *Dual process theories in social psychology* (pp. 41–72). New York: Guilford Press.

Petty, R. E., Wheeler, S. C., & Bizer, G. Y. (2000). Attitude functions and persuasion: An elaboration likelihood approach to matched versus mismatched messages. In G. R. Maio & J. M. Olson (Eds.), *Why we evaluate: Functions of attitudes* (pp. 133–162). Mahwah, NJ: Erlbaum.

Pfau, M., & Louden, A. (1994). Effectiveness of adwatch formats in deflecting political attack ads. *Communication Research, 21,* 325–341.

Pierce, J. P., & Gilpin, E. A. (2001). News media coverage of smoking and health is associated with changes in population rates of smoking cessation but not initiation. *Tobacco Control, 10*(2), 145–153.

Pingdom.com. (2011). Internet 2010 in numbers. Retrieved from http://royal.pingdom.com/2011/01/12/internet-2010–in-numbers/

Pingree, S. (1983). Children's cognitive processing in constructing social reality. *Journalism Quarterly, 60,* 415–422.

Pingree, S., & Hawkins, R. P. (1981). U.S. programs on Australian television: The cultivation effect. *Journal of Communication, 31*(1), 97–105.

Ploughman, P. (1984). *The creation of newsworthy events: An analysis of newspaper coverage of the man-made disaster at Love Canal* (Unpublished doctoral dissertation). State University of New York at Buffalo.

Poe, E. A. (1902). Richard Adams Locke. In J. A. Harrison (Ed.), *The complete works of Edgar Allan Poe* (Vol. 15, pp. 126–137). New York: Thomas Y. Crowell.

Poindexter, P. M., & Stroman, C. (1981). Blacks and television: A review of the research literature. *Journal of Broadcasting, 25*(2), 103–122.

Pollard, P. (1995). Pornography and sexual aggression. *Current Psychology: Developmental, Learning, Personality, Social, 14*(3), 200–221.

Pool, I. De S. (Ed.). (1977). *The social impact of the telephone.* Cambridge, MA: MIT Press.

Popkin, S. L. (1991). *The reasoning voter: Communication and persuasion in presidential campaigns.* Chicago: University of Chicago Press.

Porpora, D. V., Nikolaev, A., & Hagemann, J. (2010). Abuse, torture, frames and the *Washington Post. Journal of Communication, 60,* 254–270.

Postman, N. (1985). *Amusing ourselves to death.* New York: Penguin.

Potter, B., & Sheeshka, J. (2000). Content analysis of infant feeding messages in a Canadian women's magazine, 1945 to 1995. *Journal of Nutrition Education, 32,* 196–204.

Potter, W. J. (1993). Cultivation theory and research: A conceptual critique. *Human Communication Research, 19*(4), 564–601.

Potter, W. J. (1994). Cultivation theory and research: A methodological critique. *Journalism Monographs, 147.* Columbia, SC: Association for Education in Journalism and Mass Communication.

Potter, W. J., & Warren, R. (1996). Considering policies to protect children from TV violence. *Journal of Communication, 46*(4), 116–138.

Potter, W. J., Warren, R., Vaughan, M., Howley, K., Land, A., & Hagemeyer, J. (1997). Antisocial acts in reality programming on television. *Journal of Broadcasting & Electronic Media, 41,* 69–75.

Powell, G. B., Jr. (1986). American voter turnout in comparative perspective. *American Political Science Review, 80*(1), 17–44.

Powell, J. A., Low, P., Griffiths, F. E., & Thorogood, J. (2005). A critical analysis of the literature on the Internet and consumer health information. *Journal of Telemedicine and Telecare, 11* (Supplement 1), 41–43.

Powell, K. A. (2011). Framing Islam: An analysis of U.S. media coverage of terrorism since 9/11. *Communication Studies, 62*(1), 90–112.

Power, J., Murphy, S., & Coover, G. (1996). Priming prejudice: How stereotypes and counterstereotypes influence attribution of responsibility and credibility among ingroups and outgroups. *Human Communication Research, 23,* 36–58.

Preiss, R. W., Gayle, B. M., Burrell, N., Allen, M., & Bryant, J. (Eds.). (2007). *Mass media effects research: Advances through meta-analysis.* Mahwah, NJ: Erlbaum.

Preston, M. I. (1941). Children's reactions to movie horrors and radio crime. *Journal of Pediatrics, 19,* 147–168.

Price, V., & Tewksbury, D. (1997). News values and public opinion: A theoretical account of media priming and framing. In G. A. Barnett & F. J. Boster (Eds.), *Progress in communication sciences: Advances in persuasion* (Vol. 13, pp. 173–212). Greenwich, CT: Ablex.

Price, V., Tewksbury, D., & Powers, E. (1997). Switching trains of thought: The impact of news frames on readers' cognitive responses. *Communication Research, 24,* 481–506.

Prince, D. L., Grace, C., Linebarger, D. L., Atkinson, R., & Huffman, J. D. (2001). Between the Lions *Mississippi literacy initiative: A final report to Mississippi Educational Television.* Starkville: The Early Childhood Institute, Mississippi State University.

Prochaska, J. O. (1994). Strong and weak principles for progressing from precontemplation to action on the basis of twelve problem behaviors. *Health Psychology, 13,* 47–51.

Prochaska, J. O., Redding, C. A., & Evers, K. E. (2002). The transtheoretical model and stages of change. In K. Glanz, B. K. Rimmer, & F. M. Lewis (Eds.), *Health behavior and health education: Theory, research, and practice* (3rd ed., pp. 99–120). San Francisco: Jossey-Bass.

Protess, D. L., Cook, F. L., Doppelt, J. C., Ettema, J. S., Gordon, M. T., Leff, D. R., & Miller, P. (1991). *The journalism of outrage: Investigative reporting and agenda building in America.* New York: Guilford Press.

Pucci, L. G., Joseph, H. M., Jr., & Siegel, M. (1998). Outdoor tobacco advertising in six Boston neighborhoods: Evaluating youth exposure. *American Journal of Preventive Medicine, 15*(2), 155–159.

Puckett, J. M., Petty, R. E., Cacioppo, J. T., & Fischer, D. L. (1983). The relative impact of age and attractiveness stereotypes on persuasion. *Journal of Gerontology, 38,* 340–343.

Putnam, R. D. (2000). *Bowling alone.* New York: Simon & Schuster.

Quackenbush, D. M., Strassberg, D. S., & Turner, C. W. (1995). Gender effects of romantic themes in erotica. *Archives of Sexual Behavior, 24,* 21–35.

Quan-Haase, A., & Young, A. L. (2010). Uses and gratifications of social media: A comparison of Facebook and instant messaging. *Bulletin of Science, Technology & Society, 30*(5), 350–361.

Rabin, R. L. (2007). Controlling the retail sales environment: Access, advertising and promotional activities. In R. J. Bonnie, K. Stratton, & R. B. Wallace (Eds.), *Ending the tobacco problem: A blueprint for the nation* (pp. 641–652). Washington, DC: Board on Population and Public Health Practice, Institute of Medicine of the National Academies.

Rachman, S. (1966). Sexual fetishism: An experimental analogue. *Psychological Record, 16,* 293–296.

Rachman, S., & Hodgson, R. J. (1968). Experimentally-induced "sexual fetishism": Replication and development. *Psychological Record, 18,* 25–27.

Radvansky, G. A., Swann, R. A., Federico, T., & Franklin, N. (1998). Retrieval from temporally organized situation models. *Journal of Experimental Psychology: Learning, Memory and Cognition, 24,* 1224–1237.

Ramasubramanian, S. (2011). The impact of stereotypical versus counterstereotypical media exemplars on racial attitudes, causal attributions, and support for affirmative action. *Communication Research, 38*(4), 497–516.

Ranney, A. (1983). *Channels of power.* New York: Basic Books.

Reese, S. D., & Danielian, L. H. (1989). Intermedia influence and the drug issue: Converging on cocaine. In P. J. Shoemaker (Ed.), *Communication campaigns about drugs: Government, media and the public* (pp. 29–45). Hillsdale, NJ: Erlbaum.

Reid, L., & Vanden Bergh, B. (1980). Blacks in introductory ads. *Journalism Quarterly, 57*(3), 485–489.

Reid, P. T. (1979). Racial stereotyping on television: A comparison of the behavior of both black and white television characters. *Journal of Applied Psychology, 64*(5), 465–489.

Reimer, B., & Rosengren, K. E. (1990). Cultivated viewers and readers: A life-style perspective. In N. Signorielli & M. Morgan (Eds.), *Cultivation analysis: New directions in media effects research* (pp. 181–206). Newbury Park, CA: Sage.

Rhee, J. W. (1997). Strategy and issue frames in election campaign coverage: A social cognitive account of framing effects. *Journal of Communication, 47,* 26–48.

Rhen, B. (2011). "School Shooter" web video game raises concerns. *Education Week, 30*(29), 1, 16–17.

Ribisl, K. M., Kim, A. E., & Williams, R. S. (2007). Sales and marketing of cigarettes on the Internet: Emerging threats to tobacco control and promising policy solutions. In R. J. Bonnie, K. Stratton, & R. B. Wallace (Eds.), *Ending the tobacco problem: A blueprint for the nation* (pp. 653–678). Washington, DC: Board on Population and Public Health Practice, Institute of Medicine of the National Academies.

Rice, M. L. (1984). The words of children's television. *Journal of Broadcasting, 28,* 445–461.

Rice, M. L., & Haight, P. L. (1986). "Motherese" of Mr. Rogers: A description of the dialogue of educational television programs. *Journal of Speech and Hearing Disorders, 51,* 282–287.

Rice, M. L., Huston, A. C., Truglio, R., & Wright, J. C. (1990). Words from *Sesame Street:* Learning vocabulary while viewing. *Developmental Psychology, 26,* 421–428.

Rice, M. L., & Woodsmall, L. (1988). Lessons from television: Children's word learning when viewing. *Child Development, 59,* 420–429.

Rice, R. E., & Atkin, C. K. (2000). *Public communication campaigns* (3rd ed.). Thousand Oaks, CA: Sage.

Rice, R. E., & Atkin, C. K. (2009). Public communication campaigns: Theoretical principles and practical applications. In J. Bryant & M. B. Oliver (Eds.), *Media effects: Advances in theory and research* (3rd ed., pp. 436–468). New York: Routledge.

Richmond, S. (2010). Angry birds: Just what makes it so popular? Retrieved from http://www.telegraph.co.uk/technology/apple/8192398/angry-birds-just-what-makes-it-so-popular.html

Rickheit, G., & Sichelschmidt, L. (1999). Mental models: Some answers, some questions, some suggestions. In G. Rickheit and C. Habel (Eds.), *Mental models in discourse processing and reasoning* (pp. 9–40). New York: Elsevier.

Riddle, K. (2010). Always on my mind: Exploring how frequent, recent, and vivid television portrayals are used in the formation of social reality judgments. *Media Psychology, 13,* 155–179.

Rios, D., & Gaines, S. (1999). Latino media use for cultural maintenance. *Journalism & Mass Communication Quarterly, 75,* 746–761.

Ritterfield, U., Cody, M., & Vorderer, P. (Eds). (2009). *Serious games: Mechanisms and effects.* New York: Routledge.

Rivadeneyra, R., Ward, L. M., & Gordon, M. (2007). Distorted reflections: Media exposure and Latino adolescents' conception of self. *Media Psychology, 9,* 261–290.

Robb, M. B., Richert, R. A., & Wartella, E. A. (2009). Just a talking book? Word learning from watching baby videos. *British Journal of Developmental Psychology, 27,* 27–45. doi: 10.1348/026151008X320156

Roberts, D. F., & Christenson, P. G. (2000*). "Here's looking at you, kid": Alcohol, drugs and tobacco in entertainment media.* Washington, DC: Kaiser Family Foundation.

Roberts, D. F., Foehr, U. G., & Rideout, V. (2005). *Generation M: Media in the lives of 8–18 year olds.* Palo Alto, CA: Kaiser Family Foundation.

Rockman et al. (1996). *Evaluation of* Bill Nye the Science Guy: *Television series and outreach.* San Francisco: Author. Retrieved from http://rockman.com/projects/124.kcts.billnye/bn96.pdf.

Rogers, E. M. (1983). *Diffusion of innovations* (3rd ed.). New York: Free Press.

Rogers, E. M. (1994). *A history of communication study: A biographical approach.* New York: Free Press.

Rogers, E. M., & Chaffee, S. H. (Eds.). (1997). *The beginnings of communication study in America: A personal memoir by Wilbur Schramm.* Thousand Oaks, CA: Sage.

Rogers, R. W. (1975). A protection motivation theory of fear appeals and attitude change. *Journal of Psychology, 91,* 93–114.

Rogers, R. W., & Prentice-Dunn, S. (1997). Protection motivation theory. In D. Gochman (Ed.), *Handbook of health behavior research: Personal and social determinants* (Vol. 1, pp. 113–132). New York: Plenum.

Ropelato, J. (n.d.) Internet pornography statistics. Retrieved from http://internet-filter-review.toptenreviews.com/internet-pornography-statistics.html

Rosenbaum, R. (1979, September). Gooseflesh. *Harpers,* pp. 86–92.

Rosengren, K. E., & Windahl, S. (1972). Mass media consumption as a functional alternative. In D. McQuail (Ed.), *Sociology of mass communications* (pp. 166–194). Middlesex, England: Penguin.

Rosenthal, T. L., & Zimmerman, B. J. (1978). *Social learning and cognition.* New York: Academic.

Roskos-Ewoldsen, B., Davies, J., & Roskos-Ewoldsen, D. (2004). Implications of the mental models approach for cultivation theory. *Communications, 29,* 345–363.

Roskos-Ewoldsen, D. R. (1997). Attitude accessibility and persuasion: Review and a transactive model. In B. R. Burleson & A. W. Kunkel (Eds.), *Communication yearbook 20* (pp. 185–225). Thousand Oaks, CA: Sage.

Roskos-Ewoldsen, D. R., Klinger, M., & Roskos-Ewoldsen, B. (2007). Media priming. In R. W. Preiss, B. M. Gayle, N. Burrell, M. Allen, & J. Bryant (Eds.), *Mass media theories and processes: Advances through meta-analysis* (pp. 53–80). Mahwah, NJ: Erlbaum.

Roskos-Ewoldsen, D. R., Roskos-Ewoldsen, B., & Carpentier, F. D. (2009). Media priming: An updated synthesis. In J. Bryant & M. B. Oliver (Eds.), *Media effects: Advances in theory and research* (3rd ed., pp. 74–93). New York: Routledge.

Roslow, P., & Nicholls, A. F. (1996). Targeting the Hispanic market: Comparative persuasion of TV commercials in Spanish and English. *Journal of Advertising Research, 30,* 66–77.

Ross, J., & Tomlinson, B. (2010). How games can redirect humanity's cognitive surplus for social good. *Computers in Entertainment, 8*(4), article 25. doi: 10.1145/1921141.1921145

Rothman, R. (2011, March). Video games take testing to the next level. *Education Digest, 76*(7), 4–8.

RRKidz.com. (2011). Launch release PDF. Retrieved from http://www.rrkidz.com/

Rubin, A. M. (1979). Television use by children and adolescents. *Human Communication Research, 5,* 109–120.

Rubin, A. M. (1981). An examination of television viewing motives. *Communication Research, 8,* 141–165.

Rubin, A. M. (1984). Ritualized and instrumental television viewing. *Journal of Communication, 34*(3), 67–77.

Rubin, A. M. (1986). Uses, gratifications, and media effects research. In J. Bryant & D. Zillmann (Eds.), *Perspectives on media effects* (pp. 281–301). Hillsdale, NJ: Erlbaum.

Rubin, A. M. (1994). Media effects: A uses-and-gratifications perspective. In J. Bryant & D. Zillmann (Eds.), *Media effects: Advances in theory and research* (pp. 417–436). Hillsdale, NJ: Erlbaum.

Rubin, A. M. (2002). The uses-and-gratifications perspective of media effects. In J. Bryant & D. Zillmann (Eds.), *Media effects: Advances in theory and research* (2nd ed., pp. 525–548). Mahwah, NJ: Erlbaum.

Rubin, A. M. (2009). Uses-and-gratifications perspective on media effects. In J. Bryant & M. B. Oliver (Eds.), *Media effects: Advances in theory and research* (3rd ed., pp. 165–184). New York: Routledge.

Rubin, A. M., & Perse, E. M. (1987). Audience activity and television news gratifications. *Communication Research, 14,* 58–84.

Rubin, A. M., & Rubin, R. B. (1982). Contextual age and television use. *Human Communication Research, 8,* 228–244.

Rubin, A. M., & Step, M. M. (2000). Impact of motivation, attraction, and parasocial interaction on talk radio listening. *Journal of Broadcasting & Electronic Media, 44,* 635–654.

Rubin, A. M., & Windahl, S. (1986). The uses and dependency model of mass communication. *Critical Studies in Mass Communication, 3,* 184–199.

Rucker, D. D., & Petty, R. E. (2006). Increasing the effectiveness of communications to consumers: Recommendations based on the elaboration likelihood and attitude certainty perspectives. *Journal of Public Policy and Marketing, 25,* 39–52.

Russell, D. E. H. (1998). *Dangerous relationships: Pornography, misogyny, and rape.* Thousand Oaks, CA: Sage.

Rust, L. W. (2001). *Summative evaluation of* Dragon Tales: *Final report.* Briarcliff Manor, NY: Langbourne Rust Research.

Ryan, E. (2010). *Dora the Explorer:* Empowering preschoolers, girls, and Latinas. *Journal of Broadcasting & Electronic Media, 54*(1), 54–68.

Ryan, E. L., & Hoerrner, K. L. (2004). Let your conscience be your guide: Smoking and drinking in Disney's animated classics. *Mass Communication & Society, 7*(3), 261–278.

Saelens, B. E., Sallids, J. F., Nader, P. R., Broyles, S. L., Berry, C. C., & Taras, H. L. (2002). Home environmental influences on children's television watching from early to middle childhood. *Journal of Developmental and Behavioral Pediatrics, 23*(3), 127–132.

Sahin, N. (1990, September). *Preliminary report on the summative evaluation of the Turkish co-production of* Sesame Street. Paper presented at the International Conference on Adaptations of *Sesame Street,* Amsterdam, The Netherlands.

Saito, S. (2007). Television and the cultivation of gender-role attitudes in Japan: Does television contribute to the maintenance of the status quo? *Journal of Communication, 57,* 511–531.

Sánchez-Martínez, M., & Otero, A. (2009). Factors associated with cell phone use in adolescents in the community of Madrid (Spain). *Cyberpsychology and Behavior, 12,* 131–137.

Sandman, P. M. (1976). Medicine and mass communication: An agenda for physicians. *Annals of Internal Medicine, 85,* 378–383.

Sapolsky, B. S., & Zillmann, D. (1978). Experience and empathy: Affective reactions to witnessing childbirth. *Journal of Social Psychology, 105,* 131–144.

Sarafino, E. P. (1986). *The fears of childhood: A guide to recognizing and reducing fearful states in children.* New York: Human Sciences Press.

Sargent, J. D. (2009). Comparing the effects of entertainment media and tobacco marketing on youth smoking. *Tobacco Control, 18*(1), 47–53.

Sargent, J. D., Beach, M. L., Adachi-Mejia, A. M., Gibson, J. J., Titus-Ernstoff, L. T., Carusi, C. P., . . . & Dalton, M. A. (2005). Exposure to movie smoking: Its relation to smoking initiation among US adolescents. *Pediatrics, 116*(5), 1183–1191.

Sargent, J. D., Wills, T. A., Stoolmiller, M., Gibson, J., & Gibbons, F. X. (2006). Alcohol use in motion pictures and its relation with early-onset teen drinking. *Journal of Studies on Alcohol, 67*(1), 54–65.

Savage, J. (2004). Does viewing violent media really cause criminal violence? A methodological review. *Aggression & Violent Behavior, 10*(1), 99–128.

Savage, J. (2008). The role of exposure to media violence in the etiology of violent behavior: A criminologist weighs in. *American Behavioral Scientist, 51*(8), 1123–1136.

Schachter, S., & Singer, J. (1962). Cognitive, social, and physiological determinants of emotional state. *Psychological Review, 69,* 379–399.

Schaefer, H. H., & Colgan, A. H. (1977). The effect of pornography on penile tumescence as a function of reinforcement and novelty. *Behavior Therapy, 8,* 938–946.

Scheufele, D. A. (1999). Framing as a theory of media effects. *Journal of Communication, 49*(1), 103–122.

Scheufele, D. A. (2000). Agenda-setting, priming, and framing revisited: Another look at cognitive effects of political communication. *Mass Communication & Society, 3*(2&3), 297–316.

Scheufele, D. A. (2004). Framing-effects approach: A theoretical and methodological critique. *Communications, 29,* 401–428.

Scheufele, D. A., Hardy, B., Brossard, D., Waismel-Manor, I. S., & Nisbet, E. C. (2006). Democracy based on difference: Examining the links between structural heterogeneity, heterogeneity of discussion networks, and democratic citizenship. *Journal of Communication, 56,* 728–753.

Scheufele, D. A., & Nisbet, M. C. (2007). Framing. In L. L. Kaid & C. Holz-Bacha (Eds.), *Encyclopedia of political communication* (pp. 254–257). Thousand Oaks, CA: Sage.

Scheufele, D. A., & Tewksbury, D. (2007). Framing, agenda setting, and priming: The evolution of three media effects models. *Journal of Communication, 57,* 9–20.

Schiffrin, H., Edelman, A., Falkenstern, M., & Stewart, C. (2010). The associations among computer-mediated communication, relationships, and well-being. *Cyberpsychology, Behavior, and Social Networking, 13,* 299–306. doi: 10.1089/cyber.2009.0173

Schlinger, M. J., & Plummer, J. (1972). Advertising in black and white. *Journal of Marketing Research, 9,* 149–153.

Schmitt, K., & Anderson, D. R. (2002). Television and reality: Toddlers' use of information from video to guide behavior. *Media Psychology, 4,* 51–76.

Schocket, A. M. (2011). Little founders on the small screen: Interpreting a multicultural American Revolution for children's television. *Journal of American Studies, 45,* 145–163. doi: 10.1017/S0021875810000630

Scholastic productions banks a best seller. (1997, July). *Broadcasting & Cable, 127*(31), 48.

Schramm, W. (1954). How communication works. In W. Schramm (Ed.), *The processes and effects of mass communication.* Urbana: University of Illinois Press.

Schramm, W. (1997). Carl Hovland: Experiments, attitudes, and communication. In S. H. Chaffee & E. M. Rogers (Eds.), *The beginnings of communication study in America: A personal memoir by Wilbur Schramm* (pp. 87–105). Thousand Oaks, CA: Sage.

Schramm, W., Lyle, J., & Parker, E. P. (1961). *Television in the lives of our children*. Stanford, CA: Stanford University Press.

Schwartz, E. I. (2002). *The last lone inventor: A tale of genius, deceit, and the birth of television*. New York: Perennial.

Scott, D. (1995). The effect of video games on feelings of aggression. *Journal of Psychology, 129,* 121–132.

Seggar, J. F., Hafen, J., & Hannonen-Gladden, H. (1981). Television's portrayals of minorities and women in drama and comedy drama, 1971–1980. *Journal of Broadcasting, 25*(3), 277–288.

Selman, R. L., & Byrne, D. (1978). A structural analysis of levels of role-taking in middle childhood. *Child Development, 45,* 803–807.

Shah, D. V., Cho, J., Eveland, W. P., & Kwak, N. (2005). Information and expression in the digital age: Modeling Internet effects on civic participation. *Communication Research, 32,* 531–565.

Shah, D. V., Kwak, N., Schmierbach, M., & Zubric, J. (2004). The interplay of news frames on cognitive complexity. *Human Communication Research, 30,* 102–120.

Shah, D. V., McLeod, D. M., Kim, E., Lee, S-Y., Gotlieb, M. R., Ho, S., & Brevik, H. (2007). Political consumerism: How communication practices and consumption orientations drive "lifestyle politics." *The ANNALS of the American Academy of Political and Social Science, 611,* 217–235.

Shah, D. V., Schmierbach, M. G., Hawkins, J., Espino, R., & Donavan, J. (2002). Nonrecursive models of Internet use and community engagement. *Journalism & Mass Communication Quarterly, 79,* 964–987.

Shanahan, J., & Morgan, M. (1999). *Television and its viewers: Cultivation theory and research*. Cambridge, UK: Cambridge University Press.

Shanahan, J., Morgan, M., & Stenbjerre, M. (1997). Green or brown? Television's cultivation of environmental concern. *Journal of Broadcasting & Electronic Media, 41,* 305–323.

Shane, P. (Ed.). (2004). *Democracy online: The prospects for political renewal through the Internet*. New York: Routledge.

Shannon, C., & Weaver, W. (1949). *The mathematical theory of communication*. Urbana: University of Illinois Press.

Shapiro, J. S. (1999). Loneliness: Paradox or artifact? *American Psychologies, 54*(9), 782–783.

Shapiro, M., & Lang, A. (1991). Making television reality: Unconscious processes in the construction of social reality. *Communication Research, 18,* 685–705.

Shapiro, M. A., & Rieger, R. H. (1992). Comparing positive and negative political advertising on radio. *Journalism Quarterly, 69,* 135–145.

Shaw, D., & McCombs, M. (Eds.) (1977). *The emergence of American political issues: The agenda setting function of the press*. St. Paul, MN: West.

Sheldon, P. (2008). Student favorite: Facebook and motives for its use. *Southwestern Mass Communication Journal,* Spring Issue, 39–53.

Shen, F. (2004). Effects of news frames and schemas on individuals' issue interpretations and attitudes. *Journalism & Mass Communication Quarterly, 81,* 400–416.

Shepard, W. J. (1909). Public opinion. *The American Journal of Sociology, 15,* 32–60.

Sherif, C. W., Sherif, M., & Nebergall, R. E. (1965). *Attitude and attitude change: The social judgment-involvement approach*. Philadelphia: W. B. Saunders.

Sherif, M. (1967). *Social interaction: Processes and products*. Chicago: Aldine.

Sherman, B. L., & Dominick, J. R., (1986). Violence and sex in music videos: TV and rock 'n' roll. *Journal of Communication, 36*(1), 79–93.

Sherman, B. L., & Etling, L. W. (1991). Perceiving and processing music television. In J. Bryant & D. Zillmann (Eds.), *Responding to the screen: Reception and reaction processes* (pp. 373–388). Hillsdale, NJ: Erlbaum.

Sherry, J. L. (2001). The effects of violent video games on aggression: A meta-analysis. *Human Communication Research, 27,* 409–431.

Shih, C.-H. (2011). A standing location detector enabling people with developmental disabilities to control environmental stimulation through simple physical activities with Nintendo Wii balance boards. *Research in Developmental Disabilities, 32,* 699–704.

Shoemaker, P. J., & Reese, S. (1991). *Mediating the message: Theories of influence on mass media content.* New York: Longman.

Shoemaker, P. J., & Reese, S. D. (1996). *Mediating the message* (2nd ed.). White Plains, NY: Longman.

Shoemaker, P. J., Wanta, W., & Leggett, D. (1989). Drug coverage and public opinion, 1972–1986. In P. Shoemaker (Ed.), *Communication campaigns about drugs: Government, media and the public* (pp. 67–80). Hillsdale, NJ: Erlbaum.

Shrum, L. J. (1995). Assessing the social influence of television: A social cognition perspective on cultivation effects. *Communication Research, 22,* 402–429.

Shrum, L. J. (1997). The role of source confusion in cultivation effects may depend on processing strategy: A comment on Mares (1996). *Human Communication Research, 24,* 349–358.

Shrum, L. J. (1999). The relationship of television viewing with attitude strength and extremity: Implications for the cultivation effect. *Media Psychology, 1,* 3–25.

Shrum, L. J. (2002). Media consumption and perceptions of social reality: Effects and underlying processes. In J. Bryant & D. Zillmann (Eds.), *Media effects: Advances in theory and research* (2nd ed., pp. 69–96). Mahwah, NJ: Erlbaum.

Shrum, L. J. (2004). The cognitive processes underlying cultivation effects are a function of whether the judgments are on-line or memory-based. *Communications, 29,* 327–344.

Shrum, L. J. (2007). The implications of survey method for measuring cultivation effects. *Human Communication Research, 33,* 64–80.

Shrum, L. J., Burroughs, J. E., & Rindfleisch, A. (2005). Television's cultivation of material values. *Journal of Consumer Research, 32,* 473–479.

Signorielli, N. (1990). Television's mean and dangerous world: A continuation of the cultural indicators perspective. In N. Signorielli & M. Morgan (Eds.), *Cultivation analysis: New directions in media effects research* (pp. 85–106). Newbury Park, CA: Sage.

Signorielli, N., & Bacue, A. (1999). Recognition and respect: A content analysis of prime-time television characters across three decades. *Sex Roles, 40,* 527–544.

Signorielli, N., & Kahlenberg, S. (2001). Television's world of work in the nineties. *Journal of Broadcasting & Electronic Media, 45,* 4–22.

Signorielli, N., & Morgan, M. (1996). Cultivation analysis: Research and practice. In M. B. Salwen & D. W. Stacks (Eds.), *An integrated approach to communication theory and research* (pp. 111–126). Mahwah, NJ: Erlbaum.

Signorielli, N., & Staples, J. (1997). Television and children's conceptions of nutrition. *Health Communication, 9*(4), 289–301.

Sigurdsson, J. F., Gudjonsson, G. H., Bragason, A. V., Kirstjansdottir, E., & Sigfusdottir, I. D. (2006). The role of violent cognition in the relationship between personality and the involvement in violent films and computer games. *Personality and Individual Differences, 41,* 381–392.

Simon, A., & Jerit, J. (2007). Toward a theory relating political discourse, media, and public opinion. *Journal of Communication, 57,* 254–271.

Simons, D., & Silveira, W. R. (1994). Post-traumatic stress disorder in children after television programmes. *British Medical Journal, 308,* 389–390.

Singer, J. L. (1975). *Daydreaming and fantasy.* London: Allen & Unwin.

Singer, J. L., & Singer, D. G. (1983). Implications of childhood television viewing for cognition, imagination, and emotion. In J. Bryant & D. R. Anderson (Eds.), *Children's understanding of television: Research on attention and comprehension* (pp. 265–295). New York: Academic.

Singer, J. L., & Singer, D. G. (1994). Barney and Friends *as education and entertainment: Phase 2—Can children learn through preschool exposure to* Barney and Friends? New Haven, CT: Yale University Family Television Research and Consultation Center.

Singer, J. L., & Singer, D. G. (1995). Barney and Friends *as education and entertainment: Phase 3—A national study: Can children learn through preschool exposure to* Barney and Friends? New Haven, CT: Yale University Family Television Research and Consultation Center.

Singer, J. L., & Singer, D. G. (1998). Barney and Friends *as entertainment and education: Evaluating the quality and effectiveness of television series for preschool children.* In J. K. Asamen & G. L. Berry (Eds.), *Research paradigms, television, and social behavior* (pp. 305–367). Thousand Oaks, CA: Sage.

Singer, M. I., Slovak, K., Frierson, T., & York, P. (1998). Viewing preferences, symptoms of psychological trauma, and violent behaviors among children who watch television. *Journal of the American Academy of Child and Adolescent Psychiatry, 37*(10), 1041–1048.

Singhal, A., & Rogers, E. M. (1989). Pro-social television for development in India. In R. E. Rice & C. K. Atkin (Eds.), *Public communication campaigns* (pp. 331–350). Newbury Park, CA: Sage.

Sintchak, G., & Geer, J. (1975). A vaginal plethysymograph system. *Psychophysiology, 12,* 113–115.

Slater, M. D. (1999). Integrating application of media effects, persuasion, and behavior change theories to communication campaigns: A stages-of-change framework. *Health Communication, 11,* 335–354.

Slater, M. D., Henry, K. L., Swaim, R. C., & Anderson, L. L. (2003). Violent media content and aggressiveness in adolescents: A downward spiral model. *Communication Research, 30,* 713–736.

Sloan, W. D. (1998). The partisan press, 1783–1833. In W. D. Sloan (Ed.), *The age of mass communication* (pp. 119–146). Northport, AL: Vision Press.

Slothuus, R. (2010). When can political parties lead public opinion? Evidence from a natural experiment. *Political Communication, 27,* 158–177.

Smith, B. L., Lasswell, H. D., & Casey, R. D. (1946). *Propaganda, communication, and public opinion: A comprehensive reference guide.* Princeton, NJ: Princeton University Press.

Smith, H. (1988). *The power game.* New York: Random House.

Smith, J. (1616). *A description of New England.* Reprinted in P. O. Barbour (Ed.), (1986), *The complete works of Captain John Smith* (Vol. 1, pp. 323–361). Chapel Hill: The University of North Carolina Press.

Smith, S. L., & Granados, A. D. (2009). Content patterns and effects surrounding sex-role stereotyping on television and film. In J. Bryant & M. B. Oliver (Eds.), *Media effects: Advances in theory and research* (3rd ed., pp. 342–361). New York: Routledge.

Smith, S. L., Granados, A. D., Choueiti, M., & Pieper, K. (2007). *Gender prevalence and hypersexuality in top grossing, theatrically released G, PG, PG-13, and R-rated films.* Unpublished data.

Smolej, M., & Kivivouri, J. (2006). The relation between crime news and fear of violence. *Journal of Scandinavian Studies in Criminology and Crime Prevention, 7,* 211–227.

Smythe, D. W. (1956). *Three years of New York television: 1951–1953.* Urbana, IL: National Association of Education Broadcasters.

Snow, D. A., & Benford, R. D. (1992). Master frames and cycles of protest. In A. D. Morris & C. McClurg Mueller (Eds.), *Frontiers in social movement theory* (pp. 133–155). New Haven, CT: Yale University Press.

Snyder, L. B., Anderson, K., & Young, D. (1989, May). *AIDS communication, risk, knowledge and behavior change: A preliminary investigation in Connecticut.* Paper presented to the International Communication Association, San Francisco.

Soh, J. O. B., & Tan, B. C. Y. (2008). Mobile gaming. *Communications of the ACM, 51*(3), 35–39.

Soley, L. (1983). The effect of black models on magazine ad readership. *Journalism Quarterly, 60*(4), 686–690.

Sotirovic, M. (2001a). Affective and cognitive processes as mediators of media influence on crime policy preferences. *Mass Communication and Society, 3,* 269–296.

Sotirovic, M. (2001b). Effects of media use on complexity and extremity of attitudes toward the death penalty and prisoners' rehabilitation. *Media Psychology, 3,* 1–24.

Sotirovic, M. (2003). How individuals explain social problems: The influences of media use. *Journal of Communication, 33,* 122–137.

Sotirovic, M., & McLeod, J. M. (2008). U.S. election coverage. In J. Stromback & L. Kaid (Eds.), *Handbook of election coverage around the world*. Mahwah, NJ: Erlbaum.

Sparks, D. A., Coughlin, L. M., & Chase, D. M. (2011). Did too much Wii cause your patient's injury? *The Journal of Family Practice, 60,* 404–409.

Sparks, G. G. (1986). Developmental differences in children's reports of fear induced by mass media. *Child Study Journal, 16,* 55–66.

Sparks, G. G., & Cantor, J. (1986). Developmental differences in fright responses to a television programme depicting a character transformation. *Journal of Broadcasting & Electronic Media, 30,* 309–323.

Sparks, G. G., Sherry, J., & Lubsen, G. (2005). The appeal of media violence in a full-length motion picture: An experimental investigation. *Communication Reports, 18,* 21–30.

Sparks, G. G., & Sparks, C. W. (2002). Effects of media violence. In J. Bryant & D. Zillmann (Eds.), *Media effects: Advances in theory and research* (2nd ed., pp. 269–285). Mahwah, NJ: Erlbaum.

Sparks, G. G., Sparks, C. W., & Sparks, E. A. (2009). Media violence. In J. Bryant & M. B. Oliver (Eds.), *Media effects: Advances in theory and research* (3rd ed., pp. 269–286). New York: Routledge.

Squires, C. R. (2011). Bursting the bubble: A case study of counter-framing in the editorial pages. *Critical Studies in Media Communication, 28*(1), 30–49.

Stack, S. (2005). Suicide in the media: A quantitative review of studies based on non-fictional stories. *Suicide & Life-Threatening Behavior, 35*(2), 121–133.

Star, S. A., & Hughes, H. M. (1950). Report on an education campaign: The Cincinnati plan for the UN. *American Journal of Sociology, 55,* 389–400.

Steinfield, C., Ellison, N. B., & Lampe, C. (2008). Social capital, self-esteem, and use of online social network sites: A longitudinal analysis. *Journal of Applied Developmental Psychology, 29,* 434–445.

Stempel, G. (1971). Visibility of blacks in news and news-picture magazines. *Journalism Quarterly, 48*(2), 337–339.

Stephenson, W. (1967). *The play theory of mass communication*. Chicago: University of Chicago Press.

Stern, S., & Mastro, D. E. (2004). Gender portrayals across the life span: A content analysis look at broadcast commercials. *Mass Communication & Society, 7,* 215–236.

Stilling, E. (1997). The electronic melting pot hypothesis: The cultivation of acculturation among Hispanics through television viewing. *The Howard Journal of Communications, 8,* 77–100.

Stobbe, M., & Johnson, C. K. (2011, March 3). U.S. teens, young adults "doing it" less, study says. Retrieved from http://news.yahoo.com/us-study-says-sex-down-among-young-adults-20110303-083300-359.html

Stodghill, R. (1998, June 15). Where'd you learn that? *Time,* pp. 52–59.

Stone, B. (2010, January 9). The children of cyberspace: Old fogies by their 20s. *The New York Times.* Retrieved from http://www.nytimes.com/2010/01/10/weekinreview/10stone.html?pagewanted=print

Stouffer, S. A. (1942). A sociologist looks at communications research. In D. Waples (Ed.), *Print, radio, and film in a democracy: Ten papers on the administration of mass communications in the public interest—Read before the Sixth Annual Institute of the Graduate Library School, The University of Chicago—August 4–9, 1941,* pp. 133–146. Chicago: University of Chicago Press.

Strasburger, V. C., Wilson, B. J., & Jordan, A. B. (2009). *Children, adolescents, and the media* (2nd ed.). Los Angeles: Sage.

Strate, J. M., Parrish, C. J., Elder, C. D., & Ford, C., III. (1989). Life span and civic development and voting participation. *American Political Science Review, 83*(2), 443–464.

Stryker, J. E. (2003). Media and marijuana: A longitudinal analysis of news media effects on adolescents' marijuana use and related outcomes, 1977–1999. *Journal of Health Communication, 8*(4), 305–328.

Subervi-Velez, F., & Necochea, J. (1990). Television viewing and self-concept among Hispanic American children—A pilot study. *The Howard Journal of Communications, 2,* 315–329.

Sullivan, C. (2003). What's in a name? Definitions and conceptualizations of teleworking and homeworking. *New Technology, Work & Employment, 18,* 158–165.

Sun, S., Rubin, A. M., & Haridakis, P. M. (2008). The role of motivation and media involvement in explaining Internet dependency. *Journal of Broadcasting & Electronic Media, 52*(3), 408–431.

Sunstein, C. (2006). *Infotopia: How many minds produce knowledge.* New York: Oxford University Press.

Surbeck, E. (1975). Young children's emotional reactions to TV violence: The effects of children's perceptions of reality. University of Georgia. *Dissertation Abstracts International, 35,* 5139–A.

Sutton, S. R. (1982). Fear-arousing communication: A critical examination of theory and research. In J. R. Eiser (Ed.), *Social psychology and behavioral medicine* (pp. 303–337). London: John Wiley.

Svenkerud, P. J., Rao, N., & Rogers, E. M. (1999). Mass media effects through interpersonal communication: The role of "Twende na Wakati" on the adoption of HIV/AIDS prevention in Tanzania. In W. N. Elwood (Ed.), *Power in the blood:* A *handbook on AIDS, politics, and communication.* Mahwah, NJ: Erlbaum.

Swanson, D. L. (1977). The uses and misuses of uses and gratifications. *Human Communication Research, 3,* 214–221.

Swanson, D. L. (1979). Political communication research and the uses and gratifications model: A critique. *Communication Research, 6,* 37–53.

Swasy, J. L., & Munch, J. M. (1985). Examining the target of receiver elaborations: Rhetorical question effects on source processing and persuasion. *Journal of Consumer Research, 11,* 877–886.

Sweeper, G. W. (1983). *The image of the black family and the white family in American primetime television programming 1970 to 1980* (Unpublished doctoral dissertation). New York University, New York.

Takeshita, T., & Mikami, S. (1995). How did mass media influence the voters' choice in the 1993 general election in Japan? *Keio Communication Review, 17,* 27–41.

Tamborini, R., & Weaver, J. B., III. (1996). Frightening entertainment: A historical perspective of fictional horror. In J. B. Weaver III & R. Tamborini (Eds.), *Horror films: Current research on audience preferences and reactions* (pp. 1–13). Mahwah, NJ: Erlbaum.

Tamborini, R., Zillmann, D., & Bryant, J. (1984). Fear and victimization: Exposure to television and perceptions of crime and fear. In R. N. Bostrum (Ed.), *Communication yearbook 8* (pp. 492–513). Beverly Hills, CA: Sage.

Tan, A. S. (1979). TV beauty ads and role expectations of adolescent female viewers. *Journalism Quarterly, 56,* 283–288.

Tan, A., Fujioka, Y., & Tan, G. (2000). Television use, stereotypes of African Americans and opinions on affirmative action: An effective model of policy reasoning. *Communication Monographs, 67,* 362–371.

Tannenbaum, P. H., & Zillmann, D. (1975). Emotional arousal in the facilitation of aggression through communication. In L. Berkowitz (Ed.), *Advances in experimental social psychology* (Vol. 8, pp. 149–192). New York: Academic Press.

Taylor, A. S., & Harper, R. (2001). *Talking "activity:" Young people and mobile phones.* Paper presented at the CHI 2001 Workshop: Mobile communications: Understanding users, adoption, and design, Seattle, WA. Retrieved from http://www.cs.colorado.edu/_/palen/chi_workshop

Taylor, C., & Stern, B. (1997). Asian-Americans: Television advertising and the "model minority" stereotype. *Journal of Advertising, 26,* 47–61.

Taylor, C. B., Winzelberg, A., & Celio, A. (2001). Use of interactive media to prevent eating disorders. In R. Striegel-Moor & L. Smolak (Eds.), *Eating disorders: New direction for research and practice* (pp. 255–270). Washington, DC: APA.

Tedesco, J. C. (2011). Political information efficacy and Internet effects in the 2008 U.S. presidential election. *American Behavioral Scientist, 55,* 696–713. doi: 10.1177/0002764211398089

Teevan, J. J., & Hartnagel, T. F. (1976). The effect of television violence on the perception of crime by adolescents. *Sociology and Social Research, 60,* 337–348.

Terlecki, M., Brown, J., Harner-Steciw, L., Irvin-Hannum, J., Marchetto-Ryan, N., Ruhl, L., & Wiggins, J. (2011). Sex differences and similarities in video game experience, preferences, and self-efficacy: Implications for the gaming industry. *Current Psychology, 30,* 22–33. doi: 10.1007/s12144-010-9095-5

Tewksbury, D., Jones, J., Peske, M., Raymond, A., & Vig, W. (2000). The interaction of news and advocate frames: Manipulating audience perceptions of a local public policy issue. *Journalism & Mass Communication Quarterly, 77,* 804–829.

Tewksbury, D., & Scheufele, D. A. (2009). News framing theory and research. In J. Bryant & M. B. Oliver (Eds.), *Media effects: Advances in theory and research* (3rd ed.). New York: Routledge.

Thayer, J. F., & Levenson, R. W. (1983). Effects of music on psychophysiological responses to a stressful film. *Psychomusicology, 3,* 44–52.

Thomas, M. H., Horton, R. W., Lippincott, E. C., & Drabman, R. S. (1977). Desensitization to portrayals of real-life aggression as a function of exposure to television violence. *Journal of Personality and Social Psychology, 35*(6), 450–458.

Thompson, K. M., & Yokota, E. (2001). Depiction of alcohol, tobacco, and other substances in G-rated animated films. *Pediatrics, 107*(6), 1369–1374.

Thompson, S. (1998). Origins of advertising, 1600–1833. In W. D. Sloan (Ed.), *The age of mass communication* (pp. 81–95). Northport, AL: Vision Press.

Thompson, S., & Bryant, J. (2000, June). *Debunking the media effects gospel: A reexamination of media effects research history and directions for researchers of the twenty-first century.* Paper presented at the International Communication Association 50th Annual Conference, Acapulco, Mexico.

Tichenor, P. J., Donohue, G. A., & Olien, C. N. (1970). Mass media flow and differential growth of knowledge. *Public Opinion Quarterly, 34,* 159–170.

Titchener, E. B. (1898). Minor studies from the psychological laboratory of Cornell University: Distraction by musical sounds; the effect of pitch upon attention. *The American Journal of Psychology, 99,* 332–345.

Tito, G. (2011a, February). Inside the sick mind of a *School Shooter* mod. *The Escapist.* Retrieved from http://www.escapistmagazine.com/news/view/108065-inside-the-sick-mind-of-a-school-shooter-mod

Tito, G. (2011b, March). ModDB shuts down *School Shooter* mod. *The Escapist.* Retrieved from http://www.escapistmagazine.com/news/view/108695-moddb-shuts-down-school-shooter-mod

Tormala, Z. L., Briñol, P., & Petty, R. E. (2006). When credibility attacks: The reverse impact of source credibility on persuasion. *Journal of Experimental Social Psychology, 42,* 684–691.

Towbin, M. A., Haddock, S. A., Zimmerman, T. S., Lund, L., & Tanner, L. R. (2003). Images of gender, race, age, and sexual orientation in Disney feature-length animated films. *Journal of Feminist Family Therapy, 15,* 19–44. doi: 10.1300/J086v15n04_02

Troseth, G. L. (1998). The medium can obscure the message: Understanding the relation between video and reality. *Child Development, 69,* 950–965.

Troseth, G. L. (2003). Getting a clear picture: Young children's understanding of a televised image. *Developmental Science, 6,* 247–253.

Tuchman, G. (1978). *Making news: A study in the construction of reality.* New York: Free Press.

Tudor, A. (1989). *Monsters and mad scientists: A cultural history of the horror movie.* Oxford, England: Blackwell.

Turner, C., & Berkowitz, L. (1972). Identification with film aggressor (covert role taking) and reactions to film violence. *Journal of Personality and Social Psychology, 21,* 256–264.

Tyler, T. R. (1980). The impact of directly and indirectly experienced events: The origin of crime-related judgments and behaviors. *Journal of Personality and Social Psychology, 39,* 13–28.

Tyler, T. R. (1984). Assessing the risk of crime victimization and socially-transmitted information. *Journal of Social Issues, 40,* 27–38.

Tyler, T. R., & Cook, F. L. (1984). The mass media and judgments of risk: Distinguishing impact on personal and societal level judgments. *Journal of Personality and Social Psychology, 47,* 693–708.

Uhlmann, E., & Swanson, J. (2004). Exposure to violent video games increases automatic aggressiveness. *Journal of Adolescence, 27,* 41–52.

Ulitsa Sezam Department of Research and Content. (1998, November). Preliminary report of summative findings. Report presented to the Children's Television Workshop, New York.

UNICEF. (1996). *Executive summary: Summary assessment of* Plaza Sésamo *IV—Mexico.* [English translation of Spanish.] Unpublished research report. Mexico City, Mexico: Author.

Univision Communications. (2005). Univision. Retrieved from http://www.univision.net/corp/en/index.jsp

U.S. Dept. of Health and Human Services. (1994). *Preventing tobacco use among young people: Report of the Surgeon General*. Washington, DC: Government Printing Office.

U.S. Surgeon General's Scientific Advisory Committee on Television and Social Behavior. (1972). *Television and growing up: The impact of televised violence* (DHEW publication No. HSM 72–9086). Washington, DC: Government Printing Office.

Valentino, N. A. (1999). Crime news and the priming of racial attitudes during evaluations of the president. *Public Opinion Quarterly, 63,* 293–320.

Valentino, N. A., Beckmann, M. N., & Buhr, T. A. (2001). A spiral of cynicism for some: The contingent effects of campaign news frames on participation and confidence in government. *Political Communication, 18,* 347–367.

Valkenburg, P. M., Cantor, J., & Peeters, A. L. (2000). Fright reactions to television: A child survey. *Communication Research, 27*(1), 82–97.

Valkenburg, P. M., Semetko, H. A., & de Vreese, C. H. (1999). The effects of news frames on readers' thoughts and recall. *Communication Research, 26,* 550–569.

Van den Bulck, J. (2004). Media use and dreaming: The relationship among television viewing, computer game play, and nightmares or pleasant dreams. *Dreaming, 14,* 43–49.

Van der Voort, T. H. A. (1986). *Television violence: A child's eye view.* Amsterdam: Elsevier Science.

Van Dijk, T. A., & Kintsch, W. (1983). *Strategies of discourse comprehension.* New York: Academic Press.

Van Gorp, B. (2007). The constructionist approach to framing: Bringing culture back in. *Journal of Communication, 57,* 60–78.

Van Rooij, A. J., Meerkerk, G.–J., Schoenmakers, T. M., Griffiths, M., & Van De Mheen, D. (2010). Video game addiction and social responsibility, *Addiction Research, 18,* 489–493. doi: 10.310916066350903168579

Vandewater, E. A., Barr, R. F., Park, S. E., & Lee, S.-L. (2010). A US study of transfer of learning from video to books in toddlers: Matching words across context change. *Journal of Children and Media, 4,* 451–467. doi: 10.1080/17482798.2010.510013

Velten, E. (1968). A laboratory task for the induction of mood states. *Behavior Research and Therapy, 6,* 473–482.

Vogel, J. J., Vogel, D. S., Cannon-Bowers, J., Bowers, C. A., Muse, K., & Wright, M. (2006). Computer gaming and interactive simulations for learning: A meta-analysis. *Journal of Educational Computing Research, 34,* 229–243.

von Feilitzen, C. (1975). Findings of Scandinavian research on child and television in the process of socialization. *Fernsehen und Bildung, 9,* 54–84.

Wagner, S. (1985). *Comprehensive evaluation of the fourth season of* 3-2-1 Contact. New York: Children's Television Workshop.

Wall, W. D., & Simson, W. A. (1950). The emotional responses of adolescent groups to certain films. *British Journal of Educational Psychology, 20,* 153–163.

Wallack, L. (1989). Mass communication and health promotion: A critical perspective. In R. E. Rice & C. K. Atkin (Eds.), *Public communication campaigns* (2nd ed., pp. 353–367). Newbury Park, CA: Sage.

Walsh-Childers, K. (1994a). Newspaper influence on health policy development: A case study investigation. *Newspaper Research Journal, 15*(3), 89–104.

Walsh-Childers, K. (1994b). "A death in the family": A case study of newspaper influence on health policy development. *Journalism Quarterly, 71*(4), 820–829.

Walsh-Childers, K., & Brown, J. D. (2009). Effects of media on personal and public health. In J. Bryant & M. B. Oliver (Eds.), *Media effects: Advances in theory and research* (3rd ed., pp. 469–489). New York: Routledge.

Walther, J. B., Loh, T., & Granka, L. (2005). Let me count the ways: The interexchange of verbal and nonverbal cues in computer-mediated and face-to-face affinity. *Journal of Language and Social Psychology, 24,* 36–65.

Wang, T. L. (2000). Agenda-setting online: An experiment testing the effects of hyperlinks in online newspapers. *Southwestern Mass Communication Journal, 15*(2), 59–70.

Wang, Y., Monteiro, C., & Popkin, B. M. (2002). Trends of overweight and underweight in children and adolescents in the United States, Brazil, China, and Russia. *American Journal of Clinical Nutrition, 75*(6), 971–977.

Wanta, W. (1988). The effects of dominant photographs: An agenda-setting experiment. *Journalism Quarterly, 65,* 107–111.

Wanta, W., & Foote, J. (1994). The president-news media relationship: A time series analysis of agenda-setting. *Journal of Broadcasting & Electronic Media, 38,* 437–449.

Wanta, W., & Ghanem, S. (2000). Effects of agenda-setting. In J. Bryant & R. Carveth (Eds.), *Meta-analyses of media effects.* Mahwah, NJ: Erlbaum.

Wanta, W., Stephenson, M. A., Turk, J. V., & McCombs, M. E. (1989). How president's state of the union talk influenced news media agendas. *Journalism Quarterly, 66,* 537–541.

Waples, D. (1942a). Communications. *The American Journal of Sociology 47,* 907–917.

Waples, D. (Ed.). (1942b). *Print, radio, and film in a democracy.* Chicago: University of Chicago Press.

Waples, D., Berelson, B., & Bradshaw, F. R. (1940). *What reading does to people: A summary of evidence on the social effects of reading and a statement of problems for research.* Chicago: University of Chicago Press.

Ward, L. M., & Friedman, K. (2006). Using TV as a guide: Associations between television viewing and adolescents' sexual attitudes and behavior. *Journal of Research on Adolescence, 16*(1), 133–156.

Wartella, E. (1996). The history reconsidered. In E. E. Dennis & E. Wartella (Eds.), *American communication research—The remembered history* (pp. 169–180). Mahwah, NJ: Erlbaum.

Watt, J. G., Jr., & van den Berg, S. A. (1978). Time series analysis of alternative media effects theories. In R. D. Ruben (Ed.), *Communication yearbook 2* (pp. 215–224). New Brunswick, NJ: Transaction Books.

Weaver, A. J. (2011). A meta-analytical review of selective exposure to and the enjoyment of media violence. *Journal of Broadcasting & Electronic Media, 55*(2), 232–250.

Weaver, A. J., Jenson, J. D., Martins, N., Hurley, R., & Wilson, B. J. (2011). Liking violence and action: An examination of gender differences in children's processing of animated content. *Media Psychology, 14*(1), 49–70.

Weaver, D. H. (2007). Thoughts on agenda setting, framing, and priming. *Journal of Communication, 57,* 142–147.

Weaver, D. H., Graber, D. A., McCombs, M. E., & Eyal, C. H. (1981). *Media agenda-setting in a presidential election: Issues, images and interests.* New York: Praeger.

Weaver, J., & Wakshlag, J. (1986). Perceived vulnerability to crime, criminal victimization experience, and television viewing. *Journal of Broadcasting & Electronic Media, 30,* 141–158.

Weaver, J. B., III, & Tamborini, R. (Eds.) (1996). *Horror films: Current research on audience preferences and reactions.* Mahwah, NJ: Erlbaum.

Webb, T., Martin, K., Afifi, A. A., & Kraus, J. (2010). Media literacy as a violence-prevention strategy: A pilot evaluation. *Health Promotion Practice, 11*(5), 714–722.

Weigel, R. H., Loomis, J., & Soja, M. (1980). Race relations on primetime television. *Journal of Personality and Social Psychology, 39*(5), 884–893.

Weinstein, A. M. (2010). Computer and video game addiction—A comparison between game users and non-game users. *The American Journal of Drug and Alcohol Abuse, 36,* 268–276. doi: 10.3109/00952990.2010.491879

Weiss, B. W., Katkin, E. S., & Rubin, B. M. (1968). Relationship between a factor analytically derived measure of a specific fear and performance after related fear induction. *Journal of Abnormal Psychology, 73,* 461–463.

Weld, H. P. (1912). An experimental study of musical enjoyment. *The American Journal of Psychology, 23,* 245–309.

Wertham, F. (1954). *Seduction of the innocent.* New York: Rinehart.

West, D. (1993) *Air wars.* Washington, DC: Congressional Quarterly Press.

Westley, B. H. (1978). Review of *The emergence of American political issues: The agenda setting function of the press. Journalism Quarterly, 55,* 172–173.

Westley, B. H., & MacLean, M. (1957). A conceptual model for mass communication research. *Journalism Quarterly, 34,* 31–38.

Wheeler, S. C., Petty, R. E., & Bizer, G. Y. (2005). Self-schema matching and attitude change: Situation and dispositional determinants of message elaboration. *Journal of Consumer Research, 31,* 787–797.

White, L. A. (1979). Erotica and aggression: The influence of sexual arousal, positive effect, and negative effect on aggressive behavior. *Journal of Personality and Social Psychology, 37,* 591–601.

White House. (1996). Excerpts from transcribed remarks by the president and vice president to the people of Knoxville on Internet for schools. Retrieved from http://govinfo.library.unt.edu/npr/library/speeches/101096.html

Wiersma, B. A. (2001). *The gendered world of Disney: A content analysis of gender themes in full-length animated Disney feature films.* (Doctoral dissertation). Retrieved from UMI. (UMI number: 99973222).

Williams, D. (2006). Virtual cultivation: Online worlds, offline perceptions. *Journal of Communication, 56,* 69–87.

Williams, D., & Skoric, M. (2005). Internet fantasy violence: A test of aggression in an online game. *Communication Monographs, 72*(2), 217–233.

Williams, M. D., Hollan, J. D., & Stevens, A. L. (1983). Human reasoning about a simple physical system. In D. Gentner & A. L. Stevens (Eds.), *Mental models* (pp. 131–153). Hillsdale, NJ: Erlbaum.

Williams, T. M. (1986). *The impact of television.* New York: Academic.

Wilson, B. J. (1987). Reducing children's emotional reactions to mass media through rehearsed explanation and exposure to a replica of a fear object. *Human Communication Research, 14,* 3–26.

Wilson, B. J. (1989). The effects of two control strategies on children's emotional reactions to a frightening movie scene. *Journal of Broadcasting & Electronic Media, 33,* 397–418.

Wilson, B. J., & Cantor, J. (1985). Developmental differences in empathy with a television protagonist's fear. *Journal of Experimental Child Psychology, 39,* 284–299.

Wilson, B. J., & Cantor, J. (1987). Reducing children's fear reactions to mass media: Effects of visual exposure and verbal explanation. In M. McLaughlin (Ed.), *Communication yearbook 10* (pp. 553–573). Beverly Hills, CA: Sage.

Wilson, B. J., Hoffner, C., & Cantor, J. (1987). Children's perceptions of the effectiveness of techniques to reduce fear from mass media. *Journal of Applied Developmental Psychology, 8,* 39–52.

Wilson, B. J., Martins, N., & Marske, A. L. (2005). Children's and parents' fright reactions to kidnapping stories in the news. *Communication Monographs, 72*(1), 46–70.

Wilson, C., & Gutierrez, F. (1995). *Race, multiculturalism, and the media: From mass to class communication.* Thousand Oaks, CA: Sage.

Wilson, T., & Capitman, J. (1982). Effects of script availability on social behavior. *Personality and Social Psychology Bulletin, 8,* 11–19.

Wilson, T. D., Lindsey, S., & Schooler, T. Y. (2000). A model of dual attitudes. *Psychological Review, 107,* 101–126.

Wimmer, R. D., & Dominick, J. R. (1994). *Mass media research: An introduction* (4th ed.). Belmont, CA: Wadsworth Publishing.

Winett, R. A., Leckliter, I. N., Chinn, D. E., Stahl, B. N., & Love, S. Q. (1985). The effects of television modeling on residential energy conservation. *Journal of Applied Behavior Analysis, 18,* 33–44.

Winn, M. (1977). *The plug-in drug.* New York: Penguin.

Witte, K., & Allen, M. (2000). A meta-analysis of fear appeals: Implications for effective public health programs. *Health Education and Behavior, 27,* 591–615.

Wittenbrink, B., & Schwarz, N. (Eds.). (2007). *Implicit measures of attitudes.* New York: Guilford Press.

Wober, J. M. (1978). Televised violence and paranoid perception: The view from Great Britain. *Public Opinion Quarterly, 42,* 315–321.

Wober, M., & Gunter, B. (1982). Television and personal threat: Fact or artifact? A British survey. *British Journal of Social Psychology, 21,* 43–51.

Wober, M., & Gunter, B. (1988). *Television and social control.* Aldershot, England: Avebury.

Wolak, J., Mitchell, K., & Finkelhor, D. (2007). Unwanted and wanted exposure to online pornography in a national sample of youth Internet users. *Pediatrics, 119*(2), 247–257.

Wolfinger, R. E., & Rosenstone, S. J. (1980). *Who votes?* New Haven, CT: Yale University Press.

Wood, R. (1984). An introduction to the American horror film. In B. K. Grant (Ed.), *Planks of reason: Essays on the horror film* (pp. 164–200). Metuchen, NJ: Scarecrow Press.

Wood, W. (2000). Attitude change: Persuasion and social influence. *Annual Review of Psychology, 51,* 539–570.

Wood, W., Wong, F. Y., & Chachere, J. G. (1991). Effects of media violence on viewers' aggression in unconstrained social interaction. *Psychological Bulletin, 109,* 371–383.

Woodruff, S., Agro, A., Wildey, M., & Conway, T. (1995). Point-of-purchase tobacco advertising: Prevalence, correlates, and brief intervention. *Health Values, 19*(5), 56–62.

Worden, J., & Flynn, B. (1999, January 2). Shock to stop? Massachusetts' antismoking campaign. *British Medical Journal, 318.* [online]. NEXIS: News Library, CURNWS File.

Worley, J. R., Rogers, S. N., & Kraemer, R. R. (2011). Metabolic responses to Wii Fit™ video games at different game levels. *Journal of Strength and Conditioning Research, 25,* 689–693.

Wortham, J. (2010). Angry birds, flocking to cell phones everywhere. Retrieved from http://www.nytimes.com/2010/12/12/technology/12birds.html

Wright, C. R. (1960). Functional analysis and mass communication. *Public Opinion Quarterly, 24,* 605–620.

Wright, J., St. Peters, M., & Huston, A. (1990). Family television use and its relation to children's cognitive skills and social behavior. In J. Bryant (Ed.), *Television and the American family* (pp. 227–251). Hillsdale, NJ: Lawrence Erlbaum.

Wright, J. C., & Huston, A. C. (1995). *Effects of educational TV viewing of lower income preschoolers on academic skills, school readiness, and school adjustment one to three years later: A report to the Children's Television Workshop.* Lawrence: Center for Research on the Influences of Television on Children, The University of Kansas.

Wright, J. C., Huston, A. C., Scantlin, R., & Kotler, J. (2001). The Early Window project: *Sesame Street* prepares children for school. In S. M. Fisch & R. T. Truglio (Eds.), *"G" is for "growing": Thirty years of research on children and* Sesame Street (pp. 97–114). Mahwah, NJ: Erlbaum.

Wroblewski, R., & Huston, A. C. (1987). Televised occupational stereotypes and their effects on early adolescents: Are they changing? *Journal of Early Adolescence, 7,* 283–297.

Wu, H. D., & Coleman, R. (2009). Advancing agenda-setting theory: The comparative strength and new contingent conditions of the two levels of agenda-setting effects. *Journalism & Mass Communication Quarterly, 86*(4), 775–789.

Wuang, Y.-P., Chiang, C.-S., Su, C.-Y., & Wang, C.-C. (2011). Effectiveness of virtual reality using Wii gaming technology in children with Down syndrome. *Research in Developmental Disabilities, 32,* 312–321.

Wyer, R. S., Jr., & Radvansky, G. A. (1999). The comprehension and validation of social information. *Psychological Review, 106,* 89–118.

Wyer, R. S., Jr., & Srull, T. (1981). Category accessibility: Some theoretical and empirical issues concerning the processing of information. In E. Higgins, C. Herman, & M. Zanna (Eds.), *Social cognition* (Vol. 1, pp. 161–197). Hillsdale, NJ: Erlbaum.

Xenos, M., & Moy, P. (2007). Direct and differential effects of the Internet on political and civic engagement. *Journal of Communication, 57,* 704–718.

Yang, H., Ramasubramanian, S., & Oliver, M. B. (2008). Cultivation effects on quality of life indicators: Exploring the effects of American television consumption on feelings of relative deprivation in South Korea and India. *Journal of Broadcasting & Electronic Media, 52*(2), 247–267.

Yang, N., & Linz, D. (1990). Movie ratings and the content of adult videos: The sex-violence ratio. *Journal of Communication, 40*(2), 28–42.

Yarros, V. S. (1899). The press and public opinion. *The American Journal of Sociology, 5,* 372–382.

Young, D. G. (2004). Late-night comedy in election 2000: Its influence on candidate trait ratings and the moderating effects of political knowledge and partisanship. *Journal of Broadcasting & Electronic Media, 48,* 1–22.

Young, K. S. (1996). Addictive use of the Internet: A case that breaks the stereotype. *Psychological Reports, 79,* 899–902.

Zeng, L. (2011). More than audio on the go: Uses and gratifications of MP3 players. *Communication Research Reports, 28*(1), 97–108.

Zero to Three/National Center for Clinical Infant Programs. (1992). *Heart Start: The emotional foundations of school readiness.* Arlington, VA: Author.

Zgourides, G., Monto, M., & Harris, R. (1997) Correlates of adolescent male sexual offense: Prior adult sexual contact, sexual attitudes, and use of sexually explicit materials. *International Journal of Offender Therapy and Comparative Criminology, 41*(3), 272–283.

Zhong, B., Hardin, M., & Sun, T. (2011). Less effortful thinking leads to more social networking? The associations between the use of social network sites and personality traits. *Computers in Human Behavior, 27,* 1265–1271. doi: 10.1016/j.chb.2011.01.008

Zhong, X., Zu, S., Sha, S., Tao, R., Zhao, C., & Yang, F. (2011). The effect of a family-based intervention model on Internet-addicted Chinese adolescents. *Social Behavior and Personality, 39,* 1021–1034.

Zhou, S., Greer, A., & Finklea, B. W. (2010, April). *Discrimination, racist events, and their effects on behavioral and evaluative outcomes of movie posters with black and white protagonists.* Paper presented at the 55th annual meeting of the Broadcast Education Association, Las Vegas, NV.

Zill, N. (1977). *National survey of children: Summary of preliminary results.* New York: Foundation for Child Development.

Zill, N. (2001). Does *Sesame Street* enhance school readiness? Evidence from a national survey of children. In S. M. Fisch & R. T. Truglio (Eds.), *"G" is for "growing": Thirty years of research on children and* Sesame Street (pp. 115–130). Mahwah, NJ: Erlbaum.

Zill, N., Davies, E., & Daly, M. (1994). *Viewing of* Sesame Street *by preschool children and its relationship to school readiness: Report prepared for the Children's Television Workshop.* Rockville, MD: Westat, Inc.

Zillmann, D. (1971). Excitation transfer in communication-mediated aggressive behavior. *Journal of Experimental Social Psychology, 7,* 419–434.

Zillmann, D. (1978). Attribution and misattribution of excitatory reactions. In J. H. Harvey, W. J. Ickes, & R. F. Kidd (Eds.), *New directions in attribution research* (Vol. 2, pp. 335–368). Hillsdale, NJ: Erlbaum.

Zillmann, D. (1979). *Hostility and aggression.* Hillsdale, NJ: Erlbaum.

Zillmann, D. (1980). Anatomy of suspense. In P. H. Tannenbaum (Ed.), *The entertainment functions of television* (pp. 133–163). Hillsdale, NJ: Erlbaum.

Zillmann, D. (1982a). Television viewing and arousal. In D. Pearl, L. Bouthilet, & J. Lazar (Eds.), *Television and behavior: Ten years of scientific progress and implications for the eighties* (Vol. 2, pp. 53–67). Washington, DC: Government Printing Office.

Zillmann, D. (1982b). Transfer of excitation in emotional behavior. In J. T. Cacioppo & R. E. Petty (Eds.), *Social psychophysiology.* New York: Guilford Press.

Zillmann, D. (1988). Cognition-excitation interdependencies in aggressive behavior. *Aggressive Behavior, 14,* 51–64.

Zillmann, D. (1991a). Empathy: Effect from bearing witness to the emotions of others. In J. Bryant & D. Zillmann (Eds.), *Responding to the screen: Reception and reaction processes* (pp. 135–167). Hillsdale, NJ: Erlbaum.

Zillmann, D. (1991b). The logic of suspense and mystery. In J. Bryant & D. Zillmann (Eds.), *Responding to the screen: Reception and reaction processes* (pp. 281–303). Hillsdale, NJ: Erlbaum.

Zillmann, D. (2000). Excitement. In A. E. Kazdin (Ed.), *Encyclopedia of psychology.* New York: American Psychological Association and Oxford University Press.

Zillmann, D., & Bryant, J. (1982). Pornography, sexual callousness, and the trivialization of rape. *Journal of Communication, 32*(4), 10–21.

Zillmann, D., & Bryant, J. (1984). Effects of massive exposure to pornography. In N. M. Malamuth & E. Donnerstein (Eds.), *Pornography and sexual aggression* (pp. 115–138). New York: Academic.

Zillmann, D., & Bryant, J. (1985). *Selective exposure to communication.* Mahwah, NJ: Erlbaum.

Zillmann, D., & Bryant, J. (1986). Shifting preferences in pornography consumption. *Communication Research, 13,* 560–578.

Zillmann, D., & Bryant, J. (1988a). Effects of prolonged consumption of pornography on family values. *Journal of Family Issues, 9*(4), 518–544.

Zillmann, D., & Bryant, J. (1988b). Pornography's impact on sexual satisfaction. *Journal of Applied Social Psychology, 18,* 438–453.

Zillmann, D., & Gibson, R. (1996). Evolution of the horror genre. In J. B. Weaver III & R. Tamborini (Eds.), *Horror films: Current research on audience preferences and reactions* (pp. 15–31). Mahwah, NJ: Erlbaum.

Zillmann, D., Hay, T. A., & Bryant, J. (1975). The effect of suspense and its resolution on the appreciation of dramatic presentations. *Journal of Research in Personality, 9,* 307–323.

Zillmann, D., Mody, B., & Cantor, J. (1974). Empathetic perception of emotional displays in films as a function of hedonic and excitatory state prior to exposure. *Journal of Research in Personality, 8,* 335–349.

Zillmann, D., & Weaver, J. B., III. (1999). Effects of prolonged exposure to gratuitous media violence on provoked and unprovoked hostile behavior. *Journal of Applied Social Psychology, 29,* 145–165.

Zimmerman, E. J., Christakis, D. A., Meltzoff, A. N. (2007). Television and DVD/video viewing in children younger than 2 years. *Archives of Pediatrics and Adolescent Medicine, 161*(5), 473–479.

Zoglin, N. R. (1984, June 25). Gremlins in the rating system: Two hit films raise new concerns about protecting children. *Time*, p. 78.

Zwann, R. A., & Radvansky, G. A. (1998). Situation models in language comprehension and memory. *Psychological Bulletin, 123,* 162–185.

Zwarun, L., & Farrar, K. M. (2005). Doing what they say, saying what they mean: Self-regulatory compliance and depictions of drinking in alcohol commercials in televised sports. *Mass Communication and Society, 8*(4), 347–371.

Index